The
Merchants
of Zigong

Studies of the Weatherhead East Asian Institute
Columbia University

Studies of the Weatherhead East Asian Institute, Columbia University

The Weatherhead East Asian Institute is Columbia University's center for research, publication, and teaching on modern East Asia. The Studies of the Weatherhead East Asian Institute were inaugurated in 1962 to bring to a wider public the results of significant new research on modern and contemporary East Asian affairs.

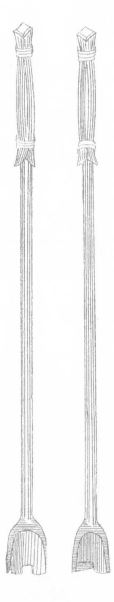

Madeleine Zelin

The Merchants of Zigong

Industrial Entrepreneurship
in Early Modern China

Columbia University Press / New York

Columbia University Press
Publishers Since 1893
New York Chichester, West Sussex
Copyright (c) 2005 Columbia University Press
All rights reserved
Library of Congress Cataloging-in-Publication Data

Zelin, Madeleine.
The merchants of Zigong : industrial entrepreneurship in
early modern China / Madeleine Zelin.
p. cm. — (Studies of the Weatherhead East Asian
Institute, Columbia University)
Includes bibliographical references and index.
ISBN 0–231–13596–3 (cloth: alk. paper)—
ISBN 0–231–50976–6 (electronic)
1. Zigong (China)—Commerce. I. Title. II. Series.
HF3840.Z54Z45 2005
338.4′76644′095138—dc22   2005046538
                                                        ⊛

References to Internet Web sites (URLs) were accurate at the
time of writing. Neither the author nor Columbia University
Press is responsible for Web sites that may have expired or
changed since the articles were prepared.

To my son,

Iain David Zelin Ware

Contents

Tables, Figures, Maps, and Illustrations

Tables

Figures

Maps

Illustrations

Chinese Weights, Measurements, and Money

CHINESE WEIGHTS, measures, and monetary denominations varied somewhat from place to place. Standard equivalents are generally calculated as follows:

Dan a measure of weight equal to 100 *jin.*
Jin a measure of weight, approximately 1.3 pounds.
Li a measure of distance equal to about one-third of a mile.
Shi a measure of grain sometimes referred to as a picul, approximately
   133.3 pounds.
Tael (Chinese = *liang*) a Chinese ounce. Sixteen *liang* equaled one *jin.*
   Uncoined silver money was measured in taels.
Yuan a Chinese dollar. Used to refer to coined silver money during the late
   nineteenth and early twentieth centuries and to paper money issued by
   the Republic of China after 1935.
Zai a standard salt shipping unit equal to between 115,000 and 120,000 *jin*
   (or approximately 75 to 78 tons).

Preface

Zigong in Chinese History

THIS BOOK recounts the one-hundred-year rise and decline of China's first privately owned high-capital, high-throughput industrial enterprises—the salt manufacturing firms that emerged in the mid-Qing dynasty in the present-day city of Zigong, Sichuan. It is a work of business history. It is also a social history of a discrete merchant community whose deployment of economic, social, and political resources has much to tell us about Chinese urban elite formation at the periphery of empire. The merchants themselves engaged in a number of trades, but their fame was for the production of salt, which by the nineteenth century was made from brine that was drawn from deep wells excavated among the local hills, then transported to furnaces via pipes that traversed the local landscape like giant bamboo roller coasters, and finally distilled in salt pans, many of which were heated by locally mined natural gas.

In their heyday in the late nineteenth and early twentieth centuries, the two towns that made up Zigong—Ziliujing and Gongjing—comprised the largest industrial center in China. Furong, the saltyard that spread across their borders, was responsible for 60 percent of the salt produced in Sichuan. Its workers were among the first men (for this was a male industry) to leave the countryside or small town to work in a factory, not just for a few years or in the agricultural slack season, but full time and for life. Its entrepreneurs, large and small, were pioneers in industrial capital formation and in the development of economies of scale and scope. The most successful built large horizontally and vertically integrated companies that dominated the southern Sichuan economy and made their shareholders among the richest men in China.

In writing about Zigong's salt manufacturers I have had two goals: to better understand the institutions that structured China's indigenous economic development and to try to resituate the history of Chinese business within the larger history of the firm in the nineteenth and early twentieth centuries. It will be clear to anyone who reads about these Chinese industrialists that their experience was only partially transferable. Their success was in part a gift of nature, in the form of rich deposits of brine and natural gas that still form the basis for Zigong's industrial development today. However, the ability of the merchants of Zigong to mobilize capital, develop and utilize new technologies, capture markets, and build and sustain corporate business organizations was only moderately dependent on fortuitous geology. Like entrepreneurs everywhere they labored within a complex of cultural resources and political realities that molded their business behavior and were manipulated by them in the pursuit of profit.

The cultural resources upon which Zigong people drew to build their firms were already important in the structuring of property rights and the organization of various kinds of corporate entities throughout the Chinese-speaking world. They remained important even after the expansion of foreign business in China and the increased movement of Chinese overseas in the latter part of the nineteenth century provided new models for Chinese industry. Inasmuch as the main period of growth at the saltyard occurred before the period of Western influence on Chinese business, the merchants of Zigong provide a rare opportunity to examine Chinese institutions in a purely indigenous "big business" context. Zigong also allows us to track changes in indigenous business organization over time, permitting a more nuanced assessment of the forces that shaped industrial organization, interaction with the regional and national economy, and the actions of business elites in an urban setting that was not dominated by the West and Japan.

Business never operates in a political vacuum. The story of Zigong's prosperous century stretches across three key political transitions in modern Chinese history—the early period of Manchu rule, the imperial political realignment of the post–Taiping Rebellion, and the warlord and Nationalist (Guomindang) republics of the postdynastic period. Although salt had long been a source of revenues for China's rulers, the early Qing government was far too preoccupied with dynastic consolidation to concern itself with extracting the maximum revenues from the salt industry in distant Sichuan. Until the mid-nineteenth century, salt producers at Furong labored under a salt administration that placed few restrictions on the manner in which they conducted their business and allowed far more freedom in the development of market opportunities than was enjoyed by salt producers in eastern and northern China. The Taiping Rebellion (1851–1864), by cutting off trade between central China and the salt production regions of the east coast, suddenly and dramatically expanded their market reach, a condition that was not reversed until the early decades of the twentieth century. Thus, in most respects Sichuan salt manufacturers operated free of external constraints. Even after the imposition of stronger state control over the sale of salt in the late 1870s, Zigong salt production benefited from an expanding market that encouraged new investment and technical innovation.

It is difficult to locate the stifling influence of the "feudal" state of popular Chinese historical narrative in the story of Zigong's Furong saltyard. As I have argued elsewhere, Qing economic policies were relatively benign, limiting neither the movement of capital and workers, nor the entrepreneurial energies of merchants and manufacturers.[1] The success of Zigong's investors in transforming their industry from one of handicraft workshops to large-scale industrial firms also belies long-held beliefs that social structure, the absence of modern banking, and cultural bias against business precluded industrial investment and development in China. As Tim Wright has noted with regard to China's late-nineteenth-century coal mining industry, where there were profits to be made in China there was investment.[2]

Where the economy is concerned, the late imperial state is more notable for what it did not do for industry than what it did to it. In the interests of central communications with the provinces, the Qing state maintained a dense network of roads and watercourses that benefited long-distance trade. However, by the eighteenth century this network fell far behind the needs of China's producers and particularly of those regions far from the centers of maritime trade. In the nineteenth century, a weakened Qing state continued its domestic tradition of economic laissez-vous faire, too late assuming responsibility for infrastructure development and the promotion of industry.

It is easy to blame the last imperial government for a lack of vision in its approach to the challenges China faced from the West and Japan. However, in key areas it performed far better than its successors. The early development of the Furong saltyard took place under conditions of relative political stability (save for the years of the Taiping wars). State enforcement of property rights and contracts compensated in large measure for the absence until the turn of the twentieth century of a state-promulgated commercial law. While salt producers blasted the introduction of commercial taxes on salt in the form of the mid-nineteenth-century *lijin* tax, the Qing tax system as a whole was relatively benign in its extraction of profits from manufacturing and commerce. And despite the demands of Sichuan's competitors, the state did not roll back the Sichuan salt market to its pre-Taiping borders.

The governments that followed the ouster of the Qing dynasty did not do as well for Zigong businessmen. Infrastructure projects that might have helped them diversify their products and participate in the more prosperous trade and manufacturing emerging in the east and northeast did not materialize. Political instability challenged their access to established markets and to inexpensive capital. And the needs of competing militarists for revenues raised the effective tax burden far beyond the limits imposed by the late imperial regime. The stresses placed on business in twentieth-century Zigong did not destroy the saltyard. But they did drive out the marginal producer and change the way business was conducted among those who remained.

Zigong and the History of the Firm

As important as Zigong is to an understanding of Chinese industrial history, it is also a valuable addition to the general investigation of early industrial development and organization worldwide. The problems that Zigong businessmen faced and the choices they made in response will be familiar to economic historians. Prior to the nineteenth century most of the world's merchants and artisans operated within a low-fixed-cost economy in which, as Langlois notes, "profitability depended not on the ownership of tangible assets but on specialized knowledge and the ability to adapt."[3] Manufactures were produced in small workshops and were sold by merchants who handled diverse products and traveled between widely dispersed markets. During the nineteenth century, parts of Western Europe and the United States experienced market growth, which in turn made possible the introduction of larger-scale manufacturing processes. In the United States this industrial development followed the expansion of the domestic market. Elsewhere, it was the result of expansion of overseas trade. Whatever the cause, this change in the size of the market made possible a shift to more capital-intensive production and the integration of the production process. The introduction of factory production, with its higher-cost machinery and larger wage and materials schedules, demanded new ways to finance business.

Zigong's remarkable expansion in the early nineteenth century and its equally swift decline in the late 1920s and early 1930s were also first and foremost the product of market expansion and later contraction. In this case it was state policies governing the regional distribution of salt markets that made feasible investment in deep drilling technologies and stimulated the refinement of those technologies to produce dramatically increased supplies of brine and natural gas. That this market expansion was not the result of improvements in transportation or other factors facilitating market integration and the flow of information would become important later on. However, in the early nineteenth century Zigong salt producers found themselves in the same situation as manufacturers of textiles, brewers, miners, and others around the world who saw the opportunities presented by expanding markets and the possibilities for exploiting economies of scale.

How these new industrial enterprises were financed depended on local conditions. For most firms fixed-capital costs were sufficiently low to allow entrepreneurs to rely on individual and joint owner financing and to retain profits for industrial growth. Merchant loans also played a role in providing long- and short-term credit.[4] In the instances where banks played an important part in capital accumulation it was most often not as impersonal lender but as participant in one or more financial-industrial networks bound by kinship. Naomi Lamoreaux has demonstrated the importance of banks as "insider lenders" to early New England textile manufacturers. During the nineteenth century, banks founded by members of prominent New England families became important sources of capital for the business ventures of bank directors and their kin. At the same time, by opening the purchase of bank shares to the general public, these financial-industrial networks were able to expand the pool of money available for industrial development.[5]

At Zigong we will see both patterns at work. In Sichuan the wealthiest merchants were those who controlled the wholesale market in salt. So it is no surprise that some of the earliest efforts at deep drilling in Zigong drew on capital from the large Shaanxi merchant houses that dominated that market. At the same time, entrepreneurs took advantage of other entrenched practices to achieve unprecedented levels of capital investment. Chapter 2 looks in detail at the utilization of kinship organization and the growth of a local share market in Zigong to combine the underemployed capital of numerous local and regional households. Whereas banks acted as intermediaries in the combination of capital in the New England case, in Zigong kinship networks operated directly as poolers of capital, while specialized middlemen facilitated the combination of capital not shared by kin and its management. The basic form of capital accumulation in both instances was the contract-based unlimited liability shareholding company.

The shareholding companies formed at Zigong display characteristics both similar to and different in fundamental ways from those of the firms formed by early-nineteenth-century industrialists in the West. Like the latter, they began as contractual partnerships in which investors shared in profits and losses in proportion to their contribution to the capital fund. A distinctive feature of the Zigong case was the commoditization of shares, which allowed the developers of wells and furnaces to use the share market to extend the life of the firm beyond either the finances or the biological life spans of the original investors. Purchase and sale of shares also gave firms control over inputs to production, which allowed greater flexibility than would outright purchase of production assets.

The absence of state involvement in setting the rules of the game for business organization in Zigong and elsewhere in China is striking. While Zigong businessmen had to contend with the state over taxes and markets, they were left an open field to utilize contracts to shape their businesses and to govern their conduct through a simple set of self-binding regulations, which in turn was enforced in the courts. Unlike England, no constraints were ever placed on the size or capitalization of a partnership. Nor did the state interfere in the relations between capital and labor. Shareholding was governed entirely through contract. As opportunities for economies of scale and from coordination became apparent, Zigong businessmen drew on forms of asset incorporation native to the extended kinship group to organize production units and ensure their longevity beyond the founding generation.

The state's uninterest in regulating the economy during the Qing turns out to have been a double-edged sword. On the one hand, Chinese businesses, in Zigong and elsewhere, were free to govern themselves. Although this gave rise to a plethora of terms for similar activities, the relative homogeneity of Chinese culture and a highly mobile merchant and official class seems to have resulted in similar business practices throughout most of China. On the other hand, without a legislative forum for debate over business practices and the legal forms that would best serve them, business practices were not elevated to the level of the law and problems shared by all businessmen were never resolved by state action. As a result, until 1904 Chinese businesses operated without a law of limited liability or a means to mitigate business debt through a law of bankruptcy.

High fixed capital was not the only distinguishing characteristic of the modern industrial firm. During the course of the second half of the nineteenth century many producers began to integrate forward into marketing and in some cases backward into raw material supply. Scholars disagree on the causes of this phenomenon. Williamson, following Coase, has argued that integration occurs to overcome transaction costs created by imperfect and often asymmetric information.[6] However, the scenario mapped out by Alfred Chandler for firms such as Standard Oil provides the most useful framework for an analysis of the evolution of the firm in Zigong. Chandler emphasizes the development of new technologies, which in turn made possible high capacity or "throughput" production.[7] In the case of the United States, innovation in both transportation and manufacturing contributed to the new business environment. As Langlois reminds us, the first was really a market revolution, "collapsing geographical barriers [and increasing the] integration of the domestic market."[8] It was this expansion of the market that in the United States and elsewhere encouraged investment in new technologies, which in turn made possible unprecedented levels of output. Integration resulted when producers of high-throughput products sought to control both supply and marketing to make optimal use of their capital investment.

In Zigong, the development of highly productive brine wells and the concurrent recognition of the potential of local deposits of natural gas occurred shortly before the advent of the Taiping Rebellion broke open the market for Sichuan salt. Investors with sufficient capital almost overnight became classic high-throughput producers with a virtually unlimited potential market. The absence of technology to store natural gas reinforced the impulse to keep brine flowing to the furnaces. Firms first brought together brine and gas wells and the furnaces that evaporated salt. Firms with brine but insufficient gas used the market to ensure gas supplies through long-term leases and the purchase of gas well shares. Some firms extended their linkages back further by investing in agricultural land to feed the buffalo that pumped the brine and by developing networks that guaranteed access to critical inputs like bamboo, timber, and cable. The largest firms extended their linkages forward as well, creating their own marketing divisions and later investing in the development of brine pipes, both of which gave them advantages over smaller producers. With all the pieces in place, many Zigong furnaces operated 24 hours a day.

Integration requires changes in management. While not all firms experienced the kind of management professionalization to which Chandler attributes the success of the American industrial giants, coordination of various functions subsumed within the integrated firm everywhere led to specialization and hierarchical organization of the various divisions within the firm. Integration also led to the introduction into the management team of persons who were neither shareholders nor shareholders' kin.[9] In Zigong we see this clearly in the hierarchical management structures adopted by large lineage-based firms and signs of a similar transformation of management practices within non-lineage partnerships for which we have fragmented data. Professionalization of managerial training lagged behind advances in organization. Managerial skills continued to be acquired through apprenticeship (not necessarily at the firm where one ultimately worked) and on-the-job experience, with many managers making their careers moving up the hierarchy within one firm. However, evidence from partnership agreements and accounting records suggests a growing recognition of management accountability to shareholders who were themselves not active participants in the activities of the firm.

While integration was responsible for the success of the first generation of salt producers who took advantage of deep-well technology, the story of the merchants of Zigong is not one of linear development. As such, it addresses questions posed by the late-twentieth-century decline of the large integrated industrial firm. The critique of the theory of the firm provided by Naomi R. Lamoreaux, Daniel M. G. Raff, and Peter Temin is useful in this regard.[10] Rather than view industrial integration as inevitable, they lay out the relative advantages and disadvantages of different organizational forms along a continuum from market-based to hierarchically based (i.e., integrated) coordination. Arguing that the choice of firm structure along this continuum is contingent upon numerous factors that change over time, the authors conclude that the large integrated firm is no longer as efficient as it once was. Langlois, who makes a similar argument that nonetheless maintains the basic framework of Chandler's, claims that one of the results of integration was the building of capacities which can later be used to diversify in ways that ultimately lead to the decentralization of many late-twentieth-century firms.[11]

The history of the Zigong saltyard prior to the outbreak of World War II underscores the importance of a multivalent theory of the firm. If we assume the choice of firm organization is based largely on an effort to reduce risk, the integrated salt conglomerate buffered producers against interruptions in supply that would impede the 24-hour-a-day, 30-days-a-month production schedules of Zigong's gas-fired furnaces. As long as they produced, wholesalers could find a market in the expanding Sichuan salt frontier in Yunnan-Guizhou to the south and Hunan-Hubei to the north. Even an increase in salt taxes and a government takeover of marketing did not lead to a structural change in the organization of the industry prior to the end of the nineteenth century.

In the early twentieth century, techniques of solution mining employed to exploit newly discovered rock-salt deposits created new economies of scale and changed the balance of power between owners of brine and owners of gas. With brine prices at all-time lows and less productive brine wells closing every day, the importance of backward supply linkages declined. At the same time, the introduction of steam engines at the yard allowed a new group of investors, latecomers to the field of well exploration, to penetrate the industry on the basis of their control of capital as well as expertise in mechanical engineering and links to pump manufacturers in Hankou and Shanghai.

Probably the most important influence on business organization was the changing political environment of the twentieth century. The fall of the Qing dynasty and its replacement by a succession of unstable military regimes added to the uncertainties under which Zigong's salt industry functioned. Frequent changes to the salt administration exacerbated their effects. By the 1920s militarist competition for salt revenues led to a radical contraction in the legal market for Zigong salt and a dramatic rise in salt taxes. All of these factors influenced the disintegration of the Zigong salt firms, diversification of investment portfolios, and the growing importance of networks in business behavior.

Sources

All students of China's historical economy must face the dilemma posed by inadequate quantitative data, both relating to the economy as a whole and to individual sectors and firms. In the case of Zigong, what survives is in large part the product of that city's special importance to the state as a source of taxes. Among our most important sources on the overall conduct of business and trade, on output, taxation, and production costs are state-sponsored compilations—salt gazetteers, salt administration histories, collections of essays on salt administration, and local and provincial gazetteers. In addition, we are fortunate to have several private surveys of the saltyard, including one large compilation from the turn of the twentieth century and another undertaken in 1928.[12] During the 1990s locally sponsored projects to compile historical gazetteers covering various aspects of Zigong's urban history, particularly during the twentieth century, have also provided valuable information on such matters as the founding of firms, the establishment of local banks, and the transformation of Zigong from a capitalist to a socialist economy.[13]

While quantitative estimates contribute to a number of arguments presented in this study, far more important has been material that contributes to a picture of institutions, associations, and practices within this business community. I was fortunate to have been able to work in the Zigong Municipal Archives, which holds an extensive collection of documents generated by the southern Sichuan salt administration and the Zigong Chamber of Commerce. The latter includes case records from the hundreds of suits filed by Zigong businessmen against the state and against each other. The Archives also has a small collection of salt business accounts and an eclectic collection of documents from the pre-1949 salt companies. Among these are a large number of contracts and other agreements, many of which have been collected in *Zigong yanye qiyue dang'an xuanji (1732–1949)* (Selected

Zigong salt industry contracts and documents [1732–1949]).[14] These have been particularly important in understanding how capital was brought together at the yard, how partnerships were structured, and how business organizations changed over time. Material from the Zigong Municipal Archives reprinted in this collection is cited by the number assigned to each contract as it appears in print. To these were added compilations of documents on specific subjects brought together by Chinese scholars.[15] The many additional materials I was able to find at the Archives are cited according to their archival catalogue number.

This book could not have been written without a third kind of source, one that is increasingly finding its way into the work of Chinese historians. Because of the special problems this genre presents it requires particular mention. Since the 1950s Zigong, like many places in China, has been the focus of intensive efforts to gather the oral (and sometimes written) recollections of people who participated in important events or activities. In the case of Zigong, the building of an industrial center was deemed worthy of such a project, even as the communist state was dismantling its firms and incorporating its personnel into the state-owned sector. Hundreds of memoirs were transcribed during the 1950s and early 1960s; many of them were published in *Zigong wenshiziliao xuanji* and *Sichuan wenshiziliao xuanji* prior to the onset of the Cultural Revolution. The oral history enterprise was halted during the late 1960s and 1970s. However, it was revived in the 1980s and continues to this day. I was fortunate to receive, from colleagues in the Zigong Salt Industry Museum and the gazetteer office, copies of the unabridged originals upon which several of these published oral histories were based, and I have made careful use of them and numerous published (compiled and edited) transcriptions.

Such materials need to be used with caution, as do indeed all materials with which we build our picture of the past. Because the subjects of these memoirs were largely former salt businessmen (including some of the most powerful of the last cohort before the revolution), we should expect that they would feel constrained by their new circumstances and anxious to present themselves in the best possible light. It is also clear that some of these memoirists had axes to grind. They each have their own take on why their businesses succeeded or failed, which government actors were pro- or anti-industry, and who was in the right in particular conflicts and disputes. In each case I have tried to avoid accepting the subjective conclusions of the author, while culling his story for clues to the institutional structures at play, the problems he and others faced, and the choices they made. The opportunity I have had to check and cross-check the information contained in oral histories against contracts, official compilations, nonofficial surveys, the records of legal cases, and the papers of the Chamber of Commerce has made me more sanguine but still cautious in their use.

Acknowledgments

This project has benefited from the friendship, advice, and wise counsel of many Chinese colleagues over the years. Ran Guangrong (Sichuan University), Lu Zijian (Sichuan Academy of Social Sciences), and Gao Wangling (People's University's Qing History Research Institute) were instrumental in the development of my initial research plan. Wu Tianying (Beijing College of Economics) helped arrange my visit to the Zigong Municipal Archives, joined me there, and spent countless hours availing me of his insights into salt technology and terminology. Ran Guangrong, Gao Wangling, and Wu Tianying also shared their knowledge with me and my colleagues as visiting scholars at the Weatherhead East Asian Institute at Columbia University.

In Zigong the staff and researchers of the Zigong Municipal Archives and the Zigong Salt Museum gave so generously of their time and knowledge. My gratitude to them cannot be expressed in mere words. Without their help this book would not have been written. I wish to extend a special thanks to Song Liangxi, who continued to correspond with me after my departure and made sure that for many years to come I received the publications being produced by Zigong's various historical research units. I also wish to thank the staff of the Number One Archives in Beijing, where I collected data on Qing grain prices in Sichuan.

Friends and colleagues outside China have also contributed much to this book. Hans Ulrich Vogel sent me photocopies of early drafts of the Cambridge History of Science chapter on salt production as well as photocopies of early editions of *Zigong wenshiziliao xuanji*. Thanks go also to research assistance provided by Emily Luo, Li Chen, and Khee Heong Koh and to Janice Duffin, Elizabeth Lacouture, Jason Petrulis, and to Anne McCoy and Irene Pavitt at Columbia University Press, for their superb editorial assistance. It was a pleasure working with Douglas Miller and Christian Brest to create the maps that appear in this study. The encouragement and support of Anne Routon, my editor at Columbia, has been priceless. Jon Ocko, David Weiman, Robert Gardella, Elizabeth Köll, Tim Brook, Brett Sheehan, and Georgia Mickey read various versions of this book, helping me to clarify my arguments and forcing me to make accessible what could sometimes be the arcane details of a very complicated industry. I also received the sage advice of members of the Columbia University Seminar on Economic History. I appreciate the effort each of them devoted to this work and hope the book does not disappoint.

Family members have played a special role in my scholarly endeavors, urging me on with their kind words and smoothing my path by living their own lives well. Thanks first to my parents, Murray and Rita, who are there for me in all ways. All single working mothers should be blessed with children as loving, helpful, and accomplished as my son Iain. I began this book when he was a garrulous, energetic toddler and dedicate it to him as he enters the world as an exceptionally promising young man. Joey, my stepson, I thank for his sweetness and for always making me laugh. Finally, I wish to thank my husband, David Weiman: economist, historian, and true friend. He has been my most acute and exacting critic and my most constant and loving supporter. To be married to such a scholar and mensch is a great blessing.

The
Merchants
of Zigong

1

Salt Administration and Salt Technology

IN THE southern Sichuan city known today as Zigong, site of the Furong saltyards, there is an often-told story of a wealthy salt manufacturer and merchant named Wang Langyun, who resisted the efforts of the Qing state (1644–1912) to tax and control the Sichuan salt market. In one version of the story, Langyun, one of the most powerful merchants in the region, and a fellow merchant named Yan, of almost equal stature, plotted to thwart an 1863 plan to levy *lijin* taxes on salt brine producers and salt evaporators.[1] While Yan hastened to the provincial capital to influence provincial officials and perhaps stave off suspicions of his own involvement, Wang's and Yan's employees set upon the newly established tax collection office and demolished it in the middle of the night. In a charming twist to the tale, the vandals would have gotten away with their crime had one of their number not gotten drunk and fallen asleep at the site with a carrying pole by his side stamped with the mark of one of Yan's salt evaporation furnaces. While Yan did all he could to influence officials in Chengdu, Wang Langyun was arrested but subsequently released for his role in the affair. According to some accounts, although Langyun showed no respect for the local officials, the magistrate was loath to hold in custody a man who had contributed so greatly in money and leadership to local defense during the Taiping Rebellion.[2]

The tax that formed the target of protest in this story was never levied, and it is possible that both the tax and the opposition recounted here were no more than the stuff of myth. But tales of the exploits of Zigong's merchant elite have had a life of their own. A second version of the Wang Langyun story takes place against a very real and dramatic change in the administration of salt revenues in late Qing Sichuan. In 1877, the state moved to limit the relatively free market for Sichuan salt that had developed during the course of the dynasty by establishing a system of salt licensing and official transport known as *Guanyun shangxiao* (Guanyun). The brainchild of the newly appointed Sichuan Governor General Ding Baozhen, the Guanyun reforms came to require that over half of all salt produced in Sichuan be sold to government transporters, which then sold the salt to licensed distributors in the territories permitted to purchase Sichuan salt.[3]

For merchants like Wang Langyun, the reforms meant the loss of an important part of their overall business, wholesale marketing, as well as the opportunity to evade taxation altogether in the movement of salt. For large producers, shipment of salt produced at their own facilities had also permitted product branding as well as a measure of control over the retail market through the cultivation of relationships with local vendors. As in the story related above, Langyun is said to have responded to the reforms first through lobbying and ultimately through violence. In a subtle twist to the tale of the Wangs and the Yans, after giving the order for his henchmen to sack the Guanyun bureau in his hometown of Ziliujing, it was Langyun who sped off to Chengdu. Traveling day and night, changing sedan chairs every 10 *li* (3.11 miles),[4] Langyun made the six-day trip in two days and two nights, establishing his alibi for the day of the attack. Having initially succeeded in deflecting the attention of investigators away from him, Langyun fled south to Guizhou province. Only after four years in exile and hefty contributions to central government coffers was Langyun able to return to Sichuan and reclaim his life as one of the empire's wealthiest businessmen.[5]

The story of these brash Zigong salt merchants can be read on many levels. It is foremost a tale of local pride in a business tradition, which to this point had converted a modest salt-producing town into one of China's great nonadministrative centers of population and wealth. Wang and Yan quite unashamedly escape by means of wealth, cunning, and political influence and are later rehabilitated by the same. Yet their resort to violence betrays ambivalence toward the state and their ability to influence its actions by legal means. Yan's and Wang's employees functioned here as both workers and private thugs, raising questions about the foundations of elite power, as well as the relationship between workers and the firm and the firm and the state. These exploits, if they occurred, did so at a turning point in the fortunes of one of China's most important early modern manufacturing towns. From the early Qing to the late 1870s politics and geography combined to give Wang and his Furong cohabitants an arena for entrepreneurship relatively free of the heavy hand of the state. Remote location spared Zigong from bureaucratic interference in economic affairs and allowed its merchants to take advantage of political upheavals in China's eastern provinces. However, by the time of this incident the state's involvement in the salt industry in Sichuan was intensifying, a fact that would change the nature of the elite and the bases for their wealth. Zigong's salt industry became an important target of state revenue extraction as the fiscal pressures on the Chinese state mounted. As we will see at the end of this study, increasing importance to the national treasury did not translate into greater state contributions to local infrastructure. Nor did it increase the role of Zigong citizens in the national political arena. By the 1930s remoteness was Zigong's greatest handicap and a major factor in its rapid industrial decline.

In this chapter we will examine the conditions that until the late Qing enabled Sichuan's salt merchants to operate in a business environment fundamentally different from that of salt merchants elsewhere in China and that make Zigong an important case in the comparative study of early industrial enterprise. We will then turn to the technology of production that developed within this relatively free market context. As marketing opportunities grew, Zigong merchants undertook innovative and often risky investments and utilized a rich merchant and kinship tradition to develop under-exploited resources and build corporate business structures. This process of institution building will be the subject of chapters 2 and 3.

Sichuan Salt and the Late Imperial State

The history of the late imperial Chinese state is one of diminishing state regulation of the private economy.[6] That Chinese dynasties took a laissez-faire approach to economic activity was reflected in the Chinese tax system, which relied largely on levies on land. The one significant exception to the state's intervention in the patterns of commerce was the salt gabelle. The universal demand for salt as a preservative, as a medicinal substance, and as a food additive made it an early item of trade and an easy target for taxation.[7] In China, a close relationship between salt and the state was well developed by the Han dynasty (206 B.C.E.–220 C.E.) and, as S. A. M. Adshead has argued, was not only a site for the working out of the proper role of government in the economy. The *Salt and Iron Debates* of 81 B.C.E. discusses how a state monopoly over salt distribution became the pretext for one of China's most renowned expressions of the tension between generalist and specialist knowledge within officialdom.[8] Despite the controversy raised by the institution of salt administration, salt taxes played an important part in Chinese statecraft up until the founding of the People's Republic.[9]

Sichuan salt, much less salt from Zigong, made only minor contributions to state coffers during the early empire. Archeological evidence points to the existence of natural salt springs in Sichuan during the early historical period. By the Qin dynasty (897–221 B.C.E.) there were three salt-producing counties in what is present-day Sichuan, rising to several dozen by the Sui (605–618 C.E.) and Tang (618–907 C.E.). Production technology at Sichuan salt wells remained primitive and labor intensive, and the Tang state was satisfied merely to levy a fixed tax on individual wells about which it had knowledge.[10] It was not until the Song dynasty (960–1279 C.E.) that new production technologies and reform of the salt administration brought Sichuan salt into the larger history of salt taxation as a mainstay of state finances.

During the eleventh century new drilling techniques improved both the output and the stability of Sichuan salt wells. Borehole (*zhuotong*) wells reached depths of as much as 400 feet, allowing exploitation of more saline brine.[11] At the same time, the Song state instituted a system of state-managed distribution that, in its varied forms, was to persist as the main form of Chinese salt administration until the end of the imperial period. This salt certificate system had three elements. Although the state continued to own some salt manufacturing facilities, the foundation of the system was private production. China's main salt production regions were divided into a number of salt administration districts known as certificate territories (*yindi*). In 1900 these territories (and their main area of coverage) were Hedong (Shanxi and western Henan); Fengtian; Changlu (Hebei and eastern Henan); Shandong; Huaibei (Anhui and northern Jiangsu); Lianghuai (most of Hunan, Hubei, and northern Jiangxi); Liangzhe (Zhejiang and southern Jiangsu); Fujian; Liangguang (Guangxi, Guangdong, parts of southern Jiangxi, Hunan, and eastern Yunnan); and Sichuan, Yunnan, and the Northwest (Gansu and Shaanxi).[12] Salt from each certificate territory could be sold only in certain sales territories (*yin'an*). Government checkpoints guarded against smuggling, which was defined as the sale of both untaxed salt and salt from outside a sales territory's designated production area.[13] Salt administration, however, was never uniform. Among and even within the producing areas the organization of salt administration could vary considerably, as we will see in the case of the Sichuan production area centered on Zigong.

Despite the introduction of the salt certificate system, for much of the period prior to the Ming dynasty (1368–1644), government benefited from the production of salt in Sichuan through the ownership of wells and control over shipment and sale of salt.[14] During the Ming, the administration of Sichuan salt remained fragmented and subject to a number of programs ranging from the exchange of salt for horses from the western border regions to the better-known *kaizhong* system, which first required merchants, wishing to sell salt, to ship grain to distant military outposts. There they received certificates allowing them to purchase salt at designated saltyards and sell salt within designated sales territories. The main goal of the state was to supply the military frontier at minimal cost.[15] While in keeping with the principles of state paternalism, the *kaizhong* system failed both consumers, by adding to the costs of salt, and merchants, by inserting an unwanted and burdensome transaction into the marketing of salt. Influenced by an increasingly commercialized economy the rulers of the Ming were finally forced to abandon *kaizhong* in the early seventeenth century.

Sichuan remained a relatively minor player in the overall Ming salt gabelle. The province ranked seventh among twelve salt administration regions in the mid-Ming, and total salt taxes generated in Sichuan were less than one-half of the average for the empire as a whole.[16] One reason for the low proportion of salt revenues collected in Sichuan was the difficulty encountered in monitoring the output of hundreds of small wells scattered over the provincial landscape.[17] Greatly reduced population and salt production further marginalized the Sichuan saltyards during the early years of the Qing dynasty (1644–1911). Between the onset of anti-Ming rebellion in the 1620s and the consolidation of Manchu power in the 1660s, as many as half of Sichuan's people are thought to have fled or died of famine, disease, or warfare.[18] At least as high a proportion of its salt wells were destroyed or fell into disuse before the imposition of the peace. Sichuan suffered again during the war against the Three Feudatories (1673–1681). Writing in the 1680s following an inspection tour of the Furong saltyard, Fushun magistrate Qian Shaokui wrote:

> In the region of Ziliujing the army comes and goes daily. The salt households that live there have all fled to Weiyuan and Rong counties, several tens of *li* away. Their beds have been turned to firewood, their rice has been exhausted, and their grain fed to the horses. It has been more than five months since the salt households ceased evaporating salt.[19]

Early Qing policy in Sichuan combined measures to rehabilitate the provincial economy and a gradual approach toward the reestablishment of long-standing forms of taxation. Efforts to restore previous levels of population and land cultivation included incentives for developers, subsidies for individual immigrants and land reclaimers, and tax holidays of six to ten years on newly registered farmland.[20] A similar approach was taken to encourage the rehabilitation of the salt industry. A modest tax was levied at the yard, either on wells, evaporation pans, or evaporation furnaces.[21] But in Sichuan and Shaanxi, no effort was made to reestablish the sale of salt by certificate. Instead, merchants with sufficient capital were allowed to purchase salt tax tickets or *piao*, which gave the bearers the right to buy and market 40 *jin*[22] of salt apiece. Small peddlers moving 40 *jin* or less were permitted to do so without a permit or tax.[23] In response to a 1667 request to resume certificate sales, the Board of Revenue reminded the memorialist that the purpose of the salt gabelle was not *only* to generate revenue. Citing the case of Jianwei, one of the most productive Sichuan saltyards during the Ming, the Board noted that for years only small merchants had marketed salt. Some borrowed the capital they needed; others pooled their capital. But they each shipped no more than several hundred *jin*, traveling overland to avoid the cost of renting a boat and paying the boatmen. Were a certificate system to be implemented now, the Board feared, not only would it be difficult to find merchants able to sell the large quantities licensed by certificate. It would have an adverse effect on permit sales as well. The memorialist's mistake was that he did not recognize that salt taxes needed to be designed in a manner suited to the time and the place, both facilitating commerce and satisfying the needs of the people.[24]

In 1686 the Board of Revenue in Beijing began to reissue certificates for Sichuan, allowing merchants the opportunity to ship salt in larger quantities. Certificates for salt shipped by river (*shuiyin*) entitled the bearer to carry 50 bundles (*bao*) per certificate. Certificates for salt shipped over land, by both human and animal labor, were for only four bundles apiece.[25] Nevertheless, during the early years of the Qing the state made no attempt to limit where Sichuan salt could be sold. It was not until the middle of the Yongzheng reign (1722–1735) that Sichuan's salt industry recovered sufficiently to warrant greater state manipulation of the market for tax purposes. In 1729 Sichuan Governor-General Huang Tinggui and Governor Xiande memorialized the emperor with a plan to reformulate the certificate system to accord with current conditions in Sichuan. Sales territories (*an*) were assigned to consume salt from specified Sichuan saltyards. The amount of salt to be sold in each territory was to be determined by the size of the local population—hence the name for this system, *jikou shouyan* or "calculate the population and confer the salt." In theory, the new salt tax administration would benefit the state's finances at the same time that state paternalism operated to ensure the markets of both salt producers and consumers.

Four main sales territories were authorized to purchase salt from Sichuan (see map 1): counties in Sichuan supplied by Sichuan salt sold by certificate (*bensheng ji'an*); counties in Sichuan supplied via land routes by peddlers holding tickets to sell Sichuan salt (*piao'an*); counties in Hubei supplied via the Yangzi by merchants holding certificates to sell Sichuan salt (*Hubei ji'an*); and counties in Yunnan and Guizhou designated to receive Sichuan salt sold by certificate (*bian'an*).[26] Counties in each category were to change over time,

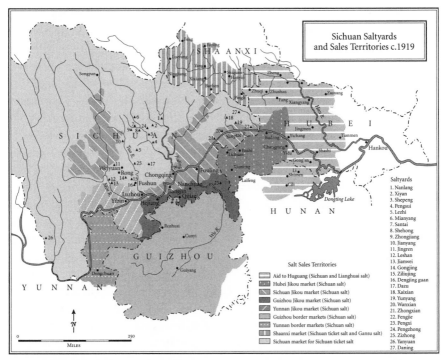

MAP 1. Sichuan Saltyards and Sales Territories c. 1919
Source: Adapted from Lin, *Essentials of Sichuan Salt,* front matter; map created by Christopher Brest.

but the basic outline of the salt sales territories remained the same until the end of the dynasty. Each saltyard was responsible for producing a quota of salt to be sold by certificate and excess production could be sold to small peddlers without tax by receipt of a ticket. In each case, merchants and peddlers continued to go directly to the saltyard to purchase salt. Government checkpoints were established along both land and river routes to prevent smuggling. At each checkpoint bundles were inspected and merchants were required to present their certificate or ticket as proof that their salt had been legally obtained and was being shipped to its designated market. The manufacture of salt remained entirely in private hands, and the market determined the price of salt both at the saltyard and at the final market destination.

Over time, the market for Sichuan salt and the administration charged with its taxation became more complex. At first no specialized agency dealt with salt. Salt matters in Sichuan were relegated to the office of the Sichuan Grain Intendant (*Duliang dao*). During the early Yongzheng period the Judicial Commissioner was put in charge of the administration of tea, salt, and the imperial post, but he was soon relieved of these duties by the appointment of a post and salt intendant (*yiyan dao*).[27] In 1778 he was replaced by a salt and tea intendant (*yancha dao*) with subordinate staff to manage the tea and salt treasury.[28] In addition, each prefecture and county containing a saltyard was assigned lower-level officials with salt responsibilities. And at the larger saltyards themselves assistant magistrates (*xiancheng*) and sub-county magistrates (*xunjian*) acted as intermediaries in the government management of salt affairs. Nevertheless, the task of preventing smuggling and continuously assessing and adjusting supply and demand proved to be too great for a small and generalist local bureaucracy already overburdened with responsibilities.[29]

The eighteenth century presented enormous challenges for government officials charged with the supervision of salt taxes in Sichuan. A decimated province at the start of the Qing, Sichuan became a major destination for internal migration as peace was restored. Immigration, combined with natural increase, contributed to an estimated fivefold growth in Sichuan's population between 1713 and 1813.[30] Aboriginal territories were brought under direct state control (*gaitu guiliu*), requiring changes in their administrative treatment, including integration into the salt gabelle. And dramatic improvements in technology and output at several salt-producing areas upset the distribution of markets among producers established by means of the original "calculate the population and confer the salt" quotas.

One of the most difficult tasks facing the Sichuan salt administration was tracking the rapid change in production taking place during the eighteenth century. Certificate quotas—the number of salt certificates carrying fixed amounts of salt from one yard to be sold in an assigned consumption territory—were regularly revised upward throughout the Yongzheng and Qianlong reigns.[31] Nevertheless, the *Gazetteer of Sichuan Salt Administration* (*Sichuan Yanfa zhi*) indicates an equally steady increase in above-quota production, particularly in the southern Sichuan saltyards of Furong and Jianwei.[32] As in the case of reclaimed land, it was in the interests of producers, who could evade tax, and local officials, who could avoid collecting an enlarged tax quota, to conceal increased output. Inasmuch as a well could turn out to be just "a flash in the pan," it was also in both their interests to wait a few years before registering new productive units.

Officials also kept increased production off the books in order to increase the tax revenues available in their own jurisdictions. During the Yongzheng reign a Fushun county magistrate devised a plan to augment his county coffers by issuing his own permits for the sale of salt produced by unregistered new wells. When Governor Xiande discovered the plan, the magistrate was impeached. But before long Xiande himself had devised a form of provincial ticket to incorporate the output of new wells into the provincial tax structure. These ad hoc *yandao yinpiao* were taxed at a rate higher than the statutory salt certificates, and, not surprisingly, had few comers. In the end the *yandao yinpiao* remained unclaimed by merchants and unregistered output continued to be sold outside the salt gabelle.[33]

Quota shifting, even in the early years of the "calculate the population and confer the salt" regime, was another sure sign that the salt gabelle could not adequately regulate supply and demand. Only four years after implementation of the new system of salt taxation, the Sichuan governor was complaining that some counties were not getting enough salt and that the certificate quotas of other yards could not be filled because merchants refused to buy their salt.[34] Inefficient saltyards, whose remote location, relatively low output, or high unit costs made it difficult to compete for salt sales with more efficient yards, petitioned to have their certificate quotas shifted to other saltyards, a practice known as *gaipei,* or reapportionment.[35] It was in this way that the Furong and Jianwei yards took over the entire certificate quotas of many northern Sichuan saltyards whose wells were no longer productive.[36] Jianwei, which experienced greater growth during the late eighteenth century, had taken over the quotas of smaller yards that served the border territories, increasing its certificate quota by more than 2,000 water-route certificates.[37]

At the same time, salt-recipient counties in remote and mountainous areas often found that merchants did not purchase sufficient certificates to serve their populations. Local officials, concerned that the people of their jurisdictions were forced to "eat bland food," petitioned the state to allow their counties to purchase salt outside the salt gabelle. The tax receipts that the state would have yielded by sale of certificates to serve these counties were then merged into the local land and head tax and paid by the counties' wealthier inhabitants. Counties receiving permission to consume salt—the tax on which was absorbed in this way—were known as *guiding* (merging the salt tax with the head tax) counties, 31 of which were recognized in 1850. Merchants supplying these areas saved the tax and were free to buy their salt on the open market, presumably enabling them to take advantage of the lower-cost surplus salt made available by more efficient yards.[38]

Merging the salt tax with the head tax and salt certificate reapportionment were admissions that the state salt-tax system could not undertake to guarantee all salt producers a market or all consumers a state-licensed salt provender. However, salt smuggling was the most dramatic evidence of the government's failure to adequately micromanage supply and demand for salt. It is impossible to determine the precise quantity of salt that slipped through the grip of the state salt administration. However, the fact that Sichuan's population increased as much as fivefold, while the land-route certificate quota, that portion of salt sold by certificate within Sichuan, grew by only about 170 percent,[39] indicates considerable seepage of surplus production into the untaxed market. The brief section on smuggling in the early Republic's salt handbook, *The Essentials of Sichuan Salt* (*Chuanyan jiyao*), begins with the words "smuggling is to salt as weeds are to seedlings, and blight is to bean plants."[40]

Smuggling was an inevitable but deadly phenomenon that had to be rooted out. But the problems facing Sichuan officials exceeded those supervising other saltyards. Although writing at the beginning of the twentieth century, the compiler of *The Essentials of Sichuan Salt* echoed the rumblings of a long line of predecessors when he noted that smuggling suppression in Sichuan was thwarted by the widely scattered locations of salt producers, the breadth of markets that ranged from the borderlands of Yunnan and Guizhou to the hills of Hubei and Hunan, the varieties of water and land transportation by which salt was shipped, and the difficulties facing a state that tried to keep track of it all. However, the problem went further than this. Almost every stage in the process of moving salt from producer to consumer held opportunities to evade the salt-tallying officials working for the state, and all opportunities were widely exploited. Salt evaporators produced their few extra *jin* without reporting them. Workers who bundled the salt for shipment sneaked in a few extra *jin* per certificate. Boatmen carried a few extra bundles per certificate. And the ever-present poor were always ready to carry away a few *jin* of salt from the yard or to buy a few smuggled *jin* from their fellows to avoid the added burden of tax.[41]

Indeed, if official reports are any indication, throughout the early Qing, official efforts to micromanage the salt market, assessing and distributing changing output to satisfy rapidly changing needs, resulted in chaos and encouraged corruption and evasion of the regulations of salt administration. In short, despite the expansion of the complement of officials and functionaries in charge of Sichuan's salt administration, state control over how much salt was produced, how much was sold, and to which markets was never complete. One could argue that market forces won out despite state efforts to maximize tax revenue and protect inefficient producers. It was in the context of this officially regulated but significantly unregulated market that the saltyards in Fushun and Rong counties fulfilled the promise of technological advance and succeeded in dominating the market for salt in the southwest and parts of central China.

Placing the Furong Saltyard

Present-day Zigong, home of the saltyards of Fushun County (aka Ziliujing) and Rong County (aka Gongjing), is a city built on salt. This is literally so. The city itself sits on the edge of what was once a vast inland sea. Changes in climate and the rise of the Sichuan basin led to the gradual recession of the sea, leaving behind much saline material in the form of brine and saline rock, as well as natural gas. According to Chinese geologists, at today's level of technology there is still enough saline material beneath Zigong to continue to mine for salt for another 2,000 years.[42]

The earliest recorded evidence of salt production in this area appears to have been in the sixth century C.E., although salt production elsewhere in the province was recorded as early as the third century B.C.E.[43] During the subsequent centuries the territory was known by various names and placed under a number of jurisdictions. However, it is likely that until the first decades of the Yuan dynasty (1271–1368), the yards known today as Ziliujing and Gongjing were treated as one salt production area and were governed by the precursors of Rong County. During the Yuan dynasty Ziliujing was made part of Fushun County, although the two yards were only ten *li* apart. During the early Qing the two saltyards were governed together, this time under the jurisdiction of Fushun County, until they were once again divided between Fushun and Rong counties in 1730 (see map 2).[44] This separation persisted for almost 200 years, perpetuated at least in part by the state's desire to maintain a disjunction between the boundaries of political and economic spheres in order to dilute the political power of economic elites.[45] During the Qing dynasty community and economic activities increasingly crossed the divide between the two saltyards, despite their separate administration. As we shall see, such was the sense of common purpose among the elites of both yards that the first Chamber of Commerce established at the saltyards was a unified organization taking its name from the first characters of the names of the two yards. The name Zigong was used again by the local elite in establishing local government institutions following the fall of the Qing dynasty. While this attempt at merchant self-rule was soon squashed, the idea of a unified city of Zigong lived on, finding legal expression at last in the incorporation of Zigong municipality in 1939.

During the late imperial period many of China's great fortunes were made in the business of salt. For centuries, leading merchants in the economic heartland had generated large profits from privileged access to the sale of salt by certificate. But while their history is vital to an understanding of late imperial merchant culture, they remained rooted in a world in which

MAP 2. Qongjing, Zilusjing, and Nearby Cities
Source: GIS work by Douglas Smith.

economic power was derivative of hereditary privilege and political ties. As much as the flat, well-watered geography of coastal China, the politics of the certificate system formed the basis for most salt merchant success in the early Qing. The merchants of Zigong prospered in a wholly different environment. From the first, geography was a handicap, located as they were in the remote, hilly western reaches of the empire. More importantly, the merchants of Zigong were manufacturers first and only later profited from the shipment and wholesale marketing of their own branded product.

Until the mid-eighteenth century neither the men who made Sichuan salt nor the men who sold it were particularly well off. The certificate system implemented in Sichuan in the late seventeenth century was not a continuation of the salt tax administration in place under the Ming. With the establishment of salt sale by certificate, native Sichuanese were recruited anew to purchase certificates and market salt. These natives, variously known as *zuoshang, benshang,* or *yinshang* (merchants in situ, native merchants, or certificate merchants), were generally from families of modest means, as were most Sichuanese in the aftermath of the wars of the Ming-Qing transition, and many purchased small numbers of certificates or undertook their purchase jointly with others (*pengling,* lit. acquisition among friends). Some of these new native Sichuanese certificate merchants, whether for lack of business acumen or lack of capital, leased their certificates to others, most notably to wealthy merchants from Shaanxi who in local parlance became differentiated from the natives as *hangshang*, a term connoting merchants engaged in commerce.[46]

The early years of the Qing Sichuan certificate system did not provide easy opportunities for profit. Sichuan officials complained that the inability to predict supply and frequent fluctuations in salt prices at the yards encouraged certificate leaseholders to press for maximum advantage when marketing salt. The resulting high consumer prices for salt were an additional factor compelling some counties to request that their supply networks be decoupled from the salt gabelle.[47] For merchants operating in northern Sichuan, with its rougher terrain and few navigable waterways, transportation costs were a major disincentive to long-distance trade. Shrinking sources of brine and fuel diminished the importance of northern yards like Shehong and Pengxi.[48] Most northern saltyards that survived into the late nineteenth century served only their own counties.[49] Southern yards had an advantage in the ready availability of water transport, and it is no surprise that the preponderance of water-route certificates were marketed from there. The shift to reliance on southern producers to fill Sichuan's domestic and export quotas was one factor in the rise of the Zigong merchant elite. Nevertheless, transportation, even for these growing southern yards, continued to be a major expense. Certificate taxes in Sichuan were kept low in comparison to those of eastern Chinese salt regions in order to offset the high costs of shipping.[50]

The Fuxi River (also known as the Yanjing or Salt-Well River), a shallow, winding watercourse on which only small sculls could navigate, carried salt from Zigong to Dengjing guan. At Dengjing guan salt was transferred to larger boats headed for Luzhou, the center of the southern Sichuan salt administration. From Luzhou salt was shipped south to Yunnan and Guizhou or was transferred to even larger boats for the trip to Chongqing. Once at Chongqing, salt was carried down the Yangzi to western border counties of Hunan and Hubei.[51] The difficulties entailed in shipping salt began at the Fuxi River, which could be crossed on foot during low water and often flooded when the water was high. In order to maintain a steady flow of goods all year round, weirs were built to raise the water level, with a specialist office of weir maintenance supported by user fees. A *zai* of salt, the standard shipping unit, weighed an average of 75 to 78 tons, less in the twentieth century. Each *zai* had to be loaded on five separate boats at Ziliujing, reloaded onto three boats at Luzhou, and reloaded again at Chongqing, each leg of the trip sustaining costs in time and money to hire packers, coolies, boats, and boatmen.[52] Goods imported to supply the saltyards and

salt workers, work animals, and supporting industries incurred high transportation costs as well, traveling inland by mule or on the backs of transport
laborers or via the narrow rivers that fed into the Tuo River.[53]

Just as the Qing state did little to interfere in the market, it did little to
further it. Zigong was too far from the centers of government to attract
much in the way of state-funded infrastructure investment. Indeed, it was
not until the War of Resistance Against Japan (1937–1945) that the main
roads linking Ziliujing and Gongjing, and Ziliujing and Luzhou, were up-
graded from dirt tracks to highways of mud and crushed stone, surfaced
with coal cinders.[54] Industrial progress in Zigong was spurred by access to
expanded markets, but breakthroughs in transportation played no role in
this process.

The Technology of Salt Production
at the Early Qing Furong Saltyard

The technology of salt production, as well as its system of taxation, distinguished Sichuan from other salt regions in China. China derived its salt
from six sources: seawater, salt lakes, gypsum mines, salt-saturated earth,
brine wells, and saline rock. Only Sichuan, Yunnan, and Gansu produced
well salt and only Sichuan and Yunnan produced salt from saline rock, an
innovation of the late nineteenth century that we will turn to in chapter 8.
During the early Qing the production of the Furong yard increased dramatically after the yard's rehabilitation following the warfare of the seventeenth
century, and later by means of improved deep drilling technology and the
development of methods to maintain the working life of wells. Deep drilling
increased the salinity and volume of brine raised. In addition, a major by-
product was the expansion of natural gas output, which resulted in dramatic
savings in fuel costs for brine evaporation. It was by means of investment in
deep drilling that the Furong saltyards in Ziliujing and Gongjing were able
to take advantage of the market opportunities that presented themselves in
the nineteenth century.

Drilling the Well

The first step in the process of salt production was to drill a well. Not unlike the myths that surround successful oilmen in the American West,
stories abound of entrepreneurs who had the instinct, who knew where to
drill. Yan Changying, one of the founders of the wealthy Furong merchant
lineage that created the Yan Guixin trust, based his fortune on his ability to

scope out good drilling sites. A grave inscription honoring Yan notes that initially he had no connection to the salt industry. He lived in the city and was impressed by the proliferation of salt wells in the surrounding country-side. Taking note of which ones struck brine and which did not, he decided to take a chance at drilling in the hills with his brother.

> If a piece of land was narrow and low lying, people would abandon it. When people saw him drilling wells there they all said he had made a bad move. After several years, when his wells had not reached a brine spring, but had hit solid stone, everyone urged him to change his strategy. [Yan] still smiled and said nothing. He drilled a few more years; the stone split and the brine came gurgling out.[55]

Not surprisingly, the success of one well often led to drilling on nearby land, with the result that certain areas of Ziliujing and Gongjing came to be known for their concentrations of wells of specific types and depth.

Once a site was selected and acquired, skilled laborers known as *shan-jiang*, who often also helped choose the site, undertook the task of constructing the well. The openings of early Qing wells were small, averaging 3 inches in diameter.[56] Before drilling began, steps were taken to shore up loose earth and prevent seepage of fresh water into the well. After breaking ground, "stone rings shaped like mortars but open at the bottom are prepared. For the first hundred feet or so, these rings are fitted into the well one above the other. Below this level and for some 320 more feet, wooden rings with hollow centers, and shaped like cylinders are fitted one above the other."[57] This sixteenth-century addition to borehole well design was one factor facilitating the construction of deeper wells during the Qing period (see illustration 1.1).

Following the laying out of the borehole a platform was erected on which a lever was built. The iron drill itself was suspended over the well hole from a cable attached to the lever. As many as ten men took turns stepping on and off the lever causing the heavy drill to fall, breaking through the rock below. Another worker guided the drill cable so that as the drill fell it created a cavity that was both round and straight. [58]

Well drilling was a labor-intensive process that could take many years to complete. According to Li Rong, writing in the late nineteenth century, depending on the condition of soil and rock a team could drill as little as an inch or as much as a foot a day.[59] At this rate wells that struck brine could take between five and ten years to produce sufficient brine to begin pumping, a condition locally known as *jiangong* (literally, seeing results). *Jiangong* was followed by sacrifices to the god of the soil and a shrine was

ILLUSTRATION 1.1. Opening the Borehole
Source: Ding, *Gazetter of Sichuan Salt Administration*, juan 2, jingchang 2, 5b–6a.

built in his honor. According to former Zigong well workers, if the well was really productive, the god of the soil was given a wife and even a number of concubines.[60]

The mere production of brine was not a signal of real success. *Jiangong* should perhaps best be seen as indicating that the drilling had struck brine. Because the depth of the well was directly correlated to the salinity of brine, even wells that struck brine were drilled to greater depths. Brine that could be pumped from depths of 2,000 to 2,300 feet was called yellow brine and had an average salinity of 13 percent by weight. Less than this was not considered worth utilizing for salt production. In the 1830s Gongjing producers began exploiting black brine, found at depths of almost 3,000 feet, which had an average salinity of 18 percent.[61] The late-nineteenth-century discovery of saline rock and the introduction of solution mining will be discussed in chapter 8.

Several improvements in well drilling technology were necessary before the widespread development of black-brine wells became possible. In addition to improvements in the strength and variety of drill bits and the use of a stone lining at the entrance to the well, skilled well artisans became adept at lining the upper reaches of the well with joined wooden cylinders constructed from hollowed-out logs of pine or cypress. In order to hoist the drill to sufficient height, these deeper wells necessitated the erection of a derrick housing a rigging of wheels and pulleys that allowed the drill to be raised once it had crashed into the rock deep within the excavated well.[62] Working at great depths and within very narrow openings, the workers and artisans who built wells also developed ingenious tools for the retrieval of rubble and lost tools and for the repair of damaged well linings.

The development of black-brine wells, which produced more concentrated brine and a greater volume of brine than yellow-brine wells, greatly increased the efficiency of the salt-production process. Statistics for the 1930s indicate that the average output of black-brine wells in Gongjing, where black-brine sources were most abundant, was between 800 and 900 *dan*[63] per month for the least productive well and 10,000 *dan* for the most productive. This is in contrast to a productivity range of 800 to 6,000 *dan* a month for the more diluted yellow brine.[64] Some black-brine wells, such as the Shuangfu jing, produced as many as 1,000 *dan* a day when they first came in.

Pumping Brine

In its simplest form, the pumping process involved the raising and lowering of a tube into the well by means of a system of pulleys and wheels. Special bamboo, imported from eastern Sichuan, was used to construct the tubes employed in the pumping process. Several lengths of bamboo were usually joined to form one tube, near the bottom of which was attached a one-way leather valve. When the tube was dropped into the well, the valve was pushed up by the pressure of the brine and brine filled the tube. Pump workers, operating from the cables attached to the tube, shook the tube in a vertical direction to hasten this process. When the tube was full it was lifted out of the well, the force of the brine pressing down on the leather valve, preventing the brine from leaking back out. The tube was then held over a large vat. Using a hook on the end of another bamboo, a worker then opened the valve and allowed the brine to spill into the vat.[65]

Most of the rigging that made up the well factory was dedicated to pumping the well. The tube through which brine was raised was attached to a cable made of slatted bamboo, hoisted on a bamboo derrick known as a *tianche*. The height of the derrick corresponded to the depth of the well, so that as deeper wells were developed the sight of derricks upward of 60 feet and more became typical of the skyline of many areas of the Furong yard. The cable passed through a wheel at the top of the derrick called the *tiangunzi* and then passed through a second wheel on the ground called the *digunzi*. Guided over the ground by a roller, the cable was attached to the wheel, or *diche*.[66] As the wheel was turned, usually by a team of water buffalo, the cable passed through this pulley system and raised the tube from the well. Once the tube was emptied of brine, a brake on the cable was released and the tube was allowed once again to plunge into the well (see illustration 1.2). According to Wallace Crawford, a scientist who visited Ziliujing in the 1920s, the entire process of lowering and raising the tube could be accomplished within 25 minutes.[67]

Improvements in the process of pumping brine from the well responded to the greater depth and productivity of Furong's black-brine wells. Many of these were designed to increase the pulling force of the pumping machine. Wheels were increased in circumference and the use of buffalo, in place of men, to turn the wheel became standard. Some deep wells kept two teams of buffalo pumping in alternate shifts. At the same time, derricks were built higher, the capacity of the brine tubes increased, and various techniques were used to strengthen well equipment.[68]

Gas Wells

Natural resources have no inherent value without the technology that makes feasible their profitable exploitation. Although the existence of subterranean gas deposits in Sichuan had been known since ancient times,

ILLUSTRATION 1.2. Turning the Wheel and Raising the Brine
Source: Ding, *Gazetteer of Sichuan Salt Administration,* juan 2, jingchang 2, 20b–21a.

their value remained locked beneath the ground without the means to transport gas. We have some evidence of the modest use of gas in salt boiling from the Song period on. However, gas evaporation technology did not have a significant impact on the structure of salt production, marketing, or investment in the province until the nineteenth century.[69] According to the Fushun County gazetteer, in the mid-eighteenth century the county had eleven gas-producing wells.[70] The local name for such gas, turf fire (*caopi huo*), indicates that it was seen more as a nuisance than as a source of fuel.

Prior to the nineteenth century, most brine in Furong was boiled using firewood, charcoal, or coal mined in Rong County and in the neighboring county of Weiyuan.[71] These same resources provided most of the fuel used in cooking and heating. The breach of rock layers at almost 3,000 feet produced not only black brine, but also an unexpectedly vast reserve of natural gas, particularly in the limestone beneath Ziliujing.[72] With greatly increased quantities of brine to refine and the solution of the less technically difficult problem of moving brine to the gas, well and furnace owners were suddenly able to achieve efficiencies only dreamed of in the past.

Gas wells produced pure gas or a combination of gas and brine. In either case the first step was to secure the gas and direct it to the evaporating pans.

> As soon as gas emerges from a well, a wood basin is placed upside down on top to hold it in. The basin is 10 feet high, 10 feet in diameter and 30 feet in circumference. The lower part [of the basin] is wide, but it becomes narrower towards the top so that the gas is controlled. Bamboo pipes are installed along the sides of the basin to carry the gas to the evaporating furnaces.* In the center of the bottom of the basin, there is also a hole 3 inches in diameter. This hole, the opening for the well, is lined with a stone ring and banked with earth. If there is also brine in the well, it can be bucketed out as usual.[73]

Once the well was capped, the gas was ignited and allowed to burn until it was exhausted (see illustration 1.3).

The gas output of wells varied, as did the productivity of individual wells over time. The earliest method of calculating the output of wells measured the number of pans that could be boiled by channeling the gas from a particular well to one or more furnaces. The unit of gas was then recorded as so many fireballs (*huoquan*). The measure word for fireballs was *kou* and saltyard contracts referred to the number of *kou* involved in a transaction. Beginning in the twentieth century, efforts were made to refine this mea-

---

*Fang translates the original *zao* as "ovens," but I prefer the term "furnaces" to refer to the often large complexes housing the pans in which brine was evaporated to produce salt.

ILLUSTRATION 1.3. The Gas Well and Gas Furnace
Note the gas well opening covered by a wooden tub at bottom center, from which six pipes
lead to the evaporation furnace and its lines of salt pans.
Source: Ding, *Gazetter of Sichuan Salt Administration*, juan 2, jingchange 2, 39b–40a.

sure by specifying the strength of the gas by indicating how much salt a *kou*
of gas could produce.[74]

The building that housed the salt pans, and to which the burning gas
was channeled, was the furnace (*zao*). Together with the business office
or countinghouse (*guifang*), the furnace and the derrick complex formed
the complete operational structures or *langchang* of a well enterprise. As
we shall see, more productive wells became complex businesses, which not
only produced brine and/or gas, but also often leased part of their output to
furnaces established by partnerships, which may themselves have also had
shares in the output of other wells. Large or small, the basic workings of the
furnaces were the same. As noted by Crawford, even in the 1920s Furong
salt producers had not contrived to pump gas to the furnaces but relied on
the lighter-than-air burning gas to rise. Furnaces were located uphill from
the source well and pans were located, one higher than the one before, in
two lines on either side of a gas intake tunnel.[75]

Gas evaporation of salt pans was a continuous process, the fires burning
24 hours a day. The product of gas furnaces was a pure white granular substance known as *hua* salt. Its manufacture required considerable expertise
on the part of *hua* salt evaporators, who were the elite of the saltyard labor

force. One of the skills of the evaporator was the ability to judge when to undertake the various steps in the refining process. At a certain point in the initial boiling phase the intensity of the heat was lowered and the state of evaporation was assessed. If the addition of a bit more brine caused the early-forming salt granules to dissolve, the brine was boiled some more. This process of boiling and adding more brine was repeated several times until the granules no longer dissolved. At this point bean-curd juice (*douzhi*), formed by soaking and then pressing soybeans, was added to the brine to clarify it. After additional boiling the impurities in the brine began to rise to the surface and were ladled out. This was repeated several times, after which the brine was judged to be relatively clean and two ladles of the bean refuse were removed, taking care not to remove too much lest the salt be too fine. The sample was then boiled until it turned into salt. This granulated product acted as a kind of catalyst to the crystallization process. Adding bean-curd juice and continuing the boiling process removed its impurities. Once it was clean, the heat was lowered to a simmer and eventually the salt began to appear on the surface like tiny snowflakes. When the brine in the main pan was dense and clean, additional catalyst was ladled in, and the remaining mixture in the pan began to produce the granulated salt from which *hua* salt got its name. One pan could produce 100 or more *jin* or about 133.3 pounds of salt. If the gas from the well firing the pan was strong, it could evaporate two pans in 24 hours. If the gas was weak, it could take two or three days and nights to produce one pan of salt.[76]

Coal evaporation of salt was far less efficient than gas evaporation and produced a different type of salt directed at a different market. Coal-evaporated, or *ba,* salt was so named because of its resemblance to the crust left on the pan when rice was overcooked. It was far less pure than *hua* salt, being boiled in closed sheds in which the smoke emitted by the coal fires mixed with the salt as it congealed. There are no records of *ba* salt undergoing the kind of purification process described above for *hua* salt. And the final product, rather than being granulated salt that was packed into bundles, was a large cake that Crawford describes as being black with "soot and dirt and debris."[77] While most *hua* salt was sold within Sichuan and in the Huguang market, *ba* salt was particularly popular in the border markets (*bian'an*) to the south of Sichuan where salt was scarce and households would buy a piece of the salt cake, bind it with string, and dip it in soup for flavor.[78]

The Rise of the Furong Saltyard

Until the mid-eighteenth century Ziliujing and Gongjing were home to two southern Sichuan yards among several serving a limited market consisting of parts of their own depopulated home province and small sections of Yunnan, Guizhou, and Hubei. In overall production they did not match the output of northern yards like Shehong and Pengxi and, with Leshan and Jingyan, fell far behind their southern rival, Jianwei.[79]

By the middle of the nineteenth century several factors had changed the conditions under which Ziliujing and Gongjing salt producers operated. A growing Sichuan population, the expansion of the border market and the drying up of wells at other yards, particularly in the north of the province, stimulated well drilling in Fushun and Rongxian. Not only did Sichuan itself achieve a fivefold increase in population during the eighteenth century. Yunnan, which produced some salt, also had increasing difficulty meeting provincial demand. Early in the dynasty two Yunnan prefectures near Sichuan, Zhaotong and Zhenxiong, were assigned to "eat Sichuan salt." By 1738 several more areas of Yunnan were given Sichuan quotas, including Dongchuan and the border counties of Nanning, Zhanyi, and Pingyi. Jianwei and Furong supplied almost all of the Yunnan border salt.[80] Guizhou produced no salt of its own. While it relied largely on Huai salt from eastern China during the Ming,[81] by the mid-Qing it was being supplied almost entirely by Sichuan. Initially high transportation costs made it difficult for Guizhou consumers to buy Sichuan salt. However, the greater proximity of Guizhou to Fushun and Rongxian and their access to both existing and restored avenues of water transportation encouraged a shift to Furong as the source of new salt supplies.[82] At the same time, *gaipei*, which allowed one saltyard to take over the markets of another, was a boon for Furong. By the 1870s Furong was responsible for more than 1,300 water-route certificates or approximately 6.5 million *jin* originally supplied by Santai, Shehong, Pengxi, Zhongjiang, Yanting, Jianwei, and Xingwen counties.

Guizhou officials requesting new shipments of salt from Furong spoke of the new wells being drilled in Furong.[83] Furong's official complement of wells rose from 298 wells and 755 pans during the 1720s to 405 wells and 1,055 pans in the late nineteenth century.[84] However, these numbers have little meaning as a measure of industrial expansion. Private contracts and other nonofficial materials indicate considerable turnover in wells during these 150 years; less productive or dried-up wells were falling into disuse while new ones were being drilled. Moreover, as we have noted, new wells drilled from the early nineteenth century on were far deeper and more productive than wells recorded in the early Qing. While Jianwei continued to rival Furong in overall salt production and had many more wells, output per well was almost twice as high in late-nineteenth-century Ziliujing and Gongjing.[85] Productivity may have been even higher than official figures indicate, inasmuch as they do not include any of the Furong salt smuggled into Huguang or taxed by methods other than the certificate system.[86]

In addition, during the process of deep drilling Furong producers not only stumbled on more saline black brine. The discovery of rich natural gas deposits at Ziliujing also released that yard from its reliance on imported coal and created a symbiotic relationship between the two Furong yards, Gongjing supplying black brine and Ziliujing dominating evaporation at its gas-fired furnaces. This combination created efficiencies that allowed Furong's superior-tasting *hua* salt to infiltrate the controlled markets of other Sichuanese salt-producing counties while Ziliujing and Gongjing *ba* salt came to dominate the salt market in Yunnan and Guizhou. When the outbreak of the Taiping Rebellion severed trade routes between eastern China and the central provinces of Hunan and Hubei, previously served largely by Huai sea salt, Furong producers were poised to move in and capture that market as well.

Thus, both technology and politics conspired to create the conditions for industrial expansion in Furong. The potential for large profits clearly accounts for the willingness of Furong entrepreneurs to invest. However, investors, particularly in the early years of well expansion, operated in an environment of limited household wealth relative to the capital requirements of the burgeoning salt industry. The story of Furong's initial rise is therefore one of organizational as well as technical innovation designed to spread risk, combine resources, protect assets, and take advantage of market opportunities and economies of scale. It is also the story of business institution-building within the context of China's late imperial political and legal regimes. For this reason, the triumphs and travails of the merchants of Zigong have much to tell us about the economic history of early modern China and its place in a comparative history of early modern business communities.

2

The Structure of Investment in Late Qing Furong

THE SIMULTANEOUS development of new technologies allowing the excavation of highly productive black-brine wells, the discovery of large deposits of natural gas at the Ziliujing yard, and the sudden expansion of Sichuan salt markets into Huguang during the early years of the Taiping Rebellion formed the background for a rapid "takeoff" in the well-salt industry in Furong. Salt output, based on taxable salt certificates filled by Sichuan as a whole, rose from an estimated 112 million pounds in 1850 to almost 390 million pounds a year during the late Guangxu reign (1871–1908).[1] When smuggled salt and salt sold by permit are added to the mix, estimates of Sichuan's total salt in the 1890s rise to almost twice that amount.[2] At the same time, the early-nineteenth-century trend toward concentration of salt capital and market shares in the southwest became an irreversible fact that even the equalizing influence of the salt gabelle could not control. By the end of the nineteenth century more than half of Sichuan's total output came from the twin saltyards in Fushun and Rong counties.[3]

How did the merchants of Ziliujing and Gongjing achieve this rapid expansion of output and market share? The potential rewards of deep drilling were great but they were achieved at a high price and with considerable attendant risk. A typical deep well in the mid-nineteenth century could cost upward of 10,000 taels; many cost several times that amount.[4] Unlike traditional enterprises, deep-well drilling did not produce immediate returns. According to Li Rong, and confirmed in dozens of well-drilling contracts, a well could take "four or five years to some ten years to [come in]. There have been cases where it has taken tens of years and passed through several changes of ownership."[5] After much investment and many years it was not uncommon for a well to be abandoned for failure to produce sufficient brine at depths of as much as 3,000 feet. Millions of taels were lost in creating empty, deep, narrow holes, and even successful wells could fall victim to hazards such as leakage, collapse, and blockage from fallen tools and debris.

Few Sichuanese households had the resources to undertake independent well exploration.* Sichuan in the early years of the Qing was a poor backwater dependent on sojourning merchants and immigrants for the importation of technical skills and capital "lost" by the native populations who survived the decades of warfare and occupation of the late Ming and early Qing.[6] During the years of recovery, which in Sichuan lasted until at least the mid-Qianlong reign (1736–1795), only two groups could be said to control large financial resources in the province: grain merchants operating out of the emerging port of Chongqing and salt wholesalers who worked within the strictures of the government salt monopoly.[7] Merchants from Shaanxi played a particularly important role in the salt market, often buying or leasing the certificates originally granted to Sichuan natives, who in the early Qing lacked the resources or experience to engage in long-distance trade.[8]

By 1752 Shaanxi merchants as a group were sufficiently prosperous to begin construction of a guildhall (*Xiqin huiguan*) in Ziliujing at the cost of more than 100,000 taels,[9] and by the early nineteenth century Shaanxi wholesale firms were among the main suppliers of goods in Ziliujing's commercial center.[10] Merchants from Shanxi, Guangdong, Jiangxi, and Fujian soon joined Shaanxi merchants in the long-distance trade in Sichuan but do not appear to have been able to break into the market in salt. Among them, only the Shanxi merchants accumulated notable wealth, and this only in the nineteenth century when they became involved in the banking and remittance business. While extraprovincial capital would play some role in the development of the Furong saltyard, most of the profits of long-distance merchants were repatriated or reinvested in commercial ventures. At least until the early nineteenth century these profits would not be a source of investment in Furong's productive capacity.[11]

If large private fortunes were not the source of Zigong capital accumulation, what role did institutional lenders play? A dearth of long-term bank

---

*The reader should keep in mind that property in China was vested in the household (*jia*) and not the individual. This legal condition prevailed until 1929 and, as was the practice of many Chinese, continued far into the twentieth century. When we speak here of individual investors we are referring to individual households unless otherwise indicated. The implications of this legal condition for investment will be discussed in chapters 8 and 9.

finance has often been cited as a factor in China's slow industrial growth.[12] However, scholarship on early modern Europe and the United States suggests that few early industrialists relied on banks to provide their initial fixed capital. Indeed, even where banking was more developed than in China, it was often bank policy to require the entrepreneur to assume the risk of fixed capital investment, providing instead short-term loans for working capital.[13] Zigong's financial sector followed this familiar pattern.

A number of institutional lenders existed in Sichuan by the eighteenth century in the form of pawnshops and native banks (*qianzhuang*). Individual moneylenders and pawnshops were the mainstay of household credit. Native banks, specializing in money exchange and short-term mercantile credit, were few in number, and well into the twentieth century these local financial institutions were poorly capitalized and sometimes operated as sole proprietorships.[14] Until the late nineteenth century the most important function of native banks was the exchange of copper coins for silver received in payment for salt and the clearing of local inter-firm accounts. During the second half of the nineteenth century Sichuan became home to a new form of financial institution. Often called Shanxi banks in recognition of the provenance of their founders, these remittance banks (*piaohao*) engaged largely in the movement of funds between urban centers. Remittance banks were initially established only in larger towns and cities. The first remittance bank in Ziliujing was not opened until 1879.[15] Neither native banks and remittance banks nor their predecessors, private moneylenders and pawnshops, provided long-term credit at low rates of interest. Although each contributed to the day-to-day operations of the salt industry, they played no part in the creation of the saltyard's physical plant.

Despite the absence of concentrated private wealth and industrial banking, investment in the productive capacity of the Furong saltyard was robust, driven by the potential for profit and for market expansion. Entrepreneurs in Ziliujing and Gongjing in the eighteenth century found the means to hire labor, acquire drilling rights, buy equipment, and wait out the long period between breaking ground and hitting pay dirt. Rather than stagnation, the Furong salt industry experienced growth and technological improvement. In the early years of saltyard development, before success produced its own fortunes, institutional mechanisms became a substitute for financial means, allowing for the combination of resources and dispersion of risk among numerous households of modest wealth and providing the industry itself with considerable flexibility to meet changing market conditions.

Well-Drilling Contracts in the Early Qing

Drilling a well was an exercise in the combination of land, capital, and labor. At many Sichuan saltyards simple shallow wells were drilled by landowners on their own property and remained a by-employment of agriculture.[16] At the technologically more advanced yards well drilling had long since ceased to be a cottage industry. As we saw in chapter 1, the excavation of borehole wells required a considerable measure of expertise, both in the placement of the well and in its construction. In their advanced form, Furong salt-yard wells became components of complex business partnerships bringing together the capital of both kin and non-kin, locals and outsiders, the management of which displayed many of the characteristics of modern industrial firms. The mechanism by which technical expertise, capital, and land were combined in the form of these complex business partnerships requires some elaboration, particularly as their evolution took place without the benefit of formalization under Qing law.

The template for the Qing agreement and the basis for its claim to recognition under law were found in the simple land contract. The use of formal contracts to divide household property, establish the marital relationship, and transfer rights to land had a long history in China. During the Qing, land contracts were recognized as the most potent form of evidence in a land dispute, by extension giving legal recognition to the written contract as a tool of property creation.[17]

In the early years of well development, entrepreneurs obtained land on which to drill wells by means of rental contracts, which shared their form and much of their language with the agricultural land lease. Reliance on leasehold was not, however, a response to ideological or legal constraints against the alienation of land. At the same time, Fushun and Rong counties had lively markets in land. Rather, the well-site lease allowed landowners without funds to combine resources with investors without rights to land in mining areas. If drilling was successful, the landowner was able to develop his property and receive a share of well output. From the point of view of the tenant/investor, rental allowed exploration of a piece of land for a minimal initial outlay, an important factor in a capital-poor environment. Moreover, during the early years of saltyard expansion, it allowed developers to acquire piecemeal the additional land needed for furnace construction, placement of a countinghouse, pipes, ponds, and storage vats, as need arose and as production provided the necessary cash. As we shall see, during the early years of well-site rental, the balance of power lay with the landowners whose good fortune had situated them on rich brine deposits.

As productivity advanced and the markets for Sichuan salt expanded, that balance shifted, and the relationship between landowner and tenant at the most developed saltyard, Furong, ceased to resemble one of tenancy at all.

Simple Tenancy on Well and Mine Lands

The earliest surviving Furong well-site rental agreements date from the Qianlong reign and already represent a sophisticated approach to factor exchange. However, mine-site leases from Sichuan's Baxian coalfields, as well as well-site leases from salt-producing areas with lower capital requirements, may provide a glimpse of the earliest stages of capital investment in extractive industry. In both cases, the derivation of the mine-site lease from a long tradition of land rental in the agricultural sector is clear.[18] As in the case of arable land in commercialized areas, leases tended to be for fixed rents. Both rents in kind and in cash were common, and in most cases a rent deposit was demanded of the tenant. For example, in 1905 Lei Hengtai rented land in Leshan County from Fan Changshou on which to drill a well. Fan received a rent deposit of five strings[19] of copper cash and a monthly rent of one *jin* of salt. The period of tenancy was fixed at 20 years.[20] Often contracts that on the surface appeared to be deeds of sale were in fact rental contracts as well. In 1915, a Jianwei landowner named Yuan Shufang agreed to sell (*chumai*) a piece of land on which Yuan Lianjiu planned to drill a well and establish a furnace. Separate terms were established for each, a deposit of 500 taels being taken for the well site, with an annual rent of 1.5 bundles (*bao*) of salt, and a deposit of 100 taels for the furnace site, with a rent of four bundles of salt a year.[21] Examples of fixed rents in cash can also be found, as evidenced by a rare surviving contract for the Jingren yard.[22]

A similar tendency can be found in the case of land rented for the excavation of coal mines in Baxian. Here the data indicate a stronger move in the direction of cash rents, prompted by the remote location of most coal mines and the difficulties encountered in the transport and sale of their product.[23] Of 43 coal mines documented in county litigation records for the late eighteenth and early nineteenth centuries, all but nine involved outside investors who leased the land on which they had opened the mine. Of these, more than half paid the landowner a fixed rent in the form of cash or coal.[24] And, like renters of land in Sichuan, most paid a rent deposit in cash, which was refundable upon breach of the contract or when the contract came to term.[25] In the case of salt, ease of sale and the location of many well sites near river transportation, particularly in southern Sichuan, probably encouraged many landowners to continue to collect rents in kind. This trend was given a further boost by the extreme inflationary pressures of the 1940s. Indeed, as late as 1947 wells could still be found in Sichuan on which rent was paid as a fixed sum in kind.[26] The Nationalist government's own policy of collecting land taxes in kind during this period undoubtedly contributed to this trend.[27]

While the form of rent payment and the existence of rent deposits underlined the close links between agricultural tenancy and tenancy on land used for extractive industry, several developments in the nineteenth century demonstrate the movement away from these earlier rural roots. First, a separation developed between the mine or well and the land itself. This distinction paralleled to some extent the development of topsoil and subsoil rights in agricultural tenancy, but had an added significance in the case of salt and coal. Separation of the mine or well from the land played an important part in the development of security of tenure in the extractive industries and encouraged the large investment in fixed capital that opening a mine or well entailed. By the nineteenth century many contracts stipulated that the tenant would not begin paying rent until production began and the well or mine was proved a success.[28] Coal mine contracts of the same period also stipulated that the tenancy extend until the contents of the mine were used up.[29] Likewise, well-site leases often contained phrases such as that in the contract signed by Zeng Guangcheng, providing that the lease would extend until "the well was old and the brine dried up" (*jinglao shuigu*).[30] Thus, the land only reverted back to the landowner when its usefulness as a well or mine had ceased. On the other hand, if production stopped for whatever reason, the landowner could recover the property and find others to work it or restore it to agricultural use.

At the same time, the owner of the land on which a mine stood gradually lost both the responsibilities and powers that rural landowners traditionally retained with agricultural land. In the case of coal-mining land, this may have grown out of the landowner's desire to avoid criminal liability for the actions of unruly miners. Several mine leases in the Baxian archives specifically state that if workers were involved in drinking, gambling, or other troublesome behavior, responsibility lay solely with the tenant.[31] In both mining and well-salt regions the practice of separating the landowner from the land was also in the interests of efficient management. Landowners in Baxian were expressly forbidden from interfering in the business of mining and could be denied the right to open a pit on adjoining land lest they try to tap into a tenant's seam.[32] In 1800 Liu Yujiang rented three mines from the Zhou family. Not only did the rental contract stipulate that the Zhous would not impede Liu's mining activities. It also provided that they would pay a fine and make up all of Liu's expenses if their actions caused Liu's mine to cease operations.[33] The *Sichuan Salt Administration History* (*Sichuan yan-zheng shi*) states that landowners in Jianwei received a rent deposit (*zumai yin*) and a fixed annual rent on their land, after which "the landowner has no say in how the well is run."[34] At Santai and Pengzhou, too, contracts came to stipulate that the landowner had no rights other than receipt of rent.[35] Even a landowner who withdrew a lease because of rent arrears might be expected to compensate his tenant for the tenant's investment in sinking the mine shaft.[36] These new protections added a degree of stability to the coal and salt mining industries in Sichuan. The separation of the land and the industrial unit located on the land became complete when relations of tenure were transformed into those of partnership in mid-Qing Furong.

The Return to Share Rents

By the beginning of the nineteenth century population growth and social stability formed the foundation for a period of economic prosperity in Sichuan that was to last at least until the turn of the next century. Coal and salt, both primary consumption goods, benefited from a growing market and the greater safety encountered by merchants trading within Sichuan. In the case of salt, the discovery of black-brine and gas deposits in the 1820s was a turning point in salt manufacturing in southern Sichuan and particularly at Furong. As the potential productivity from a single successful well soared, landowners began to regret the advances which had brought them fixed rents and had removed them from involvement in the actual operation of extractive enterprises. Thus, in all but the most backward areas, we begin to see attempts to return to a form of percentage rents, which would give the landowner a larger share of production.

In the coal-mining industry share rents generally took two forms. In some cases the landowner required a fixed fee in cash or loads of coal for every hundred loads produced.[37] Since productivity was difficult to verify, other landowners claimed a fixed cash payment for every worker on the coalface. This was called paying by the pickax.[38] In either case, the landowner was able to benefit from improvements in coal output and was encouraged to maintain conditions conducive to the smooth operation of the mine. In the more advanced saltyards a similar transformation of the landowner's relationship to the mine took place. In 1886, when Dai Tongde drilled four shafts on a piece of leased land in Leshan, he paid a small rent deposit of 10 taels to the owner of the property and promised him 1 percent of the total output from his wells.[39] When four investors entered into partnership to drill at the Jingren yard, they paid a deposit of six strings of cash per well to open four wells and build a countinghouse on leased land. Once production began, their lease required that they pay the owner of the land 500 cash for every 1,000 *jin* of salt they produced as well as a fixed payment of 50 *jin* of salt per well each year.[40]

The introduction of share rents on leased mineral lands proved to be only a transitional form in the development of more productive wells and mines. In the salt industry, the shift to share rents soon evolved into a sophisticated system of partnerships. By the turn of the nineteenth century it became possible for the possessors of land, capital, drilling equipment, technical expertise, and managerial talent to each partake of rights to a well in proportion to the value of their particular contributions.

The Marriage of Land and Capital at Furong

Simple Well-Drilling Partnerships

In 1779 Wang Jingan, the owner of a plot of land in Ziliujing, entered into a contract with Cai Canruo. The object of their agreement was to drill a well, which was to be called the Tongsheng. By the terms of the agreement Wang received 7.5 shares in the well and Cai received 22.5. The initial costs of drilling were to be borne by Cai, who would sell any brine produced in the early stages of drilling to help offset these expenses. Once production reached a certain level (in this case between 20 and 40 *dan*), the landowner, Wang, would join Cai in the cost of bringing the well into full production. Once the well was complete landowner and investor would share both the profits and any taxes and expenses according to their shares in the well. The term of the lease was for 11 years. When the lease was up, the well would revert to the landowner.[41]

The Tongsheng well contract is the earliest surviving example of what was to become the basic structure of well-drilling investment in Furong prior to 1949. The landowner (*dizhu*) contributed the land needed to start the new enterprise, usually designated as *yijing sanji*. This consisted of the parcel on which the actual well was drilled, the minimum area necessary to erect the derrick and wheel and, in most cases, the furnace in which the brine produced was evaporated. The landowner was not responsible for contributing any money to the drilling of the well. This was the task of the lessee(s). Their designation in the surviving contracts as the "guest partnership" (*kehuo*) was indicative of the expectation that they would constitute a stable group of investors in the anticipated enterprise.

Under the terms of the Furong well-site leasehold each of the parties involved received shares in the well they hoped to bring into operation.

The number of shares in each well was determined by custom and not by the number of investors. Landowner shares were called *dimo* shares. Those of investors can be found under several appellations, the most common being *gongben* shares, *ke* shares, and *kaiguo* shares. At the Ziliujing yard most contracts called for the division of the well into 30 shares, while at Gongjing the majority of contracts distributed 24 shares among investors and landowners.[42] Several terms applied to shares in general. While the term *kouguo* or *shuifen* used at Gongjing most likely originated in a measure of productivity, the use of *ban*, *tian*, or *rifen* to refer to shares at Ziliujing probably dated back to a time when shareholders took their profits by actually running the well in turns for a fixed number of days each month, an issue to which we will return shortly.[43] Once large numbers of investors began entering partnerships in wells in this area, it was not uncommon to see some with entitlement to only a few "minutes" or a few "seconds" of the well's monthly productivity.

The number of shares obtained by the landowner and the investors was set by custom, but shifted over time as the relative value of land versus capital changed. In the case of the Tongsheng well the landowner received 7.5 and the investors 22.5 shares in a 30-share well. By the early 1800s the distribution seems to have moved slightly in favor of the investors, with most 30-share wells having a split of between 5–25 to 7–23 (giving the landowner a 20–30 percent share) and most 24-share wells having a split of 6–18 (giving landowners a 33 percent share). However, by the end of the century, the high costs of drilling black-brine and, later, rock-salt wells[44] seem to have encouraged encroachment on the landowner's share, with many contracts reducing the landowner's share to less than 15 percent. Accompanying this loss of shares was a corresponding increase in the contribution the landowner was expected to make toward the development of the well. Although all contracts stipulated that the landowner would not pay for the drilling of the well, costs beyond the original excavation could be funded in a number of ways. At the same time, the point at which the well was deemed to have "come in" determined what share of the profits was applied toward the actual development of the well and how soon the landowner would begin to receive dividends from his shares in the enterprise.

Before reaching their optimum depth, most wells began producing small amounts of brine or gas (*weishui*, *weihuo*). Profits from the sale of this early product were almost universally applied toward the costs of further drilling.[45] Thus, in effect, the landowner did pay for part of the drilling by deferring participation in profit sharing. In some contracts this was made explicit, with cautions against any attempt by the landowner to distribute the profits at this early stage.[46] The level of productivity that would be considered *weishui* or *weihuo* was often stated in the contract as well, ranging from production of enough gas to run one evaporation pan to enough gas or brine to supply two or three pans in most contracts from the 1820s on.[47]

The appearance of *weishui* or *weihuo* was a good predictor of the ultimate success of the well and often marked the beginning of construction of the pumping facilities and other components of the physical plant by the investors in the well. It is in the investment expectations that arose when the facilities were built that we can see the first signs of the erosion of the landowner's position in well-drilling partnerships. Many early well-drilling contracts stated explicitly that the construction of the derrick, wheel, and other basic facilities would be the sole responsibility of the investors in the well.[48] In others, this was implicit, and undoubtedly understood by the parties to the contract. However, by the middle of the nineteenth century delayed division of profits was increasingly used to enable investors to draw on the proceeds of the well itself to pay for increasingly expensive equipment and to offset the already large expenses incurred to drill a well.

Formal entry of the landowner or holder of landowner shares into the well partnership took place only once the well "came in" (*jiangong*). At this point the landowner entered the partnership (*fenban, qiban,* or *jinban*) and, unless otherwise stated, his rights and obligations were the same as those of any other partner. Most contracts did not make explicit the bar that had to be crossed before the gestation period of the well was considered complete, which must have caused conflicts between holders of landowner and investor shares. Landowners were often anxious to begin sharing in the profits, particularly when wells could take five or more years to drill. Investors, on the other hand, had an interest in extending the gestation period as long as they could to enable them to utilize the product of the well to finance its development.[49] During the late Qing some contracts set the standard for entry of the landowner into the partnership at the point when the well began pumping,[50] while others marked this event by the arrival of large amounts of brine or gas (*dashui, dahuo*).[51] In a few instances, partners in well-drilling enterprises set a specific standard for *jiangong*.[52] Indeed, in the Tongzhi edition of the *Fushun xianzhi* (Fushun County gazetteer) four pans worth of brine, or about 80 *dan*, are given as the customary limit, after which dividends would be paid on wells rented for a limited period. By the Republic period the standard had risen considerably, as a function of increased well productivity and costs of well drilling, as well as a general decline in the power of saltyard landowners.[53]

Any expenses incurred in the development of the well once the landowner entered the partnership were borne equally by all 24 or 30 shares. This included rental of any additional land that the enterprise might require, repairs to the well or equipment, and any costs incurred to drill deeper if the well should go dry.[54] Operating expenses, taxes, the construction of sheds for the water buffalo, purchase of buffalo, and the offering of sacrifices and theatricals in thanks for the good fortune of reaching brine or gas were all among the items included in lists of payments to be deducted from income before profits were shared. By the middle of the nineteenth century this long list of joint expenses came increasingly to include the costs of constructing the facilities as well, adding a major expense originally borne by the investors alone to those of the constituted partnership.[55] Even the decision whether or not to redrill an abandoned or damaged well resided with the investors. Thus the landowner entering a well-drilling partnership committed himself in advance to expenditures that he could not control.[56]

Indeed, by the time the landowner entered the partnership, he had relinquished almost all rights to determine how his land would be used. As early as the 1850s contracts appeared such as the one signed by Mrs. Li nee Zou and her son Wenhua. Not only was Mrs. Li cautioned "whether the well comes in or not, it is the sole purview of the investors to operate." She was also warned not to send someone to the site to manage things, lest she "mess up well affairs."[57] In two of our surviving contracts from the 1860s the size of the plot being leased was left open-ended, and the managers of the well were given full power to determine the final boundaries required.[58] Perhaps in response to pressures of this kind some contracts specified that the site boundaries were to be marked in stone and that any additional land would have to be rented separately from the landowner.[59] Even the disposal of the land for purposes other than the needs of the well in question could be lost when a well-drilling contract was signed.[60]

What little leverage landowners had depended on their ability to charge for land use other than that specified in the contract concluded with investors. Landowners at the Wutongqiao saltyard in neighboring Jianwei County exercised this prerogative by charging fees for everything from piling coal on their land to crossing their land to carry the brine from well to furnace.[61] However, higher capital costs in the development of a well at Furong diminished the bargaining power of Ziliujing and Gongjing landowners. By the 1850s a standard litany of proscribed behavior appeared in their leases, including the levy of extra fees for the use of rights-of-way over the land to move coal, pans, men, or animals, or to lay pipe or construct vats for the storage of brine. Landowners were called upon to permit the construction of any necessary buildings or other structures, and ponds to provide fresh water for buffalo or to irrigate rock-salt wells. They could not prohibit the investors from drilling for earth or stone on the land or from piling slag or coal on the site. Indeed, some contracts simply covered everything by enjoining the landowner to permit any use of the land for which the site was sufficiently large.[62] One contract even stated that if the landowner obstructed use of the land for any purpose and it became necessary to rent land elsewhere, he would be charged for the rent.[63] Implicit in these agreements was the understanding that land was purely a productive input and held no value beyond its contribution to the enterprise.

The transformation of relations of production from leasehold to shareholding and the shift in the balance of power from landowners to investors represented moves in the direction of more efficient, unified management and ensured the greatest possible levels of capital investment before profit sharing began. The same trend can be seen in the changes that took place in the way in which landowners and investors enjoyed their shares. When early contracts used the term *fenban* to indicate that the landowner had begun to share in the profits of the well, a literal division of management usually took place. In the most primitive arrangements the landowner and each of the investors began to pump the well and extract the brine for a certain number of days each month.[64] A modest advance on this system saw unified pumping and division of the brine. By the time the terms *qiban* and *jinban* came into use in the mid-nineteenth century, most partnerships evaporated brine at furnaces built with well funds and from wells managed by the partnership as a whole (*hetui hejian*).[65]

Although well-drilling agreements were similar in many ways to partnership contracts, we must not forget that they were fundamentally designed to establish the leasing of mineral rights. During the early phase of development, it is likely that most of these leases were for fixed terms. Sites rented for a limited tenancy were called "guest wells" (*kejing*), and according to the Tongzhi *Fushun County Gazetteer* they were generally set for 12 to 20 years. Arrangements of this kind could survive only as long as capital costs of opening a well were relatively low. During the early expansion of wells, when productivity was modest and wells were often no more than a thousand feet deep and cost at most several thousand taels, it was possible to attract the necessary capital with a promise of only limited tenure. The investors in the Yiliu each paid 114 taels, for a share in the well. With 18 investor shares this meant initial costs of only 2,052 taels. The Dehou cost slightly more, approximately 4,904 taels, but this sum too could easily be earned back within a couple of years at a successful well.[66]

Limited-tenure agreements encouraged landowners to convert land for agricultural or forestry use to extractive use. At the same time, they enabled landowners with little capital to enter the salt industry as merchants themselves. A landowner not only reaped a share of the profits from successful wells drilled on his land. When the lease was up, the well, all well shares, and most of its facilities also reverted to him. This generally included the

wheel and derrick, and often the furnace, countinghouse, and other structures as well. The investors retained movable property such as buffalo, tools,
and sometimes salt pans that could be used in new ventures.[67] Several of
the wealthy salt-producing lineages of the late Qing period began as petty
salt operators and landowners in Ziliujing and Gongjing. Wang Langyun,
the architect of the Wang Sanwei lineage trust (*tang*) fortune, started his
empire in the 1840s by redrilling one well that had been operated as a yellow-brine well and by renting lineage land to both local and Shaanxi merchants to open new wells.[68] Stories of the rise of the Li Siyou trust invariably open with a chance meeting between Li Weiji and a Shaanxi salt and
tea merchant named Gao, which led to the latter's investment of 3,000 taels
in the Li family's rather unproductive shallow wells.[69] During the 1840s and
1850s Xiao Zhihe and Zhang Sanhe were well known for their ability to attract investors to drill on their land, a practice that resulted in rapid profits
for both and a reputation, along with Hu Yuanhe, as the "three rivers of
Gongjing" (*Gongjing santiaohe*).[70]

Few examples of limited-tenure contracts for the late Qing period have
survived. By the 1850s investors were no longer willing to accept conditions
in which growing capital expenditure resulted in only short-term returns.
The expansion of exploration of black-brine wells, with well depths of approximately 3,000 feet, heralded a dramatic increase in productivity and
also in the costs of drilling wells. *Essentials of Sichuan Salt* estimates that
even a well of about 2,500 feet would require an initial investment of at least
40,000–50,000 taels.[71] As a result, more and more wells were drilled under
conditions of permanent tenancy. Shares in these so-called son-and-grand-
son wells (*zisunjing*) were passed on to one's descendants in perpetuity and
represent an implicit separation of the landowner from his land as land.[72]

Not all of the protections built into these agreements served the explicit
interests of investors in brine wells. As leasing agreements, most of these
contracts continued to require a rent deposit. Many of the contracts that
do not mention rent deposits involved the recapitalization of earlier projects, arranging for redrilling of earlier sites or for additional investors to
contribute to the costs of drilling. During the Qing period rent deposits
seem to have averaged around 100 taels, although by the last years of the
dynasty, figures of three, four, or even five hundred taels were probably not
uncommon.[73] These increases no doubt reflected the greater profitability of
wells as black-brine and, later, rock-salt wells became widespread. During
the early Republican period boom at the Furong saltyard some well-drilling
contracts record deposits as high as 1,000 to 2,400 taels,[74] figures which
were topped again in the 1930s and 1940s when a second boom and the
beginnings of the Nationalist inflation brought deposits at some wells to

10,000 yuan and beyond.[75] This inflationary trend caused serious problems for salt-well developers, particularly because, as we will see, most rock-salt wells were developed on fixed-term leases with refundable deposits. The devaluation of deposits by the time leases were up led the writers of some contracts to stipulate that the refund be adjusted for inflation.[76] The collection of large rent deposits was in keeping with the pattern we find in the disposal of agricultural land in Sichuan.[77] Since the majority of rent deposits were nonrefundable, it is likely that they originated as a concession to landowners who might have considered putting their land to agricultural or forestry use and would now realize no income from their property for many years to come. However, a number of contracts called for return of the deposit once the well came in.[78] Where landowners had more leverage, particularly because successful wells were known to have been drilled in their vicinity, this served as a strong incentive to investors to undertake expeditious drilling of the well.

A further concession to the interests of landowners was the stipulation that any suspension of drilling would result in the return of the well and all its shares to the landowner. If drilling was not resumed before the landowner took action, the investors stood to lose everything they had already put into the well. In early contracts this action was often taken immediately if drilling did not commence with the signing of the contract.[79] The difficulties encountered in raising capital, particularly as the costs of drilling rose, resulted in a modification of such clauses by the 1850s, with an increasing number allowing a grace period of from two or three months to 18 months.[80] In the case of wells drilled during the Republican period an exception to this clause was sometimes made in the event that warfare brought a halt to excavation.[81]

What is important about these clauses is not their protection of landowner rights, but the role that they played in the development of the salt industry as a whole. As in the case of items that encouraged investor confidence in salt partnerships, these landowner-centered stipulations helped to bring more land into industrial use at the saltyard. More important, they served to protect the development of the well itself against ineffective or bankrupt partnerships by promptly penalizing those who did not get on with the business of well excavation as quickly as was technically feasible.

The Expansion of Well Partnerships

Regardless of how conducive the conditions set out in well-drilling contracts were to the formation of cooperative relationships between landowners and investors, few investors were able to manage the high costs of well excavation on their own. This was particularly true after the middle of the nineteenth century when black-brine and gas wells began to dominate well development. Indeed, even by the time of the late Ming, partnerships appear to have been the most common form of well management in the technologically more advanced areas of Sichuan. According to a memorial by Fan Jian dated 1536, the construction of a well in Sichuan required "the combined resources of several families, accumulations of hundreds of taels, and many years to accomplish."[82] The *Sichuan Salt Administration History* cites partnerships as the primary form of well management in Yunyang, Daning, Zhong County, Wan County, and Yanyuan in addition to the two saltyards at Furong.[83] Examples of partnerships can be found for Jianwei, Nanbu, and Yanting as well.[84] At Furong, the institutions of partnership were developed to their highest level and provide an excellent opportunity to examine the ways in which investors sought to overcome limited household wealth relative to the capital requirements of the salt industry. There, many partnerships combined the resources of ten or more investors, including investment partnerships operating furnaces, and retail or wholesale companies.[85] Lineage trusts played a particularly important role in bringing together capital in the southern Sichuan salt-producing region and were among the most active investors in saltyard partnerships. These trusts found their institutional form in the ancestral estates established by Chinese common descent groups to generate income in support of ancestral rites. As we shall see, among merchants they became a mechanism for the pooling of business shares, as well as land and other assets, in a form that was not subject to household division or predation.[86]

By the twentieth century almost all wells were partnerships. Furnaces, which were themselves owned by large numbers of households and lineage trusts, appear to have been the dominant investors in wells by this time, although diverse combinations of shareholders can also be found. The Tianlong well, a rock-salt well in Guojia ao, was opened by a firm owned by an individual household in partnership with a lineage trust, four other households, a business firm, and four other lineage trusts.[87] The complexity of this partnership was not unusual. Although it may have resulted in part from the difficulties encountered in opening the well, which was refinanced twice before it became operational, it also reflected the multiplication of investors, both household and corporate, in the Zigong region.

Chengshouren and the Management of Well-Drilling Enterprises

Resource pooling was not new to China. The creation of joint property among members of a common descent group has a long history. Earth god, temple, burial, and other forms of associations, in which rural households purchased shares in return for various social, economic, and religious returns, are known to have been a common feature of rural life.[88] Richard Belsky's detailed study of Beijing native-place (*huiguan*) associations points to an understanding of urban associations of people of common provenance or occupation (or what we commonly call guilds) as shareholding associations as well.[89] In Zigong, investors came together through friendship or kinship. As we shall see, some of the most important corporate groups were based on institutions developed within the system of lineage property holding. However, in Zigong we also see the development of partnerships among holders of capital (corporate and household) with no prior personal relationship. The ability of large numbers of unrelated people to come together and continue over many years to finance the construction of an enterprise as complex and fraught with difficulties as a brine well necessitated new organizational and management techniques. One of the most important organizational innovations in the development of the Furong saltyard was the *chengshouren*. In our sample of 84 well-drilling contracts, 37 mention the existence of one or more of these men in their discussions of the initial formation of the well partnership.[90] Thirty-two, or about two-thirds of these, date from the Qing period.

The *chengshouren* performed several vital functions during the phase of well drilling. In most cases he was a middleman and broker in the development of well sites. Although some investors in brine wells came together at the behest of a landowner or themselves approached an owner of prime well land with a proposal to drill, this was not possible in every case. More often, a landowner sought out a broker or vice versa, and it was the job of the broker to find investors to drill the well. Indeed, many of the well-drilling contracts we have for the nineteenth century are agreements not between a landowner and his "tenants," but between the landowner and the *chengshouren*. The investors remain unknown to us because they were not yet "invited" when the agreement was signed. It was the *chengshouren* who paid the deposit, which became an incentive for him to quickly find investors to pay him back.[91] In a few instances the investors are named and the *chengshouren* is not. In these cases it is likely that the investors and landowners came together and sought out a *chengshouren* to manage the well, pointing to the importance of the *chengshouren* as a manager as well as a middleman.[92]

Chengshouren fell into two main categories. Some were men who knew the salt business but had no capital. This, as we will see in a moment, was a way into a well partnership without putting up either land or capital of one's own. Some *chengshouren* were able to make enough money in this way to become investors in their own right and show up on later well or furnace contracts as partners in other ventures. The second group consisted of already established saltyard merchants with good connections and a record of success in well development. Zhang Lesan was such a man. During the early twentieth century he was the main partner in at least two highly profitable wells in Gongjing. In 1919 the investors in the Hungchuan called upon Zhang first to manage their well-drilling venture and ultimately to take it over and refinance it under a new investment group that he brought together.[93] *Chengshouren* could be men of considerable local influence, as in the case of Huang Yushu. While listed as *chengshouren* of the Deshan well, Huang was also a primary investor in at least one other well and a member of the Rong County local elite group that supported the anti-Manchu revolutionary movement in Sichuan.

When acting in his capacity as broker, the *chengshouren* would put up no capital, receiving instead a share in the well. Known variously as *tuanshou rifen, ganrifen,* or *fuguo rifen,* these shares were usually allocated from the landowner's portion.[94] The number of broker shares seems to have increased with the difficulties of opening a well. Throughout the Qing period most *chengshouren* received between half a share and one share, but several from the 1860s on acquired three and even four *chengshouren* shares.[95] Like the landowner, the *chengshouren* received no income from his shares until the well came in. From then on he was a full partner in the well and was even expected to put up capital if the well had to be redrilled.[96] When limited-tenure wells were returned to the landowner, the *chengshouren* and the landowner split the investor shares.[97] In the case of perpetual lease wells, the *chengshouren*'s shares, like those of other partners, could be passed on to future generations.[98] Moreover, there is evidence that while the well was being drilled, the *chengshouren* was paid a small salary for supervising the process.[99]

Many *chengshouren* were men with considerable technical skill, whose contribution to the actual drilling of the well may be likened to that of the architect or engineer at a building site. Some had their own sets of tools (*jiahuo gunzi*) used in drilling and other aspects of well construction. The frequent reference to *chengshouren* shares as *jiahuo gunzi* shares is a clear indication of the importance placed on the consideration of these tools in lieu of capital investment.[100] It was the *chengshouren*'s job to make certain that the well was properly drilled and that drilling continued unabated as long as it took for the well to come in. Some contracts included a clause that underlined the *chengshouren*'s personal responsibility in this regard. When Liu Kunlun and Zhang Shimian undertook to find investors in the Tianyuan well, one of the conditions of tenure was that they refund double the investors' capital if drilling were halted on the well.[101] In the case of the Tianshun well the *chengshouren* received several reminders that he was solely responsible for the successful opening of the well and would have to return his two shares if drilling stopped.[102]

The key to maintaining drilling schedules and avoiding funding shortages lay in skillful financial management of the investment group. This too was the task of the *chengshouren*. High startup costs, frequent unexpected additions to cost, and the long time periods involved before a well came in meant that few partnerships could put up all the necessary capital when drilling began. It was therefore essential that mechanisms existed to ensure the continuous flow of cash into the partnership. The principle that profits should be reinvested in well development was established early, in standardized contract clauses requiring that income from *weishui* and *weihuo* be plowed back into the drilling of the well. It was also vital that investors continue to contribute on a regular basis to the opening of the well and the construction of the facilities needed to pump and evaporate salt. The importance of tight financial controls in the early stages of well development gave rise to a set of management techniques that appear to have been common to the saltyard as a whole.

Investors were responsible for two kinds of funds. Many wells required an initial payment, or *diqian*, designed to cover the costs of drilling the first level of the well and constructing the stone lining around the soft soil layers at the uppermost section of the well wall.[103] Most of the capital used to open a well was paid by the investors in monthly installments called *yuefei* or *shifei qian*. In some cases the amount was stipulated in the initial well-drilling lease.[104] More often, contracts simply called for the payment of a monthly levy by each holder of investor shares.[105]

From an examination of account books now in the Zigong municipal archives, the compilers of *Selected Zigong Salt Industry Contracts and Documents* (Zigong yanye qiyue dang'an xuanji) have determined that these levies were based on calculations of the previous month's expenses.[106] This is confirmed by the discovery of monthly investor levy tickets or *jiepiao* in the same collection of documents. These tickets were mass-produced by woodblock printing. Each month an investor levy ticket was sent by the *chengshouren* to every active investor in the well. On it were spaces for the *chengshouren* to fill in the total expenses incurred at the well that month, how much had been spent from the day drilling began until the end of that month, how much the investor in question was required to pay as his monthly levy, how much the investor in question had paid to date, how much of his total obligation the investor in question was in arrears, and the depth to which the well had been drilled during the preceding two months.[107] Thus, the investor levy ticket served not only as a mechanism to dun the investor for his monthly contribution. It also functioned as a monthly shareholders report, keeping all concerned informed of the financial condition of the enterprise and how far they still had to go to hit gas or brine.

The resemblance of these tickets to government tax receipts was probably not an accident, given the close connections between government and the salt industry as a whole. Indeed, in the style of government tax receipts, the investor levy tickets had printed on them the customary rules of the saltyard governing the handling of investors who failed to pay their monthly fees. After a one-month grace period it was the responsibility of the *chengshouren* to deprive investors with arrears of their shares and find someone who would put up the capital and to whom the shares could then be transferred. Only when the well came in would the delinquent shareholder receive back, without interest, the capital he put into the well.[108]

In practice well partnerships seem to have dealt even more harshly with problem members. In some cases the *chengshouren* was authorized to find a new partner to take over their shares with explicit instructions never to refund the money already spent.[109] In others the original partner was saved from loss of all his capital by means of a share reapportionment system known as *taizuo*. If one or more investors proved unable to continue paying their share of the drilling costs, the rest of the partners would take over paying their contributions. When the well came in, the actual paid-up capital of each shareholder was calculated and shares in the operating well were reapportioned on this basis.[110] Finally, a shareholder could sell his shares in the well outright. This was not always easy before a well came in, but evidence of several cases has survived.[111] All of these methods protected a well from being abandoned if a small number of investors could not keep up their responsibilities to the group. Moreover, many well-drilling contracts anticipated such problems and stipulated that in the event of share sales, the shares would be offered to partners before outside investors were sought. The language used in such clauses—no one may *privately* (my emphasis) sell shares to an outsider (*bude siding wairen*)—suggests that the partnership was seen not simply as a collection of rent-takers but as a corporate entity with collective rights.[112]

Shangxia jie Transfers

The techniques that evolved to handle arrears by a small number of investors could not solve the problems of many well partnerships in the late nineteenth and early twentieth centuries. As wells began to take a decade or more to drill, often eating up tens of thousands of taels before even reaching small amounts of brine or gas, it was not uncommon for the whole partnership to run out of funds before a well came in. It is impossible to determine what proportion of the total number of wells excavated at Furong experienced such problems. However, in our surviving collection of well-drilling contracts, 29, or over one-third, involve the transfer of an entire partnership to other hands. In the techniques devised to handle such contingencies, we can see once again the resilience of Furong's capital markets and the development of institutions that encouraged investment under conditions of weak capital accumulation. While many wells were abandoned as a result of poor management, technical difficulties, or bankruptcy, the evolution of the practice of *shangxia jie* transfers guaranteed that, at least during periods of prosperity at the saltyard, funding became available for most of the potentially productive wells.

As early as the mid-nineteenth century, *shangxia jie* transfers were part of the customary rules of the Furong saltyard. The Tongzhi *Fushun County Gazetteer* describes the practice in this way:[113]

> If, after a long period of time, a well does not come in, or it produces meager results and requires further drilling, those without the means to put up more money may transfer their shares to others. They are called the *shangjie* and the persons who take over their shares are called the *xiajie*. From that time on, all funds to drill the well are put up by the *xiajie*. If the transfer is total, when the well comes in the *shangjie* will not get a share in the profits. If it is not total, that is, if the *shangjie* has not recovered all of his investment, once the well comes in the *shangjie* sometimes gets a certain amount of capital. [In other cases] he may split the profits 50–50 with the *xiajie*, or the *shangjie* may get 20 or 30 percent and the *xiajie* 70 or 80 percent. If the *shangjie* did not drill very deep and his expenses were not great, he receives a small share of the profits. If the *xiajie* drilled the well deep and spent a lot of money, then he gets a large share of the profits. If, after a long period of time the well does not come in and the *xiajie* is also unable to pay out any more money, he may transfer his shares to someone else. Then the former *xiajie* becomes the *zhongjie* and the person presently putting up money to drill the well becomes the *xiajie*. When the well comes in, the *zhongjie* too might take back a certain amount of the startup expenses or share in the profits.

A number of factors could impel the original developers of well land to transfer their property to a new partnership (*diuxiajie*). The investors in the Wufu well began redrilling what was already an abandoned well in 1904. By 1907 they had reached around 1,800 feet and were able to pump some brine, indicating the well would probably come in. However, just as success appeared possible, they ran out of funds. In order to save what they had already invested, they transferred half the shares in the well to Lu Zishou to finish drilling the well.[114] Huang Yushu, whom we have already encountered as a *chengshouren*, rented land from the Li Rulian hui (most likely a revolving credit association) to drill a well. After finding investors, the partnership drilled for 10 years, spending well over 30,000 taels. Although the primary facilities were built and the well was now producing a few *dan* of brine and enough gas to fire five pans, the original developers no longer had the funds to continue drilling to a depth that would make the well competitive in the era of solution mining in the 1920s. As a result, they were forced to transfer their shares to a *xiajie* partnership to finish the drilling and share in the profits when the well came in.[115] In other cases work was proceeding well when an unexpected accident, such as the collapse of the well wall or something falling in the well, left a partnership unable to go on.[116] Finally, a sharp decline in the market for Sichuan salt in the late 1920s and the disruption of the market under warlord rule were responsible for suspension of drilling by many partnerships, which later had to call in a *xiajie* partnership to finish the well.[117]

One reason for the large number of *shangxia jie* contracts was that despite clauses in most well-drilling agreements that investors would relinquish their shares if drilling ceased, shareholders often maintained their interest in wells that had been abandoned for failure to produce brine.[118] Repeated *shangxia* transfers, in an attempt by investors to recover the funds they had already spent and bring a well in for future profits, created extremely complex relations of partnerships at many Furong wells. Both the distribution of shares and the management of the well were greatly altered by a decision to call in a *xiajie*.

Redistribution of Well Shares

As we have already seen in the saltyard rules cited previously, the most immediate effect of the transfer of well-drilling responsibility to a *xiajie* was the redistribution of shares in the well. How these shares were allocated among the original landowners, the original investors, and the new investment group depended on the particular conditions at that well site. An examination of the types of transfer possible confirms that every effort was made to ensure that the shares one held reflected one's capital investment in the well.

According to the compilers of *Selected Zigong Salt Industry Contracts and Documents*, the most common form of transfer was one in which the total shares in the well were divided equally between the old and the new investment group.[119] However, not all *shangxia jie* agreements were this simple. If the *shangjie* had been drilling for some time, or had already drilled to a considerable depth, the *shangjie* would often retain more than half the well shares. This was frequently the case among wells where the original investors ran out of funds after reaching small amounts of brine or gas, or when there was some other reason to believe the well would come in soon.[120] On the other hand, a well which had experienced considerable difficulties in drilling, which was located on a layer of particularly hard rock, or which had to be relocated could cost the *xiajie* quite a lot before brine or rock salt was reached. In cases such as this the *xiajie* could receive two-thirds or even more of the well shares.[121]

Whether the *shangjie* had demanded an up-front cash payment (often called a transfer payment, or *dingjia*) could also influence the distribution of shares. Although contracts do not indicate the reasons for these payments, they may have been a way for *shangjie* to pay off debts to suppliers and workers at the well. The shareholders in the Fenglai well relinquished two-thirds of their shares, but in return received a transfer payment of 1,400 taels. The high potential profits from rock-salt wells were an added stimulus to increase *xiajie* shares. Even transfer to a *xiajie* did not guarantee that a well would be supplied with adequate funding to reach gas or brine. In order to encourage *xiajie* to increase their investment when progress was slower than anticipated, a *shangjie* might cede additional shares after the original agreement went into effect. In 1934 the Wang Sanwei trust signed a contract with two *chengshouren* who were charged with finding investors to redrill the Delong well. By the following year the *xiajie* had drilled to over 2,800 feet at great cost and with no sign of increased productivity at the well. They therefore called a meeting with the managers of the Wang Sanwei trust and requested another two shares as an incentive to continue excavating the well. This they received in return for an additional 300-yuan cash payment. In 1938 they reported expenditures of over 40,000 yuan and a well depth of over 3,600 feet. The well had still not come in and at this time the *shangjie* ceded another two shares, bringing the distribution between *shangjie* and *xiajie* to 8:22.[122]

Not all arrangements were so simple. As the active partners became increasingly removed from those who first opened the well, the division of shares became more and more complex. During the Qing dynasty the Mao Zhiyuan trust and the Gao Jingshe trust, under the name Dehe company (*hao*), bought the Lianhai well and changed its name to the Tianlong well.[123] They got 20 shares in the well and the landowners, the widow Yuan nee Luo and her sons, appear to have received 10. In 1910 they transferred their shares to a *xiajie*, the Li Wumei trust, a lineage trust involved in several well deals for which contracts survive. The *shangjie* kept four shares and the *xiajie* took possession of 16. In 1927 they transferred one share of their remaining four to Li Boquan. The Li Wumei trust also bought five landowner shares from the Yuans, bringing their total to 21 shares. In 1927 they transferred eight of these shares to the Liao Zhonghou trust, leaving them with 13 shares. Then, in 1928, the Li Wumei trust transferred another eight shares to what appears to be the partners in the Xiuyang furnace: Li Sijiu, Li Shengjiu, Li Jinghou, the Li Wumei trust, the Li Boxing trust, Yan Niantao, Yan Chongfuyong (a firm), and Chen Boqun. This left the Li Wumei trust with five *xiajie* shares. Table 2.1 lists the shareholders in the well when it came in, in 1933.

Not only was the distribution of shares influenced by the degree of work already undertaken on a well. The ability of the new investment group to fulfill its obligation to bring in the well could also easily rest on accurate information regarding the condition in which the well was being transferred. Responsibility for any preexisting debts, disputed title to land, and so on was almost always contractually disclaimed by the *xiajie*.[124] All previous agreements with the landowner for access rights and building rights also had to be reaffirmed.[125] Many redrilling contracts also stipulated the depth to which the well had already been drilled and the state of the equipment being turned over with the well.[126] In the case of long-abandoned wells, almost nothing might be left standing on the site. Where the *shangjie* had recently run into difficulties, the well might already be provided with a derrick, wheel, furnace, countinghouse, and essential tools. At least by the twentieth century, the developers of each well appear to have kept a log of the day's drilling, the depth achieved, and conditions at the well. These

TABLE 2.1 Shares in the Tianlong Well, 1933

Shareholder	Shares	Shareholder	Shares
Dehe Company	2	Li Jinghou	1
Gao Jingshe trust	1	Yan Niantao	0.5
Li Wumei trust	6	Yan Chongfuyong Company	1
Li Boquan	1	Chen Boqun	0.5
Li Siyou trust	5	Yan Xianyang	1
Liao Zhonghou trust	8	Li Zixing trust	1
Li Sijiu	1	Li Shengjiu	1
		Total Shares	30

Source: Zigongshi dang'anguan, Beijing jingjixueyuan, and Sichuan daxue, eds., *Zigong yanye qiyue dang'an xuanji (1732-1949)* [Selected Zigong salt industry contracts and documents (1732–1949)] (Beijing: Zhongguo shehuikexue chubanshe, 1985), contract 58.

wellhead registers (*yankou bu*) may have provided the data for filling out the investor levy tickets mentioned earlier and provided prospective new investors with data on the progress of the well and its potential success. At least one contract stipulates that these well-head registers be turned over to the investors upon completion of the contract. Once drilling resumed under the new partnership, the investors would turn the registers over to the landowner at the end of each year to show how far the well had now progressed.[127] At the same time, new investors sometimes included clauses in the transfer contract that allowed them to stop drilling and pump the well, regardless of its productivity, once a certain depth was reached. The limit was usually set at 3,000 feet—below this depth no well was known to have struck brine.[128]

All of these clauses protected the *xiajie* and encouraged their investment in wells that had a history of trouble. Such protection was important given the division of responsibility once a share transfer deal was closed. In effect, all previous owners took on the role of landowners and almost all we have said about landowner shares now applied to their shares as well. They no longer made any contribution to investment capital and took no share in the profits until the decision was made to have the landowner "enter the partnership" (*jinban*). At the same time, they lost all say in the management of the well, both during drilling and once production began.[129] It was now up to the *xiajie* alone to apply his money and managerial skill to bringing the well into production and ensuring that all shareholders see a profit in the end. The transfer of complete managerial control to one investment group worked against management disputes between what could often be several groups with competing interests. At the same time, it could leave earlier investors quite vulnerable in the event that the wrong *xiajie* were found. Perhaps the most interesting example of this can be seen in the case of the Taohai-Taisheng well. In 1872 the Yan Guixin trust, one of the great salt-manufacturing fortunes at Zigong, and a group of investors first began drilling the Taohai well. By the late 1880s they had run out of money and transferred the well to Yan Jihou, also a prominent member of the saltyard community. As *xiajie* Yan changed the name of the well to Taisheng. Soon after taking over the well, Yan died and his sons stopped drilling. In accordance with the original contract the *shangjie* allowed a grace period of three months and then took back the well. Without money to continue drilling, the *shangjie* left the well idle for several years. However, in 1911, Yan's sons tried to restore their claim, establish themselves as *zhongjie*, and bring in a new *xiajie* investment group. In the end the original developers (*shangjie*) were able to thwart their erstwhile collaborators' plans and the well yielded an average output of gas sufficient to evaporate 280 pans.[130]

The difficulties faced by Furong well developers were not unique to the Chinese business environment. An interesting comparison can be made to the plight of American railroads in the late nineteenth century, many of which were shareholding entities heavily burdened by debt and, like the Furong well developers, facing liquidation if they could not raise new capital. As Peter Tufano has pointed out, firms with "debt overhang" had difficulty raising any new capital because the incremental value of new capital would be absorbed by senior claimants.[131] In the American case two institutions played a role in rescuing railroads from financial disaster and devising new legal frameworks for firm reorganization: the courts and the investment bank, particularly that of J. P. Morgan. At Furong a set of commonly accepted practices provided a legally enforceable framework to ensure the continuous infusion of capital in well excavation. *Shangxia jie* share restructuring resolved most of the issues raised by debt overhang by giving new investors a stake in the profits of the new firm commensurate with the risk and debt they absorbed and by contractually establishing the responsibility for preexisting debt. Holdout by inside investors was also dealt with by internal share restructuring, reducing the shares of reluctant insiders. Tufano also points to information asymmetry and the high transaction costs of investment restructuring as impediments to the infusion of new capital. Furong wells were far less dispersed or complex entities than railroads, and it is likely that new investors, most often local residents, were able to acquire the information they needed from inspection of the wellhead register and interrogation of well-drilling crews. On a much more limited playing field, the *chengshouren* then played much of the same role of informed "honest broker" performed by investment bankers like J. P. Morgan.

Well development in Furong was certainly not without problems. Even the existence of mechanisms such as *shangxia jie* could work against the success of a well. By the late Qing and early Republic some wells had so many partners, and had experienced so many permutations of ownership, that it was not always possible to know who the shareholders were. Some of the lawsuits that reached the Fushun County magistrate were concerned with disputed shares and conflicts over rights to wells.[132] By the middle of the nineteenth century the problem of multiplying stakes in individual wells had already been mentioned in the *Fushun County Gazetteer.*[133] Nevertheless, institutions such as those of the *chengshouren* and *shangxia jie* played a vital role in building up the Furong saltyard. Both institutions depended on the rich culture of contracting in both rural and urban China. Parties to agreements of the kind we have examined above could rely on both informal and formal adjudication to uphold the commitments they freely made. Contracts established relationships of partnership and were critical in the redistribution of risk, investment, and debt. They also gained widespread acceptance by memorializing practices that had emerged in the early years of well development before the salt boom of the 1850s. Thus contract, courts, and custom worked together to support capital investment on a scale rarely seen in China prior to the twentieth century.

3

Fragmentation as a Business Strategy

THE SUCCESSFUL drilling of a gas or brine well was only the first step in the establishment of a business for the manufacture of well salt. Many partnerships formed for the excavation of a well continued as production units, pumping brine and disposing of the product by selling it. A smaller number set up their own furnaces to evaporate salt. However, as much as half of the brine and gas produced at Furong during the late Qing period was redistributed, largely through leases and subleases, to partnerships formed solely to operate finished wells and independent furnaces.[1]

The partnerships formed to produce salt at Furong represent a wide variety of solutions to the problem of organizing human, capital, and natural resources to evaporate the brine produced by Furong's several hundred salt wells. These included partnerships organized to rent an entire well and its output of brine, partnerships organized to lease a percentage of the output of a well, partnerships formed to start a furnace and lease brine and/or gas, partnerships between owners of furnaces and owners of wells, and partnerships formed by two or more furnaces to promote more efficient operations. Along with the partnerships formed to invest in well digging, salt-production partnerships served in part to overcome the problem of limited household wealth relative to the capital requirements of salt production. Reducing various elements within the production process to discrete firms also served to minimize risk in an extractive industry subject to political as well as economic and technical pressures, as demonstrated by the participation in such partnerships by even the most successful salt entrepreneurs.[2] Finally, organizational fragmentation also helped to overcome some of the supervision problems inherent in an industry based on large numbers of investors. This was particularly important before 1904, when China first adopted a legal framework to register firms as limited-liability corporations. Organizational fragmentation was partially reversed from the 1920s on, as the exploitation of the rock-salt layer, the use of mechanized pumps, and the consolidation of warlord power stimulated concentration under a new group of salt industrialists. Thus, technological, legal, and political factors all played a role in shaping the industry.

The leasing out of productive assets was most likely initially prompted in part by the enormous productive capacity of the Furong wells. At the Leshan and Jianwei saltyards, furnaces were almost always built by the operators of a well. Because fuel for the furnaces, in the form of coal, was elastically supplied in the market, the only limit on the size of the furnace was the amount of brine the associated well produced.[3] Even the largest operators had only two or three pans at any one furnace.[4] By contrast, an average yellow-brine well at Furong produced between 100 and 200 *dan* of brine a day, and a middling gas well could operate at least fifty and some even as many as several hundred pans.[5] The organizational structure of the salt industry was particularly affected by the fact that the most productive gas wells did not produce brine[6] and, more importantly, that gas production was concentrated at Ziliujing, while Gongjing maintained a position of dominance in brine production until the discovery of the rock-salt layer in the late nineteenth century.

Equally decisive in the formation of the relations of production was the shortage of capital, which encouraged small units of production and risk-averting behavior even among the larger salt-producing groups. Rental permitted salt producers to respond creatively to changing market demand and allowed groups with small capital reserves to open furnaces and evaporate salt without having to invest in the actual process of well excavation. At the same time, fragmentation exacted a heavy price, impeding capital accumulation in the long run and contributing to the perpetuation of small and sometimes inefficient production units.[7] Finally, the existence of multiple claims to wells and furnaces encouraged the development of an elaborate and detailed body of customary law designed to preserve the increasingly complex partnership relations that evolved during the last half of the nineteenth century.

Partnerships in the Production of Well Salt

Salt-Production Partnership Contracts

Before the promulgation of company law in 1904 and 1929, the regulation of Chinese business was wholly dependent on the dynamic interaction of "customs of the trade" and a highly developed tradition of written contract.

Partnership agreements structured the Furong salt industry, governing resource distribution, maintenance, and construction, and the management of operating well and furnace sites. Enforced by the state through the institutions of the magistracy and the office of the Sichuan salt controller, partnership agreements accounted for both the stability and the flexibility of the Furong business environment.[8]

The main function of a partnership agreement was to document who the partners were and their initial financial contribution to the firm. Most partnership agreements began with a list of the partners and the exact number of shares held by each. Careful examination reveals that in many cases the partners were not individual households, the primary property-owning unit in China, but corporate groups, lineages, furnaces, or wells themselves.[9] In a minority of contracts the statement of shares is replaced by a delineation of each partner's initial capital investment, a practice influenced by the growing importance of intrapartnership credit (discussed later). The original contract occupied a critical space in the history of a firm, establishing every aspect of its identity, its goals, and the means by which these goals would be achieved. Contracts began with a description of the business and its holdings and often included a history of how it came to control, through purchase or rental, the production facilities now at the partners' disposal. If facilities were leased, it was important to state the exact tenure period, as this often served as the life span of the partnership itself.[10] In part because of the detailed information contained in the partnership contract, changes in the structure of the partnership, transfers of shares, and other important new information were often registered by means of an addendum to the original rather than by drawing up supplementary agreements.[11]

Almost all partnership agreements contained a section dealing with management issues. The division of managerial responsibility was often outlined in the original partnership contract. In some cases this meant joint management by a small partnership group.[12] In others it entailed the selection of one partner as manager with overall responsibility.[13] However, even in the 1940s many partnerships retained overall strategic and planning responsibilities as a function of the partnership as a whole.[14] Others simply retained the right to replace the manager if the shareholders were dissatisfied with his performance.[15]

Among the most important duties of the management group was the handling of accounts. Partnership contracts often detailed the kinds of accounts to be kept in addition to naming an officer in charge of cash accounts and a separate officer with bookkeeping responsibilities.[16] The importance of fiscal transparency was affirmed in the requirement that accounts be cleared at least once a year and often at intervals of several months. Partners were sent a report on the finances of the business annually (*nianjie*), quarterly, or even monthly (*yuejie*), depending on the protocols established in the partnership agreement.[17] Some partnership contracts designated a fixed amount or a percentage of the profits of the business to be set aside for managerial or other operating expenses.[18]

Daguan Management Organizations

During the early twentieth century we see the development of more sophisticated management organizations known collectively as *daguan*.[19] The *daguan* was an attempt to address two separate structural problems. The first emerged from the tendency of well-drilling partnerships to dissolve after the well came in. Prior to the introduction of vacuum evaporation in the second half of the twentieth century, large capital requirements and economies of scale were limited to drilling and extraction. Processing, by contrast, could be efficiently conducted on a smaller scale. For this reason, each partner or small group of partners in the well-drilling partnership took his share of the brine or gas produced by the well to operate his own salt pans. As the industry matured, many well-drilling partnerships continued to break up either as a result of conflicts with the *chengshouren*, who had originally brought the investors together,[20] or because the investment group was itself now a complex collection of investment units with diverse portfolios, whose goals for use of the well's output did not always coincide.[21] In this case the *daguan* served as the overall management structure for the operation of the well itself, overseeing daily operations and maintenance, major repairs, care and feeding of oxen, workers' issues, fire and flood prevention, and security. The *daguan* also drew up regulations for the distribution of the product of the well, maintained its own countinghouse with a permanent staff, and acted as the contact point for the well with the outside.[22]

Somewhat different were *daguan* which evolved to handle the increasing complexity of partnership portfolios. An excellent example of this form of *daguan* was the Jiyuanchang, established in 1930 to oversee the 10 wells owned by the Shuanghongyuan, a partnership of Shaanxi merchants and lineage estates that had broken away from a larger group in 1923. In this case, the *daguan* played an intermediating role between the *daguan* of individual wells and partners in the Shuanghongyuan, while making certain that each partner in the Shuanghongyuan received his share of profits and refrained from abusing the resources of the partnership for personal gain.

From these brief descriptions it is clear that the *daguan*'s most important function was to be the impartial arbiter of competing and intersecting interests, productivity being the main determinant of its decisions. As such, it was one of the main organizations devised to handle the complex supervision problems that emerged from the intensification of shareholding partnerships at the saltyard. Indeed, according to one source, the term *daguan* arose from the perception that this organization functioned like a strategic pass or *guankou* at which many roads met.[23] While many *daguan* had "managers" chosen from among the shareholders themselves, they functioned largely as a board of directors. The day-to-day management of the *daguan* was undertaken by a paid manager and his staff, chosen either from among the technical staff who had supervised the drilling of the well or from among outsiders with management and technical expertise.[24] The importance of both technical and accounting skills was underscored by the *daguan*'s responsibility for coordinating the leasing of brine and gas belonging to different shareholding groups and destined for different furnaces, calculating the amount of gas and brine accruing to each share over time, adjusting leases as well output changed, and controlling the size of the well opening, the equipment that channeled the gas, the changing character of the well's internal structure, and well safety.[25]

Perhaps the most important characteristic of *daguan* was the way in which their diverse activities were funded. Two patterns appear to have prevailed, each of which represents an advance in the history of the firm in China. In some cases the contract that established the *daguan* set aside a number of shares or a certain amount of gas for the *daguan* itself, the income from which was used for management expenses.[26] In others, the furnaces served by the well being managed by the *daguan* were expected to pay a monthly assessment to cover the *daguan*'s costs, a sort of management fee.[27] In both cases, it was the duty of the *daguan* to make certain that shareholders did not interfere in the operations of the facilities it managed and, in particular, that they did not draw on the resources of the *daguan* for their own purposes. At the same time, the *daguan* was held accountable to the shareholders, submitting financial reports on a quarterly, semiannual, or annual basis and meeting with shareholders on an irregular basis as well if major decisions regarding the *daguang*'s constituent units had to be made.[28] The *daguan* gave continuity to a business in which shares might frequently change hands, and because it controlled the technical side of the operation, the *daguan* facilitated new cash infusions into the industry by people with little experience in salt production. Thus, *daguan* were both an outcome of the commoditization of salt-production shares and contributors to the growth of the share market.

Partnership Restructuring Contracts

It was not until the implementation of China's first company law in 1904 that Chinese firms had the option of incorporation as a limited liability company. The company law was further refined in 1929. Yet only a small proportion of Chinese businesses took advantage of the new legal framework.[29] Few Zigong enterprises appear to have availed themselves of the opportunity to incorporate, retaining unlimited liability and distributing liability in the original agreement, most often according to the number of shares held.[30] Contracts clearly stated the pecuniary obligations that would be triggered by an agreement of partnership, including payments beyond initial investment for construction, acquisition of assets, and so on.

Unlimited liability and the instability of the business environment, a subject to which we will return in later chapters, prompted serious attention to the maintenance of the integrity of the original investment group. Outside takeover of the firm was barred in some contracts by stipulations that any partner desiring to dispose of his shares must first offer them to his fellow shareholders.[31] Where there were only a small number of partners, the need to prevent casual withdrawal from the business was also crucial. At least one surviving contract required that partners could leave only under absolutely inescapable circumstances and even then, the guarantee of the local *baojia*[32] head was necessary to validate the partner's claim.[33] Some contracts tried to avoid conditions that might drive out a partner by specifically allowing for the contracting of loans should the initial capitalization prove inadequate.[34]

By the twentieth century, the expansion of local banking and the development of a variety of private loan-making organizations widened the credit options available to salt-manufacturing firms.[35] However, evidence from lawsuits indicates that even in the 1920s large partnerships tended to borrow from many small lenders. The acrimonious breakup of the earlier-mentioned Shaanxi merchant Shanghongyuan partnership provides an excellent example of the problem of credit at the yard and the reason many management groups were loath to go outside the partnership even in periods of financial stress.[36]

The earliest extant contract attributed to this partnership is dated 1869, although, given the profile of Shaanxi merchants at Ziliujing, it is possible that the partnership existed even earlier. By 1911 the partnership was deeply in debt, and an arrangement was worked out whereby its six lineage trusts regrouped into three subsidiary partnerships for the purpose of paying off their creditors. Their total obligation, in both unpaid bills and loans, came to approximately 41,803 taels, considerably more than the cost of digging the average rock-salt well. More important, however, is the fact that this sum was composed of 94 separate loans, the largest being 5,642 taels and the smallest only six taels. The creditors themselves consisted of private individuals, lineage estates, other firms, and even local fraternal associations like the Huoshen hui, originally founded to make sacrifices to the god of fire, who protected the gas wells and furnaces.

Credit had not been difficult to obtain. Indeed, individual partners had found it far too easy to borrow small amounts of money on the collateral of the firm. However, when it came time to pay off this large debt the firm was forced to rely on what can only be called private scrounging by individual shareholders in the absence of public credit institutions. The alternative would have been recourse to debt consolidation with the help of a private "credit group" (*zhaituan*) of the kind we will see did bail out some of the larger salt firms in the early twentieth century.[37] Although we do not have any contracts memorializing the founding of credit groups, they appear to have been partnerships made up largely of merchants and bankers who came together to provide private medium-term credit to small industrialists. Resort to a loan from a credit group meant relinquishing partial or total managerial control over one's business interests, particularly if one were unable to meet the agreed-upon payment schedule. Having succeeded in avoiding bankruptcy by breaking up the original partnership, the constituent parts of the Shanghongyuan then assigned management of all assets to a *daguan,* the charter of which expressly prohibited partners from private borrowing from outside sources on the assets of the firm.[38]

An alternative to the partnership division undertaken by the Shanghongyuan was recapitalization within the partnership. Internal recapitalization amounted in effect to a restructuring of the partnership, in which rights and obligations were reallocated in recognition of changing contributions to capital. Nevertheless, by avoiding the breakup of the firm, the physical plant was kept intact, and ties to suppliers, management expertise, goodwill, and market position were maintained.

Partnership restructuring appears to have followed two patterns. As early as the 1860s we have examples of partners formally buying out part of the holdings of fellow shareholders who could not put up the additional capital required to successfully dig a well. For example, in 1864 six investors formed a partnership to drill the Jinhai well on land belonging to Wang Yugu. When drilling stopped in 1889 one of the partners, Zhou Xiangji, bought out two-thirds of every share held by the other partners and continued digging the well.[39] The arrangement settled on here was similar to that found in those cases examined in chapter 2, in which the partnership as a whole took on the contribution of delinquent shareholders and redistributed shares on the basis of real investment after the well came in. In fact, the funds Zhou put up were in the form of a loan secured by well shares. The other partners had the option to buy back their alienated shares by repayment of the funds advanced by Zhou to bring in the well.

By the twentieth century we see variations in the system of intrapartnership credit that involved some members breaking off and managing part of the company independently while keeping the partnership as a whole intact. In 1944 six of the original partners who had come together six years earlier to establish the Dafa furnace broke away to start their own salt-evaporating business under the name Deji dafa furnace. Their purpose in breaking away appears to have been a desire to augment the capital invested in the part of the business they controlled. However, the *daguan* management organization that ran the furnace itself remained in operation and the newly organized branch of the larger furnace complex continued to follow the regulations of the parent partnership.[40] A similar agreement was reached among the three partners in the Tongsheng futong furnace. Over a period of three years these men had managed to lease or buy ten shares in gas wells producing enough gas to fuel seven pans. In 1945 they decided to form two separate shareholder groups, each managing half of the holdings of the original partnership. Nevertheless, cooperation between the two groups remained strong. Once again, the *daguan* continued to function, and each side agreed to reallocate its gas if one or the other's share of output diminished in strength.[41]

We can only guess at the reason for such arrangements. Most likely they came about because one or more members of a partnership wished to expand the business or improve the facilities and others were unable to put up the cash for which their shares would be assessed. Rather than break up the business or hold up the proposed investment program, shareholders devised what some scholars have called subsidiary partnerships such as the ones already described.[42] Their purpose was not the destruction of the partnership but its preservation under conditions where the financial resources of partners were unequal and the weaker partners either did not want to sell or were unable to find outright purchasers for their shares. Fragmentation thus allowed production to expand and prevented the dissolution of management groups.

Another common solution to the problem of recapitalization of working wells and furnaces was to bring in outside investors, often for a limited tenure. During the course of these delimited partnerships the original owners remained active members of the management and profit-sharing group. An excellent example of this kind of arrangement is the contract entered into by Li Zizhang and Li Yuhua. In need of money to expand his business Zizhang invited Yuhua to join him in a partnership for an initial period of two years. Yuhua put up a deposit, or "goodwill" money (*xinyongqian*), amounting to 100,000 yuan. Both partners then equally shared all costs for construction or other expenses. The same criterion was applied to the allocation of profits and losses. In addition, as long as the contract was in effect, the original owner and investor jointly managed all aspects of the business. Once the time limit was up, Zizhang was bound to refund Yuhua's deposit without interest and their relationship was considered dissolved. However, if both parties desired, signing a new agreement could renew the partnership.[43]

A similar arrangement was worked out between Zhang Xinghua, Zhang Jingzhong, and Cui Yuzhi. The Zhangs had a two-thirds share in a gas well, which gave them sufficient gas to operate seven pans. In the past these had been leased out, but in 1942 they decided to operate their own furnace. Cui was invited to join them for an initial sum of 50,000 yuan, while the Zhangs put up their gas. During the three-year life of the contract Cui would receive 40 percent of all profits. However, out of their profits, the Zhangs were expected to pay back prior debts as well as Cui's capital investment. Management passed largely into the hands of men appointed by Cui, although the Zhangs kept control of the company books and had the right to send a man to oversee the activities of the furnace.[44] A similar arrangement can be found in contract 282, where the investor was brought in because the owner of a coal-burning furnace did not have adequate funds to buy both the brine and coal needed to begin operations. Once again, the bulk of the money was put up by the investor, who took on responsibility for running the furnace, while in this case both parties received an equal share of the profits.

In each of these cases, the owner of the means of production received an infusion of capital, either to expand his business or pay off prior debt. In return, the investor received part of the profits of the business and input into how it was run. Contracts of this kind were designed to deal with short-term financial needs, but allowed the original partners in a salt-production unit greater flexibility and a longer loan period than would be available if they had to turn to a usurer or native bank. Many of the investors were men who had not been involved in the salt industry before, and this was a way of expanding the field from which capital could be drawn.[45] Moreover, the extraction of interest in the form of profit sharing may have been seen as a hedge against inflation inasmuch as profits would be linked to the market, while interest would remain linked to the amount of the initial loan.

Distribution and Redistribution of the Means of Production

Furnace-Based Management at the Minor Sichuan Yards

Once formed, salt-production partnerships utilized a variety of means to obtain brine and gas for their furnaces. While local custom played an important role in defining salt-production regimes, a comparison of agriculture, mining, and salt production throughout Sichuan demonstrates the importance of technology in the evolution of property relations during the early modern period. At the advanced manufacturing centers of Ziliujing and Gongjing, the commoditization of shares, a phenomenon documented in many parts of China by the late Qing, played a dominant role in structuring production and alleviating problems of capital shortage. Together with a sophisticated system of brine and gas leasing, the market in well shares guaranteed flexible access to brine and gas. At the same time, it encouraged fragmentation within the industry and frequently discouraged capital improvement.

Salt producers in Sichuan obtained access to brine and gas in four ways: by excavation or purchase of entire wells, by direct purchase of brine, by purchase of shares in wells, and by lease of a portion of the production of a well. In most parts of Sichuan well productivity was low. This encouraged the organization of production around individual furnaces. In order to guarantee adequate and reliable sources of brine, each furnace would attempt to control between 10 and perhaps 100 wells. Fuel, on the other hand, was obtained by direct purchase from nearby coal mines, as gas was of limited importance as a fuel outside Zigong. The system of production wherein the main investment unit was the furnace, which in turn controlled the wells, was known in the industry as *yizao tongjing*.[46] Local variations, especially at smaller yards, were numerous. Among the most interesting was that which prevailed at Fengjie, where the brine in the wells was public property and the target of investment was the furnace. Low and seasonally variable productivity discouraged large capital investment in the industry there.

With the small sample of contracts now available for saltyards outside Furong, it is impossible to make any statement about long-term trends in contractual relations. However, several points are clear. First, at minor yards it appears to have been common to sell wells, furnaces, land, and equipment as a package.[47] Well sites were handled in much the same way that coal-mine sites were handled in the Baxian hills.[48] The well and the land itself were often treated separately. Purchasers received only the subsoil rights. Some sale contracts stipulated that the land would be returned when the well dried up, while others were sold for fixed periods of time, usually generational in scale, as in a contract from Leshan that was valid for 40 years. Landowners maintained certain ties to these lands that further distinguished them from final sales. In some cases the landowner demanded payments of salt, and in others there was a stipulation that an additional fee be paid if additional wells were drilled.[49] At those saltyards based on natural salt springs, such as Yunyang and Daning, there were few wells, and wells themselves were never sold. In these cases either brine was sold outright or pumping rights were rented if the owner did not wish to evaporate brine himself.

Well rental was also common in northern and eastern Sichuan and even among well owners in the highly developed saltyards at Leshan and Jianwei. From surviving tenancy contracts we can see that most tenancies were for entire wells. Tenancies could be for as little as one and as many as 20 years. Many contracts provide examples of families renting several wells and all equipment as a package, an indication of the ease of drilling wells in these areas and their low productivity and life expectancy. Most contracts required a rent deposit, an annual payment in salt, and a cash rent, though variations may also be found. There is some indication that payments in salt were declining in the Republic period, although by the 1940s the extraordinary escalation of China's rate of inflation accounts for the fact that many contracts reverted to rents in kind or at least rents stated in salt and converted to cash at market rates. Landowners also continued to demand many of the by-products of salt production, particularly a portion of the coal slag left over after salt was evaporated and of the manure left by the buffalo who pumped the brine. Both were extremely valuable sources of fertilizer and in part confirm our impression that most landowners of brine wells outside Furong still obtained a substantial portion of their income from agricultural pursuits. According to a much-cited article on corruption at the Wutongqiao saltyard, Jianwei had more than 6,000 buffalo turning brine pumps in 1943, producing products of excreta valued at more than 100,000 yuan. Over 70 percent went to the landowners who rented out the well sites.[50]

Although owner management was the preferred option, rentals were made available when individual well owners experienced financial difficulties that made it impossible for them to manufacture salt or when an individual's wells were not productive enough to warrant the construction of his own furnace. It is also likely that competition from larger producers forced smaller producers to sell or rent their wells, contributing to the increasing concentration of brine reserves we see in areas like Yunyang and Daning.[51] Nevertheless, most rented wells probably fell within the category of supplementary wells (*bangjing*), acquired by furnace owners whose own wells did not produce adequate brine for their needs. As such they played a subordinate role in the operations of the well yards.

Furong and the Sale of Salt Shares

Circumstances prevailing at the Furong saltyard were quite different from those elsewhere in Sichuan. At Furong, the extraordinary productivity of wells meant that one well could supply numerous furnaces. Although Furong was commonly said to operate according to a system of "well control of furnaces" (*yijing tongzao*) to distinguish it from the situation elsewhere in the province, in fact management and distribution of brine and gas was highly fragmented and called for a very complex system of sales and rentals.

The most important characteristic differentiating Furong from the salt-yards described above was the fact that wells were almost never rented or sold in their entirety. The system of partnerships that enabled well developers to bring together sufficient capital to dig wells also determined the way in which brine and gas would be dispersed among those furnace operators who did not possess large well holdings of their own. Putting aside for a moment the special conditions obtaining in the rental of gas, we may say that the produce of wells was almost always obtained by rental or purchase of well shares. Inasmuch as most well shares were held in small denominations, rental or purchase to obtain brine was almost always in small amounts as well. Thus, one of the responsibilities of the men putting together a partnership to evaporate salt was the highly delicate task of obtaining rights to well shares, often from a wide variety of owners.[52]

Share purchase was the simplest way to put together the productive resources necessary to evaporate brine and produce salt. The terms of share purchase contracts were not unlike those of contracts for the sale of land. Most important was a statement of the number of shares for sale and the accompanying facilities at the well.[53] The new owner of the shares would own and be responsible for only that proportion of the facilities, such as pumping equipment, vats, access roads, buffalo sheds, and countinghouses, to which his shares entitled him. In the absence of a reliable system of title registration, contracts not only stipulated in great detail what property rights were being transferred. They also assigned liability for subsequent title or boundary disputes and residual claims against the property being transferred to the "seller" in the transaction.[54] Often stated in the form of a disclaimer of liability by the purchaser, these clauses were routinely upheld in Qing and Republican courts.

The derivation of share contracts in familiar land-sale contracts is further confirmed by the care with which contracting parties indicated the finality of share sales. In Sichuan, as in other parts of China, it was common to find contracts of land sale that were really in the nature of conditional sales, "living contracts" (*huoqi*),[55] or long-term tenancies.[56] However, by the late Qing, well-share purchase agreements in Furong were invariably in the nature of final sales, and buyers went to great lengths to ensure that no subsequent claims could be made by the previous owners of shares. Following the list of equipment and buildings found on the site, phrases such as "not a hair is retained," "not a yard, a foot, or an inch is retained," and other such picturesque language were appended to demonstrate to the judges in future lawsuits that nothing was being held back by the owner.[57] Equally important in this regard was the inclusion of a disclaimer of any rights to *guahong*, or subsequent increased compensation on the part of the party alienating his shares.[58] In the agrarian sector, conditional sale, among other things, compensated the original owner for an increase in value accrued to a parcel of land over time. Sellers of land would demand extra payments lest they exercise their right of redemption.[59] Likewise, *guahong* was sometimes demanded by previous owners of wells whose productivity rose, as compensation for their failure to exact the full value of the well in the original sale price. Finally, as a further expression of the fact that this was a final sale, some contracts added the provision that the seller would never try to redeem his shares, as some undoubtedly wished they could, when profits at the wells began rolling in.[60]

In an area like Furong, where salt production was such an important part of the local economy, salt shares had much the same importance to their owners that landed property did in other parts of the country.[61] Indeed, the role played by shares in the portfolios of households and lineages belies theories of Chinese "cultural preference" for land as the most secure store of wealth. As we shall see, it was not uncommon for a lineage to sell its agricultural land in order to protect its salt assets against creditors' demands. Nevertheless, shares in wells and other saltyard assets were subject to many of the same customs that attempted to conserve property within the kinship group. Many contracts note that shares were first offered to members of the seller's lineage before tender on the open market was allowed.[62] Indeed, such stipulations were as common as those acknowledging prior offers to fellow partners in a well.[63]

An examination of the reason for well share sales also indicates that well shares were seen as valuable assets to be sold with great reluctance. Sellers often explained their decision to sell in the contract of sale, alerting any interested parties that they had little other choice. Of 56 surviving contracts of sale, 17 indicate that shares were sold to pay debts, three note that the shares' owners had run out of money to contribute to the completion of the well, and seven claimed that the owner, while not in debt, was in urgent need of money. Thus over 48 percent of all sales were due to what Chinese sources often call "unavoidable causes." This percentage is even higher, a full 56 percent, if we exclude those contracts for which no cause is given. This can be compared to 12 cases in which the owner stated that he had better use for the money he would obtain, one case in which the owner felt the property was too far from his home to keep an eye on, and three cases in which small profits and poor market conditions drove investors to bail out while they could.

Although similar to the practices we find in the sale of land in Sichuan, the peculiar nature of well partnerships did bring complications to transactions in well shares. The first emanated from differences in property rights accruing to investor and to landowner shares, depending on whether the original well-digging agreement had been for a fixed term or perpetual lease. In the former case, investor shares would eventually revert to the landowner, and the value of shares was influenced greatly by the number of years left in the lease. Likewise, the small number of landowner shares in a fixed-term well would some day be worth two or three times their present value. On the other hand, investor shares in either type of well could be seriously affected by *shangxia jie* transactions at the well. Landowner shares were not always diminished in such deals, but the purchaser did well to make very certain that family divisions had not led to a diminution of the shareholdings for which he was negotiating. This was a particular concern in the case of landowner shares inasmuch as many of the original landowners in the area were corporate bodies.

Many operating wells were already leased to groups or individuals engaged in the production of salt. Whereas tenants on agricultural plots subject to purchase negotiations often found themselves removed from the land, salt industry tenants appear to have enjoyed absolute security of tenure. The enormous investment involved in operating and maintaining a well or furnace is undoubtedly responsible for this improvement in tenant rights at the saltyards. Sale contracts involving wells already under lease to someone else included clauses stipulating that possession of the product of the well would have to wait until the tenant's lease was up.[64] However, the new owner would receive any rent due his shares.

Of course our sample is too small to draw any conclusions regarding the frequency of share sales beyond the kinship group. Likewise, we can never know how many shares were sold over and over again. Nevertheless, the similarity between attitudes toward land and attitudes toward well shares meant that purchase of shares could never serve as an adequate mechanism for the redistribution of the factors of production among those actually manufacturing salt. It is in part for this reason that we see such a lively market in the rental of well produce and well shares.

Rental of Brine

Both direct purchase and rental of well shares played a role in the redistribution of brine. Methods involving direct purchase, or purchase through a middleman, dominated the market in brine between the yellow- and black-brine wells of Gongjing and the gas furnaces of Ziliujing.[65] However, for those operating furnaces close to the sources of brine, and particularly for small and medium-sized producers who did not command large, independent holdings in wells, some form of well-tenancy agreement was preferable.

In the case of brine, the most common method was rental of well shares for a fixed period.[66] While most tenancies outside Furong required a rent deposit and some payment in kind, in Furong we see a new system uniquely suited to the high profits and high demand business transacted at brine wells. Rents were always paid in cash, save for a short period in the late 1930s and 1940s when inflation was extremely high. Tenure ranged from six to 12 years during the late Qing and Republican periods. At the same time the need for rent deposits was eliminated by the unusual requirement that the entire rent be paid in advance or within a short time after the contract was signed.[67] While some Chinese scholars have suggested that the system arose as a result of the desire of shareowners to get money to buy land, the situation was clearly far more complex. During the early twentieth century several large Furong salt-producing lineages took advantage of this practice to rent out their considerable facilities as a means to pay off their mounting debts.[68] On the one hand, as we have seen, rental allowed people with limited capital to enter the business of salt production without having to bear the risk and expense of opening a well. Many of the parties to well-share leases were wholesale merchants and firms, and the owners of businesses in fields other than salt production in Furong and elsewhere in Sichuan. Rental brought shareowners considerable immediate gains and as we will see in later chapters, some owners used these to diversify their holdings, expand into related businesses, and increase the vertical integration of salt enterprises.[69]

The biggest problems posed by brine-share tenancy arrangements arose from distribution of responsibility for maintenance of wells and changes in the productivity of a well during the life of a lease. Most contracts stipulated that neither side would make any claims against the other if productivity rose or fell.[70] However, the compilers of the *Selected Zigong Salt Industry Contracts and Documents* have noted that many landowners included clauses in their leases designed to encourage tenants to redrill the well if productivity declined. Incentives included rent-free extension of the tenancy period and cession to the tenant of any increase in productivity achieved during the life of the lease.[71] Repairs to well equipment and to the well itself were generally paid for by the landowner, who would reclaim control of the property within a short time. In practice, landowners rarely made a cash grant for this purpose. Rather, the tenant carried out necessary repairs and was reimbursed either by means of a deduction from rent or by extending the length of the lease.[72] Although this system served the interests of tenants, practices relating to the construction of new equipment may have discouraged capital improvements in operating wells. With the exception of very costly machinery, such as steam-driven pumps, most equipment and facilities reverted back to the landowner when the lease was up.[73]

What the well-share leases do not reveal is how wells were operated and repaired when large numbers of people had varying claims to their productivity and shared responsibility for their repair. At any one well there would be holders of landowner shares and investor shares and persons who had rented either type of shares for a limited time. It is unlikely that each undertook to pump the brine accruing to those shares, particularly as some may have controlled as little as several minutes of pumping time each month. Rather, some form of unified management must have obtained at each well. This management organization, which in the twentieth century fell under the rubric of the *daguan* (discussed previously), would allocate brine and assess those with shares, rented or owned, for the various expenses the well incurred in accordance with the terms of their individual contracts.

Rental of Gas

Although some furnaces in Furong were fueled by coal, by the early twentieth century coal furnaces were declining both in numbers and in their relative influence among salt producers. As we shall see, during the periods of the so-called salt glut in the mid-1920s and early 1930s many coal-burning furnaces were shut down and their numbers strictly limited by government decree. Thus, the control of gas became a major source of income and power in the Furong saltyard and the practices governing its distribution were even more complex than those found in the sale and rental of brine.

Unlike brine, gas was never sold directly to the furnaces that evaporated salt but had to be rented from gas wells. The basic unit of gas in Furong was the fireball (*huoquan*). This misnomer extended to the appellation of gas sources as well, commonly known as fire wells (*huojing*). One fireball may be simply understood as the amount of gas necessary to boil one pan of brine to produce fine-granulated salt (see illustration 3.1). Henceforth this quantity of gas will be referred to as a pan unit of gas. However, the uniformity in well output that this definition implies was not found in the real world of salt production. The number of pan units of gas produced by a well varied over time and the risk of a diminution of gas strength during the life of a tenancy was always present. As a result, the methods of leasing gas continued to be refined and changed up until the time the PRC established its authority in Sichuan.

The earliest and simplest method of gas rental found in surviving contracts was the rental of a fixed number of pan units for a fixed period of time. The *Selected Zigong Salt Industry Contracts and Documents* contract 375, dated 1791, called for the rental of four pan units for a period of five years at a total rent of 1,200 taels. As in the case of brine rental, a portion of the rent for gas would typically be paid in advance and the rest within a year after the tenancy began.[74] One variation on this form of contract was the rental of a number of gas well shares. Some of these contracts stated the number of pan units the shares would entail. Others simply said that the tenants would be entitled to that number of pan units accruing to the shares being rented. The latter form of contract was more flexible and could account for rises and falls in well productivity without any further negotiations on behalf of the parties involved.[75] Nevertheless, by the late Qing it was one of the customs of the saltyard to charge around five taels per month for a pan unit of gas.[76]

All of these methods suffered from an inability to take into account differences in the strength of gas (*huoli*) from different wells. To put the matter simply, a pan unit from one well might take 24 hours to evaporate one pan of brine, while a pan unit from another might take only 12 hours to produce

ILLUSTRATION 3.1 Brine Pans at a Zigong Furnace
Photograph by Madeleine Zelin.

the same pan of brine, much as the strength of the fire differs on a gas stove turned to low or to high. In order to remedy this, many gas rentals in the Republican period began to be based on a measure of the productivity of the pan unit. In some we see calculations based on the amount of brine a pan unit could evaporate into salt within a 24-hour period.[77] Inasmuch as brine itself varied in concentration, this measure of productivity also had its shortcomings and a more accurate method of measurement was devised at some furnaces based on the amount of table salt actually produced with gas rented from a given well.[78] A very few contracts even began to stipulate the kind of brine upon which the measure of productivity was based.[79] Variable rent meant that rent could no longer be paid as a lump sum in advance. By the 1940s an even more progressive form of rent was introduced by which leaseholders paid a deposit per pan unit and a monthly rent based on a calculation of 15 percent of the official price being paid for the salt the gas in question produced.[80] In this way quality, productivity, and inflation were taken into account in a manner that balanced the interests of both the owners of gas well shares and the furnace owners who leased their output.[81]

As in the case of brine leases, the balance of power shifted between those who developed the well and those who leased its product. Contracts detailed all items of equipment included in the gas lease and the tenant was compensated for any repairs or additions he made to the physical plant by extensions to the lease period.[82] Nevertheless, the well developers retained considerable power over the disposal of gas well resources. The most striking indication of this is the institution of *dipi huo* or rent of the land on which the furnace itself was constructed. *Dipi huo* could be paid to the original owner of the land or to the owners of well shares, to which group the landowner belonged. *Dipi huo* could be quite high, ranging from 10 to 20 percent of the gas utilized at the furnace.[83] In either case, all facilities built to house the furnace and store brine reverted to the landowner when the well dried up.

Although a small number of gas wells were rented in their entirety, most, like brine wells, were rented in small portions to a large number of separate furnace partnerships. Contracts drawn up by the shareholders of the Hai-sheng-Taisheng-Xinglong well provide an example of one well that rented gas to a number of different furnaces under different terms of tenure. It took over a quarter of a century to bring this well into production, and the changes in name noted above are an indication of the infusions of new capital required as a result. However, according to a sociogeography of the saltyard compiled in 1916, by the early Republic the well was producing 260 pan units of gas, rented out by its many shareholders in a variety of ways.[84] When Li Xueqiao and Li Yunqiao rented four shares yielding twelve pan units in 1941 they paid a rent of 40,000 yuan per pan unit for a total of 160,000 yuan. When the productivity of the well increased three years later and their shares entitled them to six more pan units, they did not have to pay any additional rent.[85]

Cai Puquan and Hu Yingshi obtained a similar arrangement in 1938. Cai and Hu rented one share for which they received eight pan units. The lease was for 13.5 years at a rent of 7,500 yuan.[86] However, in 1939, when the Pufeng furnace, managed by Cai Puquan and Li Xubai, leased a separate share of the production of the well, their rent was calculated by the number of bundles of salt the gas could produce each month.[87] An earlier contract entered into by this same furnace, dated 1920, stipulated payment of a 1,300-tael rent deposit and rent of 135 cash per *dan* of brine boiled. It was this same well that pioneered the signing of contracts giving the landowner a percentage of profits from the final sale price of salt, as already mentioned. Arrangements such as these could be further complicated when pan units of gas were subleased from the original tenant in a gas well and when one furnace put together gas from several different wells.

Although saltyard regulations held that neither side would make any claims on the other if the strength of the gas increased or decreased,[88] in practice the high degree of likelihood that over time the gas in a well would diminish in its power to heat pans led to a number of accommodations to tenant interests. The simplest solution was to add more pan units rent free in order to restore the furnace to its original productive capacity.[89] Other well developers and their tenants agreed to a decrease in rent and/or compensatory extension of the lease.[90] More important were those cases in which the well developers took measures to increase lost capacity by investing in further drilling of the well themselves or providing the tenant with incentives to carry out such work. Provisions of the latter variety included rent-free use of any increased productivity that resulted from tenant investment or stipulations that the rent would be raised, but the tenant would keep any additions he made to the plant when the tenancy was up.[91]

Profit Sharing Among Brine and Gas Stakeholders

Well drilling and the distribution of the brine and gas that wells produced were only the first steps in salt production. It was this phase of production that the largest numbers of Zigong residents invested in, often in the form of small numbers of shares. It was also in this phase of production that the initial fortunes at the yard were made, fortunes which, as we will see in chapter 4, allowed a small Zigong elite to utilize retained earnings to develop highly profitably brine evaporation furnaces, as well as wholesale firms that marketed salt throughout the southwest and much of central China. It was also early entry into this phase of production that allowed the wealthiest investors to develop vertically and horizontally integrated firms combining all aspects of the salt business under one management structure.

Surviving contracts are of only limited use in determining the profitability of share ownership, sale, or lease. Given the variations possible in a single transaction, ranging from the length of a contract to the number of shares involved, the productivity of the well, and the concentration of brine and/or strength of gas, it is not surprising that it is difficult to compare incomes per share. Changes over time in taxation, conditions of production, market access, and the relative supply of brine versus gas also influenced the value of well shares. Unfortunately the small number of account books and ledgers that have survived have not provided the kind of information that would make calculations of average returns to shares possible. Therefore any analysis of the profitability of well drilling and shareholding can be only an approximation.

The most direct data for such an estimate come from Qiao Fu's 1916 local sociogeography mentioned above. It provides brief snapshots of various aspects of business in Ziliujing immediately following the 1911 revolution. As we will see in chapter 10, this was a period of open markets, similar to the first well-drilling boom of the second and third quarters of the nineteenth century. Table 3.1 summarizes Qiao's data on the average costs of production at a brine well which turned out over 100 *dan* of brine a day.

According to Qiao, at this time a *dan* of unprocessed concentrated black brine brought on average 0.47 taels. Profitable black-brine wells during the early 1900s produced between 100 and 300 *dan* of brine per day. Using a conversion rate of 0.42 taels per string of cash, it is possible to get a rough estimate of the net monthly income of a black-brine well (see table 3.2).

The *Essentials of Sichuan Salt*, an official gazetteer published in 1919, estimates the cost of drilling at this time to range from 30,000 taels for a well of medium depth to 40,000–50,000 taels for the deepest black-brine wells.[92] At this rate, a successful well producing brine alone could take four to seven years to recover the costs of excavation. From that time on, depending on whether the well was a 24- or 30-share well (Qiao does not make this distinction in his calculations), each share could net upward of 240 taels a year. Of course such calculations do not take into account the money the same shareholder may have lost in several other well ventures that did not succeed. We do not have sufficient longitudinal data on individual investors to determine how much unsuccessful drilling efforts and the opening of wells that soon went out of production contributed to the real costs of

TABLE 3.1 Average Monthly Cost of Major Inputs at a
Ziliujing Brine Well Producing Over 100 *dan*/Day c. 1916

Input	Cost in strings of cash*
Buffalo feed	1,903
Rope	302
Bamboo	1,224
Hemp	1,536
Labor	320
Buffalo medicine	30
Miscellaneous	66
Total	5,381

*Conversion of taels to strings for the price of bamboo and hemp is based on Qiao's estimate of a
1:0.42 conversion rate between copper cash and taels in 1916 Ziliujing.
Source: Fu Qiao, *Ziliujing diyiji* [Ziliujing, volume one] (Chengdu: Quchang gongsi, 1916), 144.

well development. Qiao Fu notes that there were thousands of well shafts
dotting the Ziliujing and Gongjing yards, but that there were at least 1,250
in operation at the time he was writing.[93] The market for well shares was
sufficiently strong in the late nineteenth century to command prices of as
much as 50 taels per share even for unfinished wells.[94]

If you were lucky enough to have invested in shares in a well that produced
gas or both gas and brine, profits could be even greater than for brine wells.
Most of the gas wells were located at the Gongjing yard. According to Qiao,
one pan unit of gas produced at such a well could be rented to a furnace for
about 100 taels a year. Gas mined in Ziliujing was weaker, and rented for

TABLE 3.2 Net Monthly Income of Ziliujing Brine Well (in taels)*

Average price of brine/*dan* in taels[a]	0.47
Average production/month in *dan*[b*]	4,050
Average income/month (a*b) in taels	1,903
Average costs of production/month in taels[c†]	1,294
Average net monthly profit (b–c) in taels	609
Average annual profit in taels	7,308

*Assuming operation 27 days per month, 150 *dan* per day.
†Based on total in table 3.1 converted to taels.
Source: Fu Qiao, *Ziliujing diyiji* [Ziliujing, volume one] (Chengdu: Quchang gongsi, 1916), 79, table 3.1.

about 50 or 60 taels per pan unit annually.[95] As of 1916 the official count of pans being fired at the Furong yard was 9,416 large pans and 913 small pans.[96] Inasmuch as each pan was fired by one pan unit of gas, we can assume that approximately 10,000 pan units of gas were leased or owned by the early twentieth century, generating income of about one million taels annually. The earnings rate on shares of gas wells varied widely. At wells producing 600–700 pan units a year, a share could return as much as 2,000 taels or more a year minus production costs. Even weaker mines with outputs of several tens of pan units produced gross gas receipts of several thousand taels a year. In an oral account of his experience working at the Gongjing saltyard between 1909 and 1936, Ji Rongqing recalled annual profits of 20,000 to 50,000 taels at wells producing both brine and gas and as much as 80,000 a year at the highly productive Tianlong well, which was first drilled as the Lianhai well in the nineteenth century and was still operating in the 1930s.[97]

High potential profits clearly compensated for the risks of well development. By contrast, the risks entailed in salt evaporation were small and the costs of opening a brine evaporation furnace were quite low. The *Essentials of Sichuan Salt* estimates that a gas-powered furnace cost an average of about 280 to 350 taels per "line" of pans. A coal-fired furnace, which did not have to overcome the technological problems of piping gas to the pans and regulating the flow of the gas to each pan, cost less than 150 taels per line.[98] These figures do not include the costs of renting the land on which the furnace was built.

The profits of furnaces, both gas and coal fired, are difficult to generalize, depending as they did on fluctuating supplies and costs of brine and gas, the costs of the furnace site lease, and the price that salt fetched at the yard. The early twentieth century was a prosperous period for salt furnaces. According to Qiao Fu, it cost 172.6 taels to produce the salt sold by one *hua* salt certificate, or 11,000 *jin*. Thus salt could be processed at a cost of about 0.016 taels per *jin*. The average gas-fired pan produced 11,760 to 23,520 *jin* per year at a cost of 188 to 376 taels. A *jin* of *hua* salt sold in 1916 for an average of 79 copper cash at Ziliujing and 74 copper cash at Gongjing, the difference most likely resulting from Gongjing's greater distance from the main river port for shipment of Furong salt. Taking the higher Ziliujing figure, at current rates of exchange the price the furnace received for a *jin* of salt was about 0.044 taels. Assuming it operated every day, the average Ziliujing furnace could gross approximately 517 to 1,034 taels per pan per year with a net annual profit per pan of 329 to 658.[99] This is based on before-tax profits. As we shall see, the system of taxation changed several times over the course of the nineteenth and twentieth centuries, but only rarely was the tax imposed at the furnace.

With profits so high and risk so low, we might wonder why more people did not invest in furnaces. The simple answer is that supply constraints gave owners of brine an advantage in the construction of furnaces and the marketing of salt. During the nineteenth century, when the salt industry in Zigong was beginning to take off, the discovery of vast stores of natural gas created an imbalance in the supply of fuel and the supply of brine. By the early twentieth century the discovery of the rock-salt layer in Ziliujing temporarily restored the balance between gas and brine. However, as we will see, new technologies for brine extraction and the increased value of gas under conditions of brine surplus would again change the conditions under which furnaces operated. Nevertheless, as long as the market for Sichuan salt remained open, both large and small producers could expect a sufficient return on investment to continue drilling wells and evaporating salt at both Furong yards.

Conclusion

The Furong saltyard provides an excellent case study of the interaction between technology and institutions in economic development. Limited household accumulation relative to the capital needs of salt exploration, combined with a strong contract culture in both agriculture and mining, provide the background for understanding the remarkable growth of the Furong salt industry in the late nineteenth century. The commoditization of well shares was a direct outgrowth of this process. Of particular importance is the apparent willingness of both small and large holders of capital to tie up their resources for long periods of time in the anticipation of profits. This experience of long-term investment challenges long-held assumptions about Chinese preferences for quick returns through usury and pawnbroking, an assertion used to explain the difficulty experienced by late-nineteenth-century "self-strengtheners" seeking investment in new Western-style endeavors.[100] Furthermore, despite claims by many scholars that China's underdevelopment can be traced in part to the absence of a commercial code, the existence of consistently applied and highly technical customs of the yard (*changgui*), having no relation to the concerns of the official salt gabelle, suggests that we have ignored regionally significant customary commercial law. The ability of businessmen to rely on the government to uphold this law, even amid the chaos of the warlord era, testifies to its traditional importance in economic life and alerts us to the need to explore this facet of China's economic and legal history in other highly commercialized regions.

At the same time, the pattern of investment and resource allocation that emerged in Furong during the nineteenth century was one that encouraged fragmentation and mirrors the development of small business elsewhere in China. While sale of well shares was limited by a traditional reluctance to sell ancestral property, a number of positive factors influenced the development of a lively rental market in brine and gas. In particular, this market enabled furnace owners to respond flexibly to market demand for salt, changing their access to well shares through relatively short-term leases as opposed to permanent purchase of well shares. This flexibility was further enhanced by the possibility of sublets and recombinations among furnaces themselves. Supplies could be protected by lease continuation contracts and advance re-lease whereby tenants renewed their tenancies in a well even before their original lease had expired.[101] Moreover, although tenancy must have discouraged large-scale capital investment, the benefits of which would revert to the landowner once the lease was up, we have seen that both brine and gas renters were provided with considerable incentives to maintain and improve levels of production. These were further enhanced by the apparent ease with which leases were renewed, often on the same terms as the original lease.

Furong provides other insights into Chinese patterns of economic development as well. While the saltyard displays a clear tendency toward fragmentation of ownership, we can detect important integrating tendencies in both management and organization. The evolution of business partnerships and the use of *daguan* management organizations to oversee the diverse interests in wells and furnaces provide a glimpse of this process. Equally important was the growth of large lineage-based firms, which both took advantage of their positions as early entrants to capture large well resources and capitalized on the rapid and extensive growth of the market for Sichuan salt in the years following the Taiping Rebellion. They were among the most important investors to benefit from the large profits to be obtained when a well did come in and were able to parlay these profits into investments in ancillary industries, marketing, and the integration of brine and gas resources.

4

Organization and Entrepreneurship in Qing Furong

FOR MOST of the investors who put their money into digging wells, pumping brine, and evaporating salt in the salt-producing areas of Fushun and Rong counties, purchase, rental, and redistribution of salt shares made up the salt business. Although the combined impact of their capital on the development of salt production in the region was great, the fragmented nature of their investment meant that as individuals they made only a small contribution to the form that development took. As important as the elaboration of a complex system of shareholding and partnership at the yard was the evolution of new, transitional forms of business organization. In an extractive industry like that in Zigong it was luck and a willingness to take risks that allowed some early entrants to amass the fortunes that have made them legends in late imperial history. What draws us to the stories of these early salt magnates is what they did with those fortunes. Besides buying for themselves and their immediate descendants an elite lifestyle to which they could never have aspired in the past, a small group of large salt manufacturers in nineteenth-century Ziliujing and Gongjing experimented with two critical advances in the structure of the firm. Driven in part by the composition of investment discussed previously and in part by a quest for economies of scale and scope and opportunities for market domination, these entrepreneurs pioneered the development of vertical and horizontal integration of production and the modernization of management in China.

Making a Fortune in Salt

By the end of the Taiping Rebellion four families had emerged as the leaders of the Furong salt community. Following in their wake, and no doubt aspiring to the enormous wealth and influence that these families had accrued during the years of war, were several hundred other large salt developers.[1] The strategies they pursued to build their fortunes were similar, although in the case of the Li Siyou, Wang Sanwei, Hu Yuanhe, and Yan Guixin lineage trusts (*tang*), the results exceeded those of almost any merchant in the land. A popular ditty in Sichuan during the Qing was suggestive of the awe in which the senior members of these merchant houses were held. "If you're not named Wang, if you're not named Li, then old man, you can't scare me."[2]

The histories of these powerful lineages were representative of Sichuan's long-standing place as a recipient of overflow population from parts east and south of its borders. The ancestors of Wang Langyun, the architect of the Wang Sanwei trust's salt empire, were among the first wave of migrants to Sichuan following the fall of the Ming.[3] Leaving Hubei and settling in Fushun County in the 1660s, they remained a family of modest means set upon a conventional course of land management combined with attempts at examination success.[4] Wang Duanhu, the great-grandfather of Wang Langyun, held a minor military rank. His grandfather, Wang Yuchuan, reached the position of expectant first-class assistant department magistrate (*zhoutong*), while his father, Wang Kai, served in government as a legal secretary (*liwen*) in a financial commissioner's yamen. During the first half of the dynasty, the Wangs accumulated a modest legacy in the form of agricultural and brine land, much of the latter apparently abandoned or relatively unproductive wells.

The Li Siyou trust had a similar history, although their ancestors are said to have come to the province during the late Yuan (1279–1368). They may also have been involved in salt production at an early date. In his biography of his grandfather, Li Jiuxia wrote that in 1628, at the age of 10, Li Guoyu was already climbing the derrick to change the cable that drew up brine.[5] During the years of Wu Sangui's rule in Sichuan,[6] in the 1660s and 1670s, Li Guoyu was often a spokesman for salt-industry interests and was instrumental in submitting at least one successful petition for salt-tax relief. Until the early nineteenth century, the family pursued the same mixed strategy followed by most upwardly aspiring families in late imperial China, applying its energies to farming while ensuring that the children of each generation received ample education to achieve modest academic success. One of Li Guoyu's brother's sons obtained the academic rank of provincial graduate (*juren*), serving in several magisterial-level posts. The next generation produced a county graduate (*shengyuan*), a provincial graduate, and an instructor (*jiaoxi*) in the plain white banner, who later served as a magistrate. One cousin even presaged a pattern that was to be common among salt industrialists in the late Qing and purchased the rank of prefectural registrar (*jingli*), but never actually served in a substantive post.

The ancestors of Yan Changying, the founder of the Yan Guixin trust, did not migrate to Sichuan until the 1730s, when they joined the waves of Guangdong migrants who came to Sichuan to take advantage of its still abundant farmland. The Yans, originally based in Weiyuan County, were farmers until the 1830s, although family lore has it that the first ancestor in Sichuan was a teacher, and Yan Changxun, eldest of the generation that entered the salt industry, is said to have studied for but failed to pass the civil service examinations. A combination of luck and an intellectual interest in the technology of salt production appears to have been behind the family's fortunes. Happening upon a natural salt spring on their own land, Changxun and Changying devoted their savings to the drilling of the Yongxing well, which came in in 1825 and continued to produce gas and brine for more than a century.[7]

While the Wangs, Lis, and Yans grounded their fortunes in the possession of land and cultivation of traditional gentry roles, the founder of the Hu fortune at Gongjing represents that other breed of immigrant so important to Sichuan's early economic development, the merchant.[8] Hu Liwei was born in Luling County, Jiangxi, of a large, but impoverished agricultural lineage. He and his kinsman, Hu Shiyun, came to Ziliujing during the mid-Jiaqing reign (1796–1820), lured there by the already strong links between Jiangxi merchants and the salt-producing regions of distant Sichuan. Liwei married in Sichuan but died soon after, leaving a wife and son who were forced by poverty to return to Jiangxi. When he grew up, the son of this union, Hu Yuanhai, borrowed some money from a relative and returned to the site of his father's dreams. Here he joined other members of the Jiangxi guild in selling cloth. Yuanhai made enough money to open a shop in Ziliujing, and soon after the owner of the new Yuanhe store married the daughter of a fellow provincial surnamed Wang.

Together Hu Yuanhai and his wife built a strong business, and it was with the money he made selling cloth that he first entered a partnership to drill for brine. Following the success of this venture, he used the more than 8,000 strings of cash he obtained in profits to buy a piece of agricultural land yielding 80 *shi* of grain a year in rents. But far more important in the purchase was the apparently barren wasteland and riverbank land that adjoined it. It was here that Hu Yuanhai opened his first gas and brine wells, and on the bank of the river, at the foot of the Zhaizi hills, that he moved his family and built his business offices.

At mid-century none of these families had yet accumulated notable wealth. With a prospering cloth business to fall back on, Hu Yuanhai was alone among the early salt giants to remain relatively independent in his business activities. After his first successful partnership Hu tended to develop his wells on his own land. The method used was known locally as "using one well to build another well" (*yijing zhuangjing*), but we would readily recognize this strategy as one of building a firm with retained earnings.[9] At Zigong, once an investor was successful in opening one well, the next could easily be developed using only the profits from the first. Even if the new venture failed, the investor's original capital was safe. And, unless the first well dried up, he would some day have sufficient profits to try again. It was this method that protected another salt capitalist, Huang Zhiqing, from bankruptcy, despite an investment of almost 70,000 taels in a well that was finally abandoned after drilling for eight years.[10] Luo Xiaoyuan, one of the leading Zigong businessmen of the early twentieth century, also applied this method to the development of furnaces. For Hu Yuanhai the method not only guaranteed profits, but also promised to relieve him and his descendants of the complications that partnerships could bring. Nevertheless, it did limit the scope of his endeavors. Unlike those of his fellow magnates, most of Hu Yuanhai's wells produced yellow brine, albeit of good quality. They tended to be shallow and took relatively little time and money to dig. At his death Hu had accumulated an estate consisting of five brine wells and 30 pan units of gas, agricultural land yielding 2,000 *shi* in rents, and liquid assets amounting to several tens of thousands of taels.[11]

For the Yans, a larger lineage with branches in Weiyuan, Fushun, and Rong counties, this investment strategy also proved attractive.[12] Yan Changying took the profits of his Yongxing well to drill the Beihai well and then used the profits from the Beihai to drill the Lailong well. By this time the income of the lineage trust was sufficient to allow a substantial distribution to each branch, which they invested in the development of wells and furnaces of their own. The primary restriction on the expansion of their holdings was land. With limited property in Ziliujing and unwilling to risk joint ventures outside of their own lineage, the Yans invested in land in the less developed Gongjing side of the saltyard. While this district did not produce gas wells, the Yans were able to expand their fortunes in the highly profitable black-brine market. Only with the discovery of the so-called rock-salt layer did they lose their competitive position.

On the eve of the Taiping Rebellion neither the Lis nor the Wangs had the resources to "go it alone," as did the Hus and the Yans. The initial strategy pursued by these two families, and by hundreds of less successful households and lineage groups, was entry into landowner-tenant relations with

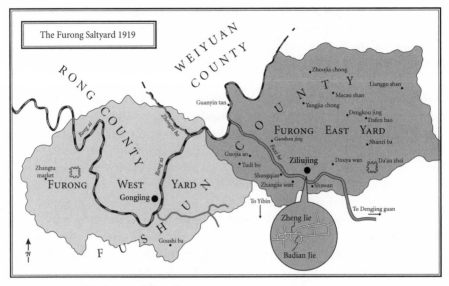

MAP 3. The Furong Saltyard, 1919
Source: Adapted from Lin, *Essentials of Sichuan Salt,* front matter; map created by Christopher Brest.

owners of capital.[13] A key source of investment was commercial capital earned by extraprovincials engaged in trade in Sichuan and its neighboring provinces in the southwest. The Hus were among these sojourners, the majority of whom were merchants from Shaanxi, Guangdong, Huguang, and Jiangxi.[14] Merchants from Guangdong, Huguang, and Jiangxi appear to have been engaged in the general merchandise trades,[15] and it is not surprising that they played a smaller role in the development of the Furong saltyard than did merchants from Shaanxi. The latter, we have seen, dominated the salt trade in early Qing Sichuan, a highly lucrative endeavor which also brought them into early contact with potential partners in Gongjing and Ziliujing. Shaanxi merchants were also prominent in the tea trade and the establishment of pawnshops throughout Sichuan.[16] It was they too who engineered the revision of salt quotas during the early nineteenth century, which allowed the supply of salt to shift to the more efficient saltyards in the southwest.[17] From this base they also entered the native banking business.[18] The shops of the eight main Shaanxi merchant houses formed the backbone of the main street in Ziliujing and the street itself was named Badian jie, or Eight Shops Road, after their establishments (see map 3). It was not until the late nineteenth century that merchants from Shanxi, too, began to play an important role in the Sichuan economy, with the development of remittance banks (*piaohao*) in the province.[19]

Until the 1830s Shaanxi merchants appear to have had little, if any, involvement in the manufacture of salt. We do not know why the investment strategy of Shaanxi merchants in Sichuan changed when it did. Luo Chengji has offered as explanation a combination of frustration with the hardships of trading in Yunnan and Guizhou, the main Shaanxi salt merchant stronghold, and the opportunities presented by new salt manufacturing technology. At the same time, Shaanxi control of the wholesale shipping market was increasingly challenged by the entry of merchants from the expanding production area of Furong and by merchants from the economic capital of Sichuan in Chongqing.[20]

It was this combination of Shaanxi capital and native land that was responsible for the first phase of the takeoff in the salt industry at Furong. The effect on the composition of capital in the industry was dramatic. By one estimate, the Shaanxi merchant share in the total capitalization of salt production in Sichuan rose from almost nothing in 1830 to as much as 70 or 80 percent by the 1870s.[21] While this may be an exaggeration, it is clear that an enormous increase in outsider investment did take place. The first major strike by salt evaporators was waged largely against the Shaanxi guild, which was said to own a dominant share in furnaces at the Furong yards.[22] Although we do not know the provenance of most investors listed in salt contracts, we do know that many of the wells we can identify in late Qing Furong were opened with the help of Shaanxi merchant funds.[23] Indeed, it was at a well owned by members of the Shaanxi guild that the first rock-salt well was drilled.[24] It was also Shaanxi merchant funds that helped transform the landed holdings of the Wang Sanwei trust and the Li Siyou trust into salt empires.

In the 1830s the fortunes of the descendants of Wang Yuchuan were on the decline.[25] They had few operating wells and only modest holdings in agricultural land. In 1838 one of their number, an enterprising and ambitious man named Wang Langyun, proposed that the property of the three existing branches of the lineage be divided and a small estate be maintained to support the sacrifices to their common grandfather. Wang Langyun took over the management of the estate and embarked on two projects that were to decide the destiny of his lineage.

With the meager resources of the lineage itself, Wang Langyun decided to redrill a well the family was already operating near Gaoshan jing. Because the Tianyi well had already been excavated to a certain depth, a richer black-brine deposit below it could be reached at far less expense than would be entailed in drilling a new well. At the same time, Langyun signed a limited-tenure lease with a Shaanxi merchant to drill another black-brine well on Wang land. The terms of this agreement, like those of the limited-tenure contracts we examined in chapter 2, gave the Wangs 12 landowner shares and the Shaanxi investor 18. Langyun and his relatives had nothing to lose if the well failed. If it came in, the Wangs would enjoy two-fifths of the profits it produced. Even more important, after 18 years the well and all immovable equipment would revert to their lineage estate.

It was by means of tenancy contracts such as these that the Wangs moved into the large-scale production of salt. Many of their investors appear to have been extraprovincial merchants looking for opportunities at the Furong yard for the quick profits that a successful black-brine or gas well could bring. But at least a few of the partners in these new Wang ventures were local merchants, such as Yan Yongxing, said to have been Langyun's partner in resistance to Qing tax policy. We must also note that a good deal of luck was combined with the business acumen that Wang Langyun brought to these deals. Popular recognition of the importance of luck is reflected in apocryphal legends such as this one about the Tianyi well mentioned before. At the time this well was being drilled the pressure of creditors became so severe that the Wangs decided to simply sell off their land at Shanzi ba. Negotiations with the Shaanxi guild were already under way and a contract was to be signed at the offices of one of the member firms on Badian jie. Langyun had begun to experience misgivings and temporarily left the discussions to give the matter further thought. At that moment, the manager of the Tianyi well ran over and announced that they had just struck brine. The deal with the Shaanxi guild was called off and Shanzi ba later became one of the most productive sites of black-brine well development.

The Tianyi was no ordinary well. At its peak of productivity it pumped between 2,000 and 3,000 *dan* of brine a month. When the well first opened, the brine gushed out to a height of over 10 feet. All the owners had to do was fix a bamboo plate over its opening and brine would run down the sides into storage vats. The high demand for brine brought about by the expanding salt market and the development of gas furnaces meant that prices for the produce of these wells were also high. With the profits from this well and the wells in which the Wangs held only landowner shares, the family began to invest its own capital in redrilling the abandoned wells it had inherited at Shanzi ba.

The Wang Sanwei trust relationship with non-kin investors can be seen as a temporary one, useful for building up the family investment portfolio, but only one of many facets of their growing salt fortune. The Li Siyou trust's early development was based more firmly on business relationships with wealthy Shaanxi merchants and grew more slowly in its early years. As late as the 1820s the Li Siyou trust had only four modestly productive brine wells.[26] When the profits from these wells were divided among the four sons of Li Shijin, little was left for investment in increasing the family business. Therefore, during the early years of the century, the Li Siyou trust as an economic unit was relatively inactive. In 1827–1828 Li Weiji went to Chengdu to take the provincial examinations. There he had a chance meeting with a Shaanxi merchant named Gao who was involved in both the salt and tea trade in Sichuan. Gao became interested in the Li family's holdings and decided to invest 3,000 taels to allow them to expand. Their first venture was to rent the Lianzhu well behind the Pearl Temple. Here again, good fortune had a hand in the family's success, for the excavation of the nearby Decheng well resulted in an increase in the productivity of the Lianzhu well from 30 to over 100 *dan* a day. Inasmuch as rental contracts contained a clause disallowing any change in the terms of tenure should productivity rise, the tenants enjoyed all the profits resulting from this windfall.

The Li Siyou trust and the merchant Gao formed a partnership in which each held 50 percent of the assets. In the wells they developed together, this meant 15 shares apiece. However, some of their ventures were in concert with other investors, such as the Shuifeng well, in which they only held 7.5 shares each, or the Falong well, in which only one-third of the shares were assigned to their collective holdings. In all, the Li-Gao partnership developed seven brine wells with a combined production of more than 200 *dan* a day. Three more wells turned out to produce gas, giving them a total of 600 pan units of gas as well.[27] With the addition of gas wells the Li-Gao partnership was transformed from a net marketer of brine to a net purchaser, a factor that encouraged their further exploration of wells.[28]

By the time of the Taiping Rebellion, families like the Lis, Wangs, Hus, and Yans were thus already becoming important producers of salt for Sichuan's domestic (*ji'an*) and border (*bian'an*) trade. But the actual marketing of that salt still remained principally in the hands of the large Shaanxi salt companies (*hao*). With the opening of the Huguang market after the fall of Nanjing due to the rebellion, this monopoly broke down. The dangers involved in shipping salt downriver before the trade was legalized and the extraordinary demand for salt in Hubei and Hunan enabled those merchants with stocks on hand and a bit of nerve to amass thousands of taels in a short time through speculation in and export of Sichuan salt. Salt that cost only a few copper cash per *jin* at the Sichuan yards could be sold for 90–200 copper cash per *jin* at the other end.[29] It was said that a man could sell a *jin* of salt in Hubei and come back with a *jin* of cotton,[30] and indeed, many salt merchants first became involved in the cotton trade in this way. Many heroic stories circulated at the time, serving as an inspiration to those with a sense of adventure and an eye toward wealth. The most famous story, and no doubt most far-fetched, was about a merchant named Liu Kunzhi, who was supposed to have personally carried a load of salt to Hubei, to have bribed the

TABLE 4.1 Brine Production of the Li-Gao Partnership, 1830s

Well Name	Approx. *dan*/day
Lianzhu	100
Shuifeng	30–40
Fengtai	40–50
Zhongxing	10
Duixi	10
Falong	30
(at Wuxing)	n/a

Source: Zilin Li et al., "Ziliujing Li Siyou tang you fazhan dao shuaiwang" [The Li Siyou trust of Ziliujing from their development to their decline], *Sichuan wenshiziliao xuanji* 4 (1962–63): 147–48.

Qing soldiers blockading the Yangzi River pontoon bridge, and, after reaching his destination, to have succeeded in getting a *jin* of gold for every *jin* of salt.[31] This was smuggled salt and, as such, beyond the constraints of the *yin* system of licensed sales. Anyone could get involved, and it was through this pirate trade that the Lis, Hus, Yans, Wangs, and other salt producers became actively engaged in marketing as well as production.

The entry of the Li Siyou trust into marketing is attributed to a faithful retainer named Five Pockmarks Zhang, who looked after the family's interests in Chongqing. As soon as news of the blockade of eastbound shipping reached Sichuan, Zhang is said to have bought up all the salt he could find in this central salt-marketing entrepôt. When salt prices rose in Huguang (Hubei and Hunan), he sold this salt, making huge profits for his employers and undoubtedly for himself as well.[32] At this time Li Xiang'an was general manager (*zongban*) of the Li Siyou trust. A marriage alliance between the Lis and the Wang Sanwei trust facilitated formation of a joint venture to market salt in Huguang. Chen Huiting, another large saltyard merchant, participated as well. However, after a while disputes among the partners led to the dissolution of the company and Li Xiang'an set up his own Xiangxingtai salt company (*hao*).[33] Wang Langyun was also involved in setting up his own trading company at this time. Called the Guangshengtong salt company, it eventually established branches in Dengjing guan, Luzhou, and Chongqing in Sichuan and in Yichang, Shashi, and Yangxi in Hubei. Most of the salt it marketed was produced at the lineage's own wells, increasing even further the profits to be made.[34]

The Hus, whose productive capacity was far smaller than that of their counterparts in Ziliujing, could never rely solely on their own wells to build up a marketing empire. Nevertheless, they too took advantage of the oppor-

MAP 4. Zigong and Upper Yangzi Cities
Source: GIS work by Douglas Miller.

tunities presented by war. Their Juyichang salt company had its head office in the Temple to the Goddess of Heaven (*Tianhou gong*) right on Badian Jie. Its branches and warehouses could also be found all along the Yangzi, with larger offices in Chongqing, Yichang, and Shashi. In later years its name was changed to the Fulinyi salt company, but its business strategy remained the same. In particular, the managers of the Juyichang salt company were famed for their ability to shift their marketing strategies to take advantage of price differentials between the yard and the sales territories and to meet the demands of seasonal production in industries such as the curing of salted vegetables, which was done in the second and third months, the brewing of soy sauce in the fifth and sixth months, and the curing of meat, largely a wintertime occupation. Without adequate salt supplies of their own, the Hus were also keen judges of the time and place to buy and sell, never restricting their purchases only to the saltyards or insisting on selling all the way to the final destination on the salt certificate. The managers of the Juyichang had a broad network for gathering market information and the skill of Hu Mianzhai in this regard won him the nickname of the "Zhuge Liang" of the salt industry, after the famous military strategist of the Three Kingdoms period.[35]

By the end of the Taiping war the Shaanxi monopoly was broken, not only in the new Huguang market, but in the domestic and border markets as well. From then on, two marketing groups dominated the trade, the so-called Chongqing group, largely extraprovincial and founded on control of financial resources in the economic capital of the province, and the Well group, whose ability to compete was based on their own enormous productive capacity at Gongjing and Ziliujing and their ability to buy up the product of many small Furong producers who could not market their salt themselves.[36] In this way, the large salt producers came to combine well development, salt evaporation, and marketing within one organizational framework. It was this integration of the business that guaranteed their dominance within the industry as a whole.

The Management of the Great Salt Empires

The Lineage as a Corporation

Scholars have long viewed traditional lineage institutions as one of the keys to the maintenance of elite status in China. However, their "familism," as well as their emphasis on the accumulation of landed wealth and examination success, has been presumed to limit their utility as engines of economic growth.[37] Among the great families of Furong it was precisely the institution of the lineage hall that permitted the consolidation of early economic successes and the development of modern management techniques. The ancestral hall and its accompanying estate became a substitute for the corporate business forms being developed in the West. For at least half a century the lineage trust was the structure within which business property was built up, diversified, and preserved against the ravages of the tax collector, the creditor, and individual family members. It was also the organization through which early concepts of limited liability and vertical integration were perfected, making it one of the most advanced business institutions of the late imperial period.

The Li Siyou trust predated the family's rise as a great salt dynasty.[38] However, by the 1850s it had been transformed largely into an institution for the organization and preservation of the family's business wealth. Under the first two successors to Li Weiji all lineage resources were reinvested to build up the collective property of the trust. Even the potential for disputes among family members, which would soon plague the Wangs, was initially avoided by granting each branch a fixed allowance of 800 *shi* in agricultural rents and a cash allowance of no more than 1,200 taels a year from the profits of the salt business. All other income from lineage enterprises was plowed back into production and sales.[39]

The Hu Yuanhe trust may also have predated the 1830s. However, as the holdings of the family grew, its structure underwent a change specifically designed to meet the needs of a large salt conglomerate. In the early years of the Hu Yuanhe trust all positions of responsibility remained entirely in family hands. We know nothing of the family rules associated with the trust, but its structure was simple, with a main office in charge of salt property, a separate department in charge of agricultural property, and one in charge of all lineage business with the world outside. This latter office was charged with cultivating lineage *guanxi*, or useful connections, with businesses and officials associated with the salt industry, the functional equivalent of today's public relations office and lobbyists. Each of these departments was run by one of the husbands of Hu Yuanhai's three daughters, Lei Xiaosong, Zhong Chunquan, and Wang Bitian.[40] Both the structure and the men who manned it remained largely unchanged until the 1890s, when Hu Yuanhai's oldest son, Mianzhai, died and was succeeded by his second son, Ruxiu. Under Hu Ruxiu the lineage rules were redrafted to include provisions that the family never live apart and that their property remain forever as a corporate whole. However, in the event that a division should become necessary, a clause was added to allow equal distribution of wealth according to the number of lines in the present generation and not the three branches that had formed the original Hu Yuanhe trust.[41] This would save the family from much of the bitterness and infighting that plagued the Wang Sanwei trust and the Li Siyou trust when they finally dissolved.

At the same time, a set of management rules was incorporated into the regulations of the trust, establishing the complex corporate structure that would continue to run the many Hu Yuanhe trust businesses and its personal affairs. Besides a general manager in charge of the main countinghouse, there were managers (*guanshi*) with special responsibility for agricultural land, the family school, sacrifices to the ancestors, the family accounts, repairs to lineage property, feed for the lineage's buffalo, warehouses, and so on—twenty in all. This hierarchy continued downward for several levels and was devoted entirely to the private needs of the lineage members. A separate hierarchy was devoted to business affairs. Moreover, by the Guangxu period (1871–1908) most offices were run by hired managers and not relatives.[42]

The Wang Sanwei trust appears to have been the only one of the four that was formed specifically to meet the needs of a growing salt empire. According to family tradition, Wang Langyun feared that his family would dissipate the property he had worked so hard to build up. Therefore, he incorporated the well and agricultural property that had grown out of the original ancestral estate and set it aside as temple land to be maintained in perpetuity. The center

ILLUSTRATION 4.1 The Wang Sanwei Lineage Hall
Photograph by Madeleine Zelin.

of the new lineage organization was a recently built ancestral temple called the Yuchuan ci, located at Bancang ba. It was there that the three branches pledged to follow the example set by Fan Wenzhang and establish a charitable estate (*gongyitian*).[43] In 1877 Wang Langyun memorialized the emperor for permission to have a stele carved and installed in the Yuchuan temple so that Wangs of future generations would all see and obey the rules of the lineage hall.

In all, the Wangs put aside 20 operating wells and 600 *mou* of agricultural land as a lineage trust.[44] This property was to be used to pay for sacrifices, the upkeep of ancestral graves, support of elderly lineage members, the expenses of lineage members taking the examinations, and aid to relatives and neighbors in time of famine. In order to achieve the lineage's goals of wealth and influence, special provisions were made to support examination success. A school was established that all male progeny of the lineage could attend and which was open to promising nonrelatives as well. Wang sons and grandsons would be given 20 taels each to help defray the costs of taking the provincial examinations and two strings if they went to take the county or prefectural exams. Those who passed would be rewarded with 100 taels. Anyone fortunate enough to qualify for the metropolitan examinations would be given 400 taels toward the trip to Beijing. And if someone was selected to enter the Hanlin Academy or the Imperial University established during the last years of the Qing, the lineage would provide him with a stipend of 400 taels a year.

The Wang Sanwei trust also provided a pension of one *shi* of rice a year for any tenant on trust land who lived to the age of sixty and put aside 240 strings of cash a year as payment for the man chosen by each lineage branch to oversee ancestral sacrifices. The trust promised to request that a memorial archway be erected in honor of chaste widows and virtuous women among its female members, contributing 50 taels to the construction of every one for which permission was granted. However, the most important passage, and that which set the Wang Sanwei trust rules apart from classic lineage admonitions, referred to the disposal of the huge surplus profits that the Wang Sanwei trust would eventually produce. It was arranged that the entire lineage would meet annually to settle the trust's accounts. At this time, half the money left over from the designated expenditures and upkeep of lineage property would be reinvested to add to the lineage's holdings. The other half would be used to buy more property for each branch, in accordance with its share of the lineage's corporate possessions. Thus half of the net earnings was reinvested in lineage businesses and the other half was available for disposal or investment by each lineage branch.

At other saltyards as well, the lineage trust became a crucial tool for managing industrial resources and ensuring the integrity and continuity of business holdings. The Wu Jingrang trust of Jianwei, one of the few salt corporations to survive the changes that occurred in the world of business under the warlord and Nationalist regimes of the early twentieth century, became a major industrial giant in southwest China. Other, more traditional lineage organizations served the interests of industrial development as well. The Yuan Hele trust was one of the largest landowners at the Jianwei yard. Their lineage regulations included a separate section on salt resource management, setting out levels of fees for various forms of tenancy and stipulating that any land sales transacted by family members be divorced from the wells and furnaces constructed on them.[45] Alienation of real estate was acceptable, but the industrial holdings of the lineage had to be maintained intact.

Business Organization at the Lineage Halls

The key to the extraordinary business success of the Wang, Li, and Hu trusts was the development of efficient management organizations which promoted expertise, centralized control of a large business empire, and allowed the expansion of the initial well business into a vertically integrated salt conglomerate.[46] Although these practices were carried out to their fullest extent among the largest salt lineages, centralized, hierarchical organization of diversified business interests was common to many of the families involved in the salt industry at this time.[47] The economic interests of the large Furong lineage trusts were based on a two-tiered management system. At the apex was a main office with overall supervisory control over the operation of each subsidiary business. At the Hu Yuanhe trust this function was performed at the Shenyi trust, established in 1867. The main office (zongguifang) was usually headed by a family member whose title was general director (zongzhanggui). Under him were five departments: (1) a countinghouse or accounting office (guifang) run by a chief accountant (zongzhang) and two assistants (bangzhang) in charge of the overall operation of the lineage's wells and furnaces; (2) a procurement department (huowugu) in charge of purchasing all supplies needed for the daily operation of the wells and furnaces; (3) an external affairs department (jiaojigu) in charge of buying brine for the lineage's furnaces and selling salt at lineage-owned retail shops; (4) a department of agricultural estates (nongzhuanggu) in charge of collecting rents and selling grain; and (5) a cash department (xianjingu) in charge of daily cash expenditures and silver-copper exchange transactions.[48]

After more than 30 years of unified management under the leadership of its founder, Wang Langyun, the Wang Sanwei trust was almost destroyed by a period of fragmentation in the late nineteenth century. Individual family members, distrustful of each other's intentions, took over operation of groups of wells, furnaces, and other family businesses. Although the family never violated the trust regulations that required maintenance of lineage holdings as an undivided estate, poor business practices, waste, embezzlement, and loss of the advantages gained by coordination of wells, furnaces, and wholesale enterprises left it in debt for almost 700,000 taels.[49] The lessons learned in the 1880s and 1890s led to a renewed attention to centralized management, and during the height of its prosperity the countinghouse (guifang) of the Jingfeng well regulated all income and expenditure, planning, and allocation of materials for Wang Sanwei trust agricultural lands, wells, furnaces, wholesale companies, and brine pipes.[50] For many years the main office was run by a man named Pan Zhongsan, whose power at the saltyard was almost as great as that of the Wang heirs themselves. Upon his death, a second layer of managerial authority was inserted between the main office and the individual production units. Known locally as the Big Four Courtiers (Sidachaochen), these new management agencies were in charge of agricultural land, large pipes, Shanzi ba wells, and the Guangshengtong wholesale company, respectively. Soon afterward, similar structures were set up to oversee wells and furnaces at Guojia ao and those at the Gongjing yard as well.[51]

Coordination between the main office and its specialized agencies and the activities of individual production units was achieved through a classic M-form (multidivisional) structure.[52] We do not know why Furong salt manufacturers chose a decentralized over a unified organizational form, particularly as lineage trusts themselves tended to employ more unified management structures with a manager in charge of each functional arena of activity. It is possible that decentralized management was seen as more flexible under conditions of rapid growth and expansion into new fields of endeavor. Moreover, at least some of the scale economies that would have been lost through decentralization appear to have been captured through centralized purchasing of well and furnace supplies and centralized marketing of the furnaces' salt.

Below the main supervisory bodies at each lineage trust was a separate management structure for each furnace, well, wholesale company, and pipe. The literature on the Li Siyou lineage trust gives the fullest picture of how these management hierarchies worked.[53] Taking as an example the organization of furnaces, we find two layers of authority (see figure 4.1). Each furnace was under the overall charge of a countinghouse, whose manager

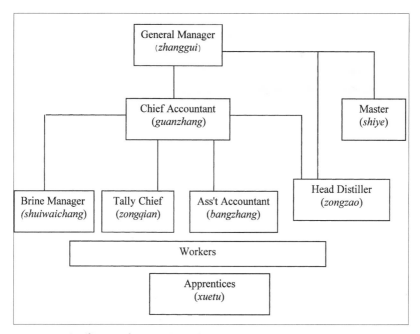

FIGURE 4.1 Staff Hierarchy at Li Siyou Trust Furnaces

Source: Zilin Li et al., "Ziliujing Li Siyou tang you fazhan dao shuaiwang. [The Li Siyou trust of Ziliujing from their development to their decline], Sichuan wenshiziliao xuanji 4 (1962–63): 170.

(*zhanggui*) took his orders directly from the main office of the lineage trust. In reality, he had considerable freedom in running the furnace, with the aid of a senior bookkeeper (*guanzhang*) and assistant bookkeeper (*bangzhang*). Besides handling the furnace's books, the head bookkeeper was the manager's assistant and in complete charge of the business when the manager was away. Together, these three men were the main decision-making group at the furnace and in charge of all purchases, sales, and planning.

Beneath the managers were a number of supervisors in charge of various specific operations at the furnace. Among them were men whose roles were similar to that of a foreman and thus somewhere between management and labor. Most important was the head distiller (*zongzao*), who was in charge of evaporation, packaging, and weighing of the salt. Below him were several furnace foremen (*zuozao*), who directly supervised the salt evaporators, the men who guarded the salt warehouse and the *tongzijiang*, among whose responsibilities was the soaking of the brine-infused soil surrounding the pan to extract additional brine to boil. The number of furnace foremen varied with the size of the furnace, most having one for every 30 or 40 pans. A similar supervisory role was played by the tally chief (*zongqian*), who, with his assistants (*sanqian*), oversaw the porterage of brine to special pre-evaporation vats and made certain that each contained brine of a uniform concentration. Every furnace also had a *shuiwaichang*, whose duty it was to negotiate the purchase of brine for evaporation, and a *paojie*, who handled the purchase of other items, including food consumed at the factory.

In addition, most furnaces also employed a "master," or *shiye*. This was a man of education and some political sophistication whose job it was to handle the external relations of the management group. Social relationships played an important part in the highly competitive world of salt manufacture and sale, and it is likely that many of these men were chosen for the connections they could bring to the business. However, they also performed another function. Most *shiye* were also high-level advisers to the lineage headquarters and were not under the jurisdiction of the management of the enterprise itself. It is likely that they were also spies, keeping an eye on operations and making suggestions when problems arose. At the same time, they undertook the task of training a number of apprentices who performed servile chores for the master while learning the ways of business, the use of the abacus, and techniques for keeping accounts.

The training of apprentices was only one of the signs of the attention the lineage trusts gave to selecting managerial staff. The middle-level staff at the furnaces of the Wu Jingrang trust of Jianwei were all chosen from among the young men sent to study business methods in its countinghouses. They went through stringent testing before being selected for these posts, and exceptional performance promised promotion to manager within a few

TABLE 4.2 Salaries of Management Staff at Li Siyou Trust Furnaces c. 1880 (in strings of cash per month)

Manager (*zhanggui*)	20–30
Accountants (*guanzhang*)	10 plus
Assistant accountants (*bangzhang)*	5–6
Head distillers (*zongzao*)	20
Furnace foremen (*zuocao)*	6–7
Tally chiefs (*zongqian*)	16
Assistant tally chiefs (*sanqian*)	3–8
Master (*shiye*)	7–8 (10 at the main office)
Paojie	6–7
Shuiwaichang	10 plus
Apprentices	1% of house take when managers host gambling parties

Source: Zilin Li et al., "Ziliujing Li Siyou tang you fazhan dao shuaiwang" [The Li Siyou trust of Ziliujing from their development to their decline], *Sichuan wenshiziliao xuanji* 4 (1962–63): 154.

years.[54] The Wang Sanwei trust and Hu Yuanhe trust often promoted their managers from among their own apprentices. Luo Xiaoyuan, one of the leading salt merchants of the mid-twentieth century, started in the salt industry when his father, a salt merchant in Nanxi County, sent his son to work as an apprentice to Wang Dazhi. Luo had already received training in both classics and business methods from his father and within three months was transferred to the Wang Sanwei trust countinghouse as a cash dispenser (*guanxianqian*). Later he was promoted to senior bookkeeper before beginning a long career as a top-ranking manager or *jingli*.[55]

The Lis, too, had a rigorous system of training and selection, with a trial period before promotion to the permanent managerial ranks.[56] It is probably for this reason that men from their own white-collar staff were much sought after by competing firms.[57] As we shall see, the business acumen and technical expertise of the men who managed the holdings of the large lineages were of a high level. Most of the great salt magnates who emerged in the twentieth century began their careers in this capacity. The value of a good manager was recognized in a system of high salaries and material incentives to encourage involvement in the fortunes of the company and efforts to increase productivity.[58] Tables 4.2 and 4.3 contain the average salaries paid to managerial staff at the Wang and Li factories. Salaries of managers at the wholesale companies were probably even higher, if the levels found at the Shaanxi guild's salt company, upon which they were modeled,

TABLE 4.3 Salaries of Management Staff at Wang Sanwei Trust Furnaces c. 1880 (in strings of cash per month)

Manager (*dazhanggui*)	30
Accountant (*daguanzhang*)	20
Assistant accountant (*bangzhang*)	7–8
Middle-level staff such as furnace foremen (*zuozao*)	5–6
Cash dispensers	3
Apprentices	0.6–1

Source: Xiaoyuan Luo, "Ziliujing Wang Sanwei tang xingwang jiyao" [The basic elements of the rise and fall of the Wang Sanwei trust], *Sichuan wenshiziliao xungji* 7 and 8 (1963): 192.

are any guide. Here a good manager received at least 100 taels a month, as well as an expense account for entertaining, for his clothing, and for the payment of his sedan chair bearers, the late imperial equivalent of the company car. At this rate he had remuneration on a par with the statutory salary of a high provincial official and one hundred times the wage of an average saltyard worker.[59]

Staff members were also fed at the offices in which they worked, a practice that was often abused by managers who prepared frequent banquets for themselves and fellow staff.[60] In addition, the Lis instituted a system of material incentives that was also modeled on practices of the Shaanxi guild. At the Xiexinglong wholesale company, in which the Lis were shareholders, 20 to 30 percent of profits were sent to the main office each year and a distribution of profits was carried out every three years. Managers received a share of these profits as a bonus, and during the height of saltyard prosperity in the late Qing other staff and workers received bonuses as well.[61] The Li Siyou trust also had a policy of assisting staff with family difficulties and contributing to the costs of weddings, funerals, and other expenses.[62] A percentage of profits was also promised the managers and staff of the various Hu Yuanhe trust enterprises,[63] and at the Wang Sanwei trust bonuses could sometimes equal six months' to a year's salary.[64]

Close bonds of loyalty were developed between managers and the leadership of the lineage trusts as well as among managers themselves. During the years of prosperity overall coordination of wide-ranging business interests was the job of the lineage head himself. Luo Xiaoyuan recalled that when Wang Dazhi was in charge of the Wang Sanwei trust, every day before breakfast he went to the head office to hear the reports of his top managers and give them instructions for the day. After breakfast he visited the lineage's wholesale shops in town and took care of other lineage business.

Long-range planning was centered on meetings of all high-level managerial staff, held at the Dragon Boat, Mid-Autumn, and New Year's festivals. Prior to these meetings, the entire white-collar staff of each business unit met for several weeks to discuss problems and prepare the reports on the basis of which Wang Dazhi made all the final decisions.[65]

At the Li Siyou trust, management conferences were held on an annual basis soon after the New Year. These meetings were attended by the head of the lineage as well as the general managers of the four departments in charge of wells, furnaces, pipes, and wholesale marketing. In preparation, the four department managers met with each of the managers of individual business units. These meetings were designed not only to tally accounts and share out profits. Like those of the other lineage trusts, they also served as a planning forum and gave the staff on the ground an opportunity to suggest ways that the business and technology could be improved.[66] Surprise visits by lineage heads such as Li Xiang'an served to keep the management on its toes and acted as a check on malpractice while giving the leadership first-hand information on business problems.[67]

The holdings of the Hu Yuanhe trust's Shenyi trust were fewer and less geographically dispersed than those of its counterparts. This allowed more direct centralized controls. Each morning each business unit was required to report the previous day's production. One copy went to the office of the Shenyi trust and the other to the headquarters of the lineage itself (*zonggui-fang*). On the first and fifteenth day of each month the director of the Shenyi trust chaired a meeting of all unit managers with the lineage head at which any production problems were discussed and solutions decided upon. An annual conference of all top management was held after the Lantern Festival[68] in order to decide on an overall plan for the following year.[69]

Coordinated action such as that favored by the large salt lineages required a sophisticated system of communication, particularly in the operation of far-flung wholesale outlets. The absence of a government-run postal system in the imperial period has been seen as a major impediment to information exchange. However, in Sichuan, in response to the needs of large salt and other trading interests, we can see the development of a number of efficient private messenger services (*dabang*) and postal companies (*minxinju*). By the 1880s seven large postal companies, established by investors from Chongqing and Hunan, served an area extending from central Sichuan to Gansu, Hubei, Yunnan, and Guizhou.[70] The Li Siyou trust, and most likely other lineages as well, also kept a number of so-called "fast feet" (*kuaijiao*) on their payroll to transmit urgent or sensitive information between the head office and branch businesses around the southwest. These men could travel between Chongqing and Chengdu in three days, traveling day and night, an indication less of their speed than of the rough terrain even in the Sichuan basin.[71] Subsidiary businesses, especially wholesale companies in distant areas, could also be used as bases from which intelligence on market conditions and the activities of competitors could be culled.[72]

Fragmentation and Vertical Integration

Fragmentation and Small-Scale Production

Most of the investors in salt at the Furong yard were engaged in small-scale production, spreading their risk by purchasing only a fraction of a share in each of a few wells and furnaces. Although we do not have records of the ownership of every well, it is likely that no more than half were under the control of the kind of integrated management organizations described above. Many were independent and could not take advantage of the benefits that we will see integrated management could bring. Indeed, it was in part the weakness of small producers that allowed large-scale salt industrialists to prosper as they did. One of the main sources of salt-lineage wealth in the early years of their development was the monopoly they achieved over marketing, especially in the border and Huguang markets. The high costs of long distance shipment of salt and the need to be able to hold large stocks until the price was favorable precluded the involvement of small-scale manufacturers and allowed the few large producers to take control of the wholesale sector.[73]

For some Zigong investors, fragmentation meant not only separation of well and furnace ownership and vulnerability to a pricing system set by the large pipe (see below) and salt wholesale company proprietors. In addition the operation of wells and furnaces could be fractionalized and divided among many units. We have already seen how the produce of one well could serve many furnaces of fewer than 10 pans. In rare instances brine too was pumped by partners in turn, with all the risks of poor maintenance and inefficient production practices which that entailed.

More common were practices aimed at saving small well owners the costs of pumping their own wells. In general, a well required one buffalo for each *dan* of brine drawn each day.[74] Therefore, a well of modest productivity would require the purchase and upkeep of between 40 and 100 buffalo. Besides employing the men who actually operated and maintained the pump, a well also had to feed and provide medical treatment for the buffalo and pay the wages of the men who drove the buffalo to turn the wheel, as well as the minder (*niupaizi*) who looked after day-to-day needs of the herd.[75]

Many small operators contracted with specialized pumpers rather than incur the capital outlay this entailed. These buffalo contractors (*niutuihu*) worked in several different ways. In the most comprehensive form of contract pumping the buffalo contractor supplied the buffalo and the drivers, and all the movable equipment used at the well, such as cable and tubes, and paid the wages of the workers we would normally think of as employees of the well. The well owner in effect divorced himself from the production process and did no more than send a man to oversee his interests. In return, the buffalo contractor received a proportion of the output of the well. If an accident occurred at the well, the buffalo contractor was responsible for the first three days of dredging. After that, he might continue the job but would have to be paid an additional fee.

Also common was a system whereby the buffalo contractor provided the buffalo and the drivers, but the well owners continued to participate in production, paying for all equipment and workers' wages. Under these conditions the buffalo contractor was paid according to the number of tubes of brine raised. Each buffalo team had four head and could be rented for 0.3 taels for each time the tube was raised to the top of the well and lowered to the bottom again. If anything fell into the well, the well owner's men were responsible for dredging. Finally, it was not uncommon to hire a buffalo contractor when problems arose at a well. In this instance payment was based on the number of buffalo used. In cases where a whole team was not needed, rent could be determined by the number of buffalo used per day. All of these fees would be adjusted for special conditions, such as turning one wheel to pump two wells.[76]

There were about 200 buffalo contractors at the Furong saltyard. In all they owned about 3,000 buffalo and their operations were capitalized at about 200,000 taels during the late Qing. This came to approximately 10 percent of the buffalo in use at the yard. Most buffalo contractors were small-scale operators themselves, able to work perhaps one or two wells at a time. However, a few enterprising men, like Li Songshan and Huang Si, who had more than 300 buffalo, and Zhou Rongtai and Yu San, who had more than 200, were wealthy men by the standards of the time. Their profits eventually allowed them to accumulate enough capital to invest in wells and furnaces of their own and eventually abandon contract pumping altogether.[77] As such, the institution of buffalo contracting fits well with the patterns of fragmentation common to many industries in late imperial times.[78] For the well owners who made use of its services, contract pumping meant lower initial capital costs but a considerable dispersion of control. Nevertheless, for smaller producers the loss in profits may have been sufficiently small to make subcontracting well operations worthwhile.[79]

An even further step away from the large-scale factory system found at the Li, Wang, Yan, and Hu wells was the institution of *banfangche*. This too was an effort to cut down on the costs of owning a herd of buffalo. In this case, rather than rent the use of animal power, well owners used human labor in the pumping of the well. For small producers human labor provided flexibility in periods of low labor costs. Once purchased, a buffalo had to be cared for and fed no matter how little brine you could sell. In some cases the human labor hired to turn the wheel was contracted as well, the labor boss taking full responsibility for workers' wages, hiring only the number of men necessary to fulfill the production quota set by the well owners.[80]

Vertical Integration at the Large Salt Lineages

The difference between the operations of small producers and those of the men we can identify as salt barons lay not simply in their scale of production but also in their ability to combine all aspects of production and sales in one company. The advantages vertical integration held in an industry such as salt in the early stages of capitalist development were numerous. They match in importance the organizational breakthrough made by the great American oil and steel companies in the formative years of its industrial revolution. By combining ownership of wells and furnaces, they could almost invariably guarantee their supplies of the key ingredients in salt manufacture, brine, and gas. By controlling the main salt wholesale companies in the province, they ensured that their salt was first to be sold in the major Sichuan salt markets. With the wealth accumulated in salt production they expanded into the development of brine pipes, which, as we shall see, gave them complete control over the marketing of a large portion of Gongjing brine and enabled them to hold the unaffiliated furnaces of Ziliujing ransom to their production requirements. Their control of large capital reserves allowed them to buy up stocks of seasonal goods or items like coal, the price of which was lower in the winter, when the pits were operating at peak production. And finally, they went on to diversify their holdings into almost every industry, including that of credit, which served the producers of salt. As a result, by the end of the dynasty, with little reduction in output, they could virtually conduct the business of salt without ever making a purchase from an outsider.

The Assets of the Wang Sanwei Trust

At its height in the 1890s, the Wang Sanwei trust was probably the richest single private owner of agricultural and industrial property in Sichuan and, according to some scholars, in China. From a few abandoned wells in Shanzi ba, it came to control an integrated empire consisting of wells, furnaces, pipes, wholesale outlets, and agricultural land. While exceptional in the value of its holdings, the estate of the Wang Sanwei trust stood as a model of Zigong business practices. The relative importance of various categories of assets, and their role over the life of the firm, also sheds light on the rise and fall of the large consolidated lineage trusts as the mainstay of Zigong salt production and distribution.

Agricultural land. By the end of his life, a life which he devoted to building up the Wang Sanwei trust fortune, Wang Langyun had expanded the agricultural holdings of his lineage to more than 9,000 *shi* a year in rents. These properties were not only in Fushun and Rong counties, but were scattered over neighboring Weiyuan and Yibin as well,[81] making the Wangs one of the largest absentee landowners in western Sichuan. Under the stewardship of his nephew, Wang Huitang, that fortune was dissipated, and during the period of fragmented management mentioned above the debts of the lineage rose to as much as 700,000 taels. It was due to their common involvement in loans to the Wang Sanwei trust that the powerful Chongqing-Shashi Credit Group was formed and one of its first acts was to sue the Wangs at the yamen of the Chongqing magistrate. It was not until the head of the official salt distribution bureau (*guanyunju*) in Chongqing intervened that the family's debts were at long last sorted out. At the suggestion of the bureau, Wang Dazhi, by far the most able of the generation following Wang Langyun's, was appointed director (*jingli*) of the lineage trust. In order to pay debts and raise capital to rescue the trust's faltering salt business, Dazhi sold land remaining in Wang hands valued at more than 2,000 *shi* in rents a year. This left the family with lands producing 3,000 *shi* in rents, greatly diminishing the importance of agricultural holdings in the total portfolio but still meriting the Wangs' inclusion among the great landowners of their day.[82]

Brine and gas wells. By the time Wang Dazhi took over trust affairs, most of the brine wells operated by the Wang Sanwei trust were under its exclusive control. At Shanzi ba, the site of their earliest strikes, the family still operated 21 modestly productive wells. These yielded an average of 1,000 *dan* of brine a day of a concentration of approximately 18 percent salt by weight. During the late nineteenth century four of these wells dried up. However, the Wangs had both the capital and the good judgment to move rapidly into investment in rock-salt wells, keeping their profits from brine production high. By the turn of the century, the Wang Sanwei trust had at least three of these extraordinarily productive wells, as well as 25 shares in the Qichang well at the center of Shanzi ba.

As a lineage with its base in Ziliujing, it is not surprising that the Wang Sanwei trust's brine holdings were unspectacular. Far more important were their furnace operations. In the region of Shanzi ba the family owned the Qingjiang, Tiansheng, Tianshen, Jinhai, and Baosan gas wells, with optimum output of 70–80 pan units each. Far more productive were the Yuxing well at Gaoshan jing, the Tongxing and Tongwang wells at Zhulin wan, and the Sihai well at Shanqiao. All produced more than 100 pan units each, the Yuxing fueling 240 pans and the Tongxing fueling 175.

In addition to evaporating salt with gas produced at its own wells, the Wang Sanwei trust was also an important gas leaser at Ziliujing. During the late nineteenth century it rented seven furnaces with approximately 10 pans at each. According to a former manager at the Wang Sanwei lineage trust, the family itself generally operated only around 700 pans, in which case some of their gas capacity must also have been leased out. However, even at this level of production, they would have had an output of around 400 bundles of salt a day, or approximately 144,000 bundles a year. At the time, the licensed quota of salt at Furong was just under 3,000 *zai*. At 450 bundles to the *zai*, the Wangs would have been producing around 320 *zai* a year, or around 11 percent of the annual licensed quota for the main salt production area in the province.[83]

Commercial enterprises. The most important component of the Wang Sanwei trust's commercial empire was the Guangshengtong salt company. This company had its origins in the move by salt producers to enter the Huguang market during the early days of the Taiping Rebellion and remained one of the most profitable units of the Wang Sanwei trust conglomerate. We know little about the operations of the Guangshengtong company, particularly during the years of the unregulated trade with Huguang. With the reinstitution of government quotas in this market the ability to expand sales independently was halted. Despite the opposition of Wang Sanwei trust leaders to the new system of official transport and merchant sales (Guanyun), large merchant houses like the Guangshengtong company may have reaped some benefits from government controls. The sale of salt under the new dispensation was divided between salt sold by certificate (*yin*) and the relatively unregulated sale of salt by ticket (*piao*). The sale of certificate salt was more profitable, and it was only by certificate that salt could be marketed in the territories beyond Sichuan. This, in effect, reestablished the monopoly of the large wholesale houses, among which the major Zigong native salt-producing companies could now claim a place. The certificate quota, which varied over time, was divided equally between the so-called transport merchants (*yunshang*), heirs to the earlier extraprovincial wholesale salt companies, and the yard merchants (*changshang*), salt merchants who had their roots in the saltyards. Each group was allocated half of the initial 600-*zai* quota destined for Huguang. Of the 300 allocated to the saltyard merchants, the Wang Sanwei trust received 72,[84] giving them 12 percent of the total Huguang wholesale market. Wang Xiangrong was also responsible for the Zhongxingxiang salt company, one of the two large wholesale companies operating in the Renhuai border market.[85]

In addition to the marketing of salt, during the course of the late nineteenth century the Wang Sanwei trust continued to expand into other fields of commercial enterprise, developing economies of scope made possible by their existing marketing infrastructure.[86] Their Fuchangsheng company was a major purveyor of rice, broad beans, soy, rapeseed oil, and other basic provisions. Purchased in Luzhou and Jiangjin, these items not only stocked the kitchens and buffalo sheds of Wang Sanwei trust holdings. They also became a source of supply for wells and furnaces throughout the saltyard. In order to guarantee their own stores of coal, the Wangs set up the Bianli coalyard at Gaotong, the main coal distribution point in Furong. At the same time, they established the Tiantang medicine shop to purchase and retail herbal medicines, particularly those used in the treatment of water buffalo.[87] Wang Sanwei trust leaders, along with members of the Li Siyou trust, and the prominent Gongjing salt merchants Huang Dunsan and Liu Huanzhai also controlled the only tannery in Furong, with a monopoly over the processing of hides from the thousands of buffalo that died at the yard each year.[88] In the years immediately following the 1911 revolution, the Wangs took a further step in the direction of unifying supply and production by investing in several bamboo yards.[89]

The Wang Sanwei trust's wholesale salt trade also involved them in several businesses with only indirect links to salt. It was not until 1907 that the first remittance shops (*piaohao*) were established at the saltyard.[90] As a result, the silver that the salt producers received for their salt at state warehouses in Chongqing run by the official salt transport administration had to be carried back to Ziliujing. In order to multiply their profits, many salt merchants began using the silver to purchase foreign cotton yarn to ship home, creating a triangular trade that extended all the way to Great Britain. The Wang Sanwei trust carved out a lucrative cotton market for itself, wholesaling yarn in Weiyuan and Rong counties and retailing the same through their Guangshenggong yarn shop on Zheng jie in Ziliujing. At the same time, they took advantage of the inadequate credit and money exchange facilities at the saltyard to open the Guangshenggong money shop on Dafenbao jie.

Assets of the Li Siyou Trust

We have far less detailed information about the assets of the Li Siyou trust. The height of its prosperity predated that of the Wangs and it is generally felt that by the 1890s the Li fortune had begun to decline. During the 1870s, when Li Xiang'an's influence was still being felt, lineage activity in all areas of production continued to expand. During his lifetime, Li Xiang'an is said to have drilled or rented more than 100 new wells, the names of only 17 of which now survive.[91] Most of these were brine wells, although the few gas wells in their possession were highly productive, allowing the Li Siyou trust, too, to evaporate more than 800 pans. Li Xiang'an's successor continued the family's involvement in well exploration, including investment in five shares of the Shuangfu well, which was to be one of the great strikes of the period.[92]

The Li Siyou trust also had extensive wholesale interests. The Dashenghou salt company, with its headquarters in Chongqing and its main branch outlets in Yichang and Shashi, was the second most important company in the domestic Sichuan (*ji'an*) and Huguang salt markets.[93] Li Siyou trust firms were also active in the border markets. The Xiexinglong salt company, a joint Li, Tian, and Liu lineage operation, was the strongest wholesale company in the Renhuai market. Its headquarters were in the Renhuai County seat, but more than 70 branches served the counties between it and the Guizhou provincial capital in Guiyang. Each branch had a business office, salt warehouse, and living quarters for staff. Large agricultural holdings in the region yielded sufficient rents to pay for all operating expenses of the branch units of the wholesale firm. In addition, the company trained and staffed its own anti-smuggling police (*yanjing*), who served as escorts for their merchant shipments and as personal guards for the company's bosses.[94] Similar conditions prevailed in the Qijiang market, where the Li Siyou trust was the sole owner of the Dashengmei salt company.[95] The Lis were also engaged in a number of retail businesses, including ownership of two medicine shops and their own lumberyard to supply materials for construction of wells, derricks, wheels, and saltyard buildings.[96]

Assets of the Hu Yuanhe Trust and the Yan Guixin Trust

Although smaller than the Li and Wang salt conglomerates, the Hu Yuanhe trust followed the same pattern of vertical integration and investment in support industries. Table 4.4 illustrates the continued expansion

TABLE 4.4 Well Development Under Three Generations of Hu Lineage Managers

Well Name	Well Type	Gas Output (pans boiled)
A. Wells opened under the management of Hu Yuanhai (1830s–early 1860s)		
Jianlong well	yellow brine	10
Yuanlong well	yellow brine	5
Linjiang well	yellow brine	none
Shuanglong well	yellow brine	none
Zhitan well	yellow brine	15
B. Wells opened under the management of Hu Chengjun (early 1860s–1892)		
Fengyu well	yellow brine	15
Zhenglong well	yellow brine	5
Encheng well	yellow brine	3
Fengcheng well	unknown	n/a
Yuchuan well	black brine	15
Deyu well	unknown	20
C. Wells opened under the management of Hu Mianzu (1892–1911)		
Independent wells		
Jicheng well	black brine	202
Yichun well	black brine	102
Zhichuan well	yellow brine	40
Fuyuan well	yellow brine	none
Yuanting well	black brine	10
Chengyuan well	black brine	none
Yuanxi well	black brine	none
Yicheng well	black brine	none
Xianxi well	black brine	4
Tianlong well	yellow brine	2
Wells opened as a xiajie *shareholder*		
Tiancheng well	black brine	4
Fuyuan well	black brine	2
Hengfu well	black brine	none
Jiangyuan well	black brine	none
Dasheng well	black brine	none

Source: Shaoquan Hu. "Gongjing Hu Yuanhe di guangzou yu shuailuo" [The rise and fall of Hu Yuanhe of Gongjing]. *Zigong wenshiziliao xuanji* 12 (1981): 78–79.

of Hu lineage holdings in primary production. Almost all the lineage's wells continued to be opened independently, with the exception of a group of wells in which the Hu Yuanhe trust bought *xiajie* shares in the last years of the dynasty, giving them half interest in exchange for completing excavation.

We know little about Hu business activities outside of salt. In addition to a company dealing in white wax in Jiading prefecture the family also opened a pawnshop in Chengdu.[97] However, the most important merchant business of this, as of the other lineages, continued to be in the wholesale marketing of salt. The Hu Yuanhe trust's Fulinyi salt company sold only salt produced at Hu-owned furnaces, giving the lineage a guaranteed outlet in the Huguang market.[98] At the time of Hu Chengjun's death in 1892, the family's salt marketing interests were capitalized at 300,000 taels.[99] With the discovery of several highly productive gas wells on their Gongjing properties, the Hus also pioneered the production of *ba* salt using gas furnaces instead of the traditional coal-fueled technology. This produced a block salt of higher quality and uniformity of color than that commonly sold by other Gongjing merchants, giving them a considerable advantage in the border markets where *ba* salt was dominant.[100]

In many ways, the Yan Guixin trust followed a business strategy similar to that of the Hus. With wells in both Ziliujing and Gongjing they were well placed to take advantage of the different productive capacities of the two yards. Reinvesting profits in salt production, rather than land, the family was able to expand its holdings during the late nineteenth century without seeking outside partners or loans.[101] Through their main office at Wujia bo, the Yans coordinated a vast salt empire with investments in wells, furnaces, and pipes. Two wholesale firms gave them a high profile in both the Huguang market and the Sichuan domestic market. The Taihezhen company, serving Huguang, had branches in Yichang, Shashi, and Hankou, while the Hengxinglong company, serving Sichuan, had offices in Jiangjin, Fuling, and Chongqing.[102] In the years following the Taiping Rebellion, Yan Juewu, fourth son of Yan Changying, established a wholesale firm for the border market in Yunnan and Guizhou.

Surviving account books do not allow us to determine which units of these vertically integrated firms were most profitable. Control over resources vital to each phase of production allowed these and other large firms economies of scale and scope with which smaller producers could not compete. The ability to boil one's own brine, raised by one's own buffalo and evaporated by one's own gas, cut out middleman costs and assured supplies of raw materials, particularly during periods when imbalances between factors of production were critical to one's productive capacity. Investment in all phases of production also allowed larger firms to hedge against shifts in the relative value of brine and gas.

Salt shipment and sale in the retail markets was probably not the most profitable phase of the salt industry. Table 4.5 lists estimated profits for each of the major Sichuan salt sales territories. The Huguang market was thus the most lucrative for salt from Sichuan during the early twentieth century. From the 1850s to the 1870s, when the great lineage-based fortunes were being made, the share of taxes in the shipment of salt was much lower than it was in the late Qing and early Republic. Indeed, during the 1830s and 1840s it was probably subject to no taxes at all and thereafter paid only *lijin* taxes levied locally to fund the resistance to allies of the Taiping uprising. Because sales to Hubei fell beyond the scope of the regular salt administration it is likely that most salt entering Hubei continued to incur no tax at all. As we will see in chapter 6, beginning in 1878 the Qing state, as well as individual provinces whose coffers benefited from salt revenues, began to target Sichuan salt shipments to Huguang. As a result, both a rise in salt taxes and intermittent contractions of the legal market in Hubei had an adverse effect on Sichuan producers, particularly those whose business strategy had been based on production and sale for the Huguang sales territory. The most prominent of these were the large lineage trusts. By cutting back on shipments of salt produced by others they could protect for a while the demand for their own output. However, such restraint of trade eventually would come under attack both by its targets and by the state.

TABLE 4.5 Profits from the Sale of Salt in Sichuan Sales Territories c. 1916 (in taels)

	Huguang market (hua)	Sichuan market (ba)	Yungui market (ba)
Main Transshipment Point	Shashi	Chongqing	Luxian/Hejiang
Price of *zai* at yard	1,512	1,800	1,800
Taxes and shipping	2,938	1,445	1,911
Price at destination	6,010	4,304	4,968
Proft/*zai*	1,560	1,059	1,257
Profit/*jin**	0.07	n/a	0.01

*The number of *jin* per *zai* varied over time and by market. Estimates here are based on observations by Qiao Fu.

Source: Based on data in Qiao Fu, *Ziliujing diyiji* [Ziliujing, vol. 1] (Chengdu: Quchang gongsi, 1916), 117–119.

Defensive Business Strategies

Business practices at the Furong yard were a response to both technological change and market opportunities. Like most late-nineteenth-century firms their financial practices reflected their reliance on retained earnings and locally available credit. However, unlike Western firms, which were benefiting from a revolution in transportation during this period, China's underdeveloped system of communications and transportation created bottlenecks, which also had a profound impact on the way in which Furong firms evolved.

In the accounts of both the Hu Yuanhe trust and the Li Siyou trust we see strict adherence to a policy of maintaining sizable cash reserves. Each of the salt companies and salt warehouses these lineages operated were expected to hold a large portion of their assets in cash. At its height the countinghouse of the Li Siyou trust always kept 300,000 taels on hand in case of emergencies, and the salt company it managed was expected to maintain reserves of about one-third that amount.[103] Even the offices of the individual wells and furnaces kept a crisis fund, and if any of this money was spent it was common to hear the leadership of the lineage bemoan the danger the business was in.[104] This insistence on a large pool of liquid capital should be viewed within the larger context of the late imperial political economy. Vulnerability to natural disaster, social disorder, and changing market conditions created a defensive mentality among even the most successful businessmen. Government agencies maintained contingency funds following the Yongzheng period fiscal reforms of the early eighteenth century.[105] The government's own capricious tax policies in the last decades of the Qing multiplied the fear of cash shortage among manufacturers and merchants. As a result, a large percentage of the available capital for industrial development may have lain idle during the Qing, not as a result of conspicuous consumption but as conscientious business practice. The disorder that followed the fall of the dynasty only intensified the fears that gave rise to these practices and make even more startling the sudden growth in the level of debt we will see among the largest salt developers in the early years of the Republic.

By contrast, the practice of building up large agricultural estates should not be seen merely in terms of traditionally conservative lineage investment strategies. By the turn of the century, Wang, Li, and Hu estates produced annual rental incomes of approximately 17,000, 5,000, and 7,600 *shi*, respectively, placing them among the largest landowners in the province.[106] Although agricultural land did provide investment security, it also served an important function as part of the integrated business holdings of the salt conglomerate. We have already seen the role that farmland could play as a substitute for secure cash holdings. When the Wang San-wei trust ran into debt in the 1880s it did not sell salt properties, but rather disposed of agricultural assets in order to shore up its industrial holdings. While invested in land, business capital yielded comfortable returns in the form of rents that could rapidly be converted into cash in the highly fluid land market of the late Qing. More important, however, was the contribution of the product of agricultural land to business investors. We have already seen the use of income from agricultural land to run the border-market salt companies of the Li Siyou trust. There is also considerable evidence that part of the landed holdings of merchants were used to feed employees of their commercial outlets. Although this does not account for all 17,000 *shi* collected by the rent agents of the Wang Sanwei trust, the fact that salt workers and staff received their food as part of their wages placed considerable pressure on large producers, whose employees could number in the thousands.[107] Equally pressing was the need to feed between 600 and 1,300 head of cattle at each lineage's factory.[108] Large well owners rented part of their landed holdings in nearby villages to tenants committed to the cultivation of grass. Under the *baoniugong* system of tenancy, the farmer had to agree to supply a certain well with an agreed-upon quota of grass every day. Periodic payment would be made to the tenant after a deduction was made for his rent. The landowner received his feed and guaranteed that the rent was paid. The tenant was tied to one buyer for his crop and was forced to sell at a low price.[109] Similar tactics were most likely pursued among growers of broad beans, another important component of the buffaloes' diet and a major item of expenditure at the wells. Thus, even agricultural land served the interests of the industry and can be seen as part of the strategy of vertical integration of supply, production, and sales at the Furong saltyard.

Brine Pipes

Along with wholesale salt companies, the operation of brine pipes was the most powerful weapon wielded by the large salt companies in their struggle for dominance in the salt market, as they gave the larger producers a transport link between highly productive black-brine wells in Gongjing and the gas wells of Ziliujing. In addition, for almost three decades they allowed their owners to control the sources of supply of wells and furnaces operated by smaller producers in both yards. The power of pipe owners exceeded that of any other actor in the late Qing salt industry, and this power was acknowledged in the special relationship they maintained with the salt authorities who determined whose salt would be sold in the most lucrative markets beyond Sichuan's borders.

The Construction of the Large Brine Pipes

Although the technology necessary for the transport of brine through pipes (*jian*) was known as early as the Qianlong reign, its development as a vital feature of the Furong saltyard can be dated no earlier than the 1850s.[110] As we have seen, it was then that the coincidence of rapidly expanding markets for Sichuan salt and the rise of gas wells in Ziliujing (commonly referred to as the East Yard) created an unprecedented demand for brine from the highly productive black-brine wells of Gongjing (the West Yard). The distance between the two yards is over 20 *li* or approximately 6.6 miles, and until the first pipes were laid the only way to feed the great furnace capacity of the East Yard was on foot by porters carrying the brine on buckets suspended by poles. About 3,000 *dan* of brine were transported in this way each day, equal to the capacity of just one of the soon-to-be-constructed pipes.[111]

At the height of their use, from the 1880s to the early years of the Republic, there were 18 large pipes constructed between the two yards, as well as a now unknown number of smaller pipes serving remote gas deposits or individual owners' needs. Running between Gongjing and Guojia ao in Ziliujing were the Datong, Yuhe, Dasheng, Dachuan, Tongfu, Jitong, Dachang, Yuanyuan, Yuanchang, and Yuantong pipes, frequently referred to as the Ten Big Pipes. Linking Dafen bao and the gas wells were the Dasheng, Quanfu, Yifu, Qingyun, Tongxin, and Enliu pipes. Along with the Datong and Yuanchang, which carried brine from both well areas, these were known as the Eight Big Pipes.[112] Brine pipes were major engineering feats, and the silhouettes of their roller-coaster-like frames against the skyline of Furong's hilly countryside makes the saltyard look like an enormous amusement park.

The pipes themselves were constructed out of hollowed-out bamboo, with one joined inside the other. The joins and outer surface of the bamboo were wrapped in fine hemp covered with putty made of lime and tong oil. Hoops composed of bamboo slats, which were changed twice a year, were then set along the entire length of the pipe to prevent splitting. The pipes followed the lay of the land. Where the terrain was flat they could be buried in the ground. However, rivers and hills presented special challenges. In the former case pipes were laid directly in the riverbed, covered with inverted troughs of stone to prevent seepage of water and disintegration of the pipe. Shallow depressions in the terrain were handled by the construction of trel-

ILLUSTRATION 4.2 Ziliujing Brine Pumps c. 1919
Source: Lin, *Essentials of Sichuan Salt*, front matter.

lises, similar to that pictured in illustration 4.2. However, transit through more rugged countryside required considerable skill. Most interesting were the techniques used to deal with mountains. In most cases, the brine had to be carried up on a frame using a series of linked wooden vats driven by a pump similar to that used to irrigate agricultural land. In very high areas two, three, or even ten sets of pumps, set up along the face of the mountain and driven largely by mules, were required to transport the brine to the top (see illustration 4.3).[113] Inasmuch as bamboo was inflexible and could not be bent, techniques also had to be developed to turn the pipe at angles to conform to the lay of the land. At the head of the angle, a large vat, called a *jianwo*, was constructed. Incoming brine was fed into the vat and exited from a new pipe set at the appropriate angle on the other side.[114]

The Development of Pipe Merchant Power

Both politics and economics played a part in determining who built brine pipes. A major pipe could extend between 10 and 40 *li* once the vagaries of topography were accounted for. Depending on its length, it could cost anywhere from several thousand to more than 100,000 taels to build, presenting considerable capital barriers to entry into the pipe market.[115]

ILLUSTRATION 4.3 Mule Pumps Raising Brine Over Rough Terrain
Source: Ding, *Gazetteer of Sichuan Salt Administration,* juan 2, jingchang 2, 30b–31a.

As a result, only the wealthiest salt producers were able to invest in these marvels of late Qing engineering. Indeed, even then at least half of the large brine pipes were the product of partnerships and not independent capital. Even the Wang Sanwei trust's Dasheng pipe was originally built in concert with other shareholders. However, Wang Dazhi's policy of plowing profits back into the company during its early years yielded sufficient income to allow him to buy out his partners and eventually gave the Wang Sanwei trust exclusive ownership of the pipe.[116]

It was not cost alone that limited the number of large pipe owners. Developers of brine pipes faced holdup by landowners, a common bottleneck when creating essential facilities. Whereas outside capital played a dominant role in the early development of wells and furnaces, pipes were almost exclusively local enterprises. In order to build a well, one needed to rent a single plot of land from a landowner often hungry himself for investment capital to bring him into the ranks of salt industrialists. In the case of a brine pipe, one had to obtain the cooperation of tens or hundreds of landowners over whose land a pipe might traverse. Many were agricultural landowners whose interests could be harmed by leaking brine and careless pipe personnel. If only one in a crucial area refused to cooperate, the pipe could not be built. Thus, most of the owners and primary shareholders in pipe projects were local landowners themselves or men with considerable local political capital who could overcome holdup by landowners.[117] The Luzhou salt merchant Wang Chengzhi tried to break into the field in the early Republic by drawing together capital from staff at a number of wells to open the Yutong pipe. The terms they were able to negotiate with local landowners were so extortionary that the pipe went under within a year. Hu Tiehua, of the Hu Yuanhe trust, took it over, renegotiated the leases, and soon made a substantial profit.[118]

The difficulties encountered in negotiating pipe contracts are highlighted by the wide variation in rents found in leases for pipe land.[119] No pattern can be discerned which would indicate the kind of "customs of the trade" that existed in so many other sectors of the industry. Instead, the rate of rent depended on the relative power of landowner and tenant, how crucial a particular piece of land was, and whether there were other connections between the parties involved. Some tracts belonged to interlocking partnerships, such as wells or furnaces participating in the ownership of a pipe. Also found were cases where the owners of wells or furnaces did not invest in the pipe itself, but granted favorable tenancy conditions to its developers in return for privileged treatment in the movement of their own brine. For example, one of the landowners of the Dasheng pipe was the Wang Six Branches, owners of numerous brine wells. Their contract stipulated that the pipe company would purchase only brine from their wells. Any change in these arrangements would require a renegotiation of the lease.[120]

The length of tenure could also affect the viability of a pipe. Whereas permanent tenancy was becoming almost universal among well investors, pipe tenancies continued to be limited to an average of seven years.[121] Once the lease was up, the pipe company had no guarantee that it would be renewed, and the power of lineage-based pipes like the Wangs' Dasheng pipe is demonstrated by the continuation of its leases over a period of more than 30 years. Contracts entered into by the Dasheng pipe demonstrate that the Wangs were able to renegotiate a large number of their leases long in advance of their expiration in the form of advance-lease contracts (*yudian*). At the same time, although the terms of tenure obtained from different landowners varied, there was little change in rents for individual sections of pipe land before the late nineteenth century. From the 1890s on, however, rents appear to have risen by as much as 100 percent, far more than could be accounted for by the long-term change in rice prices during this same period (see figure 4.2).[122]

The ability of large lineages to wield both the economic and political capital needed to open large pipes gave them dominance in the field. Until the early Republic, Li, Wang, and Hu capital controlled six of the main pipes at

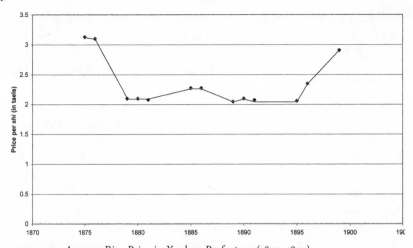

FIGURE 4.2 Average Rice Price in Xuzhou Prefecture (1875–1899)

Source: Number One Historical Archives, Beijing, Junji chu lufu zouzhe, nongye lei, yuxue liangjia, bundles 75, 79, 88, 92, 95, 105, 112, 117, 121, 125, 137, 140, 142, 146.

Dafen bao and managed an additional two in partnership.[123] This not only gave them a source of considerable new profits. It also guaranteed their supremacy in the production and marketing of salt.

Most brine pipes were initially developed by owners of large wells and furnaces to serve their own productive requirements. By the late nineteenth century large combinations of brine wells and furnaces were organized under the name of the pipe that served them, and it was the pipe name that was used as the brand when the salt was sold.[124] Owners of the larger pipes also began to establish relationships with other brine producers to ship their brine as well. Brine belonging to other well and furnace owners was transported across brine pipes in two ways. Some pipe owners purchased the brine outright and simply charged a markup based on their own costs and the market price of the salt the brine would ultimately produce. Less concentrated brine was more expensive to move because it produced less salt. Thus, while furnace owners paid less for such brine, well owners in effect paid a premium for its shipment in disproportionately lower prices per *dan*.[125]

However pipe companies obtained brine, they controlled most of the brine that was purchased for evaporation at gas-fired pans and enjoyed the benefit of inventory storage within the pipes as well.[126] Furnaces without pipes could obtain brine through the equivalent of a spot market, with the advantage that they could adjust their orders to suit the market for salt and the changing strength of their gas supplies. However, the fixed capacity of pipes made this a riskier mode of supply than contracting with a pipe for a certain volume of brine each year. A sign of the relative power of pipes was the practice by which furnaces paid for their yearly contracts with pipes in advance, while wells received payment for their brine from the pipes approximately once every four months.[127] In addition to their profits, this in effect gave the owners of pipes an annual interest-free loan of considerable size.

Of course, not all brine sales were intermediated by pipes. Some furnaces were owned by brine-producing partnerships that supplied their own raw materials. Others bought brine directly from wells in Gongjing. In such cases, they might still move their brine by pipe, paying a straight transport fee (*guojia*).[128] The profitability of simple transport was not as great as that which could be obtained when pipes inserted themselves between brine producer and brine evaporator. It is not surprising, then, that pipe owners were accused of trying to increase their take and discourage wells from selling directly to furnaces. Pipes collected large "wastage fees" on the grounds that brine inevitably was lost as it moved through the labyrinth of bamboo that was a pipe system. More disreputable pipe managers were known to dilute brine or even use different-sized measures when well owners brought brine to the pipe than when it was carted away by the recipient furnace.[129]

The attraction of pipe ownership lay not simply in the discount at which brine was purchased and the markup at which it was sold. During the period when the great salt lineages were establishing their firms, the demand for brine at Furong's gas furnaces continuously exceeded the capacity of its pipes. If we assume that all 4,895 gas-fired pans were operating every day, that each pan produced about 32 *jin* of salt, using a combination of 75 percent black brine and 25 percent yellow brine, the two main gas furnace sites would have consumed over 380,000 *dan* of brine a day (see table 4.6). No more than a tenth of this amount was carried by pipes. Thus, pipes were virtually assured of a source and a market for their brine. Moreover, except for a small staff of men to check the pipe for leaks, operate the occasional pump, and supervise the introduction and exit of brine, brine pipes had few employees and low labor costs. Nevertheless, it was the control that pipe ownership gave one over brine that was the main advantage of pipe development. During the years before the exploitation of the rock-salt layer, brine was continuously in short supply at the Ziliujing gas furnaces. Although brine could be stored if one had the facilities, gas escaped whether one used it or not. Idle pans meant lost profits, and many furnaces unable to maintain constant supplies were forced to close down. During the period before 1920, when gas was still in ample supply and brine still difficult to obtain, pipe owners always supplied their own furnaces before filling their outside contracts. Likewise, during the

TABLE 4.6 Estimates of Brine Requirements at Main Gas Furnace Sites c. 1916

	Guojia ao	Dafen bao	Total
Number of large pans	4,311	584	4,895
Jin of salt produced/pan/day	32	32	
Total *jin* produced/day	137,952	18,688	156,640
Dan of brine boiled per *jin*			
(black brine)	2.31	2.31	
(yellow brine)	3	3	
Average *dan* boiled/day	342,467	46,393	388,860

Sources: Zhenhan Lin, *Chuanyan jiyao* [Essentials of Sichuan salt] (Shanghai: Shangwu yinshu guan, 1919), 214, 248; Wei Wu, ed., *Sichuan yanzhengshi* [Sichuan salt administration history]) (China: Sichuan yanzhengshi bianjichu, 1932), juan 2, pian 2, changchan, 56; juan 3, pian 2, changchan, 1.

brief periods of brine surplus in the mid-1890s and the 1920s and early 1930s, they also gave priority to the brine from their own wells.[130]

Because they were the only producers who could guarantee levels of production, the large well, pipe, furnace combinations developed special relationships with the salt wholesalers in Sichuan. Salt was generally sold on advance contracts to the big salt companies at markets held three times a year: at the time of the Dragon Boat, Mid-Autumn, and New Year's festivals. Pipe owners were among the few merchants able to contract these consignments. With the institution of official transport and merchant sales (*Guanyun*), to be discussed in chapter 6, salt for sale by certificate was registered with the government at the thrice-yearly markets and pipe merchants came to control supplies of salt to the Huguang and border markets. In addition, pipe merchants alone were able to negotiate with the government over price. According to one expert on pipe management in Furong, pipe merchants were given the opening price (*kaipan*) when negotiations began with the Guanyun bureau each season. Smaller producers received the lower *genpan* rate and were subject to cutbacks in their quota if the market was bad.[131]

Management Practices at the Large Pipes

The management of large pipes was organized in much the same fashion as wells and furnaces. At the Li Siyou trust's Dasheng pipe, a single manager (*zhanggui*) had overall responsibility for operations. Under him were an accountant (*guanzhang*), an assistant accountant (*bangzhang*), and a man in charge of cash transactions. Also operating out of the countinghouse of the pipe was a *shuiwaichang* whose duty it was to negotiate the purchase and sale of brine and a *mashuizhang* who kept the accounts of brine movements. In addition, two foreman-level positions can be considered to be at the lowest levels of management, a general supervisor and four subordinates whose duty it was to supervise the movement of brine in and out of the pipes. The labor contingent at the pipe was small compared with that of a well. Ten men were employed to run the pumps that lifted brine over high mountains, and one man was in charge of caring for the mules that operated the pumps. Two men tested the concentration of brine brought in by the well owners for transportation, and one skilled craftsman was kept on salary to repair the pipe. In addition, a number of miscellaneous workers served the needs of the staff in the capacity of sedan-chair bearers, cooks, and handymen.[132]

A similar structure was implemented at the countinghouse of the Dachang pipe, operated by the Wang Sanwei trust. Here two general managers (*zongli*) and two assistant managers (*bangban*) were in charge and had the power to appoint and fire all administrative personnel. The partners took an active role in the business, meeting every 20 days to discuss problems, examine accounts, and suggest ways to improve pipe operations. However, the ultimate authority in the running of the company lay with the managerial staff. Even in cases where wells or furnaces operated by partners dealt with the pipe, no preferential treatment was given in the rates charged or the measures used. We know little else of the progress of the business. However, by 1918 the pipe itself operated 163 pan units and had cash reserves of 35,525 taels.[133]

Organizational Innovation and Capital Accumulation

Salt merchants have held special fascination for historians due to their enormous wealth at a time when the development of non-landed assets in China was in its infancy. However, for most analysts, it was the salt merchants' access to government monopoly privileges that lay behind their ability to accumulate capital. The provenance of their wealth, tied as it was to bureaucratic connections, helped explain the propensity of wealthy salt merchants to imitate the landed elite in both lifestyle and investment practices. Likewise, their familism, reinforced by the fact that the right to purchase government certificates to sell salt was often hereditary, exemplified the feudal nature of their wealth. No foundation for structural change is thought to be found here.[134]

Although engaged in the production and sale of salt, the Furong merchants provide a very different window on the development of modern Chinese business practices. To look only as far as their ties to the salt gabelle and the kinship roots of many of their business dealings would be to miss the real significance of their achievements. While we would feel more comfortable generalizing about the bases of their business success in the presence of accounting records of some temporal depth, even the anecdotal data that we do have merits a reevaluation of capital accumulation and business consolidation in early modern China.

Family was an important factor in the business success we have documented so far. The major salt firms all had lineage trusts as their organizational foundation. An examination of the hundreds of contracts that survive from the Furong yard demonstrates that the majority of investors in wells, furnaces, and pipes were lineage trusts. In the case of the most successful salt entrepreneurs, the development of vertically integrated holdings, managed under a lineage trust and with minimal outside investment, was the ideal form of business organization. The lineage trust was a surrogate for incorporation in the modern business environment, protecting company assets from division through inheritance or succession and regulating the redistribution of income through the trust's internal rules. Lineage trusts, by bringing together the assets of many kin, were an important source of investment funds. At the same time, the organizational potential of the lineage trust was great. Experience in managing diverse holdings was translated into the development of vertically and horizontally integrated firms that in turn provided important opportunities for efficiencies of scale and aided these firms in capturing a greater market share.

While family feeling and, more importantly, the power of the family hierarchy to direct the activities of family members was important in the development of the Furong yard, one should not overemphasize the particularly Chinese character of the investment and management strategies undertaken by Zigong salt enterprises. That they did not rely on outside capital markets does not distinguish them from their counterparts in the West. Nor does their preference for retaining ownership of their firms within a narrow group of family and associates. As Smith and Sylla, speaking of the United States, make clear, "Before 1890, the business landscape was still rather simple. Few corporations apart from railroads were large enough to require long-term financing from outside sources."[135]

Alfred Chandler's seminal work has shown that most of the manufacturers who developed mass markets for such commodities as cigarettes, matches, flour, soup, and even photographic film in the United States in the 1880s found both their working capital and the funds to expand their plants and equipment largely internally, from the profits generated in earlier ventures. While they did rely on local businessmen and commercial banks for both long- and short-term loans, they did not have to rely on outside capital markets, which meant that they did not have to relinquish control of their firms as they grew. "Thus, although day-to-day operations had to be turned over to full-time salaried managers, long-term decisions as to investment, allocation of funds, and managerial recruitment remained concentrated in the hands of a small number of owners."[136]

At Zigong some investors chose to deal only with members of their own kinship group. But the evidence from contracts demonstrates that most productive resources were developed by groups of investors of diverse surnames. The Wang Sanwei trust, which in its later years was a large consolidated lineage corporation, began to amass its fortune by seeking partnerships with unrelated investors, often with people who were not even natives of Sichuan but with whom the Wangs had developed business associations. It is one of history's great coincidences that civil war visited both China and the United States at mid-century. However, it is no coincidence that war provided the shock that opened new markets on both continents and gave many fledging industrialists the profits on which their future business fortunes were based. Like those in the United States, the merchants of Zigong capitalized on these new market opportunities. Over time, advances in technology and the shifting political map of the late nineteenth and early twentieth centuries would contribute to continuing structural change in the salt industry. Furong businessmen cultivated political and social capital as a means to preserve both their personal fortunes and their industry's market share. In doing so, they cultivated traditional gentry roles as well as contributing to the development of modern commercial and legal institutions as part of an emerging modern Chinese business elite. It is to this transition that we will turn in chapter 9.

5

The Growth of an Urban Workforce

THE SALT industry was the single largest employer of labor outside of agriculture in early modern Sichuan. Toiling at its furnaces, drilling and pumping its wells, caring for its livestock, supplying it with construction materials
and food, carrying brine, fresh water, and coal, shipping salt from furnace
to customs point, and from port to port was an army of men whom writers from as early as the nineteenth century have estimated to number in
the hundreds of thousands at Furong alone. As we have seen, during the
nineteenth century, salt production in Sichuan as a whole increased by at
least 350 percent, with less conservative estimates running as high as 650
percent. A disproportionate percentage of this growth was concentrated
at the saltyards in southwestern Sichuan, most notably those in Jianwei,
Fushun, and Rong counties. This dramatic expansion in output could not
have taken place in the absence of conditions often ignored in the analysis
of China's economic development.

Most important was a relatively mobile free labor force. At least by the
late Ming, and probably earlier, the majority of Chinese were free of any
legal or social encumbrances to their movement between places and between occupations. Many of the salt entrepreneurs whose histories we have
already examined came to Sichuan after migrating to one or more intermediate points and pursuing several paths to family fortune along the way.
The hundreds of thousands of men who ended their days as workers at the
saltyards could tell similar stories. Most of them came from a distance. Even
when their backgrounds were rural, which most of them were, they already
had experience as wage earners, as day laborers, peddlers, transport work-

ers, and miners. Despite the harsh conditions of employment at wells and furnaces, many Zigong workers found in their new home opportunities to defend their interests by means of the same institutional structures through which their employers pursued theirs—native place associations, religious associations, guilds, and secret organizations of various kinds.

Immigration and Industrialization

Sichuan has been the subject of a number of important studies on Chinese demographic history.[1] While most studies are concerned with aggregate growth, Paul Smith's work on the seventh to twentieth centuries traces a long-term shift in Sichuan's demographic center from the northeast to the southwest of the province.[2] These population movements may reflect the growing importance of salt production in the Sichuan economy, which from the middle period was increasingly concentrated in the southwest. For our period the pull of a growing salt industry is unmistakable. The "Reports on Household and Male and Female Population" of the Sichuan financial commissioner, housed in the Number One Historical Archives in Beijing, provide an opportunity to compare overall growth in Sichuan's population with that of the key salt-production areas. These statistics were compiled by the Sichuan financial commissioner from county-level reports and were referred annually to the Board of Revenue in Beijing. For the period 1822 to 1887 they show overall population growth for Sichuan province at 66 percent or approximately 0.78 percent annually. However, for the counties in which were located the three most important Qing saltyards, average annual population growth ranged from 1.02 percent to 1.37 percent.[3]

During the early Qing, the most important source of population growth was immigration, which would continue to be an important factor in growth in the late Qing as well. However, as Skinner and others have pointed out, by the end of the dynasty the pull of rich uncultivated agricultural land had diminished as Sichuan itself "filled up" and the Taiping devastation of the Lower and Gan Yangzi provided new and less distant targets of migration for the farmers of China's densely populated eastern and southeastern provinces.[4] Qualitative confirmation of the role of migration in the Furong labor market can be found in discussions of the provenance of certain types of specialized salt workers.[5] Salt evaporators at Leshan largely originated in Hubei and Guangdong, while Yan Ruyi found that most of the skilled workers who drilled wells in Jianwei were from Guizhou.[6] Merchants and transport workers frequenting the trade route between Furong and the eastern Sichuan Yangzi River port city of Chongqing carried news of employment opportunities to both Sichuan and Lower Yangzi communities. Salt evaporators at Furong during this period often migrated from Jiangjin and Nanchuan counties in Chongqing prefecture.[7] The economy of Jiangjin itself relied in part on the manufacture of salt pans for the Furong market and the export of agricultural produce to the yard.[8] Indeed, by the early eighteenth century, Furong was drawing on a third wave of immigration originating largely from within Sichuan. This consisted predominantly of peasants from agriculturally less productive areas along the periphery of the Upper Yangzi macroregion. By the late Qianlong period, these areas, which had been extremely important in the second wave of immigration into marginal and highland areas, were also becoming "filled up." Therefore it is not surprising to hear that many moved to the saltyards of the southwest as the needs of production in that area began to dramatically expand during the 1830s and 1840s. Nanchuan was typical in this regard. A poor mountainous county that relied largely on coal and iron extraction, it saw its agricultural land use ratio drop to only 13 percent by the twentieth century.

Chinese scholars have suggested that climatic conditions also contributed to the factors that drove peasants off the land and into the saltyards. Sichuan experienced widespread drought followed by floods in 1864, 1873, and 1884–85.[9] Grain price data for the late nineteenth century confirm the existence of a series of food crises corresponding to these dates.[10] Over this same period, grain prices in Sichuan's mountainous peripheral prefectures recovered far more slowly than in the core areas surrounding Chongqing and Chengdu.

We know very little about how workers came to Furong.[11] It is likely that two patterns dominated. First, as in the case of the salt evaporators, native place ties to merchants dealing in the Furong market and investing in Furong wells and furnaces enabled some men from the counties along the Sichuan border with Guizhou to migrate, often in groups, to the saltyards. During the early Qing many men from western Hubei entered the province as rope pullers, towing boats making the trip upriver through the Yangzi River gorges to Chongqing. Far fewer boatmen were needed for the return trip than were needed to guide the boats against the upstream currents and through the rapids between Hankou and the Kui pass. Thousands of these men remained in the province, many finding their way to marginal agricultural areas along Sichuan's border with Hubei and Shaanxi and from there to the saltyards at Furong and Jianwei.[12]

Second, workers were probably recruited by labor bosses who operated in the villages of nearby counties. We know that many of the workers at the lumberyards in Fushun were brought to the yard in this way from Yibin, and from Shuangshi pu, Dengjing guan, and Maotou pu in Fushun County.[13] The use of labor bosses who went into distant areas to attract men to the wells is also documented. Men brought in to work in this way were often drawn into indentured status through loans made by local strongmen contracted to undertake labor recruitment. Practices such as this were outlawed in Leshan in the late 1820s and were probably more common in the early years of well development when labor was relatively scarce.[14]

The presence of so large and heterogeneous a group of unattached men was a natural concern for agents of the state. Like miners, charcoal burners, and migrant agricultural laborers, salt workers were a potential source of social disorder and a natural pool of recruits for secret societies and bandit gangs. In the case of salt, the location of the wells in densely populated agricultural regions easily accessible by rivers made exploitation of immigrant labor less risky. However, there is evidence that the immigrant status of most salt workers was a great worry to officials during the early nineteenth century. These concerns were only intensified with the outbreak of the Taiping uprising in the east. A stele dated 1853 ordered furnace owners in parts of Jianwei to investigate the background of every salt worker they hired in order to avert infiltration of the yard by bandits.[15] Similar orders may well have been issued at Furong. If they were, they did not stave off the large-scale defection of salt workers to the side of the enemy when the rebel army of Li Yonghe and Lan Chuanshun occupied the Furong yard in 1859.[16] The early years of the nineteenth century were turbulent ones in these rapidly developing industrial areas. They were also years of active organizing among workers themselves. For much of the Qing period these two forces would come together to provide a remarkably stable labor environment, one that served the interests of permanent workers and employers alike until the transformation of the industry in the late nineteenth and early twentieth centuries.

The Size of the Salt Industry Workforce

Just as it is difficult to trace with any precision the movements of men into the saltyard, it is almost impossible to calculate how many men were directly employed in the Furong salt industry during its golden age. The estimates of contemporary observers place the total population dependent for their livelihood on the salt industry at between several hundred thousand and a million people. During the 1880s, Sichuan Governor-General Ding Baozhen estimated that at least a million men worked at the wells and furnaces, with several hundred thousand more operating as boatmen in the transport of salt.[17] Li Rong, also writing in the late nineteenth century, set the figure somewhat lower, at 300,000–400,000, including peddlers of saltyard supplies and workers in ancillary industries such as stonemasons, metal workers, and the like.[18] The gazetteers of Fushun and Rong counties, compiled in the early twentieth century, noted that official estimates of population for their counties as a whole during the last years of the dynasty were 898,356 and 482,513, respectively. These figures did not include minors and can be assumed, like most late Qing census figures, to undercount population by at least 10 percent.[19] Therefore it is not inconceivable that the saltyard itself was home to almost a million permanent and transient residents during the course of a year.

Only a minority of the Furong labor force was engaged in pumping brine, boiling salt, and supervising the movement of brine through brine pipes. Two of the leading experts on the Sichuan salt industry, Ran Guangrong and Zhang Xuejun, have estimated that an average of 50 to 70 men were employed at each well, 14 to 23 men at each furnace, and 28 men at each pipe in Furong. If we take the total number of wells, furnaces, and pipes named in the early Republic's Ziliujing guidebook compiled by Qiao Fu in 1916, we would arrive at a total primary workforce at the larger section of the saltyard of between 70,000 and 100,000 men.[20] Assuming a somewhat smaller workforce at the Gongjing section of the yard, it would appear that approximately one-third of the population of the yard was directly employed in the production of salt. The remainder consisted of either dependent women, children, and the elderly or those engaged in agriculture, in subsidiary industries, or in the various commercial and financial enterprises to be discussed in chapter 10. By the 1930s, higher levels of mechanization led to a decline in the number of men employed at any one production unit (see table 5.1). As we shall see, the number of production units also fell during the mid-Republic as a result of the development of high-productivity rock-salt wells and a reduction in overall demand during the warlord period. The resulting unemployment at the yard altered the delicate balance established between labor and management in the nineteenth century and provided a fertile ground for labor organizing among modern political parties.

The Growth of a Modern Free Labor Force

From the viewpoint of size, concentration, and organization, few places in China in the late nineteenth and early twentieth centuries could compare with the labor conditions found in Furong. As late as 1933 (and probably up until the 1950s), workers in modern industry, defined as factories, mining, and utilities, constituted less than 1 percent of an overall workforce of

TABLE 5.1 Average Number and Types of Employees at Furong Wells, Furnaces, and Pipes c. 1932

Wells	
Job	Number of Employees
Well division manager (*jingli*)	1
Bookkeepers (*guanzhang*)	3
Ass't bookkeepers (*bangzhang*)	2
Unit managers (*guanshi*)	2
Chief well artisans	2
Drill supervisor (*jingkou guanshi*)	1
Buffalo handler (*niupaizi*)	1
Well cleaners (*shimiejiang*)	3
Gas handlers (*shenghuogong*)	3
Pump workers (*kaichegong*)	3
Ass't pump workers (*dabangche*)	2
Treadle drill operators (*daoduijiang*)	20+
1st-level unskilled workers (*dazagong*)	3
2nd-level unskilled workers (*zagong*)	3
Apprentices	6+
Total	55+
Furnaces*	
Job	Number of Employees
Furnace division manager (*jingli*)	1
Bookkeepers (*guanzhang*)	3
Ass't bookkeepers (*bangzhang*)	2
Unit managers (*guanshi*)	2
Foreman (*zaotou*)	1
"Adobe-salt" handler (*tongzijiang*)	1
Salt evaporators (*shaoyangong*)	10
1st-level unskilled workers (*dazagong*)	2
Apprentices	6+
Total	28+

*Assumes a furnace with approximately 50 pans.

(continued)

TABLE 5.1 *(continued)*

Large Pipes	
Job	Number of Employees
Pipe division manager (*jingli*)	1
Bookkeepers (*guanzhang*)	5
Brine intake supervisor (*jianlugong*)	1
Site managers (*zuomatou*)	2
Brine vat supervisors (*zuohuangtong*)	2
Pipe workers (*jianjiang*)	6
Leak technician (*xunjianguanshi*)	1
Brine handlers	8
Mafu	3
Freshwater carriers	4
Apprentices	6+
Total	39+

Source: Wei Wu, ed., *Sichuan yanzhengshi* [Sichuan Salt administration history] (China: Sichuan yanzhengshi bianjichu, 1932), juan 3, 82a–85b.

approximately 200 million people in China. If we add to this handicraft workers of all kinds, as well as modern and traditional transport workers and people engaged in trade and service industries, the combined nonagricultural workforce was still no more than approximately 25 percent of workers and 13 percent of the overall Chinese population.[21] By contrast, the proportion of peasant to nonpeasant households in early 1930s Fushun and Rong counties was 49 percent.[22] During the second half of the nineteenth century, when the Furong saltyard was experiencing its greatest growth, the percentage of overall households in China deriving the majority of their income from nonfarm labor would have been lower still. For most Chinese, opportunities for wage labor continued to be combined with non-industrial employment. This was true of most Chinese salt workers as well. At the saltyards in Daning, Kai County, Fengjie, and Pengshui the brine was too dilute to support full-time labor, and salt workers remained part-time agriculturalists. At the marginal saltyards in northern Sichuan, salt processing was largely an occupation of the agricultural slack season, as was labor in other extractive industries throughout China.[23] The large Mentou gou coal mines west of Beijing only operated between the eighth and the fifth months of the lunar calendar. During the warm-weather hiatus, when poor ventilation technology forced a halt to production, most workers returned to their native places to join their families in work on the farm.[24] This cycle of industrial and agricultural labor set limits on the catchment area from which workers could be drawn and allowed much greater flexibility in employment practices than would evolve at Furong.

Unlike most of their counterparts elsewhere in Sichuan, the wells and furnaces of Furong operated 24 hours a day, every day of the year, except New Year's day. The high level of investment in digging wells, the fact that gas escaped whether used or not, and the risk that the well would collapse if pumping were halted for any length of time meant that new forms of labor utilization had to be devised at the saltyard. Almost all of the workers who came to the Furong yard severed their ties with the land. Those who came as immigrants also relinquished any possibility of periodic return home. The Furong salt worker was thus one of the first examples of the genuine proletarianization of the workforce in China.[25]

Perhaps the only comparable industrial environment in China at this time was that which prevailed at the large quasi-official manufacturing complexes like the Jingdezhen porcelain works and the imperial silk works of the early Qing. Here state direct investment and imperial orders were responsible for the initial growth of labor concentration in large-scale factory settings. Both the development of the Furong saltyard and the evolution of business practices at the imperial silk and porcelain works represent a movement toward privatization during the late imperial period. However, whereas the opportunities for private market expansion led to a process of business consolidation in Furong, the large silk and porcelain factories experienced fragmentation, as government funding was withdrawn and labor management came under a system of private subcontractors and small workshops.[26]

Division of Labor and Specialization of Skills

The large number of full-time wage laborers at Furong did not necessarily engender worker solidarity. The number of workers employed by any one salt producer could be considerable. The Li Siyou trust is said to have had at least 2,000 employees by the 1830s, while the Wang Sanwei trust had a workforce of at least 1,200 men.[27] However, most of these men worked in small groups at individual wells, furnaces, and pipes. The strength of workers' associations and the ability of workers to protect their jobs through native place and other associational affiliations of workers in particular tasks hampered the movement of individuals between jobs. Nevertheless, the ability to transfer workers where needed within their category of work was one of the advantages of large-scale production. In general, it was the fore-

TABLE 5.2 Wages at the Wang Sanwei Trust in Late Qing (in strings of copper cash per month)

Job	Wage
Managerial Staff	
Managers	30
Bookkeepers	20
Foremen	5–6
Cash dispensers	3
Apprentices	0.6–1
Workers	
Chief well artisans	2.4
Skilled salt evaporators	4
Pump and drill operators	0.8–1.2
Unskilled furnace workers	1.8
Buffalo handlers	1.2
Freshwater carriers	1

Source: Xiaoyuan Luo, "Ziliujing Wang Sanwei tang xingwang jiyao" [The basic elements of the rise and fall of the Wang Sanwei trust], *Sichuan wenshi ziliao xuanji* 7 and 8 (1963): 192.

man in charge of a particular job who hired the men at his work unit. At the wells that responsibility fell to the chief well artisan (*shanjiang*). At furnaces, it was most often the furnace foreman (*zaotou*) who took on the long-term laborers who evaporated the salt.[28] As labor recruiters foreman were powerful figures at the yard. A letter from the Zigong Chamber of Commerce dated 1929 indicates that at least by the early twentieth century foremen took a cut of the wages of workers, indicating relations of dependence between workers and foremen common in the early modern Chinese factory system.[29] Nevertheless, the ultimate responsibility for production lay with the unit managers hired by the main office of the lineage or company, and it was they who determined manning levels and presumably could shift workers from one unit to another if necessary.

A high degree of specialization among workers was evident by the eighteenth century, as is testified to by Wen Duanbo's early Qing memorial on the organization of the salt industry in Sichuan. His list of the jobs available to workers contains references to at least 12 different specialized functions.[30] Tables 5.1, 5.2, and 5.3 provide an indication of the division of labor that had evolved at the wells, furnaces, and pipes of Furong by the end of the nineteenth century. The *jingli, guanzhang, bangzhang,* and *guanshi* were all members of the management team at the wells and were

TABLE 5.3 Wages at the Li Siyou Trust in Late Qing (in strings of copper cash per month)

Furnace Personnel	Wage
Manager	30
Operations head	21
Bookkeeper	16
Tally chief	13
Brine procurer	13
Master	8
Supply procurer	7
Foreman	7
Assistant bookkeeper	6
Management apprentice	2
Skilled worker	2 to 4
Unskilled worker	0.5 to 1.5
Pipe Personnel	**Wage**
Manager	24
Brine procurer	16
Bookkeeper	10
Master	7
Supply procurer	6
Assistant bookkeeper	5
Tally chief	5
Lower-level clerk	3 to 4
Management apprentice	1
Skilled worker	4 to 5
Unskilled worker	0.5 to 1

Source: Zilin Li et al., "Ziliujing Li Siyou tang you fazhan dao shuaiwang" [The Li Siyou trust of Ziliujing from their development to their decline], *Sichuan wenshiziliao xuanji* 4 (1962–63): 169–170.

discussed in chapter 4. The chief well artisans were the most important workers at the wells. The most respected among them were said to be able to select a well site by the smell of the grass and soil in an area. The role of the chief well artisan continued after the well was completed. At wells that were pumped by the owners, he was in charge of general maintenance work and the dredging of the well.[31] The tasks performed by the *dabangche* and *shenghuogong* are unclear. However, it is likely that the former worked with the *kaichegong* to operate the derrick and windlass in pumping the well, while the latter specialized in operating the gas pipes at gas wells. The *shimiejiang* was probably one of the workers whose job it was to keep the well clean of debris, while the *niupaizi* was the man who drove the buffalo to turn the wheel. When a well was being drilled or redrilled after having been abandoned or when the decision was made to attempt an increase in productivity, a new team of skilled workers was brought to the site. Under the supervision of a *jingkou guanshi*, who was trained to move the drill bit to ensure a perfectly round well opening, 20 or more *daoduijiang* were needed to operate the treadle drills.

At the furnaces there were fewer specialized jobs, the main division being between those who handled the brine and those who ran the furnaces. The furnace foreman not only supervised the evaporation process, but was also in charge of the construction of the furnace itself.[32] Under him were two groups of workers, the salt evaporators (*shaoyangong*) and the workers who carried the brine, under the supervision of the tally head and his assistants. In addition, men known as *tongzijiang* were employed to soak the adobe used to raise the sides of the pans with fresh water in order to prepare the salt dissolved in it for evaporation as well.

The number of staff at the pipes was smaller, but the differentiation of functions among them was no less fine. The *jianlugong* appears to have been responsible for receiving the brine from the owners of the wells, a job that required some skill in determining brine concentration, one of the factors considered in setting the shipping price. The site manager (*zuomatou*) was in charge of input and outflow of brine at the pipe, while the *zuohuangtong* supervised activities at the brine vats along the pipe route. General laborers at the pipe were called *jianjiang* and the number varied with the length of the pipe. At least one man worked as a *xunjiang guanshi*, touring the pipe route looking for leaks or other problems, while others concerned themselves with the operation of the pumps set up along the route to raise the brine, served as general handymen, carried freshwater to workers and animals, or toiled at the vats where brine from many wells was mixed to obtain a standard concentration of salt.

Conditions of Employment

The men who held the positions described before were permanent employees. A case from Jianwei County in the Routine Memorial Cases in the Board of Punishments (*Xingke tiben*) suggests that salt workers were hired by contracts that stipulated wages and other conditions of employment.[33]

During the Qing period, before the effects of warlord currency manipulation were felt at the yard, wage levels were stable and real wages remained relatively high, particularly at management and supervisory levels (see tables 5.2 and 5.3).[34] Both workers and supervisors also appear to have received food on the job.[35] Workers at Furong also did well compared to their counterparts in extractive industries around the country. Workers at the Mentou gou mines were paid on a piecework basis. However, Deng To has calculated that on average a miner made 1.5 taels a month and a pit porter made between 0.6 and 0.8 taels.[36] Similar wage rates are found among miners in Baxian in Sichuan.[37] Thus, while the lowest-paid workers in Furong lagged somewhat behind coal miners, skilled and semiskilled workers at the saltyard did very well indeed.[38]

At Furong the requirements of skill and experience, the stability of employment, and the higher level of worker mobilization created a three-tiered hierarchy among laborers. Skilled drill and furnace foremen were very well paid by late imperial standards and were given a great deal of responsibility in the organization of production. They were also the main non-management beneficiaries of bonuses in years when productivity and profits rose. According to one elderly well driller, skilled craftsmen such as these were able to leverage their specialized tools and skills into job security and privileged treatment. So precious were their trade secrets that some craftsmen would construct their own tools for the job and would allow no witnesses to be present while they were being used. Below the small ranks of foremen was a large pool of workers whose skills and access to guild support also earned them job security and relatively high wages. Salt evaporators were the most privileged of this group, and their guild will be discussed in detail below. Their income was 2.5 times that of coal miners and unskilled salt workers. On the lowest rung of the labor ladder were menial workers, odd job men, and the large number of temporary workers who toiled on a piecework basis, did not receive their food, and could not rely on employment throughout the year. The difference in status and wages is clear in a photo from the early twentieth century in which unskilled well-drilling workers and their skilled supervisors posed in front of a drill rig (see illustration 5.1).

By contrast, the workers in ancillary industries serving the needs of salt production appear to have enjoyed wage levels comparable to those of the lowest tier of laborers at the saltyard. Workers in the factories producing the twisted bamboo cable used to raise and lower the brine tubes in the wells were paid for piecework, although the exact rate of their wage is no longer known.[39] Most of the employees at lumber yards were odd job men who stacked wood, erected scaffolding, and built simple structures like warehouses, which did not require the skills of an experienced carpenter.

ILLUSTRATION 5.1 Drill Workers Posing at Their Rig
Source: Lin, *Essentials of Sichuan Salt,* front matter.

Paid for work done, they made no more than 24 to 32 copper cash a day, less than some of the worst-paid pump operators. Those fortunate enough to get outside work delivering lumber to the wells could expect to make two or three times this amount but were required to return 10 percent to the labor bosses who got them their jobs.[40]

It should not be inferred from this discussion that salt workers lived a comfortable life. The environment of the saltyard itself was debilitating. Fumes from the brine wells mixed with escaping gas that Li Rong claimed could suffocate a man if he got too close.[41] Cholera, malaria, and dysentery were endemic to the area.[42] It was to escape the foul influence of the yard, as much as to protect their families from rebels and bandits, that wealthy salt merchants built estates on the high ground in the hills surrounding the yard.[43] Most Chinese accounts of labor conditions speak of the workers living in sheds like the cattle that worked alongside them, sleeping on straw, and eating unhusked rice.[44]

The worst off were the temporary laborers paid on a piecework basis. Brine porters at the furnaces spent their days balancing loads of up to 300 *jin* from vat to pan. A very strong man could make an average of one string of cash a month in this way, but his employment was likely to be intermittent and he received no food from his employer.[45] A less muscular man might elicit the aid of his wife and children, a practice called "carrying the water off the surface" (*tao mianzi shui*). Well drillers were required to jump as many as 40 times a minute to raise and lower the lever that pounded the drill into the rock at the well opening.[46] Even less fortunate were the men who worked on the *renbanche*, human substitutes for the labor of the buffalo that turned the wheel to lift the brine tube from the well. This practice, banned in some areas during the 1830s, was revived in Furong, Jianwei, and Pengshui during the last years of the Qing. Chinese scholars attribute the rise in this use of human labor to natural disasters that drove large numbers of peasants into the cities looking for work. Equally important were the instability of the salt market during the 1890s and the first decade of the twentieth century and a series of outbreaks of rinderpest, culminating in a major epidemic toward the end of this period. According to a Republican period Fushun gazetteer, "Buffalo feed is composed largely of broad beans. [Buffalo] also require men to herd them and drive them [to work]. The costs are considerable, and the rise and fall in the price of salt generally hinges on it. If you use fewer buffalo and the energy of poor people is employed [to raise the brine], you can pay them a few cash, and there will be hordes who come to earn a living in this way."[47]

Under conditions of fluctuating demand, purchase and maintenance of a large herd of buffalo was impossible for many smaller owners. A quality water buffalo cost an average of 80 taels. Whether or not it was used at the well, it had to be fed and one handler was kept on the payroll for every 25 head. Well owners who switched to human labor could hire and lay off workers as the market demanded. Some hired workers directly, while others contracted with a labor boss to raise a fixed volume of brine. The men employed in this way were paid by the number of times the brine tube was raised, a tally being issued at each instance, converted to cash in the evening. In the late nineteenth century a man could make about 30 to 50 cash a day in this way.[48]

Even the notion of job security was relative. High levels of production and large demand for labor all year round meant that workers hired for permanent positions could expect to keep their jobs as long as their performance was good and they avoided industrial accidents. We have no record of the frequency of such mishaps. However, it was not uncommon for a man to lose a leg jumping on the trestle drill or suffer burns at the furnaces. Owners took no responsibility for industrial accidents, although it was the practice at the saltyard for the boss to contribute eight strings of cash toward a worker's funeral.[49] It is therefore not surprising that a far more common reason for loss of employment was simple deterioration of health after years of ceaseless hard physical labor. It was the fear of joblessness when old that most plagued the men dependent for work on the salt entrepreneurs. And these fears are echoed throughout the songs they chanted while working at the wells and furnaces, songs with lines such as "If you work as a migrant worker all your life/ when you're old you will have to beg" and "Owners don't want the old or the young/ they just want your middle years/ Get sick or reach your declining years/ and only heaven will see your tears."[50]

Many permanent workers belonged to successive generations of family members employed at the saltyard.[51] Expanding production and the need to hire vast armies of temporary workers on a daily or monthly basis also led to the growth of a permanent labor market in Furong. By the 1820s and 1830s there were markets at four locations. We know little about their operations during the Qing period. However, testimony taken at a meeting of elderly salt workers in 1963 gives an indication of what it was like during the labor surplus years of the Republic.[52]

A worker who wanted to carry water or work on the treadle hammer of the drills used in drilling wells, each day before dawn had to take a torch, and with a worn-out garment wrapped around him, run to the labor market. There he stood and waited for the man who handled the external affairs of the well to arrive and call out names. Because there were too many men at the labor market, the external affairs officer would not call out real names, but would call out nonsense sentences…. Those who understood what he said would seek him out and perhaps get work. Those who could not understand would end up standing there for nothing and would not find work.

The supervisor in charge of hiring at the Linhai well had an equally idiosyncratic method for selecting unskilled labor. He would go to the labor market with a bag of tallies, one for each man he hoped to hire. Once there he would scatter them around the yard and whoever could scramble to get one was employed.[53]

These practices were demeaning for workers and also hint at the continuation of practices by which workers relied on patronage by men who controlled access to jobs. They also add credence to claims of secret society influence in the labor market by the end of the dynasty. The use of secret passwords that would have significance only to the initiated society member would help explain what the worker quoted above called the bizarre chanting of "nonsense sentences." Some of these workers may also have been hired through labor bosses or *batou* with connections to the warlord government of the area.[54] Labor bosses figured prominently in the control of salt transport during the 1920s to 1940s, taking over the role of the earlier confederation of boat owners that had controlled this aspect of the business during the Qing period.[55]

Worker Organization and Worker Unrest

Information on workers' associational activity in the Qing period is scarce. Most of what we know has been transmitted as the memory and lore of more recent workers and by a small number of stele which have memorialized in stone worker actions and the rules that they set for their organizations.

We know that during the Ming dynasty collective action by salt evaporators at the Daning yard in northeastern Sichuan played a part in the empire-wide rejection by artisans of hereditary occupational classification of households.[56] The Daning strike itself was most likely a spontaneous reaction to government policy and was carried out largely by independent artisans for whom salt evaporation was a household industry. It is not until the mid-Qing, when the expansion of salt production began to bring together large numbers of salt workers, particularly at yards in the southwest of the province, that we begin to see the formation of associations dedicated to the concerns of saltyard workers.

The members of Furong's labor force drew on a long tradition of association (*hui*) formation. Founded on the designation of patron gods and the raising of money to conduct rites in their honor, by Qing times such *hui* could be found in both rural and urban communities and among members of all social classes.[57] The development of *hui* among workers in Furong reflected several characteristics of the yard: a large immigrant population, a growing division of labor, and an increasing differentiation between skilled and unskilled labor.

According to the recently completed *Zigong Municipality Salt Industry Gazetteer,* Furong workers were already served by a broad range of job-specific *hui* by the late eighteenth century. While it is not certain when most of these associations were founded, by the mid-nineteenth century the Yandi hui, formed by salt evaporators, appears to have been joined by the brine porters' Huazhu hui, the well drillers' Sisheng hui, the brine pump operators' Menglan hui, the bamboo cable makers' Qiaosheng hui, the coopers' and woodworkers' Luzu hui, the blacksmiths' Laojun hui, and the chief well artisans' Puxian hui in providing support for fellow workers.[58] Each association was named after a patron god, often invented by the association's members to resonate with their sense of connection to their trade. This is particularly striking in the case of the buffalo handlers' association, the Niuwang hui, named after the buffalo god.[59]

The Dala hui

The first major Qing salt workers' strike in southern Sichuan for which we have data took place not in Furong, but in Jianwei's Wutongqiao yard. This was due in part to the earlier development of this yard and to the economic pressure exerted on merchants at the yard as a result of growing competition from Furong. The action by workers at Wutongqiao was led by the Dala hui, or Large Lamp Society, which served as the main organization of salt workers at this yard. Unlike the organizations that were to evolve in Furong, this society was open to all salt workers and began as a religious foundation among workers who gathered to worship at the Guanyin temple on a hill on the outskirts of the yard. During the early 1820s a group of workers joined together to formally collect subscriptions from the main categories of workers in order to purchase oil and incense for the temple. In addition, the practice evolved of setting out 20-foot lamps at the foot, middle, and top of the mountain on which the temple stood. These lamps were lit every day at dawn, and it is from them that the society derived its name. By the 1840s it had already become the practice of the society to hold a special ceremony every year on the occasion of the Festival for the Deliverance of Hungry Ghosts, on the 15th day of the seventh month of the lunar year. For the most part the occasion appears to have been limited to rituals of popular religious significance, particularly the lighting of incense and chanting of prayers.

The occasion for the strike by the Wutongqiao salt workers was the 1850 celebration of the Festival for the Deliverance of Hungry Ghosts. Two leaders of the Dala hui, Xiong Silun and Lü Wenzhong, took advantage of the large number of workers assembled to light incense on this occasion to incite the workers to stop salt production. The strike appears to have been called largely to redress economic grievances. The workers' only demands were that wages be raised and working conditions improved. After several hundred workers responded to the first call to stop salt evaporation, the owners, through their own representative association, the Yanzong hui, called for a meeting with workers' leaders. Xiong and Lü presented their demands to the owners and warned that if they were not met, they would release a group of more than 100 pigeons they had been raising at the temple as a signal to the workers of the whole yard to go on strike. In the end their demands were rejected and approximately 2,000 workers joined in the action against the well and furnace owners.

The government's handling of the Dala hui conformed to general government policy toward private associations seen to threaten imperial order. The first move by the local administration was to call a meeting of the strikers at which they were admonished by the local officials and told to return to work. As evening drew near the Leshan magistrate and the Jiading prefect invited one of the workers' leaders to return to the county yamen for further talks. Along the way, Xiong Silun was arrested for inciting anti-state activity, and it is alleged that he was beaten to death while in custody. Lü Wenzhong was arrested soon after and sentenced to death. Workers were then offered the option of returning to their posts without penalty for participation.

Arresting the leaders and granting amnesty to the followers, a technique widely used in the Qing to deal with unrest, was a success. The work stoppage ended almost immediately as the threat of intervention by government troops was made known. The same group made a second attempt at a strike in 1852. However, their plans were leaked before action could be taken and their leader, Song Laoba, was captured and killed.[60]

The Yandi hui

The most powerful of the hui organized by workers at the Furong yard was the Yandi hui. Most of what we know about its origins, organization, and dealings with employers is a result of worker memoirs and one stele commemorating its founding. The Yandi hui appears to have begun as a mutual-aid association formed by salt evaporators at the turn of the nineteenth century. Most Furong salt evaporators came from Sichuan's Jiangjin or Nanchuan counties and a large number of them were already members of the Jiangjin *bang*, a native place association. It was that tie that facilitated the organization of a subscription loan group or *fangduijin hui* among a small group of salt evaporators in the late eighteenth century. Dues were paid into the association coffers and were loaned out at interest to other workers. The sums involved must have been tiny, for it took some time to amass even the 100 taels that enabled the workers to build a small hall to house their organization.[61] The pretext used for construction of this building was the erection of a temple to the Earth God (*tudi miao*). Earth God temples were routinely constructed by investors at the site of wells and were the location of banquets and other rituals of thanksgiving when a well came in. It was at this particular temple, on Banbianjie in Ziliujing, that salt evaporators congregated during the early 1800s. For men who worked shifts consisting of 24 hours on and 24 hours off, the Earth God temple became a home away from the mere pallets they enjoyed at the furnace. Dues, in the form of enough cash to purchase three *jin* of firewood, were paid by each member. As membership grew, the group decided to expand its activities, build a larger hall, and change its name to that of the patron god they had chosen for their association.

The reliance on the heat of the fire as they toiled at the furnaces naturally inspired the workers to call on the help of the Fire God or Huo Shen as the patron for their expanding organization. The fact that there was no Huo Shen in the traditional Chinese religious pantheon appears to have been of little concern to the workers themselves. However, legend has it that it did worry a local lower-degree holder who was friendly with the workers and acted as a secretary for their organization. Deng Keyu suggested that they change their name to the Yandi hui. Yandi was another name for Shennong, the legendary Chinese ruler among whose gifts to his people was the invention of agriculture. The only connection with the salt evaporators was the character for Yan, which means "huge fire" and consists of one character for fire poised above the other.

Deng also suggested that the workers learn from the experience of lineage associations and use the money they had saved to buy a piece of land from which rents could be generated as an endowment for their temple. With a plot yielding 30 *shi* of rice a year they began to build their Yandi temple. The first section went up during the teens of the nineteenth century and additions continued to be made in 1825, 1854, and 1855 as money became available. Members supplied all of the labor, so that the entire structure cost less than 10,000 taels to build. According to one source, the Yandi hui itself was formally inaugurated in 1842.[62]

The Yandi hui, as it finally evolved during the 1850s, was as sophisticated as any of the guild structures in late imperial China. Zhang Xuejun's seminal article on the activities of southern Sichuan salt workers' associations transcribes the Yandi hui rules that were carved in stone in the early nineteenth century.[63] The association had six heads (*zongshou*), each serving a three-year term. Below them were ten assistant heads, each serving for one year. The heads were divided into three pairs, one to handle association economic affairs, one to manage the temple itself, and one to deal with relations between the association and the outside world. The ten assistant heads were also paired off and given special responsibilities for external affairs, accounts, the kitchens run by the association, purchases, and miscellaneous business. New heads were chosen by the old heads, with the approval of the entire membership, from among the people who had served as assistant heads.

It is not clear how one was selected to become an assistant head. To become a member one had to be presented by a guarantor and approved by both the mass membership and its leaders. As we shall see in a moment, guild membership became essential to obtain the highly paid senior evaporator positions at the Furong yard. As jobs became scarcer, the association resorted to infrequent intake periods to limit the number of members. The process of enrollment in the Yandi hui was called *kaibu*. This "opening of the registers" was probably an annual event during the last years of the Qing. By the mid-Republican period it was limited to a 16-day period at irregular intervals of several years depending on the demand for new workers.

When a new worker joined the Yandi hui he had first to pay an entry fee, approximately 2.8 strings of cash when the organization was first founded, rising to as much as 6.8 strings toward the end of the dynasty and leveling off at 8.8 for much of the Republican period. This was equivalent to one or two months' wages for a skilled evaporator. In addition, annual dues, in the form of incense money, were collected from each salt evaporator, with guild members (*shangshou*) paying half that of nonmembers (*xiashou*) for the privilege of obtaining work.[64]

The ability of the Yandi hui to enforce its discipline over the activities of salt evaporators was the result of one of the most interesting imperial period labor struggles for which we have a record. After its founding, the association devised a set of rules for working at the pans. They included the following items:

1. Each guild member will be paid to operate no more than 5 pans. Each nonmember may only operate 3 or 4 pans.
2. Two guild members may form a team and operate 10 pans together. Nonmembers may only work as individuals.
3. Members will work shifts of 24 hours on and 24 hours off (*shiwu ban*). Nonmembers will work a shorter shift every day of the year. (*sanshi ban*).

Rules were also established to govern personal conduct. No gambling, opium smoking, brawling, smoking, cursing, or excessive drinking was allowed.[65] Members caught exhibiting such behavior were fined the cost of a certain number of theatrical performances, or a certain number of spirit lamps, or *jin* of oil. Men caught stealing or engaging in other serious offenses were expelled from the association. The latter punishment was extremely serious inasmuch as loss of guild membership meant loss of one's job. A system of mutual responsibility appears to have been enforced among guild members, allowing the leadership to mete out punishment to anyone failing to report an offender as well as to the culprit himself.

The association also established rules for mediation of disputes among members. Whenever serious disagreements arose, the instigator of the "suit" was required to pay *yaxijin* of 3,200 cash, the estimated cost of a two-table banquet, attended by all the parties to the disagreement, witnesses, and the mediator himself. After the banquet, the mediator would hear testimony from all sides and his decision on the case would be binding. Strict procedures for hearing cases were also laid out in the guild rules. Ritual obeisance would be made to the patron god. The rules of the association relating to the case would be read, and anyone creating a disturbance during the proceedings would be fined. If the "plaintiff" was found guilty, in addition to any damages, it was his duty to repay the man who had brought the suit for the banquet.

From these regulations it is clear that the Yandi hui sought to play a dual role. On the one hand, it continued to be a "surrogate family" institution, enforcing discipline and mediating disputes in much the way that lineages defended the interests of the group. On the other, it acted as an artisans guild, struggling to set work rules on the shop floor and guarantee the jobs and wages of its members. In addition to rules governing their own members, the Yandi hui sought to establish levels of remuneration for skilled workers at the furnaces, one tael per pan per month, in addition to a monthly allowance of 0.15 *shi* of rice, one *jin* of oil for cooking, and a daily ration of four cash for vegetables.[66] This would have meant a considerable increase over the two to four strings that appear to have been standard wages at Wang and Li furnaces in the late nineteenth century.

It is not clear when the Yandi hui decided to present these demands to management. Some accounts claim it was soon after the founding of the organization. However, it is more likely to have been around the time the stele commemorating the completion of its temple was struck. This was 1859. The institution through which the Yandi hui sought to reach an agreement with the managers of the hundreds of furnaces around the saltyard was the Bada hui, the Eight Big Guilds of Shaanxi salt merchants whom we have already seen were probably the largest investors in salt development at this time. The merchants were not at all interested in acquiescing to the workers' demands and negotiations went on for months. When the discussions finally broke down, the Shaanxi Eight Big Guilds petitioned the magistrate to punish the Yandi hui for unlawful rebellion against one's employer.[67] Contrary to expectations, the salt evaporators did not walk off the job but fought their case through the courts. The workers engaged their old friend Deng Keyu to argue their side of the case. There is no record of violence, although several years intervened before a decision was reached. By this time the case had gone all the way to the provincial seat, where Deng Keyu was forced to move, leaving his daughter in the Yandi hui's care. In the end the Shaanxi merchants acquiesced to the workers' demands, and the rules they so brazenly carved in stone became the basis for labor relations at every furnace in Furong. It is this stele that provides most of our knowledge of the case.

The victory of the salt evaporators is the only instance we have of a worker's guild establishing work rules as well as a virtual monopoly over jobs in the trade. The highly skilled nature of the salt evaporation process, upon which the owners' profits ultimately rested, the recent boom in gas well production, requiring an expansion in the numbers of evaporators at the furnaces, and the powerful organization built up by the workers were undoubtedly behind the decision by the employers and the magistrate to yield to the Yandi hui's demands. But we should not overlook the role that the Yandi hui played in disciplining labor and supplying the yard with the reliable, skilled workforce required by the high-throughput industry of salt evaporation. Local officials had an interest in supporting local industry, both as a source of tax revenues and to provide employment for a growing (and potentially disruptive) population of skilled and unskilled men. The working relationship between the Yandi hui and Furong's emerging industrialists appears to have remained in place down to the twentieth century. Indeed, until the twentieth century large-scale worker actions were remarkably few.[68] The only reliably documented strike before the end of the Qing dynasty took place in 1884. Led by the organization of Furong well drillers, the Sisheng hui, it was joined by both skilled and unskilled laborers and lasted about a month. The precipitating event was a fight between a well driller and a well manager.[69] However, the proximate cause was most likely wage cuts prompted by rising taxes and growing political pressure to restore to Lianghuai salt manufacturers the Hubei markets lost to Furong during the long Taiping war.

Conclusion

Salt production in Furong created a labor environment that differed greatly from that of traditional manufacturing in China. At its wells, furnaces, and pipes we see the emergence of many of the conditions associated with modern industry: a permanent, full-time workforce, division of labor, and substantial hierarchical managerial control over labor. At the same time, workers took advantage of a rich Chinese organizational repertoire to ease the shocks of industrial and urban life. As was true of workers throughout China, native place remained a strong organizational logic, especially for skilled laborers.[70] Through local recruitment networks and guild rules protecting access to skills, salt evaporators, drillers, and well artisans maintained near monopolies in skilled jobs for workers from particular regions of Sichuan. Unskilled labor was more heterogeneous, but the concentration of permanent workers also facilitated the formation of associations drawing on popular religious and guild traditions. These in turn fostered internal solidarities and enabled even unskilled workers to occasionally protest wage and worksite conditions.

The late nineteenth and early twentieth centuries was a time of considerable change within the Sichuan salt industry. Government efforts to increase revenue extraction from Sichuan salt sales and better control Sichuan access to its newly acquired markets resulted in insecurity for both owners and workers. However, the introduction of new pumping and drilling technology during this same period dramatically increased the output at

Sichuan wells and brought new sources of brine to Furong's furnaces. By the fall of the Qing dynasty it was clear that government efforts to control the market had failed and that new technologies had brought with them new investment opportunities. Nevertheless, transformations in production and government policy left their mark on the organization of business and labor. It is to these changes that we now turn.

6

Official Transport and Merchant Sales

THE END of the Taiping Rebellion and the pacification of the numerous other challengers to Manchu rule during the second half of the nineteenth century precipitated efforts at reform and regeneration throughout China and at every level of the political hierarchy. Patterns of commerce and modes of doing business disrupted by the northern progress of insurgence were only partially restored to the status quo antebellum. Particularly in the regions of China hardest hit by anti-Qing violence both political and material reconstruction provided new opportunities for elite activism and new demands for revenue. Efforts to join "self-strengthening" to "restoration" ordained a struggle for control over taxes between central and provincial governments and the survival and elaboration of wartime taxes long after the fighting stopped.

For the salt manufacturers and merchants of Sichuan and those who consumed their product this had two important consequences. The first was the effort by officials in the region of the Lianghuai salt administration to drive Sichuan out of former Lianghuai markets. The urgency with which this goal was pursued was tied to income, from the sale of Lianghuai salt and from taxes levied on that salt. *Lijin*, a tax on goods in transit, which had been imposed on commerce of all kinds during the Taiping Rebellion, continued as an important source of income for both the center and local authorities. During the war, *lijin* had been the main source of revenues from salt shipped from Sichuan into the Huguang market, consisting of parts of Hunan and Hubei (see map 1 on page 7). Who was to benefit from revenues on salt shipped to the Huguang market now became a matter of great significance, both to the authorities in Sichuan, Hunan, and Hubei and to the governments of Zhejiang and Jiangsu, where the Huai salt that had served the Huguang market before the war was manufactured. For the latter the question of the status of Sichuan salt in this market had implications for both its ability to fulfill its salt certificate quotas and its ability to amass new forms of income from *lijin*. For Sichuan the stakes were similar. Would Sichuan be able to serve this new market, and would the government of Sichuan continue to reap the benefits of the *lijin* levied on this lucrative trade? For consumers as well as producers there also loomed the question of how large the flexible *lijin* tax would be allowed to grow. Pegged too high, *lijin* and other new nonstatutory taxes could price Sichuan salt out of the market, even if eastern Chinese salt interests did not succeed in barring well salt from the old sea salt sales territories.

New taxes were not the only threat to Sichuan's salt industry to evolve out of post-Taiping reconstruction. New institutional arrangements calculated to make up for central government revenue shortfalls also changed the nature of the game for Sichuan salt producers. In the face of the Taiping onslaught many provincial governments ceased to send their full quota of land and head taxes up to the center in Beijing. Following the war, as provincial officials sought to rebuild infrastructure, restore agriculture, and take early steps in the direction of what would later be called "self-strengthening," few hurried to restore levels of prewar revenue sharing. Confronted by rising costs for security, foreign debt, and a diminishing central tax base, the government in Beijing could ill afford to let any source of income at its command go untapped. Hence the abolition of Sichuan's relatively benign salt administration and the introduction of a radical form of state-controlled commerce known as "official transport and merchant sale" (*guanyun shangxiao*) (hereafter cited as Guanyun).

Considerable work has been done by scholars in Taiwan and China on the imposition of salt *lijin* and the implementation of Guanyun. Most of the material from which these descriptions are drawn may be found within several official compilations on salt administration and a small number of accounting reports by provincial and salt administration officials that are now housed in the Number One Historical Archives in Beijing. Because these scholars are working from a common set of documents that largely deal with the impact of salt taxes on state revenues, one should not be surprised to discover that all of these studies agree in their basic assessment of salt policy during the final decades of the Qing. As we shall see, both the increase in tax rates and the greater control that Guanyun gave the state meant that the Qing benefited from increased revenues from salt at a time when such income was critical to the survival of the state. It is also clear that salt became more expensive for consumers in Sichuan and in the Sichuan salt sales territories in Yunnan and Guizhou. What is not clear is how Guanyun, *lijin*, and market restrictions affected salt *producers* in Sichuan, especially those at the most advanced yards. It would be wrong to assume, as most writers have, that their impact was wholly negative or that their effect was uniformly felt. In this chapter we will examine the main components of Sichuan salt administration as it was reshaped in the late Qing. We will then evaluate the impact of the new rules of the game on output, market access, and the structure of business before turning in chapter 7 to the role of new production technologies in the further transformation of salt manufacturing in late Qing Zigong.

The "Aid to Huguang" (*jichu*) Market

When Sichuan salt was introduced into the salt market in Hubei and Hunan in the 1850s, it was without the restraints that limited the sale of salt in other markets in China. Although this was still a licensed trade, inasmuch as the collection of revenue was of primary concern to the government, no quotas were set on the volume of Sichuan salt that could be exported. Indeed, as originally envisioned, the opening of the Huguang market would absorb the already large excess productive capacity of the largest Sichuan saltyards, Furong and Jianwei, thereby relieving Sichuan officials of the burden created by large stores of unsold salt certificates. Salt destined for the Huguang market was to be of two types. The first was the unregulated "surplus salt" which, as we have seen in chapter 1, merchants could already purchase at the saltyards for sale without a license in the Sichuan domestic market. The second was salt that had been designated for sale by certificate but for which the certificate had never been sold (*jiyin*).[1] Although the sale of surplus salt had already led to the development of an unregulated (or smuggling) trade parallel to the designated marketing system established under the salt gabelle, the opening of the "aid to Huguang" market heralded the elimination of specified sales territories for certificate salt as well. Officials in Huguang were simply instructed to set up tax collection stations at which merchants from Sichuan paid a single fee, set at between 10 and 20 percent of the market value of the salt, and received a certificate entitling them to sell their salt anywhere in the "aid to Huguang" region.[2]

Beginning in 1854 *lijin* was also levied on salt shipments to Huguang. The first *lijin* bureau to collect transit taxes on Sichuan salt was set up at Yichang (see map 4 on page 83), the main Yangzi River port east of Sichuan in Hubei. For every *jin* of salt passing through the Yichang customs barrier, a tax of

0.0015 tael was collected, yielding a total of more than 20,000 taels during the first year and several months. Not satisfied with this level of revenue, the government established a branch *lijin* bureau at Shashi, the flourishing nonadministrative market town downriver from Yichang, linking both the overland and riverine trade routes from Sichuan. With the establishment of this second tax barrier, salt shipped to Huguang was first taxed 2.5 copper cash at Yichang. Salt shops in Shashi then collected another 4.5 copper cash from the consumer, providing the government with a total of 7 copper cash per *jin*. In 1861 the *lijin* tax at Shashi was raised another 2 copper cash and at Yichang the bureau added 1 copper cash to bring the total levy to 10 copper cash per *jin*. By 1864 further increases in the tax and manipulation of the exchange rate between silver and copper cash brought the total *lijin* impost on salt shipped to Huguang to 18 copper cash per jin.[3]

Most of the salt on which the above *lijin* was levied was salt for which the certificate had never been sold (*jiyin*). In 1855 the government also instituted measures to tax surplus salt. In order to catch this salt before it left Sichuan, a checkpoint was set near Kuizhou and a *lijin* of 0.13 taels was imposed on every 100 *jin* destined for export. An additional checkpoint was established at Kongwang tuo in Wushan County to catch salt from Daning, located below the Kui pass. At the same time, *lijin* bureaus were situated at the main saltyards in order to tax both certificate and surplus salt at the point of production.[4] Smaller saltyards did not merit bureaus of their own. Instead the collection of this new *lijin* was left to the local bureaucracy. Areas where the salt gabelle had already been merged into the land and head taxes were required to establish salt depots to which furnaces sold their surplus salt.

By 1860 the increasing importance of Chongqing as a central entrepôt for both the domestic and export trade in salt led to the consolidation of internal salt *lijin* collection there. The charge was 650 cash for every bundle of *ba* salt and 1,350 for every bundle of *hua* salt.[5] A much lower rate of taxation, only 2 taels per *yin*, was imposed on salt destined for sale within Sichuan itself.[6] Despite the increase in *lijin* imposts, much of the income from which was used to supplement the military budgets of both Huguang and the Lianghuai region, the volume of Sichuan salt entering Huguang continued to grow. Of particular concern to the government was the rate of tax evasion that a system of branch *lijin* bureaus encouraged, and within a few years all external *lijin* taxes on Sichuan salt were consolidated and collection limited to the main port of entry at Yichang.[7]

On the basis of certificate equivalents recorded by the salt administration, Ran and Zhang estimate that approximately 86,400,000 *jin* of Sichuan salt was shipped into Huguang each year.[8] Contemporary estimates taking into account the likely rate of illegal shipments put the total even higher. Corruption within the *lijin* bureaus was considerable and merchants were quite adept at evading the tax barriers, shipping the salt by river past Chongqing and then carrying it by land over the Huguang border to avoid taxes at Yichang. So high were the prices they could obtain for salt during the war years that even the costs of porterage could easily be absorbed by an enterprising merchant. Officials at the time deduced that the equivalent of at least 800 Sichuan water-route certificates found their way into Huguang each month. To estimate total sales we assume that certificates allowed the bearer to sell the standard weight established in 1850; a *ba* certificate would have allowed the sale of 8,000 *jin* and a *hua* certificate 10,000 jin. Inasmuch as Huguang consumers, used to the granular sea salt shipped by Lianghuai merchants, preferred granular *hua* salt to the darker, "saltier" *ba* variety, we may assume that approximately three-fourths of certificates were used to sell *hua* and one-fourth to sell *ba*, for a total of as much as 91,200 *jin*.[9]

What portion of Furong output contributed to the "Aid to Huguang" market? Tang Jiong, in a memorial dated 1877, reported that Furong produced more than a million *jin* of salt a day during the peak productivity months in autumn, winter, and spring. If the summer drop in production, when the water table fell, was taken into account, daily average output was still at least 800,000 *jin* per day or 292 million *jin* per year.[10] If we assume that most of the salt shipped through Yichang came from Furong then approximately 30 percent of Furong output was oriented toward Huguang.[11] Even if we assume some contribution from Jianwei, at least a quarter of Furong production was directed toward this new market.

The opening of the Huguang market was a boon not only to the most advanced sectors of the salt economy. Small producers also flourished as a result of the sudden expansion of demand for Sichuan salt. As we noted in chapter 1, during the first half of the nineteenth century many smaller yards saw their markets swallowed up by the more efficient producers at Furong and Jianwei. During the 1850s victims of *gaipei* and *guiding*, by which the licensed salt quotas of "mom and pop" producers were redistributed to their more efficient competitors, saw their fortunes temporarily reversed. Anecdotal evidence reveals a significant resurgence in production throughout the province. The Taiping years saw the emergence of 100 new salt-producing families in Luoquan, an area whose salt industry was in ruins during the late Daoguang reign (1821–1850).[12] Fengjie had had its entire production quota removed and was an area designated for consumption of Yunyang salt. However, during the 1850s so many people turned to digging wells and boiling salt that "the vapors from salt manufacture filled the air"[13] (see map 1 on page 7). A similar phenomenon was noted in Nanlang, while the Gazetteer of Sichuan Salt Administration recorded that at She-Peng "unregistered wells opened daily. Now they are everywhere, and it is beginning to be impossible to know which wells are private and which salt is illegal."[14]

The Struggle Over the Huguang Market

Salt administration, as we have seen, was a matter for central government legislation. However, the structure of this second most important source of state revenues was a matter of intense regional interest as well. Salt merchants had always been important contributors to the informal revenue streams of local and provincial officials. However, by the nineteenth century, and increasingly after the Taiping Rebellion, revenues from the salt gabelle itself became a source of discretionary funding for Qing governors and governors-general in their efforts to reconstruct infrastructure damaged by war and undertake reforms inspired by Western contact. So, while the central government's fiscal interests would have been served whoever met the consumption needs of the people of Huguang, whether the salt would flow from the east or the west became a matter of passionate concern to many within the Qing bureaucracy. The political struggle over the lucrative Huguang market is, for our purposes, less important for what it tells us about late Qing politics than as the background against which we can begin to evaluate the response of the Furong industrial system to the mounting political distortions of the market in the late nineteenth and early twentieth centuries.

The first challenge to the relatively free market within which Furong salt manufacturers had initially flourished was the attempt of Liangjiang Governor-General Zeng Guofan to recover the lucrative tax revenues formerly generated by the salt gabelle of the Lianghuai region. Following the fall of the Taiping and the restoration of trade links between the lower Yangzi and central China, Zeng, the universally acknowledged architect of the military victory, approached the court with a plan to wean back the Huguang population to the consumption of Huai sea salt from eastern China. In 1864 he received approval for a rise in the rate of *lijin* on Sichuan salt and undertook measures to flood Hubei shops with what was hoped would be a cheaper Huai product. After five years this plan proved unable to alter the consumption habits of the target population, in part because high levels of smuggling activity had maintained a relatively competitive price for the better-quality Sichuan salt.

In 1868 Zeng began a new campaign to ban Sichuan salt from the Huguang market, which included a proposal to circumvent the market by forcing the closure of Sichuan wells and limiting legal exports from Sichuan.[15] Vigorous opposition to the plan was voiced from both Sichuan and Huguang. Sichuan Governor-General Wu Tang's arguments against the closures focused both on tax revenue and the economic impact of market interference. Not only would Sichuan be deprived of its main source of *lijin* revenues. These changes would also have devastating effects on an industry that was both a major employer in the province and a target of considerable investment. As Wu Tang tactfully put it, it would be difficult for the people who opened wells to reconcile themselves to such a policy.[16] Li Hongzhang was also worried about the vast unemployment a ban on exports to Huguang would cause. His five-point memorial raised the likelihood of increased smuggling should such a ban be carried out. In addition he pointed to the importance of Huguang as a transshipment point to parts of Guizhou and speculated on the effect a ban would have on supplies of salt to this longstanding Sichuan market. His memorial closed with his own observation, as governor-general of Huguang, that the people under his jurisdiction preferred Sichuan salt and no amount of coercion would force them to buy what they did not like.[17]

Lin Dihuan has suggested that officials in Huguang defended the Sichuan market because salt smuggled into Huguang was subject to Huguang *lijin*, while salt imported from Lianghuai yards was taxed before reaching Huguang's borders.[18] Whatever their motivation for defending Sichuan's market in Huguang, Sichuan was allowed to retain a share of the Huguang market. Zeng Guofan was able to win support for more vigorous measures to curtail smuggling of Sichuan salt and for sealing off unregistered wells and furnaces. Apparently these measures had little effect, and in 1869 Li Hongzhang memorialized again with the suggestion that the Huguang market be divided between Sichuan and Huai salt producers, with Sichuan retaining 80 percent of sales.[19]

Huai salt proved unable to control even the 20 percent share of the market set aside for its exploitation and in 1871 Zeng Guofan resumed his campaign to recapture the Huguang market. Among the solutions he proposed were an increase in the Huai share of the market to 60 percent, designation of a fixed quota for Sichuan salt exports to Huguang, and a realignment of the salt gabelle territories to limit access of Sichuan salt to eastern Huguang counties and departments. In the end the latter approach was adopted. Beginning in 1873 the Shashi office for the collection of *lijin* on Sichuan salt imports was closed. Wuchang, Hanyang, Huangzhou, and De'an were required to sell only Huai salt, while parts of western Hubei including Xiangyang, Yichang, and Jingmen were designated as Sichuan salt territories to which Huai salt could also be sent. Vendors of Huai salt also recovered their markets in Yuezhou and Changde in Hunan. Li independent department was temporarily assigned to Sichuan because of its proximity to the Sichuan sales territories in Hubei. Zeng also issued a set of five regulations designed to lower the price of salt, dismantle redundant tax bureaus and checkpoints, reform anti-smuggling operations, and improve the quality of Huai salt in order to enhance its ability to compete in the mixed markets opened to both Sichuan and Huai producers.[20]

Legal access of Sichuan salt to Huguang markets continued to be eroded over the next few years. In 1876 Liangjiang Governor-General Shen Baozhen succeeded in winning back control over Anyue and Xiangyang in Hubei and independent Li prefecture for the salt administration under his control. This was followed by a memorial by the censor, Zhou Shengshu, that the entire Huguang territory be ceded to the Lianghuai salt administration. Sichuan Governor-General Wenge vigorously resisted Zhou's request. Most convincing was his argument that diminished certificate sales for the border market made it essential that Sichuan retain a revenue stream from Huguang salt sales in order to meet its military security obligations at home and its responsibility to provide grain rations for the military in Yunnan, Guizhou, Shaanxi, and Gansu.[21] During the ensuing year, Shen Baozhen continued to press for a complete restoration of the Huai salt region's Huguang market while officials in Sichuan and Huguang offered unrelenting opposition to the measures proposed.

The Guanyun Reforms

The implementation of a new system of salt administration for the Sichuan region is usually linked to the above-mentioned effort to regulate Sichuan exports to Huguang in the years after the Taiping Rebellion. The radical nature of state intervention undertaken to protect its share of salt revenues has helped perpetuate the impression that the market for Sichuan salt was drastically reduced in the postwar years, contributing to a slump in demand from which producers never recovered. Salt merchants, whose participation in certain aspects of the industry was seriously curtailed by the new policies, reinforced this belief. As we will see, demand for Sichuan salt did not decline during the last years of the nineteenth century. The reform of the Sichuan salt gabelle did, however, change the structure of the industry, driving out small producers and many who relied on haulage of small amounts of salt as a by-occupation. Of greater significance to our study of business organization, the new system of salt administration curtailed an important source of profits for large vertically integrated firms. Whether it eliminated smuggling, one of its main goals, is doubtful.

The implementation of Guanyun was initially a targeted response to a particular problem. Neither the problem nor the response was directly related to Huguang. Rather, Guanyun was a reaction to the accumulation of unsold salt certificates (*jiyin*) entitling merchants to sell salt in parts of the Sichuan domestic market (*ji'an*) and the so-called border markets in Yunnan and Guizhou (*bian'an*). By the mid-1870s failure to sell more than 800,000 of these salt certificates to wholesalers of Sichuan salt had resulted in over a million taels in lost government revenues. Ding Baozhen, a Guizhou native with many years of experience in provincial government, was charged with solving the problem of unsold salt certificates.

Ding Baozhen was appointed to the post of Sichuan Governor-General in 1877. In his memorial laying out the plan for reform of the Sichuan salt administration Ding directed the Board of Revenue's attention to what were really two separate problems affecting the ability of the state to obtain revenue through the sale of salt certificates. The first was the disruption to commerce in general as a result of secret society uprisings coincidental with the Taiping Rebellion. This was a major factor in the withdrawal of the large Shaanxi firms that dominated the border market. Equally important was the overall underdevelopment of Guizhou. One of the poorest provinces in China, Guizhou was also a mountainous province with inferior communications that made it difficult for high officials to monitor the activities of either their subordinates or local residents. Indeed, these geopolitical factors were among the reasons for the establishment of designated markets and the salt certificate system in Guizhou in the first place, for without it the state feared few merchants could be induced to provide salt to all of the province's remote communities. According to Ding, since the withdrawal of the Shaanxi salt firms from the Guizhou market, smaller firms, comprising Sichuan and Guizhou natives, were taking over the movement of salt into the border market. Lacking the networks or the capital of their larger predecessors, they were less able to deal with potential losses and less able to resist the proliferation of *lijin* and other fees imposed by government functionaries and local strongmen. Moreover, those who did weather these storms still had to face intense competition from less scrupulous coprovincials who took advantage of the difficult-to-patrol border between Sichuan and Guizhou, which Ding likened to the interlocking teeth of a dog, to smuggle lower-taxed Sichuan domestic market salt into the border market.[22] It was no wonder that Sichuan had experienced difficulty selling its quota of Guizhou border certificates.

Ding's solution to the problem of unsold certificates was to take the wholesale shipment of salt out of private hands and consign it to a new centrally supervised bureaucracy. Salt production and the retail sale of salt remained as before in private hands. Now, however, the state would purchase salt directly from the manufacturer, ship it to designated markets, and sell it to merchants *in situ* who would deal directly with consumers. This was a fundamental change in the relationship between the salt industry and the state. Under the mixed system of administration prevailing before the Taiping Rebellion, bulk shipments of salt were taxed when a merchant or merchant firm purchased a certificate (*yin*) that entitled the holder to buy a fixed amount of salt directly from the furnaces. Each certificate authorized its holder to sell that salt, produced in that yard, within a specified sales territory. Surplus production beyond that sold by certificate and salt sold to areas no longer enrolled in the gabelle could be purchased in small amounts and sold by ticket (*piao*) after the payment of a fee. In both cases the government played little role in the salt market and only influenced the price of salt to the extent that the burden of tax was passed on to the consumer. In principle, the regulation of sales by means of certificates assured smaller yards a share of the market and made certain that the purveyors of this essential commodity did not neglect remote areas. However, even before the Taiping Rebellion, the allocation of markets was breaking down under pressure from the large wholesale merchants operating in the more efficient saltyards of the southwest.

The system of official transport and merchant sales was initially sanctioned for the Guizhou market and sales of Sichuan domestic market salt in those areas of Sichuan near the border market, including Xuyong independent ting, Yongning, Lu zhou, Nanxi, Hejiang, Jiangjin, Qijiang, Nanchuan, Qianjiang, and Pengshui (see map 1 on page 7).[23] In 1878 the Yunnan market was also enrolled in the Guanyun system along with 12 Sichuan counties and departments near the border of that province. Within a few years most of the territories along the main trade routes to Yunnan and Guizhou were also subject to Guanyun, as well as those areas of Huguang still entitled to Sichuan supply.[24] As a result of these reforms, by 1880 the Guanyun system had control of the entire market for Sichuan salt in Yunnan, Guizhou, and Hubei as well as domestic consumption of salt in 33 Sichuan counties, departments, and subprefectures. In all 19,571 water-route certificates and 56,046 land-route certificates were now sold through the new administrative structure. This accounted for approximately 58 percent of total legal Sichuan salt sales.[25] By carefully monitoring the sale of salt at the point of production, the state was able to capture a vastly larger share of the salt sold and make it subject to official levies. As table 6.1 so dramatically demonstrates, the capacity of its legal markets to absorb Sichuan salt was considerable. By the mid-1890s the accumulated unsold certificates as a percentage of new certificates sold had dropped from a high of 76 percent

TABLE 6.1 Accumulated Unsold Certificates in the Yunnan and Guizhou
Salt Sales Territories as a Percentage of Current Certificate Quota Sold (land
certificates converted to water equivalents)

Year	A. Certificate Quota	B. Accumulated Unsold Certificates	B as % of A
1878	13,523.88	10,284.84	76.00
1879	19,078.80	6,953.24	36.40
1880	20,611.88	7,403.60	35.90
1881	24,022.68	5,094.00	21.20
1882	24,054.68	5,297.32	22.00
1883	24,054.68	5,571.24	23.20
1884	24,054.68	5,904.24	24.50
1885	24,054.68	5,665.12	23.60
1886	24,054.68	5,757.00	24.00
1887	24,054.68	5,906.00	24.60
1888	24,054.68	5,759.20	24.00
1889	24,054.68	5,760.80	24.00
1890	24,054.68	5,906.96	24.60
1891	24,054.68	5,762.40	24.00
1892	24,054.68	5,907.04	24.60
1893	24,054.68	5,760.60	24.00
1894	24,054.68	4,000.00	16.60

Source: Data derived from accounting reports (qingdan) housed in the Grand Council Archives of
the Number One Historical Archives in Beijing, cited in Guangrong Ran and Xuejun Zhang, Ming
Qing Sichuan jingyanshigao [A draft history of the well-salt industry in Sichuan during the Ming and
Qing period] (Chengdu: Sichuan renmin chuban she, 1984), 138–39.

to a low of 16 percent. Of course these official figures do not speak to the
amount of salt that most likely continued to be smuggled into legal and
unauthorized sales territories.[26]

It is important to keep this in mind when we examine the new administrative structure established under the leadership of Ding Baozhen. The
Guanyun system not only eliminated the role of private merchants in the
wholesale shipment of Sichuan salt. It also recognized the increasing concentration of production that had taken place since the mid-eighteenth century.
When it was decreed that henceforth no private merchant could buy salt
directly from salt producers, what was really meant was that licensed salt
would be purchased by state agents from the most productive yards, leaving
the insignificant percentage of overall production attributable to "mom and

pop" operations in less advanced areas to continue to supply local consumers as before. Six Guanyun branch bureaus were established; the most important were in Ziliujing, for buying salt at the Furong yard and in Wutongqiao, which had the largest concentration of furnaces in Jianwei. Other branch bureaus dealt with salt evaporators at Shehong, Yunyang, Daning, and Pengshui.[27] Some excess production beyond the quota was permitted, and private parties could purchase this salt as well as salt from marginal production areas in small amounts after payment of the *lijin* tax.[28]

In practice, the state did not attempt to undertake all phases of purchase and shipping by government personnel. Nor did it maintain a permanent presence at the yards. Instead, three times a year the agents of the branch bureaus went to the yards, purchased salt, and contracted local companies to wrap the salt and ship it to the various sales territories. In the case of Furong, private shipping contractors handled the salt purchased at Ziliujing as far as Dengjing guan, at which point it was transferred to larger Yangzi River craft.[29] In order to control smuggling by these private boat owners, Ding promulgated detailed regulations for monitoring members of the boat guilds. Boats were registered and the size of cargo recorded on permits that could be checked by antismuggling officers along the shipping routes. Shipping rates were set for each *jin* of salt carried, including adjustments for loss in shipping and to account for the greater difficulty navigating Yangzi tributaries and their branch rivers during the dry season.[30] The main depots for the distribution of salt in the sales territories (*anju*) were the same as those used under the old system, except that now it was government agents who sold salt to local merchants. Salt entering Guizhou was distributed by branch bureaus at the Ren *an*, Fou *an*, Qi *an*, and Yong *an*. That destined for Yunnan was handled at branch bureaus in Zhangwo and Nanguang. All salt to be sold in Hubei passed through a central collection point in Wan County. Substations scattered throughout the countryside beyond these distribution points continued the task of inspecting the salt, supervising riverine shipments, and guarding against smuggling. In addition to controlling the actual movement of salt between the point of production and point of sale, the Guanyun bureaus attempted to resurrect the strict system of designated marketing territories. Smaller saltyards were permitted to supply their local communities. However, larger production areas were linked once again to specific distribution centers.

Once the salt arrived at the government warehouses associated with the designated sales territory depots, it was sold to merchants who actually marketed the salt to the consumer. Whereas under the certificate system a further demarcation of sales territories was made at this point, now merchants were free to sell their wares at any point under the jurisdiction of the sales territory from which they made their purchases. However, price was no longer entirely determined by market forces. The difficulties involved in transporting salt within the mountainous regions of the border territories led to an unregulated market within Yunnan and Guizhou. Having paid the salt bureau for their supplies, merchants in these areas could set their own retail price. The price of salt sold within Sichuan was more closely controlled. The rate at which merchants in this market were permitted to sell salt was officially determined based on the cost of salt at the well, transportation expenses to the point of distribution, all taxes and levies, and a formula for transportation costs within the designated sales territory that differed from place to place. Those selling near the Yunnan and Guizhou borders were allowed a profit of 20 taels per certificate on *ba* salt and 22 taels per certificate on *hua* salt. In other areas profit margins were generally calculated on the basis of an additional one copper cash per *jin* for the first 40 *li* and an additional two copper cash for each 50 *li* thereafter.[31]

The main office of the Guanyun administration was set up in Luzhou, the central distribution point for salt from the southwest and an important economic center for its close proximity to the Furong, Leshan, and Jianwei saltyards. Headed by a general manager (*zongban*) with the rank of expectant circuit intendant, it supervised all salt affairs for the province and was under the direct authority of the Board of Revenue in Beijing. This new specialized fiscal institution took the place of the joint administration of salt affairs by the governor-general and the salt and tea intendant, a move clearly calculated to lessen provincial control of salt revenues. Assisting the general manager were four departments: the Department of Records and Correspondence (*wen'an suo*), the Department of Income and Expenditure (*shouzhi suo*), the Certificate Department (*yinmu suo*), and the Ticket Department (*piaoju suo*). The last two were particularly important inasmuch as they handled the issue of certificates for the sale of salt and it was to these departments that the used certificates and tickets were returned as a record against which to check income, regulate quotas, and prepare the annual report (*zouxiao*) to the Board.[32] While the details of salt administration would change frequently over the next 70 years, the general framework established by Ding Baozhen remained as the basis for salt administration in Sichuan.

One of the main goals of the Guanyun reforms was the rationalization of salt taxation in order to increase government revenues and discourage evasion by merchants. The most efficient means by which to accomplish this was to consolidate all previous taxes into one lump sum. Rather than levy this as a tax, it was incorporated into the price that wholesale merchants paid for the salt in the sales territory. Only the well tax continued to be collected by local officials at the yard. In this way no component of the tax could be evaded, and new levies could easily be added to the mounting burden on both merchant and consumer. Indeed, this new policy accounts in large measure for the increasing importance that officials in need of cash during the late nineteenth century placed on the salt gabelle.

During the Yongzheng reign, when the system of allocating certificates on the basis of population was first implemented, only two taxes were levied on salt, the certificate tax and a wastage fee (*xianyu*). This was the case until the 1850s, when the need for revenue to fight rebel armies led to the introduction of *lijin* and a number of additional legalized fees. Vigorous efforts by Ding Baozhen enabled the salt administration to bring irregular fees and graft under control for a time. Imitating the reforms undertaken by the Yongzheng emperor almost 150 years before, all customary fees (*lougui*) were outlawed and a fixed fee of 15 percent of the certificate tax was added to the cost of salt in order to pay the salaries of those who worked in the Guanyun bureau, its branches, and its associated offices. In 1880 and 1883 respectively, arrangements were made to remit a portion of this fee to cover the administrative costs of officials in Guizhou and Yunnan.[33]

During the last decades of the Qing the need for new income to pay foreign indemnities, fund the New Army, pay for border defense, and raise militia led to many new taxes being tacked on to the rates paid for salt by merchants in the sales territories.[34] More than half of the new taxes collected on salt under the Guanyun administration were first introduced in 1895, the year that China signed the Treaty of Shimonoseki obligating the payment of a 200 million tael indemnity to Japan following its defeat of China in the Sino-Japanese War. Reformers in the early twentieth century identified 25 different fees and surtaxes levied on Sichuan salt.[35] The impact of these charges on the price of Furong salt in its various markets can be seen in table 6.2.

While not all fees were levied on salt sold in each market and the rates varied within each tax and fee category, over the course of the late Qing fees and surtaxes soon dwarfed the regular statutory salt tax. While the regular imposts remained relatively stable throughout the late Qing, the new taxes steadily grew. Even *lijin*, which had been the scourge of salt merchants during the 1860s and 1870s, remained relatively stable as new and increasing fees for special purposes were added to the price of salt at the point of sale to merchants. Most important was the rapid rise in "added price," the main category under which special taxes to pay for foreign indemnities, the New Army, and late Qing local government reforms were grouped.[36] By the end of the dynasty miscellaneous taxes on Furong salt accounted for approximately 95 to 98 percent of total taxes collected on salt manufactured at Sichuan's most productive yard (see table 6.2). According to Qiao Fu, in 1916

TABLE 6.2 Taxes per Salt Certificate for Furong Salt According to Designated Market c. 1911 (in taels of silver)

Tax	Yunnan and Guizhou Markets		Sichuan Domestic Market	Huguang Market	
	Furong ba	Furong hua	Furong hua	Furong Guanyun	Furong Merchant
Regular tax	3.405	3.405	3.405	3.405	3.405
Wastage fee	4.495	4.495	5.595	4.323	4.323
Yard *lijin*	19.500	18.000	18.000	18.000	18.000
Added price	35.000	43.750	43.750	0.000	0.000
Guizhou *lijin*	10.400	10.400	0.000	0.000	0.000
Guizhou *lijin* added price	9.000	9.000	0.000	0.000	0.000
New Army training fee	10.000	12.500	12.500	12.500	12.500
Diyao(?) added price	20.000	25.000	18.750	6.250	6.250
Yunnan *lijin*	0.600	0.600	0.000	0.000	0.000
Yunnan militia fee	1.087	1.087	0.000	0.000	0.000
Chongqing *lijin*	2.000	2.000	2.000	25.000	25.000
Guanyun bureau fee	5.000	5.000	5.000	0.000	0.000
Administrative expense fee	0.000	0.000	3.000	0.000	0.000
Gaidai fee	0.000	0.000	0.000	0.000	3.000
Military preparedness fee	0.000	0.000	0.000	0.000	1.000
Militia fee	0.000	0.000	30.000	0.000	0.000
Border defense fee	5.000	5.000	0.000	0.000	0.000
Huben (military-related)	1.000	1.000	2.000	1.000	0.000
Added *huben*	1.000	1.000	0.000	1.000	0.000
Certificate exchange fee	1.000	1.000	1.000	0.000	0.000
Artillery boat fee	0.500	0.500	0.000	0.000	0.000
Aid to Shi and Kang	0.500	0.500	8.000	0.000	0.000
Inspection fee	0.600	0.600	0.600	0.750	0.000
Interest fee	0.000	0.000	0.000	0.000	0.000
Totals	130.087	144.837	153.600	72.228	73.478
Miscellaneous taxes as % of total tax	97.663	97.649	97.783	95.285	95.365

Source: Zhenhan Lin, *Chuanyan jiyao* [Essentials of Sichuan salt] (Shanghai: Shangwu yinshu guan, 1919), 5.5. These data appear to be copied directly from an earlier compilation by Xi Zhang, *Sichuan yanwu baogao shu* [Report on the Sichuan salt administration], printed in 1911.

the amount of *hua* salt that could be shipped by purchase of one certificate cost approximately 140 taels. Thus, depending on its destination, miscellaneous taxes more than doubled the price of salt sold in Sichuan and the border markets and added a bit over 50 percent of the purchase price to salt marketed in Huguang.[37]

Measured in revenue generated and volume of taxed sales, the Guanyun reforms were a resounding success. As early as 1878 Ding Baozhen could triumphantly announce that for the first time in years the entire quota of Sichuan certificates had been sold, as well as a record number of certificates left over from previous years. By the end of the century Sichuan's salt administration was producing at least 3 million taels in taxes and Sichuan's certificate quota to Yunnan and Guizhou alone had been almost doubled (see table 6.1). The revenues generated by the Guanyun administration benefited both the central and provincial governments, with a fixed share sent to the Board of Revenue, and the remainder divided between Sichuan itself and Yunnan and Guizhou, the majority of the latter being used for military expenses. The ability of the bureau to reassign certificates to different areas in response to changes in market demand was in part responsible for the dramatic recovery in certificate sales. However, equally important was the restoration of peace in the border territories and the vigorous efforts made by officials to eliminate the corruption that had blighted the prereform administration. The practice of selling off unsold certificates continued until 1894, when disposal of the entire quota from the years before the institution of Guanyun was finally achieved. In that year the Guanyun bureau began to authorize the sale of salt produced beyond the established quota. These so-called surplus certificates allowed the level of sales to continue at approximately the same rate (or 125 percent of the regular quota) that had prevailed during the period up to 1894 (see tables 6.1 and 6.3).

There is some evidence that early in the twentieth century the Guanyun administration began to encounter difficulties filling its quotas. According to the editor of the *Essentials of Sichuan Salt,* this problem reached serious proportions between 1906 and 1908. Rising prices, triggered in part by an inflated copper–silver ratio, increased the cost of coal and other producer goods.[38] However, escalating taxes were of greater import. High taxes meant high prices for the consumers, who, the author laments, were forced to cut back on salt consumption.[39] Most of these consumers were in the Yunnan and Guizhou markets, where the efforts of the Guanyun administration remained concentrated.

If we are to understand the response of salt manufacturers to the Guanyun system, it is important to note that the declining effectiveness of the salt administration did not signify a contraction in the industry itself. In addition

TABLE 6.3 Surplus Certificates Sold in the Yunnan and Guizhou Salt Sales Territories as a Percentage of Current Quota Sold (land *yin* have been converted to water-route equivalents)

Year	A: Certificate Quota	B: Surplus Certificates Sold	B as % of A
1894	24,054.68	4,000.00	16.62
1895	24,054.68	1,960.00	8.14
1896	24,054.68	5,194.00	21.59
1897	n/a	n/a	n/a
1898	23,641.88	5,906.90	24.98
1899	23,641.88	5,715.80	24.17
1900	23,641.88	5,726.80	24.22
1901	23,641.88	5,717.80	24.18
1902	23,641.88	5,720.80	24.19
1903	23,641.88	5,723.80	24.21
1904	23,641.88	5,729.80	24.23
1905	23,641.88	5,741.80	24.28
1906	23,641.88	5,918.80	25.03
1907	23,641.88	5,744.80	24.29
1908	23,641.88	5,744.80	24.29
1909	23,641.88	5,823.80	24.63

Source: Data derived from accounting reports (*qingdan*) housed in the Grand Council Archives of the Number One Historical Archives in Beijing, cited in Guangrong Ran and Xuejun Zhang, *MingQing Sichuan jingyanshigao* [A draft history of the well-salt industry in Sichuan during the Ming and Qing period] (Chengdu: Sichuan renming chubanshe, 1984), 140.

to the salt sold by certificate, Sichuan salt makers, particularly those in more backward areas, were permitted to sell some salt by ticket to small private merchants who only paid relatively small *lijin* taxes to the state. Moreover, throughout the period after 1877, a portion of the Sichuan salt sold in Huguang continued to be shipped by private merchants, making the volume of sales impossible to track. Finally, in 1894 the government reversed its policy of relatively uniform treatment of the entire Sichuan market and eliminated the Guanyun administration's jurisdiction over the shipment of Sichuan salt within Sichuan—the *ji'an* market. One indicator of sales, and hence of production, is the figures for salt *lijin* paid at Yichang, the central entrepôt for the entry of Sichuan salt into Huguang. On the basis of these figures Alexander Hosie, who served as British consul general in Chengdu at the turn of the century, calculated shipments of Sichuan salt into this market at about 86 million *jin* per year. If we compare Hosie's estimate to the figures cited earlier in this chapter for sales of Sichuan salt to Huguang at the end of the Taiping Rebellion, it would seem that the "aid to Huguang" market held steady during the last decades of the century despite the drastic cuts in Sichuan's designated sales territory there. Moreover, as Hosie also indicates, the 1906 Yichang Customs Trade Report found total Sichuan salt exports to Huguang to be almost 97 million *jin*, raising suspicions that the earlier figures were underreported and shipments to Huguang actually rose.[40] This impression is furthered by the insistence of some of Hosie's informants that smuggling increased the volume of Sichuan salt available to consumers by as much as 50 percent of the state-controlled market.[41]

The Impact of Guanyun on Furong Salt Producers

If increased state market regulation did not result in a reduction in Sichuan salt sales, how should we evaluate the impact of Guanyun on producers?

First, the contraction of the "aid to Huguang" market and the coincident implementation of Guanyun appear once and for all to have wiped out the small Sichuan saltyards, except as producers of salt for their own local inhabitants. Zhang Xi's Reports on Sichuan Salt Administration, printed during the first year of the Republic, lists all the counties and departments in Sichuan, Yunnan, Guizhou, and Huguang served by Sichuan salt. Of these, the vast majority had their quotas met by salt from Furong and Jianwei, with Shehong, Leshan, Nanbu, Zizhou, Santai, Pengxi, Kuizhou, Jingyan, and Jianzhou picking up small quotas here and there.[42] Indeed, one of the striking facts uncovered by Alexander Hosie in his investigation of Sichuan salt production during the early twentieth century was the enormous shift in the proportion of total output that came from just a few yards. At the top of the list, with 58 percent of the provincial total, was Furong, while the top four producing yards contributed 92 percent of overall Sichuan output (see table 6.4).[43]

The changes wrought in the "aid to Huguang" market and the administration of the salt gabelle both benefited and hurt businessmen operating at the Furong yard. The Furong merchant resistance to government salt policies related at the beginning of this study dates from this period. Luo Xiaoyuan, a former officer of the Wang Sanwei trust, tells of a lengthy strike against the Guanyun bureau in 1908.[44] While these tales of merchants and workmen joining forces to oppose the state may be somewhat apocryphal, and certainly contain elements of family lore culled from many efforts to resist the Manchu regime, Furong salt producers clearly had every reason

TABLE 6.4 Estimated Output of All Sichuan Yards by County c. 1900

Salt Yard	Output in *jin*	% of Total Sichuan Output
Fushun/Rongxian	274,400,000	58.46
Jianwei	83,872,320	17.87
Leshan	51,100,000	10.89
Yunyang	25,427,250	5.42
Medium-size producers (*n*=7)	27,515,750	5.86
Small producers (*n*=14)	6,592,500	1.40
Marginal producers (*n*=13)	479,400	0.10
Total	469,387,220	100.00

Source: Alexander Hosie, *Szechuan, Its Products, Industries, and Resources* (Shanghai: Kelly and Walsh, 1922), 181–82.

for outrage at the switch from a system of relatively free trade and low taxes to the system that prevailed after 1877. However, not all participants in the industry or all aspects of the production and marketing process were adversely affected by the new relationship between state and society.

The first thing one notices when looking at the Furong yard as the Qing drew to a close is the disappearance of Shaanxi merchants as the dominant force in the marketing of salt in the southwest. The withdrawal of this powerful commercial influence began during the Taiping Rebellion, when warfare interrupted trade in the salt-marketing territories of Yunnan and Guizhou dominated by the Shaanxi guild. By the 1860s high taxes, corruption, and smuggling had already decimated the market in salt sold by certificate and provided the first cause for the policy of government control over long-distance transport.[45] Denied the profits accruing to what had been a virtual monopoly market for Shaanxi merchants, and faced with losses as a result of Muslim uprisings in their home region in the northwest, Shaanxi merchants began to shift their investments in new directions, including the growing credit market in Sichuan and elsewhere.[46] In the 1890s changes in the technology of salt production (see chapter 7) would complete the eclipse of the Shaanxi guild by indigenous Ziliujing and Gongjing merchants.

The Ziliujing and Gongjing salt companies that led the yard into the twentieth century were themselves transformed by the new system of salt administration. Guanyun fell particularly hard on smaller producers. Purchasing quotas were established by the branch Guanyun bureaus, which determined which salt would reach the lucrative certificate territories. According to Luo Xiaoyuan larger producers were given preferential treatment in negotiating with the bureaus, inasmuch as they could guarantee delivery of the stocks for which prepayment was issued months in advance.[47] Smaller furnace owners may have had to negotiate with their larger competitors to include their output in the latter's transactions.

Both gas and coal furnaces produced finished salt and it was the business offices of the furnaces that dealt directly with the purchasing agents of the Guanyun bureaus. In order to simplify their own task, bureau officials granted larger furnaces and furnaces of more powerful firms permanent quota shares or *paizi*. Furnaces with a *paizi* had to maintain production levels lest the *paizi* be revoked. In practice, a lively rental market in *paizi* developed, allowing furnaces to adjust to temporary changes in output without relinquishing the valued quota that guaranteed them a market.[48] Thus, just as certificates had become a commodity in the past, leased by small local merchants to powerful Shaanxi merchants (see chapter 1), *paizi* became a commodity to be rented and perhaps even bought and sold like shares in wells. Coal furnaces were disadvantaged under the quota system. Only when the output of gas furnaces could not meet the quota did the Guanyun administration buy coal-evaporated salt.[49] The ease with which coal furnaces could be built and put into production injected a degree of flexibility into industry. However, numerous coal furnaces were closed in the early years of the reforms, disadvantaging Gongjing brine producers as well. It was only a temporary fall-off in Ziliujing gas output that saved Gongjing from permanent decline.

While Guanyun favored larger producers it also ate into the profits of these firms and eroded the advantages of the vertical integration in which they were so heavily invested. The combination of brine pumping, evaporation, and wholesale and retail marketing had allowed the large firms to take advantage of the opportunity to sell a branded product. The Wangs, Lis, Yans, and Hus, and many of their somewhat smaller competitors, wrapped and marketed their own salt, which was then sold through their own agents who developed lasting relationships with retailers throughout the sales territories. Now that the government mixed all the salt it purchased together prior to shipment to distant markets, the incentive to maintain retail networks was diminished, as were the profits to be gained from improving the quality, uniformity, and name recognition of one's product.[50]

The larger producers also suffered from the sudden imposition of price controls, both at the saltyard and at the collection points for retail distribution. Salt producers now had to accept a fixed rate of return, established by the bureau at each sales period.[51] The large integrated salt companies had already been forced out of the wholesale market everywhere except Huguang. But Huguang, and later the unrestricted Sichuan market, retained considerable potential for making deals. Price controls not only lowered their profits on every sale of salt to the branch bureau at the yard. They also set the markup that could be passed on to the consumer. Any remaining advantage to be gained by maintaining information-gathering networks and agents in the retail markets was lost, and with it one of the major sources of profits for the aggressive merchants of the large lineage-based firms. Surviving account books do not allow us to evaluate the extent to which the loss of price-setting power contributed to the decline of the pioneers of the modern Furong saltyard. We do know that by the 1880s the Li Siyou trust had completely closed down its wholesale operations, even those based in Huguang.[52] And in the twentieth century, vertical integration and the combination of production and marketing ceased to be the hallmark of Furong entrepreneurs.

7

Technological and Organizational Change, 1894–1930

BY THE turn of the twentieth century, the Furong saltyard was one of the most prosperous communities in China. Despite its remote inland location it was a major source of government revenue in the form of salt taxes and an important target of investment for both native and extraprovincial merchants. Despite the changes imposed on Furong salt producers by reform of the salt gabelle, the production and marketing of salt still promised enormous profits for those with the capital, the know-how, and the nerve to get involved in this often volatile industry. In the early 1890s, the four great families of Zigong were at the apex of their fortunes, and the business techniques developed at their wells and those of their less prosperous fellow businessmen exemplified the potential for integrated professional management in early modern China. The economic importance of Zigong was such that it would become the most sought-after prize of dozens of Sichuan and extraprovincial warlords following the fall of the dynasty. Yet, within a few decades, an economic system that had been a century in the making would crumble. And champions of a new China looking backward from amid the rubble would see little of the structure that had once stood on this site.

In a novel written in the 1940s,[1] Wang Yuqi, a fourth-generation descendant of the founders of the Wang Sanwei trust, would depict his lineage's rapid decline in much the same way as would most Chinese historians. Intralineage feuding, feudal thinking, and rapacious government brought about the downfall of the Wangs, as they brought about the downfall of China. In fact, the Wangs et al., and China for that matter, did not so much fall down as get rearranged. And the forces that propelled that rearrangement can only be tenuously attributed to feudal thinking and greed. For Zigong, changes in production technology and the persistence of a poorly developed financial sector dealt the first blow, bringing with them their own logic and opportunities. Politics also played a role, first in the fall of the Qing and then in the development of new institutions through which both business and the state contended for control of Zigong's productive potential. And finally, war took its toll, first in setting Zigong up as a cash cow in an increasingly fragmented Sichuan and then by cutting the yard off from the markets that had been at the root of its original takeoff in the dark days of the Taiping uprising. It is to these factors and the manner in which the merchants of Zigong responded to the challenges they posed that we now turn.

Li Bozhai and the Discovery of the Rock-Salt Stratum

In 1894 Li Bozhai, a salt merchant with modest investments at the Furong yard, was invited by an acquaintance to take over development of a well that had recently been abandoned by a group of Shaanxi merchants.[2] The Guangyuan well was to be a black-brine well, as were most of the brine sources under excavation in the Dafen bao district of Ziliujing.[3] Dafen bao was a relatively undeveloped production area, supplying the furnaces of Ziliujing with an average of approximately 800 tons of brine a year.[4] It was also an area in which drilling teams frequently encountered problems, particularly as a result of the highly friable "beancurd residue" stratum (*dousha yan*) located at between 2,200 and 3,000 feet.[5] When earlier investors had drilled in Dafen bao and nearby Yangjia chong, a mixture of tong oil and lime was applied to this layer of rock in order to prevent collapse of the interior wall of the well.[6] A similar process would have been carried out at the Guangyuan well, now called the Fayuan well under its new owners, had workmen dredging the shaft at around 3,000 feet not begun to note the appearance of a white granular substance mixed in with the mud and rock removed from the well. At first these particles of salt were ignored. But as the team dug deeper, their volume increased.[7] According to most accounts of the discovery of the rock-salt stratum, Li Bozhai began to suspect that the process of drilling, in which water was introduced periodically to assist in the removal of debris, had caused a layer of salt somewhere other than the bottom of the shaft to begin to dissolve. The practice of deep drilling to levels of 3,000 feet or more in the construction of black-brine wells undoubtedly made it difficult to conceive of an even more concentrated source of salt several hundred feet above. However, as he experimented with various techniques for dissolving the source of this concentrated salt deposit, it became increasingly clear that the origin was not below, but at level of the "beancurd residue" stratum where the original developers of the well had ceased digging due to collapse of the well wall. This deposit was approximately 93 percent pure sodium chloride. At Dafen bao alone it extended over half a square mile at a width of 13 to 20 feet, with a potential productive capacity of almost 10 million tons of brine.[8]

Li Bozhai's initial efforts to dissolve the rock-salt layer involved pouring boiling water into the well and drawing out the brine.[9] In order to increase the salinity of the water, he combined this with a process known as *shan-shui*. As we have seen in chapter 2, the basic equipment for pumping a well consisted of the wheel and the derrick. On the top of the derrick was a wheel or pulley (*tiangunzi*) on which the cable that raised and lowered the brine tube was threaded. The cable ran from the well, up over the *tiangunzi*, down to the *digunzi* on the ground, and then on to the wheel. In order to agitate the mud at the bottom of the well two workers were employed to alternately press down on and release the *guojiang*, the length of cable that extended between the wheel and the derrick. This made the tube move up and down in the well. As it moved up, the piston at its lower end was forced open and brine entered the tube. As it moved down, the fresh water, which had been introduced into the well, was driven out the top of the tube and more concentrated brine was forced in. Within a short time it was discovered that cold water would work as well as hot, and the first economically feasible exploitation of the rock-salt stratum was begun.

The modest success of the Fayuan well experiment encouraged Li and other saltyard merchants to reopen a number of abandoned black-brine wells with a history of problems with "beancurd residue" layers. Among these were the Tianquan well at Yangjia chong and the Wanfu, Jixian, and Hengsheng wells at Dafen bao. In 1900–1901 six more wells were opened in this area.[10] The productivity of these wells was low and operations were highly labor intensive. Each well was irrigated individually; those at a distance from a freshwater source employed hundreds of laborers to carry in water from the nearest river or pond. Wells without a water source on their own land had to lease water rights, paying an annual fee based on estimates of yearly requirement, or purchase water as used, at rates as high as 400–500 copper cash per load.[11] However, inasmuch as most rock-salt wells were constructed from abandoned black-brine wells or by extending yellow-brine wells, startup costs were relatively small. Knowledge of the history of a well, recorded in the drilling records[12] kept by most late Qing investors, almost guaranteed success. The most difficult engineering task

ILLUSTRATION 7.1 Agitating the Brine
Source: Ding, *Gazetteer of Sichuan Salt Adminitration*, juan 2, jingchang 2, 14b–15a.

was the removal of the tong oil and lime sealant applied to the rock-salt stratum to prevent it from crumbling when deep drilling was under way.[13]

Men like Wang Ziheng, Deng Bingxuan, Wang Ju, and others were able to make a start in the salt business with little capital investment during the early years of rock-salt development.[14] All that was needed was sufficient cash to hire workers, buy buffalo, and, if necessary, rebuild the derrick and wheel complex. According to Nie Jicheng, a former member of the managerial staff of the Wanfu well, the largest single expense when this well was put into operation in 1903 was for buffalo. A herd of 80 could cost as much as 10,000 taels and allowed the well to pump approximately 2,000 *dan* of brine a month. Later, mules were substituted for buffalo at a cost of 120 taels a head, raising the monthly production figures to between 3,000 and 4,000 *dan*.[15]

The output from these early wells was not exceptional. In part their attraction for late entrants into the industry was a result of the large imbalance between gas and brine output during the last years of the Qing. As already noted, whether captured to boil salt or not, the gas tapped at Ziliujing wells continued to escape. Unable to store it or transport it any distance, owners had either to cap the well or find more brine, to boil. It was thus a seller's market for brine, and some well owners were even able to contract for advance payment as furnaces scrambled to guarantee their supplies.[16] More important, however, was the latent potential if this rock-salt layer could be efficiently mined. Brine from these wells had a saline concentration that averaged between 25 percent and 33 percent. This was almost twice the 17–18 percent concentration of brine from the average black-brine well.[17] In addition, rock-salt brine contained fewer impurities than yellow or black brine, requiring less processing before evaporation and resulting in less salt loss. Salt made from this brine was therefore far more economical to produce.

Most of the early rock-salt brine wells were independent operations in which irrigation of the rock-salt stratum was accomplished by introducing fresh water into the well being pumped. Li Bozhai undertook several such projects during the years between 1894 and 1900. One of these, the Tianquan well, was opened about 140 meters away from the original Fayuan well. About a year after production began, the erosive force of the fresh water created a channel connecting the rock-salt stratum below the two wells. From that point on, water could be poured into the less productive Fayuan well and the brine from both wells pumped from the Tianquan well alone. This wholly fortuitous event marked the real beginning of high-profit exploitation of the extensive layer of rock salt which lay below the districts of Yangjia chong, Dafen bao, Zhoujia chong, and Shanzi ba, an area extending across the yard for several miles (see map on page 83). By the early twentieth century most rock salt was pumped from interlinking wells. In 1902 the Huaifeng well became the entry point for irrigation of 20 wells forming the Yangjia chong–Zhoujia chong production area. In 1913 investors began introducing water into the Jirong well belonging to Wang Hefu and irrigating 22 wells forming the Jinyan ba-Macao shan-Xindian production area. In 1916 the same process was followed at the Wufu well, allowing the efficient pumping of five wells forming the Diaoyu tai-Shanzi ba production area.[18]

The inauguration of solution mining of rock salt resulted in dramatic changes in the management of brine production and opened up the possibility of greater mechanization and efficiency in salt production. An examination of the innovations that were adopted and the opportunities that were lost tell us much about the evolving business environment in Zigong in the early twentieth century.

The first change was a result of the structural reality that rock-salt wells could no longer be treated as wholly separate entities. As wells began to merge via underground channels well owners found it economical to form cooperatives for the joint irrigation of their wells. Cooperative agreements also avoided a potential nightmare of competing legal claims to underground wealth that could no longer be easily linked to above-ground land rights. The supply and transport of water played a role in the development of these initial cooperative arrangements. The availability of large quantities of water had not been a major concern in the early development of the yard. Most wells not near freshwater maintained ponds to bathe and water their buffalo but little more. Soon after the discovery of the rock-salt layer, entrepreneurs founded specialized companies that provided the water to irrigate rock-salt wells. Where there was no nearby water source, well owners paid such firms to supply water from distant reservoirs or ponds, with rates assessed either by the load[19] or by annual contract.[20]

While many wells continued to be pumped by their owners, some irrigation companies took on broader roles, both irrigating wells and pumping brine. Wang Hefu, a distant cousin of the Sanwei trust Wangs, pioneered the development of the rock-salt pumping business. The Master Hefu Rock Salt Irrigation Office, in which he was the majority shareholder, specialized in bringing contiguous wells together, managing the water supply, and irrigating the wells on a contract basis. The irrigation office's profits came from fees paid by each well owner on the basis of his annual brine production.[21] Wang's control of the water source essential to the operation of a number of wells at the Jinyan ba-Macao shan-Xindian production area was a major factor in the development of his fortune and also contributed to his rise as a leader within the salt community.[22]

From the start, the business of pumping rock-salt brine was far more volatile than that associated with successful black- and yellow-brine wells. As more rock-salt wells came into production, the process of irrigation and pumping itself changed the geology of the yard. The first district to be so affected was Dafen bao. During the initial stage of development, the water table in this area was quite deep and brine had to be raised a considerable distance, necessitating large outlays for pumping equipment, wages, and buffalo. Wells in this area were far less profitable than those owned by investors at Yangjia chong. However, within a few years the barrier between the wells in these two areas dissolved, the water table at Yangjia chong fell, and irrigation was carried out through a contiguous channel between the two areas. According to reports at the time, the final destruction of the barrier was felt as an underground explosion of tremendous force, the nearest analogy to which appears to be a giant underground avalanche.[23] Once the channel was complete, the location of a well along its many branches determined in large measure how profitable the well would be. Wells closest to the point where the water was introduced or on the direct path taken by the water as it flushed a group of wells invariably had lower yields.[24] Some wells were so adversely affected that their owners withdrew them from their irrigation cooperative and redrilled the wells to be pumped for black brine.

TABLE 7.1 Wells by Type at the Furong Yard c. 1932

Well Type	Number	% of Total
Rock salt	76	10
Black brine	94	13
Yellow brine	91	13
Black brine/gas	207	28
Yellow brine/gas	117	16
Dry gas	143	20
Total wells	728	100

Source: Wei Wu, ed., *Sichuan yanzhengshi* [Sichuan salt administration history] (China: Sichuan yanzhengshi bianjichu, 1932), juan 3, pian 2, zhang 10, jie 2, 72b–73a

Lai Mingqin and his colleagues recount one of the most dramatic examples of shifting fortunes in the rock-salt brine business. The Da Zhenghai well, originally drilled in the late Qing dynasty, began as an independent well. Water was introduced into the well through the nearby Lailong well and the pressure of the water raised the brine level by about 1,200 feet. As a result, the Da Zhenghai became one of the most productive of the yard's wells. However, not long after it went into production its rock stratum dissolved, bringing it into a direct line with the main irrigation channel of a large contiguous well system. Not only did its water level drop. The effect of direct line irrigation also washed much of its salt to the lower reaches of the channel and concentration levels fell. At the same time, the way in which the salt layer had dissolved led to repeated collapse of the well wall, and in a few years the well was closed.[25]

Over time rock-salt wells would become increasingly important to the overall productivity of the yard. Comparing official output totals, Zigong produced an average of 3,193,832 *dan* of salt between 1914 and 1919.[26] This figure had increased to about 4,120,000 by the early 1930s.[27] However, Zigong salt output in the early 1930s was generated by far fewer wells, and the majority of the overall output was by then the product of rock-salt brine wells. We do not have official figures for the number of rock-salt wells operating during the earlier period. However, according to the Essentials of Sichuan Salt there were a total of 1,004 brine-producing wells and 199 gas wells at that time.[28] As we will see later, mechanical pumping developed as a result of the opening of the rock-salt brine layer. The *Essentials of Sichuan Salt* does inform us that a survey taken in 1919 determined that only 38 wells were being pumped using steam and of these 32 were rock-salt brine wells.[29] We may therefore assume 32 was close to the number of rock-salt brine wells being pumped at this time, keeping in mind that many wells linked

TABLE 7.2 Estimated Output by Well Type in *dan* c. 1932

	Total Wells[a]	Average Brine Output/ Well/Day[b]	Total Brine/ Day	Total Brine/ Year	Total Salt/ Year[c]	% of Total Salt Output
Rock salt	76	300	22,800	6,840,000	1,778,400	57%
Black brine	94	150	14,100	4,230,000	761,400	25%
Black brine/gas	207	50	10,350	3,105,000	558,900	18%
Total[d]					3,098,700	100%

[a] See Table 7.1.

[b] Zhenhan Lin, *Chuanyan jiyao* [Essentials of Sichuan salt] (Shanghai: Shangwu yinshu guan, 1919), 228; Rongqing Ji, "Gongjing yanchang fazhan yipie" [A glance at the development of the Gongjing saltyard], *Sichuan wenshiziliao xuanji* 11 (1964): 193–196.

[c] Calculated as the percent of salt solids per unit of brine multiplied by the brine produced per year. For brine concentrations see Xu, Dixin, and Chengming Wu, eds., *Zhongguo zibenzhuyi fazhanshi* [A history of the development of the sprouts of capitalism in China] (Beijing: Renmin chuban she, 1985), 591 and Lin, *Essentials of Sichuan Salt*, 238.

[d] It is assumed that the remaining output can be attributed to yellow-brine wells whose brine concentration could range from 4 to 13 percent and whose output ranged from 40 to over 200 *dan* a day.

to rock-salt channels were being irrigated together and pumped through a terminal well. This is compared to the breakdown of wells documented in the Sichuan Salt Administration History in 1932 (see table 7.1).

Not only were there far fewer wells by the 1930s. By then, rock-salt brine wells were also producing about 57 percent of all salt at the Furong yard (see table 7.2). While the shift in production from black-brine to rock-salt brine was not the only factor in the eclipse of the nineteenth-century elite at the Furong yard, it certainly played a part. Most early entrants were deeply invested in black-brine wells. As we have seen, until the discovery of the rock-salt layer theirs was a seller's market. By the 1920s the expansion of production of the rock-salt layer would reverse the terms of trade between producers of gas and producers of brine. Moreover, as will be discussed below, the discovery of the rock-salt layer led to other changes in technology and relations of production, to which the holders of assets developed in the Taiping period and after had difficulty responding.

The Introduction of Steam-Driven Pumps

The story of the adaptation of steam power to the workings of the Furong saltyard is revealing not only of the new forces that would affect its business community. It also provides an interesting case study with which to evaluate the dominant narrative of Chinese modernization. We have already engaged this narrative of failure in its more benign form in our discussion of salt merchant entrepreneurship in the mid-nineteenth century. In this case a sudden change in the size of the market and the ready availability of underutilized technology sparked a takeoff in industrial investment and output. The commonly cited barriers to development—the imperial system of rule, lack of a commercial law, low levels of capital accumulation, and so on—all proved easy to surmount when the opportunity for profit was of sufficient size and duration. As it has been applied to China in the late nineteenth and early twentieth century, the narrative of failure becomes a tale of opportunity rejected. Western technologies abounded, and the few forward-looking officials who appreciated their potential could persuade neither the central state nor the private sector to finance their development in China. Hence the piecemeal construction of railways and the scattershot investment in arsenals, mines, textile works, and steamships sponsored by provincial governments.[30] Once again, the experience of Furong salt producers allows us to complicate this picture and draw attention to the factors at work in shaping China's early modern economic trajectory.

Until the 1890s the outside world had little to offer the salt producers whose entrepreneurship had for the past 40 years both fired the growth of the Sichuan economy and filled the coffers of the region's bureaucracy. The percussion drill technology used at Furong, as well as the craftsmanship behind the construction and maintenance of wells, was as advanced as any available in the nineteenth-century Western world.[31] And with the development of the rock-salt layer China became one of the first large-scale employers of solution mining of salt. However, Furong's technological isolation was to change as the century drew to a close. In the early 1890s, as a result of persistent foreign pressure, foreign shipping was extended up the Yangzi River to its farthest navigable point, where the city of Chongqing was newly designated as a treaty port (see map on page 12). Not long afterward the rock-salt layer was discovered at the Furong yard. Saltyard merchants appear to have become aware of the existence of steam power as soon as it traveled upriver into Hubei and Sichuan.[32] Experiments in the application of steam to the process of hoisting brine from deep wells began almost immediately. The concentration of the industry within a small geographic area facilitated the spread of the new technology. And, as in the mid-nineteenth century, both internal and external capital was brought together for the purpose of industrial investment.

The move toward mechanization of salt extraction and well irrigation was the result of a timely coincidence of knowledge and need. Whereas the productivity of yellow- and black-brine wells was limited by the abundance of the brine source tapped, it soon became apparent that the only limit on the output of rock-salt wells was the volume of water introduced into the well and the speed at which it could be pumped. If steam engines could pump brine more rapidly and in greater volume than buffalo or mules, their potential for the developers of this new brine source was incalculable. By 1932 most of Furong's rock-salt brine wells and several of its more productive black-brine wells were equipped with mechanical pumps. Nevertheless, the road to universal application of steam power had not been a smooth one, and factors external to the production process would continue to hamper mechanization until the end of the decade.[33]

As best as we know, the first person to attempt to apply steam technology to the problems of raising brine was not a salt manufacturer but a cotton merchant by trade. Ouyang Xianrong was a resident of Tongliang County, northeast of Zigong.[34] He worked for a merchant company with branches in both Chongqing and the commercial town of Neijiang, on the Zhong River, a major tributary of the Yangzi that joins the Xihe at Fushun. As we have seen, cotton yarn became a major commodity in the trade system that developed between Zigong and Huguang, and it is likely that through this commodity Ouyang developed ties to Furong salt producers. We do know that he, like others with capital, had some investments in salt wells in Zigong.

As a cotton merchant Ouyang Xianrong's business frequently took him to Hankou, the main commercial entrepôt in central China and, before the opening of Chongqing as a treaty port, the nearest port of call to Sichuan for foreign products.[35] Ouyang's trips to the port of Hankou and its sister industrial city, Hanyang, introduced him to the use of steam power and in 1894 he began to play with the notion of mechanized pumping at the saltyard. Upon his return to Chongqing he contacted an acquaintance with overseas experience and some knowledge of mechanical engineering named Zhang Peicun.[36] Together they traveled to Ziliujing to explore the feasibility of using steam-driven cranes to raise salt at the yard. Satisfied that it could be done, the two men returned to Chongqing and sought out a Japanese employee of the Chongqing branch of the Nissei Foreign Trading company. Ishii Takeo appears to have had some skill in working with machinery and was enlisted by Ouyang and Zhang to draw up blueprints for the adaptation of steam engines to use at wells. While waiting for the final plans to be completed, Ouyang Xianrong and Zhang Peicun formed the New Sichuan company (*Xinshu gongsi*). In all, 50 shares were sold at a cost of 60 taels apiece, making the start-up capital of the new firm a mere 3,000 taels.

The distribution of shares is not clear, although Ouyang and Zhang may have held a large portion themselves. Other investors were drawn largely from the Chongqing business community, including members of the newly formed Chamber of Commerce like Zeng Yuqing.[37] With the backing of the new company Ouyang and Zhang then took the blueprints to Hanyang, one of three cities making up the Wuhan complex in Hubei, where a small machine industry had begun to emerge. There the partners approached the Zhouhengshun foundry to build a steam-driven hoist that could be used to pump brine wells. The prototype was probably finished in 1902.[38] Its initial trial was at the Shixing well in Douya wan, a substandard producer whose owner, Zhong Xinzhi, was convinced to participate in the experiment because he had little to lose. In his short memoir Ouyang admits that he had to guarantee Zhong against damage to his well.[39] What he fails to acknowledge is that he did not simply pump Zhong's well; he leased it, assuring Zhong a fair rate of return and promising to restore the well to its original condition should the experiment fail.[40] The experiment did fail, in part because the output of the well was too small to demonstrate the real potential of steam and in part because the engine itself was too weak. Realizing that much tinkering would have to be done to make the mechanical hoist practical, Ouyang and Zhang returned to Hanyang and hired four experienced machinists from the Zhouhengshun foundry to work with them in Ziliujing refurbishing and repairing the engines and their hoists.[41] A second model was tried out at Wang Hefu's Shenghong well and was able to produce brine at a rate sufficiently in excess of that produced by buffalo to convince Ouyang and Zhang that their efforts were not in vain. However, corrosion of the engine from constant contact with brine soon forced a cessation of production here as well.[42]

Despite these early setbacks Ouyang continued to experiment with steam power at the wells. In 1904 he sold his stake in the cotton business for 20,000 taels to set up the Huaxing company, a firm devoted entirely to the manufacture of mechanical hoists. Soon afterward he registered a patent on his machine with the newly formed Ministry of Industry and sent Zhang to Hanyang to purchase parts and equipment that would allow Huaxing to repair its own pumps. According to Ouyang, Zhang died during this trip, but with other investors Ouyang continued to develop steam technology, eventually substituting steel cable for the less durable bamboo in common use and altering the design of his steam engines to accommodate steel's greater weight and capacity.[43]

Ouyang Xianrong's story is a complex one. Commercial networks facilitated the spread of technology and supplied both the know-how and much of the capital for his new venture into steam. The existence of a latent market for brine also contributed to his and his successor's "inventive" behavior.[44] The state was no obstacle to innovation and even provided the opportunity to patent Ouyang's design, although it is not clear that the Ministry of

Industry at this time had the infrastructure to enforce intellectual property claims. Nevertheless, slow progress in the development of rock-salt wells, the high cost of shipping coal from Weiyuan and Rongxian, social unrest in the years leading up to the 1911 revolution, numerous problems with the engines, and suspicion over the efficiency of mechanized pumps and their effect on well integrity continued to hamper the ability of Ouyang and his fellow investors to bring the new technology to the masses of well owners.

It was not until after the fall of the Qing that mechanization took hold at the Furong yard. In 1913 a Chongqing-based merchant named Dong Jingying brought together a group of investors to ship several steam-driven hoists to Ziliujing and established the Xiecheng company to pump brine.[45] By 1915 Dong's company was ready to pump its first well, the Fengwang rock-salt well, with a derrick driven by a 14-horsepower steam engine purchased from the same Hanyang company that had served Ouyang Xianrong's earlier efforts. According to the Sichuan Salt Administration History the pump, which cost the Xiecheng company between 2,000 and 3,000 yuan, was operated on a profit-sharing basis with the well's owner, the company, and the well each taking half of the overall output of the well.[46]

Dong was not the only non-local to invest in the new technology. Mechanized pumping provided an opportunity for outside capital at a time when the shrinking number of wells and the consolidation of brine production along the rock-salt vein made entry into the salt industry difficult for newcomers. Among Dong's partners were Zhou Zhongxuan of the Hanyang Zhouheng-shun foundry; Huang Fuji, an engineer for the Sichuan Electric Light company; Wang Zixiang, a prominent Sichuanese degree holder; and Zeng Yujing, who had already invested in Ouyang Xianrong's Xinshu company. Together they raised 10,000 taels, with which they put a down payment on five pumps to be purchased from the Zhouhengshun foundry.[47]

At the same time, Zigong salt producers also began to enter the contest for a share of the mechanized pumping market. In 1915 Fan Rongguang organized the Fuchang company with a capitalization of 30,000 taels. Deng Hongru was named manager and at least five pumps were purchased in Hanyang and Shanghai. Most of the wells Fan pumped were ones in which he himself had shares. However, he also pumped two belonging to the Yu family at Lianggao shan and Yangjia chong. Lai Mingqin and Xiong Zuo-zhou formed a partnership to pump the Fengwang well. Yang Duxing and Wang Zixiang, one of Dong Jingying's investors, organized the Hefeng and Zhengyi factories. Among their investors were Huang Fuji and Han Youren of the Wanfeng native bank. It was Huang who arranged for the purchase of the first pumps from Shanghai at half the price of those manufactured in Hanyang.[48] Zhong Xingxiang and Wang Hefu founded the Zhongxingchang and bought eight pumps in Hanyang and Shanghai, many of them to pump wells they themselves owned. In 1917 Wang Zixiang set up another company, the Fulongchang, with four pumps from Shanghai, while on a smaller scale men like Yan Xinshe and Li Zihui formed partnerships to pump only one or two wells.[49]

While the main concern of investors was profits, civic leaders had an added interest in the new technology. As the compilers of *Essentials of Sichuan Salt* put it, Zigong was a crowded town with more than 100,000 workers and several tens of thousands of livestock. The stink of mule and buffalo manure was unbearable. The more steam pumps were installed, the fewer the work animals and the cleaner the streets.[50] An outbreak of rinderpest[51] in Gongjing in 1916 helped speed up the process of change as well owners chose to switch to steam rather than replenish their costly herds.[52] Nevertheless, three dramatic engine explosions in 1917 and 1918 also served to discourage owners from risking installation of the new technology at their wells.[53]

By 1919 there were 32 wells being pumped with the aid of steam engines owned by 15 different companies or individuals, most of them in Dafen bao. The majority of them pumped one well and may only have had one steam-driven hoist. The largest was the Zhongxingxiang company, owned by Zhong Xingxiang and Wang Hefu, which in 1919 was operating at nine wells, followed by Dong Jingying's Xicheng company and the Fan Rongguang's Fuchang company, pumping six wells each.[54] These numbers were not large. But by the middle of the decade demand for brine and the rising price of salt were beginning to provide incentives that would lead to the conversion of all rock-salt brine wells to steam during the next decade.[55] Merchants acting as middlemen between salt producers and foundries in Hanyang and Shanghai opened offices in Zigong. And a number of investors in mechanized pumping opened their own foundries and machine shops to provide parts and repair steam engines and mechanized hoists.[56] Skilled machine operators, many originally from Jiangsu and Zhejiang, took up residence in Ziliujing and Gongjing and schools were established to train indigenous workers as well.[57] In 1926 a machine pump workers' association was founded with a little over 300 members.[58] Moreover, as the pumps themselves were improved and well construction altered to take advantage of the opportunities created by steam, output began to reach levels never even dreamed of before the turn of the century.

Reorganization of Relations of Production

When Ouyang Xianrong first developed the idea of mechanized pumping, it was his intention to rent his pumps to the wells and allow them to operate the new technology themselves. Instead, Ouyang was forced to rent the wells to carry out his experiments with steam. In his earliest contracts we already see the separation between well pumper and well owner that was to characterize the rock-salt wells of the Republican period. According to the contract between Ouyang Xianrong and the Shixing well, the Xinshu company paid the owner of the well 40 taels a month for its use. Once the rent was paid, all profits from the sale of brine belonged to the lessee alone. If anything happened to the well, it was the responsibility of the lessee to undertake dredging or repairs. Thus Ouyang assumed all the risk associated with extraction and marketing of brine.[59]

Ouyang Xianrong was forced to rent the wells he pumped because steam was a new and untested technology. But there were many other possible ways steam pumping could have been applied to Furong's brine wells. One was for well owners to purchase their own pumps. Some did so, often by building pumping companies that tended their own wells and wells not in their own portfolios.[60] Wells could also lease pumps and operate them themselves. However, this arrangement was rare. Although the surviving contracts perpetuate the language of the lease, calling the owner of the pumping equipment *ke* or guest and the owner of the well *zhu* or property owner, in fact, the relationship between most well owners and pump owners did not follow the standard pattern of landlord and tenant. Rather, it became something more complex that reflected the relative financial power and expertise embodied in the assets of each party to the transaction.

The system of mechanized brine extraction that came to dominate the saltyard by the 1920s was called contract pumping (*baotui*).[61] Whereas under the lease signed with the Shixing well Ouyang Xianrong had paid a fixed rent to the well owners and kept all the brine he pumped, under *baotui* the well owner paid the pump owner a fixed fee in the form of a deposit and agreed to a share of the output from his well. In exchange the owners of the pump took over responsibility for operating the well, fitting out the derrick, paying the workers, and making any repairs that became necessary during the time they had charge of production. While we do not have many examples of well pumping contracts in the 1920s and 1930s, the memoirs of former saltyard personnel all point to the dominance of *baotui* from this early period.[62]

In the beginning, the costs of installing the pump, as well as a rent deposit to guard against damage to the pump, loss, or nonpayment of pumping fees, were paid by the owners of the well. Once operation began, the well paid the pump owners a percentage of every *dan* of brine produced. Rather than measure the brine, the number of tubes of brine raised was counted and converted to brine at a fixed rate per tube. These were the terms applied when the Xiecheng company began to pump the Fengwang well and in most other *baotui* agreements during the teens and probably the twenties.[63]

In effect, pump contractors and well owners entered into limited-term partnerships. Well owners controlled a critical asset, the brine itself, and this is reflected in their share of output. Contract pumpers were rewarded for their technical expertise and their access to distant pump manufacturers and machine shops employing workers skilled in pump repair. In 1916 Qiao Fu compared the two types of operations from the viewpoint of the well owner (see table 7.3).

Although not mentioned by Qiao, well owners would no longer have to purchase and maintain buffalo or mules, nor would they have to bear the costs of repair and replacement of machinery. If output could be increased by 50 percent or more and well owners were spared all production costs save a relatively small rent deposit, sacrifice of half the brine could still result in a profit as big or bigger than that obtained by pumping the well oneself. Moreover, for well owners experiencing cash flow problems, as many did in the early twentieth century, the *baotui* arrangement eliminated the need to come up with funds for wages and raw materials before receiving payment for brine.[64]

TABLE 7.3 Advantages of *Baotui* for Well Owners

Animal Power	Machine Power
Buy 100–120 buffalo	Use one machine owned by pumping company
Buffalo feed	Coal purchased by pumping company
Wages for buffalo keepers	Wages of well workers paid by pumping company
Pollution of water by buffalo feces	No equivalent
Continued upkeep of buffalo and handlers' wages even when production interrupted	No equivalent
Use bamboo-cable, which is easily broken	Use steel cable, which rarely breaks
Average output of 100 tubes per day	Average output of 150 tubes or more per day
Pumping stopped by hot-weather exhaustion of buffalo	Can pump in any weather

Source: Fu Qiao, *Ziliujing diyiji* [Ziliujing, vol. 1] (Chengdu: Quchang gongsi, 1916), 147.

While saltyard elders recall that early contracts called for a fairly even division of brine output between well owners and pumping companies, by the 1930s control over operation of the well and over well output had shifted dramatically in the direction of partnerships formed to purchase and operate mechanized pumps. The earliest surviving example of such a contract was one entered into by the partners in the Tianhai well and the owners of the Tongxing furnace, which undertook to pump the well. The agreement, signed in June 1930, calls for the Tongxing furnace to install a steam-operated pump at the Tianhai well, absorbing all costs for equipment, workers' wages, and so on. Maintaining the language of a lease, it allocates to the well owners "brine rent" (*zushui*) in the amount of 16 percent of overall brine raised, the remaining 84 percent going to the furnace partnership that was to pump the well. Each party is left free to sell its share of the brine with no interference from the other, most likely a concession to the well partners, who would not wish to be forced to sell to a particular furnace.[65] Except where the pump owner is clearly at fault, the well owner gets no brine if there is a decline in production. Moreover, if the well is damaged, the pump owners will undertake the repairs as the management unit on site, and the well owners will be required to repay them on presentation of all bills.

The terms of trade between well owners and pump owners did not improve over the course of the next two decades. Almost all of the contracts that now survive, dating from the 1940s, demonstrate this. While beyond the scope of this study, they paint a picture of a relationship that remained relatively stable despite the rising demand for Sichuan salt during the Sino-Japanese War when most of China was cut off from the salt-producing regions along the northeast and southeast coasts. In a few cases, such as the agreement drawn up to pump the Yuanfeng well, the division of the brine between the two parties was to vary along a sliding scale depending on the output and salinity of the brine. In all cases, the well owners received the minority share of the brine, ranging from 6 and 14 percent, with only one surviving contract allotting the well owners 30 percent. Most contracts also called for payment of a deposit to the pump owners to be refunded at the termination of the contract.[66]

This separation of ownership and operation of brine wells in the twentieth century was the result of new technology, which unlike well and furnace technology initially entered the yard from outside. In the first instance, it was outside capital that enabled mechanized pumping to take off at the yard. Many of the earliest pumps in use at the yard were purchased by groups of outside businessmen, most of them drawn from the ranks of the modern banking and industrial community emerging at this time in Chongqing. The pumping companies formed by these men did not own wells, but took advantage of their knowledge of the emerging machine industry downriver at Hanyang and Shanghai and the long history of trade between Chongqing and Zigong. Modern banking was in its early stages in China in the teens and branches of eastern banks, which could have served to vet the credit of Zigong entrepreneurs, were only beginning to be established beyond Chongqing (see chapter 10). Within a few years, local well and furnace own-ers began to purchase steam pumps as well, investing profits made in the salt industry and taking advantage of the development of machine manu-facturing and repairs at Zigong. At existing wells where only a portion of the investors were able to commit to large new infusions of capital, subsets of partners formed separate companies to manage the pumping of the well, occasionally also extending their business to contracts with other wells. At others, the well partners entered into pumping agreements with specialist pumping firms that gradually eroded the well owners' share of output and eventually their control over the operation of the well itself.

Wide-Diameter Wells and the Improvement of Well Productivity

The discovery of the rock-salt layer, the development of wide-diameter wells, and the introduction and improvement of mechanized pumping pro-vide an excellent example of what Nathan Rosenberg has called technologi-cal interdependence, the phenomenon whereby advances in one technology often lead to advances in multiple phases of production.[67] The volume of brine in a well lost its relevance with the introduction of solution mining. The only limits on output now would be the amount of fresh water that could be pumped into the well, the saturation level of salt, and the capacity and number of tubes of brine that could be raised in a day. Because they were established within the shafts of earlier black- and yellow-brine wells, the diameters of most of the early rock-salt brine wells were small, ranging from 2.8 to 3.2 inches. The threshold diameter for wells was determined entirely by the width of bamboo used to construct the tubes that lifted the brine. Larger and heavier tubes were not feasible as long as the main source of power at the well derricks was teams of buffalo and mules.

The increased pumping power of steam engines encouraged some inves-tors to experiment with openings of up to 3.6 inches. However, the increased productivity brought about in this way was limited. Sometime between 1917 and 1918 Zhang Xiaopo joined forces with a group of local investors to dig a new rock-salt well at Yangjia chong.[68] The Zehou well appears to have been the first wide-diameter (*dakoujing*) well, measuring 4.8 inches.[69] The value added by the Zehou's additional width disproved the view of early skeptics that greater width and larger tubes could not be accommodated at the Furong yard. Almost immediately, Zhang Xiaopo's wide-diameter well became the catalyst for experiments with new and more powerful engine designs. The size and capacity of the boilers were increased, boilers were made thicker and stronger, and gear ratios were altered, all to increase the horsepower of the engine and the lifting power of the derrick.[70] The introduction of steel cable was a response to this greater lifting power, and the market in this new commodity provided an additional opportunity for enterprising newcomers to enter the salt business.[71]

As pumps and pumping equipment improved, the cost of outfitting a well for pumping soon surpassed the costs of drilling the well. When Niu Jicheng dug the Jianglong well between 1919 and 1921 total costs for equipment, buildings, and drilling came to over 35,000 taels, only 15,000 of which was spent on well excavation.[72] At the same time, the combination of wide well shafts, allowing larger tubes, and pumps operated by 250-horsepower engines, revolutionized brine production. When it began production in 1922 the Jianglong well yielded between 14,000 and 15,000 *dan* of brine a month, compared to the 2,000–3,000 *dan* a month we saw in the first years of mechanization. Examples such as this led to widespread investment in wide-diameter wells and horizontal boiler pumps.

At the same time, new companies were formed to import the improved pumping technology from factories in Hanyang and Shanghai. In 1919 Yang Duxing, who had been working for the Zhengyichang, formed a new partnership composed largely of Chongqing merchants. The Qiancheng company invested in the Shanghai Baochunfu factory, which was their main supplier of pumps and also bought 17 horizontal boiler engines for sale in Zigong.[73] The Zhouhengshun company also began shipping the new pumps to Ziliujing, largely supplying its old customers at Dafen bao. At the same time individual well developers like Yan Xinshe and Li Jingcai began to purchase pumps directly from the factories in Hanyang and Shanghai. According to Yang Duxing, by the 1920s most of the older pumps in use at Ziliujing were sold off to less productive wells in Gongjing. Eventually these too were replaced by large-horsepower horizontal boiler pumps and some of the original engines used at Dafen bao were sold to wells at Wutongqiao and a small number of coal mines in Weiyuan County.[74]

Many of the investors in the new wide-diameter wells were the same men who had been instrumental in the spread of mechanized pumping. Fan Rongguang, Wang Hefu, Yan Xinshe, Wang Wentao, and Xiong Zuozhou had all invested in steam engines as early as the mid-teens. Of those others whose activities are known, Huang Zhiqing was a salt merchant who also invested in the pawnshop business, Huang Chunwu came from a long line of bamboo merchants, Zhang Shaofu was the manager of the Yushang bank, and Li Yunxiang was a descendant of one of the powerful Li salt lineages. With the exception of Li Yunxiang, these were all men whose fortunes were made in the twentieth century, in large part because of their participation in the early history of steam at the yard.

The Effect of Wide-Diameter Steam-Pumped Wells at the Furong Saltyard

The opening of wide-diameter wells utilizing horizontal boiler pumps raised the average productivity of rock-salt brine wells in Ziliujing to around 15,000 *dan* a month. By 1931, a total of 48 wells at Ziliujing and 46 at Gongjing were pumped using steam.[75] Between 1920 and 1925, at Dafen bao alone brine output rose to an average of 156,333 tons a year, with a peak production of 202,000 tons in 1925. A grand total of 983,000 tons were pumped during these years, accounting for 9.61 percent of total reserves. The costs of exploitation also fell as the number of interlocking channels grew. By 1920 there were only two main systems. Water that entered the Lailong well allowed the pumping of five wells, while the introduction of water into the Jirong, Xinfa, and Shenyong wells irrigated 93 wells, only 71 of which were pumped.[76]

The dramatic expansion of output from the rock-salt sector of the Furong yard affected the economy of the yard in several ways. Its most far-reaching, and by no means inevitable, contribution was to the growth of industrial engineering in Sichuan.[77] The installation of steam pumps stimulated the machine repair and manufacturing business at the yard. As early as 1914 Wang Hefu set up a pump repair and spare parts workshop near Zhoujia chong in Ziliujing. This was the first machine factory in Zigong and drew on the services of a number of skilled blacksmiths and metal workers brought in from Shanghai. According to the *Gazetteer of the Zigong Machine Industry* (*Zigongshi jixiegongye zhi*) Wang's factory soon employed over 40 workers and was fitted with two belt-driven lathes, a vertical drill, a shaping machine, four cupola furnaces, and four bellows. Wang received technical assistance from Wang Dahong, a graduate in machine engineering from the recently established engineering department of Tongji Medical and Engineering School in Shanghai. In 1915 Fan Rongguang also hired engineers from Shanghai and established a foundry and repair workshop to service both his own and other companies' pumps. At the same time, Chu Yasan founded a workshop at Dafen bao and Wu Maochang opened a repair shop and spare parts factory in Dongkou jing.[78] By the 1930s Zigong had numerous large and small hardware and machine repair establishments, as well as around 28 foundries, which allowed the salt community to service most of its own equipment.[79] Skills acquired at this time formed the basis for a flourishing machine-tools industry in contemporary Zigong.

At the same time new technology increased Zigong's dependence on distant markets, domestic and foreign, that the new technology created. Steam engines were imported from Shanghai and Hangyang until the outbreak of the Sino-Japanese War in 1937, when Japanese occupation barred access to the east coast. The introduction of wide-diameter wells also led to the substitution of steel cable for bamboo-slat cable and iron tubes for the hollow bamboo that had once held the brine raised from the wells.[80] While tubes appear to have been manufactured domestically, drawing on Rong County's rich iron deposits, cable was imported from abroad. The earliest purveyor of these goods in Sichuan was the foreign trade division of the Juxingcheng bank. Around 1915 the Zhouhengshun company, whose Hanyang factory supplied most of the earlier pumps used in Zigong, set up an outlet in Ziliujing to sell spare parts, steel cable, and metal tools. In 1919 Yang Duxing opened his own Chengkang metal shop to engage in similar trade, followed by the establishment of Li Jingcai's Shushan company and Yan Xinyu's Foyuancheng company.[81] The installation of steel cable for the first time made Zigong dependent on foreign markets. The cable first sold by the Juxingcheng bank came from Germany, while later companies also imported cable from England and the United States. Dependence on foreign trading companies based in Shanghai limited the ability of native companies to control the quality and quantity of supplies. It also intensified the vulnerability of Zigong manufacturers to volatile exchange rate shifts between Sichuan currencies and those of eastern treaty ports.

The introduction of mechanized technology also dramatically altered the relationship between Zigong and its hinterland. As we will see in chapter 10, almost all of the inputs employed at the saltyards were purchased from within a several-hundred-mile radius of Zigong. Nearby counties supplied the bamboo, lumber, tong oil, coal, and animal feed upon which the wells and furnaces depended. Rural communities in Sichuan and across the nearby Guizhou border specialized in raising buffalo for the salt derricks. And many of the growing number of underemployed men in rural Sichuan and its surrounding provinces found employment at the yard or in transport and handicrafts serving the industry. That embeddedness, the trickle-down effect that it had on the surrounding economies, and the advantages it gave to the old salt elite disappeared in the twentieth century.

The introduction of steel cable and iron brine tubes was a serious blow to the bamboo industry serving the wells.[82] By one estimate, the number of lengths of bamboo purchased each year declined by more than 10,000 in the 1920s.[83] While we do not have a record of the number of lengths of bamboo used at the yard in the days before iron tubes, we do know that a bamboo tube generally required 10 lengths of *banzhu* and 20 lengths of *nanzhu*. If we assume that each well in production in 1916 changed tubes once a year, then Zigong would have purchased more than 15,000 lengths a year for tubes alone. In fact, accidents and decomposition of tubes meant they had to be changed more frequently than once a year. According to the Sichuan Salt Administration History, by 1932 Zigong was importing only 4,368 lengths of *nanzhu* and no mention is made of *banzhu*. We can compare this to Jianwei at the same time, where more than 11,000 lengths of *banzhu* and 11,000 of *nanzhu* were still being purchased for manufacture of pipes and bamboo slats.[84] Bamboo continued to play a modest role at the Furong yard, in the construction and repair of brine pipes, and in small amounts in the pumping of wells.[85] Moreover, some of Zigong's bamboo merchants, most notably Wang Desan and Huang Chunwu, had already diversified, investing in wide-diameter wells and other aspects of the salt business. For the cultivators of bamboo forests, the porters and transport workers who moved the bamboo to Zigong, the skilled workers who manufactured the tubes and cable at the yard, and the small craftsmen who fashioned handicrafts out of the bamboo ends that could not be used at the wells, alternative opportunities were few.

Indeed, while profits rose for those fortunate merchants with large investments in wide-diameter wells, pumps, and furnaces, the effect of mechanization on most of those previously dependent on the salt industry was unemployment and loss of subsidiary income. Hardest hit were those with investments in or employed at yellow- and black-brine wells, particularly those at Gongjing. Black-brine wells opened at enormous expense to meet the needs of the Ziliujing gas furnaces in the 1890s, and the early twentieth century gradually closed as rock-salt wells began to supply more than the furnaces could evaporate.[86] Of the 87 deep wells drilled in Gongjing at the turn of the century, at least 46 closed between 1910 and 1930, most of them as a result of diminishing demand for Gongjing brine.[87] According to Ling Yaolin the number of black-brine wells still in production during the 1940s had declined to no more than 20, and almost no yellow-brine wells remained.[88] The 1914 edition of the Fushun County Gazetteer also indicates a decline over the 1911 total.[89]

By the turn of the century the large salt merchant lineages of the nineteenth century had already begun their withdrawal from salt marketing as a result of the new taxes and surcharges levied on salt destined for the border and Huguang markets in the late Qing. The discovery of abundant sources of brine in Ziliujing and the subsequent decline in demand for Gongjing brine were serious blows to the brine pipe industry as well. Of the ten big pipes running from Gongjing to Ziliujing, six were completely destroyed and four were dismantled and moved to Ziliujing to carry rock-salt brine to the areas of high gas output. In response to declining productivity a number of pipe merchants attempted a merger of their formerly highly competitive businesses. The first to attempt a pipe merger was Wang Hefu, whose Yuan-chanxin pipe joined forces with Hu Tiehua's Tongxin pipe under the name Yuanxin pipe. Their efforts were soon imitated by Li Yunzhi, the assets of whose Yifu pipe were combined with those of the Quanfu pipe owned by Gao Yuncong and Fan Rongguang.[90]

In none of these cases was the pipe itself the main target of consolidation. Far more important were the brine wells and furnaces operated under its name. It was to ensure access to evaporation pans that most of the mergers took place. This was most apparent in the case of the Li Siyou trust's Qingyun pipe, which by the 1920s had only a few gas fires of its own. By moving its pipe equipment to Ziliujing to take advantage of the rock-salt market, it was able to lure a number of furnaces with no pipe facilities into a merger under the name Dasheng pipe. These adaptations to changing circumstances notwithstanding, most pipe owners in the 1920s and 1930s found it increasingly difficult to deal with the surplus in brine supplies and the growing power of independent furnace partnerships. By the mid-1920s there were only six pipes in Ziliujing, most of these owned by investors new to the Furong yard. Many of the wells dependent on the old pipes also found their markets cut off and were forced to close. The effect of this phenomenon on the old salt fortunes will be examined further in chapter 9.

While mechanized pumping provided an opening into the salt industry for a new generation of investors, many of them new to the yard, it had one benefit enjoyed by all. Mechanized pumping brought a dramatic decrease in the number of buffalo in Zigong and an immediate improvement to Zigong's chronically polluted water supply. It also brought stability to the production regime at the yard, as machine pumps were not affected either by changes in weather or by disease. However, the substitution of mechanical for animal power also had a serious negative impact on those not directly engaged in salt production. The mountain areas that supplied buffalo to the saltyard were hardest hit. To this must be added the loss of subsidiary income to peasants who worked as peddlers of buffalo, although many would find employment as transport workers or marketing other products. Areas of southern Sichuan that specialized in the production of broad beans, the mainstay of buffalo feed, also saw their market diminished, as did local farmers whose income depended in part on the provision of straw to the wells.

Employment at the yard was also affected by these changes in the mode of production. The closure of less productive wells and the elimination of jobs associated with the supervision and care of buffalo altered the structure of employment in Zigong. According to a survey of land use in Ziliujing in the 1930s, only about 6 percent of the population was employed directly in the production of salt, the vast majority of workers being engaged in occupations serving the salt industry. Although rock-salt brine had meant a decrease in the number of wells, employment at rock-salt wells was high, as many as 60 workers per well, as compared to a maximum of 30 for black-brine wells.[91] Nevertheless many of the unskilled workers previously used in well pumping were now replaced by mechanics and skilled workers able to deal with steam pumps, many of whom came from outside the province.[92] Some of the unskilled were charged with the new task of irrigating the wells, a job whose only qualification was brute strength. According to an elderly ex-water carrier at the Jiuda company, a salt-producing conglomerate established at Zigong during the Sino-Japanese War, the only qualification an unskilled worker needed at the great rock-salt wells was callused hands and the ability to carry a load of 300 *jin* without getting winded or turning red.[93] Even great prowess ceased to guarantee employment as the productivity of rock-salt wells rose and fewer and fewer wells were needed to meet the demand for Sichuan salt. Mechanization, however, had little effect on the structure of employment at pipes and furnaces, where the technology of production had changed not at all since the mid-nineteenth century.

The cost of technological advance to Zigong's enormous labor force would be felt most strongly in the late 1920s and early 1930s when politics intervened and the market for Sichuan salt collapsed. Traditional labor unions and modern political parties would both play a role in pressing for the rights of workers in an increasingly unstable economy and salt producers would find themselves pitted against one another as they struggled for a piece of the market that remained. The end of the dynasty, the weakness of China's early republican state, and the rise to power in Sichuan of a series of military governors would reshape the relationship between Zigong businessmen and the state. At the same time, new institutions such as the Chamber of Commerce, trade associations, and the short-lived local assembly would create new arenas for the exercise of local power and new platforms for the expression of business interests. When conjoined with the transformation in production we have just examined, they would herald yet another change in the way that business was conducted at the yard.

8

The Changing of the Guard at the Furong Saltyard

THE SCIONS of the old lineage-based salt fortunes continued to play a role in the economy and politics of Zigong well into the twentieth century. However, by the 1920s they were eclipsed by a new group of businessmen at the yard, some of whom we have already met as drillers of wide-diameter wells and investors in contract-pumping firms. In many respects the old guard were greater innovators than their successors. In the years when well drilling was the key to business success, the combination of local ties and ownership of land enabled the earlier generation of men of middling wealth to parlay their assets into significant industrial and commercial empires. Contract as a means to redistribute rights to agricultural resources was transformed into a means to accumulate capital for industrial investment. The lineage trust as a largely landed endowment for ancestral rites became the legal and managerial framework through which assets were combined and protected from multiple claimants to property rights. And expanding markets encouraged the refinement of old technologies and the development of new ones. Through their trading firms they opened new markets for their salt and became the conduit through which new products—machine-spun cotton yard and, later, steam engines—were introduced to southern Sichuan.

The new business elite was more varied in their backgrounds and their interests, and they operated within a far more complex social, political, and economic arena. The institutional arena within which they operated broadened as well, with the creation of local assemblies, Chambers of Commerce, trade associations, yet another salt administration, and a new and still evolving modern legal system. In response, their investments became more diversified and dispersed and politics took on an importance it never had in the late imperial period. Although networks played a role in the earlier development of the saltyard, in the twentieth century vertically integrated firms as the dominant route to business success gave way to firms that relied largely on networks, not simply of business relationships but of political relationships as well.

Chinese scholars have most often linked the decline of the nineteenth-century saltyard elite with an inevitable degeneration of feudal traditions. Without discussing at length the misuse of the concept of feudalism in such writings, it is important to note that neither their temporal existence during the last years of the last Chinese dynasty nor their manipulation of existing family institutions for economic ends merit the equation of the Wang, Li, Yan, and Hu generation with feudalism, even taken in its broadest sense as used in China as a synonym for "backward." Clearly, in their willingness to take risks, make long-term investments, and exercise entrepreneurship in seeking new markets, new sources of capital, new technologies, and new forms of business organization the nineteenth-century Zigong elite were an important part of the story of modern Chinese business.

At the same time, we should not expect to see a linear progression in business practices from the nineteenth to the twentieth centuries. The economic and political challenges of the Republic led businessmen in the latter period to retreat from what some might think of as more "modern" practices. However, vertical and horizontal integration, the hallmarks of the great salt conglomerates of the nineteenth century, were also responses to market weaknesses, modes of business organization brilliantly designed to ensure control of inputs and quasi-monopolies over sales territories. As the technologies of production changed, this advantage was lost and new entrants were able to capture the most profitable phases of production. The business plans of these new entrepreneurs responded to a very different business environment, one in which the market extended as far as Shanghai and beyond, and in which declining markets for Sichuan salt encouraged not vertical integration but cartelization.

Rather than attempt a comprehensive study of twentieth-century business in its many contexts, this chapter will examine the decline of the old guard and the rise of a new business elite in Zigong against the background of two major changes to the business environment. First, we will look at the signs of business decline in surviving accounts of the four big lineage trusts and propose a working theory for that decline. For this purpose the case of Zigong is an interesting one precisely because it takes place at a distance from the more dramatic influences of foreign politics and trade in

China. Nevertheless, as we have already seen, even in Zigong the impact of the West, in the form of new technologies, was being felt. Second, we will look at a representative group of new businessmen in order to discern the way they differed from their predecessors in the conduct of business. In chapter 9 we will then turn to the political and institutional factors that affected both pre- and post-imperial businessmen in Zigong in an attempt to develop a more nuanced picture of the forces influencing business organization and business performance in early modern China.

The Decline of the Old Saltyard Elite

With only scattered remains of firm account books and shareholders' reports, it is difficult to map the process by which the major players of the nineteenth century became the "coupon clippers" of the twentieth. Oral histories, contracts, and correspondence preserved within the offices of the salt administration and local government provide our best clues to the forces that brought down the houses of Li, Wang, Hu, and Yan. While they leave many questions unanswered, they do point to a common pattern among the old salt elite. Years of high profits and dividends created a business culture that spurned the accumulation of reserves and assumed that business would always be as it had been. While entrepreneurial within their local domain, the businessmen of nineteenth-century Zigong did not think in terms of new markets or new products. And when changes in technology and market share challenged the status quo they were ill prepared to respond. While the outcome for each firm differed in its details, in each case it was accompanied by rising debt, internecine struggle, and fragmentation of jointly managed property.

The Signs of Decline

The first assault on the large salt conglomerates was the introduction of Guanyun (official transport and merchant sale) in the 1880s (see chapter 6). The Lis withdrew from direct marketing in Huguang soon after Guanyun was established.[1] The impact on the Li Siyou's shareholders was to throw the lineage trust into its first struggle with debt. In order to keep its southwestern wholesale firms open, the lineage is said to have borrowed large sums from remittance banks in Chongqing, the emerging financial capital of the southwest. By the turn of the century the Li Siyou trust may have had as much as 900,000 taels in outstanding obligations. These were not industrial loans, but loans to cover lost inventory, pay taxes, and purchase current stock.

The Yan Guixin trust was also forced to downsize during the last years of the Qing. As with all early entrants into well development, the output of a number of their yellow- and black-brine wells was declining and pumping was curtailed. Like the Lis, they also experienced problems in the wholesale marketing portion of their business, especially the Qianfengtai. Chroniclers of the Yan Guixin trust attribute the demise of the Qianfengtai to agency problems resulting from poor communications between its headquarters in the Sichuan border town of Fengdu and the mostly native Guizhou staff who undertook the transport and sale of Yan salt in the Guizhou border market. In this case the cause of decline was not new technology or the state, but the poor communications infrastructure of the southwest region. According to one account, once news reached Guizhou that the home office was considering closure of its Guizhou operations, the local Guizhou staff walked off with the existing stocks of salt, leaving the mother company to pay taxes and absorb lost revenue from sales.[2] Left deeply in debt, the Yans raised part of the over 300,000 taels owed the government by selling off salt in their warehouses. They also borrowed from close business associates, such as the Li Taoshu trust descendants of Li Ji'an, partner of the Yan Guixin trust's founder, and from individual lineage branches which had entered the salt business in their own right.[3]

The fact that the Lis and the Yans had to borrow heavily to cover shortfalls in their wholesale marketing operations suggests that by the end of the century other profit centers were not doing well either. We are told that the Li Siyou trust closed between 20 and 30 yellow-brine wells and nine black-brine wells during the last decade of the nineteenth century. In order to pay its debts, it was also forced to sell off all but three of its gas wells just as the discovery of the rock-salt layer was making these an even more valuable productive asset than before. The picture at the Yan countinghouse is less clear. After their initial success in attracting investment on their modest holdings in Ziliujing the Yans concentrated on development of black-brine wells in Gongjing. By the end of the century many of these wells were reaching the end of their productive lives. We know of few additions to the trust's assets in the last years of the century. The Haisheng well was initially drilled by Yan Juewu, son of the founder of the Yan Guixin trust. A highly productive gas well, which later went by the name Xinglong, it appears to have been one of the last remaining salt assets shared by the lineage in the early twentieth century.[4]

The Li Siyou trust experienced a brief period of renewed prosperity between 1899 and 1911 under the management of Li Xingqiao. A young man of twenty when he took over the position of general manager, Xingqiao pursued an aggressive policy of debt consolidation, eventually reducing the

trust's obligations from 960,000 taels to around 200,000 through installment arrangements with its two largest creditors, the Chongqing-based
remittance banks, Dadeheng and Dadetong. The trust drilled at least one
new well during these years, the Zhenglong well, which is said to have produced 390 pan units at its height. In the aftermath of the Boxer Rebellion
(1900–1901) Li Xingqiao made the daring move of opening a new wholesale
marketing firm, the Dingtongchang, to reenter the Huguang market. As a
sign of the low level of output to which the once mighty Li Siyou trust's
wells and furnaces had fallen, Xingqiao was forced to rely on salt from other
producers in order to stock his Huguang outlets.[5]

In addition to dealing with creditors and slightly expanding the trust's
business, Li Xingqiao attempted to deal with one of the weaknesses in the
legal framework within which Chinese businesses functioned. Although
the lineage trust was effectively an unlimited liability company whose assets were distinct from those of the lineage members who participated in
shareholder profits, protection of collective assets required strict managerial supervision. Under Li Xingqiao each lineage branch was allowed only
1,200 taels a year for feasts and sacrifices, beyond which no further cash
could be drawn on the trust's accounts. Most importantly, lineage members
were barred from arranging discounts for their own furnaces when buying
brine or renting gas from Li Siyou trust wells. It was these injunctions that
appear to have strained his relations with the senior members of the other
branches of the lineage. In 1911 the confrontation between Xingqiao and his
cousins was mediated by Huang Zhiqing, a ranking manager at the Siyou
trust. Li Xingqiao stepped down as general manager and was for the first
time replaced by a non-family member.

Du Dingshan ran the Li Siyou properties for a total of three years. With
little experience in salt manufacture—he appears formerly to have headed a
salt-pan factory—he was an attractive compromise candidate for manager
of the trust because of his connections with the financial community at the
yard.[6] During his short time in office Du borrowed heavily from local native
banks as well as Zigong's newly established modern banks to solve the Li
Siyou trust's cash flow problems and revitalize two of its wholesale firms.
Within a short time he came into conflict with the lineage leadership, who
accused him of pilfering the borrowed funds to support his own business
ventures.

Between 1914 and 1927 the Li Siyou trust was run by a succession of family members, none of whom seem to have had the experience or interest
necessary to maintain profits under the difficult conditions that obtained
at the end of the Quig dynasty and the imposition of military rule in Sichuan. Internal problems also increased. Staff loyalty is said to have been

shaken by layoffs during Du Dingshan's tenure. Without reserves to invest in new wells, supplies of brine and gas began to dry up.[7] By 1927 the lineage had lost control of all its marketing interests and their pipes were all but defunct. As we have seen, the Dasheng pipe, which carried brine from Gongjing to Ziliujing's Guojia ao, was dismantled in 1918. The rebuilt Qingyun pipe, installed to carry rock-salt brine between Da'an jie and Guojia ao, did well for a time, carrying over 2,000 *dan* a day in 1919. However, by 1927 only a few hundred *dan* passed through the pipe each day, hardly enough to justify its operation.

Li Siyou trust well holdings also experienced a sharp decline. At Ziliujing the only brine wells that remained in Li Siyou trust hands were the Shenghai and Honghai wells, each producing no more than 80 to 90 *dan* a day at a time when rock-salt wells were turning out an average of 15,000 *dan* a day. Li Shitai, not related to the family, held half the shares in the Shenghai well, while the lineage had sole rights to the Honghai well. At Gongjing they also had a one-third share of the Jisheng well, a far more productive machine-pumped operation, yielding over 1,000 *dan* a day. Involvement in the pipe industry and several highly productive gas wells allowed the family to maintain a far more respectable portfolio of gas-fired furnaces. Drawing on gas from the Zhenglong well opened by Li Xingqiao and others, the Li Siyou trust still evaporated more than 470 pans in 1927.

Debts would dog the Lis and the Yans throughout the early years of the twentieth century and would ultimately lead to the dissolution of their business organizations. The Yan Guixin trust's debts to the Li Taoshu trust were the subject of continuing lawsuits between the two lineages, despite their long history of intermarriage and joint investment. The final settlement with the Li Taoshu trust was reached by selling off most of the Yan Guixin trust's remaining productive wells. Within a few years the trust was dissolved, each branch of the lineage receiving a modest annuity in the form of agricultural land and some mostly defunct wells.[8]

The Li Siyou trust, with greater assets, lingered on. Their considerable gas output in a time of brine surplus should have enabled them to weather the political storms of the 1920s and 1930s. By this time, however, their total debt was so high that annual profits could not pay all the interest due to modern financial institutions such as the Junchuan bank and numerous native banks with which they had dealings over the years. In 1927 Li Dewen and Li Sicheng consigned the entire agricultural holdings of the lineage trust to the Junchuan bank in order to protect the salt interests that remained. Nevertheless, each year the inability of the Li Siyou trust to pay its interest in full led to increasing conversion of interest to principal and an escalation of the lineage's outstanding collective obligations.

In 1931 it was decided to dispose of the remaining property to clear debts and provide a small allowance for lineage members. Even the resolve to divide the property became a major source of intra-lineage feuding. Outright sale of the property was never considered. Members of the lineage who were also creditors of the lineage trust, such as Li Deqian, favored mortgage. This would provide them with a lump sum repayment and still allow redemption of the property at a future date. Others, such as Li Dewen, whose interests no longer lay solely within the saltyard, favored a leasing arrangement which would yield a small but constant income over the years. In the end a contract was signed in which a newly created firm, the Jirongxiang, leased 108 pan units for a period of 14 years for the bargain price of only 172,000 yuan. A low overall rent was offered in exchange for payment of most of the rent up front, enabling the trust to pay its debts and eliminate future interest payments.[9] Among the investors in this new company were two descendants of the old lineage elite, Li Deqian and his frequent business partner Yan Xianyang, the rising salt developer Luo Xiaoyuan, and Li Dewen, who was drawn into the deal to obtain his vote. Thus, among the main beneficiaries of the agreement were members of the lineage acting on their own behalf.

By the time of the alienation of its operating gas wells to the Jirongxiang company, the Li Siyou trust was a mere shadow of its former self. Its agricultural properties now yielded only 160 *shi* in rents and with the sale of shares in its pipe to Li Jinghou, it had only a one-quarter interest in its last operating pipe, the Datong. It was in this state that it existed until 1948, when pressure from family members led to a final division of the trust.

The Li Siyou trust died a slow and painful death, its members still agonizing over the future of the lineage less than a year before the Communist victory would make all decisions moot. The dissolution of the Hu Yuanhe trust was far cleaner and swifter. In 1913, distrust of the lineage leadership led to a decision to divide the family's agricultural holdings into several branch lineage estates. Lands yielding 2,000 *shi* in rents were set aside for sacrifices and land with rents of 2 *shi* were set aside for the education of each son and grandson. Land with an annual income of 600 *shi* was allocated to general lineage expenses, leaving lands worth 1,000 *shi* a year in rents for each branch of the Hu lineage.[10]

It is significant that the salt holdings of the estate were not divided at this time. Among the properties still operated by the Hu Yuanhe trust were the highly productive Jicheng well, a rich black-brine well called the Deyu well, the Yuchuan well, producing abundant brine of a concentration inferior to that of the new rock-salt wells, and the Yichun, Yifeng, Yuanxiang, and Hongxi wells, producing brine and gas, as well as several relatively unproductive wells the names of which no longer survive. The management of each well was placed under a trusted employee and centralized control of the wells appears to have been abandoned at this time. At the same time, shipping interests were maintained in Gongjing, Chongqing, Yichang, and Shashi. Under the vigorous leadership of Jiang Zihe, a professional salt-well manager who had been trained at the Li Siyou trust, the Yuchuan well was converted to steam and the gas pipes at the Jicheng well were improved to allow unimpeded gas flow and ensure that the fire at each pan was uniform in strength.

Despite the apparent vitality of the Hu Yuanhe trust during the early Republic, in 1917 the decision was made to divide that portion of the agricultural estate that had been left intact in 1913. In 1919 the salt holdings were distributed as well. Each well was divided into 24 shares. Four shares were turned over to each branch, and four were kept as communal property in the form of landlord shares. The fortunes of the Hus declined rapidly once division had taken place. Pursuit of individual interest led to poor business practices. Moves to increase the immediate output of gas from the Jicheng well led to a sharp drop in production within a few years. Branch members with shares in furnaces neglected to pay for the brine they drew from lineage wells. The brine wells were forced to borrow money to continue pumping and the Hu Yuanhe trust's remaining collective holdings were soon encumbered by debt. A brief effort was made in the mid-1920s to remedy the problems brought about by fragmentation of the trust's assets when Hou Ceming, a rising salt developer, was brought in to manage the wells. However, after two years conditions deteriorated, and the debts of Hu Yuanhe trust members continued to grow. Land producing almost 200 *shi* in rents was sold from the lineage's charitable estate, and the lineage homes in Chongqing and Rong County were mortgaged to repay the money that Hou Ceming had personally invested in their wells. In the end the Hu Yuanhe trust opted to rent out its properties, as had the Li Siyou trust. From this point on the constituent branches of the lineage drew income from salt, but few had any personal involvement in the daily operations of the industry.[11]

The experience of the Wang Sanwei trust contained elements of all three of its competitors. The trust entered the Republican period already burdened by debt and intra-lineage conflict. During the 1890s a combination of the declining productivity of black-brine wells and poor management of lineage assets led to almost 700,000 taels in liabilities, most of them covered through loans from a consortium of merchants from the Yangzi ports of Chongqing and Shashi (*yusha zhaituan*). By 1910 the lineage trust still owed the credit group between 170,000 and 180,000 taels,[12] and over the next 12 years the Wangs filed a series of unsuccessful suits at the Chongqing civil tribunal (*shenting*), the Fushun magistrate's yamen, the Zigong civil tribunal, the Ziliujing civil tribunal, the Chengdu court of appeals, and the Supreme Court in Beijing to try to clear the debt at terms favorable to themselves.[13] At the same time, the private interests of individual branches and family members led them to exert considerable pressure to dissolve the lineage estate. For many family members the fall of the Qing signaled the end of an institution whose founding was sanctioned by imperial edict and whose survival relied on traditions no longer applicable in a Republican age. The Wang Sanwei trust might have met its end in 1911 had the family been able to decide on a formula for division of the shares.[14] Instead, suspicion of the management of the lineage trust was expressed by reorganizing its constituent parts. Each of the main components of the Wang Sanwei trust—agricultural property, brine wells, pipes and furnaces, marketing companies, and external affairs—was placed under independent management, with Wang Sufeng acting as general manager of the whole.

The first branch of the lineage business to suffer from the breakup of the integrated firm was marketing. Unlike the Li Siyou trust, the Wang Sanwei trust continued to be an important exporter to Huguang during the early twentieth century. Even after 1911 it shipped a quota of 10 *zai* to that market via Chongqing every year. According to Luo Xiaoyuan, who worked for the Wangs during these years, their Guangshengtong salt company suffered from cash flow problems that forced the scaling back of salt shipments to eastern markets.[15] The source of the cash flow problem is not clear but may have been linked to changes in the administration of the salt gabelle, which required prepayment of taxes before salt could be shipped. The decoupling of salt manufacture and salt shipping also required an increase in real cash transactions between previously related firms.

The already large debt load carried by the trust itself left spinoff firms in a vulnerable position vis-à-vis upper Yangzi institutions of credit. Prior to 1929 Chinese law vested all rights of property in the household. While the 1904 Qing revision of the legal code and the 1914 Ordinance Concerning Commercial Associations provided a mechanism by which to limit shareholder liability, Zigong firms were no more disposed to take advantage of this law than were firms in other parts of China.[16] As a result, even the fragmentation of Wang Sanwei trust firms could not protect them from the claims of creditors as long as the shareholders in any one firm continued to be members of lineage branches and their member households. Thus, the debts held collectively at the main lineage countinghouse, the functional equivalent of the trust's head office, continued to place a burden on all lineage assets.

In the case of the Guangshengtong, with business throughout the upper Yangzi, this was particularly destabilizing. Fears that profits made in Huguang would be impounded by creditors in Chongqing led to a contraction of Wang Sanwei trust marketing interests to nearby districts of Sichuan. At some time during the 1910s a dummy company called the Rongjixiang was set up to market Wang Sanwei trust salt through Wan County in an effort to evade the long arm of the Chongqing financial community. However, little could be sold through this port and the business was soon closed. By the 1920s the salt marketing branch of the lineage's interests was shut down, and only the companies dealing in associated products remained. However, before long even these suffered from the fragmentation of the Wang Sanwei trust's holdings, which no longer guaranteed the kind of monopolistic hold they had had over certain products in the days of the consolidated firms.[17]

Wang Sanwei trust wells and furnaces fared little better during the early Republic. When Wang Zuogan took over as general manager following Wang Sufeng's death, he attempted to lower Wang Sanwei trust interest payments by selling off some of its productive assets to pay down the principal. Most of the purchasers were independent salt development companies or lineage trusts set up by branches of the Wang lineage itself. The Shengcai well was sold to Wang Zuogan's Dasheng trust. The Qingjiang well was sold to Wang Defu, a nephew of Wang Dazhi. The Tianshen, Dicheng, and Baosan wells were sold to Wang Faqin, a cousin of Wang Sufeng. And more than 20 pan units from the Yuxing well's Shuangfa furnace, along with other well shares, were purchased by several cousins in the middle branch. In addition, agricultural land valued at approximately 1,000 *shi* in rents a year was mortgaged to members of the lineage who had not invested in salt industry shares.[18] Nevertheless, as early as 1914 the Wang Sanwei trust was back in litigation with its largest creditor, the Chongqing-Shashi credit group.

Despite their financial difficulties, the trust drilled at least two rock-salt wells during this period. The Wangs were also among the first to try out the newly introduced mechanized pumps brought to Zigong by Ouyang Xiangrong and Dong Jingying.[19] Efforts to dig additional gas wells also paid off during the mid-1910s. In 1916 the Shuanghai well came in, giving the Wang Sanwei trust 257 new pan units and another 20 pan units from landowner shares. The Shuanglong well, which yielded 140 pan units, and shares in the Longsheng and Longwang wells, fueled another 107 pans to evaporate salt. However, shortages of brine forced the family to lease out many of its pans, reducing the profits to be had from these new finds.[20]

Efforts to further expand capital investment were thwarted by the control exercised over the Wang Sanwei trust by the representatives of its creditors at the wells. Wang Rudong's attempt to borrow 80,000 taels to restock the buffalo herds at the trust's black-brine wells was blocked when the financial group that owned the Wangs' outstanding notes commandeered the money to reduce the Wang Sanwei trust's debt. Indeed, coping with creditors was the main concern of the managers of the lineage trust throughout the 1920s.

During the latter part of 1921 sales at the yard picked up, and in 1922 the Chongqing-Shashi credit group signed an agreement with the Wang Sanwei trust aimed at solving the debt issue. Responsibility for management was placed under a business manager (*yingye zhuren*) supplied by the Wangs and business supervisors (*yingye jiangdu*) sent to the yard by the credit group.[21] Each year the lineage trust was allowed a certain share of income to cover the operating expenses of the business. The remainder was to be divided, 80 percent going to the credit group and 20 percent to be handed over to the Wangs.[22] By the time of the 1922 credit agreement, the Wang Sanwei trust owed approximately 649,544 taels. Its wells at Shanzi ba, the site of its first well projects in the 1830s, were reduced to only four. Its buffalo herd was still too small to relieve all its wells from dependence on contract pumpers. The two rock-salt wells it opened, the Chusheng and Shengsheng wells, began to decline in concentration and were soon closed. And the overall decrease in brine production from Wang Sanwei trust properties prompted the family to lease out much of its gas, while leases were allowed to lapse on gas it had rented from the outside.[23] Once the most important investor in well development, the Wang Sanwei trust was reduced to renting out land on which others might invest in the drilling of new wells, content to settle for the much smaller stake due the holder of landowner shares.

In 1928 a final settlement was arranged with the Chongqing-Shashi credit group through the mediation of several prominent members of the new saltyard elite, including Li Jingcai and Wang Hefu.[24] In order to conclude the agreement, the leadership of the lineage trust conducted its own agonizing negotiations with its 300-odd shareholders, obtaining majority support without which it could not go forward. The final agreement divided the lineage trust's properties into those to be sold outright (largely salt pans), those to be leased for 14 years, those to be leased for 21 years, and those to be jointly managed by the trust and the credit group until the proceeds paid off the entire debt. Table 8.1 displays the assets dealt with in this agreement. The complexity of the agreement resulted not only from the variety of property rights already attached to Wang Sanwei trust assets, but also from the existence of earlier agreements with the credit group concerning these same properties and the existence of other creditors not party to the agreement.

In addition to allocating rights over assets, the agreement's 23 clauses covered liability for loss during lease periods, management issues, compen-

TABLE 8.1 Assets Covered by the 1928 Wang Sanwei Trust Debt Liquidation Agreement

Asset	Amount	Value (in taels)
Wholly owned gas	300 pan units	460,500
Leased gas	31 pan units	21,700
Datong pipe	6 shares	18,000
Salt pans	331 pans	99,000
Rock-salt wells	15 shares	9,000
Black-brine wells	30 shares	6,000
		560,500

Source: Zigongshi dang'anguan, "Zigong yanye susong dang'an zhuanti xuanzepian—(1) Ziliujing Wang Sanwei tang yu Yusha zhaiquantuan zhaiwu jiufen an" [Selected documents on special topics from the archives of Zigong salt lawsuits: (1) The case of the debt dispute between the Ziliujing Wang Sanwei tang and the Chongqing-Shashi creditor group.], *Yanyeshi yanjiu* 2 (1993): 78.

sation for access rights, noncompensation for improvements undertaken by the credit group, responsibility for normal wear and tear, and so on. To avoid future disputes the contract was signed by the parties and mediators, while copies were also deposited with the main governmental authorities at the yard.[25] In the end, the Wangs were left with just over 50 pan units of gas, dispersed among lineage branches or leased to nonlineage furnaces. Most of the remaining property consisted of abandoned wells and potential well sites, few of which appear to have been developed collectively by 1949.

Credit and Decline

How was it that business groups which had dominated the industry for much of the nineteenth century slid so quickly into oblivion in the twentieth? The immediate cause was the transformation of the market and production technology. The proximate cause was debt.

Prior to the 1880s none of the partnerships engaged in salt manufacture and sale appear to have carried any significant external debt. As we have seen, households and firms engaged in short-term commercial borrowing through pawnshops and native banks. Most of the large conglomerates operated their own native banks as well, oriented toward the commercial needs of their own constituent firms. Firms maintained reserves to pay for repairs and maintenance. Industrial capital was raised through the contracting of shares in a specific enterprise, and capital improvements were financed through levies on the shareholders themselves or the splitting of shares to allow subsets of shareholders to increase their investment when others could not. In effect, this pattern continued when better-capitalized subsets of well investors joined to purchase steam engines and set up companies to pump theirs and others' wells.

As we have seen, the first problem encountered by the old salt conglomerates was falling profit margins, brought about by new taxes, state marketing, and the development of a new generation of wells whose brine was cheaper to pump and cheaper to evaporate (due to higher saline concentration) than those in which they were heavily invested. Even after the discovery of the rock-salt layer black- and yellow-brine wells continued to produce a significant portion of the brine evaporated at Furong. In the 1910s, Furong still had more than 900 operating black- and yellow-brine wells.[26] Strong demand for Furong salt and excess demand for brine created by Furong's large gas capacity meant that until the 1920s brine of all kinds could still find a market, though at prices considerably below that of rock-salt brine. At the same time, steam technology shifted the terms of trade at the yard in favor of those who pumped brine and away from those who drilled for it.[27] This, too, meant smaller profits for black- and yellow-brine well owners. Thus by the twentieth century these owners had become marginal producers.

The old salt conglomerates could have entered the rock-salt and steam-pump sector. The Wangs certainly did. However, with profits down, equipment to maintain, and staff to pay, and with a new system of state-controlled marketing, it was unlikely that the growth strategies of the past would work in the present. Using the profits from one well to build another, cornering the wholesale market to guarantee high profits for the sale of one's own branded salt, controlling large agricultural estates to feed one's buffalo, using one's brine pipes to guarantee privileged access to brine supplies for one's own gas furnaces—none of these techniques made possible by horizontal and vertical integration worked any longer in the world of Guanyun, rock salt, and steam. Nor could one rely on the sale of shares to cover temporary shortfalls in capital or to weather periods of market decline. Investors with new capital, including some individual members of old lineage firms, were putting their money into new wells or pumps.

Faced with unexpected tax bills, reduced profits, embezzlement by distant agents, costly repairs, and so on, salt manufacturers did what they always did when cash reserves were low. They borrowed. Their business decline is reflected not in the fact that they resorted to short-term credit. What was new was the difficulty they had in repaying their loans. The fact that most of the funds borrowed by the old Zigong salt manufacturers were of external provenance was not a sign of decline but of the growing integration of financial markets among towns and cities along the upper Yangzi.

By the late nineteenth century Zigong had developed strong ties to the higher-level marketing community centered on Chongqing. Chongqing, the westernmost major Yangzi River port in the southwest, had become in the nineteenth century the financial center of the Upper Yangzi region and the main clearinghouse for salt transactions to the east as well as to Yunnan and Guizhou to the south. Here, as elsewhere in the early modern world, payments clearing and lending were closely related.[28] Remittance banks and merchant houses in Chongqing (and Shashi downriver) had access to information about the businesses for which they made payments and often held deposits for them as well. By the turn of the century a complex network of relationships existed among the remittance banks, native banks, and wholesalers based in Chongqing. Remittance banks, through which the profits from sales in Huguang were transferred to Sichuan, became important sources of short-term loans to both native banks and large merchant companies throughout the region.[29]

If the experience of the Chongqing-Shashi credit group is any indication, even though all of these loans remained in arrears for decades they were a source of substantial profits for the lenders. The Wang Sanwei trust agreed to an interest rate of 15 percent per annum for the first loan they contracted with the Chongqing-Shashi credit group. According to Chen Benqing, the Wangs were never able to pay down their principal, as the Lis at one point did. As a result, over the 27 years that they carried their original 600,000- to 700,000-tael loan, they paid over 3 million taels in interest.[30] We do not know the precise combination of factors that made repayment of the initial loan difficult. However, by 1914 a new agreement was negotiated that designated the income from certain wells and furnaces to pay off the debt to the Chongqing-Shashi credit group. Moreover, although the trust owed money to many commercial creditors, payment of interest to this credit group was given first claim on profits from these assets.

As we have seen, conditions at the yard were such that we do not have to blame the trust's managers for the continued difficulty the trust had in paying even the interest on its loans. Within a few years of the 1914 agreement many of the wells that had been earmarked for credit group repayments were already closed.[31] In 1922 the trust again restructured its debt, this time entering into a joint-management agreement with the Chongqing-Shashi credit group. The status of the Wangs' business manager and the business supervisors who represented the interests of the credit group were to be equal. In a lengthy governance agreement, the two parties established protocols for the management of wells, furnaces, pipes and other assets, budget and accounting, personnel management, procurement of supplies, and so on. Of particular interest are the clauses that refer to the participation of

Wang Sanwei trust shareholders in day-to-day details of the business. In addition to the co-equal managers, the agreement called for designation of two mutually acceptable members of the credit group to serve in effect as auditors. The agreement then went on to say:

> The debtors should also designate one member of their trust as the *yingye zhuren* [the same position as the business manager noted above] and another as an investigator (*diaocha*). If anyone from the Wang Sanwei trust not designated in this agreement tries to interfere in the business or embezzle, or obstruct the authority of the business supervisor it will be the sole responsibility of Wang Zuogan [the head of the lineage trust] to handle him. If he is unable to stop him, then both the credit group and the Wang Sanwei trust will ask the officials in charge to punish him.[32]

In addition, the two auditors could raise questions regarding the activities of the two co-equal managers, and vice versa, and any officer designated in accordance with the agreement could be removed by a majority vote of the shareholding bodies of both parties to the agreement.[33] Despite the meticulous efforts to ensure good management and avoid dishonest practices on either side, as of 1928 the Wang Sanwei trust still owed the credit group over 900,000 taels.

The 1922 agreement, which in effect put the Wangs' properties in receivership to the credit group, was just an extreme version of the relationships which often developed between debtor and creditor in late imperial and early Republican China. While the use of written contracts and the state's enforcement thereof was a matter of routine in the late imperial period, debt posed a special problem. The Qing code did not outlaw usury; in fact, it allowed rates of up to 3 percent a month. However, it did ban the collection of interest in excess of the original principal, in effect putting a ceiling on interest if the term of the loan exceeded more than a few months.[34] The state upheld credit agreements and occasionally helped work out payment plans that would allow both parties to continue intact. However, it did not, as a rule, follow up by imposing sanctions on debtors who continued in arrears. Inability to collect would require the creditor to file a second suit.[35] This explains the continued reliance on physical collateral and guarantors in Chinese lending well into the twentieth century.[36] However, in cases where large loans were involved, particularly if they extended over long periods, it was common for the lender to send a representative to keep watch over the collateral. The Dadeheng remittance bank sent the manager of its Chongqing branch office to take up residence at the main office of the Li Siyou trust's Dasheng pipe during the time that its loans to the trust were in ar-

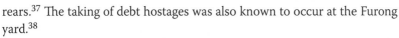

rears.[37] The taking of debt hostages was also known to occur at the Furong yard.[38]

Large creditors were not only concerned that borrower firms would abscond with profits before making their payments. This is a problem faced by all creditors whose borrowers are in arrears. They were also worried that individual shareholders would make off with assets and profits. Their anxieties were shared by the members of the trusts themselves.

A Failure of Property Rights

The oral histories recounting life and business at the Furong saltyard make much of the extravagant habits of the members of the large salt lineages as the source of corporate decline. At the same time, they often lay the blame for the company's failure at the feet of lineage members who, by the turn of the century, were engaged in business dealings of their own. Some lineage members undoubtedly exploited collective assets to obtain advantages for their own firms or simply to feather their own nests. Second- and third-generation family members are notorious everywhere for their failure to maintain the business acumen and ruthless hunger for company expansion that drove the cohort of founding fathers. What makes the story of the lineage trusts of Zigong important to our understanding of Chinese history and of business history in general is not that the children of Zigong's salt moguls were more greedy or more corrupt than children of the rich elsewhere. It is that they operated within a system of property rights that made partnerships increasingly unstable as they grew in size and generational depth.

The lineage trust provided an excellent structure through which to bring together and preserve capital. In the agricultural world in which most Chinese lived, lineage trusts which produced dividends at all—many simply financed lineage functions—were based largely on cultivated land yielding rents in kind or cash, the proceeds from which were divided at intervals, generally of one year. Lineage regulations might call for expenditure of a fixed amount or percentage of income to buy more land. However, most lineage trusts and their nonfamilial counterparts such as temple associations were very simple constructs. If a trust survived for generations such that the total number of members or shareholders numbered in the thousands, as have some of the oldest trusts in Guangdong, it simply meant smaller dividends for each member or each member branch.

Because they evolved into complex businesses combining varied assets and requiring sophisticated financial management of large staffs and labor forces, wholesale and retail firms, and productive assets that required repair, maintenance, and development, the lineage trusts at Zigong confronted increasingly difficult agency and coordination problems. These problems arose first in the distant wholesale markets, where branch managers with local knowledge were among the first non-kin employed in high lineage trust posts. As business became more complex, we have also seen the employment of increasing numbers of non-kin managers such as Luo Xiaoyuan and Luo Huagai. At the same time, as these trusts grew, in both the range and the number of their investments, and temporally in their generational depth, they encountered problems inherent in China's system of property rights.

The first problem arose as individuals within households, households within lineage branches, and branches within lineage trusts began to engage in business activities on their own. Common property implied common liability. Because property belonged to the household (*jia*) and not the individual, the debts of the father became the debts of the sons,[39] who themselves could be held accountable for each other's bad business dealings. Prior to the implementation of a new civil code in 1929, some businessmen tried to separate ownership of their business interests from those of their families by making shares appear to be part of their wives' dowries. However, across the economy this could not provide a surrogate for individual property rights.

The issue of who had authority to dispose of property, including shares, was one that was never satisfactorily addressed in the Republic. Its impact on business confidence and the enforcement of contracts was considerable. One illustrative case involved several leading investors at the yard. Zhang Xiaopo, one of the rising stars of the well community, leased two wells from the Wang Sanwei trust.[40] In 1924 the two wells were closed because of an accident, and Zhang sued at the Chamber of Commerce for compensation of lost income, as provided for in his contract. Zhang claimed to have signed the lease with Wang Zuogan and Wang Shouwei. Wang Shouwei filed a countersuit at the chamber claiming that Zhang's lease was invalid. His charge held that neither he nor Wang Zuogan had the authority to sign such a lease. These two wells were the property of the lineage as a whole and could only be disposed of by the manager of the lineage's business department, who at the time was Wang Deqian.

Likewise, by 1928, the dispute that ensued between the Wang Sanwei trust and the Chongqing-Shashi credit group no longer centered around how the mounting debts of the lineage trust would be paid off. More important was who had the authority to dispose of lineage property, and specifically, whose seal could be affixed to a contract.[41] In August 1928 the local garrison command[42] approved an agreement by which an official seal for the business office, a personal seal for the holder of the office, an official seal for the office of the Chongqing-Shashi credit group supervisor of Wang Sanwei trust wells, furnaces, pipes and wholesale companies, and a personal seal for the holder of this awkwardly named office would have to be affixed to any contract relating to Wang Sanwei trust properties for it to be valid.[43]

While the drama and the economic significance of this dispute were amplified by the importance of the Wangs to the history of the yard, the issue of authority to sign a contract was at the heart of a large number of the legal disputes decided in Zigong during the early twentieth century. In 1924 Liao Rongzhai drew up a will in the presence of members of his lineage and other close relatives. In it he divided his property, not between his two sons, but between his sons' sons.[44] His rationale was sound. The younger son was dead, and the elder "spent money like it was water." Afraid that his wealth would soon be dissipated, Rongzhai named the widow of the younger son manager of the property and turned all the deeds over to her before his death. Following his demise the two branches of the family quarreled, and mediation was begun under the guidance of family members. Unable to resolve the issue, the lineage association appealed to the local Chamber of Commerce for assistance in two areas. First, it sought to deprive Mrs. Liao (née Chen) of her stewardship on the grounds that she was a woman. Second, it requested that the chamber help oust a certain Mr. Yang, who had made a private deal with the profligate older son to lease the Ronghai well. Despite the son's lack of authority to dispose of the well, Mrs. Liao had been unable to get Yang to leave.[45] The action of the surviving son was symptomatic of the intrafamilial dispute over who should inherit Liao's wealth. Here the younger generation appears to have been taking advantage of new laws relating to family property that allowed sons a more immediate claim to personal inheritance of their father's estate. The challenge to Mrs. Liao as manager of the estate had more traditional roots and does not seem to have succeeded.[46]

As firms became more complex and lineage trusts that invested in one firm invested in other firms, serious problems also arose sorting out the liabilities of the firm, as distinct from the liabilities of the investors, who themselves were not individuals. When the Tongli company was formed to buy goods in Chongqing for sale at the saltyard, the Yonghexiang company made a small investment in the firm and acted as its agent in Zigong. The Yonghexiang went bankrupt in 1929, and its creditors took possession of all the goods in its warehouses, including goods shipped by the Tongli company that had not yet been sold. Because the Yonghexiang was a partner in the Tongli company, the former's creditors in Zigong argued that these were joint assets that could legitimately be sold to pay the Yonghexiang's debts. The Tongli company did not challenge this principle. Instead it went to great pains to demonstrate that the Yonghexiang owed it sufficient money to have negated any relationship of partnership that was originally intended between the two firms.[47] Cases such as these could tie up Zigong's courts and institutions of commercial mediation for years. As we will see in chapter 9, this, coupled with increasing competition among local administrative, judicial, parapolitical, and military organizations for jurisdiction over business disputes, suffused the business environment of the 1920s and 1930s with an uncertainty that had not existed under the Qing.

The Rise of the New Salt Elite

Whereas the late Qing saltyard merchant elite rose to economic dominance by owning well sites and later by developing these sites, the new elite relied largely on rental and purchase of operating wells and furnaces, often acquired as a result of the debt restructuring schemes of lineage trusts. The large lineage fortunes were consolidated by means of vertical integration of well, furnace, pipe, and wholesale operations. Some of the new elite benefited from investment in the new pumping technology, which yielded large profits in its own right and gave them control of the furnace industry in a period of brine overproduction. However, most of the important names in Republican Zigong salt production rose to prominence because their political connections and acumen allowed them to take on leadership roles in a period of crisis that far exceeded their economic position in the yard. This becomes clear when we look at the struggles surrounding voluntary cuts in production during the period of the brine glut between 1924 and the beginning of the Sino-Japanese War. The contraction of Sichuan's salt markets and the resulting decline in overall profits during this period led to a change in the investment strategies of men like Luo Xiaoyuan and Hou Ceming. No longer do we see single-minded engagement in salt production and marketing. Instead, many of the new entrepreneurs had diversified manufacturing and commercial portfolios. Many became involved in banking as well, which brought them into closer contact with the economic center of the province in Chongqing. Moreover, in their relations with each other and with the agents of authority, there emerged a distinct pattern of clientelism, which replaced lineage as the organizing framework within which business was conducted. This was true even though some of these men began their careers as managers in the large lineage-based conglomerates we have been examining throughout much of this book. The importance of the lineage trust as a mode of organizing business relations declined during the twentieth century. Large numbers of lineage trusts continued to appear as investors in wells and furnaces during the Republican period, but often they showed up as landlord shareholders or as corporate shareholders within a diversified investment group. The lineage trusts of Sichuan were still investing in wells, as they continued to invest in land. But we no longer see great, integrated salt empires organized around the institution of the lineage estate.

Wang Hefu and the Heirs to the Large Lineage Trusts

Wang Hefu is a transitional figure in the story of Zigong business. Wang's grandfather Wang Xiangyun was of the same generation of Wangs as Wang Langyun, the founder of the prominent nineteenth-century lineage trust. Although his economic success was less spectacular than that of his relations, he followed the family model in combining wells, furnaces, pipes, and wholesale firms in one family firm. At the same time, Wang Hefu represented precisely the kind of individual entrepreneurship that scions of the large lineage trusts came to suspect of undermining their collective fortunes. His wealth was generated through innovation and entrepreneurship and maintained through gentry politics. By the end of his life, the vertically integrated company that he had almost singlehandedly created met the same fate as that of his Wang Sanwei trust kin.

Wang Hefu's career took off in the 1890s with the introduction of solution mining at the yard. He was the first salt producer to set up pipes to carry fresh water to irrigate the newly developed rock-salt wells during the late nineteenth century. When the wells began to merge he set up his well as an irrigation point, assessing each connecting well for the costs of irrigation according to its average productivity. However, it was not as a well developer that Wang initially made his fortune. Joining forces with Zhong Xingxiang, Wang was one of the early pioneers in the use of steam pumps at the yard. His firm, the Zhongxingxiang, was a partnership in which Zhong Xingxiang, after whom the firm was named, was most likely initially the larger investor. However, within a short time Zhong disappears from the historical record. The firm purchased eight pumps in 1915, making it one of the largest investors in steam technology in Zigong (see chapter 7), and many of the wells it initially pumped belonged to Zhong.[48] With the profits from this enterprise, Wang went on to invest in furnaces as well as rock-salt brine and black-brine wells. Wang was also one of the first to use steam engines to pump water from the nearby river and then transport it to his and other firms' irrigation-point wells by means of bamboo pipes.[49]

Recollections of the saltyard during the early twentieth century often refer to Wang as one of Zigong's most powerful businessmen. At its height, the Zhongxingxiang owned the Yuanchang pipe and 13 brine wells, and operated about 400 gas-fired pans. It also operated a shipping company, coal mines, foundries, and several machine repair shops. Although we have little information on the degree of integration among these firms, it is likely that he followed the model of the nineteenth-century lineage-based business empires, using his own pipes and wells to ensure a steady supply of brine to his furnaces and outfitting his wells with machines and parts provided by his own factories. Wang is even known to have entered the salt wholesale market during the brief period of free trade that followed the fall of the Qing dynasty.[50]

However, the glory years of the Zhongxingxiang were few. An inventory of its assets undertaken following Wang Hefu's death shows the firm to have divested itself of most of its units by 1930. In addition to some unnamed "smaller properties" the Zhongxingxiang now had two furnaces and three gas wells producing more than 100 pan units. It was still the sole owner of the Yuanchang pipe, which was valued at 40,000 yuan. Despite Wang Hefu's pioneering role in the exploitation of rock-salt brine wells and steam pumps, in 1930 his firm appears to have owned only one rock-salt brine well and two black-brine wells, all three pumped by machine.[51] We know of these assets because Wang left the firm deeply in debt when he died, and the value of a combination of leases and outright sales only netted sufficient funds to clear the firm of its over 300,000 yuan in outstanding obligations.

Like that of the Wang Sanwei trust, the bankruptcy of the Zhongxingxiang was a matter of concern to the entire saltyard community. The several hundred parties with claims against the firm included both members of Wang's lineage, the Baoxinglong Wangs, and outside creditors, most of whom, again as in the case of the Wang Sanwei trust, were from Chongqing and Shashi.[52] The measures taken to discharge the debt were arrived at through negotiations supported by leading members of the saltyard elite. Luo Huagai, whose personal business history we will discuss, acted for the Zhongxingxiang and Wang Jieping, Wang Hefu's nephew, represented the interests of the Baoxinglong Wangs. The organization of Zhongxingxiang creditors also sent an agent, who together with Luo Huagai, Wang Jieping, the head of the Chamber of Commerce and prominent salt businessmen Hou Ceming, Luo Xiaoyuan, and Xiong Zuozhou formed the Zhongxingxiang Debt Payment Committee (*dichang weiyuanhui*). The Debt Payment Committee worked under the supervision of the Chamber of Commerce (see chapter 9). Together they negotiated a combination of leases and sales that within a short time cleared the firms' debts and for all intents and purposes brought an end to the Zhongxingxiang as an active Zigong firm.[53] In addition, by limiting the liability of each of the constituent units of the

Zhongxingxiang to its own creditors, the chamber made it possible for shareholders in the firm to retain those assets which were not part of the Zhongxingxiang combination.[54]

Despite its foundation in the more advanced technologies of rock-salt solution mining and mechanized pumping, the Zhongxingxiang and others became the victims of market forces that integrated management could not control. As a result of political decisions that excluded Sichuan salt from many of its previous markets (see chapter 9), Sichuan salt producers in the 1920s were faced with unprecedented excess capacity. The contraction of the Sichuan salt market was particularly damaging to brine producers, who, under the system described in chapter 7, included both the owners of rock-salt brine wells and pumping companies that took their profits by selling brine to evaporation furnaces. To address this brine glut, Wang Hefu joined forces with Yan Xinshe and Yan Xianyang to found the Rock Salt Well Agency (*yanyanjing banshichu*), a cartel of brine producers united to limit production and stabilize prices. One of many production and marketing cartels founded in China during the interwar years,[55] for three years the agency organized member wells to restrict their output and negotiate brine sales as a group. Following the collapse of the Rock Salt Well Agency, Li Jingcai used his influence to establish a similar organization with warlord support (see chapter 9).

Wang Hefu's business strategy may initially have resembled that of his wealthier Wang relatives, but his involvement in the political life of the yard placed him soundly within the ranks of the twentieth-century business elite. Indeed, to relate the story of Wang Hefu's public life is to tell the story of Zigong's political evolution in the first third of the twentieth century. In 1911, Wang was one of the first Zigong luminaries to join forces with the anti-Qing armies to declare the secession of the yard from the empire. It was at a banquet hosted by Wang that the first discussions were held, which led to the establishment of an independent administrative structure for the yard.[56] Only one source places Wang among the members of the short-lived provisional assembly founded by Zigong's civic leadership in December 1911.[57] However, Wang's role in the newly emerging public security apparatus of the saltyard is widely noted by his contemporaries. Wang himself may have contributed to the military effort that secured southern Sichuan for the 1911 Revolution. He and Hu Tiehua (of the Hu Yuanhe trust) founded and commanded the yard's first merchant militia (*shangtuan*) since the time of the Taiping Rebellion.[58] Wang continued to play an important role in this area, taking on the position of head of the public security militia in 1916 and serving as a fund-raiser for the merchant militia training office during the military governorships of Zhou Junji and Zhou Daogang.[59]

By the 1920s Wang Hefu was also deeply engaged in the informal governance of the salt merchant community. In 1926 he was elected head of the Chamber of Commerce. He was also a leading member of the committee organized to raise funds for the construction of a motorway between Fushun and Ziliujing in 1927.[60] In 1927 Wang was asked to be a founding director of the Zigong local council of the Guomindang. And in 1929 Wang was appointed head of the education department of the newly reorganized Chamber of Commerce. We can only speculate where his political connections would have taken him had his career not been cut short in 1930 by his death at 63 years of age.

Like many of his peers in the interwar years, Wang's associations consisted of both civilian and military figures. However, Wang's connections with several people were particularly strong. Dating back at least to the days of the militia formed in the wake of the 1911 Revolution, Wang Hefu and Hu Tiehua developed a bond that led them frequently to collaborate in civic activities.[61] Joining them in the 1920s was Li Jingcai, a scion of the Li Taoshu trust. The source of their friendship may have been their common association with Fan Rongguang, pipe owner, developer of wide-diameter wells, and founder of the Fuchang steam pump company.[62] Li, Hu, and Wang served together as mediators on the Wang Sanwei trust debt case and as members of the local Chamber of Commerce.[63] Indeed, one of Wang's last public acts was to arrange the release of Li and Hu following their arrest by warlord Wang Xuanxu.[64] So close were these three men that each was nicknamed after one of the animal sacrifices commonly found at Chinese family altars, a shoulder of pork (Wang Hefu), a rooster (Li Jingcai), and a carp (Hu Tiehua), and like these three were said always to be found together.

Wang, Hu, and Li each share the distinction of being members of large lineage trusts whose economic power was on the wane but whose investment in political capital in the last years of the Qing enabled a number of their young men to survive as powerful individuals in postimperial China. As long as the Qing dynasty maintained a laissez-faire policy with regard to the market for Sichuan salt, Zigong's salt producers invested little in the formal trappings of gentry status. Political influence remained local and relied on traditional displays of wealth in the form of real estate, weddings, funerals, and ancestral halls. The main exception was their expenditure in support of local defense during the period of the Taiping Rebellion and in the establishment of several defensive redoubts, which later became popular upland retreats for Zigong's wealthy business elite. Sale of titular degrees and official positions was a major fund-raising device during the Taiping years, and several members of Zigong's salt merchant community received such rewards in repayment for their contribution to the war effort.[65]

This pattern changed with the introduction of Guanyun. With a new salt administration setting limits on the range of Zigong's market and a far more draconian system of taxation affecting the profits of producers and marketers alike, lineages like the Wangs, Hus, Lis, and Yans began investing in markers of status that gave entrée to power at the level of the state. In the 1880s and 1890s this continued to entail the purchase of official titles or degrees, easily achieved as the Qing sank ever deeper into debt to foreign powers.[66] But it also meant more substantial efforts to network with men with political influence. The Wang Sanwei trust was involved in the founding of two Confucian academies during the late nineteenth century.[67] While only one member of the four great lineages won a high degree—Li Xinzhu is listed in the Fushun gazetteer as the holder of an 1874 *juren* degree[68]—investment in education nevertheless facilitated the creation of political networks whose utility for some lineage members extended well into the twentieth century.

The lineage school founded by Hu Tiehua's father, Hu Ruxiu, not only trained Hu and his brothers and male cousins in the classics but also created through its employment of eminent scholars, what was to become a new link between Zigong's salt manufacturers and the political elite of China. The most useful was with Zhao Xi, a Rong County man who rose to the rank of Hanlin compiler and censor before the end of the dynasty. Hu Ruxiu became a patron of Zhao Xi, providing him with financial assistance, at one time even housing his family within the Hu compound.[69] In 1909 Zhao Xi took Hu Tiehua and his two brothers with him to Beijing, where they purchased degrees, networked with capital officials, and may even have held minor positions in government.[70] Even after returning to Zigong, Zhao Xi's ties to reformers provided Hu Tiehua and his associates with the opportunity to mingle with reformers and literati, particularly those in Sichuan's political and economic capitals, Chengdu and Chongqing.

Li Jingcai also brought powerful connections to his friendship with Hu and Wang. A member of the Li Taoshu trust, Li Jingcai made his fortune in the same way as Wang Hefu. A developer of wide-diameter wells and an early entrant into the steam-pumping business, Li also invested in provisioning wells with steel cable and other metal goods and owned a number of local companies, including the Fuyuanqing, which hired out sedan chair bearers.[71] Li's older brother, Tonggai, was the scholar in the family. Jingcai is said to have ignored his studies until his twenties. In 1900, at the age of 26, Jingcai was sent to Chengdu to deliver a donation of grain to assist the government in supplying military rations. On the strength of his family's largesse he was awarded the rank of circuit intendant and came to know the Sichuan governor, who is said to have later recommended Jingcai to the

Ministry of Finance. There Li worked for several years under Yan Anlan, who later became Sichuan salt commissioner.[72] This experience enabled Li Jingcai to develop his own list of powerful political contacts and also won him a short stint in the salt commissioner's office in Chengdu.

The density of their links to officials and degree holders aided in their rise to power within the saltyard elite and explains the very early role that Wang, Hu, and Li played in the emerging civil society of the yard. However, equally important to the security of their business and their influence was their cultivation of ties to Sichuan's new warlord leadership. As we will see in chapter 9, Sichuan became a battleground for competing militarists almost as soon as the Qing dynasty fell.[73] Zigong, with salt to tax and wealthy businessmen to ransom, became a prized territory in the warlord scramble for resources. It was during one such battle, between troops of the Sichuan and the Yunnan warlord armies in 1918 or 1919, that Zhao Xi is said to have arranged for the three friends to meet the warlord at that time in control of Chongqing.[74] Their relationship with Liu Xiang, although not without its tensions, lasted well into the 1930s, long after Liu Xiang himself had become warlord of all of Sichuan. In 1920 Li Jingcai was put in charge of Liu Xiang's tax remittance office, a post that allowed him to enhance his position among the saltyard elite by protecting merchant interests against warlord excesses.[75] Li Jingcai served in this capacity for three years and remained an adviser to the powerful warlord even after stepping down. In 1926 Wang Hefu took over the post.[76] And in 1930, when Wang died during a trip to Chongqing to rescue Hu Tiehua and Li Jingcai from arrest by Liu Xiang's renegade underling, Wang Xuanxu, it was Liu Xiang who arranged for Wang Hefu's body to be returned under military escort for burial at Zigong.[77] This relationship led some of their fellow businessmen to refer to Wang, Hu, and Li as local strongmen in their own right, and we will see in chapter 9 that warlord ties certainly facilitated the promotion of some of their own causes. It afforded all three men privileged access to loans from banks with warlord ties and notably aided them in the struggles between brine-well owners and furnace owners in the 1920s.[78] However, they were not alone in combining warlord politics and business in the troubled years between the two world wars.

Zhang Xiaopo and the Enliu Pipe

Despite the difficulties faced by Zigong salt producers after the fall of the Qing, there was still room for men with no ties to the large nineteenth-century lineages in the business of manufacturing and marketing salt. The latter's declining fortunes and the existence of a lively market in well shares made entry possible even by relatively poor men like Zhang Xiaopo. By no means the only new entrant into the field of salt manufacture, Zhang Xiaopo represents in every respect the talents of the new twentieth-century Zigong businessman, politically networked and quick to innovate in both technology and organization.

Zhang Xiaopo was born in 1877 at Yanxi in Fushun County, across the Fuxi River, where his father ran a modest business shipping salt downriver to Dengjing guan. Sometime during the 1890s his father invested in an operating well that later began to produce natural gas as well as brine. With the aid of this small windfall, Zhang was given a classical education and, with the support of his in-laws, continued his studies long enough to take and pass the examination for the *shengyuan* degree.[79]

By the turn of the century a new kind of political activism was spreading among China's urban elite. Although Zhang followed his father's example and dabbled in salt investments, his real passion in the early years of the century appears to have been the revolutionary cause. Zhang was involved in the Railroad Rights Recovery Movement, which shook Sichuan from 1910 to 1911 to the point of raising a military unit against the throne.[80] Luo Xiaoyuan maintains that Zhang even joined the Revolutionary Alliance (*tongmenghui*), and his activities in later years certainly point to deep ties with certain members of the revolutionary party.[81] Although only a newcomer to the Furong yard, Zhang Xiaopo's activism earned him a place as one of 60 delegates to the local deliberative assembly formed to govern Ziliujing and Gongjing immediately after the fall of the Qing, and he served as the head of its transportation department.[82] Zhang Xiaopo continued to play an important part in local politics throughout the 1910s. He was involved in a 1915 plot against Yuan Shikai's deputies in Sichuan, and his later participation in the garrison government organized by these "rebels" culminated in his appointment as Bandit Suppression Commander (*qingxiang siling*) for southern Sichuan. Zhang's policies in this office, particularly his recruitment of "former" bandit leaders to his army, led to his dismissal. However, throughout the 1920s he continued to hold a variety of middle-level posts within the warlord regimes of men like Lu Shidi and Shi Qingyang. In this capacity, he was drawn into the world of modern banking in Chongqing and Zigong and acted as spokesman for Sichuan salt interests with the governments of Hubei and Hunan.[83] Although at the time Zhang was not one of the wealthiest men at the yard, his prestige was considerable. Zhang was the chief negotiator in the Li Siyou trust debt settlement case, for which he was amply rewarded.[84] Indeed, such was his influence within both business and warlord circles that it was Zhang Xiaopo who was chosen to represent the interests of Zigong's salt producers at the Chengdu conference on salt administration convened in 1925 by Liu Xiang.[85] Zhang was even briefly involved in Guomindang politics, heading the Ziliujing branch of the party in 1926.

Although Zhang Xiaopo shied away from party politics after the split between the Guomindang left and right wings, he continued to play an active role in politics at the yard. In 1927, when Liu Xiang's rival, Li Wenhui, sent his minions to violate the salt tax agreement that Zhang had helped to formulate, Zhang played a pivotal role in the formation of a merchant army to drive out the warlord tax collectors. Indeed, Zhang Xiaopo was remarkably lucky in his dealings with the shifting forces that controlled the Zigong area. Only once, in late 1927, was he arrested and detained for a considerable period.[86] And in 1930, following Liu Xiang's unification of Sichuan, Zhang Xiaopo once again took advantage of his warlord ties to win a lucrative position as a "specialized merchant," making him one of a limited number of licensed wholesalers of Sichuan salt.[87]

Zhang began investing in wells in 1901, but it was not until the next decade that he entered the ranks of wealthy businessmen at Zigong. In the mid-1910s he was one of the first well owners to invest in the purchase of a steam engine, to pump the Yanyuan well in which he was a partner with Li Yunzhi.[88] Luo Xiaoyuan recalls that by introducing the use of an improved engine with greater horsepower, iron brine tubes, and steel cable at this well Zhang was able to achieve output of over 13,000 *dan* of brine a month, an extraordinary amount in the days before the use of wide-diameter wells.[89] As we noted in chapter 7, Zhang was a pioneer in this area as well, his Zehou wide-diameter well inaugurating a new phase in the development of rock-salt brine and the mechanized technologies that wide-diameter wells accommodated.

However important these contributions to the salt industry in Zigong, Zhang Xiaopo is best remembered by his contemporaries and later commentators as the founder of the Enliu pipe. During the nineteenth century brine pipes gave some salt producers control over the scarcer resource, brine, and allowed them to build up the most efficient and productive furnaces at the yard. The reliability and large volume of salt manufactured in pipe-owned pans gave pipe-furnace combinations a tremendous advantage in contracting for certificate quotas and ensuring that their salt would be sold. Because furnace owners saved money by transporting the brine they needed through pipes, pipe owners were able to gain control over most of the brine supply in Gongjing. Large profits were made by buying up brine and selling it at a premium to furnaces that did not have investment ties to pipes. Moreover, by cornering the market in a scarce resource, pipes were able to guarantee the first supply to their own furnaces.[90]

Only four of the 10 big pipes survived the changeover to solution mining. The Wang Sanwei trust was the dominant investor in the Datong pipe, which was rebuilt in Ziliujing. The Yuanchang pipe, owned by a branch of the Wang lineage descended from the brother of the founder of the Wang Sanwei, was similarly relocated. The Jitong pipe, owned by a branch of the Li Siyou trust headed by Li Xingqiao, went bankrupt around 1919. The Dasheng pipe, which had originally been built by the Li Siyou trust, survived but by 1916 had been sold to a new group of investors. And the Tongfu pipe continued operation in Ziliujing under the ownership of a partnership headed by Li Maolin, who does not appear to have been related to the Li Siyou trust.

The remaining pipes retained control over the distribution of much of the brine produced in Ziliujing. The ability of pipe owners in this new market to control the movement of brine was the same as it had been in the nineteenth century. The factors that enabled them to relocate pipes were also not unlike the factors that had allowed them to build the Ziliujing-Gongjing pipes in the nineteenth century. It was not merely a matter of money. Few investors had the social capital to put together a deal to build a pipe requiring lease or purchase of long contiguous tracts of land fulfilling exacting requirements.

The power of the pipe owners was finally broken by Zhang Xiaopo. By the 1920s Zhang had complemented his investments in rock-salt brine wells by leasing several hundred pan units of gas at bargain rates when the Wang Sanwei trust and Li Xingqiao's Jitong pipe went bankrupt.[91] Nevertheless, in 1922, when Zhang's Zehou well came in, he found himself forced to rely on the existing pipes to move his brine to his furnaces. He therefore turned to the Li Siyou trust, which he had recently assisted in negotiations with its creditors. The Li Siyou trust leased Zhang Xiaopo land and made available spare materials from their dismantled pipes. With it he laid the Enliu pipe, the only wholly new pipe constructed since the 1911 Revolution.[92]

The Enliu pipe allowed Zhang Xiaopo to transport his own brine from the Zehou well to the gas furnaces at Guojia ao. However, without additional clients from among the brine wells in Ziliujing's Da'an district he could not make a profit from his investment in the pipe. Most of the rock-salt brine in Ziliujing was being moved through the reconstructed pipes recently brought in from Gongjing. In order to break the monopoly of the old pipe owners, Zhang developed an entirely new system of brine transport that forever changed the balance of power at the yard.

The difference between the Enliu and the other pipes at Ziliujing lay in their methods of payment. Instead of forcing brine producers to sell their brine to the pipes, which then took their transport fee as a large markup when selling brine to the furnaces, Zhang took his cue from the world of finance. He called his payment system brine remittance (*huidui lushui*). Owners of rock-salt wells could bring their brine to the Enliu pipe and pay a single passage fee (*guojia*) for its transport to Guojia ao. This fee was set at half the effective price charged by the existing pipes, 0.08 tael per *dan*. Moreover, because he was not buying the brine from well owners, but only transporting it, Zhang's method did not interfere with the ability of well owners to negotiate their own deals with furnaces. The brine remittance system became extremely popular. Brine transported in this fashion was turned over to the furnace or agent of the well owners every day, while payment of the passage fee could be made twice a month. Moreover, as Zhang was a relatively small owner of gas furnaces, neither well nor furnace owners feared that he would try to commandeer the brine he was transporting were there ever to be a brine shortage.[93]

A short time after the completion of the Enliu pipe, the other pipes operating in Ziliujing were forced to imitate the payment system established by Zhang Xiaopo. Increased competition brought the price of moving brine down to 0.06 tael per *dan*. However, far more important was the loss of power to the large salt lineages. The shortage of brine noted by memoirists as a major factor in the decision to rent out Li and Wang wells can be traced in part to the destruction of their monopoly over brine transport. The demise of the large pipes also meant a considerable reduction in profits, although no accurate profit statistics are known to have survived. Pipes had been a high-cost investment whose profitability rested in large part on the local power and influence that allowed only a small group of men to engage in their operation. The end of the pipe component in the lineage trusts' business portfolios was the last great blow to their power and opened the way for the fragmentation of salt industry investment and the entry of a younger generation of businessmen at the yard.

Hou, Xiong, Luo, Luo

Hou Ceming, Xiong Zuozhou, Luo Huagai, and Luo Xiaoyuan rose to prominence at the saltyard during the downturn in the salt industry in the 1920s and 1930s, and it was not until the expansion of the market during the War of Resistance against Japan that their real fortunes were made. Nevertheless, their activities during the interwar years tell us much about the business environment and business strategies during the early Republic. All four were self-made men in a city that comes alive in their biographies as teeming with men on the make in a world of petty trade. While their family backgrounds could not have been more different, each followed a similar path to business prosperity. By the 1930s the names Hou, Xiong, Luo, and Luo became linked in what we would now call a business group, based on dense networks of friendship, interlocking investment, and mutual advantage.

Hou Ceming's personal rise was the most dramatic of the group.[94] Born in 1885 to a poor farm family, Hou spent his early years at the outskirts of the Furong yard, where his father had taken up truck farming on Wang Sanwei trust land. For a short time Hou's father worked as a laborer at the Haiyuan well in Gongjing and at age 15 Hou was apprenticed to the well, where he acquired some degree of literacy and numeracy as well as firsthand experience of well operations. Soon after marrying at age 18 he became discouraged with the low wages paid at the well and began gambling and working part-time at the Taiyuanxuan teahouse owned by a migrant from Shanxi. With occasional financial assistance from his wife's father, Hou then moved into petty trading, frequenting the rural markets in Rong County to buy agricultural goods for sale at the wells and furnaces. In 1916 he and his father-in-law formed a partnership with a Gongjing silk merchant to open a dry goods store in Ziliujing, with Hou again combing the rural market towns for goods. In 1922, after the failure of this retail undertaking, Hou entered into a partnership with Wang Jixing and Chen Pangtao to open a native bank. As we have seen, such ventures required little startup capital, and Hou's Yiji native bank probably began with no more than 500 yuan. Within a short time the partners decided there was more money to be made by selling salt in Chongqing and repatriating the profits, so they reorganized their firm and renamed it the Qianxin Salt Shipping company.

The Qianxin Salt Shipping company provides an interesting example of the opportunities and dangers that existed for men like Hou. The biggest profits to be made in shipping salt were not in salt itself but in remittance banking. According to Hou's biographers there was considerable money to be made by taking advantage of the differences in interest rates between Chongqing, where the existence of a burgeoning money market made money cheap, and Ziliujing, where unmet capital demand kept interest rates high.[95] As a result, salt merchants, who did a high-volume cash business in Chongqing, often developed remittance businesses between the two cities. Local merchants needing cash to purchase cloth, medicinal herbs, or other goods in Chongqing would purchase a "Chongqing receipt" (*yupiao*—a form of bill of exchange) from a salt shipper in Ziliujing and redeem it for cash with a banker or merchant house in Chongqing. The profits to be made on such transactions relied on each party's ability to obtain accurate information on interest rates and the changing demand for cash. The Qianxin company appears to have done quite well until 1926, when embezzlement by its manager in Chongqing forced the company to close.

A business failure again, Hou looked for the first time toward the production end of the salt industry. This time the opportunity came as a result of the decline of the large lineage trusts mentioned above. Hou's rapid repayment of the Qianxin's creditors appears to have attracted the attention of Hu Tiehua, who was looking for a manager for his lineage's Jicheng gas well. Hou ran the well's *daguan* (see chapter 3) for two years, during which time he and two partners founded yet another native bank through which he managed all purchases for the *daguan*. When the Hu Yuanhe trust began divesting itself of its gas wells, Hou took advantage of his inside knowledge of the firm to win the contract to rent the Hus' Tongxin pipe. When a drop in the price of salt destroyed the pipe's profit margin, Hou and his partners attempted to return the pipe. But when the Hus were unable to come up with the large refundable deposit stipulated in the original agreement, they were forced to sell the pipe to Hou.

From 1930 on Hou parlayed the profits from his earlier investments into a growing portfolio of salt industry assets. Many of these took advantage of his and his partners' ability to buy out older firms and continued to reflect Hou's talents at judging the market and taking advantage of price differentials. With Xiong Zuozhou, Luo Xiaoyuan, and Luo Huagai he opened the Ruchu salt company to compete against Huai salt purveyors in the Huguang market. In 1931 he took over half ownership of the Wangs' Yuanchang pipe and combined it with his own to form the Yuanxin pipe. As a reward for the mediation of a large lawsuit involving Wang Hefu's Zhongxingxiang company, the Wangs granted Hou a giveaway lease to 13 pan units of gas at their Huilong well. When Sichuan's salt producers won a suit against the salt administration and used the money to open the Yushang bank, Hou Ceming was named the bank's manager (*jingli*) and, on his recommendation, Luo Xiaoyuan became head of the Income and Expenditure Department.

We do not know the full extent of Hou's assets. His biographers have uncovered records of 92 pan units of gas, though Hou's autobiography lays claim to 120. Many of these assets were developed with Xiong, Luo, and Luo, including the Baozhen well, which came in two years after they began drilling in 1936. When Japan instituted its blockade of eastern China in 1937, Sichuan became the main source of salt for free China and even the least productive of Zigong's resources were mobilized in the interests of national salvation. During the war Hou not only opened new wells but also re-entered the business of buying materials for use in salt production, purveying coal from Weiyuan and Luzhou and selling salt throughout the Sichuan salt-shipping market. In a manner reminiscent of the old lineage trusts of the nineteenth century, the flourishing market of the war years once again encouraged integration. Only now it was unrelated entrepreneurs, combining assets through interlocking investment, who formed Zigong's powerful 1940s business groups.

Like Hou, Xiong Zuozhou[96] also came from a poor farming family. Also like Hou, his father supplemented his meager earnings with casual labor at the Furong yard. With his small savings from carrying brine and water at the furnaces, Xiong Wanquan eventually opened a small shop selling glutinous rice cakes while renting rooms upstairs. In the late nineteenth century Wanquan joined the Catholic Church, which is said to have provided him with financial assistance enabling him to move to a prime business location and open a shop slaughtering buffalo and selling buffalo soup. When the Ziliujing Catholic Church was attacked in the aftermath of the Boxer Rebellion, Wanquan's was among the congregants' homes that were destroyed. Wanquan himself received a share of the indemnity paid to the Catholic Church, and it is with these funds that he is said to have entered the salt industry itself.

Xiong Wanquan was thus like hundreds of other petty investors in turn-of-the-century Zigong. He put some of his cash into land and became an investor in a well-drilling venture that never came in. By the time he died in 1915 he had little more than some land and an undisclosed amount of cash that was somehow earning interest.[97] His children could easily have divided his estate and continued life as small shopkeepers and traders. His younger daughter became a Catholic nun and received a share of his estate for maintenance in lieu of the dowry due an as-yet-unwed daughter. Of his five sons, one died young and two others joined Xiong Zuozhou in trying their hand at the business of salt, pooling their inheritance under the Xiong Sihe trust.

Xiong Zuozhou appears to have gotten his experience in the salt business as a white-collar employee at the wells of the prominent turn-of-the-century salt manufacturer Huang Dunsan.[98] Zuozhou was one of the early developers of mechanized pumping, using the money he and his brothers had inherited to form a contract pumping firm with Lai Mingxing.[99] He also joined the ranks of older salt developers like Li Jingcai, Wang Hefu, Fan Rongguang, and Yan Xinshe, traveling to Shanghai and Hankou to purchase machinery and tools used at the wells and market them at a profit at the yard.[100] In the early 1920s Xiong was among the first to follow Zhang Xiaopo's lead and drill wide-diameter rock-salt wells.[101]

We no longer have a record of all the wells with which Xiong was involved. Not all of his business activities were linked to Hou, Luo, and Luo. However, by the early 1930s these four came together in a number of ventures, some of which were jointly invested and managed and some of which were managed separately but were linked through purchase of each other's brine, use of Hou Ceming's pipe,[102] or other business ties. In addition to a number of gas wells,[103] Xiong and the others each opened salt wholesale firms that were jointly managed. In 1936, with Hou, Luo, Luo and others, Xiong opened the Qianfuxiang to attempt to break the Huai salt monopoly in Yichang and Shashi.[104] And with the improvement of the market in the 1940s, Xiong joined Hou and the others in consolidating their investments under a vertically integrated management structure. At its founding the Tongxinghe well and furnace management office (*Tongxinghe jingzao banshichu*) provided centralized financial and production supervision for five brine wells, three gas furnaces (with approximately 340 pans), two coal furnaces, one salt wholesale company, and a newly founded modern chemicals factory. It also undertook unified purchasing for all Hou, Xiong, Luo, and Luo assets. At the same time, each of the four continued to engage in ventures outside the group, including Hou Ceming's investments in native banks, Luo Xiaoyuan's Zhengde well and furnace management office (*Zhengde jingzao banshi chu*), and Luo Huagai's Jihua furnace management office (*Jihua zao banshi chu*).[105]

Luo Xiaoyuan began his career as a white-collar employee of the Wang Sanwei trust. His father, a salt wholesaler in nearby Leshan, is said to have interceded on behalf of the Wang Sanwei trust in a lawsuit filed against them by fellow merchants in Nanxi County. The relationship of friendship cemented between Luo's father and the Wangs enabled Luo to apprentice at the Wang Sanwei trust, where he remained as a manager until 1928.[106]

Luo Xiaoyuan's first venture into private enterprise involved a scheme to loan money to businesses and individuals dealing with the Wang Sanwei trust. Starting with little capital of his own, Luo formed a traditional group loan association known as a *hui*. For 10 months the 10 members of the *hui* each put up 10 taels for a total of 100 taels. Every month a different member of the *hui* had use of the 100 taels put up that month. Once one borrowed the 100 taels, one would also put up a certain amount of interest in the subsequent months during which the *hui* was operational. Thus the first person to take the money paid the highest interest and the last to make use of it paid no interest at all. Luo, as the founder of the *hui*, took the first month's accumulation and, with the addition of a small nest egg from his father, began a number of business projects. These included rental of a gas well and development of the Rizheng furnace with Wang Gengyu and others, investment in the Tongshengmei money shop founded by Yu Shuhuai, and the formation of the Dashengxiang salt wholesale company with Wang Gengyu, Yu Shuhuai, and Niu Jigao. The Dashengxiang and a second salt-marketing firm founded with two acquaintances from Leshan did not last long, and with the closure of the Rizheng furnace Luo was left only a modestly well off man.[107]

In 1916, with the restoration of Sichuan's markets in Huguang, investment in the wholesale marketing of salt once again became an avenue to wealth. Luo Xiaoyuan and Wang Gengyu borrowed money and bought

10 *zai* of salt that they shipped to Chongqing. Luo's share of the profits from this small transaction was 1,600 taels, and with it he invested in the Baoshengrong money shop. In partnership with other merchants, he began shipping rice and broad beans from the production regions to the yard. That same year, on a trip home to Leshan for the funeral of his father, Luo decided to form another marketing firm with the dual purpose of providing a much-needed vehicle for the remittance of funds within the Chongqing-Leshan-Zigong triangle and to take advantage of the triangular trade among these three commercial centers. With Feng Shusen and Zeng Hanzhang he formed the Hengfengyu company, with branches in Leshan, Chongqing, and Ziliujing. It shipped Leshan silks and white wax to Chongqing, cotton yarn from Chongqing to Leshan, and Leshan silks to Zigong.[108] According to Luo himself, both the highly speculative nature of the business and low initial capitalization led to failure of the firm. A last-ditch effort to save the Hengfengyu by borrowing money to smuggle opium from Leshan to Chongqing also resulted in disaster when the bags became wet and the opium was ruined. One partner, Zeng Hanzhang, committed suicide under the pressure of debt, and Luo himself fled to Lezhi, where he worked as a clerk in the local salt tax offices of Wutongqiao, Lezhi, and Tuqiaogou.[109]

Luo's questionable dealings resulted in his dismissal from the Wang Sanwei trust in 1917.[110] In 1920 Wang Rudong took over leadership of the Wang Sanwei trust and invited Luo to return. In addition to his job for the Wangs, Luo turned once again to private investment at the yard. In partnership with men like Wang Yecong (of the Wang Sanwei trust) and others, he built up his holdings in gas wells to over 80 pan units. At the same time, he, Wang Shouwei (of the Wang Sanwei trust), Pan Xiaoyi, and others invested 15,000 yuan in two steam engines from Shanghai and entered the business of contract pumping. Once again, the cash-poor Luo Xiaoyuan resorted to the traditional *hui* to raise the 1,000 yuan needed to obtain his share in the new enterprise.[111] In 1925 the Zhengxiong well in which he and a group of partners had invested exploded, and lack of funds to rebuild the derrick and drill led to its closure as well. Another drilling venture was also closed for lack of funds, and in 1927 a partnership to operate the Tongxin pipe and its gas was closed when its brine and gas supplies declined.[112]

Luo Xiaoyuan tried throughout the 1910s and early 1920s to make his mark by developing new salt resources. After the explosion of the Zhengxiong well he decided that the way to wealth was to rent already operating wells and furnaces. While continuing to keep his hand in the wholesale trade, buying and selling hemp, bamboo, lumber, oil, rice, and other items needed at the yard, Luo Xiaoyuan formed a partnership with Zeng Shaobo and the then head of the Wang Sanwei trust, Wang Shouwei. Together they

rented a total of 15 pan units of gas. With the price of salt temporarily rising, they were able to make a substantial profit, and it is on the basis of this
investment that Luo's fortune was finally made.[113]

Following his departure from the Wang Sanwei trust, Luo took over as
manager of the Datong pipe, now under the joint control of the Chongqing-
Shashi credit group and the Wang Sanwei trust.[114] At the same time he,
Huang Zidong, and Xie Huanzhang formed the Yuminxin furnace and
rented 27 pan units of gas from the Jinhai well. Moreover, with investments
from friends and fellow managers at Wang lineage operations, Luo founded
the Liqun native bank in Ziliujing. Like the native banks to be discussed in
chapter 10, the Liqun profited largely by making purchase loans to wells
and furnaces and providing them with needed supplies of rice, oil, and so
on. With the profits from the bank, Luo expanded his holdings in salt production with the purchase of approximately 100 new shares in four Zigong
furnaces.[115]

By 1927 Luo Xiaoyuan was still no more than one of many entrepreneurial small investors who made their way by scrambling from deal to deal,
many of which failed due to shortages of funds or uncertain markets in early
Republican Sichuan. Much of his success was the result of access gained
through his ties to the Wang Sanwei trust, which was on its last legs by the
end of the decade, and to his ability to use the resources of the Liqun bank
to invest in other ventures.[116] It may have been as a member of the native
bankers' association that Luo first came to know Hou Ceming.[117] And it was
as a result of his long experience at the Wang Sanwei trust that he established a strong relationship with the Chongqing-Shashi credit group, which
controlled much of the trust's remaining assets.

The youngest of the Xiong, Hou, Luo, Luo group, Luo Huagai was born
into a poor lower-gentry family in nearby Jianyang County, his father having
passed the *shengyuan* exam during the late Qing.[118] While working at an
uncle's medicine shop Luo Huagai was brought to the attention of an agent
of Wang Hefu, whose duties included buying goods in Jianyang for Wang's
wells and furnaces. On the recommendation of the agent, Luo Huagai received an interview with Wang and at the age of 17 became an apprentice at
Wang's corporate headquarters, the Zhongxingxiang.

Unlike Hou and Xiong, Luo Huagai was neither an innovator nor a risk
taker. He does not appear to have had any significant investments at the
yard before launching his collaboration with Hou, Xiong, and Luo. Com-
ing from a gentry family, Huagai was probably better educated than most
apprentices and certainly very hard-working, as evidenced by his rapid rise
within Wang Hefu's organization. Before finishing his three-year term of
apprenticeship, Luo Huagai was promoted to cash clerk, from which posi-

tion he rose to assistant accountant, accountant, and then head accountant, ending his career at Zhongxingxiang as its general manager by the time of Wang Hefu's death.[119] In gratitude for his role in negotiating the settlement with Wang Hefu's creditors following his death, Wang's relatives gave Huagai six shares in the Juyuan well and over 24 pan units at the Jusheng gas furnace. These assets formed the basis of Huagai's entry into the ranks of Zigong businessmen.

❖ ❖ ❖ ❖ ❖

How was it that in a matter of a decade these four men went from such humble beginnings to the pinnacle of power and wealth at the Furong yard? And what can their story tell us about the transformation of the business environment in the twentieth century? Of course, luck had something to do with their success. One thing that their stories make clear is that Zigong was awash in business opportunities ranging from small commercial ventures to the purchase of industrial shares. Investment in a well that came in could change one's fortunes overnight. However, none of these men hit a gusher until long after their position at the yard was established.

The most important factor in their individual and collective success was their opportunity to work within the large lineage-based firms before the latters' demise. These men went from management to ownership and represent the nineteenth-century change in business structure that introduced career managerial staff to coordinate the assets of increasingly large firms.[120] It was as managers that they learned the business and acquired contacts among salt merchants and manufacturers and the men who supplied the city with consumer and producer goods. Moreover, as the large lineage-based firms declined, these men were able to use their relationships with the firms themselves literally to pick off their still profitable assets as the foundation of their own business empires. Luo Huagai had virtually no business assets before he assisted in the dismantling of Wang Hefu's Zhongxingxiang. Luo Xiaoyuan traded on his position within the Wang Sanwei trust to take rebates from suppliers and is said to have made loans with trust cash in his charge. While still employed by the Wang Sanwei trust, Luo entered a trade partnership with the representative of the Chongqing-Shashi credit group dealing with the trust's debts,[121] and with money put up by his father he entered a furnace partnership in which one of the partners was Wang Xunjiu of the Wang Sanwei trust. Luo entered into several other deals with members of the trust, including a furnace in partnership with Wang Shouwei,[122] and parlayed his position at the Wang Sanwei trust into partnerships with Yu Shuhuai to supply goods at the wells and later to ship salt during the period of the free market. When the Wang Sanwei trust finally leased out its assets to cover its debts, Luo took over management of the Datong pipe.¹²³ Hou Ceming's role as manager of the *daguang* at Hu Tiehua's Jicheng gas well was a source of considerable prestige and profits for Hou's native bank, and when Hu was forced to divest himself of his own holdings Hou was able to lease Hu's Tongxin pipe. Only Xiong Zuozhou does not appear to have had insider access to the salt empires he and his partners would someday replace.

Each of these men also developed a variety of networks through which they advanced their business interests, raised money, and protected themselves from the insecurities of doing business in warlord-period Sichuan. Luo Xiaoyuan was a devoted Buddhist and held a high post in the Zigong Buddhist Study Society. He was also a member of the Buddhist Jingang Study Society, which met in members' homes on a rotating basis on the first and fifteenth of every month.¹²⁴ Hou Ceming was a member of the Elder Brother Society (*gelao hui, paoge hui*) from his early days in the retail trade and is said to have been a sworn brother, among others, of the prominent banker Ni Jingxian.¹²⁵ Although we have no evidence of Xiong Zuozhou's religious commitments, his father's dedication to the Catholic Church and the continued commitment of his relatives suggests that he, too, was able to combine faith with an opportunity to build relationships of trust that served him in his business dealings.

For men who came to the yard as outsiders, relationships of trust developed through associational behavior would have played an important role in enabling them to participate in and develop deals of their own. The Catholic Church, Buddhist associations, and the Elder Brother society each provided an alternative sense of kinship and fostered strong obligations of mutual aid and commitment by members to each other. One mechanism for such mutual support was the revolving credit association (*hui*). We have already noted Luo Xiaoyuan's use of *hui* to raise money to lend out at interest and to invest in the purchase of steam pumps. When Hou Ceming became manager of the Jicheng well, he used a *hui* to raise the surety he was required to deposit with the well's owners.¹²⁶ While much of the literature on rotating credit associations deals with third world populations excluded from borrowing from formal lending institutions,¹²⁷ *hui* could also provide capital for men like Luo and Hou, whose only tangible asset at this stage in their careers was their dense networks of personal ties.

In addition to religious and symbolic associations, these men were deeply involved in the political and parapolitical world of their day. Whereas their predecessors became partisans in the competition among rival militarists, utilizing their warlord ties to consolidate their power within business circles, Xiong, Hou, and Luo Xiaoyuan appear to have amassed political capital by operating within the business community itself. The one exception to this strategy was a brief flirtation with the left wing of the Guomindang by Luo Xiaoyuan and possibly Hou Ceming, when in 1926 the party attempted to establish a foothold at the yard in preparation for the Northern Expedition to unify China against warlord power.[128] With party support Hou Ceming and his sworn brother Ni Jingxian, among others, joined in the formation of a party-sponsored mass organization, the Merchant's Association (*shangmin xiehui*), which apparently disbanded after Chiang Kai-shek's attack on the Guomindang left in 1927. Whether or not this association helped bolster their influence among their fellow businessmen, by the end of the decade all four were playing an increasingly prominent role in formal and informal advocacy for merchant interests. At the urging of the Chongqing-Shashi credit group, which, like Luo, had invested heavily in gas evaporation pans, Luo Xiaoyuan joined and became one of the representatives of a newly formed furnace merchants' association. In this capacity he led furnace merchant resistance to the formation of the Rock Salt Brine company organized by Li Jingcai.[129] All four men participated in lobbying against the "designated merchant" system of wholesale salt marketing established in 1930 under Liu Xiang's chosen salt controller Wang Zuanxu, making the rounds between Chongqing and Chengdu to lobby the financial and political leaders of the province in support of the salt merchants' cause.[130]

Although the influence of the Guomindang in Sichuan remained weak until late 1932, some components of its policies for reorganization of society and the economy were carried out even at a distance. In winter 1930 the national government promulgated its new Chamber of Commerce Law as well as a law governing the founding and administration of industrial and commercial trade associations.[131] Hou Ceming, Luo Huagai, and Xiong Zuozhou served on the committee charged with the reorganization of the Zigong chamber, and in 1931 Hou and Ni Jingxian became members of the chamber's standing committee.[132] In 1932 Hou was elected the body's chairman. And in January 1933 Xiong Zuozhou was elected by the standing committee to head the chamber's important Office of Dispute Arbitration.[133] Around the same time Luo Xiaoyuan was elected head of the East Yard (Ziliujing) Furnace Merchants' Association. After his retirement from this position Luo won the leadership of the newly organized Furong Certificate Salt Shippers Merchant Trade Association.[134] And in 1937, on the eve of the War of Resistance against Japan, Luo Xiaoyuan, in addition to his other positions around the yard, won election to the chamber and to its standing committee.[135]

The importance of political and parapolitical activism to success at the yard can best be understood in the context of the challenges that faced participants in the salt industry during the interwar years. That men like Wang Hefu and Zhang Xiaopo asserted their influence through association with leading militarists reflected both the latter's greater power during the first two decades of the Republic and the former's own history as participants in the anti-dynastic struggles of the early twentieth century. The cohort of Xiong, Hou, Luo, and Luo, still only modestly successful in business, was largely barred from the game of politics during these years. Establishing their reputations during the 1920s through audacious business practices and defense of merchant interests against shifting warlord regimes, they were able to solidify their political influence through leadership in the business associations sponsored by the Guomindang in the 1930s and 1940s.

In chapter 9 we will return to the Furong saltyard in the early twentieth century and examine some of the key events that shaped the business choices of these two generations of salt producers. In the process, we will revisit some of the most controversial issues in Chinese economic history: the role of culture, competition, and the state in the formation of business practices.

9

Politics, Taxes, and Markets:
The Fate of Zigong in the Early Twentieth Century

IT IS no accident that our discussion of merchant business practices during
the Qing period made little reference to politics. The cultivation of political capital by eighteenth- and nineteenth-century Zigong businessmen was
limited in both its geographic range and its institutionalization. Sponsorship
of merchant militia and local academies provided an important context for
the solidification of local elite ties. These same organizations served as the
rubric for occasional and short-lived efforts to promote merchant interests
with the salt administration. Extraprovincial merchants had their guildhalls,
such as the Shaanxi guildhall, which still dominates the old part of the city
(see illustration 9.1). These continued to play an important role in the promotion of parochial interests, but were not matched by similar collectivities
that could act for the local entrepreneurs who increasingly dominated the
saltyard economy. Until the turn of the century, the most important institutions, at the yard were the lineage trusts and their countinghouses. And
the most important venues for political consultation in Zigong, as in most
Sichuan cities, were the teahouse and the house of pleasure.

This relatively undifferentiated political landscape was to change dramatically at the turn of the century. The changing technology of salt production
was one factor in the rise of new political configurations. The breakdown
of integrated firms provided the context for the first specialized trade associations for furnace merchants, well merchants, and vendors of various
yard supplies. External politics was the next factor to have an impact on the
institutions of the saltyard community. At the instigation of the imperial
government in Beijing, both Chengdu and, rather belatedly, Zigong estab-

ILLUSTRATION 9.1 The Shaanxi Guildhall Today Houses the Zigong Municipal Salt Industry Museum
Photograph by Akiko Nakano.

lished Chambers of Commerce. Almost immediately thereafter, the saltyard became drawn into the politics of the 1911 Revolution. The response of the business community to the changing political environment was remarkable for its swiftness and for the degree of independent political initiative it displayed. The founding of the Zigong Provisional Local Assembly provides an important example of local civic mobilization during the transitional period between the Wuchang Uprising* and the solidification of central government authority, such as it was, in 1914. Nevertheless, the activities and interests of both the chamber and the assembly are clear evidence of the rather narrow business orientation of even these important media for political expression. And the inability of the merchant community to resist the dictates of the state alerts us to the rather weak development of civil society in these early years of the Republic.

The rapid onset in Sichuan of what we now call warlordism created special conditions for the merchants of Zigong. It is to the effects of warlord-

---

*Beginning on October 10, 1911, the Wuchang Uprising marked the onset of the revolution that overthrew the last imperial government of China.

ism on merchant fortunes, business practices, markets, and politics that we now turn. As already noted in chapter 8, warlordism was a factor, but only one of many, in the decline of the large lineage-based firms founded in the nineteenth century. It was more important for the way it shaped business practices in the twentieth century, encouraging clientelism and injecting new uncertainties into business decision-making as a result of the rapid turnover of Sichuan's local military rulers.

1911 and Zigong Self-Government

By early 1911 dissatisfaction with the Manchu government of China had affected people of every class and status group and could be found in almost every province. While often inchoate and by no means the product of a distinct revolutionary movement, anti-Qing feeling was strong enough for a minor uprising in October of that year to set in motion the collapse of a political edifice that on and off and in different forms had ruled China for more than 2,000 years. For most historians the proximate cause of the dynasty's final collapse was the movement in opposition to the state's nationalization of China's infant railways. In Sichuan the Railway Protection Movement (*baolu yundong*) was sufficiently strong to precipitate riots in the provincial capital so large that they required the transfer of New Army troops from Hubei to quiet the unrest in Chengdu. Less well known is the degree of antigovernment feeling in Sichuan generated by frustration with imperial salt administration. Smaller saltyards driven out of the salt market by policies seen to favor more efficient yards like Furong and Jianwei had long since become centers of anti-Qing agitation and recruitment sites for White Lotus and Boxer rebels.[1] Late Qing policies regulating salt taxation and distribution in Sichuan helped extend dissatisfaction to the merchant community as well. In 1903 this resentment intensified when Guanyun (official transport and merchant sale) was extended to include the Sichuan domestic salt market in addition to the markets for salt in the border provinces. According to S.A.M. Adshead, "By 1911 the unpopularity of the salt administration was second only to that of railway nationalization."[2]

Scholars of modern China have found it very difficult to gauge the political attitudes of local elites during the last years of the Qing. As a group the leaders of local communities do not seem to have turned away from the imperial state until the final days of 1911, when it was clear that a change would take place and the expedient course would be to find a place within it.[3] The Zigong elite were no exception. Despite their anger at government salt policies and the fact that some had lost money on railway bonds when the Sichuan–Hankou Railway was nationalized, there is little evidence of their participation in revolutionary politics prior to late 1911. Only a handful of locals appear to have participated in the formation of the Railway Protection Comrades Association (*baolu tongzhihui*) or its military incarnation, the Comrades Army (*tongzhijun*).[4] Zhang Xiaopo was the only important member of the business elite with a record of participation in the Revolutionary Alliance (*tongmenghui*), although a number of local degree holders harbored revolutionary sympathies.[5] Hu Tiehua's experience in Beijing brought him into contact with reformers like Liang Qichao. Collaboration between members of the revolutionary movement and the Elder Brother Society holds open the possibility that other members of the elite with secret society ties may have supported overthrow of the dynasty as well. Nevertheless, it was not until the Comrade Army unit based in Rong County moved to challenge the Qing at Gongjing that the saltyard was formally drawn into the revolution.

The Rong County revolutionaries declared independence in late September 1911.[6] Soon afterward they formed their own military unit, which was active throughout the counties of southern Sichuan surrounding the Furong yard. According to participants in the revolution, the unit made contact with members of the local elite in Gongjing, including at least one we know to have been a large owner of black-brine wells, Huang Yushu.[7] However, it was not until early November that they made their first attack on Zigong itself. The Qing military presence in Ziliujing and Gongjing was large, consisting of local militia, county troops, and security forces under the jurisdiction of the Guanyun bureau, and this first contact between anti-dynastic forces and the state at the saltyard ended in the rebels' defeat.[8] However, as province after province declared its independence, the ability of the Qing to hold its army and bureaucracy together declined. By the end of the month Zigong, like many other places, was without a government or a security force. Angry mobs and former Qing troops attacked shops and banks and throughout the province raided salt administration treasuries, warehouses, and en route shipments of salt. With all authority gone, those left to manage local affairs freely raided government stores of salt *lijin* taxes, while merchants found ways not to pay the *lijin* they owed. The salt merchants themselves faced looters and extortion from whatever group momentarily held power in their midst.[9] Thus, even before the fate of the dynasty was settled, the chaos of revolution created burdens to be borne by the salt industry for years to come. As Zhang Xi put it in 1912, "Not a day goes by when the old merchants do not cry out their distress within the halls of the salt administration."[10]

For the business community the fall of the Qing clearly meant the hope of an end to rising salt taxes and restrictive marketing policies and the opportunity to govern their own community. Although their dating of events is sometimes implausible, Lin Yuecong and his fellow memoirists have no doubt that among the first demands of the local elite once the Qing assistant magistrate fled was the abolition of the Guanyun administration and the establishment of a deliberative assembly.[11] During the last years of the dynasty, self-governing (*zizhi*) institutions had been authorized by the state as part of a process of constitutional reform designed to strengthen the state through the mobilization of elite participation in the governing process. The formation of deliberative assemblies, limited in membership largely to degree-holding members of the local population, had given members of the state-sanctioned elite at the county and provincial levels some experience in the collective management of local affairs, albeit within the strict confines of imperial bureaucratic governance.[12] The privilege of forming such councils had not been extended to a place like Zigong, which had no standing within the Qing bureaucratic structure.[13] In addition, its territory also cut across two county jurisdictions. Nevertheless, almost as soon as the Qing authorities vacated the yard, members of both the degree-holding and merchant elites participated in the formation of a self-governing body that would restore order and civilian rule to what they clearly saw as a unified political entity.

The lack of controversy accompanying the establishment of the Zigong Provisional Assembly (*linshi yishihui*) suggests that even on the eve of the founding of the Republic there was a consensus on who represented the interests of the saltyard elite. Liu Yuecong and his co-authors recall a suggestion by one of the advisers to the revolutionary army that first occupied Zigong to call a meeting of the yard leadership to declare independence. Following the meeting at the Temple of the Well God, Wang Hefu invited the participants to a feast at his Baoxinglong salt company at which the idea of a provisional assembly was first raised.[14] The provisional assembly itself was founded on December 30, 1911.

With 20 representatives from Gongjing and 40 representatives from Ziliujing, the composition of the assembly reflected the relative population and affluence of the two sectors of the yard. Of the members we can identify, between 19 and 22 held Qing *shengyuan* degrees and at least two held higher degrees within the Qing examination system. Another eight had studied in Japan or at one of China's new modern schools.[15] Salt businessmen like Wang Enpu, Wang Tiesheng, Wang Zuogan, Wang Wenqin, Zhang Xiaopo, and Chen Xiangtao also held important positions in the assembly, although in the absence of a complete membership roster identifying business as well as educational status, it is difficult to gauge the relative power of businessmen versus literati elites. Indeed, if anything, the composition of the new provisional assembly was living proof of the interpenetration of elites in Zigong. Chen Xiangtao, the assembly's first chairman, was originally from Yibin and was perhaps the only member of the assembly who held the highest degree (*jinshi*) in the old imperial examination system. His credentials for this position, however, included more than his experience as a former Qing local official. Chen was also in the salt business in Zigong.[16] The vice-chairman was Wang Enpu, a member of the powerful Wang Siyou lineage, while his fellow lineage-man and assemblyman Wang Zuogan had recently returned from studying in Japan. At least two other members, Wang Yulin and Wang Yuhuai, were also related to the powerful salt lineage.[17] In March 1912, when the provisional assembly was made permanent, Wang Enpu became chair, and another powerful businessman, from the Gongjing side of the yard, Liu Jingxian, became vice-chair. The rest of the membership remained largely the same.[18]

The organizational structure created by the founders of the assembly reflected their intention to establish themselves as a general government for the territory covered by the saltyard. A 12-man standing committee guided overall policy. Day-to-day administration was managed through three departments (*bumen*) and four administrative sections (*ke*). How they differed in their relationship to the assembly is not clear. The three departments were Investigation, Documents and Correspondence, and Business Affairs. The four administrative sections were Education, Finance, Salt Administration, and Transportation. In addition, the assembly voted to establish a local administrative office, a militia office, a local court, and a local procuracy.[19] The importance of the salt industry to the assembly's agenda is clear from its organizational structure alone. A glance at the leadership within the departments confirms this view. According to Lin Jianyu, who was given access to the surviving records of the assembly, Wang Wenqin of the Wang Sanwei trust served as head of the Salt Administration section, Wang Hefu was head of the Finance section, and the vice-head of the Transportation section was the lower-degree holder and rising well and pipe entrepreneur, Zhang Xiaopo.[20]

The Zigong local assembly issued hundreds of proclamations during its less than two years in existence, reflecting at least on paper a mature understanding of the demands of modern government. The Record of the Proceedings of the First Month of the Southern Sichuan Zigong Provisional Assembly makes clear that one of the main goals of the assembly was to restore public order and encourage the resumption of business. For this purpose it called for the establishment of a genuine people's militia and a militia bureau to be controlled by the assembly. The assembly also called for the rehabilitation of business, not only as a means to improve the economy of the yard, but also as a way to reduce the disorder that resulted from unemployment in the wake of the revolution. Taxes were to be lowered and a variety of customary fees eliminated. Like many local Chinese reformist governments in the early twentieth century the assembly also called for measures to regulate opium addiction, prostitution, and other social ills. And in an effort to foster community trust, it pledged openness in its fiscal dealings and its commitment to using revenues for the public good.[21]

Although the Zigong local assembly represented an important moment in the development of a nonofficial voice in Zigong public affairs, its achievements during its two-year life span were few. The rapid movement of military units into and out of the yard made the task of maintaining public order and civilian governance difficult. Moreover, for much of its existence the assembly appears to have been caught up in a struggle to give substance to political unification through the creation of a new county with Zigong at its center. The battle to create Xinhe County was waged on two fronts and provides considerable insight into the politics of the assembly itself. Xinhe was to combine pieces of four surrounding counties, Fushun, Rong, Weiyuan, and Yibin. The proposal was submitted to the Sichuan provincial assembly as well as to a meeting of representatives of the relevant counties early in 1913. In May, the Zigong assembly elected Liao Zekuan and Liu Jingxian to represent it when the provincial assembly convened in July. Lobbying on both sides of the issue was fierce. Representatives of the affected counties opposed the loss of territory, particularly rich tax-producing land. A militant anticounty faction from within Zigong, led by Li Jingcai, opposed the power that a new administrative unit would give to rival businessmen like Wang Enpu.

In the end the plan for political consolidation of the Furong yard failed. The territories that would have made up the new county remained under their original jurisdictions. A civilian administrator answerable to the provincial government was chosen from among the members of the local assembly. And in late 1914 both the administrator and the assembly were abolished and assistant magistrates were once again posted to Ziliujing and Gongjing, each under his respective county government.[22]

Salt Administration During the Warlord Years

For the business community in Zigong, the fall of the Qing meant the opportunity to sell salt in a free market unfettered by the constraints of the imperial salt gabelle. The Zigong local assembly represented an alliance of

Zigong degree holders and Zigong's most powerful businessmen. During the first two years of the Republic both groups labored to remove the restrictions they perceived as limiting the ability of Zigong's salt industry to expand. Two influential bureaucrats who held high positions within the Sichuan salt administration, Lin Zhenhan and Deng Xiaoke, most vigorously promoted the interests of salt producers. The greatest monument to their efforts was the publication of *Essentials of Sichuan Salt*, issued in 1914 and in a revised edition in 1919.

In addition to statistics on the salt industry, its manufacturing techniques, taxation, and markets, Lin and Deng, in their role as lobbyists for salt administration reform, produced a series of policy papers published as part of *Essentials of Sichuan Salt*. Most important among these was Deng's "Vigorous words on leaving office in the salt administration" (*Lici yangzhengbu zhishu*).[23] In it he attacked the high taxes recently levied on salt and advocated what he saw as the Western "enlightened" practice of nontaxation of essential consumer goods. Given the need to tax salt under the conditions of fiscal crisis prevailing in China, Deng advocated a low tax designed solely to obtain revenue. He was particularly vehement in his condemnation of the notion of *siyan*, or smuggled salt. Pointing out that under present conditions the term "smuggled" referred not to any criminal act such as theft or tax evasion, but most often to the sale of salt outside designated sales areas, he made a strong plea for open markets in this vital commodity. Rather than milk the merchant and destroy the industry, Deng called for a policy of nourishing merchants to increase their income and the volume of tax derived therefrom. Such a policy would allow only a single salt tax, at the point of production, leaving all other aspects of manufacture and commerce to conform to the demands of the market. Reform would also require a simplification of salt regulations and elimination of the separate rules governing salt sold by certificate and by ticket.

Advocates for Sichuan salt producers also suggested investments to broaden the range of manufactures and the uses of salt and salt by-products. Among the most interesting were Lin Zhenhe's proposed programs to expand the market for Sichuan brine by developing chemical, pharmaceutical, military, and agricultural applications of saltyard technology. These included the use of salt and salt by-products in animal feed and the development of Sichuan's sylvite and potassium resources.[24] One indication of the toll that warlord rule would take in Sichuan was the failure to implement any of these proposals prior to the end of the Second World War.

The political decentralization brought on by the 1911 revolution exacerbated the already severe fiscal problems that had faced the late Qing state. Salt as a stable source of central government revenue became a primary target of a state that exercised little control over land and commercial taxes. Deng Xiaoke was able to put some of his ideas into practice as the newly appointed head of the Sichuan salt administration. By December 1911 he had eliminated designated sales territories and replaced the old certificate and ticket systems with a single tax paid at the yard by the merchant purchasing salt for sale.[25] For a short time tax rates were lowered as well and, with the exception of *lijin*, which was critical to local administration, the levy of fees and surcharges was banned. Moreover, the institution of a uniform tax on salt produced throughout Sichuan gave the more efficient producers of Furong salt an added advantage in the domestic Sichuan market.[26]

This system remained in effect for only two years. In 1914, China's salt revenues were pledged toward repayment of President Yuan Shikai's newly negotiated £25 million Reconstruction Loan from a consortium of Western lenders. A new Sino-foreign bureaucracy known as the Salt Inspectorate was established to operate alongside the Chinese salt administration. Its role was to rationalize salt tax collection and guarantee the flow of salt taxes into the foreign banks that administered China's national loan and interest repayments. According to item five of the Reconstruction Loan agreement, "The Chinese government shall establish a Salt Administration Office (*yanwushu*) in Beijing, under the head of the Ministry of Finance. Within the Salt Administration Office a General Inspectorate shall be established, under the leadership of one Chinese and one foreign officer."[27] These two men, in principle of equal rank, were in charge of all reports, records, taxes, and allocation of certificates and tickets. The power of the foreign inspector was extended in the 1914 regulations to the operation of the General Inspectorate. He was made an adviser to the Salt Administration Office, and the head of the administration office was required to consult with him on all important matters, including the operation of the salt administration and its reform, salt revenues, and the hiring and firing of salt officials.[28]

The General Inspectorate was authorized to set up branch inspectorates under joint Chinese and foreign management in each salt-producing region. At first the Sichuan branch inspectorate was established at Luzhou, but was later moved to Ziliujing to be closer to the center of salt production. In 1915 a second branch was established in Mianyang to handle northern yards and subsequently was moved to Santai (see map 1). Subordinate to these were numerous sub-branches and salt collection districts. In the main sales areas, as well as important mountain passes, inspection districts (*jihe chu*) were also laid out to guard against evasion of the salt tax. A merchant wishing to sell salt by certificate went to an authorized bank and paid the certificate tax. In return he received a certificate called a *jinku dan*. The presentation of a *jinku dan* at the local branch office of the Salt Inspector-ate entitled the merchant to a permit to buy a certain amount of salt. In the early years of the inspectorate the merchant had two months from the time he purchased the *jinku dan* to arrange his financing and reach the yard at which he bought his product. When he transported his salt through a cus-toms point he also received a shipping certificate to verify that his tax was paid.[29] By increasing the number and quality of officers in the field, enlisting the cooperation of modern banks, and introducing modern methods of ac-counting and supervision, the inspectorate greatly reduced tax evasion and facilitated greater central control over the revenues produced.[30]

Despite the efforts of the inspectorate to introduce uniform practices, the details of salt administration continued to have a provincial character. In Si-chuan, where the authority of the central government was not established until well into the 1930s, both the level and method of taxation were overseen by a succession of military rulers. As S. A. M. Adshead has shown, the officers of the Sino-Foreign Salt Inspectorate were remarkably successful at maintain-ing the integrity of their administration in Sichuan, in large part because they paid out most of the revenues they collected to the military commanders of each salt district.[31] As a result, the data produced by the inspectorate and the salt administration provide a fairly accurate picture of the *official* taxes paid. However, neither the inspectorate nor the central salt administration could control the organization of salt collection and transportation or the imposi-tion of extra burdens on producers and shippers of salt.

The founding of the inspectorate was accompanied by a reorganization of the structure of tax collection in Sichuan. The free market established under Deng Xiaoke was abolished and the requirement that salt be sold in designated sales areas was restored. The justification for this return to Qing tax principles was the danger that a free market and uniform tax rates pre-sented to less-efficient saltyards. The newly appointed Sichuan salt commis-sioner, Yan Anlan, was deluged with petitions from salt producers at smaller yards complaining that their markets were being taken over by salt from Furong.[32] The organization of a Salt Industry Company by a consortium of Zigong businesses only deepened fears of Furong yard dominance.

In addition to restoring the tax structure of the late Qing Guanyun ad-ministration, the commissioner moved to consolidate marketing and limit tax evasion. Salt to be marketed within Sichuan was purchased by the salt administration directly from the furnaces and sold to merchants and ped-dlers through official warehouses. Only 18 salt companies (*gongsi*) were au-thorized to purchase certificates with which they could go to designated yards to buy salt for distribution in a specified sales territory.[33] Merchant input was limited to the establishment of appraisal offices (*pingyi gongsuo*) at major yards, the main purpose of which was to inform the salt administration of conditions of production.[34] According to the magistrate of the Santai yard, the real purpose of the appraisal offices was "to improve the mutual surveillance organizations [*baojia*], investigate the wells and furnaces for tax evasion, examine actual levels of production and prohibit smuggling."[35]

Yan Anlan's program lasted about a year. Objections came from many quarters. Zigong merchants opposed the monopoly control exercised by the salt wholesale companies, arguing that the price they received for their salt was affected and that they were themselves squeezed out of certificate-based commerce in salt. The need to bring together large amounts of capital three times a year for the salt sales season suggests that many of the wholesale companies were composed of investors with access to capital in Chongqing.[36] It was also feared that large companies would be more risk averse under the dangerous conditions prevailing in Sichuan than would be local merchants carrying smaller shipments. This latter concern seems to have been borne out by a decline in salt revenues collected under Yan's leadership.[37]

In 1916 the system of taxation and sales initiated under Deng Xiaoke was restored with the exception that salt from specific yards had to be sold in specified sales territories. Salt wholesale companies were abolished, and the market was opened to all who wished to pay the tax and buy and ship salt. Moreover, in order to reduce the competitive advantage of wealthy wholesalers, the new system eliminated the requirement that a wholesaler purchase the large quantities of salt authorized by a certificate, allowing even small quantities of salt to be moved by ticket. And although designated sales territories still existed, merchants were given a choice of destinations so that disruptions to one trade route could be overcome by selling elsewhere.[38]

While the salt administration still complained of merchants paying taxes to sell salt in low-tax areas and then selling in high-tax areas, overall the system worked well. The most persistent problem facing Sichuan's salt administration was the effect that warfare had on shipments to Sichuan's border markets and to the designated market in Hubei. The Yangzi was often impassable, and a merchant could find himself sitting with a shipment of salt for months, unable to reach his destination. According to the *Sichuan Salt Administration History,* the leaders of the Sichuan and Yunnan armies active in southern Sichuan had even established protection bureaus in Ziliujing and Chongqing, charging merchants 600 yuan and 300 yuan, respectively, per *zai* of salt to guarantee safe passage, only to dun merchants again once they were on the road.[39] As a result, Huai salt was moving into Sichuan's long-distance markets.

Despite these problems, between 1916 and 1920 the salt gabelle in Sichuan remained relatively stable. Salt taxes continued to be collected as described above. In 1918 a system of power sharing was established among the military garrisons in Sichuan. In an agreement signed by the inspectorate and General Xiong Kewu, except for the costs of operating the salt bureaucracy, all salt revenues were to be turned over to the heads of the several garrisons.[40] In addition, though the inspectorate continued as an independent bureaucracy, the government of Sichuan now appointed the salt commissioner. Beginning in 1920 the truce that existed over salt broke down and control of salt revenues became part of the booty over which Sichuan's militarists fought. By 1921 the salt administration itself became a regular target. Moreover, whereas the salt administration staff had previously been appointed by the central government, even if revenues were never remitted to Beijing, now each commander filled local posts with his own men and kept the money raised for his own coffers.[41]

The effect of these changes to the salt administration was to further intensify the demands placed on salt producers and merchants to supply the military with cash. As the source of more than half of Sichuan's salt, Zigong became a particular target of warlord activity. In 1923–1924 salt revenues at Zigong and Chongqing were partially commandeered and merchants were forced by invading troops of the Guizhou army to turn over indeterminate amounts of money.[42] To meet their needs for revenue from Zigong, Sichuan military commanders established a system of contract merchants (*baoshang*) whose role appears to have been that of tax farmers. In 1930 contract merchants were replaced by a reconfigured system of monopoly merchants, many of whom were friends or relations of the military commanders.[43] It was not until 1934, and the institution of Guomindang rule in Sichuan, that spokesmen for the Zigong salt producers were able to convince the new provincial government to abolish restrictions on who could market salt.[44]

Calculations of Sichuan salt tax collected provide little insight into the impact of salt taxation on the industry. The *Sichuan Salt Administration History*, published in 1932, provides Furong's tax quota for each of its markets as set in 1915 (see table 9.1). Tax per certificate was set at different rates, and certificates entitled one to sell different quantities of salt in each market. However, on average the tax per 100 *jin* of salt in the Huguang market was 0.625 taels, while the tax in the remaining markets ranged from 1.375 to 1.50 taels per 100 *jin*. Moreover, converting all land-route certificates to sale by ticket eliminated the differential that had existed in the Qing between water-route and land-route certificates.[45]

How close did the salt administration come to collecting the quotas set under Commissioner Yan in 1915? At first glance, the correlation appears very close indeed. Table 9.2 summarizes the taxes collected in both the cer-

TABLE 9.1 Furong Certificate Tax Quota by Market (in taels)

Market	Total Tax Quota
Huguang	618,750
Ji'bian	457,995
Renbian	463,775
Foubian	394,840
Yongbian	200,880
Lunan	487,220
Fouwan	247,670
Quhe	386,100
Total	3,257,230

Source: Wei Wu, ed., *Sichuan yanzhengshi* [Sichuan salt administration history]
(China: Sichuan yanzhengshi bianjichu, 1932), juan 8, pian 4, zhang 2, jie 2,
11b–12b.

tificate and ticket markets. Since there was no quota for ticket sales we can compare only the data for revenue collected on salt sold in certificate markets. While the original tax quota was set in taels, the longitudinal data on tax revenues collected are presented in yuan, which became the dominant unit of account in the Republican period.[46] Assuming the exchange rate remained stable between 1915 and 1916, the total tax collected in certificate markets that year, 4,755,556 yuan, would have closely approximated the original quota. Moreover, although there are quite considerable fluctuations in the absolute level of taxes collected, in only one year, 1917, did the overall taxes collected fall below that 1915 benchmark quota.

If this was so, how do we explain the perception of salt manufacturers and their representatives that conditions at the yard were declining during the years between 1916 and the start of the Sino-Japanese War? One possible explanation is that the figures for overall taxes collected represented not simply the base rate but a rising base rate and perhaps a number of additional taxes which became institutionalized during the interwar years. Then total taxes would have remained steady even if salt sold declined. This is suggested by data provided by the Salt Inspectorate in its 1933 publication *Veritable Records of the Chinese Salt Administration* (*Zhongguo yanzheng shilu*). There the regular tax rate recorded in yuan had risen dramatically over the rate set in 1915, over 600 percent for salt sold in the Huguang market and 166 percent to 182 percent for salt sold in all other markets. Moreover, included in the taxes collected are the regular tax quota, the surtax allowed by the ministry, and surtax rates agreed upon for collection by local military units (see table 9.3).

TABLE 9.2 Furong Certificate and Ticket Taxes
Collected, 1916–1929 (in yuan)

Year	Certificate	Ticket
1916	4,818,064	1,253,992
1917	4,603,348	1,188,647
1918	5,220,118	1,325,303
1919	5,225,122	1,220,181
1920	6,394,120	1,430,460
1921	4,975,600	1,557,012
1922	6,342,250	1,380,892
1923	5,794,300	1,357,101
1924	6,255,650	1,447,912
1925	4,792,600	1,490,140
1926	6,027,800	1,477,974
1927	8,197,700	1,628,872
1928	5,771,550	1,638,054
1929	6,177,000	1,686,646

Source: Wei Wu, ed., *Sichuan yanzhengshi* [Sichuan salt administration history] (China: Sichuan yanzhengshi bianjichu, 1932), juan 8, pian 4, zhang 3, jie 7, 25a–26b.

TABLE 9.3 Authorized Furong Tax Rates c. 1933 (yuan per 100 *jin*)

Market	Regular Tax	Ministry Authorized Surtax	Local Military Surtaxes	Total
Huguang	3.5	0.015	5.11	8.63
Chuhe	2.5	0.0	1.56	4.06
Lunan	2.5	0.0	1.56	4.06
Fouwan (Huguang border)	2.5	0.0	1.66	4.16
Fouwan (Sichuan border)	2.5	0.0	1.66	4.16
Jibian	2.5	0.0	1.15	3.65
Foubian	2.5	0.0	3.76	6.26
Yongbian	2.5	0.0	1.6	4.1
Renbian	2.5	0.0	0.99	3.49
Piao	2.0	0.0	0.0	2.0

Source: Caizhengbu yanwushu yanwujihezongsuo [Ministry of Finance, Salt Administration Office, General Salt Inspectorate], ed., *Zhongguo yanzheng shilu* [Veritable records of the Chinese salt administration] 2 (Taibei: Wenhai chubanshe, 1933), 891.

Finally, it has been suggested that one reason Sichuan's salt inspectors were able to fulfill their quotas throughout the warlord period was that they greatly reduced the volume of salt that was smuggled out of Sichuan or that seeped into the domestic market without paying tax. Thus, while earlier figures for salt revenues may have missed a large volume of salt that was marketed and that generated income and jobs at the yards, it is possible that the interwar figures are closer to representing actual salt sales. Both scenarios likely contributed to the continued smooth functioning of the salt administration at the same time that salt manufacturers and less privileged salt merchants felt the deleterious impact of warlord rule.

Warlordism and the Fate of the Salt Industry in Zigong

For most of the period from 1914 to 1936 real power at the yard, and in Sichuan as a whole, emanated from the barrel of a gun. If warlordism signified the continuous jockeying for control of territory and resources, then Sichuan experienced warlordism more intensely than perhaps any other province in China. From the fall of the Qing dynasty in 1911, Sichuan was the site of almost continual warfare accompanied by disruption of its once-thriving economy and an almost complete absence of unified provincial-level government.[47] For Zigong, the effects of warlordism were particularly severe. As Sichuan's great economic prize, the saltyards and the salt administration under which they operated were recurring targets of warlord advances. During the early years of the Republic, before the division of Sichuan among six main warlord factions, Zigong became a battlefield more than once a year (see table 9.4). Qiao Fu's guidebook provides a poignant snapshot of the effects of warfare in Ziliujing between 1911 and 1919. Following severe disruptions to its economy in the wake of the revolution, by the middle of 1915 the Zigong area was beginning to recover. Trade was resuming, new banks were opening, goods flowed into the city, the number of "singsong girls" was increasing, and theaters were providing much needed entertainment. And then the fighting began again:

> Banks have stopped remitting funds, salt wholesalers have stopped shipping salt, furnaces have stopped evaporating brine. Fearing the armies, messenger services and sedan-chair shops have closed their doors. For fear of conscription, coolies have run away. Because the roads are blocked there is a shortage of oil and rice. Because of banditry few goods are shipped. Theaters are not holding performances because of all the soldiers. For fear of the armies, prostitutes are pretending to reform. Because of forced contributions, the price

TABLE 9.4 Outside Military Presence in Zigong, 1911–1932

Date	Army	Commander	Affiliations
November 1911	Comrade army	Zhou Hongxun	Local revolutionaries
December 1911	Yunnan army	Qin Shengsan	
January 1912	Sichuan army	Li Biao and Long Zhuosan	Sichuan military government in Chengdu
1913	Sichuan army (1st division/2nd regiment)	He Zhongxi and Zhong Mingsan	
1914	Sichuan army (1st division)	Fang Bin (w/Zhou Zhizong and Liu Cunhou)	Sichuan military government in Chengdu
	Capital Garrison (1st battalion)	Zheng Jiting	Beijing government
1915–1916	Sichuan army (1st division)	Du Shaotang and Zhang Qingyun	Under Liu Cunhou
April–June	*Warfare between Yunnan and Sichuan armies*		
June	Yunnan army (5th brigade)	Liu Fakun	National Protection Army (anti-Yuan Shikai)
1917	Yunnan army (5th brigade)	Liu Fakun	National Protection Army (anti-Yuan Shikai)
September	Sichuan army (3rd division)	Zhang Pengwu	
	Warfare and stalemate between Yunnan and Sichuan armies		
1918	Sichuan army	Wang Weigang	
	Yunnan army	Jin Hantang	Originally under Liu Fakun
1919	Yunnan army	Jin Hantang	Originally under Liu Fakun
	Sichuan army	Zhao Zongfan	

Date	Force	Commander	Under
1920	Sichuan army (8th division)	Cheng Hongfang	
Year's end	*Yunnan army driven out of Zigong*		
1921	Sichuan army (3rd army)	Hong Yousan	Under Liu Chengjun
	Zigong Merchant Militia		
1923	Sichuan army (9th division)	Zhang Qingping	Under Liu Wenhui
1924	Sichuan army (9th division)	Zhang Qingping	Under Liu Wenhui
		Fei Dongming	Under Liu Wenhui
1925	Sichuan army (9th division)	Zhang Qingping	Under Liu Wenhui
		Fei Dongming	Under Liu Wenhui
Spring	*Warfare between armies of Yang Sen and Liu Wenhiu*		
	Sichuan army	Guo Rudong and Bai Ju	Under Yang Sen
Fall	*Warfare between armies of Yang Sen and Liu Wenhiu*		
1927	Sichuan army	Luo Zijiu	Under Liu Wenhui
1930	Sichuan army	Cai Yulong	Under Liu Xiang
1931	Sichuan army	Huang Chaopan	Under Liu Wenhui
Winter	Sichuan army	Liu Rongjiu	
1932	Sichuan army		Under Liu Wenhui
Late fall	*Liu Xiang attacks Liu Wenhui's forces in Zigong*		
	Sichuan army	Ma Yongquan and Cai Wuqing	Under Liu Xiang

Source: Chen, Kaichong et al., "Xinghai geming zhi jiefang qianxi Zigong difang zhujun qingkuang" [The troops garrisoned in Zigong from the 1911 Revolution to the eve of liberation], *Zigong wenshiziliao xuanji* 1–5 (1982): 121–31.

ILLUSTRATION 9.2 Entrance to the Sanduo zhai (fortress), 1989. Sanduo zhai was one of several fortresses built by merchants as a refuge during the rebellions of the mid-Qing dynasty and maintained by them into the twentieth century.
Photograph by Madeleine Zelin.

of pork is rising. Shops are taking down their signs and the rich are fleeing to fortresses [see illustration 9.2].[48]

The situation became so severe that banks burned their bills of exchange so they would not fall into the hands of the armies. The gentry resorted to wearing guns at their waists. Pressing the people to use military scrip, the armies punished people for using banknotes. People were shot for refusing to be impressed into labor service. Women of good families were debauched. And peddlers were even stabbed because they did not understand the dialects of the soldiers barking orders. When the head of the provincial salt administration came to Ziuliujing, he came with a capital guard.

Qiao's account continues at some length, taking us to the year his guidebook was published. As he recounts, in late 1915 General Chen Chengwu sent Liu Xingcun to be general commander of Zigong with his headquarters in the assistant magistrate's yamen. The commander of the Fifth Brigade of the Beiyang army was stationed at the Baihua market. There were Sichuan army troops at Wujia ba. The general also sent commanders to set up the first southern Sichuan army base. Despite the flood of military in the town, business was lively, until early in 1916, when the military stopped buying local goods. On May 10 the Beiyang brigade commander, Feng Yuxiang,[49] who had been stationed in Xuzhou prefecture, was suddenly transferred and passed through Zigong on the way to his new post. Large numbers of men and horses followed him, filling up all the temples in the town:

> On the 14th or 15th Fushun sent out an announcement of an emergency. All the gentry and officials telegraphed Chengdu for military reinforcements. Then we heard that the brigade commander Li Bingzhi was being transferred from Qijiang to Fushun-Zigong. On the afternoon of the 19th Regimental Commander Zhang saw them coming and he and the assistant magistrate realized they could not resist. So they went into hiding. You could hear gunfire into the middle of the night and there was chaos. Some soldiers acting on their own shot dead three members of the regiment. But they did not hurt any of the civilians. The people of Zigong were really scared. On the morning of the 20th the infantrymen stationed in Ziliujing said that Zhang had not followed orders and they elected the commander of the first battalion, Xiang Yulin, to take his place as regimental commander. Then they declared independence. In fact Chengdu had declared independence two days earlier. At this point the Bank of China closed its doors. There was no way to exchange anything for cash and no one would accept bills of exchange. That night the commander of the first regiment of the first division of the Southern army, Lei Shiruo, came to Zigong from Xuzhou. He set up his headquarters in the Shaanxi guildhall. The infantry stationed in Ziliujing was reorganized. On the 29th the commander of the Sichuan National Salvation Army, Liu Jizhi, also sent an army to be stationed in Ziliujing. Its headquarters were in the assistant magistrate's yamen. On the 30th more troops of the Southern army came. Two battalion commanders under Regimental Commander Du also brought their troops. When the Southern army arrived, soldiers were no longer allowed to walk the streets with their guns. So the town became peaceful. On May 15th we received word that commander Xiong Jinfan was also moving from Fushun to Ziliujing. The commander-in-chief of the first army left flank of the Yunnan army, Luo Peijin, was coming to Ziliujing from Xuzhou.

In June alone the Liu army was transferred to the Jiading-Meizhou region and another Southern army infantry, the fifth brigade, under Liu Fakun, was transferred to Ziliujing. This is today's Ziliujing.[50]

Qiao's account conveys the breathless anxiety with which residents of Ziliujing experienced the parade of armies through their town. Occupied first by the Yunnan army, then by the Sichuan army, by coalitions of both, and then fought over by various factions within the Sichuan army itself, Zigong's merchants experienced the full range of warlord depredations, from extortion, to kidnapping for ransom, to demands for special taxes, to outright looting and pillage of the town's fine shops and guildhalls.

After 1925, a truce between the two most powerful militarists in southern Sichuan, Liu Xiang and Liu Wenhui, brought peace to the saltyard, although the number of occupying troops was by no means reduced. Both Lius stationed armies in Zigong to protect their interest in southern Sichuan salt revenues. Each sent agents to try to squeeze additional sums from both producers and wholesalers of salt. In 1927 Liu Wenhui established the Yutong bank as a repository for salt taxes and remittances to Chengdu in the hope of capturing a larger share of this lucrative revenue stream.[51] In 1932, renewed fighting between these two powerful warlords drew Zigong once again into the center of warlord violence. Liu Wenhui's defeat provided the opportunity to completely replace his military machine in Zigong, as well as the native heads of local security units and the local militia. Liu Xiang's men remained unchallenged at the yard until 1936, when the Guomindang, which had held the central government of China from 1928, was finally able to dispatch its own security forces to this economic center of inland China.

The effect of warlord rule on the salt industry defies quantification. We would expect no record to be kept of salt looted and countinghouses raided, of surtaxes collected and merchants extorted. Just as scholars have had difficulty gauging the impact on Shanghai's capitalists of Chiang Kaishek's ascent to power,[52] we can only grope for a narrative of the environment within which the Zigong business community functioned during the warlord years.

Revenue from the salt gabelle played an important part in the ability of Sichuan's warlords to maintain their armies and stabilize their territorial positions. However, as Adshead has convincingly shown, the salt gabelle alone was not adequate to support the burgeoning numbers of troops under warlord command.[53] Unable to secure other forms of regular tax revenue, armies at every level of the military hierarchy relied on extortion, looting, and other forms of coercion to garner resources. Moreover, absent a regular revenue stream, what few local government functions were performed were paid for with ad hoc levies that soon became regular contributions, more often than not supplemented by additional gifts when budgets could not be met. Because there was no local government to speak of, levies were apportioned through the Chamber of Commerce and collected from constituent guilds. While the level of burden and the ability of the business community to bear it cannot be judged from surviving chamber records, the level of frustration created by ad hoc levies is clear.

Correspondence between the Chamber of Commerce and various local authorities about support of the Zigong police provides a useful example of the way in which local finance operated under the warlord regime. By the 1920s a police force had been created in the vicinity of the saltyard for the purpose of guarding its main access roads. A 10 percent levy on salt sales was earmarked for support of the police, with an agreement to lower the levy to 7 percent in 1922. In late 1922 the chief of police informed the Chamber of Commerce of a shortfall in his budget of approximately 1,000 yuan, urgently needed to buy winter uniforms for his men. Rather than raise the levy back to 10 percent he requested a lump-sum contribution of 1,000 yuan to tide him over into the new year. The chamber complied, and the following November the chief wrote again, this time asking for 2,000 yuan.[54] Again the chamber came through, only to receive a letter from the chief a month later complaining that the police could not pay their bills and needed the chamber to establish an office of police affairs to raise more funds. By 1926 the chamber was still fighting with the warlord regime over irregular levies for police uniforms and had refused to make any more payments until irregularities in the operations of the police force and the level of officer pay were investigated.[55]

Demands for funds were also cloaked in special fees, such as periodic fines for growing opium poppies, to which the chamber responded in 1931 that

the saltyard is long and narrow. It is no more than 12 or 13 *li* wide. The streets are filled with row upon row of houses. If there is any space between them it is wasteland, long soaked by brine. This soil is no longer suitable for growing grain. Growing poppies would be even more difficult. This is why rich and poor, everyone at the yard makes his living from pumping brine and evaporating salt. No one farms. For generations people have made their living from commerce alone. Households that make their living by manufacturing pay taxes on manufacturing. They pay these continuously, regular taxes and surtaxes. Each year these come to almost 100 million yuan.... [It is absurd] to fine yard merchants—where at the wells and furnaces are they going to grow poppies?[56]

Levies such as these constituted community extortion. Harder to evaluate is the effect of extortion on individual merchant households and firms.

Pressure came in many guises. When Fang Bin's army occupied Zigong in 1913 he accused Wang Ziheng and Wang Taozou of hiding firearms and harboring bandits. As punishment Wang lineage wells and furnaces were confiscated and sold to Fan Rongguang for about 200,000 yuan. Fan, whose family had already established itself in the wholesaling of Zigong salt, may have became a major player in the production side of the business as a result of such deals. Li Xingchao of the Li Siyou trust was also accused of opium smoking and the family fined 100,000 yuan, although local legend has it that they only paid half that amount.[57] A similar ploy was used in 1917, when the Sichuan army reoccupied Zigong and accused Wang Zuogan of collaborating with the enemy. Wang was arrested, and only a "fine" of 100,000 yuan appears to have saved him from death by firing squad.[58]

When the Yunnan army fought its way back into Zigong, these same families were accused of aiding the Sichuan army from their redoubt at Sanduo zhai. The commander of the fortress managed to escape, but the Li lineage was held accountable to the tune of 100 *zai* of salt, valued at approximately 200,000 taels.[59] By 1919 the Zigong Chamber of Commerce was appealing to the central government for assistance against Zigong's warlord governors, citing confiscation of public property, harassment of private citizens, and thefts of domestic animals. According to the chamber, over the previous eight years millions of taels in money and salt had been stolen and the people forced to exchange bullion for worthless military scrip. Wells and furnaces became poor borrowing to pay off the armies. And in the autumn of 1917, during the fighting between Yunnan and Sichuan, factories and markets were looted and burned, while goods, shops, property, and streets were destroyed at a cost of at least 2 million taels.[60]

For more than a decade after the fall of the Qing, successive warlord commanders dunned Zigong merchants for funds purportedly owed to the old Qing Guanyun bureau. Technically not a tax at all, these funds were collected from merchants who had received advances of cash for future delivery of salt to the bureau's shipping depôts and were accused of having reneged on their deliveries in the political disorder that surrounded the revolution. Merchants so charged could not prove fulfillment of their contracts because looting had destroyed the bureau's records in the months surrounding the overthrow of the dynasty. An office was established, the sole purpose of which was to collect these funds, and a special official was sent to Ziliujing to supervise the collection process. In 1921 a report by the Salt Inspectorate stated that "many merchants have gone out of business because of military demands, or have been borrowing money from the military officers at heavy rates of interest."[61] In early 1924, the head of the independent brigade of the Sichuan Bandit Suppression Army, Wang Weigang, received an urgent telegram from his superiors saying that the military was in need of funds. Wang was ordered to contact the Bureau of Old (Guanyun) Debts and charge it with the collection of 100,000 yuan. A list of delinquent individuals was sent to the Chamber of Commerce, which was given the duty of investigating the debts and ensuring that all were paid by the end of the year. The accompanying list of offenders, while possibly reflective of real arrears, was also a roster of the best targets, consisting as it did of some of the richest men at the yard: Wang Deqian (of the Wang Sanwei trust), Wang Hefu (Wang Baoxinglong), Hu Tiehua (Hu Yuanhe trust), Li Shancheng, Li Dewen (Li Siyou trust), Zhu Shanxiang (Dachuan pipe), Zhang Jiucheng, Wang Zishan, and Wang Wenkui.[62]

The warlord presence produced indirect consequences for Zigong's salt producers as well. Warfare influenced market access and appears to have affected the overall Sichuan commercial economy. During the struggles between China's northern and southern governments in the 1910s Zigong was cut off from its lucrative market in Hubei.[63] In the late 1920s, although the Hubei market had been statutorily restored, high taxes on Sichuan salt shipped to these districts discouraged wholesale merchants from purchasing salt from Zigong. Moreover, regulations lessening the time that merchants had between purchasing salt and paying taxes due in Hubei further limited the number of monopoly merchants willing to move Sichuan salt into the Huguang market.[64] And the introduction of an open market under conditions of constant warfare periodically deprived Sichuan of much of its former border market in Guizhou and parts of Yunnan.[65]

Whereas Sichuan and Hubei had worked together to maintain Sichuan's market in Huguang during the Qing, by the 1920s the configuration of warlord alliances fostered Hubei's support of increased Huai participation in their territory.[66] In 1922 an effort by a Shashi-based salt company in concert with the head of the salt administration for Hubei to bring Changlu salt into Sichuan's sales territory was blocked after vigorous protests to the central government by the Sichuan salt administration.[67] In 1923, when warfare in Sichuan blocked the shipment of salt to Huguang, Huai merchants obtained a one-year license to ship 200,000 Changlu and 200,000 Jinan certificates worth of salt to that region. An effort to extend this license for another year was obstructed by a campaign of telegrams to Beijing. However, by the end of 1924 the salt administration in the capital had granted permission for 40 million *jin* of Jinan salt to be sold in Sichuan's marketing area. The Maritime Customs Administration, fearful that such action would reduce revenues from Sichuan, limited the inflow to only 10 million *jin* and imposed a time limit of one year on each certificate. However, a Sichuanese appeal to the government in Beijing backfired and led to a repeal of the order and a judgment that Huguang was open to salt from both Sichuan and the Huai region.

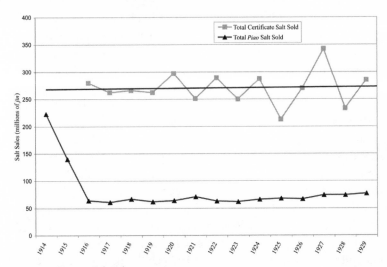

FIGURE 9.1 Furong Salt Sales, 1914–1929
Source: Based on Wei Wu, ed., *Sichuan yanzhengshi* [Sichuan salt administration history] (China: Sichuan yanzhengshi bianjichu, 1932), juan 3, pian 2, zhang 9, jie 2.

Inasmuch as southern Huai production was declining, northern Huai salt was formally authorized to enter these markets. This was followed in April 1925 by an order allowing the Huai Shipping Company (*Huaiyun gongsi*) to sell 10 million *jin* of salt from Changlu to Huguang.[68] By the 1930s advantages in wastage allowances, tax rates, and the ease of shipping by steam along the open reaches of the middle Yangzi continued to put Sichuan salt at a disadvantage.[69] Zigong was able to make up for some of its lost market by selling more salt within the domestic market, but only at the expense of less efficient smaller Sichuan yards.[70]

Figure 9.1 depicts the trend in Furong certificate and ticket salt sales after the reintroduction of salt certificates. Although there is almost no fluctuation in the sales of Furong ticket salt, fluctuation in the volume of certificate salt sales is considerable. Inasmuch as ticket salt was sold on the domestic Sichuan market and generally was handled by small merchants and peddlers, we can assume that the fluctuations in salt sales reflected obstacles to the transport of salt at long distances. The overall trend line for certificate sales is also relatively flat, which reinforces this impression. In terms of cash flow, however, the vagaries of this market affected Furong more seriously than other yards since most of Sichuan's salt exports were produced in Furong.

If we map the rise and fall of salt sales against the movements of warlord armies, the correspondence is quite close (see table 9.4). This is not surprising. Most of Furong's certificate salt moved along major roads and waterways linking southern Sichuan and Chongqing over which Sichuan's militarists vigorously fought during these years. Between 1916 and 1919 the volume of Furong certificate salt sold was relatively flat, rising again during the relative peace that prevailed in 1920 and then falling and rising during the early 1920s, reaching a post-Qing low in 1925—when military control of the yard changed hands three times—only to rise again during the ensuing stability under the command of Liu Wenhui.

As we have already noted, although the records of the Salt Inspectorate indicate that salt taxes were being collected at rates comparable to those of the late Qing, official data reveal a marked decline in the volume of Furong sales, as well as considerable excess capacity at the yard. Between 1914 and 1919 Furong produced an average of 319 million *jin* of salt per year.[71] In 1932 the compilers of the *Sichuan Salt Administration History* reported average Furong output between 1914 and 1929 to have been approximately 415 million *jin*.[72] However, the same study puts Furong's salt sales at a high of only 362 million *jin* in 1929.[73] Thus, by 1929, when salt tax revenue was on the rise, Furong was able to sell only about 88 percent of the salt it produced. Conditions did not improve in the early 1930s. According to Zhang Xiaomei, the Salt Inspectorate reported sales of Furong salt in 1933 at the lowest level since the Qing, only 281 million *jin*.[74]

The capricious nature of surtaxes interfered with trade in other goods as well. In 1925 the Chongqing salt wholesalers' guild announced that henceforth it would cease conducting trade with Ziliujing. The reason for its action was simple. Goods taxed in Ziliujing were not recognized as such in Chongqing and vice versa, with the result that merchants were double taxed and goods became too expensive to sell. Noting that such policies were carried out in total disregard for their effect on the food supply, costs of production at the saltyards, and merchants' ability to make a profit, the guild lay down the gauntlet at the feet of their warlord masters:

> We merchants have no way to continue doing business under these conditions. So we all met and decided to stop business until the warfare is over. If both sides wake up and open up the transportation routes and each recognizes the taxes collected by the other, then the producers will restore their business and there will be salt on which to pay tax. Only then will the wholesalers meet and decide to package and transport salt. Otherwise, if the government wants to commit suicide, why should we merchants sacrifice ourselves along with them?[75]

The fighting in the mid-1920s also affected Zigong's sources of producer goods. Most directly, taxes on key items could obstruct shipments into the yard. Double taxing of coal limited Zigong's supply of fuel, not only for coal-fired furnaces, but for steam-powered pumps as well.[76] More importantly, the obstruction of trade and the dangers of moving goods and money between Zigong and markets to the east dramatically raised the cost of money and credit at the yard.

The late Qing Guanyun system of official transport of salt did away with one leg of the remittance exchange, eliminating the need for transport merchants to repatriate the profits from selling salt abroad. The state paid producers in silver that was deposited in local native banks and drawn on in copper as purchases were made for materials and food required at the wells, furnaces, and pipes. Banks acquired copper through exchange by peddlers and merchants of supplies and foodstuffs and by acting as agents for these goods themselves in the surrounding hinterland.[77]

The end of Guanyun provided an opportunity for Zigong merchants to participate once more in the wholesale trade and led to a temporary boom in banking at the yard. However, the increase in military activity along the major water and land routes led the branches of provincial and national banks to close and interfered with the movement of money between Zigong and Chongqing. In 1915 both the Bank of China and the Junchuanyuan bank opened branches in Ziliujing, largely to engage in the remittance trade. These and other modern banks were all closed by 1916. Warfare also caused the collapse of many native banks critical to the provision of short-term commercial credit. In 1927 the Yutong bank was opened under the control of Liu Wenhui's 24th army as a repository for taxes and to take advantage of the possibility for profits from remittance services.[78] However, it was not until the mid-1930s that independent modern banking began to recover at the yard and Zigong was once again well serviced by note-issuing institutions.[79]

As early as 1919 complaints of tight credit and tight money were being lodged at the Chamber of Commerce. In January 1920 the suicide of a desperate Ziliujing businessman intensified public discussion of the issue. Merchants reported that, unable to get credit, "businesses are toppling and families are going bankrupt one after the other."[80] Tight credit was linked to a contraction in the money supply. Beginning as early as 1911 the armies that moved through the yard forced the exchange of bullion for military scrip and banned the use of hard currency in the marketplace or to pay taxes. As bullion was drained out of the yard, the remaining banks could no longer redeem their notes and note value rapidly declined. Many banks closed their doors and ceased providing commercial loan or remittance services. Moreover, as different armies moved in and out of the yard they brought ever new currencies, barring use of the old and making their own worth little in anticipation of its future replacement.[81]

In 1925 the Remittance Guild estimated the cash requirements of Zigong at 200,000 to 300,000 yuan a month.[82] As we have seen, remittance banks with branches in both Chongqing and Zigong provided low-cost services allowing merchants who sold salt or traded in Chongqing to draw on their accounts to make purchases or to remit cash home as necessary. Under normal conditions a balance of trade existed between the two cities that guaranteed that banks in neither had an excess of the other's notes. Thus remittance fees remained stable and merchants were easily able to calculate the costs of clearing.

By the 1920s this balance was disrupted in several ways. According to a report by the Sichuan Salt Wholesalers' Research Association dated 1925 the dangers on Sichuan roads made it difficult for both their own members and the members of the Remittance Guild to move cash between Zigong and Chongqing.[83] Merchants needing to remit profits back from Chongqing had either to take their gains in goods, which themselves were difficult to move along unsafe trade routes, or to purchase Chongqing bills of exchange. However, because of the shortage of hard currency at the saltyard, Chongqing bills could be exchanged in Zigong only at a deep discount, as much as one-third of their face value in the late 1920s.[84]

Political instability in western China also gave rise to a growing trade imbalance between Sichuan and Shanghai, resulting in mounting remittance costs between Sichuan and its main source of foreign goods. Prior to 1911 Sichuan had an export surplus with Shanghai. The excess of Shanghai bills in Chongqing meant that a Shanghai note for 1,000 taels was discounted to as low as 950 taels in Chongqing.[85] During the early years of the Republic continuous unrest resulted in a steady decline in Sichuan exports to Shanghai and a consequent reversal in the balance of trade. According to the General Inspector of Customs in Shanghai, high taxes also hindered trade with Sichuan, causing exporters in Yunnan, Shaanxi, and Gansu to bypass Chongqing and move their goods via the Han River to Hankow or directly to Shanghai.[86] As a result, Shanghai, held an excess of Chongqing notes and was buying them well below par by 1924.[87] Between 1929 and 1931 speculation in Shanghai bills of exchange increased, and following the Japanese invasion of Manchuria and later of Shanghai, it became almost impossible for Sichuanese to conduct business within the Shanghai money market.[88] We have no firm figures on the impact of the new terms of trade at Zigong. However, as steel cable and machinery from Shanghai came to constitute a growing proportion of Zigong's fixed capital costs, the rising price of money and disrupted access to this market must have contributed to the declining profits about which Zigong's businessmen increasingly complained.

TABLE 9.5 Basic Commodity Prices in Ziliujing, 1915 and 1919 (in copper cash)

Item	Unit	Price in 1915[c]	Price in 1919[c]	% Increase
Silver	1 yuan	1,500	2,300	53
Rice	1 dou	1,850	3,000	62
Rape oil	1 jin	140	280	100
Kerosene[a]	1 vat	2.75	4	45
Tong oil	1 jin	160	320	100
Coal	100 jin	1,000	2,000	100
Pork	1 jin	148	340	130
Beef	1 jin	172	300	74
Coarse cloth	1 bolt	3,450	6,850	99
Raw cotton	1 jin	645	1,600	148
Buffalo[b]	1 high quality	45	75	67
Broad beans[b]	1 shi	4	5.85	46
Sedan chair bearer	Wage/station	900	1,500	67
Salt evaporator	Wage/month	4,000	5,000	25

[a]Price quoted in yuan.
[b]Price quoted in taels.
[c]Where a price range is given, the average price is recorded.
Source: Zhenhan Lin, *Chuanyan jiyao* [Essentials of Sichuan salt] (Shanghai: Shangwu yinshu guan, 1919), 597–600.

Trade disruptions also led to inflation. We have only sporadic price data for Zigong during the period under consideration. Table 9.5 gives some sense of the rapidity of rising prices in basic food and producer goods. Unit prices are given in copper cash unless otherwise indicated. We have 1932 price data for only a few items. According to the *Sichuan Salt Administration History*, the ratio between silver yuan and copper cash was 1:2,000 in that year. However, the price of rice had risen to 2,000 cash per *dou* and tong oil, a key component of well tubes and pipes, was selling for 400 cash a *jin*. Indeed, the only commodity that seems to have fallen in price by 1932 was coal, which was selling at about 900 cash per 100 *jin*, a price most likely reflecting the depressed state of the salt market and the overproduction of both gas and brine.[89]

Finally, tight credit was most clearly manifested in the difficulty manufacturers experienced in obtaining capital, both to cover problems of short-term liquidity and to improve their operations. Tightening credit was not directly linked to the flight of modern banks, most of which did not make loans to local industry. As we have seen, most capital in Zigong was raised by the sale of investment shares, and infusions of working capital, when needed, were largely obtained through shareholder assessments. However, by the 1920s, owners of productive assets, such as wells and furnaces, appear to have been caught in a trap in which costs were rising, investment capital was drying up, and industrialists needing cash, even for operating expenses, were forced to turn to high-interest short-term loans. Early in 1925 the Chamber of Commerce declared a moratorium on the collection of interest payments. However, by June it received a petition from 18 Furong furnaces requesting help again:

> The salt industry is stagnating, prices are too low and we are forced to sell cheap. Our losses are great and our [debt] burden increases. Moreover, all of our credit is obtained from the marketplace. The greater our debt becomes, the higher interest rates rise. This is the way it is in business and need not be discussed further. But although our saltyard is a commercial center, because of its special characteristics, credit in our area is very different from that in other commercial centers. When interest rates are low they are around three percent. When they rise, they can go as high as seven or eight percent and you still cannot find any money to borrow. Moreover, you are expected to pay the first interest payment in about a half a month. Otherwise it becomes part of the principal and subject to interest.... We know that [short-term loans] are like drinking poison to ease our thirst. Originally we had hoped that when conditions improved we could quickly pay them off. But they keep building up, and we cannot pay them off.[90]

Without funds to evaporate salt, they had no salt to sell and could not pay off their debts. The furnace owners urged the chamber to appeal to the provincial government for relief. While officers of the chamber promised to do all they could, the tone of their reply makes it clear that there was little else they could do.

As early as 1922 a report by the Salt Inspectorate noted that "the rich Szechuan salt merchant is a rarity today, a large proportion of his money having passed into the hands of the military officers; or it might be said that the military officers are becoming rich salt merchants."[91] Faced with rising taxes, declining markets, rising costs, and tight credit, Zigong's salt manufacturers developed a number of strategies for survival. The elaboration of civic roles and civic institutions played an important part in maintaining business assets, as did an intensification of business and political networks.

The Zigong Chamber of Commerce

The disbandment of the local assembly left Zigong businessmen with only one institution from which to collectively defend their interests. The Zigong Chamber of Commerce originated as a branch of the All Sichuan Chambers of Commerce, founded under imperial auspices only eight months before the outbreak of the revolution. Unlike the local assembly, its members were drawn entirely from the business community and, not surprisingly, were dominated by representatives of salt well, pipe, and furnace interests.[92] Like the local assembly the chamber also acted in the name of both the east and west yards, and as such was the one institution that continued to represent both Gongjing and Ziliujing.

Chambers of Commerce played an ambiguous role in early Republican politics. Composed of representatives elected by the various guilds within a city, they were elite bodies by definition. Chambers of Commerce were never autonomous, and during the 1930s they came increasingly under the grip of the "partification" policies of the Guomindang.[93] However, as the only broadly representative nongovernmental organ in Republican China, chambers came to play a variety of roles in defense of community interests.

The organizational structure of the Zigong body was relatively simple. In addition to its guild representatives, the chamber had a chair and a vice-chair, a standing committee, and four departments: Accounting, Business Affairs, Documents and Correspondence, and Arbitration.[94] During the two decades between the founding of the Republic and the consolidation of Guomindang power in Sichuan, it was the Chamber of Commerce that stood as best it could between the merchant community and the demands of warlord tax collectors. It was the Chamber of Commerce that managed local relief efforts and kept local order through its merchant militia. And it was the Chamber of Commerce that, albeit with only partial success, became the voice of Zigong salt producers relentlessly pressing their cause with the Chinese salt administration. Officers of the chamber were unpaid, and its total budget never exceeded 10,000 yuan.[95] However, from a position as chairman of the chamber or of its arbitration board one could influence the outcome of negotiations with the authorities or the results of litigation among businessmen. Thus, within the relatively narrow political universe of Zigong, a position within the chamber became a source of considerable prestige and at times of real power.[96]

The chamber wielded its greatest influence from within the offices of the Arbitration Board. Individuals and firms could bring a case directly to the board; cases were also referred to the board by the civil courts and other government agencies.[97] Some cases involved straightforward contract disputes, such as failure to vacate a well on expiration of a lease, that could also have been dealt with in the courts. However, the board played a special role in more complicated cases, particularly those that involved the interpretation of customary law, relations among guilds, and bankruptcies involving large numbers of creditors. For example, in 1912 the board ruled against a single shareholder who had failed to consult with other shareholders before disposing of well property, noting that proper procedures among shareholders had not been observed.[98] In early 1932 it settled a dispute between the Liquor and Foodstuffs Trade Association and the Oil-Tobacco-Hemp Trade Association over division of responsibility in the payment of the Tobacco and Liquor License Taxes that cut across their arenas of business.[99]

Of the approximately 58 cases brought before the board in 1932, at least 12 involved debt and requests that the board assist in the development of a payment plan.[100] The most famous instances of board arbitration of disputes between debtors and creditors were those involving Wang Hefu's Zhongxingxiang company, the Li Siyou trust, and the Wang Sanwei trust. An announcement midway in the Zhongxingxiang case provides clues to the exhaustive procedures followed in such matters as well as the personal familiarity that must have prevailed among members of this business community:

We find that previously we called a meeting of all the creditors to discuss a solution with regard to the case of the Zhongxingxiang's debts. The debts had to be classified and representatives of the creditors had to be elected to take part in the investigation and discussion, to examine and verify and rank the debts. Then on the 4th and 9th of this month we called meetings to discuss classification [of the debts] and decided that the first group of debts [to be paid] would be those owed the government [including] the most recent brine and salt payments, the monthly fee for support of orphans and widows and most recent transactions such as wages for workers, and so on. In the second rank were placed short-term loans and transactions from this year. In the next rank were put long-term loans and transactions from past years. We find that although these rankings have already been agreed upon and tabulated, until we check them one by one we do not know the nature of each of these debts, whether they are as they are claimed, and whether among the creditors there are any with special circumstances who have raised objections.[101]

Once this process was completed, the board announced it would hold two more meetings and then compile a register in which all debts would be listed and ranked. All with creditor relationships to the Zhongxingxiang were notified to show up at one of these two meetings before noon to check the register for accuracy and their position in the payment schedule. If they had no objections, they were to indicate their agreement by signing the register next to their names on the list of ranked debts. Anyone who disagreed with the list could register his objection next to his name and his concerns would be discussed later that day. If any issues remained unresolved, the chamber would hold an open forum to complete the process. As we have already seen, the board's procedures worked well in this case, and all Zhongxingxiang debts were cleared within a year. However, some problems, among them the Wang Sanwei trust's debts to the Chongqing-Shashi credit group, occupied the energies of the chamber for years.

The record of the chamber, in its role as intermediary between the state and the business community, can be characterized as consistent but mixed. Chambers throughout China found themselves in the uncomfortable position of being a convenient agency through which government in its many manifestations could press its demands. We have already seen that Sichuan's warlord authorities used the Zigong chamber to funnel merchant contributions to their armies and to discipline chamber members.[102] However, the stature of the chamber and its members was also served by strong stands against such demands, as when it resisted surtaxes and the collection of "old Guanyun bureau funds."

Despite its willingness to go head to head with the rulers of Sichuan, at least in a war of words, the chamber had little power to change the conditions affecting the Furong yard. The extent to which its members served at the will of outside powers became clear in 1928 when the new Guomindang central government, now in alliance with Liu Wenhui's 24th army, ordered the reorganization of the chamber and new elections for general members and committee chairs. Under the new structure the chamber elected a 25-member executive committee, which in turn elected a smaller standing committee. The members of the latter were also named heads of the chamber's new departments—Education, Propaganda, Organization, Arbitration, Accounting, and General Affairs. Little changed within the chamber's structure of power. In 1929 Li Jingcai was elected the head of the new Zigong City Chamber of Commerce, and among his standing committee were the powerful Wang Hefu and Hu Tiehua.[103]

In 1930 the Guomindang promulgated a new Chamber of Commerce Law and an Industrial and Commercial Trade Association Law that required the reorganization and registration as trade associations (*tongyehui*) of all former guilds. It was trade associations, and in some cases individual shops, that would constitute the membership of the new chamber. Formation of the new chamber was in fact delayed by the difficulties many guilds had in drawing up regulations and transforming themselves into modern trade associations. In 1930 the roster of new trade associations included: East yard furnace merchants association; East yard well merchants association; West yard furnace merchants association; East yard well merchants association; East yard warehouse merchants association; West yard warehouse merchants association; Ziliujing boat merchants association; East yard furnace merchants piao salt association; Mountain products and sauce and pickle shop merchants association; Butchers association; Medicinal herbs merchants association; Gaotong coal merchants association; Pipe merchants association; Zigong salt company; East yard well company; East yard furnace merchants salt-manufacturing company; West yard furnace merchants salt-manufacturing company; Satin and silk guild; Millet and grain guild; Bamboo guild; Pawnshop guild; Labor contractors guild; Paper guild; East yard coal-burning furnace guild; West yard coal-burning furnace guild; Lumber merchants guild; Tobacco guild.[104] Familiar names among the newly elected representatives of these organizations were Xiong Zuozhou, Luo Huagai, Hou Ceming, Hu Tiehua, Li Yunxiang (later to head the chamber and hold a position in the judiciary), Zhu Ziyan (a powerful wholesale merchant originally from Jiangjin County), Ni Jingxian (prominent banker and sworn brother of Hou Ceming), and Yan Xiangyang and Yan Xinshe (of the Yan Guixin trust). Most striking is the absence of the various organizations that had represented modern bankers, native banks, and remittance services, all of which had been devastated during the 1920s.

In the shakeup of the 1930s the influence of the old turn-of-the-century elite appears to have been broken. Li Jingcai was ousted from power, and although Hu Tiehua continued to serve as a delegate his influence appears much reduced. In their manifesto of early 1931, the newly installed delegates to the chamber reflected upon the political chaos in which they operated and lamented the fact that the old chamber had been little more than a office for adjudication of disputes and an agent to raise money and corvée labor for the government. Pledging themselves to help improve conditions in the industry that dominated the city and its several hundred thousand inhabitants, the members of the chamber took an oath to strive together with the national government to pluck out corruption and those lacking in real commitment.[105] Despite their show of loyalty to the Guomindang and to Guomindang rhetoric, in December 1932 they received orders from the prefectural and provincial governments to reelect half their membership by the end of the year. In the new chamber class, up-and-coming businessmen like Yu Shuhuai gained seats, and Hou Ceming of the Hou, Xiong, Luo, Luo group was elected chamber chair.[106]

Industrial Wars and Saltyard Decline

The Guomindang reorganization of the chamber was part of a general effort on the part of the new regime based in Nanjing to manage the institutions of civil society and wrest control of civil affairs from the military regimes at whose sufferance it ruled China. It was also an expression of the party's ambition to squeeze out any Communist influence among reformist elements in the ranks of labor and business. However, Zigong was becoming a poor prize for the Guomindang and its warlord competitors. Weak markets and the dominating output of a few rock-salt wells meant economic catastrophe for both producers and their labor force. The process by which nonworkers' guilds were restructured into trade associations was telling of conditions at the yard, marking in organizational form the growing fragmentation of interests between Ziliujing and Gongjing, between producers and wholesalers, and between well owners and furnace owners. Zigong's economic decline was dramatically played out in the late 1920s and early 1930s as both manufacturers and workers struggled to deal with new economic circumstances.

The Great Brine Glut

The biggest challenge facing the owners of salt wells and furnaces was to deal with what later commentators would call the great brine glut of the late 1920s. For the first time since the 1850s Furong had more brine than it could profitably turn into salt. Excess brine output was a result of many factors. The first, as we have seen, was the enormous increase in productive capacity unleashed by the development of rock-salt brine wells using mechanized pumps. The far greater efficiency of these wells, as well as the drying up of earlier yellow- and black-brine wells, had already lowered the number of wells in production. However, a decline in the number of wells was not an indication of decreasing capacity to produce brine. Bankruptcies in the early 1920s were the result of declining demand for salt and rising costs brought on by inflation and the high cost of credit. The real indicator of Furong's decline was the falling number of pans being fired, rather than the number of wells in operation. Whereas the salt administration recorded 10,329 pans in 1916, only 8,055 were recorded in 1929.[107]

Overcapacity and falling demand led to declining prices for brine even as prices for basic producer goods and food were rising. While workers did not feel that wages kept pace with inflation, the fact that most workers received food on the job meant that rising rice prices affected costs of production as well. The price of brine was determined by its concentration, the cost of transportation to the furnace, and the going rate for processed salt. The price of brine appears to have fluctuated between 0.6 and 0.8 yuan per *dan* during the 1910s, reaching a high of 0.82 taels during the first selling session of 1922 and dropping to 0.7 in the second. By 1923 brine could be had for 0.642 taels.[108] In 1924 the bottom fell out of the brine market. The officially quoted price continued to be 0.69 taels throughout the year. But Chen Zhongxuan's Xianhai well and the wells belonging to Wu Zonghan were selling brine as low as 0.33 taels per *dan*. Both men were forced to cease operations, as the price they had received did not allow them to cover their production costs. According to records examined by Lai Mingqin, some wells were accepting as little as 0.2 taels per *dan*, one-third of what they had received two years before. By 1925 the average price of brine stabilized at around 0.472 tael per *dan*. However, some wells were known to barter their brine for oil, hemp, rice, and even iron from damaged saltpans.[109] In an effort to boost the concentration of their brine and increase the sale price, some well owners even resorted to irrigating their rock-salt wells with yellow and black brine.[110]

The struggle to survive under new political and market conditions exacerbated tensions within the industry itself. We have already seen that the new technology of mechanized pumping had created a new player in the salt industry, the owner-operator of mechanized pumps. Many of these were associated with furnaces, creating a sharp division between producers of brine and producers of salt. This division was reflected in the new civic organizations that emerged at the yard and in the appearance of organizations specific to producers in Gongjing, where gas wells were concentrated, and Ziliujing, with its higher number of brine wells. In 1926 Fan Rongguang, one of the new generation of salt producers and a pioneer in the use of steam pumps, attempted to bring together owners of rock-salt brine wells to market their brine collectively and strengthen their bargaining power with Furong's furnace owners. His initial effort was not a success, and after two months of soliciting participants to join his own Tongsheng and Tongyong wells, he gave up. In 1927 the idea was taken up once again. This time the brothers Yan Xinshe and Yan Xianyang elicited the help of Wang Hefu, the influential well and furnace owner and head of the main rock-salt well irrigation firm. Together they set up the Rock Salt Well Agency (*yanyanjing banshichu*). Wells that joined the agency agreed to sell their brine collectively. Wang Hefu acted as manager, assisted by Yan Xianyang. Their main responsibility was to arrange contracts with furnaces, guaranteeing a market and a reasonable price for their brine. At the same time they encouraged voluntary production cutbacks in order to drive up the price that furnaces had to pay for brine that was extracted.[111]

The Rock Salt Well Agency survived for almost three years. During this time it was able to obtain an average price of around 0.7 yuan (or 0.5 taels) per *dan* for those owners whose wells were enrolled in the scheme. In addition, the agency contracted loans from large Chongqing credit institutions and reloaned the money to member wells with financial difficulties but less ready access to distant sources of funds. In the end two interrelated factors brought about the demise of this first attempt at cooperative marketing at the wells. First, considerable tension was created among the membership when weaker wells defaulted on loans and repayment fell to the collective as a whole. At the same time owners of more productive wells and firms with both brine wells and furnaces tired of voluntary limits on output. Men like Zhang Xiaopo and Wang Hefu continued throughout the life of the cooperative to independently market some of their brine.

Brine producers whose operations could not sustain falling prices turned to another of the new leaders of the saltyard elite, Li Jingcai. As we have seen, Li, like Wang, fell within the category of transitional leaders. A close friend of Wang Hefu and Hu Tiehua, Li nevertheless derived much of his influence from his warlord connections. One of his closest contacts within the warlord camp, Zhang Fuan, was in control of Fushun County at the time. With Zhang's assistance Li was able to win the support of the head of the Sichuan salt administration in issuing a directive requiring all rock-salt brine wells to join the new Rock Salt Well Brine Extraction company (*yanyanjing cailu gongsi*).[112]

The Rock Salt Well Brine Extraction company operated as a cartel. Member wells continued to function as independent firms, holding shares in the company based on their output potential determined at the time of the company's formation. The Rock Salt Well Brine Extraction company set production ceilings and established a system of alternate pumping to limit overall output. Brine was then pooled and marketed by the company, which also arranged cooperative irrigation of wells to cut down operating costs. Individual wells took their profits as dividends on their shares, with extra payments made to those wells that continued to pump.[113]

Not everyone at the yard was happy with the arrangement. Alternate pumping led to large-scale layoffs of well workers and was one of the issues prolonging worker unrest at the yard.[114] The activities of the cartel also ate into the profits of furnace owners and contract pumpers. The Chongqing-Shashi credit group, which held most of its assets in furnace shares, also had much to lose if the Rock Salt Well Brine Extraction company continued to control the market in rock-salt brine.[115] Wang Hefu, whose fortune rested largely on gas wells, furnaces, and mechanized pumps, and Hu Tiehua, with large gas well holdings, also opposed the company. Together these powerful furnace interests supported opposition by a coalition of small and middling furnace owners, including Luo Xiaoyuan, Yang Xiaofang (a member of the staff of Fan Rongguang's Tongdexiang company), Liao Shuqing (a middling furnace owner), Chen Jieyu (a manager working for Hou Ceming), and Wang Jiliang. The coalition, led by Luo Xiaoyuan, began with a political campaign, contacting by letter and telegram leading figures at the local and national levels in government and the salt administration.[116] They also moved to undermine the basic premise of the cartel, control of brine supplies. In the name of their newly formed Equal Benefit group (*junyi tuanti*) member furnaces collectively entered into three-year-term contracts with small- and medium-output wells, promising a minimum purchase price of 0.52 yuan per *dan* for a fixed commitment of brine.

Among the wells that signed with the Equal Benefit group were Niu Jicheng's Jiangliu well, Wang Yongzhi's Ruhai well, and Wang Mutao's (Wang Hefu's nephew) Jiangyuan well, none of which threatened the cartel's market control. However, when Yan Boshi, a member of the powerful Yan Guixin trust and one of Zigong's most powerful mechanized pumping contractors, decided to allow his highly productive Tongchuan well to sell directly to the Equal Benefit group, Li Jingcai mustered all his political resources to stop him. For violating the order that all rock-salt brine wells join the cartel, Yan Boshi was thrown in jail and an injunction was issued against his pumping firm forbidding him from engaging in brine extraction lest his firm supply brine pumped from other wells. Unfortunately for Li Jingcai, by the end of the 1920s the forces within the warlord regime upon which he relied were trumped by those of associates of the furnace group. While Li had the support of Fushun-based Brigade Commander Zhang Zhifang, the Equal Benefit group had Liu Runqing, the Chongqing-Shashi credit group manager at the Wang Sanwei trust and a close friend of the southern Sichuan garrison commander Cai Yulong.[117] After hearing the appeal of the Equal Benefit group, Cai ordered Yan Boshi released and his pumping business restored; after wiring for permission from his superiors, he disbanded the Rock Salt Well Brine Extraction company.[118] In an effort to maintain the livelihood of brine producers Cai also ordered a 0.52 yuan floor on all brine purchases, matching the offer made in the contracts signed by the furnace representatives.[119]

The struggle over the Rock Salt Well Brine Extraction company was a vital turning point in the careers of several Zigong businessmen. Prior to 1929 Luo Xiaoyuan was just one of many struggling furnace owners seeking to establish himself during difficult economic times. His role in the battle with Li Jingcai gained him prestige that soon situated him among the major players at the yard and appears to have influenced his ability to make the deals that later created his fortune. The Rock Salt Well Brine Extraction company affair benefited other participants as well. Wang Yongzhi, who remained a relatively small investor in salt assets, was soon elected to the Chamber of Commerce and later tied with and then defeated Hu Tiehua for a seat on its standing committee.[120] Liao Shuqing appears to have improved his position as an investor in the 1930s and Chen Jieyu also held a number of positions within the reorganized Chamber of Commerce.[121]

Despite their shifting fortunes, furnace owners were soon forced to face the fact that without some form of price controls the brine industry would collapse and their own fortunes would be dragged down as well. In August 1929, at the behest of brine-well interests, the newly appointed Sichuan salt controller, Guo Changming, agreed to come to Zigong to investigate conditions at the wells. Following his visit he announced a plan whereby both well and furnace owners would be organized into marketing cooperatives designed to cope with some of the repercussions of declining markets and high productive capacity.

In place of the Rock Salt Well Brine Extraction company, Guo Changming authorized the organization of a new Rock Salt company (*yanyan gongsi*). All wells were required to join and receive a share in the company based on their output at the time of the company's formation. In order to produce salt as cheaply as possible, wide-diameter wells that produced less than 8,000 *dan* a month and narrow-diameter wells that produced less than 5,000 *dan* a month were retired and their shareholders granted a fixed payment of 100 yuan per month for the life of the company. Wells whose yields exceeded this amount were paid an extra 200 yuan for every 1,000 *dan* in excess of the quota that they contributed each month. The company as a whole bore the cost of pumping. The Rock Salt company took sole charge of marketing the brine produced at the yard. After deductions were made for the costs of production and the standard payments to each well, any additional profits were divided among the members according to their shares. The corresponding organization governing the activities of evaporating furnaces was the Ziliujing Salt Manufacturing company (*zhiyan gongsi*), headed by Luo Xiaoyuan. The company had sole authority to buy brine from the wells. As such, it held the balance of power at the yard. The salt administration required that the price of brine be pegged to the market price of salt, but the company determined how much brine could be purchased and thereby determined how many wells would remain in production.[122]

The problems faced by Zigong salt producers in the late 1920s were not unlike those faced by manufacturers in refining and distilling elsewhere at similar stages in the development of their industries. The introduction of new, relatively simple improvements in production technologies that resulted in rapidly rising output often led to plummeting prices. In the 1870s, the Standard Oil Company, the largest U.S. oil refiner, attempted to create a cartel within which oil refiners would cut back on output and control prices. This initial National Refiners Association failed, in large part because it could offer no incentives to free riders who chose to take advantage of the price rises induced by voluntary output limitations. The cooperation of smaller oil refiners was ultimately achieved through the offer of reduced shipping rates on regional railways to those who joined the Standard Oil cartel. In addition, John D. Rockefeller and his associates purchased sizable holdings in former competitors within the new Standard Oil group, ensuring their effective control over member firms.[123]

In the case of the Rock Salt company no attempt was made to purchase shares in rival wells. Instead, incentives were offered to compensate wells, in the form of payments calculated to reimburse them for the net value of the brine they did not pump, much as some American farmers are paid not to grow crops on rich farm land. Wells with complete production facilities were paid 600 yuan a year not to pump brine, and those wells that would have required some work to go into production were paid half this amount. Owners of wells with low output but whose investment in machinery and other equipment would have allowed operations under conditions of greater demand for brine were given 100 yuan in compensation each year for shutting down. In theory, this system of shares and subsidies allowed the well-owning community to make the most efficient and cost-effective use of the resources they had developed.

Soon after the founding of the Rock Salt company, conflicts among well owners began to threaten its survival. The main source of contention was the criteria by which wells were deemed inefficient. Productive capacity was established on the basis of inspections undertaken in the winter of 1929 and after examining production records kept by the wells themselves. Neither could accurately reflect a well's true capacity. Inasmuch as rock-salt wells had no brine as such, the season in which they were irrigated was a key factor in determining their output. Measurements taken in winter, when the water level in Zigong is low, led to complaints by many owners whose wells were deemed below standard. Other owners, including Li Jingcai, claimed that records kept by wells could not be taken as an indication of capacity because output had already been cut back in response to low prices and high production costs. Many well owners insisted on higher base payments to reflect what they held to be true normal output. At the same time, those owners whose wells were earmarked for closure worried that their wells would collapse and their equipment rust if not used. If the Rock Salt company went bankrupt or a rise in demand made it no longer necessary to limit output, they would be left without subsidy or a well to pump.[124] Moreover, under the new system a large producer with both wells and furnaces was prevented from benefiting from his investment in vertical integration by circumventing the Rock Salt company's restrictions and evaporating his own brine.[125]

The well owners who opposed the new system filed suit against the Rock Salt company, first with the salt controller, and then with the Ministry of Finance in Beiping, under which the salt administration of the whole country was supervised. In the end, the system of selective pumping was abandoned and a program of rotating production, which included many inefficient wells, was instituted in its stead. The name of the company was changed to the Xin District Rock Salt Well Brine Pumping company (*Xinqu yanyanjing cailu gongsi*). Following approval of its regulations by the salt controller, it began operations in May 1930.[126]

The General Strike of 1928

Mechanization at the Furong saltyard replaced buffalo with machines. The gradual phasing out of yellow- and black-brine wells for more productive rock-salt wells reduced the number of workers at the wells, in large part by reducing the number of wells in production. As the well and furnace owners toiled to find a way to cut back supply without bankrupting their members, the number of workers employed at the wells continued to decline. Whereas we have calculated that over half a million people were directly employed at the yard during the late Qing, labor statistics compiled in 1931 indicate only 215,661 men in all categories of work.[127] For the same year the *China Daily* (*Zhongguo ribao*) reported that unemployment at Zigong was above 300,000.[128] However, salt production still relied largely on human labor to build and maintain the wells, pipes, and furnaces; man the pumps; and evaporate, wrap, and transport the salt. Wages made up a large part of operating costs and were the one line on manufacturers' balance sheets that was somewhat under their control. As food prices rose and increasing numbers of workers were laid off, how to deal with the saltyard labor force became a challenge equal to that of fending off the demands of one's opposite at the wells or the furnaces.

As we have seen, skilled workers at Furong had been organized since the nineteenth century, and several actions by workers for higher wages anticipated the discontent that would erupt in 1928. In 1915 the makers of bamboo cable in three counties joined in a strike for higher wages that appears to have ended in victory for the workers. Citing rising prices, these members of the Qiaosheng hui stopped work at least two more times between 1915 and 1923 in order to extract concessions from the factories that supplied the Furong yard.[129] In 1917 a strike by salt evaporators, whose highly exclusive workers' guild was one of the most powerful of the surviving nineteenth-century workers' associations, resulted in a 20 percent raise for this skilled workforce.[130]

Each of these labor disputes was finally settled by means of negotiations between the workers' guilds and the Chamber of Commerce. Although workers' guilds were not represented on the chamber they were often invited to meetings to work out labor disputes. It was clearly with an expectation that meaningful dialogue was possible that 45 well drillers petitioned the chamber to intercede on their behalf in June 1927. They began by noting that commodity prices and the price charged by manufacturers for salt had risen in recent years, but they had not had a wage increase for some time. In the most deferential language they made their case, imploring "the honorable Chamber of Commerce to expand their broad benevolence and generous virtue and approve our plea to slightly increase the wages of workers in consideration of the livelihood of our families, fathers, elders, wives, and children."[131]

In a note at the bottom of their letter, the chamber secretary acknowledged the accuracy of their claims about rising prices and forwarded the petition to the whole chamber for discussion.[132] However, the well merchants' association rejected the workers' claims on the grounds that they had struck earlier in the year and already received adequate increases. Moreover, they confirmed the well drillers' claim that other workers at the yard, including evaporators and cable makers, had also received raises in response to rising prices in basic goods.[133]

Well drillers did not have a powerful organization behind them, which may explain why they felt left behind by the gains other workers had made. However, the expansion of the well drillers' strike into a general strike that lasted for almost two months can only be explained by the overall decline in conditions at the yard. Although salt manufacturers were never voluntarily generous with their workers, all of the incidences of worker job action for which we have documentation were settled within several weeks through the auspices of the Chamber of Commerce. Moreover, documents collected by the Zigong archives and the Zigong General Labor Association demonstrate that earlier initiatives taken for higher wages by more powerful workers' organizations generally resulted in across-the-board increases in response to inflation. This did not happen in 1927 and 1928. Furong salt sales dropped dramatically in 1925 and 1928. As we have seen, by the beginning of 1927 salt producers were combining their resources to maintain the price of salt in the face of a declining market for brine. Driven by a collapsing credit market and continued warlord pressure for taxes, salt producers also tried to hold the line on wages. In August 1927 brine pumpers joined in their action. By the new year rickshaw workers had joined them as well.

According to Chen Ran, who had access to Zigong party archives, the transformation of the strike from one involving the weakest of Furong's workers to one involving most workers at the yard could be credited to a brief period of Communist Party activism at the yard.[134] While it appears that the party did provide leadership and organizational expertise, the gathering frustrations induced by rising prices, job losses, and the sudden intransigence of the beleaguered salt producers provided the growth medium for a crises of unprecedented proportions. Prior to 1928 the Chinese Communist Party had had little influence in Zigong. According to *Zhonggong Zigong dixia dang zuzhi gaiguang* (A Survey of Chinese Communist Party Organization in Zigong), early contacts were limited to brief visits to the city by party personnel, including organization of a Marxist study group in 1924. In 1926 the Chongqing branch of the party sent Liu Yuanxiang and Liao Enbo to Zigong to establish a Ziliujing special branch.[135] Liu and Liao made contact with workers' leaders and were therefore in a position to work with the strikers when talks with the well owners broke down. However, the Zigong party branch appears to have suffered the same repression meted out to other leftist organizations as the right wing of the Guomindang, in the course of the Northern Expedition, prepared for consolidation of its hold over the fragile First United Front.[136] Chiang Kai-shek's faction within the Guomindang was in contact with the Sichuan warlord government, and in early 1927 a crackdown on Communist operatives in that province led Zigong's small party presence to go underground.

The events leading up to the general strike are shrouded in mystery. We have no documentation of negotiations between workers and employers until January 1928. On January 30, members of the Caishen hui, an organization uniting pipe owners at the yard, reported to the Chamber of Commerce that leaders of the well workers' guild had met with a man named Liu (most likely the Communist Liu Xiangyuan) and planned a strike by mid-February.[137] In February the workers issued a set of nine demands, including the release of an arrested labor leader; medical expenses for workers injured during the strike; wages, food, and medical expenses when work was halted by management; specific wage increases for different categories of workers; and strike pay and restitution of employment for all dismissed workers.[138]

By February, what had begun as a guild strike for wages was taking on a broader agenda led by the local Chinese Communist Party. In documents relating to this strike we see the first references to a broad association of Furong's salt workers, referred to as the General Workers Association (*Zonggonghui*). Broadsides containing slogans such as "Down with white terror policies," "Down with all capitalists and large landlords," "Down with the feudal large and small warlords," and "Long live the liberation of oppressed peoples," produced by an organization calling itself the Youth Work League, were distributed to picketing workers.[139] Workers were encouraged to see themselves as part of a larger movement whose momentum the party traced to the May 30 movement of 1925.[140] Party leadership aided the original well workers and the rickshaw workers who joined them around the new year to expand their support and enlist at least the sympathy of shopkeepers, militiamen, and other workers' groups. And party support may have acted to prolong the strike by keeping up worker morale.

The strike clearly worried Zigong's salt producers. The pleas and warnings of Zhang Xiaopo, the leading Guomindang member among the well owners, reflected the attitudes of owners desperate to get their workers back on the job and frightened by the prospect of Communist organizing in their midst. As a Guomindang member Zhang had visited Wuhan, the headquarters of the left wing of the Guomindang, and knew firsthand what had happened to workers who joined the left and the Communists in the wave of strike action that accompanied the Northern Expedition. In early February he met with workers and told them:

One day the workers of every trade gloriously went on strike and the next day they demonstrated. It was really lively. Soon afterward was the Party Cleansing Movement (*qingdang yundong*). The government ordered every place to expel the Communists. The workers in each trade were out of luck. Millions of Communists were killed in Hunan and Hubei, and most of them were workers. If you do not believe me, ask our engineers who are from Hubei and they will tell you I am not lying.

Zhang also tried to divide the workers at the yard by warning that halting work at the wells would lead to unemployment of other workers whose wages were even lower than their own. And barely disguising his threats as well-intentioned advice, Zhang spoke for all well owners when he pointed out that there was no lack of unemployed men ready to take the strikers' jobs.[141]

While the local military police appears to have sympathized with the workers' plight, they could do nothing but caution the strikers to work through the Chamber of Commerce to reach a negotiated solution.[142] The southern Sichuan garrison commander, concerned that no salt production meant no salt taxes, threatened military action if the workers did not go back to their jobs.[143] Appealing to the fear of communism, the owners and the chamber continued to insist that the workers' demands went beyond the bounds of reason, and could only be the responsibility of outside agitators whose capture by the military was of paramount importance.[144]

Throughout the month of February proclamations flew back and forth between the workers, who were fixed in their demands; the chamber and owners' associations, which threatened to fire all workers who did not return to their jobs; and the garrison commands, which promised military action if the strike continued. Almost a month after the onset of the general strike, the Chamber of Commerce announced receipt of an anonymous offer from the workers to negotiate a solution to their demands. Announcing its inability to respond to a nameless correspondent, the chamber issued an invitation to the workers' guilds to send representatives to the chamber. Pressure from the salt controller may have hastened a settlement.[145]

By the end of February an offer of increased wages was on the table, accompanied by a stipulation that if prices went down wages would also be reduced.[146] It was not until the end of March that all workers returned to the yard, some having sought support at their natal homes during the long wageless months of the strike. Military action against Communist operatives, blamed for the longevity of the strike, continued into the ensuing months, while the party itself appears to have suffered a loss of both members and worker support.[147]

Zigong on the Eve of the War of Resistance Against Japan

Rotational pumping remained in effect until the fall of eastern China to Japan in 1937. When it began approximately 40 narrow- and wide-diameter wells were enrolled. Because the equipment and productivity at each well differed, profits were allocated monthly by shares granted to each well in accordance with the contribution it could make. Within a short time, 15 wide-diameter wells closed voluntarily due to weaknesses in their interior walls or a decrease in brine concentration. Soon afterward, the narrow-diameter wells also ceased pumping brine. A fixed monthly subsidy of 4,500 yuan was budgeted to support inactive wells, and each well received between 200 and 500 yuan a month. In the end only 14 large-diameter wells were actually kept in production. These were divided into two groups, alternately pumping brine for two months at a time. Most of these wells had among their investors men we have identified as the upper echelon of the brine merchant elite.[148]

The continuing recession guaranteed that labor unrest would be a recurring problem at the wells. In 1929 a dispute over layoffs at one well led to a general strike of workers at Dafen bao. Unlike the strike a year before, the action resulted in few worker gains. Following the arrest of 21 workers' representatives by the Southern Sichuan Garrison Command, the *Citizens Bulletin* (*Guomin gongbao*) reported:[149]

> Even though they forced the workers to return to work, there were still many who did not, so the future does not look bright. As for the 21 workers' representatives that were arrested, they are still incarcerated within the battalion headquarters. We have heard that they are being severely questioned. Several are intellectuals and are not workers. The workers are demanding that they all be released and they will not stop until they achieve their goal. The government is also holding fast to its position so it is not clear how this will be resolved.

In a subsequent article the paper noted that following a meeting between workers and owners the workers agreed to defer any raises until conditions at the yard had improved. But strike actions continued to be a feature of saltyard life each year thereafter as food prices rose and employers' profits fell.

Only the War of Resistance against Japan halted Zigong's economic decline. By 1937 the Furong saltyard had only 170 operating wells. Many were pumped intermittently to produce about 150,000 tons of brine, compared to an output of more than 202,000 tons of brine at Dafen bao alone in 1925.[150] In one respect, the Japanese invasion of eastern China did for Furong salt producers what the Taiping Rebellion had done for their predecessors almost a century before. By July 1939 Japan had occupied all the major salt-producing areas of eastern China, leaving Zigong to ensure that the masses in free China did not have to "eat bland." However, unlike the rulers of the Qing, who had remained in their capital in Beijing throughout the wars of the mid-nineteenth century, the Guomindang was forced to leave eastern China for a new capital in Chongqing. Furong not only became the main source of salt for what remained of free China but was also now the main source of taxes for a nearby national government at war that had few revenue streams. The state for the first time became a major investor at the yard, and outside capital fleeing occupied China provided the rest. In order to better administer the saltyard, its two parts were finally combined and the city of Zigong created in 1939.[151] Although many of the men we have been studying took part in the revival of Zigong after 1937, their story was no longer a part of the entrepreneurial history of the merchants of Zigong. It was now part of a general move toward state capitalism, which would overtake Zigong and continue to dominate its development until at least the 1990s.

Zigong: Industrial Center or Handicraft Enclave?

QIAO FU, the most prodigious contemporary chronicler of urban life at the Furong saltyard, called turn-of-the-century Zigong the source of Sichuan's wealth, the manufacturer of its main product (salt), and a generator of more than 9 million yuan in taxes each year. During Ziliujing's golden age

> from Badian street and up town, the salt companies, extravagantly decorated in brilliant colors and gold leaf, were packed together like the teeth of a comb. From the moment the sun went down in the west, [the singing girls] put on their makeup, took out their instruments and sang, the sound of their music overflowing and filling everyone's ear. The activity of the money markets, the flow of currency, could come to several tens of millions. Itinerant traders and retail merchants were all in close contact with each other in a town that was equal to the greatest commercial ports. This was the Ziliujing of the days before Guanyun [official transport and merchant sale].[1]

By the time Qiao was writing in 1916, the changing salt policies of the late Qing and early Republic had begun to eat away at the Furong saltyard's markets. But the importance of the yard to commerce and finance in the southwest had not diminished. Zigong stood out as a new city whose growth was a product of the salt industry. Unfortunately, the Qianlong period Fushun gazetteer does not contain maps. However, from the maps of saltyards included in the 1882 *Gazetteer of Sichuan Salt Administration* we can conclude that urban structures at Zigong were still few in number. The only significant buildings noted in Gongjing were the office of the assistant magistrate and the office maintained by the salt administration in the town. In Ziliujing, in addition to these two structures, the map notes the location of the town (represented by another small building) as well as the assistant magistrate office, salt administration office, and buildings at Dengjing guan, the main transshipment point for Furong salt. Both maps contain what looks like a city wall. However, examination of later maps shows these to be fortresses (*zhai*), walled strongholds built at higher elevations to protect salt merchants and their families during the Taiping Rebellion. The only other structures indicated on these simple maps were small crosshatches, which are the Chinese character *jing*, meaning "well." Since most of the offices of salt firms at this time were located at the wells themselves, while wealthy investors continued to live and do business in the countryside surrounding the locale of the assistant magistrate and salt administration, this was all that was felt to be needed to give a sense of these growing yards.

By the turn of the century the demands of map readers as well as the subjects of mapping in southern Sichuan had changed. The *Essentials of Sichuan Salt*'s maps of Gongjing and Ziliujing indicate not only thriving centers of business with many streets (see map 3) but also the sites of numerous smaller market towns scattered throughout the yards, ranging from one to several streets each. Street names in the main cities revealed their connection with the salt industry: Badian Street (eight shops), named after the eight large Shaanxi wholesale firms that helped develop salt production at the yard; Yandian Street (salt shops); Shaanxi miao (Shaanxi temple); Wangjia Embankment (Wang family); Niushi Street (buffalo market); Jingshen miao (Well-god temple); as well as numerous streets named after firms whose offices stood there or other landmarks once familiar to residents. The location of both Ziliujing and Gongjing on either side of the watercourse leading to Dengjing guan was also testimony to the importance of commerce to their survival (see illustration 10.1). Zigong's shallow rivers had always presented an obstacle to wholesale merchants. As long as a free market gave the saltyard a competitive edge, its merchants found ways around the problems of low seasonal water levels. When government policy aided Furong's competitors cheaper transport became an issue for all at the yard. In the mid-twentieth century the leaders of Zigong's business community would try to overcome their dependence on water transportation by building a modern highway from Fushun to Zigong. However, Qiao Fu notes that arguments for a rail link to run the approximately 30 miles to Dengjing guan were put to the prefectural government as early as 1906.[2]

Despite the limited development of transportation in the environs of Zigong and throughout southwest China, Zigong's influence extended far into the agricultural hinterland of the province. Much of the agriculture

ILLUSTRATION 10.1 Salt Junks Anchored at Shawan, Ziliujing, c. 1919
Source: Lin, *Essentials of Sichuan Salt*, front matter.

and handicraft industry of southern Sichuan was geared to the needs of the saltyards, while production, packaging, shipping, and marketing provided a major source of employment for the tens of thousands of immigrants who flocked to the region during the early and mid-Qing. Three of the industries that depended on the saltyard and developed to fill its orders will now be discussed: the manufacture and sale of salt pans, the processing and sale of bamboo and timber, and the rearing of buffalo as work animals at the wells.

Ancillary Industries and Trades

The expansion of the salt industry in Zigong led to the establishment of numerous ancillary industries whose main clients were the salt wells and furnaces of the region. Many of these were themselves located in Zigong, while a few became important in the regional economies of areas closer to their sources of supply. According to the *Gazetteer of Sichuan Salt Administration*, the Furong yard depended on supplies of 23 basic commodities in addition to salt pans, bamboo, timber, and buffalo. These included warming pans used in the evaporation process, made by craftsmen in Luzhou and Hejiang who marketed them themselves at the yard. More than 5,000 were purchased each year. Coal was imported from Rong and Weiyuan counties, while hemp was shipped in by merchants from Wenjiang. Merchants from Luzhou, Zizhou, and Jiangjin sold Zigong retailers over 500,000 *shi* of rice annually, while neighboring counties provided animal feed, miscellaneous grains, and tong oil. In addition to processing many of the raw materials purchased outside, Zigong and its environs also supplied many of its own needs, such as lime, bricks, and wooden pan covers. By the 1920s, more than 500 spools of steel cable were being imported from Shanghai for use in machine pumping of brine.[3]

The Manufacture and Sale of Salt Evaporation Pans

One of the most important ancillary industries serving the needs of salt producers was the manufacture of salt evaporation pans. The center of the salt pan industry was Qijiang County in eastern Sichuan.[4] Here and in Nanchuan County, large deposits of iron ore and the ease of obtaining coal from Chongqing prefecture and charcoal from nearby Guizhou encouraged the growth of a large-scale industry making pans to the differing specifications of salt producers throughout eastern and southwest Sichuan. Salt-pan manufacture was an important industry all along the Qijiang River, which enters the Yangzi at Jiangkou, southeast of Chongqing. Iron ore from Nanchuan County was also shipped to Luzhou and distributed to pan factories along the Tuo River.[5]

Unlike other industries serving the salt manufacturers, pan construction and marketing remained largely in the hands of specialized merchants based outside the saltyard. The pans used at gas furnaces weighed approximately 1,000 *jin* apiece and quickly cracked under the intense heat of evaporation. Because of their short life span and high cost, pans during the early Qing were often paid for in installments and later were leased at an annual fee and replaced periodically by the manufacturer.[6] People who bought new pans were required to turn in the old ones, which were also recycled by the pan merchants. The pans used by coal-burning furnaces did not have to withstand as much heat as those used by gas furnaces. They were generally cheaper, constructed of lower-quality iron, and discarded when broken or sold for iron scrap.[7] Customs governing recycling also served to protect the monopoly of pan merchants over the manufacture of their product. In Leshan, and probably Furong as well, it was illegal to gather the remains of shattered pans or attempt to manufacture one's own supply at the yard.[8] During the 1880s a pan could be had for between 40 and 50 taels.[9] By the 1910s this figure had risen to 65 taels for the best-quality pans.[10]

By the late 1700s, merchants from Jiangjin County were already begin-ning to play an important role in the distribution and marketing of pans to Zigong. Many owned their own factories, from which they met the growing needs of the saltyard. Dai Gengxiao manufactured and shipped between 700 and 1,000 pans a year to Ziliujing, and was said to have al-most 40,000 taels in capital invested in his business. By the 1850s the Dais were joined by other countrymen. The Yuans established the Wanxing pan factory and set up a marketing outlet at Ziliujing that flourished for three generations. During the last years of the dynasty, Jiangjin men took over the pan business formerly run by Shaanxi merchants. Their factories manufac-tured approximately 300 pans a year, and each went out of business in the late 1920s as a result of the dramatic decline in the Furong salt industry.[11]

During the late Qing, the existence of a flourishing community of Jiangjin merchants in Zigong acted as a lure for others from the county. The end of the dynasty and temporary elimination of licensed sale of salt were particu-larly influential in causing enterprising Jiangjin men to buy and market *ba* salt from Furong in the Qijiang and other Sichuan markets, filling the gap left by the impoverishment of many of the more established Qing firms. This was followed by a new wave of migration to Zigong of both laborers and entrepreneurs. According to one estimate, by the late 1940s factories owned by Jiangjin businessmen produced approximately one-third of all salt manu-factured in Zigong.[12] In their role as industrialists Jiangjin entrepreneurs were also instrumental in the introduction of new production technology and new forms of factory management.[13] As we will see, Zigong was a lure not only for industrial investors. Both traditional and modern banking institutions were drawn to the yard in the twentieth century, and Jiangjin businessmen were among those involved in these enterprises as well.

Lumber and Bamboo Suppliers at the Furong Saltyard

Before the introduction of machine pumps and metal tubing, most of the equipment used at saltyards throughout Sichuan was made of bamboo and wood. Pine and China fir were used in the construction of derricks, wheels, and all the numerous buildings that made up a salt-manufacturing complex. These included housing for the wheels and derricks, buffalo sheds, countinghouses, furnace buildings, warehouses, and storage vats, as well as the miles of bamboo pipes that traversed the yards. On average, between 20,000 and 24,000 logs of pine were floated downriver to Zigong each year, and even greater quantities were necessary to meet the large demand for China fir.[14] One derrick for a wide-diameter well could require more than 200 logs, all brought into Zigong from the distant forests of western

Sichuan, Yunnan, Guizhou, and Hunan.[15] Even more varied applications were found for central and western China's abundant output of bamboo. Requisitions for the construction of brine pipes, pumping tubes, bamboo splints (*mie*) used in the drilling and dredging of wells, and slats used in the construction of cord, for wrapping salt and so on brought demand for bamboo to as much as 100,000 lengths a year in the early 1920s. At least four different kinds of bamboo were employed for specialized tasks and purchase of these supplies in mountainous areas of Sichuan, Yunnan, Guizhou, Shaanxi, Hunan, and Hubei created important links between the saltyard and these distant regions.

The purchase, processing, and sale of these commodities were undertaken by large bamboo yards and lumberyards (*zhuchang, zhupengzi, muchang*) along the waterways that served Zigong. At the height of the salt industry in Sichuan there were approximately 20 bamboo yards in Zigong.[16] According to the *Sichuan Salt Administration History*, an entire street in Ziliujing was devoted to the marketing of bamboo.[17] Lumberyards were concentrated in three main areas: 14 at Douya wan and 14 at Shang qiao in Ziliujing, and around 20 at Matanzi in Gongjing. Several of these yards were owned by the same or interlocking partnerships.[18]

The purchase of timber at the forest was controlled by merchants known as *shanke* (literally, mountain guests). As their name implies, these appear to have been investors who purchased mountain land and tenanted it to immigrants and seasonal laborers (*pengmin*) for the cultivation of fast-growing timber crops and other mountain products.[19] There is evidence that *shanke* were not able to control mountain property merely by means of commercial transactions. The absence of a strong government presence in remote mountain areas required that *shanke* also have power of another kind. Most can be identified as local strongmen and, in the twentieth century, men with warlord connections. Among the *shanke* who shipped logs to the Hejiang timber market, Ye Peilin was a brigade commander in the Guizhou army, and at least four others were also military officers.[20] The *shanke* operating in the areas of bamboo cultivation often had close ties with the Elder Brother Society.[21]

Zigong itself was served by large timber markets in Hejiang, Luzhou, Jiading, Dengjing guan, and in Matanzi in Gongjing. The best derrick poles were made of China fir from Hunan. During the Qing, some well owners may have sent their agents directly to select these important components of well construction.[22] More often, agents of the lumber merchants called *zhuangke* selected the timber at the large timber markets and either loaded it onto boats or floated it as rafts back to their Zigong lumberyards where it was processed into the various qualities and forms of lumber needed at the wells and furnaces.

The processing and marketing of bamboo was far more concentrated than that of lumber, and the more powerful bamboo merchants of Zigong were among the only distributors to have direct access to sources of supply for mountain products. Bamboo merchants without sufficient capital to finance the purchase of bamboo directly at the growing site had to buy bamboo brought to the central bamboo market at Luzhou by the *shanke* of bamboo forests. This product was of lesser quality, and the profits from its sale were not as high as those commanded by the large bamboo yards. The two largest bamboo yards were the Yongshengheng and the Tiantaihe. The Yongshengheng alone controlled half the bamboo sold in Zigong. Every year it employed three or four men to go into the mountains and select bamboo. These men left the saltyard in February to negotiate directly with the owners of the bamboo forests. The exact stands from which they wished their supplies to be cut would be marked, and they would return to the yard in time for the Dragon Boat Festival in late May or early June. In late summer they returned to the mountains to supervise the cutting of the four-year-old bamboo, a task that was not completed until late September. Then, depending on the depth of the river and the quantity of their purchase, they shipped the bamboo by boat, on rafts, or by land back to Zigong in time for the celebration of the New Year. The timing of these shipments was critical, for a store of bamboo that arrived too late would have lost too much of its moisture content to be useful for construction at the yard. That destined for slats would often have to be thrown away, and tubes made from such a consignment could not be guaranteed not to split.[23]

Although by no means as important as wells and furnaces, the lumber- and bamboo yards of Zigong were major employers and an important source of investment within the saltyard. The Yongshengheng employed a supervisory staff of more than 30 and at least three times that number of skilled and unskilled workers. During the 1920s the 14 lumberyards at Douya wan employed 30 to 50 men each just to move lumber into and out of the yard.[24] Both bamboo yards and lumberyards also provided seasonal employment for men who signed up as boatmen, raftmen, and porters conveying the unprocessed materials from the mountains to the saltyard. The annual exodus of bamboo from the forests along Sichuan's borders must have been an important source of income for peasants in marginal areas. In some places, the bamboo poles had to be carried as much as 30 miles from the mountains where they were cut to the nearest source of water transportation.[25]

It took far less money to open a lumber- or bamboo yard than a furnace or well. Recollections by several former lumberyard employees place the initial capitalization of lumberyards during the Qing at several hundred to between 3,000 and 4,000 taels. These were labor-intensive industries with high potential profits if the right contacts with suppliers and buyers could be established. According to one estimate, a well-managed yard could make at least a 30 percent profit, while the sale of materials for a derrick could yield profits of as much as 300 percent.[26] Zeng Zihua began his career as a member of the staff of the Dechangxiang lumberyard. In 1918 he was able to attract 3,300 yuan in investor capital and opened the Jiyichang lumberyard. During the 10 years he ran the business he distributed dividends totaling over twice that amount and probably pocketed a considerable amount as well. In 1928, holders suspicious of Zeng's sudden purchases of land and his acquisition of the Fulai lumberyard for his brother, Shaoqing, ordered an independent audit of the Jiyichang's books. Despite evidence of embezzlement by its manager, the company still showed total assets valued at over 30,000 taels.[27]

We know little about the finances of the large bamboo companies at Zigong. The *Sichuan Salt Administration History* simply comments that the owners of bamboo yards were wealthy merchants with capital totaling several tens of thousands of taels. The high salaries paid their managerial staff, and the long list of official titles purchased by bamboo yard owners and managers, confirm the fact that their profits too were considerable.[28] The money made in processing and marketing bamboo and lumber found a number of outlets, including the purchase of agricultural land and official posts. However, there is evidence that many of the main suppliers of the saltyard became investors in wells and furnaces themselves.

A prime example is Wang Desan. Wang was trained as a carpenter and spent the first years of his working life cutting firewood. When the Quanxingchang closed down during the last decade of the Qing, Wang took over the site and converted it from producing firewood to producing lumber. After struggling for several years, he was able to accumulate enough money to expand his operations and begin competing in the market serving the saltyard. In 1918 he won a government contract to build a granary in Zigong, and the profits he made allowed him to hire a full-time buyer of timber. By 1923 his Dechangxiang was one of the main suppliers for the salt industry. Among the investments Wang made with his profits was agricultural land at Lianggao shan yielding 50 *shi* a year in rents. Much of this land was given over to well exploration, and we know that at the very least he owned shares in the Yongchao, Guangfu, and Wufu wells. The site of the Yongchao well was developed with investor capital from Zhang Xiaopo and was one of the most productive black-brine wells to be drilled at Lianggao shan.[29] Following the 1911 Revolution we see the opposite phenomenon as well. Many of the richest saltyard merchants began to invest in their own bamboo yards and lumberyards. Wang Dexian and Wang Ziheng became partners in the Changfaxiang bamboo yard. The Wang Sanwei trust opened the Guangyigong bamboo yard, and Wang Hefu, Li Xingqiao, Li Jingxiu, and Huang Dunsan all ran their own lumberyards.[30]

In addition to pans, and large items like structural timbers and bamboo poles, the specialized needs of the salt industry also spawned small-scale manufacturing in the vicinity of the yard. Among the equipment produced was twisted bamboo cable.[31] The twisted bamboo cable industry occupied an intermediate stage between cottage industry and the factory-style production found at the saltyard itself. Salt producers purchased approximately 1 million *jin* of twisted bamboo cable each year during the Qing period, largely for use as cable at the wells. Although the product was extremely strong, exposure to brine and the stresses of both cable drilling and the raising and lowering of the brine tube meant that bamboo cable had to be frequently replaced.

There is evidence that during the late eighteenth and early nineteenth centuries most of the bamboo brine tubes used at the Furong saltyard were produced on site as a cottage industry. Even in the early Republican period expert artisans traveled from well to well to cure the bamboo to be used in lifting brine. The artisans were joined by other craftsmen, whose job it was to peel and notch the hollow bamboo pipes and wrap them in hemp to protect them from water damage.[32]

In other crafts a system of mixed handicraft and factory production had developed by the late Qing. For example, there were approximately 100 twisted bamboo cable factories, employing a total of around 3,000 to 4,000 workers in workshops of between 20 and 80 workers each. Unlike the salt industry as a whole, which became a magnet for both extraprovincial and Sichuanese immigrants, this industry helped absorb the underemployed labor of the local agricultural population. Profits in the twisted bamboo cable industry were high, but demand was volatile. Merchants employed a two-tiered system, using a large peasant workforce in factories on a part-time basis and filling excess demand when necessary by putting-out. By the twentieth century, female and child labor constituted about 10 percent of the labor input in both systems.[33]

The importance of the factory system is evident in the correspondence between factory owners and the salt administration during a 1915 strike by cable workers over employer efforts to reduce the traditional food component of wages. Some 40 firms were affected by the walkout, including factories in three counties, Fushun, Rong, and Yibin. Appealing to the salt commissioner's duty to remit salt taxes to the central government, the owners pointed out, "If there is no cable, one cannot draw brine; if there is no brine one cannot make salt; if there is no salt, one cannot fill the tax quota. They are intimately related and this is no small matter."[34] The letter indicated that the workers were organized into an association much like the patron-god associations discussed in chapter 5. The ability of their Qiaosheng hui (literally, skilled sage association) to unite workers in the same trade across three counties clearly frightened the owners and the salt administration, the latter recommending that the two parties to the dispute sit down together at the local branch office of the salt administration and work out their problems.

In the end, the urgency of the yard's need for twisted bamboo cable led to the breakup of the strike and the arrest of the strike leaders. It was not until the 1920s that declining orders for salt combined with two changes in the structure of production began to challenge the power of twisted bamboo cable merchants. The first was the growing dominance of wide-diameter rock-salt wells, which pushed the lifting capacity of bamboo cable to its limits. The second was the introduction of steam engines to pump the wells, creating an immediate demand for steel cable to replace bamboo.[35]

Buffalo Power and Buffalo By-products

One of the biggest businesses in Qing Zigong was the buying, selling, and recycling of buffalo. An estimated stock of 30,000 worked at the wells and furnaces at any one time, pumping brine, carting goods, and turning the dredging wheels. Approximately one-sixth were simply there as a reserve in the event of the death or disability of their fellows.[36] Most were common water buffalo. However, a small number of oxen (huangniu) were used for hauling the unending supplies of coal, rice, beans, and salt that moved in and out of the yard each month.

The reason for this huge reserve force, nearly 5,000 head, is not difficult to find. Although a few of this army of cattle were raised locally, the vast majority of the buffalo employed at the Furong saltyard were imported from counties in Guizhou along the Sichuan border and from mountainous counties of Sichuan. Small peddlers purchased the buffalo at source and drove them to central buffalo markets in Longshi zhen in Longchang County, in Maotou zhen in Fushun County, and in Shang qiao in Ziliujing. By the late Qing these markets operated daily, although a periodic buffalo market still operated in Dashan pu near the city of Gongjing.[37] The trade in buffalo was a fragmented one; peddlers would drive the cattle a certain distance and then sell them to other peddlers who themselves took them only part of the way to Zigong or the Jianwei and Leshan yards. Indeed, several important intermediary markets thrived during the Qing period on the profits from this trade, in particular the market in Lishi ba in Jiangjin County, which specialized in the sale of buffalo from nearby Guizhou province.[38]

The working life of a healthy buffalo averaged 10 years,[39] so that 10 percent of the stock had to be replaced annually. In general, another 5 percent died of disease, so that approximately 4,500 head were sold to the yard each year. The enormous volume of this trade provided rich opportunities for the cattle brokers who regulated their sale. Buffalo were classified into three grades. During the early Republic, the highest quality in terms of health and stamina fetched between 80 and 100 taels each, with the other two grades costing 60 to 70 taels and 30 to 50 taels, respectively.[40] The negotiations between buyers and buffalo peddlers were carried out entirely by the specialized brokers who worked the buffalo markets. When a well owner spotted a buffalo he wanted, he would call in a broker who ran back and forth between buyer and seller until a satisfactory price was agreed upon. The interested parties in the sale never exchanged words themselves. When a reasonable figure was achieved, the broker would write it on the back of the buffalo in red pigment and bow to the prospective owner, offering the salutary wish that the animal pump brine for 10,000 years. If at this point the seller dropped the buffalo's lead and the buyer picked it up, the sale was made. If not, the pigment was wiped off and the search for a buyer began again.[41]

The job of the broker went beyond arranging the sale. For his few taels he was expected to collect the payment from the buyer and act as a guarantor of the animal's fitness. If within three days the animal proved ill, or would not eat and drink, it was the broker's responsibility to return the buffalo and terminate the deal. Sales of 4,500 head could yield at least 13,500 taels in brokerage fees for the few who were fortunate to obtain the government license that gave them a near monopoly in the trade. Some of the most successful brokers hired other men to help in negotiations, increasing the volume of sales they could handle each year. As a result, a number of buffalo brokers became quite rich and invested in other local businesses as well.[42]

Buffalo were big business at the saltyard. Several thousand men were employed as their handlers, doctors, and drivers. In addition, a large number of secondary industries grew up around the large buffalo herds. We have already seen the development of specialist shops catering to the medical care and feeding of cattle at the wells. Cultivation of grass for buffalo consumption occupied a large percentage of the farms in the less fertile lands surrounding the saltyard, while broad beans, a staple of the buffalo diet, were imported from as far away as Jiangjin and south central Sichuan.[43] The collection and processing of buffalo manure also developed into a large handicraft industry at the wells. Buffalo pats were made into cakes, and then dried and sold as fuel (see illustration 10.2). During the Qing they cost between six and ten cash strings apiece and were the preferred source of heating and cooking fuel in the vicinity of the yard.[44] Workers at the wells could earn an extra string

ILLUSTRATION 10.2 A Worker Dries Buffalo Pats on a Ziliujing Hillside c. 1919
Source: Lin, *Essentials of Sichuan Salt,* front matter.

of cash a month by processing and selling buffalo dung in their spare time. The gathering of this by-product of well operation may have developed into a monopoly of well workers, as we have evidence of some hiring even less fortunate men to do the collecting for them at low pay.[45]

Another, more lucrative monopoly evolved out of the need to dispose of the thousands of carcasses of buffalo that died each year. Wells required a reliable supply of buffalo hides, particularly for use as valves at the base of brine tubes.[46] In order to guarantee the supply of this material, it became the custom at the saltyard to require that all old and dead buffalo be sold to licensed slaughterhouses. They sold the meat and sinews, the processing of which was an important industry in Zigong as well. The hides, bone, and horn were then sent for a low fee to one of four monopoly tanneries (*piju*) established around the saltyard.[47] Here, hides were prepared for use in the industry, as well as for chair cushions, mats, and so on. Glue manufactured at the tannery was sold as far away as Chengdu and Chongqing, and the bone and horn supplied a flourishing handicraft industry specializing in items of decorative and daily use.[48] The tanneries themselves were designated charitable trusts, and the use to which their profits were put was decided collectively by the heads of the various local salt merchants' associations.[49] The introduction of steam pumping led to the consolidation of the tanneries, and with the founding of the Zigong Chamber of Commerce this umbrella organization of yard businessmen took over the distribution of tannery philanthropy.[50]

Thus, not only did buffalo become a link between Zigong and the prosperity of mountain areas throughout Sichuan and the Guizhou border, but the processing of buffalo by-products and feeding of living stock were major sources of peasant and artisan income within the perimeter of the saltyard and its environs. It is no wonder that a cult of the buffalo king (*niuwang*) developed in Zigong. The fate of the industry rested on the health of these animals, whose feed and care cost more than the wages of the men whose employment depended on them. Buffalo literally overran the yard. Their manure covered the hillsides, and the pollution of the local water supply from bathing livestock led to annual epidemics of cholera and dysentery. Along with the fumes from the wells, these lumbering creatures, present in their thousands, were the main factor making Zigong such a wonderful place to make money and a less than pleasant place to live.

Credit and Banking

While the Furong yard led to an intensification of trade and manufacturing in southern Sichuan, its impact on banking and credit was modest. As we have seen, banks did not finance the initial spurt of investment that built the Furong yard. Like early industrial developers elsewhere, Furong's salt producers addressed the high capital costs of drilling wells and constructing furnaces by developing complex systems of shareholding and partnership and by incorporating kin-based wealth to produce stores of capital from which new capital could be generated. Despite the demand for long-term capital generated by the discoveries of black brine and natural gas, and later by the exploitation of rock salt, the growth of the Furong salt industry continued to be fueled by private investment. Where banking and financial services were critical to the development of the yard was in the realms of commercial credit and remittance. In these areas China already had considerable experience by the 1800s. Moreover, the demands of the salt industry for financial services made Chongqing and southern Sichuan centers for the development of provincial modern banking, particularly after the turn of the century. At the same time, business methods such as vertical integration and interlocking investment, advance payments, and credit purchasing helped firms overcome shortages of current capital.

Trade Credit

Among the advantages enjoyed by the larger salt producers was privileged access to sources of producer goods and credit. As we have seen, large vertically integrated firms could not only guarantee supplies of brine and gas but, by operating their own wholesale goods firms, also ensure their own wells and furnaces access to coal, oil, foodstuffs, hemp, animal feed, and so on, often at low or zero interest. Wholesale merchandizing also kept active the capital of larger salt producers with their own salt-marketing companies. Rather than deal with the remittance of large stores of silver, by the second half of the nineteenth century payments for salt shipped to Chongqing and Hubei ports such as Shashi were often used to purchase cotton yarn and other goods for resale in Zigong.[51] Integration and diversification thus provided most of the larger salt producers with valuable economies of scope.

Large producers were also able to benefit from the establishment of special relationships with firms supplying producer goods such as bamboo and timber. Interlocking investment linked the interests of major purveyors of producer goods and their main clients at the wells and furnaces. During the early twentieth century, large well and furnace merchants like Wang Hefu, Li Xingqiao, Li Jingxiu, and Huang Dunsan were principal investors in lumberyards.[52] A number of the main suppliers of bamboo and lumber included high-level management staff from the salt conglomerates in their partnerships. For example, one of the main investors in the Yongshengheng bamboo yard was the general manager of the Wang Sanwei lineage trust's salt businesses, Pan Zhongsan.[53] Cui Ruhua and his son-in-law Yu Shuhuai were initially able to attract business to their Xiehesheng mountain products firm by allowing customers to draw on their accounts at the Yuanchang pipe, where Cui was an accounts manager, to pay for items like oil and hemp.[54]

Both large salt producers and large purveyors of producer goods maintained special offices of external affairs, the sole purpose of which was to gather market information and establish relationships with customers and suppliers. At the lumberyards, young men were employed whose only task was to wander the saltyard and listen for gossip about new wells about to be drilled.[55] The bamboo industry relied on long-standing ties to established wells and furnaces. At the Yongshengheng bamboo yard, a close friend of Wang Dazhi was in charge of business with the Wang Sanwei trust. Mao Aiqin and his brother handled all transactions with the wells at Jinhua wan, and Li Huiting was liaison man for wells belonging to Huang Dunsan, Wang Dexian, and the Li Siyou lineage trust. Gao Yuncong, himself an investor in pipes, kept up business with the Tongfu pipe, and Jing Shaotang handled all orders from wells and pipes owned by members of the Shaanxi guild.[56] In one sense, these men operated as professional salesmen, and the services they performed differed only slightly from those performed by some accounts officers today. Gifts of chickens, ducks, hams, sugar, tea, or opium were sent routinely to the managers and owners of the main wells and furnaces at the time of the three main festivals of the Chinese ritual year. When buyers were sent from the salt factories they were always lavishly entertained. In the absence of any state regulation of business, the cultivation of clients often exceeded what we would now consider acceptable practices.

After the institution of Guanyun, salt furnaces were placed at the mercy of state salt purchasing units. Particularly in the 1920s and 1930s, when the productive capacity of the yard exceeded the legal market for Sichuan salt, negotiations over price and contracts for sale as licensed salt were crucial to the success of any producer. A handful of large producers were able to establish guaranteed quotas and did not have to engage in an annual struggle for a share of the licensed market. However, medium-size and small furnaces competed vigorously for the share of the quota that remained. It was common for them to spend considerable sums cultivating officials of the government marketing bureaus and their underlings. Houses of prostitution, traditional venues for the social gatherings of officials, scholars, and businessmen, were clustered around the districts where meduim-size furnace merchants anxious to escape the power of the large pipes congregated. Indeed, by the 1910s Ziliujing was said to have between 2,000 and 3,000 professional prostitutes, some of them recent immigrants from Chongqing, where business of the kind they offered was not as good.[57]

Business-to-business short-term credit arrangements offset the underdevelopment of banking and monetary shortages at this inland industrial town. Under the free market system that prevailed until the 1880s and for brief periods during the twentieth century, salt was typically contracted to wholesalers in advance of production at markets held at the time of the three main festivals of the year. Not only did this enable producers to calculate with considerable accuracy the amount of salt they should produce. Far more important, the institution of advance sale (*yushou*) also provided the salt furnaces with a portion of the working capital for their operations. For every *zai* that was contracted under this system, the producer received an advance payment (*jiaoguanyin*) of about 1,000 taels.[58] When the Guanyun bureau took over purchase of the output of the yard this practice was continued, although large pipe owners appear to have had an advantage in these transactions.[59]

A similar arrangement existed between pipe and furnace owners and the purveyors of brine. Indeed, cash flow was the main problem facing those who pumped the wells. Any interruption in payment schedules left small and medium-size owners without funds to pay workers and unable to feed their livestock.[60] Salt producers also benefited from the credit arrangements available from suppliers of vital materials. Whereas bamboo merchants had to pay in advance for the goods they received from the owners of bamboo forests, their dealings with wells and furnaces worked in the opposite manner. The more prosperous wells, such as those belonging to the Wang Sanwei trust or members of the Shaanxi guild, received delivery of their goods in the eleventh month and remitted payment in installments at the three main festivals of the Chinese calendar.[61] Deferred payment constituted a loan to the wells and furnaces. According to Luo Xiaoyuan, suppliers were willing to accept such practices in exchange for interest-free loans from the head clerks of the wells and furnaces or inflated valuations of the goods received.[62] Accounts at the lumberyards were also cleared at the thrice-a-year festivals.

If private share investment was the key to initial capitalization, trade credit was the grease that kept the wheels of production turning. The reach of the Sichuan market, particularly its links to Chongqing and Shashi, cycled capital back into the yard not only through salt sales, but also through profits from a variety of retail and producer goods. As long as business was good, merchants and producers could accommodate the seasonal character of the salt market through installment payments, short-term credit, and a variety of reciprocal credit arrangements. However, the slump in demand for Sichuan salt in the mid-1920s led to a gradual contraction of credit. Merchants began to insist on payment within two months of delivery, and by the mid-1930s cash purchases became the rule in most business transactions.[63]

Traditional Credit Institutions

Although banks did not finance the development of Furong's wells, furnaces, and pipes, a variety of financial services were available during the Qing period through three types of firms: pawnshops, remittance banks (*piaohao*), and native banks (*qianzhuang*). The earliest repositories of capital at the yard appear to have been pawnshops opened by extraprovincial merchants as a means to invest the profits they accumulated from leasing salt sales certificates and wholesaling salt in Yunnan and Guizhou.[64] By the middle of the eighteenth century a number of pawnshops are also known to have existed that largely relied on local capital or investment by merchants from nearby Weiyuan County. Many of the owners whose names we can identify were either salt merchants or salt producers. The Lis opened the Hengfu pawnshop in mid-century and later used the profits to establish three others under the shop name Chengmeigong. Several of the prominent pawnshops during the late Qing expanded into the credit markets of other saltyards as well. The Luos of Guanyin tan, themselves an important well-land-owning lineage, opened the Qianyi pawnshop, later extending their business to Fengjie and Wan counties. The Gous, originally from Weiyuan County, had pawnshops in Rong, Fushun, and Leshan counties.[65] In the absence of financial records from Zigong's Qing period pawnshops, it is difficult to determine their precise relationship to the business credit market in Zigong. We do know, however, that their fortunes rose and fell with those of the salt industry itself, a clear indication of the close ties between the two. Following the 1911 Revolution, few of the old Qing pawnshops survived. It was not until the early 1920s that a new group of pawnshops appeared, largely opened by prosperous investors in salt manufacture. In all, ten new pawnshops opened around 1920. Salt merchants owned all but three.[66]

By 1927 to 1928, the decline in demand for Sichuan salt and the start of the great brine glut were greeted by the closure of many of the pawnshops that had opened earlier in the decade. Banditry and the debasement of copper currency were also important factors in the failure of these money-lending institutions. However, equally important was their own corporate investment in well shares. Whereas industry-wide layoffs and production cutbacks would normally lead to an expansion of business for pawnshop owners, their own involvement in the industry meant that any dramatic change in its overall fortunes brought disaster for them as well.[67]

The development of native banking at Zigong was also a product of the expansion of salt production. By the early eighteenth century the flow of capital from long-distance merchants from Shaanxi, Shanxi, Guangdong, Fujian, and Guizhou was sufficient to stimulate the establishment of a number of native banks in Ziliujing.[68] Circulating capital at the yard came almost entirely from the sale of salt, largely in Chongqing. Particularly in the early years, merchants shipped silver back home. Because commodity transactions in Zigong were largely in copper coins, most of the banking business in Zigong was initially in the form of money exchange.[69] Among native banks, by far the largest concentration of capital belonged to Shaanxi and Shanxi merchants, whose Pufengheng, Sidaxiang, and Baofenglong were the most powerful native banks in Zigong, engaging in both money exchange and deposit/loan transactions.

The rhythm of the salt industry also accounted for the presence of a number of remittance banks in Zigong. Sichuan, with its remote but highly profitable export market in hemp, herbs, skins, and dyes, saw the establishment of remittance banks at least as early as the 1700s and is thought by some to have been the site of the first remittance businesses in China.[70] Nevertheless, remittance banks did not appear in Zigong until the salt boom of the early nineteenth century, and even then they controlled only part of the remittance business between Zigong and Chongqing. The coincidental development of the Huguang market for Sichuan salt and the introduction of foreign manufactured yarn through the port of Hankou provided a lucrative opportunity for many native Zigong salt wholesalers to substitute trade for remittance. The shortage of capital, even among the large remittance banks, was also significant in their limited expansion into southwest Sichuan. Even as late as the Guangxu reign (1875–1908) remittance banks in Chongqing frequently ran short of money, periodically importing cash from less commercialized areas.[71] Beginning in 1877 with the institution of Guanyun, the money for purchase of salt was brought into Zigong by the state under military escort, diminishing the need for remittance until the end of the dynasty and the abolition of the Guanyun system in 1911.[72]

Besides money changing and remittance, the most important role played by all three of these credit institutions was the extension of short-term credit for working capital. Thus, while they played no role in the development of producer capital at the yard, they were vital to its use in the production process itself.

We know little about institutionalized commodity financing during the early Qing. However, following the introduction of Guanyun, data on banking activity become more plentiful, providing a picture of the interpenetration of banking and commerce at the saltyard. Most remittance banks also engaged in some trade in cotton yarn, kerosene, and tong oil.[73] Far more important to the daily operations of the wells and furnaces were native banks and the main offices of large salt conglomerates, which often operated both money-changing and commodity purchase departments. From the mid-nineteenth century on, the Wang Sanwei trust's Guangshentong was the prototype for the latter. With branches in Dengjing guan, Luzhou, Chongqing, Yichang, and Shashi, it engaged in salt shipment, money exchange, and the trade in cotton yarn. It also issued notes (*qianpiao*) that were accepted as far away as Yichang, in Hubei, and could be exchanged for hard currency at full face value.[74] By the late nineteenth and early twentieth centuries native banks of this type were being established by many of the larger salt manufacturing lineages, including Li Xingqiao's Baotongchang, the Li Siyou trust's Xiexingxiang, and Huang Dunsan's Jiqingheng.[75] At the same time, the intimate relationship between commodity purchase and native banking encouraged many men whose business was in supplying the wells and furnaces with lumber, bamboo, oil, hemp, coal, and other products to form partnerships to found small native banks themselves. They were often joined by men who worked as managers and accounting personnel for the wells and furnaces.

Under the Guanyun system, furnaces producing finished salt received payment for their quota of salt three times a year, in the fifth, eighth, and twelfth months of the lunar calendar. Payments were made in silver. After paying the wells or pipes from which they had received their brine, the remainder of the silver was deposited in native banks and accrued interest of between 0.8 and 1.2 percent per month. When the furnace (or well or pipe, which each had similar arrangements with the banks) needed to purchase supplies of oil, hemp, rice, and so on, it drew against its account at the native bank.[76] Often no cash changed hands, as the commodity supplier would simply have his account credited by the bank. By the twentieth century it was common for the larger native banks themselves to trade in these commodities, providing storage in their own warehouses, often sending their own staff to production areas to buy supplies and ship them to Zigong.[77]

During the late 1920s and early 1930s, as profits at the yard contracted, native banks found it necessary to advance producers the funds they needed for commodity purchases. The interest rate on these loans, which were increasingly secured by liens on future salt production, was a source of great concern to all Zigong inhabitants. The rates themselves were set daily by the managers of the main native banks at a meeting at the Yiyuan teahouse on Zheng Jie in Ziliujing. Known as "going to the tea market" by the locals, this meeting allowed the native banks to set the bank interest rate, on the basis of which individual native banks set the rates they charged their customers. Factors influencing the bank rate included the rates being charged by Chongqing remittance banks, cash on hand at the local Zigong banks, and a calculation of the demand for loans. The last depended in large part on the state's own timeliness in paying salt producers for their salt.[78]

Although the role of the state salt administration and modern banks in the movement of funds led to the demise of the remittance banks in the early twentieth century, native banks continued to play an important role in the money-changing and short-term credit market in Zigong. Reaching their height prior to the brine glut, 50 native banks operated at the yard, almost as many as did business in the financial center of the province in Chongqing.[79] However, both their business methods and their internal structures made them extremely vulnerable to the shifting politics and business environment of the Republican period. Most were small and relied on local investment and local business. Even in the late 1930s their paid-up capital was far less than that of their counterparts in Chengdu and Chongqing (see table 10.1).

As unlimited liability partnerships, native banks were held hostage to the business dealings of their shareholders. At times individual infusions of cash could raise their reserves as high as 100,000 yuan, but as the volume

TABLE 10.1 Paid-Up Capital at Native Banks c. 1939 (in yuan)

City	Average	Median
Ziliujing	11,666	10,500
Chengdu	45,176	30,000
Chongqing	83,304	54,000

Source: Xiaomei Zhang, *Sichuan jingji cankao ziliao* [Reference materials on the Sichuan economy] (Shanghai: Zhongguo guomin jingji yanjiu suo, 1939), D46.

of business at the saltyard declined, many native banks saw both deposits and paid-up capital decline. According to Zhang Xiaomei, the volatility of Shanghai and foreign banknotes in local currency exchange markets provided an opportunity for native banks to engage in speculation as a means to survive. Arbitrage of public debts provided another. Nevertheless by 1939 at least two-thirds of native banks in Zigong had closed their doors.[80] Efforts by the Guomindang government in Nanjing to unify the currency by issuing a national bank note (*fabi*) in 1935 and by banning the private holding of silver specie most likely also contributed to the collapse of many of the native banks that relied on currency exchange as a major part of their business.

Modern Banking

Although the twentieth century saw the establishment of a number of modern banks in Zigong, they contributed little to the credit needs of the average producer. Modern banks (*yinhang*), even branches of the large modern banks based in Chongqing during the 1920s and 1930s, based most of their business on the deposit and transport of salt tax revenues. Under the Qing, Ziliujing had a branch of the Imperial bank[81] and of the Junchuanyuan bank. After 1911 both of these early efforts at Chinese modern banking closed. In 1915 the Imperial bank, now resurrected as the Bank of China, reopened its branch bank in Ziliujing and was joined by a branch of the privately operated Juxingcheng. Branches of the Railway bank (*Tiedao yinhang*) and the Zhibian bank followed later that year, along with several other small banks that closed within a few months.[82] According to Qiao Fu, the catalyst for this migration of branch banks to the yard was the transfer of the salt administration's main office in southern Sichuan from Luzhou to Ziliujing. Once settled there, the competition among these banks for a share of the salt revenue remittance business was intense. Every two weeks the salt administration would ask each bank to submit its remittance rate and the size of the remittance it was prepared to undertake. The bank would then telegraph its office in Shanghai to deposit that much money to the Bank of China branch in Shanghai for transfer to the foreign banks that received Chinese salt payments as security for Chinese loan and indemnity payments. Shanghai informed the salt administration that the money had been received, and the latter would issue a check in the amount of the transfer and its remittance fee to the branch in Ziliujing.[83] This was a lucrative business for the several banks that had established offices at the yard. However, an uprising by the Yunnan army against forces loyal to President Yuan Shikai resulted in disruption of business and communications in southern Sichuan, and by 1916 all four banks at the yard had closed their doors.

It was not until the 1930s that modern banks—or at least banks that called themselves *yinhang*, as opposed to money changers (*yinhao*) or native banks—began to multiply at Zigong. Most were connected in one way or another with the state or its surrogates, as was the returning Bank of China, the Yutong yinhang (opened by the militarist Liu Wenhui in Chongqing in 1927 with a branch in Zigong),[84] and the Chuanyan yinhang (Salt Bank of Sichuan).

The history of the Salt Bank of Sichuan is illustrative of the tangled web of private, state, and regional military interests at play in the Sichuan financial world of the early twentieth century. The bank was founded in 1930 with its main office in Chongqing and a branch in Ziliujing. Earlier that year the warlord Liu Xiang appointed Wang Zuanxu to the post of Sichuan salt commissioner. Ostensibly to address the needs of well and furnace merchants, Wang authorized the establishment of the Salt Bank of Sichuan. The capital for this bank was obtained both from private investors and from a fee levied on every *zai* of salt shipped by Sichuan salt wholesalers.[85] The move to create a capital fund targeted at Sichuan salt producers was in part an attempt to placate well and furnace owners faced with government-mandated cutbacks in salt production during the early 1930s. Although some commentators consider this to have been a merchants' bank, the appointment of Zeng Ziwei, a military man and Ziliujing native,[86] as director is evidence of the bank's strong ties to the warlord regime. The bank's ability to attract business in Zigong was limited, and the Chongqing branch itself was reorganized in 1933. At this same time, a breakaway group of Zigong salt producers and merchants founded their own bank in Ziliujing, the Yushang bank.[87]

By 1935, although the yard was no longer as prosperous as it had been in the 1910s and early 1920s, it would appear to have been well served by modern banks. In addition to those mentioned earlier, an article in *Sichuan*

Economic Monthly (*Sichuan jingji yuekan*) notes that seven modern banks operated in the city, all of which, save the Yushang bank, had their main offices in Chongqing. The Local bank (*difang yinhang*) had recently been established with branches throughout the province to aid in the regulation of local banking practices. Besides handling remittances for the salt administration, the Local bank undertook money exchange, handled deposits and loans, and discounted promissory notes. The remaining three banks, the Bank of Chongqing (*Chongqing yinhang*), Commercial bank (*shangye yinhang*), and Common People's Bank (*pingmin yinhang*), were largely engaged in remittance.[88]

Although the existence of seven modern banks allowed Ziliujing to organize a bankers' association under the rules of the Guomindang government, the focus of most of these banks on traditional remittance and money exchange and the undercapitalization of most of the city's native banks left the saltyard short of circulating currency and still without access to long-term, low-interest bank finance.[89] Competition among warlord groups for control of bank assets further weakened the role of banks in monetary stabilization, as witnessed by the monetary crisis experienced in Zigong in the late 1920s.[90] The credit needs of the yard therefore continued to be met by native banks, and increasingly by credit groups (*zhaituan*) composed of regional businessmen, often from larger downstream cities like Shashi and Chongqing.

Inland Industrial City

At the end of the nineteenth century, the residents of Zigong, native and sojourner, worker and businessman, had crafted an industrial system unique in China. Unlike its urban rivals such as Shanghai and Hanyang, Zigong was wholly Chinese in its conception and execution. It stood as an example of technological and organizational innovation in the service of production. Its links to the agricultural economy of the surrounding countryside gave rise to a dense marketing network employing tens of thousands of transport workers and supported in Sichuan's forests thriving timber, bamboo, and tong oil industries. Prior to the introduction of Western industrial technology, Zigong itself was home to the largest concentration of nonagricultural workers in China.

Zigong merchants broke new ground in the use of contracts and other instruments to raise capital and organize business relationships. In the period from 1877 to 1937 significant changes took place at the Furong yard in production technology, including the development of wide-diameter wells, rock-salt extraction, and mechanical pumping. Its businessmen took maximum advantage of opportunities to develop new markets and demonstrated flexibility and creativity in response to the structural constraints posed by poor communications and the obstacles posed by changing and increasingly predatory political regimes.

Ultimately, however, the industrial system we have been studying could not be sustained. As we saw in chapter 9, by the late 1930s those salt manufacturers who had not already abandoned their wells and closed down their furnaces were faced with challenges that would soon have overtaken them. While "state capitalism" during the War of Resistance provided a short reprieve, by 1949 the Furong saltyard, its financial institutions, and all of its ancillary industries had collapsed. In the end, socialism saved the Furong yard and preserved both its history and the store of skills upon which its future role in China's economy will be based.

Epilogue

The Furong Saltyard and Chinese Industrial Development

THE BUSINESS practices that emerged in Zigong during the mid-Qing followed patterns of organization and investment familiar to economic historians. Faced with similar opportunities and constraints, Zigong businessmen devised solutions that were not all that different from those of contemporary American entrepreneurs. To illustrate this point, let us briefly examine three aspects of the Furong salt industry in the nineteenth century.

Classic studies of late-eighteenth- and early-nineteenth-century U.S. textile manufacturing focus on the role of new technology, new methods of business organization, and bank financing. All three have relevance to our study of Zigong. Whereas the technology for the development of textile manufacturing was imported (the power loom), Furong's technological breakthrough was indigenous. Both the Furong salt industry and the textile industry of New York, New Jersey, and New England relied on the continuous improvement of their initial technological foundation. It was the nature of these improvements that determined to a large extent the geographic location of factory sites away from existing centers of commerce.

Business organization in both of these cases was centered on partnerships that initially drew on private merchant capital. Shaanxi merchants and others engaged in the salt trade helped finance Furong's expansion, and textile import-export merchants footed most of the bill for the development of the eastern U.S. textile industry. The need for credit in both emerging industries was high. However, one should not assume that in Zigong entrepreneurs depended on one another, while in the eastern United States, manufacturers had access to cheap, impersonal bank credit. Indeed, in Zigong as in Lowell, kinship and personal ties were critical to business development. In the Zigong case the problem of cheap credit was solved by means of lineage estate incorporation, familial lending, and shareholding arrangements that allowed partners to expand their capital by bringing in new partners (*shangxia jie*). In the United States the growth of banks and credit societies appears to have been a function of the manufacturers' need for credit. Successful textile manufacturers invested in banking and borrowed at low interest from these same institutions.[1] Even more striking is the kinship basis of most of the early New England banks. According to Naomi Lamoreaux, in New England "banks did indeed have an important role to play in economic development, though not as the independent intermediaries of economic theory. Rather, as the financial arms of kinship groups, they raised capital primarily for their members' diverse investments. At the same time, they provided these groups (commonly regarded as premodern institutions) with a corporate base, permitting them to survive and prosper long into the industrial era."[2]

Zigong also adopted common organizational solutions to the problems of early industrial entrants. Most Zigong firms began as family firms or simple partnerships. By the late nineteenth century all of the larger Zigong manufacturers had made the transition to complex, hierarchically organized firms with separate accounting departments that handled the overall management of the companies' many units. While the organization of these accounting departments still mirrored that of large merchant houses, the increasing use of non-kin experts to staff these administrative units represented an important step toward professionalization of management.[3] The division of labor within the yard, some of which existed prior to the mid-Qing, also became increasingly complex. Systems of worker training were paired with shop-floor supervision by foremen and capped by the cultivation of a new class of managers who were neither workers nor owners, the blue-gown equivalent of the West's white collars.

The impetus for this innovation in management was the development of vertically integrated firms. As we have seen, by the mid-nineteenth century Zigong's larger salt manufacturers had moved to capture all aspects of the salt business under one roof. Well drilling, evaporation furnaces, and wholesale salt distribution were joined with agricultural properties dedicated to the provision of food for buffalo and employees and with commercial firms whose task it was to market those goods brought back from major salt markets like Chongqing and to supply the wells and furnaces with most of their everyday needs. Those goods not made or sold by the units of the main company were often purchased from firms with which the company had interlocking shareholding relationships not dissimilar to the interlocking directorships and partnerships maintained by New England's textile manufacturers.

Vertical integration was both an advance and a sign of market underde-velopment that drove manufacturers to try to obtain a monopoly over in-puts. Just as New England textile manufacturers came to combine carding, spinning, weaving, and dyeing, while Standard Oil combined refining and marketing with the extraction of crude,[4] Zigong salt producers used verti-cal integration to guarantee sources of supply in order to make the most efficient use of their production capacity. The more efficient they became in producing brine and gas, the more critical it was to be able to maintain the 24-hour operation of their physical plant and guarantee that their salt enjoyed an expanding market. In the Zigong case, poor transportation and the importance of agricultural inputs in the production process put produc-ers who could not integrate at a considerable disadvantage. Even so, salt manufacturers could not guarantee all inputs, as was demonstrated by the panic engendered among them in 1918 when the makers of bamboo cord went out on strike.[5]

In seeking to understand Zigong's place in industrial history, it is also important to note its kinship with the cotton plantation system of the American South. This may seem an odd analogy following our description of Zigong's similarities to some of the most advanced sectors of American industry. However, not only does the key to Zigong's ultimate fate lie in its technological, financial, and managerial innovations, but Zigong must be understood as an example of industrial "monoculture."

We have already noted in a qualitative way the importance of Zigong as a market for agricultural goods in southern Sichuan. More difficult to esti-mate is the quantitative importance of Zigong in the overall provincial economy.[6] We have no reliable data on nonagricultural output in Sichuan for the late Qing. However, a leap into the early twentieth century can give us some insight into the dominating role of salt in Sichuan. In his analysis of economic growth in Republican China, Thomas Rawski has estimated gross provincial product in Sichuan in 1933 to be approximately 5,010,000,000 yuan, of which 3,553,000,000 yuan, or 70 percent, repre-sented the value of Sichuan's agricultural output.[7] In the absence of com-prehensive 1930s survey data for Sichuan, Rawski based his estimates on national data and read back from the 1950s the relative distribution of ag-ricultural and nonagricultural GDP.[8] By his calculations the value of non-farm output, including mining, in Sichuan in 1933 was approximately 1,457,000,000 yuan. These figures are probably low. Data collected by the Sichuan salt administration allow us to calculate the total value of salt sold at the yard in 1933. This figure, 2,756,112,417 yuan, is considerably higher than the value of overall industrial output estimated by Rawski.[9] Some double counting of agricultural output as inputs to salt may be partly re-sponsible for this discrepancy, as is no doubt some underreporting of GDP in figures upon which Rawski based his calculations. In any case, a reasonable adjustment to the data would attribute the majority of industrial output value in Sichuan to salt.

This is confirmed by other sources that note the low levels of industrialization in Sichuan. For example, according to the report of the inspector general of customs in 1933, Sichuan had made few advances during the previous decade in the use of machinery. Cotton spinning was still a cottage industry, with only one weaving factory experimenting with the use of electric looms. Only one mechanized dye works and four flour mills existed in the whole province. Of 86 silk-reeling factories only 17 had modern machinery. In addition, Sichuan had a handful of knitting factories, tanneries, steam filatures, and a soap factory, as well as one rice mill, two cement works, a declining number of match factories, two modern ice works, and a small number of factories for making dry batteries.[10] Many of these so-called factories were cottage industries scattered throughout the province. Thus, as late as the 1930s salt continued to be the main manufacture in the province and Zigong the largest manufacturing center.

What does this mean for our analysis of Zigong's contribution to industrial development? It suggests that Zigong, while enormously successful in raising capital for its own purposes, became a sponge, soaking up scarce capital seeking an outlet in the province. Rather than repatriating profits, many merchants from Shanxi, Shaanxi, Jiangsu, Hubei, and elsewhere invested in wells and furnaces. Merchants from counties in Sichuan, like Jiangjin's pan manufacturers, invested in businesses serving the yard and eventually in salt production as well. Natives of Ziliujing and Gongjing had even less reason to go far afield in seeking business opportunities, and by the late nineteenth century a powerful Ziliujing-Gongjing guild (*jing bang*) joined the guilds of extraprovincial merchants in business at the yard. The Furong yard not only became a target for investment capital. It also became a training ground for human capital. Many of the managerial personnel at wells and furnaces came from merchant families outside the yard, sent to Zigong as apprentices, sometimes remaining as staff and later as investors themselves. While there is no way to determine whether this human and capital flow could have been directed elsewhere, there is no question that up to the end of the nineteenth century the development of the Furong yard and its system of partnerships spurred an unprecedented migration of men and money down the Tuo River to southern Sichuan.

The fuel that fed the Zigong salt boom came not only from commercial capital like that generated by Shaanxi merchants engaged in the wholesale salt trade. The main target for the investment of profits from Zigong salt manufacture was also Zigong. Profits were invested in shares, and the profits from shares were invested in more shares. Large producers started as small producers, like the Yans of the Yan Guixin lineage trust, whose principle of using the profits from one well to drill the next well resulted in one of the four great fortunes in nineteenth-century Zigong. In the chronicles of Zigong's wealthiest late Qing salt conglomerates there is no record of investment outside of the industry. Agricultural assets were acquired to feed the firms' employees and buffalo. Commercial firms were founded to market salt and acquire the goods needed for its manufacture. Wells and furnaces invested in firms selling bamboo and timber. Indeed, there is even evidence of large salt conglomerates borrowing from the funds originally raised for construction of the Sichuan-Hankow railroad at the turn of the century to further their opportunities for profits from salt.[11]

The concentration of investment in the Zigong salt industry is easy to understand. Zigong was like a fountain in a desert. Depopulated at the beginning of the Qing, the rich Red Basin of central Sichuan was an agricultural land of opportunity. But the province as a whole was mountainous and surrounded by some of the most underdeveloped regions in China: northern Yunnan, Guizhou, western Hubei, eastern Tibet, and the dry lands of the northwest. The Yangzi River, its link to the outside world, was difficult to navigate upriver, limiting the commerce in goods from the east. But the ease of downriver travel facilitated Sichuan's export of bulk items like grain, herbs, agricultural oils, and salt. It was this riverine network, which took goods from Chongqing to Yichang in Hubei and beyond, that allowed Furong salt to break into the Huguang market during the height of the Taiping Rebellion.

Sichuan in the late Qing became the breadbasket of China, furnishing rice to feed a growing population and to replace the staples no longer grown in the emerging handicraft centers of the east. Zigong remained the only industrial game in town, isolated in the far south of the province. Moreover, the nature of the industry guaranteed that at least in the short run it would not generate new industries in its wake. Until the 1890s the potential of large gas reserves to absorb seemingly unlimited amounts of new brine discouraged investment in anything but new wells. Moreover, this expansion of production had no effect on industrial development through either backward or forward linkages. Down to the end of the century, most of the inputs to the industrial works at Zigong came from agriculture. Zigong stimulated the iron works of eastern Sichuan by demanding a constant flow of pans and drill bits and other tools. Coal mining also received a boost from the small number of wells that produced coal-evaporated *ba* salt. But the multitude of derricks that pierced the Zigong sky, as well as the wheels that operated their pulleys, were made of timber, as were the countinghouses, brine vats, and cow sheds that dotted the countryside. Pumping tubes and brine pipes were made of bamboo, as was the coil that lifted the tubes. Hemp and tong oil lined the brine pipes, and bamboo baskets were used to bind the salt for market. Leather valves regulated the movement of brine in and out of the pumps. It was not until the twentieth century that a shift to wide-diameter wells and the introduction of steam-driven pumps linked the Zigong salt industry to an industry based on inanimate energy and forced the replacement of natural products with metal hoists and coils and tubes.

Zigong also provided few chances for forward linkages. With an industry based on mineral extraction and refining, Zigong's only hope in this direction was the diversification of refining to include other minerals present in its rich brine deposits. These include lithium, barium, cesium, magnesium, potassium, chromium, iodine, borax, and strontium.[12] We have seen that as early as 1916, proponents of salt industry reform such as Lin Zhenhan had promoted alternative industrial and agricultural uses for Furong's rich brine resources. However, little progress was made in this direction during the prewar period. During the first two decades of the twentieth century, innovations in well technology and mechanized pumping attracted most of Zigong's investment capital. During the political and military unrest of the 1920s and 1930s, disruptions to Sichuan's market economy and declining profits in the salt industry discouraged outside investment and scientific investigation at the saltyard.[13] Nor was any significant progress made during the interwar years to improve Sichuan's transportation infrastructure and links to northern and eastern Chinese industry and coastal export markets. Thus, on the eve of the war with Japan, the city built on salt remained a city built on salt, vulnerable to the risks of monoculture and contributing little to industrial development beyond its borders. According to one estimate, it was producing around 150,000 tons of brine, which was all that it could sell.[14]

The outbreak of war in 1937 changed Sichuan's economy. With free China cut off from its eastern sources of supplies, the Sichuan salt industry was once again called upon to satisfy a vast population's culinary and industrial demands. Unable to rely solely on market forces to revitalize the flagging industry, the Guomindang government reinstituted a system of state purchase and distribution of salt. To stimulate the reopening of defunct wells and furnaces the state also implemented a program of low- and no-interest loans to producers. Within a short time Furong's output exceeded the highest levels of the previous decades, topping out at approximately 260,000 tons of salt a year.[15]

The Japanese occupation of eastern China also set off an exodus of Chinese companies to the West. Among them were firms like the Jiuda Salt Industries Company, Ltd., the Yongli Soda-ash company, and the Huanghai Chemicals Industry Research Institute.[16] Each brought to Zigong new production technology, equipment, and research personnel, enabling the yard to move into the manufacture of salt byproducts such as potassium chloride, boric acid, calcium carbonate, and magnesium carbonate. At the same time, the needs of the military and relocated Chinese industries created a new market for Zigong's new chemical products. While their level of technology and output remained inferior to those of their eastern Chinese models, by the end of the war 15 local firms were also invested in this area.[17]

Building on almost half a century of experience in machine construction and repair, Zigong's machine tool industry also flourished during the war years. By 1940 the nine machine factories of the prewar period had increased to 15. According to the registration records of the Zigong Machine Industry Trade Association (Zigongdichu jiqigongye tongyegonghui), by the end of the war there were 32 such firms serving the machine tool industry: 12 were foundries, and 20 were repair and spare parts workshops.[18]

In 1946, with the cessation of fighting and the restoration of China's eastern territories, China's eastern industrialists marched back to the coast and the Furong market again collapsed. By 1949 Furong was evaporating only 979 pans and producing only 1,920 tons of salt.[19] The small operation Jiuda maintained in the yard after the war stopped production in August of that year. By then most of Zigong's foundries and machine shops had shut down.[20]

Zigong under communism remained an industrial backwater, handicapped by poor transport links to China's coastal economy and by limited markets for salt and salt by-products. In the immediate aftermath of the Communist takeover, private firms in Zigong, as elsewhere in China, were allowed to coexist with nascent state-run enterprises, some of the latter being legacies of "state capitalism" initiated by the Guomindang. The remains of the Jiuda plant in Zigong became a state-private joint enterprise in 1951 employing many of Zigong's now-bankrupt salt entrepreneurs. In 1954, state pressure resulted in the creation of the joint state-private Jianhua Salt Manufacturing company (*Jianhua zhiyan gongsi*), whose "investors" included Luo Xiaoyuan, Hou Ceming, Luo Huagai, Xiong Zuozhou, and Zhang Kaiming.[21] In 1957 Jianhua became part of the newly established Number 1, 2, and 3 factories of the state-owned Zigong Salt Manufacturing company (*Zhiyan gongye gongsi*). Private entrepreneurship was over in China. As for the merchants of Zigong, their legacy became their history, and the industry they built the object of museum, archive, and memory.

❖ ❖ ❖ ❖ ❖

Before we close this part of the Zigong story, it is worth taking a brief look at Zigong today. The city created in 1939 by the combination of the east and west yards is now a booming metropolis of more than 3 million people. Bamboo derricks have been replaced by tall tower blocks as the dominant image on the skyline (see illustration E.1). Zigong's producers now reach out to markets throughout China and beyond. Search the Internet for the word "Zigong" and

ILLUSTRATION E.1 Contemporary Zigong—New Development in the Huidong Area
Photograph by Matthew Malloy.

you will be taken to the sites of dozens of firms seeking foreign business and foreign investment. In 1992, as part of the Chinese government's plan to "develop the west," Zigong was designated a "high-tech industrial development zone." Since that time it has benefited from the restructuring of government business services, the launch of a high-tech industrial park across the Fuxi River from the old city, and, perhaps most importantly, major transportation projects linking Zigong to Chengdu and Chongqing by modern highway and rail services. According to the Web site of the high-tech zone, Zigong in the summer of 2004 boasted 1,812 industrial firms, of which 49 were large- and medium-size state-owned enterprises.[22]

Zigong industrialists today benefit from access to both national and international capital markets, as well as government support in the form of infrastructure development. They operate within a very different (and still evolving) legal and international business environment from that of their predecessors. Zigong is now home to a technical college and more than 60 scientific research institutes. And technical, engineering, and management staff receive training at numerous colleges and technical schools in China and abroad.

Whether Zigong's industrialists will succeed in the highly competitive environment taking shape in contemporary China will depend on very different factors from those that affected their forerunners. But the roots of industrial Zigong in the reform era still lie in the achievements of the nineteenth-century salt industry, an industry that continued to thrive in the early twentieth century and was kept alive in state enterprises and modest research institutions throughout the Maoist years. Natural resources—brine and natural gas—still form the basis for Zigong's prosperity. And its dominant industries continue to be salt and salt by-products and a machine tool industry that grew up in their service.

Notes

Preface

1. Madeleine Zelin, "The Structure of the Chinese Economy During the Qing Period: Some Thoughts on the 150th Anniversary of the Opium War," in Kenneth Liberthal et al., eds. *Perspectives on Modern China, Four Anniversaries* (Armonk, NY: M. E. Sharpe, 1991).

2. I will leave it to others to explain why other industries did not present similar opportunities for profit in the first instance and remained embedded in the rural economy well into the twentieth century. Most explanations of this phenomenon turn on the economics of the small peasant economy and focus on cottage industry, notably in textiles and tea. See, for example, Robert Paul Gardella, *Harvesting Mountains: Fujian and the China Tea Trade, 1757–1937* (Berkeley: University of California Press, 1994); Lillian Li, *The Chinese Silk Trade* (Cambridge: Harvard University Press, 1981); and Kang Chao, *The Development of Cotton Textile Production in China*, Harvard East Asian Monographs, no. 74 (Cambridge: East Asian Research Center, Harvard University, 1977). Mark Elvin focuses attention on a number of factors, including, as Philip Richardson succinctly notes, "the combination of low labor costs and the absorption of low-level modern technology" that "served to reinforce the competitiveness of the pre-modern economic system and strengthen its hold." Philip Richardson, *Economic Change in China, c. 1800–1950*, New Studies in Economic and Social History (New York: Cambridge University Press, 1999), 11, commenting on Mark Elvin, *The Pattern of the Chinese Past* (Stanford: Stanford University Press, 1973). The most recent contribution to this discussion, particularly as it relates to the role of the peasant economy in the equation, is the vigorous debate between Philip Huang, who sees in the Chinese countryside a case of agricultural involution, and Kenneth Pomeranz, who has argued for the existence of an industrious revolution that does not follow patterns found in England due to differences in China's access to energy

resources and overseas trade. See Philip C. Huang, "Development or Involution in Eighteenth Century Britain and China? A Review of Kenneth Pomeranz's *The Great Divergence: China, Europe, and the Making of the Modern World Economy*," *Journal of Asian Studies* 61, no. 2 (2002), and Kenneth Pomeranz, "Beyond the East-West Binary: Resituating Development Paths in the Eighteenth Century World," *Journal of Asian Studies* 61, no. 2 (2002).

3. Richard Langlois, "The Vanishing Hand: The Changing Dynamics of Industrial Capitalism," *Industrial and Corporate Change* 12, no. 2 (2003): 357.

4. Sidney Pollard, "Fixed Capital in the Industrial Revolution in Britain," *Journal of Economic History* 24, no. 3 (1964); Langlois, "Vanishing Hand"; Joel Mokyr, "The Industrial Revolution in the Low Countries in the First Half of the Nineteenth Century: A Comparative Case Study," *Journal of Economic History* 34, no. 2 (1974): 377 states, "Capital markets in nineteenth century Europe were so imperfect, that industrialists, for the most part, were unable to obtain long-term credit from savings generated in other sectors." Pollard notes that short-term bank loans did play an important role in providing circulating capital.

5. Naomi Lamoreaux, "Banks, Kinship, and Economic Development: The New England Case," *Journal of Economic History* 46, no. 3 (1986): 647, 663.

6. Oliver E. Williamson, "Comparative Economic Organization: The Analysis of Discrete Structural Alternatives," *Administrative Science Quarterly* 36 (June 1991).

7. These arguments are worked out in Chandler's seminal works: Alfred Dupont Chandler, *The Visible Hand: The Managerial Revolution in American Business* (Cambridge: Belknap Press of Harvard University Press, 1977), and, with Takashi Hikino, *Scale and Scope: The Dynamics of Industrial Capitalism* (Cambridge: Belknap Press of Harvard University Press, 1990).

8. Langlois, "Vanishing Hand," 358.

9. Chandler faults British firms for continuing to allow personal ties to outweigh the importance of professional managerial skills in the promotion of managers. Chandler and Hikino, *Scale and Scope*, 242.

10. Naomi R. Lamoreaux, Daniel M. G. Raff, and Peter Temin, "Beyond Markets and Hierarchies: Toward a New Synthesis of American Business History," *American Historical Review* 108, no. 2 (2003).

11. Langlois, "Vanishing Hand," 358–71.

12. Rong Li, "Ziliujing ji" [A record of Ziliujing], in *Shisanfeng shuwu quanji* [The collected works of the Thirteen Peaks Library] (Longan shuyuan, 1892); Fu Qiao, *Ziliujing diyiji* [Ziliujing, volume one] (Chengdu: Quchang gongsi, 1916); Shuzhi Zhang, "Ziliujing tudi liyong zhi diaocha" [An investigation of land use in Ziliujing], in Zheng Su, ed., *Minguo ershiniandai zhongguo dalu tudi wenti ziliao* [Materials on the land question on mainland China in the 1930s] (Taibei: Chengwen chubanshe, 1938).

13. Many of these have been published as part of the series Zigongshi difangzhi congshu [Zigong municipal gazetteer collection].

14. Zigongshi dang'anguan, Beijing jingjixueyuan, and Sichuan daxue, eds., *Zigong yanye qiyue dang'an xuanji (1732–1949)* [Selected Zigong salt industry contracts and documents (1732–1949)] (Beijing: Zhongguo shehuikexue chubanshe, 1985). The editors' introduction to this collection proved invaluable as a guide to the specialized vocabulary of Zigong's salt merchant community.

15. Most important to this study were Zigongshi dang'anguan, "Zigong yanye susong dang'an zhuanti xuanzepian—(1) Ziliujing Wang Sanwei tang yu Yusha zhaiquantuan zhaiwu jiufen an" [Selected documents on special topics from the archives of

Zigong salt lawsuits: (1) The case of the debt dispute between the Ziliujing Wang Sanwei tang and the Chongqing-Shashi creditor group], *Yanyeshi yanjiu* 1 and 2 (1993); Zhiyi Peng, ed., *Zigongshi zhi—Shanghui zhi, ziliao changpian* [(Draft) Gazetteer of Zigong city—Chamber of Commerce gazetteer, long compilation of documents] (Zigong: Zigongshi gongshangye lianhehui, 1989); and Zigongshi dang'anguan and Zigongshi zonggong hui, eds., *Zigong yanye gongren douzheng-shi dangan ziliao xuanbian (1915–1949)* [Selected documents on the history of the struggles of Zigong salt workers (1915–1949)] (Chengdu: Sichuan renmin chubanshe, 1989).

1. Salt Administration and Salt Technology

1. *Lijin*, a tax on goods in transit, was introduced in central China shortly after the onset of the Taiping Rebellion as a way to finance local and provincial military expenditure. This new levy would have extended *lijin* to include manufacturing as well as commerce and would have been particularly contentious in 1863, as fighting against the Taiping and associated rebels was drawing to a close.
2. The author was told this story many times during her stay in Zigong in 1989. This particular version is recorded by a former high-level manager of the Wang estate in Xiaoyuan Luo, "Ziliujing Wang Sanwei tang xingwang jiyao" [The basic elements of the rise and fall of the Wang Sanwei trust], *Sichuan wenshiziliao xuanji* 7 and 8 (1963): 171–73.
3. A detailed discussion of the reasons for and implications of the implementation of *guanyun shangxiao* may be found in chapter 7.
4. A traditional Chinese measure equal to about one-third of a mile.
5. This version of the Wang Langyun story is related both by Xiaoyuan Luo and in a novel written by Langyun's great-grandson, Wang Yuqi. See [pseudo.], Manyin *Ziliujing* (Chengdu, 1944), 18–19.
6. For a fuller exploration of the argument for a laissez-faire economic regime in late imperial China, see Madeleine Zelin, "The Structure of the Chinese Economy During the Qing Period: Some Thoughts on the 150th Anniversary of the Opium War," in Kenneth Lieberthal et al., eds., *Perspectives on Modern China, Four Anniversaries* (Armonk, NY: M. E. Sharpe, 1991).
7. Two works that delve into the role of salt throughout time are S.A.M. Adshead, *Salt and Civilization* (New York: St. Martin's Press, 1992), and Mark Kurlansky, *Salt: A World History* (New York: Walker, 2002).
8. Adshead, *Salt and Civilization*, 44.
9. Vogel notes that by the late Yuan dynasty 80 percent of state tax revenues were derived from salt. Hans Ulrich Vogel, "The Great Well of China," *Scientific American*, June 1993. The relative importance of salt revenues diminished greatly during succeeding dynasties due to the increasing capacity of the state to tax other sectors of the economy, particularly cultivated land. According to Wang Yeh-chien, taxes on salt constituted 11.9 percent of total tax revenues in 1753. This figure rose to approximately 15.4 percent by 1908 as a result of the central government's declining ability to collect taxes on the land. Yeh-chien Wang, *Land Taxation in Imperial China, 1750–1911* (Cambridge: Harvard University Press, 1993), 80. Of course, none of these figures takes into account extralegal levies on salt merchants and producers by local and provincial officials. For a discussion of the salt gabelle as a source of local revenues, see Madeleine Zelin, *The*

Magistrate's Tael: Rationalizing Fiscal Reform in Early Ch'ing China (Berkeley: University of California Press, 1984), 62–65, 119, 142–46, 154, 198, 201, 204–8, 218–19.

10. Guangrong Ran and Xuejun Zhang, *MingQing Sichuan jingyanshigao* [A draft history of the well-salt industry in Sichuan during the Ming and Qing period] (Chengdu: Sichuan renmin chubanshe, 1984), 1–2.

11. Vogel, "Great Well," 119.

12. S. A. M. Adshead, *The Modernization of the Chinese Salt Administration, 1900–1920* (Cambridge: Harvard University Press, 1970), 11. There was little change in these territories during the late imperial period.

13. As Adshead has noted, while the government invested considerable resources to prevent smuggling, it was largely the balance between cost of salt and quality that maintained the salt monopolies of each *yindi*. State efforts to alter that balance through differential taxation were generally ineffective. Ibid.

14. Ran and Zhang, *Draft History*, 2–3.

15. Adshead, *Salt and Civilization*, 74; Ran and Zhang, *Draft History*, 19–25.

16. Total salt revenues during the Hongzhi reign (1488–1506) converted from certificates and tickets to *jin* came to 500,780,395 *jin*. Of this, Sichuan's quota was only 20,666,850. By far the most prosperous salt-producing area at this time was the Lianghuai salt district in Jiangsu, where the annual tax quota was 141,030,500 *jin*. Raw data are based on Chen Renxi, *Huang Ming shifa lu*, juan 28, yanke, as converted and recorded in Renyue Tang et al., eds., *Zhongguo yanye shi* [A history of the Chinese salt industry] (Beijing: Renmin chubanshe, 1997), 648–49.

17. Ran and Zhang have estimated that during the late Ming Sichuan's actual output was 10 times the quota of salt its various production areas were obliged to provide the state tax administration. Ran and Zhang, *Draft History*, 10.

18. Robert Entenmann, "Sichuan and Qing Migration Policy," *Ch'ing-shih wen-t'i* 4, no. 4 (1980): 59.

19. *Fushun xianzhi* [Fushun County gazetteer] (1777; reprint, Guangxu), juan 3.

20. Entenmann, "Migration"; Madeleine Zelin, "Government Policy Toward Reclamation and Hidden Land During the Yongzheng Reign" (Manuscript, 1986).

21. Zijian Lu, "Qingdai Sichuan de yanque yu yanxiao" [Sichuan's salt gabelle and salt smugglers in the Qing period], *Yanyeshi yanjiu* 1 (1987): 56; Ziyi Peng, "Qingdai Sichuan jingyan gongchang shougongye de xingqi he fazhan" [The rise and development of the well-salt handicraft industry in Qing Sichuan], *Zhongguo jingjishi yanjiu* 3 (1986): 27–28; Ran and Zhang, *Draft History*, 102–3.

22. A *jin* was approximately 1.3 pounds, or 16 Chinese ounces.

23. Baozhen Ding, ed., *Sichuan Yanfa zhi* [Gazetteer of Sichuan salt administration] (China, 1882), juan 16, yinpiao, banxing 2b–4a.

24. Ibid., 3b–4a. See also Dedi Zhang, "Sichuan yankeshu" [A discussion of the Sichuan salt tax], in Hao Changling, ed., *Huangchao jingshi wenbian* [Essays on statecraft of our dynasty] (Taibei: Guofeng chubanshe, 1826; reprint, 1963), juan 50, huzheng, yanke xia, 70.

25. The weight of a *bao* changed over time. The base for establishing the *bao* was a bundle of salt weighing 100 *jin*. To this was sometimes added varying allowances for salt that was inevitably lost in shipping and for the weight of the wrappings and straw padding in which the salt was bound for transport. Thus one certificate entitled a merchant to ship over 5,000 *jin*, considerably more than the earlier *piao*. Ran and Zhang, *Draft History*, 103.

26. Adshead, *Modernization*, 21. The *bian'an*, or border markets, were particularly important as part of the state management of distribution. Guizhou, which produced no salt of its own, was thought to depend on a mandated market to encourage merchants to make the long and arduous trip to serve it.

27. Guoli gugong bowuyuan, *Gongzhongdang Yongzhengchao zouzhe* [Palace memorials of the Yongzheng reign], 32 vols, (Taibei: Guoli gugong bowuyuan, 1977), Shensi governor-general Yue Zhongqi, YZ 5, 8, 19, vol. 15.

28. Lu, "Salt Smugglers," 57.

29. As early as 1729 Sichuan governor Gao Weixin noted that inadequate supervision by prefectural officials resulted in widespread salt smuggling. While certificate quotas existed for each sales area, no systematic effort was made to track the output of hundreds of small wells deep in the province's mountainous regions. Guoli gugong bowuyuan, *Palace Memorials*, Sichuan Financial Commission Gao Weixin, YZ 8, 3, 7, vol. 15, p. 823.

30. Skinner places Sichuan population at approximately 4.5 million in 1713 and 17.7 million in 1813. G. William Skinner, "Sichuan's Population in the Nineteenth Century: Lessons from Disaggregated Data," *Late Imperial China* 7, no. 2 (1986): 66. As we will see, many of these new immigrants found work in Sichuan's burgeoning salt industry. Indeed, Paul Smith has argued that salt production was the single most important factor in transforming the Sichuan basin into the province's demographic center. Paul Smith, "Commerce, Agriculture, and Core Formation in the Upper Yangtze, 2 A.D. to 1948" (paper presented at the Conference on Spatial and Temporal Trends and Cycles in Chinese Economic History, 980–1980, Bellagio, Italy, 1984), 60.

31. According to the *Salt Administration Gazetteer*, Sichuan added more than 25,000 water-route certificates and 116,000 land-route certificates during the 73 years of these two reigns. Ding, ed., *Salt Administration Gazetteer*, juan 17, yinpiao 2, 22b–27a.

32. Ibid., juan 19, yinpiao 4, 1a–4b.

33. Lu, "Salt Smugglers," 59–60.

34. The Intendant attempted to shift certificate quotas from one place to the next, but the paperwork involved was confusing and difficult to keep under control. Guoli gugong bowuyuan, *Palace Memorials*, Xiande, YZ 11, 8, 2, vol. 21, pp. 881–84.

35. Ding, ed., *Salt Administration Gazetteer*, juan 18, yinpiao 3, 1a–1b.

36. Lu, "Salt Smugglers," 50; Ruyi Yan, "Lun Chuanyan" [On Sichuan salt], in Changling He, ed., *Huangchao jingshi wenbian* [Essay on statecraft of our dynasty] (Taibei: Guofeng chubanshe, 1826), juan 50, huzheng.

37. Ding, ed., *Salt Administration Gazetteer*, juan 17, yinpiao 2, 1a–17a.

38. Ran and Zhang, *Draft History*, 111–13, citing *Qingyan fazhi*. Thirty-seven more *guiding* counties were recognized by the end of the dynasty.

39. Ding, ed., *Salt Administration Gazetteer*, juan 17, yinpiao 2, 21b–29a.

40. Zhenhan Lin, *Chuanyan jiyao* [Essentials of Sichuan salt] (Shanghai: Shangwu yinshu guan, 1919), 410. To highlight the last point Lin used a familiar refrain among China's overly stretched local bureaucrats—*ermu nanzhou* (it is difficult for the eyes and ears to be everywhere).

41. Ibid., 410–11.

42. Renyuan Wang, Ran Chen, and Fanying Zeng, eds., *Zigong chengshi shi* [The history of Zigong city] (Beijing: Shihui kexue wenxian chubanshe, 1995), 17.

43. Tianying Wu, "Yinli juren, Yinren chengyi—Cong yandu Ziliujing kan gongshangye chengshi de xingcheng jiqi tedian" [People gather to make a profit, Cities

are founded because there are people—An examination of the formation and characteristics of the industrial-commercial city from the example of the salt capital Ziliujing] (manuscript), 3.

44. Lin, *Essentials of Sichuan Salt*, 202.

45. For a discussion of the Qing practice of drawing political boundaries so as to cut across the boundaries of economic communities, see ibid., 274–345, and G. William Skinner, *The City in Late Imperial China* (Stanford: Stanford University Press, 1977).

46. Ding, ed., *Salt Administration Gazetteer*, juan 22, zhengque 3, 7a.

47. Ibid., 7ab.

48. Vogel, "Great Well," 120.

49. Ding, ed., *Salt Administration Gazetteer*, juan 17, yinpiao 2, 1a–17a.

50. Tao-chang Chiang, "The Salt Industry of China, 1644–1911: A Study in Historical Geography" (Ph.D. diss., University of Hawaii, 1975), 64.

51. Fu Qiao, *Ziliujing diyiji* [Ziliujing, volume one] (Chengdu: Quchang gongsi, 1916), 113.

52. Chiang, "Salt Industry," 22.

53. Ibid., 7.

54. Sichuansheng Zigongshi Ziliujingquzhi bianzuan weiyuanhui, "Zigongshi Ziliujingquzhi" [Gazetteer of Ziliujing district, Zigong city] (Chengdu: Bashu shushe, 1993), 207.

55. Liangxi Song, "Shilun Qingdai Sichuan yanshang di faren" [A preliminary discussion of the beginnings of the Sichuan salt merchants], *Jingyanshi tongshun* 1 (1984): 36–37.

56. Measurement presents difficult issues for the historian of China. All references to inches and feet in this study are conversions from Chinese to U.S. measures. According to Lai Mingqin, the measures used at Furong were not standard even by local criteria. Furong feet were 2 or 3 inches longer than the feet used in the marketplace in Fushun County, and Lai estimates that they were approximately equal to about 1.2 feet. Mingqin Lai et al., "Yanyanjing fazhan gaikuang" [A survey of the development of rock-salt wells], *Zigong wenshiziliao xuanji* 6–10 (1982): 5.

57. Rong Li, "Ziliujing ji, an Account of the Salt Industry at Ziliujing," *ISIS* 39 (1948): 230. The translator has relied on the version of the "Ziliujing ji" located in the 1890 woodblock edition of Li Rong's collected works, entitled *Shi sanfeng shuwu quanji*. This original edition can be found in the collection of the Starr East Asian Library at Columbia University, and the author has consulted both versions in compiling this section on salt technology. Ding, ed., *Salt Administration Gazetteer*, juan 2, jingchang 2, 1a–45b, also contains useful selections from various works on salt technology, some dating back to the Ming. The illustrations accompanying this discussion are taken from the *Salt Administration Gazetteer*.

58. Li, "Ziliujing ji," 230; Vogel, "Great Well," 119.

59. Li, "Ziliujing ji," 230.

60. Conversation with retired well workers in Zigong, May 1989.

61. Chiang, "Salt Industry," 109. Chen Ran, a leading expert on the Zigong salt industry, places the beginning of the run on black brine at 1835. Ran Chen, "Ziliujing de jueqi ji qi fazhan" [The rise and development of Ziliujing], *Yanyeshi yanjiu* 1 (1987): 141.

62. Ran and Zhang, *Draft History*, 55.

63. One *dan* equals 100 *jin*, or approximately 133 pounds.
64. Wei Wu, ed., *Sichuan yanzhengshi* [Sichuan salt administration history] (China: Sichuan yanzhengshi bianjichu, 1932), juan 2, pian 2, zhang 4, jie 1, 50b.
65. Vogel, "Great Well," 120; Wallace Crawford, "The Salt Industry of Tzeliutsing," *China Journal of Science and Art* 4 (1926): 226.
66. Qiao, *Ziliujing*, 143.
67. Crawford, "Salt Industry," 227.
68. A brief discussion of these improvements can be found in Ran and Zhang, *Draft History*, 61–64.
69. Yuanxiong Lin, Liangxi Song, and Changyong Zhong, *Zhongguo jingyan keji shi* [The history of Chinese salt technology] (Chengdu: Sichuan Kexuejishu chubanshe, 1987), 385–88.
70. *Fushun County Gazetteer,* juan 2, shanchuan xia.
71. According to the Qianlong edition of the *Weiyuan xianzhi,* the development of the Weiyuan coal industry was due in large part to the first expansion of the Ziliujing saltyard in the Ming dynasty. Cited in Chen, "Rise and Development," 138.
72. According to Li Rong, the most productive well in the nineteenth century, the Haishun well, could boil 700 pans at a time. Rong Li, "Ziliujing ji" [A record of Ziliujing], in *Shisanfeng shuwu quanji* [The Collected Works of the Thirteen Peaks Library] (Longan shuyuan, 1892), juan 1, 3b.
73. Li, "Ziliujing ji," 231–32.
74. Zigongshi dang'anguan, Beijing jingjixueyuan, and Sichuan daxue, eds., *Zigong yanye qiyue dang'an xuanji (1732–1949)* [Selected Zigong salt industry contracts and documents (1732–1949)] (Beijing: Zhongguo shehuikexue chubanshe, 1985), 151–53.
75. Crawford, "Salt Industry," 284.
76. Lin, *Essentials of Sichuan Salt*, 222–23.
77. Crawford, "Salt Industry," 284.
78. Li, "Ziliujing ji," 234.
79. Shouji Wang, *Yanfa yilue* [A brief discussion of salt administration] (Beijing, 1877), juan xia.
80. Ding, ed., *Salt Administration Gazetteer*, juan 9, zhuanyun 4, 2a–2b. While we do not have eighteenth-century Yunnan certificate quotas for each Sichuan saltyard, by the 1870s Jianwei was expected to supply 4,381 water certificates and 83 land certificates. Rong County had a quota of 2,086 water certificates and Fushun 3,986 water certificates. In addition, Fushun had taken over the quotas of Neijiang and Zizhou for an additional 222 water certificates and 56 land certificates. This does not include an unknown amount of Sichuan salt being smuggled into Yunnan, a problem for Yunnan officials at least from the mid-eighteenth century. Ibid., 6b.
81. Ibid., juan 10, zhuanyun 5, 1b.
82. Ibid., juan 10, zhuanyun 5, 20b, 38b–39a.
83. Ibid., juan 10, zhuanyun 5, 39a.
84. Ibid., juan 5, jingchang 5, 1a–18b.
85. According to the *Salt Administration Gazetteer,* Jianwei had a quota of 11,858 water-route certificates and 51,608 land-route certificates in the 1880s. Converted to *jin*, Jianwei therefore produced a minimum of 79,933,200 *jin* per year. Jianwei is reported to have had 1,195 wells. Thus average well productivity was 66,889 *jin*

per year. The same calculations for Furong produce an average productivity per well during this period of 118,642 *jin*. See ibid., juan 17, yinpiao 2, peiyin biao, and juan 5, jingchang 5, yange xia, 1a–18b.

86. As we will see, part of this market can be traced through the levy of *lijin* on Sichuan salt sold to Huguang during and after the Taiping Rebellion. Most of this salt came from Furong.

2. The Structure of Investment in Late Qing Furong

1. Baozhen Ding, ed., *Sichuan Yanfa zhi* [Gazetteer of Sichuan salt administration] (China, 1882), juan 11, zhuanyun 6, 1a–34b; Guangrong Ran and Xuejun Zhang, *MingQing Sichuan jingyanshigao* [A draft history of the well-salt industry in Sichuan during the Ming and Qing period] (Chengdu: Sichuan renmin chubanshe, 1984), 136, based on figures from the Number One Historical Archives in Beijing.

2. Alexander Hosie's estimate of total output, including smuggled salt and salt sold by ticket, came to 560 million *jin* or almost 730 million pounds. See Alexander Hosie, *Szechuan, Its Products, Industries and Resources* (Shanghai: Kelly and Walsh, 1922), 181–82.

3. Ibid. Hosie's figures on salt output by county were obtained from the Sichuan provincial administration and attribute 58 percent of total provincial output to Fushun and Rongxian combined.

4. Ding, ed., *Salt Administration Gazetteer*, juan 2, jinchang 2, jingyan tushuo, 19b.

5. Rong Li, "Ziliujing ji, an Account of the Salt Industry at Ziliujing," *ISIS* 39 (1948): 230. Modifications to the translation are my own.

6. For a general discussion of the destruction wrought by competing armies in Sichuan during this period, see James B. Parsons, "The Culmination of a Chinese Peasant Rebellion: Chang Hsien-chung in Szechuan, 1644–46," *Journal of Asian Studies* 16 (1957), and Robert Entenmann, "Sichuan and Qing Migration Policy," *Ch'ing-shih wen-t'i* 4, no. 4 (1980).

7. See chapter 1.

8. Ding, ed., *Salt Administration Gazetteer*, juan 19, yinpiao 4, 12a; Ruyi Yan, "Lun Chuanyan [On Sichuan salt], in Changling He, ed., *Huangchao jingshi wenbian* [Essays on statecraft of our dynasty] (Taibei: Guofeng chubanshe, 1826), 13. A mid-eighteenth-century stele erected at the Shaanxi guildhall (*xiqin huiguan*) in Zigong claims that Shaanxi merchants deployed 10,000 boats to sell salt to Yunnan and Guizhou.

9. See the Qianlong 17 (1752) stele of the Shaanxi guildhall, Zigong, Sichuan.

10. Liangxi Song, "Zigong diqu de qianzhuang, piaohao yu yanye fazhan" [The development of native banks, remittance banks and the salt industry in the Zigong region], *Yanyeshi yanjiu* 2 (1994): 13–22.

11. Some Chinese scholars have argued that Shaanxi capital was critical to the development of deep brine wells in Zigong. Luo Chengji has made the strongest argument against early Shaanxi merchant investment in production, noting that prior to the nineteenth-century discovery of natural gas at Zigong, profits from the sale of salt were far greater than those from production, which limited the incentive for outsiders to invest in the risky business of well drilling. Luo also cites the 1752 Shaanxi guildhall stele, which makes no reference to the production side

of the salt business. Most important, he surveys the existing contractual record and maintains that the first Zigong contract involving Shaanxi merchants in a well-related transaction is dated 1839. As we shall see, several earlier investments can be documented, but none before 1827. See Chengji Luo, "Shaanshang zai Zigong yanchang de qiluo" [The ups and downs of the Shaanxi salt merchants at the Zigong saltyard], in Ziyi Peng, Renyuan Wang, and Zigong yanye chuban bianjishi, eds., *Zhongguo yanyeshi guojixueshu taolunhui lunwenji* [Theses from the international symposium on Chinese salt industry history] (Chengdu: Sichuan renmin chubanshe, 1991).

12. The absence of modern banking is raised at the very beginning of *The Cambridge History of China* volume on the Late Qing dynasty by Albert Feuerwerker, one of the leading scholars of China's modern economy. Albert Feuerwerker, Denis Crispin Twitchett, and John King Fairbank, *The Cambridge History of China*, vol. 11, *Late Ch'ing, 1800–1911* (Cambridge: Cambridge University Press, 1978), 14.

13. Lance E. Davis, "The New England Textile Mills and the Capital Markets: A Study of Industrial Borrowing 1840–1860," *Journal of Economic History* 20, no. 1 (1960); L. S. Pressnell, *Country Banking in the Industrial Revolution* (Oxford: Clarendon Press, 1956); Naomi Lamoreaux, "Information Problems and Banks' Specialization in Short-Term Commercial Lending: New England in the Nineteenth Century," in Peter Temin, ed., *Inside the Business Enterprise: Historical Perspectives on the Use of Information*, A National Bureau of Economic Research Conference Report (Chicago: University of Chicago Press, 1991), 161–95.

14. Xiaomei Zhang, *Sichuan jingji cankao ziliao* [Reference materials on the Sichuan economy] (Shanghai: Zhongguo guomin jingji yanjiu suo, 1939), D50. As late as 1939 the average capitalization of a Zigong native bank was only 11,666 yuan, and the highest-capitalized native bank had assets of only 20,000 yuan. Ibid., D46.

15. Ibid., D50. Tian Maode claims that the first native bank was not opened in Furong until 1907. Maode Tian, "Piaohao zai Sichuan di yixie huodong" [Some of the activities of remittance banks in Sichuan], *Sichuan wenshiziliao xuanji* 32 (1984): 59.

16. See, for example, the general descriptions of well and furnace operations and landlord-tenant relations in Wei Wu, ed., *Sichuan yanzhengshi* [Sichuan salt administration history] (China: Sichuan yanzhengshi bianjichu, 1932), juan 3, pian 2, jie 1, dizhu, and jie 2, jinghu, zaohu. In Leshan, Mianyang, Lezhi, and Jianyang owner-operated wells appear to have been quite common. It is also likely that furnace operators drilling wells at the ShePeng, NanLang, Lezhi, Santai, Pengzhong, Shehong, Nanyan, Xiyan, and Zhongjiang yards also purchased at least a portion of the necessary land. Even in Furong, some examples of land purchase for the purpose of well drilling can be found. See, for example, Zigongshi dang'anguan, Beijing jingjixueyuan, and Sichuan daxue, eds., *Zigong yanye qiyue dang'an xuanji (1732–1949)* [Selected Zigong salt industry contracts and documents (1732–1949)] (Beijing: Zhongguo shehuikexue chubanshe, 1985), contracts 9, 60, 86, 102, 103. Hereafter cited as *Zigong Contracts*.

17. Madeleine Zelin, "A Critique of Rights of Property in Pre-War China," in Madeleine Zelin, Johnathan Ocko, and Robert Gardella, eds., *Contract and Property Rights in Early Modern China* (Stanford: Stanford University Press, 2004), 17–36.

18. For a detailed discussion of the evolution of agricultural tenancy in one area of Sichuan, see Madeleine Zelin, "The Rights of Tenants in Mid-Qing Sichuan: A Study of Land-related Lawsuits in Baxian," *Journal of Asian Studies* 45, no. 3 (1986).

19. Minted copper coins were the common currency of the marketplace in China, whereas unminted silver was used for large transactions and was the main unit of taxation. The ideal exchange relationship between silver and copper cash was 1 tael to 1,000 cash, the latter often being strung on a cord for ease of use. Thus, a string of cash was 1,000 cash.

20. Leshan local archives, document number 69–7–7502–93, quoted in *Zigong Contracts*, 35.

21. Leshan local archives, document number 69–7–7494–4, quoted in ibid., 36.

22. Leshan local archives, document number 69–7–7502–189, quoted in ibid.

23. Madeleine Zelin, "Obstacles to Economic Development: The Mining Industry in Late Imperial Sichuan" (paper presented at the annual convention of the American Historical Association, New York, 1985), 4–5.

24. See, for example, Baxian Archives 6.6.38886 and 6.3.17218.

25. Ibid. 6.2.642, 6.3.17168, 6.5.14437, 6.6.38874, 6.5.14456, 6.5.14453, 6.3.17218, 6.3.17162, 6.3.17171, 6.6.38859, 6.5.14437.

26. *Zigong Contracts*, 35, 37–38.

27. On the Nationalist government's tax policies in Sichuan during the 1940s, see Lloyd E. Eastman, *Seeds of Destruction: Nationalist China in War and Revolution, 1937–1949* (Stanford: Stanford University Press, 1984). The editors of *Zigong Contracts* note that the government during the 1940s controlled rents on salt well sites. For example, in 1944 well-site owners in Leshan were forced to petition the government for permission to revert to rents in kind as a way to combat inflation and the rising value of taxes levied in kind. *Zigong Contracts*, 37–38.

28. For the mining industry, see, for example, Baxian Archives 6.6.38886, 6.3.17223, 6.5.14468, 6.6.38874. For salt, see, for example, Leshan local archives, document number 69–7–7502–223. See also *Zigong Contracts*, contracts 38, 86, 87. Although few examples are available for the salt industry, the stipulation that landlords not begin receiving a share of the profits until the well comes in indicates that it must have been a common condition in earlier share rent contracts as well. Ibid., 52.

29. Zelin, "Obstacles to Economic Development," 6.

30. Leshan local archives, document number 69–7–7502–189, cited in *Zigong Contracts*, 36. See also Leshan local archives, document numbers 69–7–7494–4 and 69–7–7502–223.

31. See, for example, Baxian Archives 6.3.2952 and 6.3.17028. Similar stipulations can be found in a small number of well-drilling contracts. See, for example, *Zigong Contracts*, contracts 76 and 78.

32. See, for example, Baxian Archives 6.5.14437 and 6.6.38886.

33. Ibid. 6.2.642.

34. Wu, ed., *Salt Administration History*, juan 3, pian 2, zhang 10, jie 1, 70a.

35. Ibid., juan 3, pian 2, zhang 10, jie 1, 70b.

36. See, for example, Baxian Archives 6.2.7099 for a contract dated 1799 containing such a clause.

37. For example, Tang Changfa rented a pit for six cash per load of coal mined. Baxian Archives 6.5.14419. Wu Jichuan's tenant paid him 16 loads for every 100 loads mined. Ibid., 6.5.14472. See also ibid., 6.5.14437 and 6.5.4454.

38. For example, Xu Chengxiu paid his landlord 1.2 taels per pickax per month. Baxian Archives 6.2.7099. See also ibid., 6.3.17223 and 6.5.13651.

39. Leshan local archives, document number 69–7–7494–135, cited in *Zigong Contracts*, 39.

40. Leshan local archives, document number 69–7–7502–223, cited in ibid., 39–40.

41. *Zigong Contracts*, contract 1.

42. Wu, ed., *Salt Administration History*, juan 3, pian 2, jie 2, 71b.

43. Guangrong Ran and Xuejun Zhang, "Sichuan jingyanye zibenzhuyimengya wenti yanjiu" [Research on the sprouts of capitalism in the Sichuan salt industry], in Nanjing daxue lishixi and MingQing yanjiushi, eds., *MingQing zibenzhuyi mengya yanjiu lunwenji* [Collected essays on the sprouts of capitalism in the Ming and Qing dynasties] (Shanghai: Shangwu chubanshe, 1981), 557.

44. For a discussion of rock-salt wells, see chapter 7.

45. Specific reference was made to the use of *weishui* and/or *weihuo* to pay for completion of initial well drilling in 43 of the 84 well-drillling contracts included in *Zigong Contracts*. These cover the period from the late eighteenth to the mid-twentieth centuries. Contracts that do not make mention of such a provision are often redrilling contracts in which reference might be found in an earlier version. See, for example, *Zigong Contracts*, contracts 8, 13, 21, 22, 35, 68. In a number of cases it was stated that all shareholders would divide any profits above the costs of drilling the well. See, for example, contracts 66, 73, and 75 dating from the 1860s and contract 84 from the Republican period.

46. See, for example, ibid., contracts 68, 69, 72.

47. See, for example, ibid., contracts 20, 21, 22, 24, 27, 34, 63, 66, 74.

48. See, for example, ibid., contracts 4, 14, 18, 19, 20, 21, 22, 23, 24, 26, 28, 60, 63, 66, 72, 74.

49. See ibid., 128–37.

50. See, for example, ibid., contracts 6, 20, 21, 25. Even as late as the Republican period some contracts continued to be this vague. See, for example, contracts 31 and 84. In a similar vein, some Republican period contracts referred to the time when drilling reached the rock-salt layer. See, for example, contract 53.

51. See, for example, ibid., contracts 19, 68, 69, 74.

52. As we have seen, the Tongsheng well contract stated that after the well produced enough brine to supply one or two pans a day, the landowner would enter the partnership and begin contributing to the costs of operations. In several cases dating from the first half of the nineteenth century similar requirements were made of the partnership after daily production reached four pans. See ibid., contracts 22, 23, 24, 27, 44.

53. Productivity limits in surviving contracts range from 30 *dan* of brine and gas for 10 pans to production of 8,000 *dan* a month and enough gas to boil 100 pans a day. See, for example, ibid., contracts 7, 8, 9, 13, 14, 15, 16, 38, 39, 49, 59, 60, 82, 83, 87. Specifications of minimum productivity to *jinban* during the Republican period could be exceedingly detailed. Contract 83 required the production of at least enough gas to fire 24 pans, each of which was capable of evaporating at least 3.5 *dan* of brine of a 2-*liang* concentration. The contract added that "using buffalo-driven pumps the well shall be capable of producing 2,400 *dan* of brine per month; using mechanical pumps it shall be capable of producing 6,000 *dan* of brine per month" before the landowner could enter the partnership.

54. So many contracts include these clauses that only a few examples can be listed here. See ibid., contracts 7, 14, 17, 20, 26, 32, 38, 40, 53, 65, 79, 85.

55. See, for example, ibid.

56. See ibid., contract 9. Some contracts did require consultation with the landowner before redrilling took place. See contracts 68 and 69.

57. Ibid., contract 64. See also contracts 51, 68, and 69.

58. Ibid., contracts 66 and 74.

59. See, for example, ibid., contracts 71, 73, 75, 78.

60. See, for example, ibid., contract 52, in which the landowner agrees that should someone else build a brine pipe across his land all 30 shares would partake of the rent.

61. Ming'an Gao, "Wutongqiao yanchang de fengjian lougui" [The feudal customary fees at the Wutongqiao saltyard], in *Sichuan Provincial Gazetteer*, Leshan editorial committee, Wutongqiao salt collection no. 2 (manuscript).

62. See *Zigong Contracts*, contracts 6, 9, 13, 14, 15, 17, 26, 28, 30, 31, 38, 39, 40, 49, 51, 55, 60, 64, 65, 67, 68, 69, 70, 71, 73, 75, 76, 78, 79, 80, 81, 82, 83, 85, 86.

63. Ibid., contract 52.

64. A chronicler of the Wang Sanwei trust recalls that the option to pump the well together or take turns pumping for a designated number of days each month was written into early leases on the lineage's land. Xiaoyuan Luo, "Ziliujing Wang Sanwei tang xingwang jiyao" [The basic elements of the rise and fall of the Wang Sanwei trust], *Sichuan wenshiziliao xuanji* 7 and 8 (1963): 166.

65. *Zigong Contracts*, 97. The editors note that in contract 17, dated 1942, the landlord and an earlier group of investors are expressly prohibited from attempting independent management of the well (*fenban*).

66. Ibid., 94 and contracts 91 and 92. The editors point out that these wells were drilled in the late nineteenth century but would not have cost less than similar wells in earlier decades.

67. See, for example, ibid., contracts 1, 4, 9, 15, 17, 38, 39, 86. The investors in the Shuangxing well divided movable goods and buffalo with the landowner party. However, this was a contract to continue drilling a well in progress in which the original developers had already invested. See contract 7. The retention of steam-driven pumps, the use of which was introduced in the early twentieth century, depended largely on who was responsible for their purchase. See, for example, contracts 13 and 83.

68. Luo, "Wang Sanwei Trust," 165–66. The lease signed with one Shaanxi merchant was for a period of 18 years, after which the Wang Sanwei trust recovered everything but the buffalo and brine pans.

69. Zilin Li et al., "Ziliujing Li Siyou tang you fazhan dao shuaiwang" [The Li Siyou trust of Ziliujing from their development to their decline], *Sichuan wenshiziliao xuanji* 4 (1962–63): 147.

70. Liangxi Song, "Shilun Qingdai Sichuan yanshang di faren" [A preliminary discussion of the beginnings of the Sichuan salt merchants], *Jingyanshi tongshun* 1 (1984): 38. This appellation relied on a pun on the last character of each of their names.

71. Zhenhan Lin, *Chuanyan jiyao* [Essentials of Sichuan salt] (Shanghai: Shangwu yinshu guan, 1919), 247–48.

72. This trend was reversed in the early twentieth century with the return to long-term leases on rock-salt wells.

73. See, for example, *Zigong Contracts*, contracts 7, 30, 45, 49. Our sample is too small and we know too little about the history of individual wells to draw any conclusions about the reasons for variations in the size of rent deposits.

74. See, for example, ibid., contracts 51, 53, 54, 60.

75. For examples of the effects of inflation on rent deposits see ibid., contracts 17, 86, 87. The exchange rate between silver taels and the yuan accounts for some of this discrepancy, but with wells like that in contract 17 (dated 1943) charging a

nonrefundable 100,000 yuan, the exchange rate factor plays only a small part in the rise in the price of a deposit.

76. See, for example, ibid., contracts 87 and 113. In contract 113 the deposit was paid in rice as a hedge against inflation.

77. Zelin, "Rights of Tenants in Mid-Qing Sichuan," 499–526.

78. See, for example, *Zigong Contracts*, contracts 4, 49, 53, 64, 70, 86.

79. See, for example, ibid., contracts 4, 6, 8, 20, 21, 25, 29, 44, 51, 52, 55, 64.

80. See, for example, ibid., contracts 23, 24, 66, 76, 78, 79, 83.

81. See ibid., contracts 53, 84, 86. Suspension of drilling without the return of the well could trigger litigation. See, for example, contract 2.

82. Jiajing *Sichuan zongzhi*, juan 16, *yanfa*, cited in ibid., 45.

83. Wu, ed., *Salt Administration History*, jan 3, pian 2, zhang 10, jie 2, 71a–72b.

84. *Zigong Contracts*, 5–46. For a reference to partnerships at the Jianle saltyard, see Duanfu Zhang, "Jianle dichu shouquyizhi di dachangshang—Wu Jingrang tang" [A Jianle area saltyard merchant lineage second to none—the Wu Jingrang trust], *Jingyanshi tongxun* 6 (1979–80): 50.

85. See, for example, *Zigong Contracts*, contracts 46, 47, 48, 49, 50.

86. See chapter 4.

87. *Zigong Contracts*, contract 58.

88. Myron Cohen, "Commodity Creation in Late Imperial China: Corporations, Shares and Contracts in One Rural Community," in David Nugent, ed., *Locating Capitalism in Time and Space: Global Restructuring, Polities and Identity* (Stanford: Stanford University Press, 2002), 89.

89. Richard Belsky, "Beijing Scholar-Official Native-Place Lodges: The Social and Political Evolution of Huiguan in China's Capital City" (Ph.D. diss., Harvard University, 1997).

90. Examples of wells with two, three, or even four *chengshouren* can be found in every period. In the twentieth century the party listed as *chengshouren* is sometimes a lineage estate or a partnership in its own right. Under these conditions it is possible that the estate or partnership had a department active in bringing together investment capital for its own projects. See, for example, *Zigong Contracts*, contracts 57, 79, 81.

91. For examples of contracts between landowner and *chengshouren,* see ibid., contracts 20, 21, 23, 27, 29, 35, 64, 66, 68, 69, 72, 73, 74, 75, 77, 78, 79.

92. See, for example, ibid., contracts 22, 25, 28, 36.

93. See ibid., contract 57. Some of Zhang Lesan's investments in wells are noted in Rongqing Ji, "Gongjing yanchang fazhan yipie" [A glance at the development of the Gongjing saltyard], *Sichuan wenshiziliao xuanji* 11 (1964): 197–201.

94. *Zigong Contracts*, 55. For specific references to the allocation of *chengshouren* shares from the landowner's shares, see contracts 22, 23, 24, 27, 66, 72, 74, 80, 81. Ran Guangrong and Zhang Xuejun indicate that these shares were sometimes taken from the investor's shares or both the investor's and the landowner's shares. Ran and Zhang, *Draft History*, 201. Two contracts survive in which the *chengshouren* shares were split between the investor and the landowner. See contracts 34 and 35.

95. See, for example, *Zigong Contracts*, contracts 37, 72, 73, 79, 80, 81.

96. See, for example, ibid., contract 35.

97. See, for example, ibid., contract 6, in which the landowner kept 20 and the *chengshouren* 10 shares after the tenants/investors returned the well.

98. See, for example, ibid., contract 24.
99. Ibid., 54. The compilers of this collection call our attention to contract 89, in which an addendum states that the *chengshouren*, Wang Shixing, received one-half share and *xinli qian* of 1,200 cash a month. This was no more than a skilled laborer might receive on a prosperous well site and should only be seen as symbolic compensation for most of the men who would undertake this job.
100. See, for example, ibid., contracts 18, 19, 20, 21.
101. Ibid., contract 18.
102. Ibid., contract 22.
103. This process was known as *zuoxiashi anquan*. We have three examples of *diqian*, all for the first two decades of the nineteenth century. In one case the amount contributed was 6,000 cash for each half share owned and in another the investors appear to have put up only 3,000 cash for each half share. See ibid., 18, 19, 34.
104. For example, investors in the Tianyuan well agreed to put up 800 cash a month for each half share they owned. Ibid., contract 18.
105. See, for example, ibid., contracts 22, 34, 35, 36. Other contracts contain statements that "each partner shall put up money according to his shares" (contract 56) or statements of penalties if a partner did not "pay the costs due from him" (contract 37).
106. Ibid., 50.
107. Ibid., document 43.
108. Ibid., 53–54.
109. See, for example, ibid., contracts 18 and 22.
110. See ibid., contract 35. Several contracts mention the optional use of this method, including 36 and 37.
111. See, for example, ibid., documents 725, 26, 27. The term often used in such cases was *jueding*, or absolute transfer, a term that can cause confusion for us. According to the compilers of *Zigong Contracts*, at the Furong saltyard the word *ding* was often used to mean "sale." However, many contracts also use it in its more conventional sense of sublet, as in contract 44, where shares were sublet to investors and returned when the lease was up. Ibid., 72.
112. See ibid., contracts 22, 32, 34, 37, 48, 58, 68, 69. Similar limitations were placed on landowners wishing to sell their shares. See, for example, contract 82. The custom that land for sale first be offered to neighbors and kin may have been the model for such clauses. While kin may be seen as having some prior stake in a piece of land that had been acquired by a distant common ancestor, by the Qing period any sense of neighbors or kin as a collectivity with residual rights to a particular piece of land was tenuous. Indeed, this restatement of custom is generally found in contracts of sale where the buyer was not a neighbor or kin. Whether one interprets the character *si* in *bude siding wairen* as private sale or illegal sale, the expression contains a strong implication that a collective decision is necessary prior to sale outside the partnership.
113. *Fushun xianzhi* [Fushun County gazetteer] (1872), juan 30, yanzheng xinzeng.
114. *Zigong Contracts*, contract 50.
115. Ibid., contract 54.
116. For example, this was the fate of the owners of the Yunzheng well described in ibid., contract 60.
117. See, for example, ibid., contracts 16, 57, 83. During the 1930s the decline in demand became so severe that the Nationalist government placed a moratorium on all new well construction, causing many unfinished wells to temporarily close

down. The effect of the contraction of Sichuan salt markets on the salt industry in Zigong is discussed in greater detail in chapters 9 and 10.

118. Ibid., contract 2, provides an excellent example of this phenomenon, resulting in disputed ownership of the well for decades.

119. Ibid., 74. Contracts 49, 50, 55, 60, 62, 98, 130, and 138 are all examples of equal division of shares.

120. See, for example, ibid., contract 54, as well as contracts 9 and 48. Similar conditions can be seen in a number of documents not directly concerned with well drilling. See, for example, documents 220, 372, 413, 482, 486, 518.

121. Contracts calling for splits of approximately 2:1 (as in ibid., contracts 5, 16, 56) and 3:2 (as in contracts 51, 52, 53, 54, 59) appear to have been common. In one case the *xiajie* bought out the landowner's shares as well as receiving a majority of the investor shares. Ibid., contract 58.

122. Ibid., contract 59.

123. Ibid., contract 58.

124. See, for example, ibid., contracts 7, 45, 47, 51, 52, 53, 54, 55, 59, 60, 61. Similar clauses may be found in contracts between original landowners and investors as well.

125. Ibid., 81.

126. See, ibid., 8, 9, 14, 17, 45, 51, 52, 53, 54, 55, 60, 61, 83.

127. Ibid., 197. See, for example, contract 83.

128. This was presumably to guard against landowner or *shangjie* efforts to repossess a well in the hope of making an extraordinary strike if the investors did not continue drilling. See, for example, ibid., contracts 15, 59, 60.

129. Ibid., 81. See contracts 59, 64, 63.

130. Ibid., 83–86. This chain of events is derived from documents 45, 46, 91, 220, and 486 as well as several other documents in the archives that were not reproduced in this collection.

131. Peter Tufano, "Business Failure, Judicial Intervention, and Financial Innovation: Restructuring U.S. Railroads in the Nineteenth Century," *Business History Review* 71, no. 1 (1997).

132. See *Zigong Contracts*, contracts 16 and 58. See also Madeleine Zelin, "Merchant Dispute Mediation in Twentieth Century Zigong, Sichuan," in Philip Huang and Katherine Bernhardt, eds., *Civil Law in Qing and Republican China* (Stanford: Stanford University Press, 1994), 268.

133. *Fushun County Gazetteer*, juan 30, yanzheng xinzeng.

3. Fragmentation as a Business Strategy

1. Ji Rongqing, who worked at the Gongjing yard for more than 40 years, beginning in 1909, recalls that the owners of wells rarely operated their property. Rather, most well operators leased their wells. Rongqing Ji, "Gongjing yanchang fazhan yipie" [A glance at the development of the Gongjing saltyard], *Sichuan wenshi-ziliao xuanji* 11 (1964): 189.

2. See chapter 4 for a discussion of Furong's salt-manufacturing elite.

3. Although the well was drilled first, it was common practice to organize the operation under the name of the furnace built to evaporate its salt. *Sichuan Salt Administration History* lists the following saltyards as combining management of a well and its associated furnace: Jianwei, Leshan, Jingyan, Zixian, Pengshui,

Kaixian, Dengguan, Fengjie, Dazu, Shepeng, Jianyang, Nanbu, Lezhi, Langzhong, Santai, Pengzhong, Suining, Mianyang, Shehong, Nanyan, Xiyan, and Zhongjiang. Wei Wu, ed., *Sichuan yanzhengshi* [Sichuan salt administration history] (China: Sichuan yanzhengshi bianjichu, 1932), juan 3, pian 2, jie 2, 73b, 75a–78a.

4. The fortune of the great Wu family of Wutongqiao was originally based on the Linjia well and its furnace at Youjing po and the Longtai well and its associated Fuxinglin furnace. Each furnace evaporated two pans. The Linjia well operation could produce 80 to 90 *dan* of salt a month, while its sister operation generally yielded 100. Duanfu Zhang, "Jianle dichu shouquyizhi di dachangshang—Wu Jingrang tang" [A Jianle area saltyard merchant lineage second to none—the Wu Jingrang trust], *Jingyanshi tongxun* 6 (1979–80): 48.

5. In a conversation in Zigong in May 1989 retired well workers agreed that one of these wells could produce enough gas to evaporate between 500 and 600 pans. As noted in chapter 1, Rong Li's "Ziliujing ji" states that one extremely productive gas well was known to fuel 700 pans. The higher concentration of black brine meant far greater salt output per *dan* of brine. Yaolin Ling, "Qingdai Zigong jingyanye zibenzhuyi mengya fazhan daolu chutan" [A preliminary investigation of the sprouts of capitalism in the Zigong salt industry], *Sichuan daxue xuebao congkan* 14 (1982): 83. Prior to the introduction of mechanical pumps, discussed in chapter 7, rock-salt wells produced little more than this per month. However with a salt concentration of 33 percent rock-salt wells were almost twice as productive as black-brine wells. Xiaoyuan Luo, "Zhang Xiaopo dui Zigong yangchang di yingxiang" [The influence of Zhang Xiaopo on the Zigong saltyard], *Zigong wenshiziliao xuanji* 12 (1981): 184; Ling, "Sprouts of Capitalism," 88.

6. Pure gas wells were found only in Ziliujing. Here a single well fueled an average of 70 to 450 pans a day. A fire and brine well could have an output of less than one gas unit to as many as 300 at the most productive wells. Most emitted only enough gas to operate a few dozen pans. Zigongshi dang'anguan, Beijing jingjixueyuan, and Sichuan daxue, eds., *Zigong yanye qiyue dang'an xuanji (1732–1949)* [Selected Zigong salt industry contracts and documents (1732–1949)] (Beijing: Zhongguo shehuikexue chubanshe, 1985), 149. Hereafter cited as *Zigong Contracts*.

7. For a discussion of fragmentation as a generalized phenomenon in the early modern Chinese economy, see Madeleine Zelin, "The Rights of Tenants in Mid-Qing Sichuan: A Study of Land-Related Lawsuits in Baxian," *Journal of Asian Studies* 45, no. 3 (1986); Madeleine Zelin, "Obstacles to Economic Development: The Mining Industry in Late Imperial Sichuan" (paper presented at the annual convention of the American Historical Association, New York, 1985); and Madeleine Zelin, "The Structure of the Chinese Economy During the Qing Period: Some Thoughts on the 150th Anniversary of the Opium War," in Kenneth Lieberthal et al., eds., *Perspectives on Modern China, Four Anniversaries* (Armonk, NY: M. E. Sharpe, 1991).

8. For a discussion of the role of the state and various parapolitical institutions in the enforcement of contracts, see Madeleine Zelin, "Merchant Dispute Mediation in Twentieth Century Zigong, Sichuan," in Philip Huang and Katherine Bernhardt, eds., *Civil Law in Qing and Republican China* (Stanford: Stanford University Press, 1994), and Madeleine Zelin, "A Critique of Rights of Property in Pre-War China," in Madeleine Zelin, Johnathan Ocko, and Robert Gardella, eds., *Contract and Property Rights in Early Modern China* (Stanford: Stanford University Press, 2004).

9. See, for example, *Zigong Contracts*, contracts 279 and 281.

10. See, for example, ibid., contracts 269 and 270.
11. See, for example, ibid., contracts 83, 85, 88, 152, 168, 172, 179. The longevity of these contracts is highlighted by the following two examples of addenda. Contract 185 was entered into in 1896 and contains an addendum dated 1924. Contract 194, written in 1901, was amended in 1948.
12. See, for example, ibid., contracts 269 and 295.
13. See, for example, ibid., contracts 270, 282, 283.
14. See, for example, ibid., contracts 278 and 302.
15. Ibid., contract 278, is typical of such agreements.
16. A recent study of the accounting methods utilized at Zigong wells notes that "these firms used the *sanjiaozhang* (three-leg bookkeeping method) to record business transactions and their cash balances were calculated using the *sizhufa* (four-pillar balancing method). Their profits were measured at regular intervals using the advanced indigenous bookkeeping methods called the *liuzhufa* (six-pillar balancing method) and the *longmen zhang* (dragon-gate bookkeeping method). Their accounts not only showed basic features of double-entry bookkeeping, but also provided evidence for depreciation calculations and some recognition of the accruals concept." Lei Fu, Zhixiang Liu, and Auyeung Pak, "A Study of Zigong Salt Mine Accounts in China" (available at http://www.deakin.edu.au/wcah/papers/Fu.pdf). The characters for these bookkeeping methods and a discussion of their place within the history of Chinese accounting may be found in Robert Gardella, "Squaring Accounts: Commercial Bookkeeping Methods and Capitalist Rationalism in Late Qing and Republican China," *Journal of Asian Studies* 51, no. 2 (1992).
17. See, for example, *Zigong Contracts*, contracts 277, 278, 284.
18. See, for example, ibid., contracts 277, 280, 848.
19. See, for example, ibid., contracts 275, 276, 284.
20. According to Luo Congxiu, many *chengshouren* operated retail shops and native banks of their own. Much of their income was derived from the markup on goods and credit supplied to the wells they operated. This caused resentment among shareholders who often pulled out once the well was completed and managed their shares on their own. Congxiu Luo, "Gongjing yanchang de jingzao daguan" [The well and furnace *daguan* of the Gongjing saltyard], *Zigong wenshiziliao xuanji* 20 (1990): 123.
21. Yuesheng Pu, "Zigong wasijingzao de daguan" [The gas well *daguan* of Ziliujing and their functions], *Zigong wenshiziliao xuanji* 20 (1990): 119.
22. Huaizhou Wang, "Ziliujing chang daguan jiqi zhineng" [The *daguan* of Ziliujing and their functions], *Zigong wenshiziliao xuanji* 20 (1990): 113–14, and conversation with Wang Huaizhou in May 1989.
23. Zeyuan Lin, "Wosuo zhidao de Zigong jingzao daguan" [What I know about Zigong's well and furnace *daguan*], *Zigong wenshiziliao xuanji* 20 (1990): 9. *Daguan* literally means "great pass."
24. Wang, "*Daguan*," 113; *Zigong Contracts*, contract 799.
25. Lin, "*Daguan*," 110.
26. Wang, "*Daguan*," 115; Luo, "Gongjing Yard," 122.
27. Wang, "*Daguan*," 113.
28. *Zigong Contracts*, contracts 284 and 799; Lin, "*Daguan*," 110–11.
29. For a discussion of the reasons for the low uptake on limited liability incorporation, see William C. Kirby, "China Unincorporated: Company Law and Business

Enterprise in Twentieth-Century China," *Journal of Asian Studies* 54, no. 1 (1995).

30. See, for example, *Zigong Contracts*, contracts 273 and 277.
31. See, for example, ibid., contracts 272 and 277.
32. An institution of local social control by which households were organized into groups of 10 for mutual surveillance.
33. *Zigong Contracts*, contract 295.
34. See, for example, ibid., contracts 282 and 848.
35. See chapter 10.
36. See *Zigong Contracts*, contracts 798–830, and Chengji Luo, "Shaanshang zai Zigong yanchang de qiluo" [The ups and downs of the Shaanxi salt merchants at the Zigong saltyard], in *Zhongguo yanyeshi guojixueshu taolunhui lunwenji* [Essays from the international conference on Chinese salt industry history] (Chengdu: Sichuan renmin chubanshe, 1991), 503. From the names of the parties signing for each member lineage trust it appears likely that the partners were not merely all Shaanxi merchants, but were all members of a Liu common descent group.
37. See chapter 8.
38. *Zigong Contracts*, contract 799, dated 1930.
39. Ibid., contract 730.
40. Ibid., contracts 277 and 292. See also ibid, 256.
41. Ibid., contract 297.
42. Ibid., contract 256.
43. Ibid., contract 295.
44. Ibid., contract 848.
45. Ibid., 253.
46. Wu, ed., *Salt Administration History,* juan 3, pian 2, zhang 10, jie 2, 73b.
47. *Zigong Contracts*, 223–25.
48. For a discussion of the Baxian mining industry, see Zelin, "Obstacles to Economic Development."
49. *Zigong Contracts*, 222–23.
50. Cited in ibid., 123–24. See original Ming'an Gao, "Wutongqiao yanchang de fengjian lougui" [The feudal customary fees at the Wutongqiao saltyard], in Sichuan provincial gazetteer, Leshan editorial committee, Wutongqiao salt collection no. 2 (manuscript).
51. Zhen'an Liu, ed., *Yunyang xianzhi* [Yunyang County gazetteer] (1935), juan 10, yanfa.
52. Many of the surviving partnership contracts begin with a delineation of the well shares they have managed to rent and upon which their production will be based. See, for example, *Zigong Contracts*, contracts 269, 289, 297, 838, 848. Although such arrangements were rare, we do have several examples of partnerships renting entire wells. See, for example, contracts 270, 283, 300. Contracts 159 and 604 provide even less common examples of the sale of all the shares in a well in one package.
53. See, for example, ibid., contracts 145, 150, 162, 180, 191.
54. See, for example, ibid., contracts 151, 152, 164, 167, 178, 182, 184, 192, 197.
55. According to Evelyn Rawski, contracts of this kind gave the original owner the right to redeem the land or demand additional compensation for sale at a later date. Evelyn Rawski, "Property Rights in Land in Ming and Ch'ing China" (manu-

script, 1985), 24–25. See also Noboru Niida, *Chugoku hoseishi kenkyu tochiho torihikiho* [Chinese legal history—land and the law of transactions] (Tokyo: Tokyo University Press, 1960), 381–82.

56. For a lengthy discussion of well sales in other parts of Sichuan based on rare local-level archival materials, see *Zigong Contracts*, 219–30.

57. See, for example, ibid., contracts 147, 150, 152, 167, 182, 185, 191.

58. See, for example, ibid., contracts 145, 148, 150, 152, 162, 181, 184, 187, 196.

59. The Qing state attempted to control conditional sales and the disputes such sales often spawned by limiting the time period within which any parcel could be redeemed and by requiring sellers of land to clearly specify in their contracts that a sale was a final sale. For a discussion of the difficulties encountered in enforcing the rules on conditional sales, see Thomas Buoye, "Litigation, Legitimacy and Lethal Violence," in Zelin, Ocko, and Gardella, eds., *Contract and Property in Early Modern China*, 94–95, 104–6.

60. See, for example, *Zigong Contracts*, contracts 171, 189, 190.

61. A similar attitude toward well sites can be found throughout Sichuan. The 1935 edition of the *Yunyang xianzhi* stated, "Those who buy salt shares exceed those who buy land because the profits are rapid and large." The same source pointed out that wells were rented or purchased on the basis of the quality and size of the property, making well sites a form of stable property investment similar to agricultural land. Liu, ed., *Yunyang County Gazetteer*, juan 10, yanfa.

62. See, for example, *Zigong Contracts*, contracts 168, 181, 186, 189, 197.

63. These statements almost always referred to prior offers to both relatives and partners. See, for example, ibid., contracts 169, 191, 192. Only one contract in our sample mentions partners alone. See contract 188.

64. See, for example, ibid., contract 187. Protection of tenants in cases where shares were subleased was a feature of the saltyard regulations, as testified to by their inclusion in the discussion of gas well rentals in Wu, ed., *Salt Administration History*, juan 3, pian 2, zhang 10, jie 3, 74a.

65. Wu, ed., *Salt Administration History*, juan 3, pian 2, zhang 10, jie 3, 74a. We will return to this subject when we examine the brine pipe industry in chapter 4.

66. Tenancy contracts, like sale contracts, clearly stated the number of shares being transferred and the precise condition of all equipment to which those shares had a partial claim. This was particularly important to the landowner, inasmuch as he would want some guarantees that the physical plant at the well was returned in the same condition in which it was leased.

67. See, for example, *Zigong Contracts*, contracts 323, 325, 363.

68. See chapter 8.

69. Of particular interest is the history of the four great salt-producing lineages, the early histories of which are discussed in chapter 4.

70. See, for example, *Zigong Contracts*, contracts 35, 88, 112, 385.

71. For examples of the different ways this could be handled, see ibid., contracts 415, 443, 446, 449, 468, 474. These conditions did not apply to gas wells, where an increase in the number of pan units produced was generally accompanied by a rise in rent.

72. See, for example, ibid., contracts 392, 443, 454. Variations were also found. For example, contract 451 stated that the landowner and tenant would enter into discussions regarding any repairs to be undertaken, depriving the tenant of the

unilateral right to decide how much would be spent. In still other cases, the landowner agreed to pay for repair of a collapsed well and the tenant took sole responsibility for leaks. *Zigong Contracts*, 136.

73. See, for example, ibid., contracts 343, 474, 477. In the last instance the landowner promised to assist in the provision of any additions made within two years of the end of the lease.

74. See also ibid., contracts 377, 380, 385. Contracts of this kind do not appear to have included rent deposits.

75. See, for example, ibid., contract 341.

76. Ibid., 151.

77. See, for example, ibid., contract 482, in which the Ronghe furnace agreed to pay 125 cash for every *dan* of brine they boiled using gas from the Taisheng well.

78. This could be measured as a fixed rate of rent per *dan* or bundle of salt produced at the furnace or as a floating sum based on the number of *jin* of salt produced each month. See, for example, ibid., contracts 486, 497, 518, 520.

79. Ibid., 165. This was made easier by the establishment of an official standard for the saline content of brine during the Republican period.

80. This method was made possible by the establishment of a government salt-purchasing agency which fixed salt prices and distributed all salt produced in Zigong during the war with Japan.

81. *Zigong Contracts*, 156. Only one example of this form of tenancy is included in the published collection. See contract 518. Other examples were examined by the compilers at the Zigong Municipal Archives.

82. See, for example, ibid., contracts 366, 376, 379, 412.

83. Wu, ed., *Salt Administration History*, juan 3, pian 2, zhang 10, jie 1, 70a, gives a short definition of *dipi huo*. Some renters of gas also obtained all or some of their pans from the landowner. *Guozu*, or pan rent, was calculated separately from that of gas and the landowner's desire to protect his own investment in pans gave rise to elaborate measures of pan specifications to ensure that the equipment returned at the end of the lease was the same as that received when the lease began.

84. Fu Qiao, *Ziliujing diyiji* [Ziliujing, volume one] (Chengdu: Quchang gongsi, 1916), 151.

85. Zigong document 8–1–728–103, cited in *Zigong Contracts*, 154.

86. Ibid., contract 413.

87. Ibid., contract 486.

88. Wu, ed., *Salt Administration History*, juan 3, zhang 10, jie 3, 73b–79a.

89. See, for example, *Zigong Contracts*, contracts 366 and 380.

90. See, for example, ibid., contract 377.

91. See, for example, ibid., contracts 415, 429, 430, 485.

92. Zhenhan Lin, *Chuanyan jiyao* [Essentials of Sichuan salt] (Shanghai: Shangwu yin-shu guan, 1919), 247. It is not clear whether or not this included the cost of setting up the well, derrick, countinghouse, and other facilities. It did not include the costs of establishing a furnace, as furnaces were generally independent enterprises.

93. Qiao, *Ziliujing*, 143.

94. See, for example, *Zigong Contracts*, contracts 144–64. Note the higher price paid for well shares, which were held in perpetuity and were not part of a short-term contract with the landowner.

95. Qiao, *Ziliujing*, 149. These figures conform well with the lease rates found in late-nineteenth- and early-twentieth-century gas lease contracts. See, for example, *Zigong Contracts*, contracts 377, 378, 379, 380, 381.

96. Lin, *Essentials of Sichuan Salt*, 214–15.

97. Ji, "Gongjing," 77–78. *Zigong Contracts*, contract 58, memorializes the restructuring of the Tianlong well in 1932, when it still produced 160 pan units of gas. Income from 10 units was set aside for the operation of the well. If each remaining unit were leased for 100 taels per year, this well could easily have netted its investors 80,000 taels a year.

98. Lin, *Essentials of Sichuan Salt*, 248. These figures were denominated in yuan, which I have converted to taels to remain consistent with the other data I have presented.

99. Based on figures supplied in Qiao, *Ziliujing*, 81, 89, 165–66.

100. For a recent example of this argument, see John King Fairbank and Merle Goldman, *China, A New History* (Cambridge: Belknap Press of Harvard University Press, 1992), 180.

101. For examples of advance lease renewal and lease continuation contracts, see *Zigong Contracts*, contracts 567–72.

4. Organization and Entrepreneurship in Qing Furong

1. According to Rong Li's "Ziliujing ji" several hundred households dominated the salt business in the late Qing. Rong Li, "Ziliujing ji, an Account of the Salt Industry at Ziliujing," *ISIS* 39 (1948).

2. Zilin Li et al., "Ziliujing Li Siyou tang you fazhan dao shuaiwang" [The Li Siyou trust of Ziliujing from their development to their decline], *Sichuan wenshiziliao xuanji* 4 (1962–63): 147.

3. Xiaoyuan Luo, "Ziliujing Wang Sanwei tang xingwang jiyao" [The basic elements of the rise and fall of the Wang Sanwei trust], *Sichuan wenshiziliao xuanji* 7 and 8 (1963): 164–65.

4. For a discussion of the civil service examination system and its role in the construction of China's late imperial elite, see Chung-li Chang, *The Chinese Gentry: Studies on Their Role in Nineteenth-Century Chinese Society* (Seattle: University of Washington Press, 1955); Ping-ti Ho, *The Ladder of Success in Imperial China: Aspects of Social Mobility, 1368–1911* (New York: Columbia University Press, 1962); and Benjamin A. Elman, *A Cultural History of Civil Examinations in Late Imperial China* (Berkeley: University of California Press, 2000).

5. Li, "Li Siyou Trust," 145–46.

6. Wu Sangui, one of the leaders of the so-called Three Feudatories, was a former Ming military commander who assisted the new Manchu empire in its conquest of China and for about two decades ruled parts of southwest China as a virtual fiefdom.

7. Xianqi Yan, Wenfang Yan, and Zuo Yan, "Yan Guixin tang yu Ziliujing" [The Yan Guixin trust and Ziliujing], *Yanyeshi yanjiu* 3 (1990): 64.

8. Shaoquan Hu, "Gongjing Hu Yuanhe di guangzou yu shuailuo" [The rise and fall of Hu Yuanhe of Gongjing], *Zigong wenshiziliao xuanji* 12 (1981): 49–51.

9. Rongqing Ji, "Gongjing yanchang fazhan yipie" [A glance at the development of the Gongjing saltyard], *Sichuan wenshiziliao xuanji* 11 (1964): 187.

10 Mingqin Lai et al., "Yanyanjing fazhan gaikuang" [A survey of the development of rock-salt wells], *Zigong wenshiziliao xuanji* 6–10 (1982): 39.

11. Hu, "Hu Yuanhe," 50.

12. Yan, Yan, and Yan, "Yan Guixin Trust," 64–66.

13. Other important landowners who made their money by renting out well sites included Zhang Sanhe, Xiao Zhihe, the Wang Ronghua ancestral temple, the Lus, the Chens, and the Liang Zhuanjing trusts. Hu, "Hu Yuanhe," 50; Lai, "Rock-Salt Wells," 38. Numerous other examples appear in *Zigong Contracts*, including the Wang Wugui, Wang Shuangfa, Xie Puzhao, Wang Shuyuan, and Wang Yuanji trusts.

14. Jiong Tang, *Chengshan laoren zi xuan nianpu* [Autobiography of the old man of Cheng mountain] (Taibei: Wenhai chubanshe, 1910; reprint, 1968), juan 5.

15. Luo Chengji has found that merchants from Jiangxi traded in general merchandise, pottery, and dried fruit. Chengji Luo, "Shaanshang zai Zigong yanchang de qiluo" [The ups and downs of the Shaanxi salt merchants at the Zigong saltyard], in Ziyi Peng, Renyuan Wang, and Zigong yanye chuban bianjishi, eds., *Zhongguo yanyeshi guojixueshu taolunhui lunwenji* [Theses from the international symposium on Chinese salt industry history] (Chengdu: Sichuan renmin chubanshe, 1991), 490–504. My own work on merchant-related materials in the Baxian Archives (Chongqing environs) has revealed Guangdong merchants trading in dry goods, notions, and other miscellaneous goods during the nineteenth century.

16. Yuemou Ouyang et al., "Zigong difang di diandangye" [The pawnshop business in Zigong], *Zigong wenshiziliao xuanji* 13 (1983): 147. Ouyang was the manager of a pawnshop in Zigong from 1925 to 1935. The 1937 edition of the *Santai County Gazetteer* notes that both pawnshops in the county were opened by Shaanxi merchants in 1697. *Santai xianzhi* [Gazetteer of Santai County] (1937), juan 12.

17. Ruyi Yan, *Sansheng bianfang beilan* [Investigation of security at the border of the three provinces] (Yangzhou: Jiangsu Guangling gujikeyinshe, 1822; reprint, 1991), juan 10, shanhuo, 13.

18. Luo, "Shaanxi Salt Merchants," 500; Xiaomei Zhang, *Sichuan jingji cankao ziliao* [Reference materials on the Sichuan economy] (Shanghai: Zhongguo guomin jingji yanjiu suo, 1939), D50.

19. Maode Tian, "Piaohao zai Sichuan di yixie huodong" [Some of the activities of remittance banks in Sichuan], *Sichuan wenshiziliao xuanji* 32 (1984): 57–58.

20. Luo, "Shaanxi Salt Merchants," 501.

21. *Qingchao xuwenxiantongkao*, juan 37, zhenggui 9, cited in Dixin Xu and Chengming Wu, eds., *Zhongguo zibenzhuyi fazhanshi* [A history of the development of the sprouts of capitalism in China] (Beijing: Renmin chubanshe, 1985), 604.

22. Wencheng Shu et al., "Ziliujing shaoyangongren di hanghui zuzhi—Yandigong" [The guild organization of the Ziliujing salt evaporators—the Yandigong], *Zigong wenshiziliao xuanji* 12 (1981): 39–40. The date of this strike is not given, but from internal evidence it must have taken place sometime in the 1850s.

23. In tracing the history of various districts within the Furong yard, Huang Zhiqing and Nie Wufang have identified numerous wells that can be attributed to Shaanxi merchant investment, including most of the more productive yellow-brine wells drilled during the 1850s; shallow and deep wells opened in Panxia gou, including

the Dexian well, which produced over 100 *dan* a day; and more than a hundred wells in the vicinity of Shangyi hao. Shaanxi merchants were particularly lucky in the Guojia ao area, where Liu Zikang's Hongyuan well spurted over 1,000 *dan* a day and had more than 600 pan units and his fellow provincials owned the Shuanglong well, with more than 400 pan units, and the Hongfu and Shihong well, with more than 200 pan units each. Zhiqing Huang and Wufang Nie, "Zigong yanchang fazhan pianduan" [Passages on the development of the Zigong saltyard], *Zigong wenshiziliao xuanji* 6–10 (1982): 523–55. Other early examples include Wang Can, who drilled the Ruhai well in 1779; another Shaanxi merchant named Wang, who invested 1,450 taels to drill the Xinghai well in 1808; and Li Tianxi and Jiang Jiren, who drilled the Shuangfu well in the following year. Yaolin Ling, "Qingdai Zigong jingyanye zibenzhuyi mengya fazhan daolu chutan" [A preliminary investigation of the sprouts of capitalism in the Zigong salt industry], *Sichuan daxue xuebao congkan* 14 (1982): 81.

24. Ling, "Sprouts of Capitalism," 88. For a discussion of rock-salt wells, see chapter 7.

25. This discussion is based largely on information contained in Luo, "Wang Sanwei Trust."

26. According to the main memoir of this lineage's history, these wells produced no more than several tens of *dan* a day each. Li, "Li Siyou Trust," 147.

27. The Haishun and Haiwang wells together produced more than 500 pan units, while the less profitable Darong well also gave them sufficient gas to run several tens of pans. Ibid., 148.

28. During this period Shaanxi merchants invested in other saltyards as well. One such man appears to have been responsible for the improvement of technology used at the Pengshui yard as early as the late eighteenth century. From a document in the office of the committee for the compilation of the Sichuan gazetteer in Guangrong Ran and Xuejun Zhang, "Sichuan jingyanye zibenjuyi mengya di tantao—Guanyu Qingdai Furong yanchang jingying qiyue di chubu fenxi" [An exploration of the sprouts of capitalism in the Sichuan well-salt industry—a preliminary analysis of Qing period Furong saltyard management contracts], *Sichuan daxue xuebao congkan* 5 (1980): 39.

29. Baozhen Ding, ed., *Sichuan Yanfa zhi* [Gazetteer of Sichuan salt administration] (China, 1882), cited in Zijian Lu, "Chuanyan jichu yu Sichuan yanye fazhan" [Sichuan salt in aid to Huguang and the development of the Sichuan salt industry], *Shehui kexue yanjiu* 2 (1984): 78.

30. Luo, "Wang Sanwei Trust," 167.

31. Retold in ibid.

32. Li, "Li Siyou Trust," 149.

33. Ibid., 157.

34. Luo, "Wang Sanwei Trust," 167.

35. Hu, "Hu Yuanhe," 53–54.

36. *Sichuan guanyun yan'an leipian* [A collection of Sichuan Guanyun salt cases] (Beijing: Caizhengbu yanwushu, 1902), juan 34, 21.

37. For an introduction to the literature on the role of the lineage in the control of communal property, see Hillary Beattie, *Land and Lineage in China: A Study of Tungcheng, Anhui in the Ming and Qing Dynasties* (Cambridge: Cambridge University Press, 1979); David Faure, "The Lineage as Business Company: Patronage versus Law in the Development of Chinese Business" (paper presented at the Second Conference on Modern Chinese Economic History, Institute of Economics, Academia Sinica,

Taipei, Taiwan, 1989); Maurice Freedman, *Lineage Organization in Southeastern China* (London: Athlone Press, 1958); and Jack Potter, *Capitalism and the Chinese Peasant: Social and Economic Change in a Hong Kong Village* (Berkeley: University of California Press, 1968). Elisabeth Köll and Sherman Cochran, in studies of the Rong and Zhang textile empires, have demonstrated that early modern Chinese firms based on lineage trusts could engage in considerable innovation, expand beyond their local environment, and develop vertically integrated management structures. Sherman Cochran, *Encountering Chinese Networks: Western, Japanese, and Chinese Corporations in China, 1880–1937* (Berkeley: University of California Press, 2000), 117–46; Elisabeth Köll, *From Cotton Mill to Business Empire: The Emergence of Regional Enterprises in Modern China,* Harvard East Asian Monographs, no. 229 (Cambridge: Harvard University Press, 2004), 16–28.

38. See "Lijianianpu" [Li family genealogy] (early Qing manuscript copy).
39. Li, "Li Siyou Trust," 193.
40. Hu, "Hu Yuanhe," 51.
41. Ibid., 56–57.
42. Ibid., 56.
43. For the significance of Fan Wenzhang as an exemplar in the establishment of lineage trusts, see Dennis Twitchett, "The Fan Clan's Charitable Estate, 1050–1760," in David S. Nivison and Arthur F. Wright, eds., *Confucianism in Action* (Stanford: Stanford University Press, 1959).
44. The provisions of the lineage hall rules as outlined in the memorial to the emperor may be found in Luo, "Wang Sanwei Trust," 176–77.
45. Guangrong Ran and Xuejun Zhang, *MingQing Sichuan jingyanshigao* [A draft history of the well-salt industry in Sichuan during the Ming and Qing period] (Chengdu: Sichuan renmin chubanshe, 1984), 232.
46. The early downturn of fortunes among the Yan Guixin trust has been attributed in part to its failure to institute professional management of the daily operations of its lineage holdings. During the late 1860s the illness of the founder of the salt empire so occupied the family that it neglected its salt business for several years. Poor management of the Yan's Guizhou salt wholesaling firm led to its bankruptcy in the early 1870s, after which large debts and disputes among lineage branches prevented the consolidated lineage trust from regaining its former stature at the yard. Yan, Yan, and Yan, "Yan Guixin Trust," 73–74.
47. According to Li Rong, writing in the late nineteenth century, there were several types of managerial staff at the saltyards. Most important were the unit managers (*guanshi*), who included the supervisor in charge of well drilling, the supervisor in charge of the brine and gas at the furnace, the supervisor in charge of transport of brine through the brine pipes, and the supervisor in charge of wholesale operations. Other management-level personnel included *jingji* in charge of the purchase and sale of salt and *waichang*, whose job it was to deal with visitors and handle relations with the outside. Rong Li, "Ziliujing ji" [A record of Ziliujing], in *Shisanfeng shuwu quanji* [The collected works of the Thirteen Peaks Library] (Longan shuyuan, 1892), juan 1.
48. Hu, "Hu Yuanhe," 56.
49. Luo, "Wang Sanwei Trust," 185–86.
50. Ibid., 191.

51. Ibid. A system composed of a main office, with four general managers in charge of wells, pipes, furnaces, and wholesaling, respectively, was in operation at the Li Siyou trust as well. Li, "Li Siyou Trust," 150.

52. On multidivisional structures, see Oliver E. Williamson, *The Economic Institutions of Capitalism: Firms, Markets, Relational Contracting* (New York: Free Press, 1985), 279–85, and Alfred Dupont Chandler and Takashi Hikino, *Scale and Scope: The Dynamics of Industrial Capitalism* (Cambridge: Belknap Press of Harvard University Press, 1990), 43–44, especially 44, fig. 2.

53. Li, "Li Siyou Trust," 152–54.

54. Duanfu Zhang, "Jianle dichu shouquyizhi di dachangshang—Wu Jingrang tang" [A Jianle area saltyard merchant lineage second to none—the Wu Jingrang trust], *Jingyanshi tongxun* 6 (1979–80): 53.

55. Hu, "Hu Yuanhe," 70; Lei Li, "Luo Xiaoyuan jiushi" [Luo Xiaoyuan's past], *Ziliujing* 1 (1983): 40–41.

56. Li, "Li Siyou Trust," 162.

57. See, for example, the case of Jiang Zihe, who was stolen away to run one of the Hu Yuanhe trust's most productive wells. It was Jiang who first convinced the Hus to switch from animal to machine power to draw brine. Hu, "Hu Yuanhe," 70–71. When Luo Xiaoyuan set up in business on his own, most of his top managers were men he brought over from the Wang Sanwei trust. Chaolan Song, "Wosuoliaojie di Luo Xiaoyuan" [What I know of Luo Xiaoyuan], *Ziliujing* 4 (1984): 38.

58. The use of highly paid expert managers was a common feature of other industries at the saltyard as well. Lumberyards placed particular value on hiring experts as buyers (*zhuangke*) who went to the forest areas to select timber. Fangbo Ma, "Zigong yanchang di mucai shangye" [The lumber business at the Zigong saltyard], *Zigong wenshiziliao xuanji* 6–10 (1982): 276. Managers at Furong bamboo yards could make around 200 strings a year, while the best paid, Wang Jujing and Gou Pingsan, are said to have made 360, a sum unequaled by any staff member save the head of the Wang Sanwei trust's main office. Chunwu Huang et al., "Qingmoyilai Zigong yanchang zhuye" [The bamboo industry in Zigong since the late Qing], *Sichuan wenshiziliao xuanji* 9 (1963): 68.

59. Li, "Li Siyou Trust," 158–59. A popular joke in Zigong was that the only things Shaanxi guild managers did not receive from the bosses were their shoes, as a result of which they always wore beautiful clothes but their shoes were full of patches.

60. The practice of supplying food for one's staff was common in late imperial China. Clerks at government offices also enjoyed this benefit. At the Wang Sanwei trust, in addition to the usual morning and evening meal, once every five days there was the major meat meal (*yaji*) traditionally provided by masters for their craftsmen. Relatives and friends of the staff were also welcomed at these feasts. During the New Year's season, numerous banquets were held. Song, "Luo Xiaoyuan," 38.

61. Li, "Li Siyou Trust," 159.

62. Ibid., 161. This policy could sometimes work against the interests of good management, as in the case of Five Pockmark Zhang, whose loyalty and contribution to Li family fortunes was rewarded after his death by the employment of a useless opium-smoking nephew who for years came to the Lis for financial help.

63. Hu, "Hu Yuanhe," 52.
64. Song, "Luo Xiaoyuan," 39.
65. Luo, "Wang Sanwei Trust," 191.
66. Li, "Li Siyou Trust," 150. Their distance from the main office required special arrangements for the salt companies. Shareholders' meetings were held every three years at the site of the main wholesale outlets in the Yungui market. It is likely that these were also opportunities for a good time, as the managers of the salt company made certain the visiting dignitaries were well entertained. Ibid., 158.
67. Ibid., 161.
68. A holiday that marks the end of the New Year's festivities and, according to the Western calendar, generally falls in February.
69. Hu, "Hu Yuanhe," 57.
70. Tian, "Activities of Remittance Banks in Sichuan," 64.
71. Li, "Li Siyou Trust," 161; Tian, "Activities of Remittance Banks in Sichuan," 64.
72. This was one of the motivations behind the Hu Yuanhe trust's purchase of a white wax company in Jiading prefecture, home of the second largest saltyard in Jianwei County. Hu, "Hu Yuanhe," 53.
73. Lu, "Aid to Huguang," 78.
74. Xiangchen Jiang and Xiaoyuan Luo, "Zigong yanchang di niu" [Buffalo at the Zigong saltyard], *Zigong wenshiziliao xuanji* 12 (1981): 108.
75. Ibid., 209; Ran and Zhang, *Draft History*, 225. For every five buffalo used, one driver also had to be employed.
76. Jiang and Luo, "Buffalo," 109–10; Ran and Zhang, *Draft History*, 225–26; Zigongshi dang'anguan, Beijing jingjixueyuan, and Sichuan daxue, eds., *Zigong yanye qiyue dang'an xuanji (1732–1949)* [Selected Zigong salt industry contracts and documents (1732–1949)] (Beijing: Zhongguo shehuikexue chubanshe, 1985), 176–78 (hereafter cited as *Zigong Contracts*).
77. Jiang and Luo, "Buffalo," 110.
78. See chapter 3. There is some evidence that buffalo contractors could raise buffalo more efficiently than could small well owners. According to a document cited in *Zigong Contracts*, buffalo owned by buffalo contractors could sometimes be fed less and incurred fewer medical costs than those owned by well owners. This would help explain the profits made by large buffalo contractors. However, wells that leased buffalo in this way still incurred higher costs than had they kept their own teams. *Zigong Contracts*, 176.
79. If we assume that one tube could draw between one and two *dan* and a *dan* of brine earned the well owner 0.47 taels, then a well paying for pumping by the tube paid the contractor between one-third and two-thirds of his income from brine sales. As we have seen in tables 3.1 and 3.2 the largest part of the fixed costs of production was the purchase and care of buffalo. Thus it was less costly to contract for well pumping at less productive wells. The larger the output of the well, the more savings one saw by operating the well oneself.
80. Ran and Zhang, *Draft History*, 172; Xu and Wu, eds., *Sprouts of Capitalism in China*, 620. According to Zhang Xuejun, *banfangche* reappeared during the 1930s when unemployment in the region was particularly high. Xuejun Zhang, "Xinghai geming yu Zigong yanye" [The 1911 Revolution and the Zigong salt industry], *Jingyanshi tongxun* 11 (1983): 16.
81. Luo, "Wang Sanwei Trust," 168.
82. Ibid., 187.

83. Ibid., 188.
84. The next two recipients were the Li Siyou trust and the Baoxinglong, a marketing company that also had large holdings in wells and furnaces. Ibid., 190.
85. Li, "Li Siyou Trust," 157. The Renhuai market, or *ren'an,* served Renhuai Independent *ting,* and Cunyi, Dading, and Guiyang prefectures in Guizhou province.
86. Luo, "Wang Sanwei Trust," 190–91.
87. With a buffalo population of 30,000 during the last years of the dynasty, the care of water buffalo could be big business. Most wells were dependent on private medicine shops, often owned by buffalo doctors who contracted with a particular well or group of wells to care for their livestock and supply them with medicines. Jiang and Luo, "Buffalo," 117–18.
88. Ibid., 121.
89. Wang Dexian and Wang Ziheng were partners in the Changfaxiang bamboo yard, and the Wang Sanwei trust opened the Guangyigong bamboo yard. Huang et al., "Bamboo Industry," 69.
90. Tian, "Activities of Remittance Banks," 59.
91. Of these 17, the Hengtong well was still operating in 1959. Li, "Li Siyou Trust," 151.
92. When first drilled, the Shuangfu well was a self-spurting well producing over 1,000 *dan* per day of the highest-concentration black brine known at the yard. At the time of the Communist revolution it was still in operation. Ibid., 151–52.
93. Ibid., 160–61; Luo, "Wang Sanwei Trust," 190.
94. Li, "Li Siyou Trust," 158.
95. Ibid., 160. The Qijiang market consisted of Qijiang and Nanchuan counties in Sichuan, and Pingyuan independent zhou and Guiyang, Cunyi, and Duyun prefectures in Guizhou. The Dashengmei's operations must have been quite large, as their main warehouse had a capacity of 20 *zai.*
96. Ma, "Lumber," 274.
97. Hu, "Hu Yuanhe," 53.
98. Ibid., 58.
99. Ibid., 54.
100. Ibid., 59.
101. The one exception was an important investment partnership developed between Yan Changying and his in-law Li Ji'an, who was not a member of the prosperous Li Sanwei trust. Yan, Yan, and Yan, "Yan Guixin Trust," 66–67.
102. Ibid., 68.
103. Li, "Li Siyou Trust," 150.
104. The manager of the Tailai furnace, Li Cuishan, is said to have commissioned the construction of two specially designed wooden cabinets in his bedroom, in each of which was stored 40,000 taels. On the policy of the Hu Yuanhe trust, see Hu, "Hu Yuanhe," 59. Besides the cash kept at the individual salt companies, the Hus's Shenyi trust maintained a reserve fund of 200,000 taels.
105. Madeleine Zelin, *The Magistrate's Tael: Rationalizing Fiscal Reform in Early Ch'ing China* (Berkeley: University of California Press, 1984), 136–90 passim.
106. Only the Yans appear to have made a conscious decision not to invest heavily in land. The exception to this was their role in the development of the merchant retreat at Sanduo zhai. Yan, Yan, and Yan, "Yan Guixin Trust," 67–68.
107. For a discussion of the number of workers at the Furong saltyard, see chapter 5.

108. At its height, the Wang Sanwei trust kept a herd of between 1,200 and 1,300 buffalo. Even during its period of decline, its wells required the maintenance of at least 600 to 700 head. Luo, "Wang Sanwei Trust," 187.

109. Jiang and Luo, "Buffalo," 119. Even where they did not directly control the disposal of farmers' grass crop, the large well owners consumed a sufficient percentage of the output to be able to dictate prices. Every saltyard had a number of grass markets (*caoshi*) where farmers not bound to particular salt producers would sell their crop.

110. Legend has it that the technology for building brine pipes was first introduced to Sichuan by a Fujian immigrant named Li Qigong during the early Qing. Ling, "Sprouts of Capitalism," 84; Xiaoyuan Luo and Xiangchen Jiang, "Zigong yanchang di jianshang" [Pipe merchants at the Zigong saltyard], *Zigong wenshiziliao xuanji* 13 (1983): 135. Also see Wei Wu, ed., *Sichuan yanzhengshi* [Sichuan salt administration history] (China: Sichuan yanzhengshi bianjichu, 1932), juan 2, zhang 4, jie 10, 87a. Pipes were utilized to transport brine at other yards as well, particularly Jianwei and Leshan. However, these pipes were short and involved neither the expense nor the technology of their Furong counterparts. Most extended no farther than the well owner's own land, although a few of the larger pipes did involve tenancy arrangements of some kind. Wu, ed., *Salt Administration History*, juan 2, zhang 4, jie 10, 88b; *Zigong Contracts*, 273.

111. Ling, "Sprouts of Capitalism," 84; Xiaoyuan Luo, "Zhang Xiaopo dui Zigong yangchang di yingxiang" [The influence of Zhang Xiaopo on the Zigong saltyard], *Zigong wenshiziliao xuanji* 12 (1981): 186.

112. Ji, "Gongjing," 190; Luo, "Wang Sanwei Trust," 189; *Zigong Contracts*, 274. As we shall see, the Enliu pipe was a late addition to the industry. Confusion can result from the fact that these pipes underwent several changes of name over the years of their use. For example, from contracts we can see that the Datong pipe was originally called the Dasheng pipe when established by the Li Siyou trust in 1876. In 1913 it was dismantled and moved to Gongjing, after which time its name was changed to the Qingyun and Datong pipes. The Yuanchang pipe was not moved. However, its name was changed, first to the Yuanxin when it was merged with the Tongxin pipe. Most of these changes took place during the 1920s and 1930s after the peak period of pipe development had passed. *Zigong Contracts*, 275.

113. According to Needham and Lo, tunnels were occasionally dug through low hillsides to allow the pipes to continue on a downward path, letting gravity carry the brine to the furnaces. Joseph Needham and Jung-pang Lo, "The Salt Industry" [draft chapter for *Science and Civilization in China*] (manuscript, 1972), 66. I would like to thank Hans Ulrich Vogel for his generosity in making this manuscript available to me.

114. Zhenhan Lin, *Chuanyan jiyao* [Essentials of Sichuan salt] (Shanghai: Shangwu yinshu guan, 1919), pian 2, zhang 5, 221–22; Xu and Wu, eds., *Sprouts of Capitalism in China*, 594; *Zigong Contracts*, 273.

115. Lin, *Essentials of Sichuan Salt*, 248.

116. Luo, "Wang Sanwei Trust," 194.

117. Luo, "Zhang Xiaopo," 187; Wu, ed., *Salt Administration History*, juan 3, pian 2, zhang 10, 69b.

118. Luo and Jiang, "Pipe Merchants," 137. An equally telling example is that of Hu Shaozhang (no relation to the Hu Yuanhe trust). Hu was a large well and furnace

owner in Gongjing during the early twentieth century. Although he managed more than 500 pan units of gas and several wells, and had his own salt-marketing company, his lack of local connections made it impossible for him to lease land on which to build a pipe. His goal was accomplished only when he hired the locally prominent Yu Shuhuai to act as a front man for the company in arranging the leases for the land on which the pipe was built. Yuzhi Cui and Shaoyuan Yan, "Gongjing yanshang Yu Shuhuai" [The Gongjing salt merchant Yu Shuhuai], *Zigong wenshiziliao xuanji* 14 (1984): 173.

119. *Zigong Contracts*, 284–85. For examples of the wide differences in rent rates, see contracts 547–72. Most contracts stipulated rental of land for a certain number of pipe joints and, if necessary, sites for vats and other equipment.

120. Ibid., 298–99.

121. *Sichuan Salt Administration History* states that pipe land leases ranged from 10 to 20 years. However, most contracts in the Furong collection are for periods of six to 10 years. Wu, ed., *Salt Administration History*, juan 3, pian 2, zhang 10, 69b.

122. *Zigong Contracts*, 296–97. Sixty-five documents have survived for this pipe for the period between 1889 and 1920. See contracts 732–97. Rice prices during the early Qing were reported within a range, a high and a low price generally being conveyed for each prefecture in the empire. The average range of prices for rice in 1850 Xuzhou prefecture, in which Ziliujing is located, was 2.1 taels per *shi*. When we compare this with rice prices during the last decades of the Qing, it is clear that rice prices remained relatively stable, rising little higher than their 1850 counterparts, except in periods of extreme flood or drought (figure 4.2).

123. Luo, "Zhang Xiaopo," 186. In another article Luo asserts that during the 1890s, 70 percent of existing pipes were owned outright or in partnership by Wangs and Lis. Luo and Jiang, "Pipe Merchants," 135.

124. Ibid., 137.

125. Luo, "Wang Sanwei Trust," 189, Luo and Jiang, "Pipe Merchants," 139.

126. A similar advantage was gained by Standard Oil when it began building long-distance pipelines to transport oil. As Chandler points out, pipelines moved crude oil more cheaply than railroads and "[t]heir existence made possible the scheduling of a much greater and steadier refinery throughput than was possible using railroad shipments." Pipes gave Standard Oil additional oil storage. The ability to capture the transport of crude oil for its own refineries depended on Standard Oil's skillful manipulation of the legal system by bringing on board local enterprises. Alfred D. Chandler, *The Visible Hand: The Managerial Revolution in American Business* (Cambridge: Belknap Press of Harvard University Press, 1977), 223–26.

127. Cui and Yan, "Yu Shuhuai," 173.

128. *Zigong Contracts*, 273.

129. Ji, "Gongjing," 190; Luo, "Zhang Xiaopo," 187; Luo and Jiang, "Pipe Merchants," 140.

130. Luo and Jiang, "Pipe Merchants," 139–40.

131. Xiaoyuan Luo, "Furong guanyunju di bihai" [Malpractices in the Furong Official Salt Distribution Bureau], *Zigong wenshiziliao xuanji* 14 (1984): 58; Luo and Jiang, "Pipe Merchants," 137–39. According to Luo Xiaoyuan, powerful pipe owners could even buy extra certificates from the Guanyun bureau. Luo, "Wang Sanwei Trust," 190.

132. Li, "Li Siyou Trust," 155.

133. *Zigong Contracts*, 276.

134. Ping-ti Ho, "The Salt Merchants of Yang-Chou: A Study of Commercial Capitalism in Eighteenth-Century China," *Harvard Journal of Asiatic Studies* 17

(1954); Man Bun Kwan, *The Salt Merchants of Tianjin: State-Making and Civil Society in Late Imperial China* (Honolulu: University of Hawaii Press, 2001).

135. George David Smith and Richard Sylla, "The Transformation of Financial Capitalism: An Essay on the History of American Capital Markets," *Financial Markets, Institutions and Instruments* 2, no. 2 (1993): 18.

136. Chandler, *Visible Hand*, 298.

5. The Growth of an Urban Workforce

1. Among the most important are Robert Entenmann, "Migration and Settlement in Sichuan, 1644–1796" (Ph.D. diss., Harvard University, 1982); Shiqiang Lu, "Jindai Sichuan renkou midu yu renkou yali de fenxi" [Analysis of modern Sichuan population density and population pressure], *Taiwan shifan daxue lishixuebao* 5 (1977); G.. William Skinner, "Sichuan's Population in the Nineteenth Century: Lessons from Disaggregated Data," *Late Imperial China* 7, no. 2 (1986); and Di Wang, "Qingdai Sichuan renkou jingdi ji liangshi wenti" [The issue of population, cultivated acreage, and grain production in Qing Sichuan], *Sichuan daxue xuebao* 3 (1989).

2. Paul Smith, "Commerce, Agriculture, and Core Formation in the Upper Yangtze, 2 A.D. to 1948" (paper presented at the Conference on Spatial and Temporal Trends and Cycles in Chinese Economic History, 980–1980, Bellagio, Italy, 1984), 10, 57–61. Smith utilizes five benchmark years, only one of which lies within our period.

3. Number One Archives, Beijing, *Sichuansheng Daoguang* 2 *nian* (1822) *Minhu nanfu dingkou shumu*, archive no. 6697; *Sichuansheng guangxu* 13 *nian* (1887) *Minhu nanfu dingkou shumu*, archive no. 7529. While these data undoubtedly contain errors, we can assume that the level of misreporting was fairly uniform for the province as a whole and their use for an analysis of comparative, as opposed to absolute, growth is justified. The breakdown of overall population growth for the three main saltyards was Fushun (Ziliujing), 94 percent; Rongxian (Gongjing), 144 percent; and Jianwei (Wutongqiao), 111 percent.

4. Skinner, "Sichuan's Population," 65.

5. For general discussions of this phenomenon by Chinese scholars, see Guangrong Ran and Xuejun Zhang, "Sichuan jingyanye zibenzhuyimengya wenti yanjiu" [Research in the sprouts of capitalism in the Sichuan salt industry], in Nanjing daxue lishixi and MingQing yanjiushi, eds., *MingQing zibenzhuyi mengya yanjiu lunwenji* [Collected essays on the sprouts of capitalism in the Ming and Qing dynasties] (Shanghai: Shangwu chubanshe, 1981), 552–53, and Dixin Xu and Chengming Wu, eds., *Zhongguo zibenzhuyi fazhanshi* [A history of the development of the sprouts of capitalism in China] (Beijing: Renmin chubanshe, 1985), 620.

6. *Leshan xianzhi* [Leshan County gazetteer] (Leshan, 1934), juan 7, jingzhi; Ruyi Yan, *Sansheng bianfang beilan* [Investigation of security at the border of the three provinces] (Yangzhou: Jiangsu Guangling gujikeyinshe, 1822; reprint, 1991), juan 10, 11.

7. Wencheng Shu et al., "Ziliujing shaoyangongren di hanghui zuzhi—Yandigong" [The guild organization of the Ziliujing salt evaporators—the Yandigong], *Zigong wenshiziliao xuanji* 12 (1981): 35.

8. Charles Hu, *The Agricultural and Forestry Land-use of Szechuan Basin* (Chicago: University of Chicago Press, 1946), 126.

9. Anonymous, "Sichuan jinbainian dashi tigang" [An outline of major events in Sichuan during the last one hundred years], *Sichuan wenshiziliao xuanji* 2 (1962); Ran Chen, "Jindai Zigong yanye gongren zhuangkuang ji qi douzheng" [The condition and struggles of salt industry workers in modern Zigong], in Jiusong Peng, Ran Chen, and Zigongshi yanye lishi bowuguan, eds., *Sichuan jingyanshi luncong* [Collected essays on Sichuan salt history] (Chengdu: Sichuansheng shehui kexueyuan chubanshe, 1985), 248.

10. In 1865 rice prices in Chongqing jumped to an average range of 2.72 to 3.78 taels per *shi* from a range of 1.2 to 2.06 taels per *shi* in 1863. Similar spikes occurred in 1874 and again in the mid-1880s. *Junji chu lufu zouzhe (nongye lei), Yuxue liangjia*, bundles 45, 49, 53, 92, 105, First Historical Archives, Beijing.

11. On the mechanisms for immigration, see Robert Entenmann, "Sichuan and Qing Migration Policy," *Ch'ing-shih wen-t'i* 4, no. 4 (1980), and Madeleine Zelin, "Government Policy Toward Reclamation and Hidden Land During the Yongzheng Reign" (manuscript, 1986).

12. Yan Ruyi calculated that 10 boats a day docked at Chongqing, each carrying a crew of 70 to 80 men. Only half of these men gained passage on the return trip, as a result of which even in the mid-nineteenth century at least 10,000 men a month were stranded in Sichuan at the height of the trading season. Yan, *Investigation of Security*, juan 10, 15.

13. Fangbo Ma, "Zigong yanchang di mucai shangye" [The lumber business at the Zigong saltyard], *Zigong wenshiziliao xuanji* 6–10 (1982): 279.

14. Wei Wu, ed., *Sichuan yanzhengshi* [Sichuan salt administration history] (China: Sichuan yanzhengshi bianjichu, 1932), juan 3, pian 2, jie 1, 24a; Xu and Wu, eds., *Sprouts of Capitalism in China*, 621–2. Xu and Wu cite similar practices among coal mine operators during the mid-Qing.

15. Stele inscription in Xu and Wu, eds., *Sprouts of Capitalism in China*, 621.

16. Chen, "Workers' Struggles," 255.

17. Baozhen Ding, ed., *Sichuan Yanfa zhi* [Gazetteer of Sichuan salt administration] (China, 1882), juan 12, zhuanyun 7, 32b, Guangxu 3, Ding Baozhen memorial.

18. Rong Li, "Ziliujing ji," in Dejun Zhang, ed., *Shisanfeng shuwu quanji* [The collected works of the Thirteen Peaks Library] (Longan shuyuan, 1892), juan 1, 5b.

19. Yongcheng Li, ed., *Fushun xianzhi* [Gazetteer of Fushun County] (1931), juan 5, 3a [figures for Xuantong 1 (1909) census]; Xi Zhao, ed., *Minguo Sichuan Rongxian zhi* [Republican Sichuan Rong County gazetteer] (1929), juan 7, 2a [figures for Guangxu 28 (1902) census].

20. Qiao's figures are more accurate than those found in the *Sichuan Salt Administration Gazetteer*. The latter lists only those wells and furnaces registered for tax during the late Qing, giving a total of 405 wells and 1,055 pans. Ding, ed., *Salt Administration Gazetteer*, juan 5, jingchang 5, 4b, 9b. Qiao lists 1,098 wells, which would have employed between 54,900 and 76,860 men. According to Qiao's estimates there were 571 furnaces at the east and 345 furnaces at the west yard, employing 3,026 and 1,404 salt evaporators, respectively. However, he indicates that this does not include all workers at the furnaces. Fu Qiao, *Ziliujing diyiji* [Ziliujing, volume one] (Chengdu: Quchang gongsi, 1916), 153–60, 167. If we take the Ran and Zhang estimate as our basis for calculation, there would have

been between 12,824 and 21,068 workers at the furnaces. Finally, taking account only of the 18 large pipes, we could add another 504 pipe workers. Therefore, the total number of workers employed in primary production was probably around 68,228 and 98,432. Ling Yaolin's estimates of the number of workers at wells and furnaces is somewhat higher for furnaces and lower for wells. Using his figures of 40 to 50 workers per well and 30 to 40 per furnace, we would still have between 71,400 and 91,540 workers at the wells. Yaolin Ling, "Qingdai Zigong jingyanye zibenzhuyi mengya fazhan daolu chutan" [A preliminary investigation of the sprouts of capitalism in the Zigong salt industry], *Sichuan daxue xuebao congkan* 14 (1982): 85. These figures correspond well to the estimate found in *Essentials of Sichuan Salt*, cited in Chen, "Workers, Struggles," 247.

21. Derived from Ta-chung Liu and Kung-jia Yeh, *The Economy of the Chinese Mainland, 1933–1959* (Princeton: Princeton University Press, 1965), 69.

22. Xiaomei Zhang, *Sichuan jingji cankao ziliao* [Reference materials on the Sichuan economy] (Shanghai: Zhongguo guomin jingji yanjiu suo, 1939), B22. In Fushun, home of the Ziliujing portion, which constituted the largest part of the saltyard, the proportion of nonagricultural households was 48 percent.

23. See, for example, Yuanyou Wei, ed., *Daning xianzhi* [Daning County gazetteer] (1886), juan 1, fengsu, and Guangrong Ran and Xuejun Zhang, *MingQing Sichuan jingyanshigao* [A draft history of the well-salt industry in Sichuan during the Ming and Qing period] (Chengdu: Sichuan renmin chubanshe, 1984), 553.

24. Duo Deng, *Lun zhongguo lishi di jige wenti* [On several issues in Chinese history] (Beijing: Sanlian shudian, 1979), 231. Tim Wright finds seasonal and intermittent operation to be characteristic of coal mining throughout China during the imperial period. Tim Wright, *Coal Mining in China's Economy and Society, 1895–1937* (Cambridge: Cambridge University Press, 1984), 163–64.

25. It was not until Western and Japanese investors introduced new capital and technologies in the late nineteenth century that industrial processes such as silk reeling, flour milling, and the manufacture of matches, armaments, and cotton textiles led to a significant spread of factory production and labor concentration elsewhere in China.

26. See, for example, the discussion of silk manufacturing in Lillian Li, *The Chinese Silk Trade* (Cambridge: Harvard University Press, 1981), 46–57. On Jingdezhen, see Michael Dillon, "Transport and Marketing in the Development of the Jingdezhen Porcelain Industry During the Ming and Qing Dynasties," *Journal of the Economic and Social History of the Orient* 35, no. 3 (1992), and Zhuofen Fang, Tiewen Hu, Jian Rui, and Xing Fang, "The Porcelain Industry of Jingdezhen" [early and middle Qing period], in Dixin Xu and Chengming Wu, eds., *Chinese Capitalism, 1522–1840* (New York: St. Martin's Press, 2000), 308–26.

27. Xiaoyuan Luo, "Ziliujing Wang Sanwei tang xingwang jiyao" [The basic elements of the rise and fall of the Wang Sanwei trust], *Sichuan wenshiziliao xuanji* 7 and 8 (1963): 192; Guangrong Ran and Xuejun Zhang, "Sichuan jingyanye zibenjuyi mengya di tantao—Guanyu Qingdai Furong yanchang jingying qiyue di chubu fenxi" [An exploration of the sprouts of capitalism in the Sichuan well-salt industry—a preliminary analysis of Qing period Furong saltyard management contracts], *Sichuan daxue xuebao congkan* 5 (1980): 40.

28. Ran and Zhang, *Draft History*, 171. Ran and Zhang refer to the skilled artisan in charge of opening the well as the *shanjiang*. This term is also used in the *Sichuan Salt Administration History*, juan 3, 82a. The *Salt Administration Gazetteer*

calls this person the *sujiang*. Ding, ed., *Salt Administration Gazetteer*, juan 2, jingchang 2, jingyantushuo, 2b.

29. Zigongshi dang'anguan, Beijing jingjixueyuan, and Sichuan daxue, eds., *Zigong yanye qiyue dang'an xuanji (1732–1949)* [Selected Zigong salt industry contracts and documents (1732–1949)] (Beijing: Zhongguo shehuikexue chubanshe, 1985), 88 (announcement from the Zigong Chamber of Commerce to the *cheshui* workers asking them to return to work), MK 18, 5, 22. See Emily Honig's discussion of the role of "Number Ones" in Shanghai textile mills. Emily Honig, *Sisters and Strangers: Women in the Shanghai Cotton Mills, 1919–1949* (Stanford: Stanford University Press, 1986), 84–87.

30. Duanbao Wen, "Yanjing ji" [Well salt chronicle], in Changling He, ed., *Huangchao jingshi wenbian* [Essays on statecraft of our dynasty] (Taibei: Guofeng chubanshe, 1826), juan 50, huzheng, yankexia, 68.

31. Ding, ed., *Salt Administration Gazetteer*, juan 2, jingchang 2, jingyantushuo, 2b; Ran and Zhang, *Draft History*, 166.

32. Dingli Wu, *Ziliujing fengwu mingshishuo* [An explanation of Zigong's local customs and products] (1871), 2.

33. Xu and Wu, eds., *Sprouts of Capitalism in China*, 620, cites a 1787 magistrate's report stating that "Yang Kailu contracted to pump brine at Liu Zehong's well. He hired Tan Zhongyi to assist him, paying him 45 copper cash a day, paid monthly. Everyone ate at the same table and addressed each other as equals." The final phrase incorporates the legal standard for a free wage laborer as per the Qing code. Philip C. Huang, *Civil Justice in China: Representation and Practice in the Qing* (Stanford: Stanford University Press, 1996), 74. Evidence of certain institutional changes at Jianwei can be used as a guide for understanding conditions at Furong. The two yards are located within a short distance of each other. As noted in chapter 2, the Jianwei yard dominated the salt industry during the period prior to the rise of the salt works at Ziliujing and Gongjing. By the early nineteenth century, Jianwei and Furong were considered the most advanced yards in the province.

34. Wage stability was a reflection of stable rice prices, as illustrated in figure 4.2, and stable copper-to-silver exchange rates. Except in years of natural disaster, rice prices in Xuzhou prefecture averaged between 2 and 2.5 taels. At least until the early Republic, copper-to-silver exchange rates remained stable in Sichuan as well. Thus a wage of one string of cash was roughly equal to 1 tael of silver. Inasmuch as most permanent workers and staff were fed on the job, these were wages largely available to support oneself and one's family. Assuming annual average adult grain consumption to be roughly 2.2 *shi*, an unskilled worker could support a small family as long as he retained his job and did not suffer debilitating injuries. Skilled workers and managers could hope for considerably more than the subsistence existence of a water porter or drill worker.

35. Shuzhi Zhang, "Ziliujing tudi liyong zhi diaocha" [An investigation of land use in Ziliujing], in Zheng Su, ed., *Minguo ershiniandai zhongguo dalu tudi wenti ziliao* [Materials on the land question on mainland China in the 1930s] (Taibei: Chengwen chubanshe, 1938), 29056, notes the continuation of this practice in the twentieth century.

36. Deng, *Issues*, 221.

37. Baxian Archives 6.2.7134.

38. This put Furong workers far ahead of landless agricultural workers. See Xing Fang, "Qingdai Jiangnan nongmin de xiaofei" [Peasant consumption in Qing

dynasty Jiangnan], *Zhongguo jingji shi yanjiu* 11, no. 3 (1996): 91–98, for a preliminary estimate of consumption patterns among landless laborers in Jiagnan.

39. Ling, "Sprouts of Capitalism," 87.

40. Ma, "Lumber," 279.

41. Li, "Ziliujing ji," juan 1, 4a. According to Yan Ruyi, the gas at the yard smelled like
sulfur. Yan, *Investigation of Security*, juan 10, 12.

42. Xiangchen Jiang and Xiaoyuan Luo, "Zigong yanchang di niu" [Buffalo at the
Zigong saltyard], *Zigong wenshiziliao xuanji* 12 (1981): 125.

43. Zhenhan Lin, *Chuanyan jiyao* [Essentials of Sichuan salt] (Shanghai: Shangwu
yinshu guan, 1919), 592.

44. See, for example, Chen, "Workers' Struggles," 253.

45. Exhibit of water-carrier vessels, Zigong Salt History Museum. According to the
exhibit each of the two brine tubs, holding approximately 155 kg of brine apiece,
would be attached to a pole balanced across the shoulders of the brine porter.
Zilin Li et al, "Ziliujing Li Siyou tang you fazhan dao shuaiwang" [The Li Siyou
trust of Ziliujing from their development to their decline], *Sichuan wenshiziliao
xuanji* 4 (1962–63): 154; Li, "Ziliujing ji," juan 1, 5b.

46. Chen, "Workers' Struggles," 250.

47. Li, ed., *Gazetteer of Fushun County*, juan 5.

48. Ran and Zhang, *Draft History*, 172.

49. *Essentials of Sichuan Salt*, cited in Chen, "Workers' Struggles," 253.

50. Quoted in Ran and Zhang, "Sprouts of Capitalism," 554.

51. According to *Chuangong gaikuang* [General conditions of labor in Sichuan], a
pamphlet issued by the Sichuan Salt Workers Association during the Republican
period, "among Sichuan's salt workers, some worked full time, generation after
generation, such as those at the Zigong [an abbreviated form of Ziliujing and
Gongjing], Jianwei and Leshan yards." Ran and Zhang, *Draft History*, 170.

52. Testimony at retired salt workers' conference, stored at the Zigongshi yanye lishi
bowuguan (Zigong City Salt Industry History Museum) and quoted in Xu and
Wu, eds., *Sprouts of Capitalism in China*, 619–20.

53. Ibid.

54. There are almost no data on the background or role played by *batou*. It is possible
that they were a post-1911 phenomenon. For a highly emotional diatribe against
one such labor boss, see Boling Yuan, "Fengjian batou dui yanye yunshugongren
di yazha" [The oppression of salt transport workers by the feudal labor bosses],
Jingyanshi tongxun 2 (1977): 59–62.

55. According to Luo Xiaoyuan, 11 families formed a confederation of scull owners known as the Futongxing hao to carry salt from Furong to Dengjing guan
during the early twentieth century. Xiaoyuan Luo, "Furong guanyunju di bihai"
[Malpractices in the Furong official salt distribution bureau], *Zigong wenshiziliao
xuanji* 14 (1984): 61.

56. For discussions of the Daning strike, see Ran and Zhang, *Draft History*, chapter 2,
and Guangpei Tang, "Ming Zhengde nianjian Sichuan Daning zaofu lingdao di qiyi"
[The rebellion led by salt evaporators in Daning, Sichuan, during the Ming Zhengde
period], in Peng and Chen, eds., *Collected Essays on Sichuan Salt History*, 191–215.

57. Many people have written about *hui* in China. The term can refer to a wide
variety of associations, including those commonly called secret societies in the
English-language literature. The *hui* discussed here are often equated with guilds

in the West and have many similarities, including reliance on a patron god as an organizing principle. Merchants, scholars, and workers were known to have formed *hui*. In Sichuan, most such organizations formed by sojourners from a particular locale were referred to as *bang*, but their organizational structures were similar to those of *hui*. On *hui* in general, see Peter Golas, "Early Qing Guilds," in G. William Skinner, ed., *The City in Late Imperial China* (Stanford: Stanford University Press, 1977), 555–80, and Bryna Goodman, *Native Place, City, and Nation: Regional Networks and Identities in Shanghai, 1853–1937* (Berkeley: University of California Press, 1995).

58. Zigongshi yanye zhi bianzuan weiyuan hui, ed., *Zigong shi yanye zhi* [Zigong city salt industry gazetteer] (Zigong, 1992), 568. The gazetteer also mentions a general salt workers' guild called the Shicheng hui. It is unclear whom this organization served in the Qing period.

59. Jian Huang, "Zigong yanchang banghui qianxi" [A brief analysis of the guilds at the Zigong saltyard] (paper presented at the International Conference on Chinese Salt Industry History, Zigong, 1990), 2.

60. Most of what we know about this uprising comes from investigations by Ke Yuwen and a stele erected in 1852 in Niuhua xi warning against such action in the future. The stele is quoted in full in Ran and Zhang, *Draft History*, 212–14. Additional information is contained in a file entitled "Dala hui yu gongren yundong" [The Dala hui and the workers' movement] in the archives of the committee compiling the new Sichuan gazetteer and cited extensively in Ran and Zhang, "Sprouts of Capitalism," 556.

61. Shu et al., "Guild Organization," 35–48. Shu's and his fellow salt evaporators' oral testimony was recorded in 1960.

62. Xuejun Zhang, "Qingdai Chuannan diqu de yanye gongbanghui huodong" [The activities of salt workers' associations in southern Sichuan during the Qing period], in Sichuan lishi xuehui, ed., *Shixue lunwenji* [Collected essays on history] (Chengdu: Sichuan renmin chubanshe, 1982), 242.

63. Ibid., 242–44.

64. According to Shu Wencheng, during the Qing members paid 280 cash a year and nonmembers paid 560. Shu et al., "Guild Organization," 38.

65. It was not uncommon for Qing period popular religious sects and secret societies to set standards of personal conduct for their members and this practice may have been a model for similar sets of rules among workers' guilds. See, for example, Carlton Lewis, "Some Notes on the Ko-lao Hui in Late Ch'ing China," in Jean Chesneaux, ed., *Popular Movements and Secret Societies in China, 1840–1950* (Stanford: Stanford University Press, 1972), 104, and Susan Naquin, *Millenarian Rebellion in China: The Eight Trigrams Uprising of 1813* (New Haven: Yale University Press, 1976), 47.

66. One account states that the workers also demanded the meat meals skilled craftsmen were traditionally provided at intervals by their master. Ran and Zhang, *Draft History*, 216.

67. It was not unusual for the Qing bureaucracy to deal with disputes between employee and employer. The Baxian Archives contain many examples of artisans requesting that the state uphold "traditional" rights, as in the case of the weavers at a Chongqing silk workshop who petitioned the state to prevent their employer from eliminating their weekly ration of meat. Baxian Archives 6.3.17179, dated 1843.

68. Chen Ran notes actions in 1873, 1884, 1886, and 1908, but it is not clear how widespread these were. Chen, "Workers Struggles," 255.
69. Li, "Li Siyou Trust," 164–65; Zhang, "Salt Workers' Associations," 246.
70. See, for example, Gail Hershatter, *The Workers of Tianjin, 1900–1949* (Stanford: Stanford University Press, 1986), and Elizabeth J. Perry, *Shanghai on Strike: The Politics of Chinese Labor* (Stanford: Stanford University Press, 1993).

6. Official Transport and Merchant Sales

1. Zijian Lu, "Chuanyan jichu yu Sichuan yanye fazhan" [Sichuan salt in aid to Huguang and the development of the Sichuan salt industry], *Shehui kexue yanjiu* 2 (1984): 77.
2. Baozhen Ding, ed., *Sichuan Yanfa zhi* [Gazetteer of Sichuan salt administration] (China: 1882), juan 11, juanyun 6, jichushang, 1a–1b.
3. Shouji Wang, *Yanfa yilue* [A brief discussion of salt administration] (Beijing, 1877).
4. Ibid.
5. Guangrong Ran and Xuejun Zhang, *MingQing Sichuan jingyanshigao* [A draft history of the well-salt industry in Sichuan during the Ming and Qing period] (Chengdu: Sichuan renmin chubanshe, 1984), 103n9, cites the *Qing yanfa zhi*, noting that in 1850 the weight of a bag of *ba* salt was 160 *jin* and that of *hua* salt was 200 *jin*.
6. According to von Rosthorn, this was one of the main reasons for smuggling and the large amount of salt destined for Hubei that masqueraded as domestic salt. Arthur von Rosthorn, "The Salt Administration of Ssuch'uan," *Journal of the Royal Asiatic Society, China Branch*, n.s., 27 (1892–93): 20.
7. Ibid., 21.
8. Ran and Zhang, *Draft History*, 120.
9. Ding, ed., *Salt Administration Gazetteer*, juan 11, juanyun 6, jichushang.
10. Lu, "Aid to Huguang," 81.
11. Jianwei, which largely produced *ba* salt, did not benefit as much as Furong from the Huguang trade. Even during the 1850s and 1860s Jianwei's largest market continued to be the so-called border trade. Von Rosthorn notes that in the 1880s Yunnan was served exclusively by Jianwei, while Furong joined Jianwei in supplying Guizhou. Von Rosthorn, "Salt Administration of Ssuch'uan," 16.
12. *Zizhong xian xuxiu Zizhou zhi*, juan 3, yanfa, 12–15, cited in Lu, "Aid to Huguang," 80.
13. Dekun Yang, ed., *Fengjie xianzhi* [Fengjie County gazetteer] (1893), juan 16, yancha, 1–2.
14. Lu, "Aid to Huguang," 80.
15. Ding, ed., *Salt Administration Gazetteer*, juan 11, juanyun 6, jichushang, 16.
16. Ibid., juan 11, juanyun 6, jichushang, 16, 23–24.
17. Ibid., 16–17.
18. Dihuan Lin, "Sichuan Yanzheng di gaige, 1895–1920" [Reform of the Sichuan salt administration, 1895–1920.] (M.A. thesis, Taiwan National University, 1983), 26.
19. Ding, ed., *Salt Administration Gazetteer*, juan 11, juanyun 6, jichushang, 26.
20. Ibid., 29–34.

21. Ibid., juan 12 juanyun 7, jichuxia, 11–13.
22. Ibid., juan 13, juanyun 8, guanyunshang, 9–11.
23. Duo Wu, "Sichuan guanyun zhi shimo" [The complete story of the Guanyun System in Sichuan], in *Zhongguo jindai shehui jingji shi lunji* [Essays on modern Chinese economic and social history] (Hong Kong: Chongwen shudian, 1971), 137.
24. The Sichuan counties, departments, and autonomous prefectures incorporated into the new system included Ba County, Jiangbei Department, Zhong Autonomous prefecture, Fengdu County, Changshou County, Shizhu Independent Department, Wushan County, and Wan County. In Hubei, Guanyun was now applied to Hefeng Independent Department and the counties of Changle, Enshi, Xuanen, Lichuan, Jianshi, Xianfeng, and Laifeng.
25. Ran and Zhang, *Draft History,* 127–28.
26. Table 6.1 documents only salt sold in the Yunnan and Guizhou border markets, which were most affected by the decline in certificate sales under the old system.
27. von Rosthorn, "Salt Administration of Ssuch'uan," 16.
28. Ibid., 17.
29. Ding, ed., *Salt Administration Gazetteer,* juan 15, juanyun 10, 5.
30. Ibid., 5–6.
31. Xiaoyuan Luo, "Furong guanyunju di bihai" [Malpractices in the Furong Official Salt Distribution Bureau], *Zigong wenshiziliao xuanji* 14 (1984): 66; Ran and Zhang, *Draft History,* 130.
32. Ran and Zhang, *Draft History,* 129.
33. Guizhou was granted 14 taels per certificate destined for that province, while Yunnan was allocated a fixed sum of 14,000 taels a year. Ran and Zhang, *Draft History,* 134–35. For a discussion of the Yongzheng emperor's handling of customary fees, see Madeleine Zelin, *The Magistrate's Tael: Rationalizing Fiscal Reform in Early Ch'ing China* (Berkeley: University of California Press, 1984).
34. For a discussion of the relationship between the rise in salt taxes and Sichuanese politics during the last years of the Qing, see S. A. M. Adshead, *Province and Politics in Late Imperial China: Viceregal Government in Sichuan, 1898–1911* (London: Curzon Press, 1984), 29–30, 45, 60, and passim.
35. Zhenhan Lin, *Chuanyan jiyao* [Essentials of Sichuan salt] (Shanghai: Shangwu yinshu guan, 1919), bian 1, 5.
36. Similar tax policies were implemented in other provinces as well. For a discussion of the effect of late-nineteenth-century New Policies on taxation in Hubei and Hunan, see Joseph Esherick, *Reform and Revolution in China: The 1911 Revolution in Hunan and Hubei* (Berkeley: University of California Press, 1976), 113–16.
37. Fu Qiao, *Ziliujing diyiji* [Ziliujing, volume one] (Chengdu: Quchang gongsi, 1916), 182.
38. The "normal" ratio between copper and silver upon which the state tax system was based was 1,000:1. According to the gazetteer of Nanxi County, in Sichuan, which contains the closest contemporary record of the copper–silver ratio at this time, one required 1,600 copper cash to purchase 1 tael of silver in 1905. This figure appears to have risen to 2,500:1 by the end of the dynasty. Lingxiao Li et al., eds., *Nanxi xianzhi* [Gazetteer of Nanxi County] (Nanjing: Jiangsu guji chubanshe, 1937; reprint, 1992), juan 2, shihuo, 33–34.

39. Lin, *Essentials of Sichuan Salt*, 19.

40. Alexander Hosie, *Szechuan, Its Products, Industries and Resources* (Shanghai: Kelly and Walsh, 1922), 180. Hosie spent most of his time in Sichuan investigating Sichuan's agricultural and industrial resources.

41. Ibid., 182.

42. Xi Zhang, ed., *Sichuan yanwu baogao shu* [Reports on the Sichuan salt administration] (China, 1912), 5a–16b.

43. The social cost of the concentration of salt production in a handful of large yards is difficult to gauge at this remove. Adshead notes that several of the less developed salt-production areas became stepping stones for the expansion of Boxer influence in Sichuan. Adshead, *Province and Politics in Late Imperial China*, 36.

44. Luo, "Malpractices," 68–69, Xiaoyuan Luo, "Ziliujing Wang Sanwei tang xingwang jiyao" [The basic elements of the rise and fall of the Wang Sanwei trust], *Sichuan wenshiziliao xuanji* 7 and 8 (1963): 1993–94.

45. Ding, ed., *Salt Administration Gazetteer*, juan 13, zhuanyun 8, guanyunshang, 3–4.

46. One of the most famous cases of a Shaanxi merchant house leaving the Sichuan salt market was the Baoxinglong. This firm had been a wholesaler of salt in the border market. When its last owner, Su Yi, left Sichuan in the aftermath of the Taiping Rebellion he turned his firm over to his old friend and client Wang Xiangyun, who changed the name of the firm to the Wang Baoxinglong. Zigongshi zhengxie wenshiziliao weiyuanhui, ed., *Ziliujing yanye shijia* [Well-known families of the Ziliujing salt industry] (Chengdu: Sichuan renmin chubanshe, 1995), 232.

47. Luo, "Malpractices," 58; Luo, "Wang Sanwei Trust," 189.

48. Luo, "Malpractices," 59.

49. Wei Wu, ed., *Sichuan yanzhengshi* [Sichuan salt administration history] (China: Sichuan yanzhengshi bianjichu, 1932), juan 3, pian 2, zhang 10, 74b.

50. An analogy to changes in the grain market following the introduction of the grain elevator would not be far-fetched. In both instances innovations in storage and marketing eliminated the advantages of branding for the producer. See William Cronon, *Nature's Metropolis: Chicago and the Great West* (New York: Norton, 1991).

51. Luo, "Malpractices," 68.

52. Zilin Li et al., "Ziliujing Li Siyou tang you fazhan dao shuaiwang" [The Li Siyou trust of Ziliujing from their development to their decline], *Sichuan wenshiziliao xuanji* 4 (1962–63): 166–67. Li Deshan cited inability to pay the large remittance fees of remittance banks (*piaohao*) as a major factor in the decision to close down the Li Siyou trust's Huguang retail outlets, but lower prices and increased taxes made it more difficult to absorb high remittance fees when repatriating profits.

7. Technological and Organizational Change, 1894–1930

1. Manyin [pseud.], *Ziliujing* (Chengdu, 1944).

2. Li Bozhai had so little influence at the saltyard that after his initial success in opening rock-salt wells he was unable to obtain permission to sell certificate salt to the Guanyun bureau in Ziliujing. According to one account, it was only through the intervention of a member of his staff with connections at the bureau that his furnace was given priority sales rights. Xiaoyuan Luo, "Furong guanyunju di bihai" [Malpractices in the Furong Official Salt Distribution Bureau], *Zigong wenshiziliao xuanji* 14 (1984): 59–60.

3. Zhiqing Huang and Wufang Nie, "Zigong yanchang fazhan pianduan" [Passages on the development of the Zigong saltyard], *Zigong wenshiziliao xuanji* 6–10 (1982): 256; Yaolin Ling, "Qingdai Zigong jingyanye zibenzhuyi mengya fazhan daolu chutan" [A preliminary investigation of the sprouts of capitalism in the Zigong salt industry], *Sichuan daxue xuebao congkan* 14 (1982): 88; Xiaofang Yang, "Zigong yanyan di fazhan" [The development of the Zigong rock-salt layer], *Zigong weshiziliao xuanji* 1–5 (1982): 154.

4. Zongyao Ma and Chengxun Nie, "Ziliujing Dafen bao yanyanti kaifa zhuangtai ji kaicai lishi jiexi" [The conditions surrounding the opening of the rock-salt layer at Dafen bao in Ziliujing and an analysis of the history of its exploitation], *Jingyanshi tongshun* 10 (1983): 37.

5. Mingqin Lai et al., "Yanyanjing fazhan gaikuang" [A survey of the development of rock-salt wells], *Zigong wenshiziliao xuanji* 6–10 (1982): 5.

6. Huang and Nie, "Development of the Zigong Saltyard," 255–56.

7. Ma and Nie, "Conditions Surrounding the Opening of the Rock-Salt Layer," 37.

8. Ibid., 36.

9. Lai, "Rock-Salt Wells," 3.

10. Ibid., 6.

11. Wei Wu, ed., *Sichuan yanzhengshi* [Sichuan salt administration history] (China: Sichuan yanzhengshi bianjichu, 1932), juan 3, pian 2, zhang 10, jie 1, 69b.

12. See chapter 2.

13. Huang and Nie, "Development of the Zigong Saltyard," 256.

14. Ibid.; Lai, "Rock-Salt Wells," 33–34.

15. Lai, "Rock-Salt Wells," 34.

16. Ibid., 13.

17. Dixin Xu and Chengming Wu, eds., *Zhongguo zibenzhuyi fazhanshi* [A history of the development of the sprouts of capitalism in China] (Beijing: Renmin chubanshe, 1985), 591; Ling, "Sprouts of Capitalism," 88.

18. Ling, "Sprouts of Capitalism," 88.

19. A load, or *tao*, is a standard measure for moving goods like water, rice, and so on, consisting of the volume of the commodity that a porter could carry in two baskets balanced on a pole carried over his shoulders.

20. Wu, ed., *Salt Administration History*, juan 2, pian 2, zhang 10, jie 1, 69b.

21. Ma and Nie, "Conditions Surrounding the Opening of the Rock-Salt Layer," 37; Zigongshi zhengxie wenshiziliao weiyuanhui, ed., *Ziliujing yanye shijia* [Well-known families of the Ziliujing salt industry] (Chengdu: Sichuan renmin chubanshe, 1995), 235.

22. By the 1910s the Jirong well and the Shenyong well at Jingui shan were irrigating 37 wells. Lai, "Rock-Salt Wells," 7.

23. Huang and Nie, "Development of the Zigong Saltyard," 256–57.

24. Ibid., 257.

25. Lai, "Rock-Salt Wells," 7.

26. Zhenhan Lin, *Chuanyan jiyao* [Essentials of Sichuan salt] (Shanghai: Shangwu yinshu guan, 1919), 248.

27. Wu, ed., *Salt Administration History*, juan 3, pian 2, zhang 9, jie 1, 59b. This figure is called an average production quota. Elsewhere in the same compilation a lower figure is given for average production, but that figure does not square with figures given here and elsewhere for taxes paid. Ibid., juan 2, pian 2, zhang 3, jie 3, 44b–45a.

28. Lin, *Essentials of Sichuan Salt*, 208.
29. Ibid., 226–28. It is unlikely that many rock-salt brine wells were still being pumped by oxen or mules, as steam pumping was introduced as early as 1905 and was especially suited to the rock-salt brine wells, as discussed later.
30. For a summary of this narrative, see Albert Feuerwerker, *China's Early Industrialization: Sheng Hsuan-huai (1844–1916) and Mandarin Enterprise* (Cambridge: Harvard University Press, 1958). Among the various explanations for the private sector's lack of responsiveness to new and innovative investment are aversion to risk, the existence of countervailing opportunities in moneylending, the absence of a tradition of long-term investment, fear of extortion by officials, restrictive guilds, and distrust of non-kin or non-coresidents.
31. Indeed, Mark Kurlansky, in his popular account of world salt history, notes that at the turn of the nineteenth century a family of salt prospectors at the Kanawha salt works in present-day West Virginia developed a method of percussion drilling and the use of an extraction tube with a valve on the bottom similar to that developed in China in the Middle Ages. Mark Kurlansky, *Salt: A World History* (New York: Walker, 2002), 250.
32. H. E. Hobson, "Chongqing haiguan 1891 nian diaocha baogao" [1891 investigation report of the Chongqing Maritime Customs Bureau], *Sichuan wenshiziliao xuanji* 4 (1962): 192.
33. Wu, ed., *Salt Administration History*, juan 2, pian 2, zhang 5, jie 3, 90b–91a.
34. The sad saga of the first and unsuccessful attempt at mechanized pumping is mentioned in *Essentials of Sichuan Salt*. Although Ouyang Xianrong is not mentioned by name, the fact of the instigator's Chongqing connection and the failure of the attempt due to the inadequacy of the pump and the subsequent hesitance of well owners fit both Ouyang's and other accounts of his pioneering activities. Lin, *Essentials of Sichuan Salt*, 235. Ouyang's own account of his role in the introduction of steam-powered pumps at the Furong yard is recounted in a letter by Ouyang to the Sichuan-Xikang Salt Supervisory Bureau (Chuankang yanwu guanli ju) written in 1941. At that time Ouyang, who was in his eighties and rather feeble, requested that the government provide him with aid in recognition of his contribution to saltyard technology. Testimonials were taken, Ouyang was given a 2,000-yuan grant, and his position as the pioneer in the use of steam power at Furong was ratified by the state. Zigong document 3–5–745, 44–48. See also Qisheng Zhou, "Dui 'Zigong yanchang zhengqijiche xiyan gaishu' yiwen di tantao'" [An inquiry into "A general discussion of steam pumping at the Zigong salt yard"], *Zigong weshiziliao xuanji* 6–10 (1982): 265; Yang, "Development of the Zigong Rock-Salt Layer," 137. Yang was himself an investor in steam pumps at the Furong yard.
35. For a discussion of Hankow as a Yangzi port and center for foreign trade, see William T. Rowe, *Hankow: Commerce and Society in a Chinese City, 1796–1889* (Stanford: Stanford University Press, 1984).
36. Zigong document 3–5–745, 44–48. Ouyang claims that his companion was an unemployed holder of a foreign Ph.D. It is unlikely that he held a doctorate. However, it was not uncommon in the late nineteenth century for the few Chinese who had received technical training overseas to find their skills underutilized upon their return home.

37. Duxing Yang et al., "Zigong yanchang zhengqijiche xiyan gaishu" [A general discussion of steam pumping at the Zigong saltyard], *Zigong weshiziliao xuanji* 1–5 (1982): 137.

38. Some accounts have placed the first experiments as early as 1897. See, for example, Ling, "Sprouts of Capitalism," 88. However, Zhong Changyong argues convincingly that this was impossible. Most important is evidence provided by an investigation of Hubei industry carried out in 1935, which dates the founding of the Zhou Hengshun factory at 1900, three years after the alleged manufacture of the first steam pump operated at Furong. See Changyong Zhong, "Furong yanchang di jiqi xilu" [Mechanical brine pumping at the Furong saltyard], *Jingyanshi tongshun* 8 (1981): 43n7.

39. Zigong Archives 3–5–745, 44–48.

40. Yang, "General Discussion of Steam Pumping," 138.

41. Zigong Archives 3–5–745, 44–48.

42. Ibid.; Zhong, "Mechanical Brine Pumping," 39.

43. Zigong Archives 3–5–745, 44–48; Zhou, "Inquiry into 'General Discussion of Steam Pumping,'" 267.

44. Economic historians continue to debate the role of market demand as a spur to invention. Classic studies in support of the demand-driven thesis include David S. Landes, *The Unbound Prometheus: Technological Change and Industrial Development in Western Europe from 1750 to the Present* (London: Cambridge University Press, 1969); Jacob Schmookler, *Invention and Economic Growth* (Cambridge: Harvard University Press, 1966); and Kenneth L. Sokoloff, "Inventive Activity in Early Industrial America: Evidence from Patent Records, 1790–1846," *Journal of Economic History* 48, no. 4 (1988). The introduction of steam pumping at Furong appears to combine both market demand and what Nathan Rosenberg has called interdependence. In the first instance we see this in the development of steam pumping to take advantage of the greater productive potential of solution mining. Later in this chapter we will see this same process at work in the development of wide-diameter wells and the concurrent design of more powerful steam pumps to take advantage of their greater output capacity. See Nathan Rosenberg, *Perspectives on Technology* (New York: Cambridge University Press, 1976); Nathan Rosenberg, "Technological Change in the Machine Tool Industry, 1840–1910," *Journal of Economic History* 23, no. 4 (1963).

45. *Essentials of Sichuan Salt*, published in 1919, puts the date of Dong's purchase at 1913. Lin, *Essentials of Sichuan Salt*, 225. *Sichuan Salt Administration History*, which was not published until 1932, gives the later date of 1915. Wu, ed., *Salt Administration History*, juan 2, pian 2, zhang 5, jie 3, 90a. The discrepancy may lie in the gap between the time the pump was purchased and the time it was finally put into production.

46. Wu, ed., *Salt Administration History*, juan 2, pian 2, zhang 5, jie 3, 90a.

47. Yang, "General Discussion of Steam Pumping," 138; Lai, "Rock-Salt Wells," 8–9.

48. Lai, "Rock-Salt Wells," 9; Yang, "General Discussion of Steam Pumping"; Zhong, "Mechanical Brine Pumping," 40.

49. Lai, "Rock-Salt Wells," 9; Yang, "General Discussion of Steam Pumping," 139.

50. Lin, *Essentials of Sichuan Salt*, 225–26.

51. Rinderpest, also known as cattle plague, is "a highly contagious disease affecting cattle, characterized by running from the eyes, nose, and mouth, fever, cessation of rumination, constipation, then diarrhea, and emphysema before death." *The Concise Oxford Dictionary* (Oxford: Oxford University Press, 2001).
52. Yang, "General Discussion of Steam Pumping," 140. It is difficult to calculate the relative costs of steam vs. animal power inasmuch as we do not know how long a pump would last (buffalo generally survived no more than 10 years at the derricks) or the relative costs of feed vs. coal. The output varied from well to well, but the *Essentials of Sichuan Salt* estimates that one steam pump took the place of approximately 200 buffalo or mules. Lin, *Essentials of Sichuan Salt,* 229.
53. Lin, *Essentials of Sichuan Salt,* 229. These accidents, which each killed or injured several people, appear to have been caused by worker error and clearly were the result of inexperience in operating and maintaining machinery during these early years.
54. Ibid., 226.
55. In 1916 to 1917 a certificate's worth of Furong's main product could fetch as much as 300 taels at the point of sale, and brine was selling for 0.6 taels a *dan*. At this rate a well producing 130 *dan* a day (and most rock-salt brine wells could produce much more) would gross around 2,340 taels a month. According to Lai Mingqin, the outlay for coal, food, and wages would still produce a net profit of 2,000 taels a month. Lai, "Rock-Salt Wells," 34. According to *Sichuan Salt Administration History,* in 1932 all rock-salt wells were machine pumped and all but yellow-brine and low-productivity wells still utilized animal power. Wu, ed., *Salt Administration History,* juan 2, pian 2, zhang 5, jie 3, 90a.
56. For example, the Zhongxingxiang maintained its own foundry and machine repair shops. Yuesheng Pu, "Zigong yanshang Luo Huagai" [Zigong salt merchant Luo Huagai], *Zigong wenshiziliao xuanji* 19 (1989): 75; Zhong, "Mechanical Brine Pumping," 42, notes that in 1915 Fan Rongguang set up a foundry and Chu Yasan set up a repair and spare parts workshop in Dafen bao. Zhong laments that this did not lead to the development of Ziliujing and Gongjing as centers of a Chinese steel industry. However, by 1945 the yard did have a small steel mill and 28 foundries for the manufacture of machine parts.
57. Wu, ed., *Salt Administration History,* juan 2, pian 2, zhang 5, jie 3, 90a.
58. Zhong, "Mechanical Brine Pumping," 42.
59. Yang, "General Discussion of Steam Pumping," 138.
60. The foremost examples of this type of arrangement were the wells owned by investors associated with Wang Hefu and Fan Rongguang.
61. My discussion of *baotui* is based on unpublished material provided by the editors of the *Zigong Contracts* as well as contracts printed in their collection.
62. Yuesheng Pu, "Zigong yanshang Xiong Zuozhou shilue" [A short biographical sketch of Zigong salt merchant Xiong Zuozhou], *Zigong wenshiziliao xuanji* 17 (1987): 4; Roude Wang and Langhua Zhong, "Luo Xiaoyuan sishinian di yanye jingying ji qi wannian shilue" [Luo Xiaoyuan's forty years in the salt industry and a short biographical account of his later years], *Zigong wenshiziliao xuanji* 15 (1985): 77; Yang, "General Discussion of Steam Pumping," 149–51.
63. Yang, "General Discussion of Steam Pumping," 150; Zigongshi dang'anguan, Beijing jingjixueyuan, and Sichuan daxue, eds., *Zigong yanye qiyue dang'an xuanji (1732–1949)* [Selected Zigong salt industry contracts and documents (1732–1949)]

(Beijing: Zhongguo shehuikexue chubanshe, 1985), 179. Hereafter cited as *Zigong Contracts.*

64. Separation of the construction and ownership of the physical plant from the firm that actually used the plant to produce a product was not unknown in Chinese business management. The most representative examples occurred in the textile industry, in which one group of investors might build a silk filature and another rent it to produce yarn. Lynda Bell, "From Comprador to County Magnate: Bourgeois Practice in the Wuxi County Silk Industry" (paper presented at the Conference on Chinese Local Elites and Patterns of Dominance, Banff, 1987), 30; Robert Eng, *Economic Imperialism in China: Silk Production and Exports, 1861–1932* (Berkeley: Center for Chinese Studies, 1986), 71.

65. *Zigong Contracts,* contract 483.

66. Ibid., contract 509. See also contracts 482–518.

67. See Rosenberg, *Perspectives,* and Rosenberg, "Technological Change."

68. There is considerable disagreement about the chronology of these events. Luo Xiaoyuan places them in 1917, Lai Mingqin in 1918, and Yang Duxing as early as 1916. Xiaoyuan Luo, "Zhang Xiaopo dui Zigong yanchang di yingxiang" [The influence of Zhang Xiaopo on the Zigong saltyard], *Zigong wenshiziliao xuanji* 12 (1981): 184; Lai, "Rock-Salt Wells," 11; Yang, "General Discussion of Steam Pumping," 140. All three were employed at the Furong yard during the period in question. For more on Zhang Xiaopo as one of the new elite at the saltyard, see chapter 9.

69. These wells are now classified as medium-diameter wells, as wells in the period after 1950 were extended to as much as three times the width of narrow-diameter wells. Wide-diameter wells during the Qing period measured approximately 3.9 to 4.5 inches. Between 1920 and 1957 the average opening was 6.8 to 7.8 inches. This has since risen to as much as 11.6 inches at some wells. Ma and Nie, "Conditions Surrounding the Opening of the Rock-Salt Layer," 40.

70. Yang, "General Discussion of Steam Pumping," 142.

71. Xiong Zuozhou, who became one of the leading members of the business community in the early twentieth century, made part of his early fortune by importing steel cable from Shanghai. Pu, "Xiong Zuozhou," 4.

72. Lai, "Rock-Salt Wells," 11–12.

73. Yang, "General Discussion of Steam Pumping," 140.

74. According to Wu, ed., *Salt Administration History,* juan 2, pian 2, zhang 5, jie 3, 90b, by 1931 Jianwei had four vertical pumps and one horizontal pump. See also Yang, "General Discussion of Steam Pumping," 140–41.

75. Wu, ed., *Salt Administration History,* juan 2, pian 2, zhang 5, jie 3, 90a–b.

76. Ma and Nie, "Conditions Surrounding the Opening of the Rock-Salt Layer," 37–38.

77. An interesting comparison is the southern U.S. textile industry, which relied on northern mill technology and technicians long after its expansion following the end of the Civil War. Bess Beatty, "Lowells of the South: Northern Influences on the Nineteenth-Century North Carolina Textile Industry," *Journal of Southern History* 53, no. 1 (1987): 37–62.

78. Zigongshi jixie dianzi gongye guanliju, ed., *Zigongshi jixiegongye zhi* [Gazetteer of the Zigong city machine industry], Zigongshi difangzhi congshu [Zigong municipal gazetteer collection], vol. 21 (Chengdu: Sichuan renmin chubanshe, 1993), 63;

Yang, "General Discussion of Steam Pumping," 145. Tongji was founded in 1907 as a medical school and added an engineering department in 1912.

79. Zhong, "Mechanical Brine Pumping," 42.
80. Ling, "Sprouts of Capitalism," 87.
81. Yang, "Mechanical Brine Pumping," 145–46; Lai, "Rock-Salt Wells," 38.
82. Wu, ed., *Salt Administration History*, juan 3, pian 2, zhang10, jie 6, 81a.
83. Chunwu Huang, et al., "Qingmoyilai Zigong yanchang zhuye" [The bamboo industry in Zigong since the late Qing], *Sichuan wenshiziliao xuanji* 9 (1963): 69.
84. Ibid.
85. Even iron tubes were fitted with three lengths of *nanzhu*. Ibid.
86. Huang and Nie, "Development of the Zigong Saltyard," 244; Rongqing Ji, "Gongjing yanchang fazhan yipie" [A glance at the development of the Gongjing saltyard], *Sichuan wenshiziliao xuanji* 11 (1964): 189–90. Ji Rongqing worked at the Gongjing saltyard between 1909 and 1936.
87. Ji, "Gongjing," 192–207. At least eight of these wells were the property of the Li Siyou trust, and others may have belonged to individual households of the Li lineage. Only one of the wells listed is said to have belonged to the Wang Sanwei trust, which was much less invested in Gongjing than the Lis. Four of the wells are associated with the Hu Yuanhe trust.
88. Ling, "Sprouts of Capitalism," 88.
89. Zeyi Peng, *Zhongguo jindai shougongye shiliao, 1840–1949* [Materials on China's early modern handicraft industry], vol. 3 (Beijing: Zhonghua shu ju, 1962), 50.
90. Xiaoyuan Luo and Xiangchen Jiang, "Zigong yanchang di jianshang" [Pipe merchants at the Zigong saltyard], *Zigong wenshiziliao xuanji* 13 (1983): 144.
91. Shuzhi Zhang, "Ziliujing tudi liyong zhi diaocha" [An investigation of land use in Ziliujing], in Zheng Su, ed., *Minguo ershiniandai zhongguo dalu tudi wenti ziliao* [Materials on the land question on mainland China in the 1930s] (Taibei: Chengwen chubanshe, 1938), 28927–48.
92. Ibid., 29056. As noted earlier, most of the skilled engineers on the wells came from Jiangsu and Zhejiang. Wu, ed., *Salt Administration History*, juan 2, pian 2, zhang 5, jie 3, 90a.
93. Zhang Xuejun Zhang, "Xinghai geming yu Zigong yanye" [The 1911 Revolution and the Zigong salt industry], *Jingyanshi tongxun* 11 (1983): 16.

8. The Changing of the Guard at the Furong Saltyard

1. See chapter 6. Zilin Li et al., "Ziliujing Li Siyou tang you fazhan dao shuaiwang" [The Li Siyou trust of Ziliujing from their development to their decline], *Sichuan wenshiziliao xuanji* 4 (1962–63): 167. The account of the fortunes of the Li Siyou trust during this period is based largely on a lengthy narrative account compiled by Li Zilin et al. While it is impossible to verify all details, the overall picture of firm debt, downsizing, and reorganization is confirmed by contemporary accounts and documentation relating to both Li and non-Li properties.
2. Xianqi Yan, Wenfang Yan, and Zuo Yan, "Yan Guixin tang yu Ziliujing" [The Yan Guixin trust and Ziliujing], *Yanyeshi yanjiu* 3 (1990): 73.
3. Ibid.
4. The Xinglong well came into production in 1910.
5. Li, "Li Siyou Trust," 201, states that the Li Siyou trust did not have the funds to purchase salt to sell in the Huguang market and thus borrowed salt from other

merchants. More likely, the trust neither produced enough salt of its own to sell nor had the cash reserves to buy salt and was therefore forced to sell the salt of other merchants on consignment.

6. Ibid., 203.

7. The life of an average well was only a few decades. Shouji Wang, *Yanfa yilue* [A brief discussion of salt administration] (Beijing, 1877), 19. However, the life of some wells could be revitalized by redrilling, as evidenced by the numerous redrilling contracts in Zigongshi dang'anguan, Beijing jingjixueyuan, and Sichuan daxue, eds., *Zigong yanye qiyue dang'an xuanji (1732–1949)* [Selected Zigong salt industry contracts and documents (1732–1949)] (Beijing: Zhongguo shehuikexue chubanshe, 1985).

8. Yan, Yan, and Yan, "Yan Guixin Trust," 73.

9. Zigong archives 17–1–193–34–35.

10. Shaoquan Hu, "Gongjing Hu Yuanhe di guangzou yu shuailuo" [The rise and fall of Hu Yuanhe of Gongjing], *Zigong wenshiziliao xuanji* 12 (1981): 70.

11. Ibid., 71.

12. Lei Li, "Luo Xiaoyuan jiushi" [Luo Xiaoyuan's past], *Ziliujing* 1 (1983): 41.

13. Zigong archives 42–3–381–1.

14. The senior and junior branches of the lineage favored an equal division of the property among the three lines. However, the middle branch, which had been far more prolific over the years, wanted a division based on the number of family members in each line. Xiaoyuan Luo, "Ziliujing Wang Sanwei tang xingwang jiyao" [The basic elements of the rise and fall of the Wang Sanwei trust], *Sichuan wenshiziliao xuanji* 7 and 8 (1963): 196.

15. Ibid.

16. William C. Kirby, "China Unincorporated: Company Law and Business Enterprise in Twentieth-Century China," *Journal of Asian Studies* 54, no. 1 (1995): 47–48.

17. One interesting example of the lineage trusts' weakening hold over various commodity markets is their loss of power over the sale of buffalo hides, which they and the other large salt conglomerates had virtually monopolized prior to 1911. Xiangchen Jiang and Xiaoyuan Luo, "Zigong yanchang di niu" [Buffalo at the Zigong saltyard], *Zigong wenshiziliao xuanji* 12 (1981): 120–21.

18. Luo, "Wang Sanwei Trust," 198.

19. At first the Xiayixing well was pumped under contract to a steam-pumping company. Later the lineage bought the pump and used it on the Chusheng well, one of its new rock-salt wells. Ibid., 198–99.

20. Ibid., 198.

21. Zigong archives 42–3381–11.

22. This agreement did not apply to agricultural lands and lands on which future wells might be drilled, inasmuch as most of this land had been disposed of in the mortgage agreements of the 1910s. The rest was retained to maintain the lineage estate, ancestral rites, and so on. Zigong archives 42–3–381–1 and 42–3–381–11.

23. Luo, "Wang Sanwei Trust" 201–3.

24. Zigong archives 17–1–558–8.

25. For a discussion of the practice of registering contracts with local government offices during the 1920s, see Madeleine Zelin, "Merchant Dispute Mediation in Twentieth Century Zigong, Sichuan," in Philip Huang and Katherine Bernhardt, eds., *Civil Law in Qing and Republican China* (Stanford: Stanford University Press, 1994), 253–54.

26. Zhenhan Lin, *Chuanyan jiyao* [Essentials of Sichuan salt] (Shanghai: Shangwu yinshu guan, 1919), 208, 226–28.

27. See chapter 7.

28. For studies of the relationship among commercial development, payments clearing, and lending in Europe and the United States, see Raymond De Roover, *Money, Banking and Credit in Mediaeval Bruges: Italian Merchant Bankers, Lombards and Money-Changers* (Cambridge: Mediaeval Academy of America, 1948); N. S. B. Gras, *An Introduction to Economic History* (New York: Augustus M. Kelley, 1969), 243–58; and Jacob Price, "Economic Function and the Growth of American Port Towns," *Perspectives in American History* 8 (1974): 123–84.

29. Maode Tian, "Piaohao zai Sichuan di yixie huodong" [Some of the activities of remittance banks in Sichuan], *Sichuan wenshiziliao xuanji* 32 (1984): 59–60.

30. Benqing Chen, "Yusha zhaituan yu Wangsanweitang zhaiwu shimo" [The whole story of the Wang Sanwei trust's debts to the Yusha zhaituan], *Zigong wenshiziliao xuanji* 22 (1992): 1.

31. Zigong archives 42–3–381–9.

32. Ibid., 42–3–381–11.

33. Ibid.

34. Yunsheng Xue, *Duli cunyi* [Concentration on doubtful matters while perusing the substatutes], in Robert Irick, ed., *Research Aids Series,* no. 8 (Taibei: Chengwen chubanshe, 1970), juan 16, 397 (Article 149.1).

35. Zelin, "Merchant Dispute Mediation," 255–63.

36. Collateralized debt dominated Western credit markets as well until the twentieth century. See, for example, Jonathan B. Baskin, "The Development of Corporate Financial Markets in Britain and the United States, 1600–1914: Overcoming Asymmetric Information," *Business History Review* 62 (Summer 1988).

37. Li, "Li Siyou Trust," 199. A humorous story is told of a Chongqing native bank owner known as Boss Aisan, who was owed money by the Lis and took up residence in their Chongqing salt shop. Discovering this on a business trip to Chongqing with his wife, Li Xingqiao had Aisan's bedding moved out of the room and his wife's moved in. On his return to the shop Aisan stumbled in on Mrs. Li, who proceeded to accuse him of improprieties, at which point the humiliated Aisan was forced to leave. Ibid., 200.

38. Li Jiezhi, father of the general manager of the Li Siyou trust, is said to have been taken debt hostage by creditors in Chongqing while on his way to take up a government post in Beijing. Li, "Li Siyou tang," 200. Wang Zigao is also said to have been taken hostage against payment of debts when he went to Chongqing to try to negotiate a settlement with one of the Wang Sanwei trust's creditors. Luo, "Wang Sanwei Trust," 187.

39. For example, Zigong archives 17–1–543–2 [1920s].

40. Ibid. 17–1–500 [1927].

41. Ibid. 17–1–240–8-9, 17–1–1–20–64–66, 1–1–20–59.

42. See chapter 9 for a discussion of governing authorities in the Republican period.

43. Zigong archives 42–3–381–37.

44. Ibid. 17–1–546.

45. Three other cases in our sample involved women who were managing family business affairs. Two women sued for recovery of loans they themselves had

made (ibid., 17–1–549–5 [1928]; and 17–1–193–41 [1932]) and one woman is listed as the owner of disputed well land (ibid., 3–5–514 [1937]).

46. A similar case of disputed authority over trust property involved the Fan lineage, owners of wharfs, warehouses, and other buildings serving the salt industry. Ibid., 17–1–514 [1928]. For a discussion of this and other grounds for lawsuits filed at the Chamber of Commerce during the early twentieth century, see Zelin, "Merchant Dispute Mediation."

47. Zigong archives 3–5–486–6–17 [1927].

48. Duxing Yang et al., "Zigong yanchang zhengqijiche xiyan gaishu" [A general discussion of steam pumping at the Zigong saltyard], *Zigong weshiziliao xuanji* 1–5 (1982): 139.

49. Zigongshi zhengxie wenshiziliao weiyuanhui, ed., *Ziliujing yanye shijia* [Well-known families of the Ziliujing salt industry] (Chengdu: Sichuan renmin chubanshe, 1995), 235.

50. Ibid., 234; Yuesheng Pu, "Zigong yanshang Luo Huagai" [Zigong salt merchant Luo Huagai], *Zigong wenshiziliao xuanji* 19 (1989): 75.

51. *Well-known Families*, 237.

52. Zigongshi zhengxie wenshiban, "Zigong yanye zibenjia Hou Ceming" [Zigong salt capitalist Hou Ceming], *Zigong wenshiziliao xuanji* 19 (1989): 59.

53. In contrast to the handling of the Wang Sanwei trust's debts, which, as we have seen, were still being battled over in 1928, the chamber established principles for debt clearance which enabled this case to be cleared within a year. Creditors were divided into three groups in order of priority of repayment. Old debts were ranked last, with priority given to small creditors whose continued livelihood depended on speedy repayment. Zigong archives 17–1–25. For a discussion of debt cases handled by the Chamber of Commerce, see Zelin, "Merchant Dispute Mediation," 255–63.

54. Luo Xiaoyuan suggests that this practice was first introduced by Zhang Xiaopo in dealing with his creditors and that they soon became part of the regulations of the yard. A form of limited liability, it is not clear how far this practice extended. Xiaoyuan Luo, "Zhang Xiaopo dui Zigong yangchang di yingxiang" [The influence of Zhang Xiaopo on the Zigong saltyard], *Zigong wenshiziliao xuanji* 12 (1981): 178. For a discussion of unlimited liability at the Zigong yard, see Madeleine Zelin, "Managing Multiple Ownership at the Furong Saltyard," in Madeleine Zelin, Jonathan Ocko, and Robert Gardella, eds., *Contract and Property Rights in Early Modern China* (Stanford: Stanford University Press, 2003).

55. Other examples of cartels formed by Chinese firms to limit production and raise prices include the Jiuda group, which joined with several producers of refined salt in eastern China to address falling sales in the 1930s, and the China Egg Produce Company, which formed a cartel with European egg wholesalers to control sales to the European market beginning in 1935. While both of these companies faced shrinking markets as a result of the Great Depression, their response to market conditions was the same as that of Furong's brine producers. Ning Jennifer Chang, "Vertical Integration and Business Diversification: The Case of the China Egg Produce Company in Shanghai, 1923–1950" (paper presented at the Business History Conference annual meeting, Lowell, MA, 2003); Man Bun Kwan, "Managing Market, Hierarchy and Network: The Jiuda-Yongli Group, 1917–1937"

(paper presented at the Business History Conference annual meeting, Lowell, MA, 2003).

56. Jianyu Lin, "Yanye zichanjieji yu zigong difang yishihui—guancang minqu lishidang'an qianxi" [Salt capitalists and the Zigong local assembly—a brief analysis of early Republican historical documents in the archives] (paper presented at the International Conference on Chinese Salt Industry History, Zigong, 1990), 3.

57. *Well-known Families*, 238. This source is also alone in naming Wang Hefu as head of the assembly's finance department.

58. Kaichong Chen et al., "Xinghai geming zhi jiefang qianxi Zigong difang zhujun qingkuang" [The troops garrisoned in Zigong from the 1911 Revolution to the eve of liberation], *Zigong wenshiziliao xuanji* 1–5 (1982): 124; Fu Qiao, *Ziliujing diyiji* [Ziliujing, volume one] (Chengdu: Quchang gongsi, 1916), 36.

59. *Well-known Families*, 238.

60. Zigong archives 17–1–144; Xiaoyuan Luo, "Jing-Fu malu de kaishi xiujian" [The beginning of construction on the Ziliujing-Fushun highway] (manuscript, 1964).

61. In addition to their role in the merchant militia, Wang and Hu served together within the Chamber of Commerce and on the Fushun to Ziliujing Road Committee and are said to have played cards together on a regular basis.

62. *Well-known Families*, 244.

63. Zigong archives 42–3–381–11.

64. One biographer claims that it was Wang's trip to Chongqing to accomplish this feat that killed an already sick Wang Hefu. Chen, "Troops Garrisoned in Zigong," 128; *Well-known Families*, 242.

65. Madeleine Zelin, "The Rise and Fall of the Furong Well-Salt Elite," in Joseph Esherick and Mary Rankin, eds., *Chinese Local Elites and Patterns of Dominance* (Berkeley: University of California Press, 1990), 99–101.

66. Listing the elite of Ziliujing in 1916, Qiao Fu notes that only four had attained examination success, but all had at least some form of title or degree, usually purchased. His list of notables consists of Wang Hefu, Li Xingqiao, Wang Wenqin, Chen Luofu, Hu Tiehua, Li Jingcai, Wang Zuogan, Huang Yushu, Li Menglin, Wang Huafu, Wang Chengzhi, Wang Xinru, Wang Zijun, Chen Jiqing, Gao Ruihua, Wang Yuncang, Zeng Ziwei, Wang Yuru, and Wang Ruizhi. Only the last two actually held positions in the Qing bureaucracy, while Zeng Ziwei served the Qing in a military capacity. Qiao, *Ziliujing*, 185–86.

67. These were the Santai and Yucai academies. Shanquan Hu and Xiaoyuan Luo, "Qingji Zigong difang wu shuyuan" [The five academies in Zigong during the Qing period], *Zigong wenshiziliao xuanji* 14 (1984): 189–90. There is no evidence that any other salt lineage contributed to the development of Confucian education to this extent. The local prestige that these investments brought to the Wang Sanwei trust was not translated into examination success. The highest degree achieved by a lineage member appears to have been the *shengyuan* degree won by a member of the third generation. Luo, "Wang Sanwei Trust," 185.

68. Yongcheng Li, ed., *Fushun xianzhi* [Gazetteer of Fushun county] (1931), 12:53b.

69. Hu, "Hu Yuanhe," 60–61.

70. Ibid., 60. Hu Tiehua clearly learned something at the lineage academy, as he is referred to by Fu Qiao as one of only two notable calligraphers in Ziliujing in 1916. Qiao, *Ziliujing*, 209. Later memoirists frequently refer to Hu Tiehua as a former Qing official, but the position he held appears to have been no higher than that of a secretary in one of the new agencies formed right before the fall of the Qing.

71. Yang, "General Discussion of Steam Pumping," 202.

72. *Well-known Families*, 199.

73. For an overview of warlord activities in Sichuan during this period, see Robert A. Kapp, *Szechwan and the Chinese Republic: Provincial Militarism and Central Power, 1911–1938* (New Haven: Yale University Press, 1973).

74. *Well-known Families*, 239.

75. Ibid., 200.

76. Ibid., 239.

77. Ibid., 242.

78. Luo Xiaoyuan's autobiography refers to Li Jingcai as a local bully. Xiaoyuan Luo, "Luo Xiaoyuan zishu" [Autobiography of Luo Xiaoyuan] (manuscript), 3, in Zigong Municipal Archives. Wang Roude and Zhong Langhua accuse Li of being a member of the clique of the Fushun Brigade Commander Zhang Zhifang, although Song Liangxi, a senior researcher at the Zigong Salt Industry Museum, notes that Li's connection to Zhang was instrumental and was probably secured to assist Li in a particular dispute with Wang Wentao over a fire at Li's well. Liangxi Song, "Sichuan junfa dui Zigong yanshang de jielue" [The Sichuan warlord's plunder of the Zigong salt merchants], in Jiusong Peng, Ran Chen, and Zigongshi yanye lishi bowuguan, eds., *Sichuan jingyanshi luncong* [Collected essays on Sichuan salt history] (Chengdu: Sichuansheng shehui kexueyuan chubanshe, 1985), 328; Roude Wang and Langhua Zhong, "Luo Xiaoyuan sishinian di yanye jingying ji qi wannian shilue" [Luo Xiaoyuan's forty years in the salt industry and a short biographical account of his later years], *Zigong wenshiziliao xuanji* 15 (1985): 94. Nevertheless, Ni Jingxian, a former employee of the 24th army's Yutong bank, claims that Wang, Hu, and Li could get immediate loans of up to 5,000 yuan without application or interest. Jingxian Ni, "Wo dui Yutong yinhang Zigong fenhang de huiyi" [My memories of the Zigong branch of the Yutong bank], *Zigong wenshiziliao xuanji* 6–10 (1982): 298.

79. *Well-known Families*, 206.

80. Ibid., 180. It does not appear that this unit ever engaged in any fighting. For a discussion of the Railroad Rights Recovery Movement in Sichuan, see En-han Lee, *China's Quest for Railway Autonomy, 1904–1911: A Study of the Chinese Railway-Rights Recovery Movement* (Singapore: Singapore University Press, 1977), and Zhili Dai and Zhongyang yanjiuyuan jindaishi yanjiusuo, *Sichuan baolu yundong shiliao huizuan* [Collected historical materials on the Sichuan railway protection movement], *Zhongyang yanjiuyuan jindaishi yanjiusuo shiliao zonggan* 23 (Taibei Shi: Zhongyang yanjiuyuan jindaishi yanjiusuo, 1994).

81. Luo, "Zhang Xiaopo," 178.

82. Yuecong Lin, "Zigong difang yishihui de huiyi" [A recollection of the Zigong local assembly], *Zigong wenshiziliao xuanji* 1–5 (1982): 168.

83. Luo, "Zhang Xiaopo," 180–81.

84. Xiaoyuan Luo and Xiangchen Jiang, "Zigong yanchang di jianshang" [Pipe merchants at the Zigong saltyard], *Zigong wenshiziliao xuanji* 13 (1983): 141. See also Zigong archives 17–1–469 (1920), in which Zhang is called upon by the local police to mediate a case between salt producers Wang Zhengzhong and Yang Shaolin. Luo Xiaoyuan claims that Zhang was also a mediator in the Sichuan-Hankow Railways suit against Li Xingqiao for unpaid loans, a suit between the Li Siyou trust and the Neijiang guild, and in one of the several suits between the Wang Sanwei trust and the Chongqing-Shashi credit group. Luo, "Zhang Xiaopo," 187–88.

85. Zigong archives 17–1–434; Luo, "Zhang Xiaopo," 189.

86. On this occasion Zhang was accused by the garrison commander resident at Ziliujing of transferring money to a rival warlord. Luo, "Zhang Xiaopo," 181–82.

87. Ibid., 190.

88. Yang, "General Discussion of Steam Pumping," 140.

89. Luo, "Zhang Xiaopo," 184. There is some disagreement between Yang and Luo on the timing of these events.

90. See chapter 4.

91. Yifu Zhang, "Enliujian duishui de jingguo" [An account of the shipment of brine through the Enliu pipe], *Zigong wenshiziliao xuanji* 19 (1989): 91–95; Luo, "Zhang Xiaopo," 188. Note that Zhang Yifu is Zhang Xiaopo's son.

92. Luo, "Zhang Xiaopo," 188; Wei Wu, ed., *Sichuan yanzhengshi* [Sichuan salt administration history] (China: Sichuan yanzhengshi bianjichu, 1932), juan 3, pian 2, zhang 10, jie 4, 79b.

93. Luo, "Zhang Xiaopo," 188–89; Luo and Jiang, "Pipe Merchants," 141–42.

94. Unless otherwise indicated, biographical information on Hou Ceming is based on Zigongshi zhengxie wenshiban, "Hou Ceming," 49–73, and *Well-known Families*, 293–322.

95. Zhang Xiaomei, the foremost chronicler of the Sichuan economy in the interwar period, describes a similar system of remittances between Shanghai and Chongqing. Xiaomei Zhang, *Sichuan jingji cankao ziliao* [Reference materials on the Sichuan economy] (Shanghai: Zhongguo guomin jingji yanjiu suo, 1939), E12–14.

96. Unless otherwise indicated, biographical information on Xiong Zuozhou is based on Yuesheng Pu, "Zigong yanshang Xiong Zuozhou shilue" [A short biographical sketch of Zigong salt merchant Xiong Zuozhou], *Zigong wenshiziliao xuanji* 17 (1987): 1–20. Pu's account appears to be based on a manuscript biography housed in the Zigong Municipal Archives: Zigongshi gongshangye lianhehui, ed., "Xiong Zuozhou zhuan" [Biography of Xiong Zuozhou]. Pu himself was an employee of the Hou, Xiong, Luo, and Luo group during the 1940s. Pu, "Luo Huagai," 74.

97. Xiong Wanquan's biographers do not indicate where these funds were invested. Given the financial environment in Zigong at the time, it is likely that the funds were lent out at interest or deposited in a local native bank.

98. Luo, "Autobiography of Luo Xiaoyuan," 28. Huang was one of the largest developers of black-brine wells in late-nineteenth-century Gongjing. Yuzhi Cui and Shaoyuan Yan, "Gongjing yanshang Yu Shuhuai" [The Gongjing salt merchant Yu Shuhuai], *Zigong wenshiziliao xuanji* 14 (1984): 174; Rongqing Ji, "Gongjing yanchang fazhan yipie" [A glance at the development of the Gongjing saltyard], *Sichuan wenshiziliao xuanji* 11 (1964): 193–96.

99. Yang, "General Discussion of Steam Pumping," 140.

100. Mingqin Lai et al., "Yanyanjing fazhan gaikuang" [A survey of the development of rock-salt wells], *Zigong wenshiziliao xuanji* 6–10 (1982): 39.

101. Ibid., 11.

102. Huaizhou Wang, "Ziliujing chang daguan jiqi zhineng" [The *daguan* of Ziliujing and their functions], *Zigong wenshiziliao xuanji* 20 (1990): 133.

103. In the 1930s, in addition to the Baozhen well, we have records that Xiong, Hou, Luo, and Luo invested in the Yunzhen well, the Weizheng well, the redrilled Hongjun well, the Chenglong well, and the Fengren well. During the 1940s Xiong participated with these three and others in the opening of several coal furnaces as well.

104. This venture failed after one year.

105. Pu, "Luo Huagai," 80.

106. Li, "Luo Xiaoyuan," 40.

107. Luo, "Autobiography of Luo Xiaoyuan," 4–5.

108. Ibid., 5.

109. Ibid.

110. Several memoirs describe Luo Xiaoyuan as having taken advantage of his position at the Wang Sanwei trust to engage in deals involving Wang assets. Li, "Luo Xiaoyuan," 40; Chaolan Song, "Wosuoliaojie di Luo Xiaoyuan" [What I know of Luo Xiaoyuan], *Ziliujing* 4 (1984): 36. Luo himself admits as much in his handwritten autobiography.

111. Luo, "Autobiography of Luo Xiaoyuan," 9.

112. Wang and Zhong, "Luo's 40 Years," 78.

113. Ibid.

114. Ibid., 79–80.

115. Song, "Luo Xiaoyuan," 37.

116. Song Chaolan, whose father was an investor in the Liqun bank, wrote bitterly about its practices, which appear to have some of the characteristics of an industrial bank; it would grant interest on deposits but place restrictions on withdrawals in order to accumulate a pool of funds for industrial investment. Song does not indicate how dividends to investors were paid or whether investment was by the bank itself or the bank as lender to shareholders like Luo Xiaoyuan. Ibid.

117. Luo, "Autobiography of Luo Xiaoyuan," 18.

118. Unless otherwise indicated, biographical information about Luo Huagai is provided by Pu, "Luo Huagai," 74–90.

119. *Well-known Families*, 234.

120. I have deliberately avoided the word "professional" in this context. There is no implication that the employment of career managers involved the development of specialist education, although as we will see, there is an increasing trend toward the creation of occupational advocacy through the Chambers of Commerce and trade associations.

121. Wang and Zhong, "Luo's 40 Years," 74.

122. Luo, "Autobiography of Luo Xiaoyuan," 20.

123. Wang and Zhong, "Luo's 40 Years," 75, 79.

124. Ibid., 100. According to Wang and Zhong, there were more than 3,000 dedicated Buddhist practitioners in Zigong, many of them merchants, industrialists, officials, and landlords.

125. Zigongshi zhengxie wenshiban, "Hou Ceming," 52. The Elder Brother Society (Gelaohui) was more commonly known in Sichuan as the Paoge hui. A secret society commonly thought to have originated in western China in the mid-nineteenth century, it claimed a large membership in early-twentieth-century Sichuan. Cai Xiaoqing, in his seminal work on the origins of the society, notes their mention by Li Hanzhang in 1866, Hunan governor Liu Kun in 1867, and Zuo Zongtang in 1896. Shaoqing Cai, "On the Origin of the Gelaohui," *Modern China* 10, no. 4 (1984): 483, 485. G. William Skinner, who conducted fieldwork in Sichuan, notes that by the 1940s the Elder Brothers "wielded supreme power" in rural counties, including in standard marketing towns. G. William Skinner, "Marketing and Social Structure in Rural China," *Journal of Asian Studies* 24, no. 1 (1964): 37. Robert A. Kapp, reviewing the literature on southwest China available in the 1970s, was deeply disturbed

by how little mention had been made of this extremely important organization. Robert A. Kapp, "Themes in the History of Twentieth Century Southwest China," *Pacific Affairs* 51, no. 3 (1978).

126. *Well-known Families,* 301. Rotating credit associations continue to be a part of China's informal banking culture. See Kellee Tsai, *Back-Alley Banking: Private Entrepreneurs in China* (Ithaca: Cornell University Press, 2002), 28–29, 72–73, 77, and passim.

127. Tsai, *Back-Alley Banking,* 112, 291–95, which provides an excellent tabular summary of the literature on rotating credit associations worldwide.

128. Wang and Zhong, "Luo's 40 Years," 92–93. Luo Xiaoyuan is said to have been a member, along with two managers who were working for Hou Ceming's Daji native bank. It is not clear what relationship the other two may have had with the Guomindang at this time.

129. Luo, "Autobiography of Luo Xiaoyuan," 22–23. On the Rock Salt Brine company, see chapter 9.

130. Pu, "Luo Huagai," 77.

131. Zhiyi Peng, ed., *Zigongshi zhi—Shanghui zhi, ziliao changpian* [(Draft) Gazetteer of Zigong city—Chamber of Commerce Gazetteer, long compilation of documents] (Zigong: Zigongshi gongshangye lianhehui, 1989), 4.

132. Zigong archives 17–1–259 and 7–1–29.

133. Peng, ed., *(Draft) Gazetteer of Zigong City,* 4–5.

134. Wang and Zhong, "Luo's 40 Years," 97.

135. Zigong archives 17–1–27.

9. Politics, Taxes, and Markets: The Fate of Zigong in the Early Twentieth Century

1. S. A. M. Adshead, *Province and Politics in Late Imperial China: Viceregal Government in Sichuan, 1898–1911* (London: Curzon Press, 1984), 36.

2. Ibid., 94.

3. Joseph Esherick, *Reform and Revolution in China: The 1911 Revolution in Hunan and Hubei* (Berkeley: University of California Press, 1976).

4. Yuecong Lin, "Zigong difang yishihui de huiyi" [A recollection of the Zigong local assembly], *Zigong wenshiziliao xuanji* 1–5 (1982): 1–3.

5. Ibid. Lin Yuecong describes himself as a Qing *shengyuan* with revolutionary sympathies. He also names Cao Du as a Furong local who participated in the Revolutionary Alliance, but he does not appear elsewhere as an important member of the merchant community.

6. The early declaration of the Rong County revolutionary forces is mentioned in a number of memoirs as well as in Lin Jianyu's study based on local archival materials. Jianyu Lin, "Xinhai zigong difang shangren yu zhengfu" [Zigong merchants and the government in 1911], *Zigong wenshiziliao xuanji* 21 (1991): 13.

7. Yuecong Lin et al., "Xinhai geming zai Zigong" [The 1911 Revolution in Zigong], *Zigong wenshiziliao xuanji* 12 (1981): 2.

8. Lin, "Zigong Merchants," 13.

9. Lin, "1911 Revolution," 6; Xi Zhang, ed., *Sichuan yanwu baogao shu* [Reports on the Sichuan salt administration] (China, 1912), pian 1, 1a–b.

10. Zhang, ed., *Reports on the Sichuan Salt Administration,* pian 1, 1b.

11. Lin, "1911 Revolution," 6.

12. For an overview of the self-government movement, see Roger R. Thompson, *China's Local Councils in the Age of Constitutional Reform, 1898–1911* (Cambridge: Council on East Asian Studies, Harvard University, 1995).

13. The importance of Furong for tax purposes was recognized by the establishment of an assistant magistrate's yamen at the yard. Similar accommodations were made in a number of nonadministrative cities of importance during the Qing dynasty.

14. This story is repeated in all accounts of the 1911 Revolution. See, for example, Lin, "1911 Revolution," and Xuejun Zhang, "Xinghai geming yu Zigong yanye" [The 1911 Revolution and the Zigong salt industry], *Jingyanshi tongxun* 11 (1983): 12.

15. Lin, "Recollection," 168.

16. Zhang, "1911 and the Salt Industry," 12.

17. Lin, "Zigong Merchants," 9.

18. Lin, "Recollection," 170.

19. Jianyu Lin, "Yanye zichanjieji yu zigong difang yishihui—guancang minqu lishidang'an qianxi" [Salt capitalists and the Zigong local assembly—a brief analysis of early Republican historical documents in the archives] (paper presented at the International Conference on Chinese Salt Industry History, Zigong, 1990), 4; Lin, "1911 Revolution," 8. The structure of legal institutions proposed by the assembly reflects the attraction of German models entering China via Japan during the first decade of the century. For a discussion of this process, see Douglas Reynolds, *China, 1898–1912: The Xinzheng Revolution and Japan* (Cambridge: Harvard University Press, 1993), 182–84.

20. Lin, "Zigong Merchants," 16.

21. Zigong archives 196, cited in Lin, "Salt Capitalists and the Zigong Local Assembly," 397–99; Tianying Wu, "Yinli juren, Yinren chengyi—Cong yandu Ziliujing kan gongshangye chengshi de xingcheng jiqi tedian" [People gather to make a profit, Cities are founded because there are people—An examination of the formation and characteristics of the industrial-commercial city from the example of the salt capital Ziliujing] (manuscript).

22. Lin, "Recollection," 169–70; Lin, "Salt Capitalists and the Zigong Local Assembly," 5–7; Renyuan Wang, Ran Chen, and Fanying Zeng, eds., *Zigong chengshi shi* [The history of Zigong city] (Beijing: Shihui kexue wenxian chubanshe, 1995), 46.

23. Zhenhan Lin, *Chuanyan jiyao* [Essentials of Sichuan salt] (Shanghai: Shangwu yinshu guan, 1919), 446–53.

24. "Jiayan shuomingshu" [A synopsis on sylvite], in ibid., 479–88; "Tichang shoule xiyan yi" [In favor of feeding animals salt], in ibid., 500–506.

25. Wei Wu, ed., *Sichuan yanzhengshi* [Sichuan salt administration history] (China: Sichuan yanzhengshi bianjichu, 1932), juan 1, pian 1, zhang 2, jie 1, 14a–16a. S. A. M. Adshead, *The Modernization of the Chinese Salt Administration, 1900–1920* (Cambridge: Harvard University Press, 1970), 81, shows that unlike Sichuan, most other salt administration regions remained under rules similar to those of the Qing.

26. Wu, ed., *Salt Administration History,* juan 1, pian 1, zhang 2, jie 1, 14a–15b.

27. Lin, *Essentials of Sichuan Salt,* 524.

28. Wu, ed., *Salt Administration History,* juan 10, pian 7, zhang 12, jie 2, 85a–86a.

29. Ibid., juan 1, pian 1, zhang 2, jie 2, 16a–19a.

30. For a detailed discussion of this issue, see Adshead, *Modernization,* 94–110.

31. S. A. M. Adshead, "Salt and Warlordism in Szechwan 1914–1922," *Modern Asian Studies* 24, no. 4 (1990): 729–39. Zigong archives 1–1–164 contains an official circular by the Northern Sichuan Garrison Command of the National Protection Army informing the Salt Inspectorate that because Yuan Shikai was no longer the legitimate ruler of China, they had declared independence and now intended to take over Sichuan's salt revenues. They assured the inspectorate that they would remit that portion of funds earmarked for the repayment of foreign debts but would retain all "surplus" salt taxes.

32. See, for example, petitions from Shepeng, Renshou, Leshan, Jianwei, Shehong, Santai, and 13 other Sichuan yards. Zigong archives 1–1–91. The arguments against the free market were the same as those put forward during the Qing: (1) smaller yards would be put out of business, creating unemployment and unrest; (2) merchants would no longer be required to serve more remote areas, which would suffer shortages of salt; and (3) an open market is harder to regulate and makes tax evasion easier.

33. Wu, ed., *Salt Administration History,* juan 1, pian 1, zhang 2, jie 2, 16a–19a. According to Song Shangze, some of these companies were really combinations of more than one group of investors, making the total number of companies involved 25. Shangze Song, "Cong xinghai zhi jiefang Sichuan xingyan jiuyiqizhi" [The nine changes in the system of salt sales in Sichuan from the 1911 Revolution to liberation], *Zigong wenshiziliao xuanji* 23 (1993): 74.

34. Wu, ed., *Salt Administration History,* juan 10, pian 7, 110a–112a.

35. Zigong archives 1–1–26.

36. See a later section for a discussion of tight credit.

37. Wu, ed., *Salt Administration History,* juan 1, pian 1, zhang 2, jie 2, 18b.

38. Ibid., juan 1, pian 1, zhang 2, jie 2, 19a–19b.

39. Ibid., juan 1, pian 1, zhang 2, jie 4, 21b.

40. Ibid., juan 1, pian 2, zhang 2, jie 5, 23a.

41. Adshead, "Salt and Warlordism in Szechwan 1914–1922," 734–35.

42. Wu, ed., *Salt Administration History,* juan 1, pian 2, zhang 2, jie 5, 23b–24a.

43. Ibid., juan 1, pian 2, zhang 2, jie 5, 23b-24a, and juan 5, pian 3, zhang 3, jie 4, 35b–36a; Yuesheng Pu, "Zigong yanshang Luo Huagai" [Zigong salt merchant Luo Huagai], *Zigong wenshiziliao xuanji* 19 (1989): 77; Zigongshi dang'anguan and Zigongshi zonggong hui, *Zigong yanye gongren douzhengshi dangan ziliao xuanbian (1915–1949)* [Selected documents on the history of the struggles of Zigong salt workers (1915–1949)] (Chengdu: Sichuan renmin chubanshe, 1989), 78, 83.

44. Roude Wang and Langhua Zhong, "Luo Xiaoyuan sishinian di yanye jingying ji qi wannian shilue" [Luo Xiaoyuan's forty years in the salt industry and a short biographical account of his later years], *Zigong wenshiziliao xuanji* 15 (1985): 95. The spokesmen included Luo Xiaoyuan and Luo Huagai.

45. Wu, ed., *Salt Administration History,* juan 8, pian 4, zhang 2, jie 3, 17a.

46. Both local and regional governments minted silver coins denominated at various multiples of the yuan. Both the tael and the yuan varied widely in their silver content. However, the rule of thumb has been that the exchange rate between the two was 1:0.72. This differs only slightly from the conversion rate given by the *Sichuan Salt Administration History* for 1915, which was 1:0.68. Using the latter figure, the tax rate in 1915 would have been 0.913 yuan per 100 *jin* of salt destined for the Huguang market and between 2 and 2.19 yuan per 100 *jin* for the remaining salt marketed by certificate.

47. Robert A. Kapp, *Szechwan and the Chinese Republic: Provincial Militarism and Central Power, 1911–1938* (New Haven: Yale University Press, 1973), 8.

48. Fu Qiao, *Ziliujing diyiji* [Ziliujing, volume one] (Chengdu: Quchang gongsi, 1916), 4–5. The fortresses were fortified towns first built during the period of the Taiping Rebellion during the 1850s.

49. For the career of Feng Yuxiang, see James E. Sheridan, *Chinese Warlord: The Career of Feng Yu-hsiang* (Stanford: Stanford University Press, 1966).

50. Qiao, *Ziliujing*, 6–7.

51. Kaichong Chen et al., "Xinghai geming zhi jiefang qianxi Zigong difang zhujun qingkuang" [The troops garrisoned in Zigong from the 1911 Revolution to the eve of liberation], *Zigong wenshiziliao xuanji* 1–5 (1982): 121–31.

52. See, for example, Parks M. Coble, *The Shanghai Capitalists and the Nationalist Government, 1927–1937*, Harvard East Asian Monographs, no. 94 (Cambridge: Council on East Asian Studies, Harvard University, 1980).

53. Adshead, "Salt and Warlordism in Szechwan 1914–1922," 739–40.

54. To get a perspective on the size of the request, note that the entire annual budget of the chamber a decade later was only about 9,800 yuan. Zigong archives 17–1–785.

55. Ibid., 17–1–440.

56. Ibid., 17–1–259.

57. Chen, "Troops Garrisoned in Zigong," 123.

58. Liangxi Song, "Sichuan junfa dui Zigong yanshang de jielue" [The Sichuan warlord's plunder of the Zigong salt merchants], in Jiusong Peng, Ran Chen, and Zigongshi yanye lishi bowuguan, eds., *Sichuan jingyanshi luncong* [Collected essays on Sichuan salt history] (Chengdu: Sichuansheng shehui kexueyuan chubanshe, 1985), 322.

59. Zigongshi zhengxie wenshi ziliao weiyuanhui, ed., *Ziliujing yanye shijia* [Well-known families of the Ziliujing salt industry] (Sichuan renmin chubanshe, 1995), 188–89.

60. Zigong archives 17–1–466.

61. Adshead, "Salt and Warlordism in Szechwan 1914–1922," 740.

62. Zigong archives 17–1–208.

63. Ibid., 17–1–466.

64. Ibid., 17–1–175; Wu, ed., *Salt Administration History*, juan 8, pian 4, zhang 14, jie 1, 97a–99a.

65. Zhang, ed., *Reports on the Sichuan Salt Administration*, pian 3, 1a–1b.

66. Wenan Chen, "Chuanyan jichu shimo" [The whole story of the sale of Sichuan salt in Huguang], *Jingyanshi tongshun* 8 (1981): 46.

67. The Changlu salt administrative region consisted of Hebei and northern Henan.

68. Chen, "Whole Story of the Sale of Sichuan Salt in Huguang," 45–46.

69. Zigong archives 17–1–214.

70. In Furong it cost between 2.5 and 2.8 yuan to produce a *dan* of salt in 1931. In Jianwei and Daning the cost was between 4.2 and 4.8 yuan, while at some of the smaller yards a *dan* of salt could cost upward of 7 or 8 yuan to produce. Wu, ed., *Salt Administration History*, juan 3, pian 2, zhang 8, jie 5, 47b–50a.

71. Lin, *Essentials of Sichuan Salt*, 248.

72. Wu, ed., *Salt Administration History*, juan 3, pian 2, zhang 9, jie 1, 59b.

73. Ibid., juan 3, pian 2, zhang 9, jie 2, 61b–63b.

74. Xiaomei Zhang, *Sichuan jingji cankao ziliao* [Reference materials on the Sichuan economy] (Shanghai: Zhongguo guomin jingji yanjiu suo, 1939), Q 83.

75. Zigong archives 17–1–245. This letter was transmitted by the Zigong Salt Affairs and Salt Wholesalers Research Association to the Chamber of Commerce informing it that the headquarters of most of the firms that shipped Furong salt were located in Chongqing. If they did not send funds with which to buy Furong salt, there would be no way for their agents at the yard to operate.

76. For example, Zigong archives 17–1–507, dated October 1925, contains an appeal by coal shippers to the Chamber of Commerce informing it that coal boats from Weiyuan County were being intercepted by inspectors sent by the military and forced to pay a double tax on their cargo. Because they refused to do so, they had been forced to weigh anchor upriver and were not permitted to proceed to the coal yards in Ziliujing and Gongjing.

77. Wufang Nie, "Qingmo yilai Zigong yanchangde jinrongye" [Banking at the Zigong saltyard since the late Qing], *Zigong wenshiziliao xuanji* 21 (1991): 81.

78. Liangxi Song, "Zigong diqu de qianzhuang, piaohao yu yanye fazhan" [The development of native banks, remittance banks, and the salt industry in the Zigong region] *Yanyeshi yanjiu* 2 (1995): 17; Zigongshi jinrongzhi bianzuanweiyuanhui, ed., *Zigongshi jinrongzhi* [Zigong financial gazetteer], Zigongshi difangzhi congshu [Zigong municipal gazetteer collection], vol. 18 (Chengdu: Sichuan cishu chubanshe, 1994), 44–47.

79. Zhang, *Sichuan Economy*, D43–D44; Zigongshi jinrongzhi bianzuanweiyuanhui, ed., *Zigong Financial Gazetteer*, 47–54.

80. Zigong archives 17–1–486.

81. Ibid., 17–1–466.

82. Ibid., 17–1–488.

83. Ibid.

84. Nie, "Banking at the Zigong Saltyard," 83. Zhang Xiaomei seems to indicate that the premium paid on Chongqing bills continued into the 1930s at least until the introduction of a uniform currency under the Guomindang. Zhang, *Sichuan Economy*, 83.

85. The rate of discount was limited by the cost of shipping the notes back to Shanghai, redeeming them for silver, and shipping the silver back to Chongqing, but also reflected the slightly higher silver content of Chongqing silver taels.

86. Inspector General of Customs, Shanghai, China, *Decennial Reports, 1922–31*, vol. 1, *Northern and Yangzi Ports*, Maritime Customs, Statistical Series, no. 6 (Shanghai, 1933), 475.

87. Ibid., 474.

88. Zhang, *Sichuan Economy*, E22.

89. Wu, ed., *Salt Administration History*, juan 3, pian 2, zhang 7, jie 2, 5a–5b.

90. Zigong archives 17–1–488.

91. Adshead, "Salt and Warlordism in Szechwan 1914–1922," 741.

92. Some members of the assembly appear on the rosters of the early chamber, particularly influential members of the Wang lineage including Wang Yulin, Wang Yuhuai, Wang Zuogan, and Wang Hefu. Zigong archives 17–1–196 and 17–1–20.

93. Surprisingly little has been written on the role of Chambers of Commerce in early-twentieth-century Chinese cities, although a number of cities have now begun publishing collections of chamber documents. For an overview of the subject, see Heping Yu, *Shanghui yu Zhongguo zaoqi xiandaihua* [Chambers of Commerce and China's early modernization] (Shanghai: Shanghai renmin

chubanshe, 1993). David Strand was one of the first to write about the activities of chambers in English. David Strand, *Rickshaw Beijing* (Berkeley: University of California Press, 1989). See also Xiaobo Zhang, "Merchant Associational Activism in Early-Twentieth-Century China: The Tianjin General Chamber of Commerce, 1904–1928" (Ph.D. diss., Columbia University, 1995).

94. Anonymous, "Shanghui de yange" [Evolution of the Zigong Chamber of Commerce] (manuscript). The Arbitration Department was the largest and most important department, with 12 arbitrators and two investigators on its staff.

95. Zigong archives 17–1–500. If the regulations of 1935 are any indication of earlier practice, administrative expenses of the chamber were raised through fixed dues paid by member guilds. To finance specific projects the membership would vote a special levy. Zigong archives 17–1–20.

96. Among the merchants who held high positions within the chamber were Fan Rongguang, Li Jingcai, Wang Hefu, Hu Tiehua, Wang Zuogan, Wang Xinru, Hou Ceming, and Xiong Zuozhou. Zigong archives 17–1–22, 17–1–234, 17–1–19; Zigongshi dang'anguan and Zigongshi zonggong hui, *Salt Workers' Struggles*, 87.

97. For a detailed discussion of the activities of the Arbitration Board, see Madeleine Zelin, "Merchant Dispute Mediation in Twentieth Century Zigong, Sichuan," in Philip Huang and Katherine Bernhardt, eds., *Civil Law in Qing and Republican China* (Stanford: Stanford University Press, 1994).

98. Zigong archives 17–1–472.

99. Ibid., 17–1–21.

100. Ibid., 17–1–27.

101. Ibid., 17–1–25.

102. For example, in 1925 Li Wenhui's ninth division headquarters ordered the chamber to collect a fine from Xiong Zuozhou for price gouging. Ibid., 17–1–434.

103. Ibid., 17–1–23 and 17–1–82.

104. Ibid., 17–1–20.

105. Ibid., 17–1–28.

106. Ibid., 17–1–81.

107. Lin, *Essentials of Sichuan Salt*, 214–15; Wu, ed., *Salt Administration History*, juan 3, 85a.

108. Mingqin Lai et al., "Yanyanjing fazhan gaikuang" [A survey of the development of rock-salt wells], *Zigong wenshiziliao xuanji* 6–10 (1982): 35.

109. Ibid., 14.

110. Duxing Yang et al., "Zigong yanchang zhengqijiche xiyan gaishu" [A general discussion of steam pumping at the Zigong saltyard], *Zigong weshiziliao xuanji* 1–5 (1982): 148–49.

111. Lai, "Rock-Salt Wells," 14.

112. Ibid.; Wang and Zhong, "Luo's 40 Years," 93; interviews with Fan Gucun (age 70 sui), Zhong yueqiao (82), Wang Huaizhou (82), and Mao Shuwu (77), May 1989.

113. *Well-known Families*, 201. In his survey of rock-salt brine wells at Dafen bao, Wang Huaizhou distinguishes between those wells that joined the company and participated in alternate pumping and those that joined, stopped pumping, and simply drew dividends. Huaizhou Wang, "Dafenbao yanyan jing shiliao" [Materials on the Dafen bao rock-salt wells], *Zigong wenshiziliao xuanji* 19 (1989): 126–31.

114. Zigongshi dang'anguan and Zigongshi zonggong hui, *Salt Workers' Struggles*, 50–51.

115. Wang and Zhong, "Luo's 40 Years," 94; Xiaoyuan Luo, "Luo Xiaoyuan zishu" [Autobiography of Luo Xiaoyuan] (manuscript), in Zigong Municipal Archives, 22.

116. Lei Li, "Luo Xiaoyuan jiushi" [Luo Xiaoyuan's past], *Ziliujing* 1 (1983): 43.

117. Lai, "Rock-Salt Wells," 15.

118. Wang and Zhong, "Luo's 40 Years," 93.

119. Luo, "Autobiography of Luo Xiaoyuan," 12.

120. Zigong archives 17–1–81 (1932).

121. Roude Wang, "Jiefang qian Zigong yanshang di fengjianxing" [The feudal nature of the Zigong salt merchants before liberation], *Jingyanshi tongshun* 10 (1983): 23; Zigong archives 17–1–20 and 17–1–81.

122. Wu, ed., *Salt Administration History,* juan 3, pian 2, zhang 10, jie 2, 71b; Lai, "Rock-Salt Wells," 21; Wang and Zhong, "Luo's 40 Years," 94.

123. Alfred D. Chandler, *The Visible Hand: The Managerial Revolution in American Business* (Cambridge: Belknap Press of Harvard University Press, 1977), 320–22.

124. Wells that were not pumped also stood to lose pumping fees under a system of contract pumping similar to that in effect before the brine glut. Lai, "Rock-Salt Wells," 21–22. For examples of individual wells challenging their ratings, see Zigong archives 1–1–203.

125. One such case involved Hou Ceming, who filed suit against the Rock Salt company with the Sichuan salt administration, claiming that its rating system was preventing him from accessing the brine from his Yongjiang well, a well that he had spent 50,000 yuan to drill and another 10,000 to repair the previous summer. Zigong archives 3–5–501.

126. Lai, "Rock-Salt Wells," 22.

127. Wu, ed., *Salt Administration History,* juan 3, pian 2, zhang 10, jie 7, 82a–86b. Unemployment at this time was entirely the result of local factors. Neither Zigong nor China as a whole experienced the effects of the Great Depression until 1932. China, as the only large country whose currency was backed by silver, benefited during the first years of the Great Depression from currency depreciation, lower prices for foreign goods, and increased foreign investment. Japan's attacks on Manchuria in 1931 and Shanghai in early 1932, combined with Great Britain's and Japan's abandonment of the silver standard, ended China's brief period of postcrash prosperity. The U.S. decision to purchase silver at artificially high rates plunged China deeper into depression in 1934. Lloyd E. Eastman, *The Abortive Revolution: China Under Nationalist Rule, 1927–1937* (Cambridge: Harvard University Press, 1974), 185–86.

128. Cited in Zhang, "1911 and the Salt Industry," 16.

129. Zigongshi dang'anguan and Zigongshi zonggong hui, *Salt Workers' Struggles,* 2–3, 12.

130. Ibid., 6. This guild continued to exercise considerable control over employment at the salt evaporation furnaces. See chapter 5 on its early history. According to a report sponsored by pipe firms in 1917, every worker engaging in salt evaporation was required to register with the guild. Registration fees and annual dues made the guild one of the wealthiest associations at the yard. Upon entering the guild a regular evaporator paid between 8 strings and over 14 strings copper cash in membership fees. A furnace foreman paid as much as 20 or more strings. In addition, each member paid a twice-a-year contribution called incense money, which in 1917 came to 960 copper cash a year. Zigongshi dang'anguan and Zigongshi

zonggong hui, *Salt Workers' Struggles*, 8. According to table 9.5, despite their being among the best organized of Zigong's workers, evaporators' wages rose only about 25 percent between 1916 and 1919, while price rises exceeded 50 percent for most key commodities.

131. Zigongshi dang'anguan and Zigongshi zonggong hui, *Salt Workers' Struggles*, 14.

132. Ibid., 15.

133. Ibid., 16.

134. Ran Chen, "Jindai Zigong yanye gongren zhuangkuang ji qi douzheng" [The condition and struggles of salt industry workers in modern Zigong], in Peng and Chen, eds., *Collected Essays on Sichuan Salt History*, 258.

135. Zhonggong Zigongshiwei dangshi gongzuo weiyuanhui, *Zhonggong Zigong dixia dang zuzhi gaiguang* [A survey of Chinese Communist Party organization in Zigong] (Zigong: Zhonggong Zigong shiwei dangshi yanjiushi, 1995), 1. I would like to thank Danke Li for bringing this work to my attention.

136. The First United Front refers to a period of cooperation between the Communist Party and the Guomindang during which many members of the Communist Party worked as members within the Guomindang with the mutual goal of defeating warlord rule in China. For a comprehensive treatment of the United Front and its breakdown in 1927, see C. Martin Wilbur, "The Nationalist Revolution: From Canton to Nanking, 1923–28," in John King Fairbank and Denis Twitchett, eds., *Cambridge History of China*, vol. 12, *Republican China, 1912–1949* (Cambridge: Cambridge University Press, 1983), especially 614–39.

137. Zigongshi jixie dianzi gongye guanliju, ed., *Zigongshi jixiegongye zhi* [Gazetteer of the Zigong city machine industry], Zigongshi difangzhi congshu [Zigong municipal gazetteer collection], vol. 21 (Chengdu: Sichuan renmin chubanshe, 1993), 19–20.

138. Ibid., 20.

139. Ibid., 21–22.

140. For a brief discussion of the May 30 movement and its role in the spread of both Nationalist and Communist allegiances among politically active Chinese, see C. Martin Wilbur, *The Nationalist Revolution in China, 1923–1928* (Cambridge: Cambridge University Press, 1984), 21–23.

141. Zigongshi dang'anguan and Zigongshi zonggong hui, *Salt Workers' Struggles*, 23–24.

142. Ibid., 29.

143. Ibid., 30–31.

144. Ibid., 32–33.

145. Ibid., 36–37.

146. Ibid., 40.

147. The Zigong special branch of the Chinese Communist Party had 40 members when the strike began and only 10 when it ended. The party itself, while calling the workers traitors, recognized that it had not undertaken sufficient preparatory work among the workers or among surrounding peasant communities. Zhonggong Zigongshiwei dangshi gongzuo weiyuanhui, *Survey of Chinese Communist Party Organization in Zigong*, 7; Zigongshi dang'anguan and Zigongshi zonggong hui, *Salt Workers' Struggles*, 42–44. In this regard the Zigong party was little different from other party branches that infiltrated workers' organizations and attempted to foment revolution during this period.

148. These were the Shuangfu well (Yan Xianyang), Yusheng well (originally owned by Wang Wentao), Duofu well (Yan Xianyang), Yufu well (Fan Rongguang leased to Zhang Kaiming), Yulong well (Fan Rongguang leased to Zhang Kaiming), Rongliu well (Deng Huanrong), Yuhai well (Fan Rongguang), Fuhai well (Fan Rongguang), Juyuan well (Wang Hefu), Huiyuan well (Zhongxingxiang senior branch member Wang Mutao leased to Hou Ceming), Santai well (Zou Weiren contract pumped by Xiong Zuozhou), Jiangliu well, Qingyu well, and Runxian well (Mao Shuwu). Lai, "Rock-Salt Wells," 23; Wang, "Dafen bao Rock-Salt Wells," 126–30.
149. Zigongshi dang'anguan and Zigongshi zonggong hui, *Salt Workers' Struggles*, 123–24.
150. Wang, Chen, and Zeng, eds., *Zigong City History*, 68.
151. Ibid., 48–52.

10. Zigong: Industrial Center or Handicraft Enclave?

1. Fu Qiao, *Ziliujing diyiji* [Ziliujing, volume one] (Chengdu: Quchang gongsi, 1916), 2.
2. Ibid., 7.
3. Wei Wu, ed., *Sichuan yanzhengshi* [Sichuan salt administration history] (China: Sichuan yanzhengshi bianjichu, 1932), juan 3, pian 2, zhang 7, jie 2, 4b–5a.
4. Ziyan Zhu, "Jiangjinbang di xingcheng ji qi zai Zigong yanchang di jingying huodong" [The formation of the Jiangjin guild and their business activities at the Zigong saltyard], *Zigong wenshiziliao xuanji* 1–5 (1982): 243; Alexander Hosie, *Szechuan, Its Products, Industries and Resources* (Shanghai: Kelly and Walsh, 1922), 189.
5. Hosie, *Szechuan*, 189.
6. Wu, ed., *Salt Administration History*, juan 3, pian 2, zhang 10, jie 6, 80b; Zigongshi dang'anguan, Beijing jingjixueyuan, and Sichuan daxue, eds., *Zigong yanye qiyue dang'an xuanji (1732–1949)* [Selected Zigong salt industry contracts and documents (1732–1949)] (Beijing: Zhongguo shehuikexue chubanshe, 1985), 161. Hereafter cited as *Zigong Contracts*.
7. Wu, ed., *Salt Administration History*, juan 3, pian 2, zhang 10, jie 6, 80b.
8. *Leshan xianzhi* [Leshan county gazetteer] (Leshan, 1934), juan 7, jingzhi.
9. Hosie, *Szechuan*, 177.
10. *Zigong Contracts*, contracts 219 and 586, dated 1917 and 1918, respectively. The price of pans is listed in order of quality at 65, 45, 30, and 15 taels in both contracts, suggesting a fairly standard price structure throughout the industry.
11. Zhu, "Jiangjin Guild," 243–44. Zhu Ziyan was a Jiangjing businessman and investor in Zigong during the 1930s and 1940s.
12. Ibid., 247.
13. Zhenguo Liu, "Xinxing zhiyanchang" [The Xinxing salt factory], *Zigong wenshiziliao xuanji* 1–5 (1982): 249–59.
14. Fangbo Ma, "Zigong yanchang di mucai shangye" [The lumber business at the Zigong saltyard], *Zigong wenshiziliao xuanji* 6–10 (1982): 271. Ma's account is based on his own memories of working in the lumber business and those of fellow lumbermen, Zeng Shuhuai, Liu Lingxiang, and Huang Chunwu.
15. Ibid., 277, 280.

16. Chunwu Huang et al., "Qingmoyilai Zigong yanchang zhuye" [The bamboo industry in Zigong since the late Qing], *Sichuan wenshiziliao xuanji* 9 (1963): 67.
17. Wu, ed., *Salt Administration History*, juan 3, pian 2, zhang 10, jie 6, 80b.
18. Ma, "Lumber," 274–75.
19. For a discussion of the cultivation of timber products by *pengmin*, see Anne Osborne, "Natural Barriers to Agricultural Intensification in the Anhui-Zhejiang-Jiangsu Border Region" (paper presented at the annual convention of the American Historical Association, December 1985).
20. Ma, "Lumber," 280.
21. Huang et al., "Bamboo Industry," 70.
22. Ma, "Lumber," 280–83.
23. Huang et al., "Bamboo Industry," 70–71. For a discussion of the specifications and processing of the bamboo once it reached the yard, see 71–72.
24. Ma, "Lumber," 274.
25. Huang et al., "Bamboo Industry," 71. According to Fu Qiao, several million taels worth of *nanzhu* were shipped to Furong each year. It required two men to carry each of the larger poles and one to carry the smaller. These men were paid on a piecework basis at a rate of 4 or 5 copper cash a pole. Qiao, *Ziliujing*, 138.
26. Ma, "Lumber," 276.
27. Ibid., 277.
28. High-level managers at the Furong bamboo yards averaged over 200 strings of cash a year, not counting any perquisites they may have taken for themselves. Wang Jujing and Gou Pingsan, managers at the Yongshengheng, made over 360 strings a year. Huang et al., "Bamboo Industry," 68.
29. Ma, "Lumber," 277.
30. Ibid., 274.
31. The main sources for this discussion are Lei Li, "Luo Xiaoyuan jiushi" [Luo Xiaoyuan's past], *Ziliujing* 1 (1983): 108–32, and Yaolin Ling, "Qingdai Zigong jingyanye zibenzhuyi mengya fazhan daolu chutan" [A preliminary investigation of the sprouts of capitalism in the Zigong salt industry], *Sichuan daxue xuebao congkan* 14 (1982): 87.
32. Qiao, *Ziliujing*, 138.
33. Ling, "Sprouts of Capitalism," 87.
34. Zigongshi dang'anguan and Zigongshi zonggong hui, *Zigong yanye gongren douzhengshi dangan ziliao xuanbian (1915–1949)* [Selected documents on the history of the struggles of Zigong salt workers (1915–1949)] (Chengdu: Sichuan renmin chubanshe, 1989), 1–3.
35. Zigong archives 3–5–745. A letter from Ouyang Xianrong to the Chuan-Kang Salt Supervisory Bureau (Chuan-Kang yanwu guanli ju). Yuesheng Pu, "Zigong yanshang Xiong Zuozhou shilue" [A short biographical sketch of Zigong salt merchant Xiong Zuozhou], *Zigong wenshiziliao xuanji* 17 (1987): 4.
36. Xiangchen Jiang and Xiaoyuan Luo, "Zigong yanchang di niu" [Buffalo at the Zigong saltyard], *Zigong wenshiziliao xuanji* 12 (1981): 108.
37. Ibid., 111.
38. Zhu, "Jiangjin Guild," 243.
39. Hosie was told that even well-tended buffalo lasted no more than five years. Hosie, *Szechuan*, 176.

40. Alexander Hosie found that buffalo cost approximately 40 to 50 taels apiece during his visit to the saltyard in 1884. Ibid.

41. Jiang and Luo, "Buffalo," 110–11.

42. Ibid., 111–13. For example, Huang Jianting made a fortune as a buffalo broker and later opened the Rongfenghou money shop at Dafen bao.

43. Zhu, "Jiangjin Guild," 243; Xiaoyuan Luo, "Ziliujing Wang Sanwei tang xingwang jiyao" [The basic elements of the rise and fall of the Wang Sanwei trust], *Sichuan wenshiziliao xuanji* 7 and 8 (1963): 190.

44. Wu, ed., *Salt Administration History,* juan 3, pian 2, zhang 10, jie 6, 81b.

45. Jiang and Luo, "Buffalo," 115. The workers hired by well laborers to gather buffalo pats were called *niushi ke.* The processed cakes sold for 100 copper cash per 100 *jin*, as compared with 300 copper cash for the same amount of coal, or 200 copper cash for the equivalent in firewood.

46. Ruyi Yan, *Sansheng bianfang beilan* [Investigation of security at the three provinces border] (Yangzhou: Jiangsu Guangling gujikeyinshe, 1822; reprint, 1991), 11.

47. Shaoquan Hu, "Zigong yanchang jigong piju shimo" [The whole story of the Zigong saltyard public assistance hides bureau], *Zigong wenshiziliao xuanji* 23 (1993): 69.

48. Jiang and Luo, "Buffalo," 119–25.

49. Hu, "Whole Story of the Hides Bureau," 69–70. According to Hu, himself a former salt merchant, the considerable profits of the tanneries were used for relief for the poor, shelters for the homeless and orphaned, and job training for the unemployed.

50. For example, Zigong archives 17-1-241, dated MK 15, 5, 31 (1926), complains that in previous years money from the tannery had been allocated to buy new uniforms for the police and questions why such funds are not available at the present time.

51. Benqing Chen, "Yusha zhaituan yu Wangsanweitang zhaiwu shimo" [The whole story of the Wang Sanwei trust's debts to the Yusha zhaituan], *Zigong wenshiziliao xuanji* 22 (1992): 6; Luo, "Wang Sanwei Trust," 167; Zilin Li et al., "Ziliujing Li Siyou tang you fazhan dao shuaiwang" [The Li Siyou trust of Ziliujing from their development to their decline], *Sichuan wenshiziliao xuanji* 4 (1962–3): 161–62.

52. Ma, "Lumber," 274.

53. Huang et al., "Bamboo Industry," 67–68.

54. Yuzhi Cui and Shaoyuan Yan, "Gongjing yanshang Yu Shuhuai" [The Gongjing salt merchant Yu Shuhuai], *Zigong wenshiziliao xuanji* 14 (1984): 170.

55. Ma, "Lumber," 279.

56. Huang et al., "Bamboo Industry," 68.

57. Qiao Fu, *Ziliujing*, 187–88.

58. Ibid., 137.

59. This advance amounted to approximately two-thirds of the official price for the salt. The remainder was turned over when the salt was delivered to the government warehouse for wrapping and shipment to the sales territories. Xiaoyuan Luo, "Furong guanyunju di bihai" [Malpractices in the Furong Official Salt Distribution Bureau], *Zigong wenshiziliao xuanji* 14 (1984): 58.

60. When the Li Siyou trust began to default on its obligations to the suppliers of its Jitong pipe, well owners could neither lay off workers, to whom they owed too much back pay, nor sell buffalo, for fear of a shortage of power in the future. The most vulnerable to a shortfall in demand, they could neither close down, lest their

wells collapse, nor get paid for what they pumped. Many continued to pump and dump their brine on the ground. Li et al., "Li Siyou Trust," 201.

61. Huang et al., "Bamboo Industry," 75; Xiaoyuan Luo, "Luo Xiaoyuan zishu" [Autobiography of Luo Xiaoyuan] (manuscript), in Zigong Municipal Archives.

62. Luo, "Autobiography of Luo Xiaoyuan."

63. See, for example, the account in Ma, "Lumber," 285–86.

64. Stele commemorating construction of the Shaanxi guildhall in Ziliujing.

65. Yuemou Ouyang et al., "Zigong difang di diandangye" [The pawnshop business in Zigong], *Zigong wenshiziliao xuanji* 13 (1983): 147.

66. Ibid. The other three were owned by a coal merchant, a silk merchant, and a paper merchant.

67. Zigongshi jinrongzhi bianzuanweiyuanhui, ed., *Zigongshi jinrongzhi* [Zigong financial gazetteer], Zigongshi difangzhi congshu [Zigong municipal gazetteer collection], vol. 18 (Chengdu: Sichuan cishu chubanshe, 1994), 28.

68. Xiaomei Zhang, *Sichuan jingji cankao ziliao* [Reference materials on the Sichuan economy] (Shanghai: Zhongguo guomin jingji yanjiu suo, 1939), D50.

69. Wufang Nie, "Qingmo yilai Zigong yangchangde jinrongye" [Banking at the Zigong saltyard since the late Qing], *Zigong wenshiziliao xuanji* 21 (1991): 79–80.

70. Maode Tian, "Piaohao zai Sichuan di yixie huodong" [Some of the activities of remittance banks in Sichuan], *Sichuan wenshiziliao xuanji* 32 (1984): 56–72; Sufu Wang, "Chongqing jinrong shichang kaolue" [A brief examination of Chongqing's financial markets], *Shangyu huzhu zhoukan*, January 29, 1925.

71. Tian, "Activities of Remittance Banks," 69, citing a document from the Baxian Archives.

72. Nie, "Banking at the Zigong Saltyard," 80.

73. Ibid.

74. Liangxi Song, "Zigong diqu de qianzhuang, piaohao yu yanye fazhan" [The development of native banks, remittance banks, and the salt industry in the Zigong region], *Yanyeshi yanjiu* 2 (1994): 15.

75. Nie, "Banking at the Zigong Saltyard," 81.

76. Ibid.

77. Song, "Zigong Banks," 16. The direct involvement of native banks in the commodity market was adopted by local modern banks during the twentieth century. Evan Erlanson, writing about the Juxingcheng bank's role in the development of the tong oil trade in twentieth-century Sichuan, notes that the business of native banks and modern banks in China was similar. However, native banks tended to rely on the paid-up capital of a few bank partners, whereas modern banks or *yinhang* based their business on the sale of shares and the accumulation of capital through the growth of their deposit business. Evan Erlanson, "Commercial Banking in Sichuan, 1915–1935: The Case of the Young Brothers Banking Corporation," *Papers on Chinese History* 6 (1997): 46.

78. Anonymous, "Ziliujing zhi jinrong Yu jinrong ye" [Finance and banking in Ziliujing], *Sichuan jingji yuekan* 3, no. 6 (1935): 71.

79. Zhang, *Sichuan Economy*, D45.

80. Ibid., D47.

81. The Imperial bank (Daqing yinhang) was founded in 1904 with both state and private capital investment. This investment structure was retained when the bank was reorganized as the Bank of China following the 1911 Revolution.

82. Zigongshi jinrongzhi bianzuanweiyuanhui, ed., *Zigong Financial Gazetteer*, 45–47.

83. Qiao, *Ziliujing*, 132.

84. Jingxian Ni, "Wo dui Yutong yinhang Zigong fenhang de huiyi" [My memories of the Zigong branch of the Yutong bank], *Zigong wenshiziliao xuanji* 6–10 (1982): 294–99.

85. Zhang, *Sichuan Economy*, D43–44; Shaozhou Ma and Zhangqing He, "Chongqing Chuanyan yinhang shimo" [The complete history of the Salt Bank of Chongqing], in *Chongqing wujia zhuming yinhang* [Chongqing's five famous banks], *Chongqing gongshang shiliao* 7 (Chongqing: Xinan shifan daxue cubanshe, 1989), 122–56. There is some disagreement over the date of the opening of the Ziliujing branch of the Salt Bank. *The Zigong Financial Gazetteer* dates the opening to September 1933. Zigongshi jinrongzhi bianzuanweiyuanhui, ed., *Zigong Financial Gazetteer*, 47.

86. Ma and He, "Salt Bank of Chongqing," 124. Zeng held the position of brigade commander in Hubei before being sent to Ziliujing to serve as an intermediary between the Liu Xiang government and Furong salt merchants. Zeng subsequently became involved in salt investments himself. For example, as mentioned in *Zigong Contracts*, document 10, Zeng was involved in a lawsuit as a result of his lease of well shares in the early 1930s.

87. Anonymous, "Finance and Banking in Ziliujing," 68.

88. Ibid.

89. Ibid., 68–70. The Bank of Chongqing had originally been authorized to issue banknotes. However, these were recalled late in 1935. Zhang, *Sichuan Economy*, D44.

90. See chapter 9.

Epilogue

1. Barbara Vatter, "Industrial Borrowing by the New England Textile Mills, 1840–1860: A Comment," *Journal of Economic History* 21, no. 2 (1961): 216–21.

2. Naomi Lamoreaux, "Banks, Kinship, and Economic Development: The New England Case," *Journal of Economic History* 46, no. 3 (1986): 648–49. Lamoreaux's study is based largely on Massachusetts and Rhode Island.

3. Albert Chandler notes the reliance upon merchant house models of management in most early American firms. The transition to true professional management did not occur until the late nineteenth century in response to the increasingly complex engineering and finance skills required to run America's railways. Alfred D. Chandler, *The Visible Hand: The Managerial Revolution in American Business* (Cambridge: Belknap Press of Harvard University Press, 1977), 130–33.

4. Ibid., 68, 335–36.

5. See chapter 5.

6. Of course, Furong's marketing networks extended deeply into neighboring provinces, while its impact on parts of western Sichuan was small. Nevertheless, its position within a provincially defined salt administration, as well as its importance to provincial revenues and its impact on provincial investment, justifies a province-centered approach.

7. Thomas G. Rawski, *Economic Growth in Prewar China* (Berkeley: University of California Press, 1989), 20.

8. This method assumes little lasting change in the industrial economy of the province during the war against Japan, a subject beyond the scope of this book. Given the ex-migration of refugees from eastern China after the war and the low level of state investment in western China during the early 1950s, this assumption appears sound.

9. Wei Wu, ed., *Sichuan yanzhengshi* [Sichuan salt administration history] (China: Sichuan yanzhengshi bianjichu, 1932), juan 3, pian 2, zhang 9, jie 2, 59a–61b, and juan 3, pian 2, zhang 11, jie 7, 107a–109a.

10. Inspector General of Customs, Shanghai, China, *Decennial Reports, 1922–31*, vol. 1, *Northern and Yangzi Ports*, Maritime Customs, Statistical Series no. 6 (Shanghai, 1933), 480–82.

11. Duanfu Zhang, "Jianle dichu shouquyizhi di dachangshang—Wu Jingrang tang" [A Jianle area saltyard merchant lineage second to none—the Wu Jingrang trust], *Jingyanshi tongxun* 6 (1979–80): 51.

12. Renyuan Wang, Ran Chen, and Fanying Zeng, eds., *Zigong chengshi shi* [The history of Zigong city] (Beijing: Shihui kexue wenxian chuban she, 1995), 18.

13. In 1934 Deng Huilin brought together investors to open the Sichuan National Construction Chemical Factory [Sichuan jianguo huaxue gongchang] at Lianggao shan, but it ceased operations the following year and did not reopen until the 1940s. Zigongshi huaxue gongye guanli ju, ed., *Zigongshi huaxue gongye zhi* [Gazetteer of the Zigong chemicals industry], Zigongshi difangzhi congshu [Zigong municipal gazetteer collection], vol. 13 (Chengdu: Sichuan renmin daxue chubanshe, 1993), 1.

14. Wang, Chen, and Zeng, eds., *Zigong City History*, 68.

15. Ibid.

16. Renyue Tang et al., eds., *Zhongguo yanye shi* [A history of the Chinese salt industry] (Beijing: Renmin chuban she, 1997), 641. On Jiuda and Yongli, see Man Bun Kwan, "Managing Market, Hierarchy and Network: The Jiuda-Yongli Group, 1917–1937" (paper presented at the Business History Conference annual meeting, Lowell, MA, 2003).

17. Wang, Chen, and Zeng, eds., *Zigong City History*, 69.

18. Zigongshi jixie dianzi gongye guanliju, ed., *Zigongshi jixiegongye zhi* [Gazetteer of the Zigong city machine industry], Zigongshi difangzhi congshu [Zigong municipal gazetteer collection], vol. 21 (Chengdu: Sichuan renmin chubanshe, 1993), 64.

19. Wang, Chen, and Zeng, eds., *Zigong City History*, 71.

20. Zigongshi yanye zhi bianzuan weiyuan hui, ed., *Zigong shi yanye zhi* [Zigong city salt industry gazetteer] (Zigong, 1992), 656; Zigongshi jixie dianzi gongye guanliju, ed., *Machine Industry Gazetteer*, 64.

21. Zigongshi yange zhi bianzuan weiyuan hui, ed., *Zigong City Salt Industry Gazetteer*, 658.

22. http://www.zggxq.com/english/brief/en_index.html

Glossary of Selected Chinese Names and Terms

An 岸
Anju 安局

Ba 巴
Badian jie 八店街
Ban 班
Banbian jie 半边街
Banfangche 班房车
Bang 帮
Bangban 帮办
Bangjing 帮井
Bangzhang 帮账
Banzhu 辩竹
Bao 包
Baochunfu 包纯富
Baofenglong 宝丰隆
Baojia 保甲
Baolu tongzhihui 保路同志会
Baolu yundong 保路运动
Baoniugong 包牛工
Baoshang 包商
Baoshengrong 宝生荣
Baotongchang 宝通长
Baotui 包推
Baoxinglong 宝兴隆

Batou 把头
Baxian 巴县
Benshang 本商
Bensheng ji'an 本省计岸
Bian'an 边岸
Bianli 便利
Bude siding wairen 不得私顶外人
Bumen 部门

Caishen hui 财神会
Cai Yulong 蔡玉龙
Caopi huo 草皮火
Changde 常德
Changfaxiang 长发祥
Changgui 厂规
Changlu 长芦
Changshang 场商
Chen Chengwu 陈成武
Chen Huiting 陈辉廷
Chen Jieyu 陈戒于
Chen Pangtao 陈仿陶
Chen Xiangtao 陈湘涛
Chen Zhongxuan 陈仲宣
Chengdu 成都
Chengmeigong 成美公

Chengshouren　承首人

Chengshan laoren ziding nianpu
　成山老人自定年谱

Cheshui　车水

Chongqing　重庆

Chongqing yinhang　重庆银行

Chu Yasan　褚雅三

Chuanyan jiyao　川盐纪要

Chuanyan yinhang　川盐银行

Chuankang yanwu guanliju　川康盐务
　管理局

Chumai　出卖

Cui Ruhua　催汝华

Da'an zhai　大安寨

Dabangche　大帮车

Dabang　大帮

Dachang jian　大昌枧

Dadeheng　大德恒

Dadetong　大德通

Dafenbao　大坟堡

Daguan　大关

Daguanzhang　大管帐

Dahuo　大火

Dai Jingxiao　戴耕霄

Dakoujing　大口井

Dala hui　大蜡会

Dan　担

Dan　石

Daning　大宁

Daoduijiang　捣碓匠

Daoguang　道光

Daquan jian　大川枧

Dasheng jian　大生枧

Dasheng jian　达生枧

Dashenghou hao　大生厚号

Dashengmei hao　大生美号

Dashengxiang　大生祥

Dashui　大水

Datong jian　大通枧

Dazhanggui　大掌柜

Dazu　大足

De'an　德安

Dechangxiang　德昌祥

Dehe hao　德合号

Deng Hongru　邓鸿儒

Deng Keyu　邓可玉

Deng Xiaoke　邓孝可

Dengjing guan　邓井关

Diaocha　调查

Dichang weiyuanhui　抵偿委员会

Diche　地车

Difang yinhang　地方银行

Digunzi　地滚子

Dimo　地脉

Ding Baozhen　丁宝桢

Dingjia　顶价

Dingtongchang　定通长

Dipi huo　地皮火

Diqian　底钱

Diuxiajie　丢下节

Dizhu　地主

Dong Jingying　董镜莹

Dongchuan　东川

Dousha yan　豆沙岩

Douya wan　豆芽湾

Douzhi　豆汁

Du Dingshan　杜鼎珊

Enliu jian　恩流枧

Fabi　法幣

Fan Rongguang　范荣光

Fangduijin hui　放堆金会

Fenban　分班

Feng Shusen　冯树森

Feng Yuxiang　冯玉祥

Fengdu　丰都

Fengjie　奉节

Fuchang　富昌

Fuchanggong　福昌公

Fuchangsheng hao　福昌生号

Fuguo rifen　浮锅日分

Fuling　涪陵

Fulinyi hao　福临怡号

Fulong chang　阜隆厂

Furong　富荣
Fushun　富顺
Fushun xianzhi　富顺县志
Futongxing　富同兴
Fuyuanqing　富源庆

Gaipei　改配
Gaitu guiliu　改土归流
Ganrifen　干日分
Gao Yuncong　高云从
Gelao hui　歌老会
Genpan　跟盘
Gongben　工本
Gongjing　贡井
Gongjing santiaohe　贡井三条河
Gongsi　公司
Gongyitian　公益田
Guahong　挂红
Guan　关
Guankou　关口
Guangshenggong　广生公
Guangshengtong　广生同
Guangxu　光绪
Guangyigong　广益公
Guanshi　管事
Guanxi　关系
Guanxiangqian　管现钱
Guanyin tan　观音滩
Guanyun　官运
Guanyun ju　官运局
Guanyun shangxiao　官运商销
Guanzhang　管账
Guiding　归丁
Guifang　柜房
Guizhou　贵州
Guo Changming　郭昌明
Guojia　过价
Guojia ao　郭家坳
Guojiang　过江
Guoko　锅口
Guozu　锅租

Han Youren　韩友仁

Hangshang　行商
Hanyang　汉阳
Hao　号
Hefeng　合丰
Hejiang　合江
Hengfengyu　恒丰预
Hengfu dang　恒福当
Hengxinglong　恒兴隆
Hetui hejian　合推合煎
Hou Ceming　侯策明
Hu Chengjun　胡承钧
Hu Liwei　胡礼纬
Hu Mianzhai　胡勉斋
Hu Ruxiu　胡汝修
Hu Shiyun　胡仕云
Hu Tiehua　胡铁华
Hu Yingshi　胡英士
Hu Yuanhai　胡元海
Hu Yuanhe　胡元和
Hu Yuanhe tang　胡元和堂
Hua　花
Huafeng　华丰
Huaiyun gongsi　淮运公司
Huang Chunwu　黄纯武
Huang Dunsan　黄敦三
Huang Fuji　黄福基
Huang Jianting　黄鉴庭
Huang Si　黄四
Huang Yushu　黄玉书
Huang Zhiqing　黄植青
Huang Zidong　黄子东
Huanghai　黄海
Huangniu　黄牛
Huangzhou　黄州
Huaxing　华兴
Huazhu hui　华祝会
Hubei　湖北
Hubei ji'an　湖北计岸
Huguang　湖广
Hui　会
Huidui lushui　汇兑卤水
Huiguan　会馆
Huojing　火井

Huoli 火力
Huoqi 活契
Huoquan 火圈
Huoshen hui 火神会
Huowu gu 货物股

Jia 家
Ji'an 计岸
Jian 枧
Jiading 嘉定
Jiahuo gunzi 家伙滚子
Jiang Zihe 江子鹤
Jiangjin 江津
Jiangkou 江口
Jiangong 见功
Jianhua zhiyan gongsi 建华制盐公司
Jianjiang 枧匠
Jianle 犍乐
Jianlugong 煎卤工
Jianwei 犍为
Jianwo 笕窝
Jianyang 简阳
Jianzhou 简州
Jiaoguanyin 交关银
Jiaoji gu 交际股
Jiaoxi 教习
Jichu 济楚
Jie 节
Jiepiao 结票
Jihe chu 稽核处
Jihua zao banshichu 济华灶办事处
Jikou shouyan 计口授盐
Jin 斤
Jinban 进班
Jing 井
Jing bang 井帮
Jing Shaotang 景绍堂
Jingang 金刚
Jingkou guanshi 井口管事
Jinglao shuigu 井老水枯
Jingli 经理
Jingmen 荆门
Jingyan 井研
Jinku dan 金库单

Jinshi 进士
Jirongxiang 集蓉祥
Jitong jian 吉(济)通枧
Jiuda 久大
Jiyichang muchang 集义长
Jiyin 积引
Juan 卷
Junyi tuanti 均益团体
Juyichang 聚义长
Junchuan (yuan) yinhang 浚川(源)银行
Juren 举人
Juxingcheng yinhang 聚兴诚银行

Kai 开
Kaibu 开簿
Kaichegong 开车工
Kaiguo 开锅
Kaipan 开盘
Kaizhong 开中
Ke 科
Ke 客
Kehuo 客伙
Kejing 客井
Kou 口
Kouguo 口锅
Kuaijiao 快脚
Kuizhou 夔州

Lai Mingqin 赖明钦
Lan Chuaoshun 蓝朝顺
Langchang 廊厂
Langzhong 闻中
Lei Shiruo 雷时若
Lei Xiaosong 雷小松
Leshan 乐山
Lezhi 乐至
Li 里
Li Bingzhi 李炳之
Li Boquan 李伯权
Li Bozhai 李柏斋
Li Deqian 李德潜
Li Dewen 李德文
Li Guoyu 李果育

Li Hongzhang　李鸿章
Li Huiting　李辉廷
Li Jingcai　李敬才
Li Jinghou　李靖侯
Li Jiuxia　李九霞
Li Rong　李榕
Li Shancheng　李善成
Li Shengjiu　李笙九
Li Shijin　李世缙
Li Sicheng　李思诚
Li Sijiu　李思九
Li Siyou tang　李四友堂
Li Songshan　李松山
Li Taoshu　李陶淑
Li Tonggai　李桐荄
Li Weiji　李维基
Li Wumei tang　李五美堂
Li Xiang'an　李祥庵
Li Xingqiao　李星桥
Li Xubai　李续白
Li Xueqiao　李雪樵
Li Yonghe　李永和
Li Yunqiao　李云桥
Li Yunxiang　李云湘
Li Yunzhi　李允之
Li Zihui　李子惠
Li Xinzhu　李新柱
Li Zizhang　李子章
Liang　两
Liang Qichao　梁启超
Lianggao shan　凉高山
Lianghuai　两淮
Liao Enbo　廖恩波
Liao Shuqing　廖树卿
Liao Zekuan　廖泽宽
Liao Zhonghou tang　廖忠厚堂
Lice yanzhengbuzhi shu　力辞盐政部
　职书
Lijin　厘金
Lin Zhenhan　林振翰
Linshi yishihui　临时议事会
Liqun qianzhuang　利群钱庄
Liu Fakun　刘法坤
Liu Huanzhai　刘焕斋

Liu Jingxian　刘景贤
Liu Jizhi　刘积之
Liu Runqing　刘潤卿
Liu Wenhui　刘文辉
Liu Xiang　刘湘
Liu Xingcun　刘杏村
Liu Yuanxiang　刘远翔
Liuzhufa　六柱法
Liwen　理问
Longchang　隆昌
Longmenzhang　龙门账
Lü Wenzhong　吕汶中
Lu　泸
Lu Shidi　卢师缔
Luo Huagai　罗华垓
Luo Xiaoyuan　罗筱元
Luzhou　泸州

Mao Aiqin　毛爱琴
Mashuizhang　马水账
Menglan hui　孟兰会
Mianyang　绵阳
Mie　蔑
Minxinju　民信局
Muchang　木厂

Nanbu　南部
Nanchuan　南川
Nanjing　南京
Nanlang　南阆
Nanning　南宁
Nanxi　南溪
Nanyan　南盐
Nanzhu　楠竹
Naxi　纳溪
Neijiang　内江
Ni Jingxian　倪敬先
Nianjie　年结
Niu Jicheng　牛集成
Niu Jigao　牛继皋
Niupaizi　牛牌子
Niutui hu　牛推户
Niuwang hui　牛王会
Nongzhuang gu　农庄股

Ouyang Xianrong 欧阳显荣

Paizi 牌子
Pan Xiaoyi 潘孝移
Pan Zhongsan 潘仲三
Paoge hui 袍哥会
Paojie 跑街
Pengling 朋领
Pengmin 棚民
Pengshui 彭水
Pengxi 彭溪
Pengzhong 蓬中
Pian 篇
Piao 票
Piao'an 票岸
Piaohao 票号
Piaoju suo 票据所
Piju 皮局
Pingmin yinhang 平民银行
Pingyi 平彝
Pingyi gongsuo 评议公所
Puxian hui 普贤会

Qian 钱
Qiancheng 谦诚
Qianfeng tai 乾丰泰
Qianfuxiang 钱福湘
Qianpiao 钱票
Qianxin 谦信
Qianyi dang 谦益当
Qianzhuang 钱庄
Qiaosheng hui 巧圣会
Qiban 起班
Qijiang 綦江
Qingdan 清单
Qingdang yundong 清党运动
Qingxiang siling 清乡司令
Qingyun jian 卿云枧
Quanfu jian 全福枧
Quanxingchang 全兴厂

Ren'an 仁岸
Renbanche 人搬车
Renhuai 仁怀

Rifen 日分
Rong 荣
Rongjixiang 荣集祥

Sanduo zhai 三多寨
Sanjiaozhang 三脚帐
Sanqian 散签
Sanshi ban 三十班
Santai 三台
Shaanxi 陕西
Shangjie 上节
Shangmin xiehui 商民协会
Shangqiao 上桥
Shangshou 上手
Shangtuan 商团
Shangxia jie 上下节
Shanjiang 山匠
Shanke 山客
Shang qiao 上桥
Shangye yinhang 商业银行
Shanshui 搬水
Shanzi ba 扇子坝
Shaoyanggong 烧盐工
Shashi 沙市
Shehong 射洪
Shen Baozhen 沈葆桢
Shenhuogong 生火工
Shengyuan 生员
Shennong 神农
Shenyi tang 慎怡堂
Shepeng 射蓬
Shi 石
Shi Qingyang 石青阳
Shicheng hui 十成会
Shifei qian 使费钱
Shimiejiang 拭篾匠
Shiwu ban 十五班
Shiye 师爷
Shouzhi suo 收支所
Shuanghongyuan 双洪源
Shuangshi pu 双石铺
Shuifen 水分
Shuiwaichang 水外场
Shuiyin 水引

Sichuan 四川
Sichuan jingji cankao ziliao 四川经济
　参考资料
Sichuan wenshiziliao xuanji 四川文史
　资料选辑
Sichuan yanfazhi 四川盐法志
Sichuan yanzheng shi 四川盐政史
Sidachaochen 四大朝臣
Sidaxiang 四大享
Sisheng hui 四圣会
Siyan 私盐
Sizhufa 四柱法
Song 宋
Suining 遂宁
Sujiang 夙匠

Taihezhen 太和贞
Taiping 太平
Taizuo 抬做
Tang 堂
Tang Jiong 唐炯
Tian 天
Tianche 天车
Tiangunzi 天滚子
Tianhou gong 天后宫
Tiantaihe 天泰和
iao mianzi shui 挑面子水
Tiedao yinhang 铁道银行
Tongdexiang 同德祥
Tongfu jian 同富枧
Tongliang 桐梁
Tongmenghui 同盟回
Tongshengmei 同生美
Tongxin jian 同新枧
Tongxinghe jingzao banshichu 同兴
　和井灶办事处
Tongyehui 同业会
Tongzhi jun 同志军
Tongzijiang 桶子匠
Tuanshou rifen 团首日分
Tudi miao 土地庙
Tuo jiang 沱江

Wan 万

Wang Bitian 王笔田
Wang Chengzhi 王成之
Wang Dazhi 王达之
Wang Defu 王德敷
Wang Deqian 王德谦
Wang Desan 王德三
Wang Duanhu 王端笏
Wang Enpu 王恩浦
Wang Gengyu 王赓余
Wang Hefu 王和甫
Wang Huitang 王惠堂
Wang Jieping 王介平
Wang Jiliang 王绩良
Wang Jixing 王吉星
Wang Kai 王楷
Wang Langyun 王郎云
Wang Mutao 王幕陶
Wang Ronghua 王荣华
Wang Rudong 王如东
Wang Sanwei tang 王三畏堂
Wang Shouwei 王守为
Wang Sufeng 王素峰
Wang Taozou 王逃走
Wang Weigang 王维钢
Wang Wenkui 王文奎
Wang Wenqin 王文琴
Wang Wentao 王问陶
Wang Xiangrong 王相荣
Wang Xiangyun 王向云
Wang Xunjiu 王浔九
Wang Yecong 王野从
Wang Yongzhi 王用之
Wang Yuanji 王元吉
Wang Yuchuan 王玉川
Wang Yuhuai 王余淮
Wang Yulin 王余霖
Wang Yuqi 王余杞
Wang Ziheng 王子衡
Wang Zishan 王子善
Wang Zixiang 王子湘
Wang Zuanxu 王缵绪
Wang Zuogan 王作甘
Wanxing 万兴
Weihuo 微火

Weishui　微水

Weiyuan　威远

Wenan suo　问案所

Wenge　文格

Wenjiang　温江

Wu Jingrang tang　吴景让堂

Wu Maochang　吴茂常

Wu Tang　吴棠

Wu Zonghan　吴宗汉

Wuchang　武昌

Wushan　巫山

Wutongqiao　五通桥

Xiancheng　县丞

Xiande　宪德

Xiangyang　襄阳

Xiajie　下节

Xiang Yulin　向玉麟

Xiangxingtai　祥光泰

Xianjin gu　现金股

Xianyu　羡余

Xiao Zhihe　肖致和

Xiashou　下手

Xie Huanzhang　谢焕章

Xiecheng　协成

Xiehesheng hao　协和盛

Xiexinglong　协兴隆

Xinqu yanyanjing cailu gongsi　新区盐
　岩井采卤

Xinhe　新和

Xingke tiben　刑科题本

Xingwen　兴文

Xinshu gongsi　新蜀公司

Xinyongqian　信用钱

Xiong Kewu　熊克武

Xiong Sihe tang　熊四和堂

Xiong Silun　熊思伦

Xiong Wanquan　熊万全

Xiong Zuozhou　熊佐周

Xiqin huiguan　西秦会馆

Xiyan　西盐

Xuetu　学徒

Xunjian　巡检

Xunjiangguanshi　巡笺管事

Xuyong　叙永

Xuzhou　叙州

Yan Anlan　宴安澜

Yan Boshi　颜伯师

Yan Changxun　颜昌训

Yan Changying　颜昌英

Yan Chongfuyong　颜崇福永

Yan Guixin tang　颜桂馨堂

Yan Jihou　颜积厚

Yan Juewu　颜觉吾

Yan Niantao　颜念陶

Yan Xianyang　颜宪阳

Yan Xinshe　颜心畬

Yan Yongxing　颜永兴

Yancha dao　盐茶道

Yandao yinpiao　盐道引票

Yandi hui　炎帝会

Yanfa　盐法

Yang Duxing　杨笃行

Yang Xiaofang　杨篠舫

Yangjia chong　杨家冲

Yangxi　洋溪

Yanjing　盐警

Yankou bu　岩口簿

Yantai　炎泰

Yanting　盐亭

Yanwushu　盐务暑

Yanyan　岩盐

Yanyan gongsi　盐岩公司

Yanyanjing banshichu　盐岩井办事处

Yanyanjing cailu gongsi　盐岩井采卤
　公司

Yanyuan　盐源

Yanzheng　盐政

Yanzong hui　盐总会

Yaxijin　押席金

Ye Peilin　叶沛霖

Yibin　宜宾

Yichang　宜昌

Yifu jian　一福枧

Yiji qianzhuang　益记钱庄

Yijing chuangjing　以井创井

Yijing sanji　一井三基

Yin　银
Yin　引
Yin'an　引岸
Yindi　引底
Yingye zhuren　营业主任
Yinhao　银号
Yinmu suo　引目所
Yinshang　引商
Yiyan dao　驿盐道
Yizao tongjing　以灶统井
Yongli　永利
Yongning　永宁
Yongshengheng　永生恒
Yongzheng　雍正
Yu San　余三
Yu Shuhuai　余述怀
Yuan　元
Yuan Hele tang　袁和乐堂
Yuan Shikai　袁世凯
Yuanchang jian　元(源)昌枧
Yuantong jian　元通枧
Yuanyuan jian　源远枧
Yucai shuyuan　育才书院
Yuchuan ci　玉川祠
Yudian　预佃
Yuefei　月费
Yuejie　月结
Yuezhou　岳州
Yunnan　云南
Yunyang　云阳
Yupiao　渝票
Yunshang　运商
Yusha zhaituan　渝沙债团
Yushang yinhang　裕商银行
Yushou　预售
Yutong jian　裕通枧
Yutong yinhang　裕通银行

Zai　载
Zao　灶
Zaohu　灶户
Zaotou　灶头
Zeng Guofan　曾国藩
Zeng Hanzhang　曾翰章

Zeng Shaobo　曾邵伯
Zeng Yuqing　曾雨青
Zeng Zihua　曾子华
Zeng Ziwei　曾子唯
Zhai　寨
Zhaituan　债团
Zhang Jingzhong　张静中
Zhang　章
Zhang Fuan　张富安
Zhang Jiucheng　张九成
Zhang Kaiming　张开铭
Zhang Lesan　张乐三
Zhang Peicun　张培邨
Zhang Sanhe　张三和
Zhang Shaofu　张少甫
Zhang Xiaopo　张筱坡
Zhang Zhifang　张志芳
Zhanyi　沾益
Zhao Xi　赵熙
Zhengde jing banshichu　正德井办
　事处
Zheng jie　正街
Zhenxiong　镇雄
Zhengyi　正谊
Zhibian yinhang　殖边银行
Zhiyan gongsi　制盐公司
Zhiyan gongye gongsi　制盐工业公司
Zhong　忠
Zhong Chunquan　钟春泉
Zhong Xingxiang　仲兴祥
Zhong Xinzhi　钟信之
Zhongguo ribao　中国日报
Zhongguo yanzhengshilu　中国盐政
　实绿
Zhongjiang　中江
Zhongjie　中节
Zhongxia jie　中下节
Zhongxingchang　仲兴厂
Zhouhengshun　周恒顺
Zhou Daogang　周道刚
Zhou Junji　周骏继
Zhou Rongtai　周荣泰
Zhou Shengshu　周声澍
Zhou Zhongxuan　周仲宣

Zhoujia chong　周家冲

Zhoutong　州同

Zhu　主

Zhu Shanxiang　朱善祥

Zhuangke　庄客

Zhuchang　竹厂

Zhulin wan　竹林湾

Zhupengzi　竹棚子

Zigongshi　自贡市

Zigong yanye qiyue dang'an xuanji
　自贡盐业契约档案选辑

Zigongdichu jiqigongye tongyegonghui
　自贡地区机器工业同业工会

Ziliujing　自流井

Ziliujing fengwu mingshishuo　自流井
　风物名实说

Ziliujing ji　自流井记

Zisunjing　子孙井

Zizhi　自治

Zizhong　资中

Zizhou　资州

Zongban　总班

Zongcao　总灶

Zonggonghui　总工会

Zongguifang　总柜房

Zongli　总理

Zongshou　总首

Zongqian　总签

Zongzao　总灶

Zongzhang　总帐

Zongzhanggui　总掌柜

Zouxiao　奏销

Zumai yin　租卖银

Zuohuangtong　坐黄桶

Zuomatou　坐码头

Zuoshang　坐商

Zushui　租水

Zuozao　坐灶

Bibliography

Archives

Baxian Archives, Sichuan Provincial Archives, Chengdu, Sichuan
First Historical Archives, Beijing
Zigong Municipal Archives, Zigong, Sichuan

Published Sources

Adshead, S. A. M. *The Modernization of the Chinese Salt Administration, 1900–1920.* Cambridge: Harvard University Press, 1970.
———. *Province and Politics in Late Imperial China: Viceregal Government in Sichuan, 1898–1911.* London: Curzon Press, 1984.
———. "Salt and Warlordism in Szechwan 1914–1922." *Modern Asian Studies* 24, no. 4 (1990): 729–43.
———. *Salt and Civilization.* New York: St. Martin's Press, 1992.
Anonymous. "Shanghui de yange" [Evolution of the Zigong Chamber of Commerce]. Manuscript, Zigong.
———. "Ziliujing zhi jinrong yu jinrong ye" [Finance and banking in Ziliujing]. *Sichuan jingji yuekan* 3, no. 6 (1935): 67–75.
———. "Sichuan jinbainian dashi tigang" [An outline of major events in Sichuan during the last one hundred years]. *Sichuan wenshiziliao xuanji* 2 (1962).
Baskin, Jonathan B. "The Development of Corporate Financial Markets in Britain and the United States, 1600–1914: Overcoming Asymmetric Information." *Business History Review* 62 (Summer 1988): 199–237.
Beattie, Hillary. *Land and Lineage in China: A Study of Tung-cheng, Anhui in the Ming and Qing Dynasties.* Cambridge: Cambridge University Press, 1979.
Beatty, Bess. "Lowells of the South: Northern Influences on the Nineteenth-Century North Carolina Textile Industry." *Journal of Southern History* 53, no. 1 (1987): 37-62.

Bell, Lynda. "From Comprador to County Magnate: Bourgeois Practice in the Wuxi County Silk Industry." Paper presented at the Conference on Chinese Local Elites and Patterns of Dominance, Banff, 1987.

Belsky, Richard. "Beijing Scholar-Official Native-Place Lodges: The Social and Political Evolution of Huiguan in China's Capital City." Ph.D. diss., Harvard University, 1997.

Buoye, Thomas. "Litigation, Legitimacy and Lethal Violence." In Madeleine Zelin, Jonathan Ocko, and Robert Gardella, eds., *Contract and Property in Early Modern China*, 94–119. Stanford: Stanford University Press, 2004.

Cai, Shaoqing. "On the Origin of the Gelaohui." *Modern China* 10, no. 4 (1984).

Caizhengbu yanwushu yanwujihezongsuo [Ministry of Finance, Salt Administration Office, General Salt Inspectorate], ed. *Zhongguo yanzheng shilu* [Veritable records of the Chinese salt administration]. Vol. 2. Wenhai chubanshe, 1933.

Chandler, Alfred D. *The Visible Hand: The Managerial Revolution in American Business.* Cambridge: Belknap Press of Harvard University Press, 1977.

Chandler, Alfred Dupont, and Takashi Hikino. *Scale and Scope: The Dynamics of Industrial Capitalism.* Cambridge: Belknap Press of Harvard University Press, 1990.

Chang, Chung-li. *The Chinese Gentry: Studies on Their Role in Nineteenth-Century Chinese Society.* Seattle: University of Washington Press, 1955.

Chang, Ning Jennifer. "Vertical Integration and Business Diversification: The Case of the China Egg Produce Company in Shanghai, 1923–1950." Paper presented at the Business History Conference annual meeting, Lowell, MA, 2003.

Chao, Kang. *The Development of Cotton Textile Production in China.* Harvard East Asian Monographs, no. 74. Cambridge: East Asian Research Center, Harvard University, 1977.

Chen, Benqing. "Yusha zhaituan yu Wangsanweitang zhaiwu shimo" [The whole story of the Wang Sanwei trust's debts to the Yusha zhaituan]. *Zigong wenshiziliao xuanji* 22 (1992): 1–10.

Chen, Kaichong, et al. "Xinghai geming zhi jiefang qianxi Zigong difang zhujun qing-kuang" [The troops garrisoned in Zigong from the 1911 Revolution to the eve of liberation]. *Zigong wenshiziliao xuanji* 1–5 (1982): 121–31.

Chen, Ran. "Jindai Zigong yanye gongren zhuangkuang ji qi douzheng" [The condition and struggles of salt industry workers in modern Zigong]. In Jiusong Peng, Ran Chen, and Zigongshi yanye lishi bowuguan, eds., *Sichuan jingyanshi luncong.* [Collected essays on Sichuan salt history]. Chengdu: Sichuansheng shehui kexue-yuan chubanshe, 1985.

——. "Lun Zigong yanyegongren yijiuerbanian chunji dabagong" [On the great Zigong salt workers' strike of spring 1928]. In Jiusong Peng, Ran Chen, and Zigongshi yanye lishi bowuguan, eds., *Sichuan jingyanshi luncong* [Collected essays on Sichuan salt history], 258–74. Chengdu: Sichuansheng shehui kexueyuan chubanshe, 1985.

——. "Ziliujing de jueqi ji qi fazhan" [The rise and development of Ziliujing]. *Yanyeshi yanjiu* 1 (1987): 137–46.

Chen, Wenan. "Chuanyan jichu shimo" [The whole story of the sale of Sichuan salt in Huguang]. *Jingyanshi tongshun* 8 (1981): 44–48.

Chiang, Tao-chang. "The Salt Industry of China, 1644–1911: A Study in Historical Geography." Ph.D. diss., University of Hawaii, 1975.

Coble, Parks M. *The Shanghai Capitalists and the Nationalist Government, 1927–1937.* Harvard East Asian Monographs, no. 94. Cambridge: Council on East Asian Studies, Harvard University, 1980.

Cochran, Sherman. *Encountering Chinese Networks: Western, Japanese, and Chinese Corporations in China, 1880–1937.* Berkeley: University of California Press, 2000.

Cohen, Myron. "Commodity Creation in Late Imperial China: Corporations, Shares and Contracts in One Rural Community." In David Nugent, ed., *Locating Capitalism in Time and Space: Global Restructuring, Polities and Identity.* Stanford: Stanford University Press, 2002.

The Concise Oxford Dictionary. Oxford: Oxford University Press, 2001.

Crawford, Wallace. "The Salt Industry of Tzeliutsing." *China Journal of Science and Art* 4 (1926): 81–90, 169–75, 224–29; 5 (1927): 20–26.

Cronon, William. *Nature's Metropolis: Chicago and the Great West.* New York: Norton, 1991.

Cui, Yuzhi, and Shaoyuan Yan. "Gongjing yanshang Yu Shuhuai" [The Gongjing salt merchant Yu Shuhuai]. *Zigong wenshiziliao xuanji* 14 (1984): 169–84.

Dai, Zhili, and Zhongyang yanjiuyuan jindaishi yanjiusuo. *Sichuan baolu yundong shiliao huizuan* [Collected historical materials on the Sichuan railway protection movement]. *Zhongyang yanjiuyuan jinda shi yanjiusuo shiliao zonggan 23.* Taibei Shi: Zhongyang yanjiuyuan jindaishi yanjiusuo, 1994.

Davis, Lance E. "The New England Textile Mills and the Capital Markets: A Study of Industrial Borrowing 1840–1860." *Journal of Economic History* 20, no. 1 (1960): 1–30.

De Roover, Raymond. *Money, Banking and Credit in Mediaeval Bruges: Italian Merchant Bankers, Lombards and Money-changers.* Cambridge: Mediaeval Academy of America, 1948.

Deng, Duo. *Lun zhongguo lishi di jige wenti* [On several issues in Chinese history]. Beijing: Sanlian shudian, 1979.

Dillon, Michael. "Transport and Marketing in the Development of the Jingdezhen Porcelain Industry During the Ming and Qing Dynasties." *Journal of the Economic and Social History of the Orient* 35, no. 3 (1992).

Ding, Baozhen, ed. *Sichuan Yanfa zhi* [Gazetteer of Sichuan salt administration]. China, 1882.

Eastman, Lloyd E. *The Abortive Revolution: China Under Nationalist Rule, 1927–1937.* Cambridge: Harvard University Press, 1974.

——. *Seeds of Destruction: Nationalist China in War and Revolution, 1937–1949.* Stanford: Stanford University Press, 1984.

Elman, Benjamin A. *A Cultural History of Civil Examinations in Late Imperial China.* Berkeley: University of California Press, 2000.

Elvin, Mark. *The Pattern of the Chinese Past.* Stanford: Stanford University Press, 1973.

Eng, Robert. *Economic Imperialism in China: Silk Production and Exports, 1861–1932.* Berkeley: Center for Chinese Studies, 1986.

Entenmann, Robert. "Sichuan and Qing Migration Policy." *Ch'ing-shih wen-t'i* 4, no. 4 (1980): 35–54.

——. "Migration and Settlement in Sichuan, 1644–1796." Ph.D. diss., Harvard University, 1982.

Erlanson, Evan. "Commercial Banking in Sichuan, 1915–1935: The Case of the Young Brothers Banking Corporation." *Papers on Chinese History* 6 (1997): 43–82.

Esherick, Joseph. *Reform and Revolution in China: The 1911 Revolution in Hunan and Hubei.* Berkeley: University of California Press, 1976.

Esherick, Joseph and Mary Backus Rankin. *Chinese Local Elites and Patterns of Dominance.* Studies on China, no. 11. Berkeley: University of California Press, 1990.

Fairbank, John King, and Merle Goldman. *China: A New History*. Cambridge: Belknap Press of Harvard University, 1992.

Fang, Xing. "Qingdai Jiangnan nongmin de xiaofei" [Peasant consumption in Qing dynasty Jiangnan]. *Zhongguo jingji shi yanjiu* 11, no. 3 (1996).

Fang, Zhuofen, Tiewen Hu, Rui Jian, and Xing Fang. "The Porcelain Industry of Jingdezhen" [early and middle Qing period]. In Dixin Xu and Chengming Wu, eds., *Chinese Capitalism, 1522–1840*, 308–26. New York: St. Martin's Press, 2000.

Faure, David. "The Lineage as Business Company: Patronage versus Law in the Development of Chinese Business." Paper presented at the Second Conference on Modern Chinese Economic History, Institute of Economics, Academia Sinica, Taipei, Taiwan, 1989.

Feuerwerker, Albert. *China's Early Industrialization: Sheng Hsuan-huai (1844–1916) and Mandarin Enterprise*. Cambridge: Harvard University Press, 1958.

Feuerwerker, Albert, Denis Crispin Twitchett, and John King Fairbank. *The Cambridge History of China*, Vol. 11, *Late Ch'ing, 1800–1911*. Cambridge: Cambridge University Press, 1978.

Freedman, Maurice. *Lineage Organization in Southeastern China*. London: Athlone Press, 1958.

Fu, Lei, Zhixiang Liu, and Auyeung Pak. "A Study of Zigong Salt Mine Accounts in China." Available at http://www.deakin.edu.au/wcah/papers/Fu.pdf.

Fushun xianzhi [Fushun County gazetteer]. 1777. Reprint, Guangxu.

Fushun xianzhi [Fushun County gazetteer]. 1872.

Gao, Ming'an. "Wutongqiao yanchang de fengjian lougui" [The feudal customary fees at the Wutongqiao saltyard]. In Sichuan provincial gazetteer, Leshan editorial committee, Wutongqiao salt collection no. 2. Manuscript.

Gardella, Robert Paul. "Squaring Accounts: Commercial Bookkeeping Methods and Capitalist Rationalism in Late Qing and Republican China." *Journal of Asian Studies* 51, no. 2 (1992): 317–39.

——. *Harvesting Mountains: Fujian and the China Tea Trade, 1757–1937*. Berkeley: University of California Press, 1994.

Golas, Peter. "Early Qing Guilds." In G. William Skinner, ed., *The City in Late Imperial China*. Stanford: Stanford University Press, 1977.

Goodman, Bryna. *Native Place, City, and Nation: Regional Networks and Identities in Shanghai, 1853–1937*. Berkeley: University of California Press, 1995.

Gras, N.S.B. *An Introduction to Economic History*. New York: Augustus M. Kelley, 1969.

Guoli gugong bowuyuan. *Gongzhongdang Yongzhengchao zouzhe* [Palace memorials of the Yongzheng reign]. 32 vols. Vol. 15. Taibei: Guoli gugong bowuyuan, 1977.

He, Changling, ed. *Huangchao jingshi wenbian* [Essays on statecraft of our dynasty]. Taibei: Guofeng chubanshe, 1826. Reprint, 1963.

Hershatter, Gail. *The Workers of Tianjin, 1900–1949*. Stanford: Stanford University Press, 1986.

Ho, Ping-ti. "The Salt Merchants of Yang-Chou: A Study of Commercial Capitalism in Eighteenth-Century China." *Harvard Journal of Asiatic Studies* 17 (1954): 130–68.

——. *The Ladder of Success in Imperial China: Aspects of Social Mobility, 1368–1911*. New York: Columbia University Press, 1962.

Hobson, H. E. "Chongqing haiguan 1891 nian diaocha baogao" [1891 investigation report of the Chongqing Maritime Customs Bureau]. *Sichuan wenshiziliao xuanji* 4 (1962).

Honig, Emily. *Sisters and Strangers: Women in the Shanghai Cotton Mills, 1919–1949.* Stanford: Stanford University Press, 1986.

Hosie, Alexander. *Szechuan, Its Products, Industries and Resources.* Shanghai: Kelly and Walsh, 1922.

Hu, Charles. *The Agricultural and Forestry Land-use of Szechuan Basin.* Chicago: University of Chicago Press, 1946.

Hu, Shanquan, and Xiaoyuan Luo. "Qingji Zigong difang wu shuyuan" [The five academies in Zigong during the Qing period]. *Zigong wenshiziliao xuanji* 14 (1984): 185–94.

Hu, Shaochuan. "Gongjing Hu Yuanhe di guangzou yu shuailuo" [The rise and fall of Hu Yuanhe of Gongjing]. *Zigong wenshiziliao xuanji* 12 (1981): 49–79.

——. "Zigong yanchang jigong piju shimo" [The whole story of the Zigong saltyard public assistance hides bureau]. *Zigong wenshiziliao xuanji* 23 (1993): 69–70.

Huang, Chunwu, et al. "Qingmoyilai Zigong yanchang zhuye" [The bamboo industry in Zigong since the late Qing]. *Sichuan wenshiziliao xuanji* 9 (1963).

Huang, Jian. "Zigong yanchang banghui qianxi" [A brief analysis of the guilds at the Zigong saltyard]. Paper presented at the International Conference on Chinese Salt Industry History, Zigong, 1990.

Huang, Philip C. *Civil Justice in China: Representation and Practice in the Qing.* Stanford: Stanford University Press, 1996.

——. "Development or Involution in Eighteenth Century Britain and China? A Review of Kenneth Pomeranz's *The Great Divergence: China, Europe, and the Making of the Modern World Economy.*" *Journal of Asian Studies* 61, no. 2 (2002): 501–38.

Huang, Zhiqing, and Wufang Nie. "Zigong yanchang fazhan pianduan" [Passages on the development of the Zigong saltyard]. *Zigong wenshiziliao xuanji* 6–10 (1982): 251–57.

Inspector General of Customs, Shanghai, China. *Decennial Reports, 1922–31.* Vol. 1, *Northern and Yangzi Ports,* Maritime Customs, Statistical Series, no. 6. Shanghai, 1933.

Ji, Rongqing. "Gongjing yanchang fazhan yipie" [A glance at the development of the Gongjing saltyard]. *Sichuan wenshiziliao xuanji* 11 (1964).

Jiang, Xiangchen, and Xiaoyuan Luo. "Zigong yanchang di niu" [Buffalo at the Zigong saltyard]. *Zigong wenshiziliao xuanji* 12 (1981).

Kapp, Robert A. *Szechwan and the Chinese Republic: Provincial Militarism and Central Power, 1911–1938.* New Haven: Yale University Press, 1973.

——. "Themes in the History of Twentieth Century Southwest China." *Pacific Affairs* 51, no. 3 (1978).

Kirby, William C. "China Unincorporated: Company Law and Business Enterprise in Twentieth-Century China." *Journal of Asian Studies* 54, no. 1 (1995).

Köll, Elisabeth. *From Cotton Mill to Business Empire: The Emergence of Regional Enterprises in Modern China.* Harvard East Asian Monographs, no. 229. Cambridge: Harvard University Press, 2004.

Kurlansky, Mark. *Salt: A World History.* New York: Walker, 2002.

Kwan, Man Bun. *The Salt Merchants of Tianjin: State-Making and Civil Society in Late Imperial China.* Honolulu: University of Hawaii Press, 2001.

——. "Managing Market, Hierarchy and Network: The Jiuda-Yongli Group, 1917–1937." Paper presented at the Business History Conference annual meeting, Lowell, MA, 2003.

Lai, Mingqin, et al. "Yanyanjing fazhan gaikuang" [A survey of the development of rock-salt wells]. *Zigong wenshiziliao xuanji* 6–10 (1982): 3–52.

Lamoreaux, Naomi. "Banks, Kinship, and Economic Development: The New England Case." *Journal of Economic History* 46, no. 3 (1986).

——. "Information Problems and Banks' Specialization in Short-Term Commercial Lending: New England in the Nineteenth Century." In Peter Temin, ed., *Inside the Business Enterprise: Historical Perspectives on the Use of Information*, 161–95. Chicago: University of Chicago Press, 1991.

Lamoreaux, Naomi R., Daniel M.G. Raff, and Peter Temin. "Beyond Markets and Hierarchies: Toward a New Synthesis of American Business History." *American Historical Review* 108, no. 2 (April 2003): 404–32.

Landes, David S. *The Unbound Prometheus: Technological Change and Industrial Development in Western Europe from 1750 to the Present*. London: Cambridge University Press, 1969.

Langlois, Richard. "The Vanishing Hand: The Changing Dynamics of Industrial Capitalism." *Industrial and Corporate Change* 12, no. 2 (2003): 351–85.

Lee, En-han. *China's Quest for Railway Autonomy, 1904–1911: A Study of the Chinese Railway-Rights Recovery Movement*. Singapore: Singapore University Press, 1977.

Leshan xianzhi [Leshan County gazetteer]. Leshan, 1934.

Lewis, Carlton. "Some Notes on the Ko-lao Hui in Late Ch'ing China." In Jean Chesneaux, ed., *Popular Movements and Secret Societies in China, 1840–1950*, 97–112. Stanford: Stanford University Press, 1972.

Li, Junting. "Qingmo yilai di xilu meisu zhizaoye" [The twisted bamboo cable industry since the late Qing]. *Sichuan wenshiziliao zuanji* 15 (1964): 423–46.

Li, Lei. "Luo Xiaoyuan jiushi" [Luo Xiaoyuan's past]. *Ziliujing* 1 (1983).

Li, Lillian. *The Chinese Silk Trade*. Cambridge: Harvard University Press, 1981.

Li, Lingxiao, et al., eds. *Nanxi xianzhi* [Gazetteer of Nanxi County]. Nanjing: Jiangsu guji chubanshe, 1937. Reprint, 1992.

Li, Rong. *Shisanfeng shuwu quanji* [The collected works of the Thirteen Peaks Library]. Longan shuyuan, 1892.

——. "Ziliujing ji, an Account of the Salt Industry at Ziliujing." *ISIS* 39 (1948).

Li, Yongcheng, ed. *Fushun xianzhi* [Gazetteer of Fushun County], 1931.

Li, Zilin, et al. "Ziliujing Li Siyou tang you fazhan dao shuaiwang" [The Li Siyou trust of Ziliujing from their development to their decline]. *Sichuan wenshiziliao xuanji* 4 (1962–63).

Lieberthal, Kenneth. *Perspectives on Modern China: Four Anniversaries*. Studies on Modern China. Armonk, NY: M. E. Sharpe, 1991.

"Lijianianpu" [Li family genealogy]. Early Qing manuscript copy.

Lin, Dihuan. "Sichuan Yanzheng di gaige, 1895–1920" [Reform of the Sichuan salt administration]. M.A. thesis, Taiwan National University, 1983.

Lin, Jianyu. "Yanye zichanjieji yu zigong difang yishihui—guancang minqu lishidang'an qianxi" [Salt capitalists and the Zigong local assembly—a brief analysis of early Republican historical documents in the archives]. Paper presented at the International Conference on Chinese Salt Industry History, Zigong, 1990.

——. "Xinghai zigong difang shangren yu zhengfu" [Zigong merchants and the government in 1911]. *Zigong wenshiziliao xuanji* 21 (1991).

Lin, Yuanxiong, Liangxi Song, and Changyong Zhong. *Zhongguo jingyan keji shi* [The history of Chinese salt technology]. Chengdu: Sichuan Kexuejishu chubanshe, 1987.

Lin, Yuecong. "Zigong difang yishihui de huiyi" [A recollection of the Zigong local assembly]. *Zigong wenshiziliao xuanji* 1–5 (1982): 167–73.

Lin, Yuecong, et al. "Xinghai geming zai Zigong" [The 1911 Revolution in Zigong]. *Zigong wenshiziliao xuanji* 12 (1981): 1–11.

Lin, Zeyuan. "Wosuo zhidao de Zigong jingzao daguan" [What I know about Zigong's well and furnace *daguan*]. *Zigong wenshiziliao xuanji* 20 (1990): 108–11.

Lin, Zhenhan. *Chuanyan jiyao* [Essentials of Sichuan salt]. Shanghai: Shangwu yinshu guan, 1919.

Ling, Yaolin. "Qingdai Zigong jingyanye zibenzhuyi mengya fazhan daolu chutan" [A preliminary investigation of the sprouts of capitalism in the Zigong salt industry]. *Sichuan daxue xuebao congkan* 14 (1982).

Liu, Ta-chung, and Kung-jia Yeh. *The Economy of the Chinese Mainland, 1933–1959*. Princeton: Princeton University Press, 1965.

Liu, Zhen'an, ed. *Yunyang xianzhi* [Yunyang County gazetteer]. 1935.

Liu, Zhenguo. "Xinxing zhiyanchang" [The Xinxing salt factory]. *Zigong wenshiziliao xuanji* 1–5 (1982): 249–59.

Lu, Shiqiang. "Jindai Sichuan renkou midu yu renkou yali de fenxi" [Analysis of modern Sichuan population density and population pressure]. *Taiwan Shifan daxue lishixuebao* 5 (1977): 423–46.

Lu, Zijian. "Chuanyan jichu yu Sichuan yanye fazhan" [Sichuan salt in aid to Huguang and the development of the Sichuan salt industry]. *Shehui kexue yanjiu* 2 (1984).

———. "Qingdai Sichuan de yanque yu yanxiao" [Sichuan's salt gabelle and salt smugglers in the Qing period]. *Yanyeshi yanjiu* 1 (1987): 56–64.

Luo, Chengji. "Shaanshang zai Zigong yanchang de qiluo" [The ups and downs of the Shaanxi salt merchants at the Zigong saltyard]. In Ziyi Peng, Renyuan Wang, and Zigong yanye chuban bianjishi, eds., *Zhongguo yanyeshi guojixueshu taolunhui lunwenji* [Theses from the international symposium on Chinese salt industry history]. Chengdu: Sichuan renmin chubanshe, 1991.

Luo, Congxiu. "Gongjing yanchang de jingzao daguan" [The well and furnace *daguan* of the Gongjing saltyard]. *Zigong wenshiziliao xuanji* 20 (1990): 121–23.

Luo, Xiaoyuan. "Luo Xiaoyuan zishu" [Autobiography of Luo Xiaoyuan]. Manuscript, Zigong Municipal Archives.

———. "Ziliujing Wang Sanwei tang xingwang jiyao" [The basic elements of the rise and fall of the Wang Sanwei trust]. *Sichuan wenshiziliao xuanji* 7 and 8 (1963).

———. "Jing-Fu malu de kaishi xiujian" [The beginning of construction on the Ziliujing-Fushun highway]. Manuscript, 1964.

———. "Zhang Xiaopo dui Zigong yanchang di yingxiang" [The influence of Zhang Xiaopo on the Zigong saltyard]. *Zigong wenshiziliao xuanji* 12 (1981): 178–92.

———. "Furong guanyunju di bihai" [Malpractices in the Furong Official Salt Distribution Bureau]. *Zigong wenshiziliao xuanji* 14 (1984).

Luo, Xiaoyuan, and Xiangchen Jiang. "Zigong yanchang di jianshang" [Pipe merchants at the Zigong saltyard]. *Zigong wenshiziliao xuanji* 13 (1983): 135–45.

Ma, Fangbo. "Zigong yanchang di mucai shangye" [The lumber business at the Zigong saltyard]. *Zigong wenshiziliao xuanji* 6–10 (1982): 271–86.

Ma, Shaozhou, and Zhangqing He. "Chongqing Chuanyan yinhang shimo" [The complete history of the Salt Bank of Chongqing]. In *Chongqing wujia zhuming yinhang* [Chongqing's five famous banks]. Chongqing: Xinan shifan daxue cubanshe, 1989.

Ma, Zongyao, and Chengxun Nie. "Ziliujing Dafen bao yanyanti kaifa zhuangtai ji kaicai lishi jiexi" [The conditions surrounding the opening of the rock-salt layer at

Dafen bao in Ziliujing and an analysis of the history of its exploitation]. *Jingyanshi tongshun* 10 (1983).

Manyin [pseud.]. *Ziliujing*. Chengdu, 1944.

Metzger, Thomas A. "The Organizational Capabilities of the Ch'ing State in the Field of Commerce: The Liang-huai Salt Monopoly 1740–1840." In W. E. Willmott, ed., *Economic Organization in Chinese Society*, 9–45. Stanford: Stanford University Press, 1972.

Mokyr, Joel. "The Industrial Revolution in the Low Countries in the First Half of the Nineteenth Century: A Comparative Case Study." *Journal of Economic History* 34, no. 2 (1974): 365–91.

Mori, Noriko. "Salt Industry Capital in Qing Dynasty Sichuan." In Kazuko Ono, ed., *Min Shin jidai no seiji to shakai* [Ming-Qing politics and society], 543–93. Kyoto: Kyoto Daigaku Jinbun Kagaku Kenkyūjo, 1983.

Naquin, Susan. *Millenarian Rebellion in China: The Eight Trigrams Uprising of 1813.* New Haven: Yale University Press, 1976.

Needham, Joseph, and Jung-pang Lo. "The Salt Industry" [draft chapter for *Science and Civilization in China*]. Manuscript, 1972.

Ni, Jingxian. "Wo dui Yutong yinhang Zigong fenhang de huiyi" [My memories of the Zigong branch of the Yutong bank]. *Zigong wenshiziliao xuanji* 6–10 (1982): 294–99.

Nie, Wufang. "Qingmo yilai Zigong yanchangde jinrongye" [Banking at the Zigong saltyard since the late Qing]. *Zigong wenshiziliao xuanji* 21 (1991): 79–90.

Niida, Noboru. *Chugoku hoseishi kenkyu tochiho torihikiho* [Chinese legal history— land and the law of transactions]. Tokyo: Tokyo University Press, 1960.

Ono, Kazuko, ed. *Min Shin jidai no seiji to shakai* [Ming-Qing politics and society]. Kyoto: Kyoto Daigaku Jinbun Kagaku Kenkyūjo, 1983.

Osborne, Anne. "Natural Barriers to Agricultural Intensification in the Anhui-Zhejiang-Jiangsu Border Region." Paper presented at the annual convention of the American Historical Association, December 1985.

Ouyang, Yuemou, et al. "Zigong difang di diandangye" [The pawnshop business in Zigong]. *Zigong wenshiziliao xuanji* 13 (1983): 146–55.

Parsons, James B. "The Culmination of a Chinese Peasant Rebellion: Chang Hsien-chung in Szechuan, 1644–46." *Journal of Asian Studies* 16 (1957).

Peng, Jiusong, Ran Chen, and Zigongshi yanye lishi bowuguan, eds. *Sichuan jingyanshi luncong* [Collected essays on Sichuan salt history]. Chengdu: Sichuansheng shehui kexueyuan chubanshe, 1985.

Peng, Zeyi. *Zhongguo jindai shougongye shiliao, 1840–1949* [Materials on China's early mondern handicraft industry, 1840–1949]. Vol. 3. Beijing: Zhonghua shu ju, 1962.

———. "Qingdai Sichuan jingyan gongchang shougongye de xingqi he fazhan" [The rise and development of the well salt handicraft industry in Qing Sichuan]. *Zhongguo jingjishi yanjiu* 3 (1986): 27–45.

Peng, Zhiyi, ed. *Zigongshi zhi—Shanghui zhi, ziliao changbian* [(Draft) Gazetteer of Zigong city—Chamber of Commerce Gazetteer, long compilation of documents]. Zigong: Zigongshi gongshangye lianhehui, 1989.

Peng, Zeyi, Renyuan Wang, and Zigong yanye chuban bianjishi, eds., *Zhongguo yanye-shi guojixueshu taolunhui lunwenji* [Theses from the international symposium on Chinese salt industry history]. Chengdu: Sichuan renmin chubanshe, 1991.

Perry, Elizabeth J. *Shanghai on Strike: The Politics of Chinese Labor*. Stanford: Stanford University Press, 1993.

Pollard, Sidney. "Fixed Capital in the Industrial Revolution in Britain." *Journal of Economic History* 24, no. 3 (1964): 299–314.

Pomeranz, Kenneth. "Beyond the East-West Binary: Resituating Development Paths in the Eighteenth Century World." *Journal of Asian Studies* 61, no. 2 (2002): 539–90.

Potter, Jack. *Capitalism and the Chinese Peasant: Social and Economic Change in a Hong Kong Village.* Berkeley: University of California Press, 1968.

Pressnell, L. S. *Country Banking in the Industrial Revolution.* Oxford: Clarendon Press, 1956.

Price, Jacob. "Economic Function and the Growth of American Port Towns." *Perspectives in American History* 8 (1974): 123–84.

Pu, Yuesheng. "Zigong yanshang Xiong Zuozhou shilue" [A short biographical sketch of Zigong salt merchant Xiong Zuozhou]. *Zigong wenshiziliao xuanji* 17 (1987): 1–20.

——. "Zigong yanshang Luo Huagai" [Zigong salt merchant Luo Huagai]. *Zigong wenshiziliao xuanji* 19 (1989): 74–90.

——. "Zigong wasijingzao de daguan" [The gas well *daguan* of Ziliujing and their functions]. *Zigong wenshiziliao xuanji* 20 (1990): 119–21.

Qiao, Fu. *Ziliujing diyiji.* [Ziliujing, volume one]. Chengdu: Quchang gongsi, 1916.

Ran, Guangrong, and Xuejun Zhang. "Sichuan jingyanye zibenjuyi mengya di tantao—Guanyu Qingdai Furong yanchang jingying qiyue di chubu fenxi" [An exploration of the sprouts of capitalism in the Sichuan well-salt industry—A preliminary analysis of Qing period Furong saltyard management contracts]. *Sichuan daxue xuebao congkan* 5 (1980).

——. "Sichuan jingyanye zibenzhuyimengya wenti yanjiu" [Research in the sprouts of capitalism in the Sichuan salt industry]. In Nanjing daxue lishixi and MingQing yanjiushi, eds., *MingQing zibenzhuyi mengya yanjiu lunwenji* [Collected essays on the sprouts of capitalism in the Ming and Qing dynasties]. Shanghai: Shangwu chubanshe, 1981.

——. *MingQing Sichuan jingyanshigao* [A draft history of the well-salt industry in Sichuan during the Ming and Qing period]. Chengdu: Sichuan renmin chubanshe, 1984.

Rawski, Evelyn. "Property Rights in Land in Ming and Ch'ing China." Manuscript, 1985.

Rawski, Thomas G. *Economic Growth in Prewar China.* Berkeley: University of California Press, 1989.

Reynolds, Douglas. *China, 1898–1912: The Xinzheng Revolution and Japan.* Cambridge: Harvard University Press, 1993.

Richardson, Philip. *Economic Change in China, c. 1800–1950.* New Studies in Economic and Social History. New York: Cambridge University Press, 1999.

Rosenberg, Nathan. "Technological Change in the Machine Tool Industry, 1840–1910." *Journal of Economic History* 23, no. 4 (1963): 414–43.

——. *Technology and American Economic Growth.* New York: Harper & Row, 1972.

——. *Perspectives on Technology.* Cambridge: Cambridge University Press, 1976.

Rowe, William T. *Hankow: Commerce and Society in a Chinese City, 1796–1889.* Stanford: Stanford University Press, 1984.

Santai xianzhi [Gazetteer of Santai County]. 1937.

Schmookler, Jacob. *Invention and Economic Growth.* Cambridge: Harvard University Press, 1966.

Sheridan, James E. *Chinese Warlord: The Career of Feng Yu-hsiang.* Stanford: Stanford University Press, 1966.

Shu, Wencheng, et al. "Ziliujing shaoyangongren di hanghui zuzhi—Yandigong" [The guild organization of the Ziliujing salt evaporators—the Yandigong]. *Zigong wenshiziliao xuanji* 12 (1981): 35–48.

Sichuan guanyun yan'an leipian [A collection of Sichuan Guanyun salt cases]. Beijing: Caizhengbu yanwushu, 1902.

Sichuansheng Zigongshi Ziliujingquzhi bianzuan weiyuanhui. "Zigongshi Ziliujingquzhi" [Gazetteer of Ziliujing district, Zigong city]. Chengdu: Bashu shushe, 1993.

Skinner, G. William. "Marketing and Social Structure in Rural China." *Journal of Asian Studies* 24, no. 1 (1964).

——. *The City in Late Imperial China*. Stanford: Stanford University Press, 1977.

——. "Sichuan's Population in the Nineteenth Century: Lessons from Disaggregated Data." *Late Imperial China* 7, no. 2 (1986): 1–79.

Smith, George David, and Richard Sylla. "The Transformation of Financial Capitalism: An Essay on the History of American Capital Markets." *Financial Markets, Institutions and Instruments* 2, no. 2 (1993).

Smith, Paul. "Commerce, Agriculture, and Core Formation in the Upper Yangtze, 2 A.D. to 1948." Paper presented at the Conference on Spatial and Temporal Trends and Cycles in Chinese Economic History, 980–1980, Bellagio, Italy, 1984.

Sokoloff, Kenneth L. "Inventive Activity in Early Industrial America: Evidence from Patent Records, 1790–1846." *Journal of Economic History* 48, no. 4 (1988): 813–50.

Song, Chaolan. "Wosuoliaojie di Luo Xiaoyuan" [What I know of Luo Xiaoyuan]. *Ziliujing* 4 (1984).

Song, Liangxi. "Shilun Qingdai Sichuan yanshang di faren" [A preliminary discussion of the beginnings of the Sichuan salt merchants]. *Jingyanshi tongxun* 1 (1984).

——. "Sichuan junfa dui Zigong yanshang de jielue" [The Sichuan warlord's plunder of the Zigong salt merchants]. In Jiusong Peng, Ran Chen, and Zigong shi yanye lishi bowuguan, eds., *Sichuan jingyanshi luncong* [Collected essays on Sichuan salt history], 314–31. Chengdu: Sichuansheng shehui kexueyuan chubanshe, 1985.

——. "Zigong diqu de qianzhuang, piaohao yu yanye fazhan" [The development of native banks, remittance banks, and the salt industry in the Zigong region]. *Yanyeshi yanjiu* 2 (1994): 13–22.

Song, Shangze. "Cong xinghai zhi jiefang Sichuan xingyan jiuyiqizhi" [The nine changes in the system of salt sales in Sichuan from the 1911 Revolution to liberation]. *Zigong wenshiziliao xuanji* 23 (1993).

Strand, David. *Rickshaw Beijing*. Berkeley: University of California Press, 1989.

Tang, Guangpei. "Ming Zhengde nianjian Sichuan Daning zaofu lingdao di qiyi" [The rebellion led by salt evaporators in Daning, Sichuan, during the Ming Zhengde period]. In Jiusong Peng, Ran Chen, and Zigong shi yanye lishi bowuguan, eds., *Sichuan jingyanshi luncong* [Collected essays on Sichuan salt history], 191–215. Chengdu: Sichuansheng shehui kexueyuan chubanshe, 1985.

Tang, Jiong. *Chengshan laoren zi xuan nianpu* [Autobiography of the old man of Cheng mountain]. Taibei: Wenhai chubanshe, 1910. Reprint, 1968.

Tang, Renyue, Zhengzhong Guo, Changqing Ding, and Zhongguo yanye zonggongsi, eds. *Zhongguo yanye shi* [A history of the Chinese salt industry]. Beijing: Renmin chubanshe, 1997.

Temin, Peter, ed. *Inside the Business Enterprise: Historical Perspectives on the Use of Information*. A National Bureau of Economic Research Conference Report. Chicago: University of Chicago Press, 1991.

Thompson, Roger R. *China's Local Councils in the Age of Constitutional Reform, 1898–1911*. Cambridge: Council on East Asian Studies, Harvard University, 1995.

Tian, Maode. "Piaohao zai Sichuan di yixie huodong" [Some of the activities of remittance banks in Sichuan]. *Sichuan wenshiziliao xuanji* 32 (1984): 56–72.

Tsai, Kellee. *Back-Alley Banking: Private Entrepreneurs in China*. Ithaca: Cornell University Press, 2002.

Tufano, Peter. "Business Failure, Judicial Intervention, and Financial Innovation: Restructuring U.S. Railroads in the Nineteenth Century." *Business History Review* 71, no. 1 (1997): 1–40.

Twitchett, Dennis. "The Fan Clan's Charitable Estate, 1050–1760." In David S. Nivison and Arthur F. Wright, eds., *Confucianism in Action*. Stanford: Stanford University Press, 1959.

Vatter, Barbara. "Industrial Borrowing by the New England Textile Mills, 1840–1860: A Comment." *Journal of Economic History* 21, no. 2 (1961).

Vogel, Hans Ulrich. "The Great Well of China." *Scientific American*, June 1993, 116–21.

von Rosthorn, Arthur. "The Salt Administration of Ssuch'uan." *Journal of the Royal Asiatic Society, China Branch*, n.s., 27 (1892–93): 1–32.

Wang, Di. "Qingdai Sichuan renkou jingdi ji liangshi wenti" [The issue of population, cultivated acreage and grain production in Qing Sichuan]. *Sichuan daxue xuebao* 3 (1989): 90–106.

Wang, Huaizhou. "Dafenbao yanyan jing shiliao [Materials on the Dafen bao rock-salt wells]. *Zigong wenshiziliao xuanji* 19 (1989): 123–37.

———. "Ziliujing chang daguan jiqi zhineng" [The *daguan* of Ziliujing and their functions]. *Zigong wenshiziliao xuanji* 20 (1990): 112–19.

Wang, Renyuan, Ran Chen, and Fanying Zeng, eds. *Zigong chengshi shi* [The history of Zigong city]. Beijing: Shihui kexue wenxian chubanshe, 1995.

Wang, Roude. "Jiefang qian Zigong yanshang di fengjianxing" [The feudal nature of the Zigong salt merchants before liberation]. *Jingyanshi tongshun* 10 (1983).

Wang, Roude, and Langhua Zhong. "Luo Xiaoyuan sishinian di yanye jingying ji qi wannian shilue" [Luo Xiaoyuan's forty years in the salt industry and a short biographical account of his later years]. *Zigong wenshiziliao xuanji* 15 (1985): 70–113.

Wang, Shouji. *Yanfa yilue* [A brief discussion of salt administration]. Beijing, 1877.

Wang, Sufu. "Chongqing jinrong shichang kaolue" [A brief examination of Chongqing's financial markets]. *Shangyu huzhu zhoukan*, January 29, 1925.

Wang, Yeh-chien. *Land Taxation in Imperial China, 1750–1911*. Cambridge: Harvard University Press, 1993.

Wei, Yuanyou, ed. *Daning xianzhi* [Daning County gazetteer]. 1886.

Wen, Duanbao. "Yanjing ji" [Well salt chronicle]. In Changling He, ed., *Huangchao jingshi wenbian* [Essays on statecraft of our dynasty]. Taibei: Guofeng chubanshe, 1826.

Willbur, C. Martin. "The Nationalist Revolution: From Canton to Nanking, 1923–28." In John King Fairbank and Denis Twitchett, eds., *Cambridge History of China*. Vol. 12, *Republican China, 1912–1949*, 527–720. Cambridge: Cambridge University Press, 1983.

———. *The Nationalist Revolution in China, 1923–1928*. Cambridge: Cambridge University Press, 1984.

Williamson, Oliver E. *The Economic Institutions of Capitalism: Firms, Markets, Relational Contracting*. New York: Free Press, 1985.

———. "Comparative Economic Organization: The Analysis of Discrete Structural Alternatives." *Administrative Science Quarterly* 36 (June 1991): 269–96.

Wright, Tim. *Coal Mining in China's Economy and Society, 1895–1937*. Cambridge: Cambridge University Press, 1984.

Wu, Dingli. *Ziliujing fengwu mingshishuo* [An explanation of Zigong's local customs and products]. 1871.

Wu, Duo. "Sichuan guanyun zhi shimo" [The complete story of the Guanyun system in Sichuan]. In *Zhongguo jindai shehui jingji shi lunji* [Essays on modern Chinese economic and social history]. Hong Kong: Chongwen shudian, 1971.

Wu, Tianying. "Yinli juren, Yinren chengyi—Cong yandu Ziliujing kan gongshangye chengshi de xingcheng jiqi tedian" [People gather to make a profit, Cities are founded because there are people—An examination of the formation and characteristics of the industrial-commercial city from the example of the salt capital Ziliujing]. Manuscript.

Wu, Wei, ed. *Sichuan yanzhengshi* [Sichuan salt administration history]. China: Sichuan yanzhengshi bianjichu, 1932.

Xu, Dixin, and Chengming Wu, eds. *Zhongguo zibenzhuyi fazhanshi* [A history of the development of the sprouts of capitalism in China]. Beijing: Renmin chubanshe, 1985.

Xue, Yunsheng. *Duli cunyi* [Concentration on doubtful matters while perusing the substatutes]. In Robert Irick, ed., *Research Aids Series*, no. 8. Taibei: Chengwen chubanshe, 1970.

Yan, Ruyi. *Sansheng bianfang beilan* [Investigation of security at the three provinces border]. Yangzhou: Jiangsu Guangling gujikeyinshe, 1822. Reprint, 1991.

———. "Lun Chuanyan" [On Sichuan salt]. In Changling He, ed., *Huangchao jingshi wenbian* [Essays on statecraft of our dynasty]. Taibei: Guofeng chubanshe, 1826. Reprint, 1963.

Yan, Xianqi, Wenfang Yan, and Zuo Yan. "Yan Guixin tang yu Ziliujing" [The Yan Guixin trust and Ziliujing]. *Yanyeshi yanjiu* 3 (1990): 64–74.

Yang, Dekun, ed. *Fengjie xianzhi* [Fengjie County gazetteer]. 1893.

Yang, Duxing, et al. "Zigong yanchang zhengqijiche xiyan gaishu" [A general discussion of steam pumping at the Zigong saltyard]. *Zigong weshiziliao xuanji* 1–5 (1982): 137–54.

Yang, Xiaofang. "Zigong yanyan di fazhan" [The development of the Zigong rock-salt layer]. *Zigong weshiziliao xuanji* 1–5 (1982): 154–62.

Yu, Heping. *Shanghui yu Zhongguo zaoqi xiandaihua* [Chambers of Commerce and China's early modernization]. Shanghai: Shanghai renmin chubanshe, 1993.

Yuan, Boling. "Fengjian batou dui yanye yunshugongren di yazha" [The oppression of salt transport workers by the feudal labor bosses]. *Jingyanshi tongxun* 2 (1977): 59–62.

Zelin, Madeleine. *The Magistrate's Tael: Rationalizing Fiscal Reform in Early Ch'ing China*. Berkeley: University of California Press, 1984.

———. "Obstacles to Economic Development: The Mining Industry in Late Imperial Sichuan." Paper presented at the annual convention of the American Historical Association, New York, 1985.

———. "The Rights of Tenants in Mid-Qing Sichuan: A Study of Land-Related Lawsuits in Baxian." *Journal of Asian Studies* 45, no. 3 (1986): 499–526.

———. "The Rise and Fall of the Furong Well-Salt Elite." In Joseph Esherick and Mary Rankin, eds., *Chinese Local Elites and Patterns of Dominance*. Berkeley: University of California Press, 1990.

———. "The Structure of the Chinese Economy During the Qing Period: Some Thoughts on the 150th Anniversary of the Opium War." In Kenneth Lieberthal et al., eds., *Perspectives on Modern China, Four Anniversaries*. Armonk, NY: M. E. Sharpe, 1991.

———. "Merchant Dispute Mediation in Twentieth Century Zigong, Sichuan." In Philip Huang and Katherine Bernhardt, eds., *Civil Law in Qing and Republican China*. Stanford: Stanford University Press, 1994.

———. "Managing Multiple Ownership at the Furong Saltyard." In Madeleine Zelin, Jonathan Ocko and Robert Gardella, eds., *Contract and Property Rights in Early Modern China*. Stanford: Stanford University Press, 2003.

———. "A Critique of Rights of Property in Pre-War China." In Madeleine Zelin, Johnathan Ocko, and Robert Gardella, eds., *Contract and Property Rights in Early Modern China*. Stanford: Stanford University Press, 2004.

———. "Government Policy Toward Reclamation and Hidden Land During the Yongzheng Reign." Manuscript.

Zhang, Dedi. "Sichuan yankeshu" [A discussion of the Sichuan salt tax]. In Changling, He, ed., *Huangchao jingshi wenbian* [Essays on statecraft of our dynasty]. Taibei: Guofeng chubanshe, 1826. Reprint, 1963.

Zhang, Duanfu. "Jianle dichu shouquyizhi di dachangshang—Wu Jingrang tang" [A Jianle area saltyard merchant lineage second to none—the Wu Jingrang trust]. *Jingyanshi tongxun* 6 (1979–80).

Zhang, Shuzhi. "Ziliujing tudi liyong zhi diaocha" [An investigation of land use in Ziliujing]. In Zheng Su, ed., *Minguo ershiniandai zhongguo dalu tudi wenti ziliao* [Materials on the land question on mainland China in the 1930s]. Taibei: Chengwen chubanshe, 1938.

Zhang, Xi, ed. *Sichuan yanwu baogao shu* [Reports on the Sichuan salt administration]. China, 1912.

Zhang, Xiaobo. "Merchant Associational Activism in Early-Twentieth-Century China: The Tianjin General Chamber of Commerce, 1904–1928." Ph.D. diss., Columbia University, 1995.

Zhang, Xiaomei. *Sichuan jingji cankao ziliao* [Reference materials on the Sichuan economy]. Shanghai: Zhongguo guomin jingji yanjiu suo, 1939.

Zhang, Xuejun. "Qingdai Chuannan diqu de yanye gongbanghui huodong" [The activities of salt workers' associations in southern Sichuan during the Qing period]. In Sichuan lishi xuehui, ed., *Shixue lunwenji* [Collected essays on history], 241–53. Chengdu: Sichuan renmin chubanshe, 1982.

———. "Xinghai geming yu Zigong yanye" [The 1911 Revolution and the Zigong salt industry]. *Jingyanshi tongxun* 11 (1983).

Zhang, Yifu. "Enliujian duishui de jingguo" [An account of the shipment of brine through the Enliu pipe]. *Zigong wenshiziliao xuanji* 19 (1989): 91–95.

Zhao, Xi, ed. *Minguo Sichuan Rongxian zhi* [Republican Sichuan Rong County gazetteer]. 1929.

Zhong, Changyong. "Furong yanchang di jiqi xilu" [Mechanical brine pumping at the Furong saltyard]. *Jingyanshi tongshun* 8 (1981): 38–43.

Zhong, Chongmin, Shouren Zhu, and Quan Li. *Zigong zhi yanye* [The Zigong salt industry]. *Gaichu jingji diaocha congkan* 2. Chongqing: Zhongguo nongmin yinhang jingji yanjiuchu, 1942.

Zhonggong Zigongshiwei dangshi gongzuo weiyuanhui. *Zhonggong Zigong dixia dang zuzhi gaiguang* [A survey of Chinese Communist Party organization in Zigong]. Zigong: Zhonggong Zigong shiwei dangshi yanjiushi, 1995.

Zhou, Qisheng. "Dui 'Zigong yanchang zhengqijiche xiyan gaishu' yiwen di tantao" [An inquiry into "A general discussion of steam pumping at the Zigong salt yard"]. *Zigong weshiziliao xuanji* 6–10 (1982): 264–68.

Zhu, Ziyan. "Jiangjinbang di xingcheng ji qi zai Zigong yanchang di jingying huodong" [The formation of the Jiangjin guild and their business activities at the Zigong salt-yard]. *Zigong wenshiziliao xuanji* 1–5 (1982): 242–48.

Zigongshi dang'anguan. "Zigong yanye susong dang'an zhuanti xuanzepian—(1) Ziliujing Wang Sanwei tang yu Yusha zhaiquantuan zhaiwu jiufen an" [Selected documents on special topics from the archives of Zigong salt lawsuits: (1) The case of the debt dispute between the Ziliujing Wang Sanwei tang and the Chongqing-Shashi creditor group]. *Yanyeshi yanjiu* 1 and 2 (1993): 64–76, 73–80.

Zigongshi dang'anguan, Beijing jingjixueyuan, and Sichuan daxue, eds. *Zigong yanye qiyue dang'an xuanji (1732–1949)* [Selected Zigong salt industry contracts and documents (1732–1949)]. Beijing: Zhongguo shehuikexue chubanshe, 1985.

Zigongshi dang'anguan and Zigongshi zonggong hui, eds. *Zigong yanye gongren douzhengshi dangan ziliao xuanbian (1915–1949)* [Selected documents on the history of the struggles of Zigong salt workers (1915–1949)]. Chengdu: Sichuan renmin chubanshe, 1989.

Zigongshi gongshangye lianhehui, ed. "Xiong Zuozhou zhuan" [Biography of Xiong Zuozhou]. Manuscript.

Zigongshi huaxue gongye guanli ju, ed. *Zigongshi huaxue gongye zhi* [Gazetteer of the Zigong chemicals industry]. Zigongshi difangzhi congshu [Zigong municipal gazetteer collection], vol. 13. Chengdu: Sichuan renmin daxue chubanshe, 1993.

Zigongshi jinrongzhi bianzuanweiyuanhui, ed. *Zigongshi jinrongzhi* [Zigong financial gazetteer]. Zigongshi difangzhi congshu [Zigong municipal gazetteer collection], vol. 18. Chengdu: Sichuan cishu chubanshe, 1994.

Zigongshi jixie dianzi gongye guanliju, ed. *Zigongshi jixiegongye zhi* [Gazetteer of the Zigong city machine industry]. Zigongshi difangzhi congshu [Zigong municipal gazetteer collection], vol. 21. Chengdu: Sichuan renmin chubanshe, 1993.

Zigongshi qing gongye guanliju, and Zigongshi gongye hezuo lianshe, eds. *Zigongshi qinggongye zhi* [Gazetteer of Zigong city light industry]. Zigongshi difangzhi congshu [Zigong municipal gazetteer collection], vol. 23. Chengdu: Sichuan daxue chubanshe, 1993.

Zigongshi yanye zhi bianzuan weiyuan hui, ed. *Zigong shi yanye zhi* [Zigong city salt industry gazetteer]. Zigong, 1992.

Zigongshi zhengxie wenshiban. "Zigong yanye zibenjia Hou Ceming" [Zigong salt capitalist Hou Ceming], *Zigong wenshiziliao xuanji* 19 (1989): 49–73.

Zigongshi zhengxie wenshiziliao weiyuanhui, ed. *Ziliujing yanye shijia* [Well-known families of the Ziliujing salt industry]. Chengdu: Sichuan renmin chubanshe, 1995.

Index

Studies of the Weatherhead East Asian Institute, Columbia University

Selected Titles

(Complete list at: *www.columbia.edu/cu/weai/studies-of-weatherhead/.html*).

Science and the Building of a Modern Japan, Morris Low. Palgrave Macmillan, Ltd., 2005.

Kinship, Contract, Community, and State: Anthropological Perspectives on China, Myron L. Cohen. Stanford University Press, 2005.

Rearranging the Landscape of the Gods: The Politics of a Pilgrimage Site in Japan, 1573–1912, Sarah Thal. University of Chicago Press, 2005.

Reluctant Pioneers: China's Expansion Northward, 1644–1937, James Reardon-Anderson. Stanford University Press, 2005.

Contract and Property in Early Modern China, Madeleine Zelin, Jonathan K. Ocko, and Robert P. Gardella, eds. Stanford University Press, 2004.

Gutenberg in Shanghai: Chinese Print Capitalism, 1876–1937, Christopher A. Reed. UBC Press, 2004.

Japan's Colonization of Korea: Discourse and Power, Alexis Dudden. University of Hawai'i Press, 2004.

Divorce in Japan: Family, Gender, and the State, 1600–2000, Harald Fuess. Stanford University Press, 2004.

The Communist Takeover of Hangzhou: The Transformation of City and Cadre, 1949–1954, James Gao. University of Hawai'i Press, 2004.

Taxation Without Representation in Rural China, Thomas P. Bernstein and Xiaobo Lü. Modern China Series, Cambridge University Press, 2003.

The Reluctant Dragon: Crisis Cycles in Chinese Foreign Economic Policy, Lawrence Christopher Reardon. University of Washington Press, 2002.

Cadres and Corruption: The Organizational Involution of the Chinese Communist Party, Xiaobo Lü. Stanford University Press, 2000.

Japan's Imperial Diplomacy: Consuls, Treaty Ports, and War with China, 1895–1938, Barbara Brooks. Honolulu: University of Hawai'i Press, 2000.

China's Retreat from Equality: Income Distribution and Economic Transition, Carl Riskin, Zhao Renwei, Li Shi, eds. M. E. Sharpe, 2000.

Nation, Governance, and Modernity: Canton, 1900–1927, by Michael T. W. Tsin. Stanford University Press, 1999.

Assembled in Japan: Electrical Goods and the Making of the Japanese Consumer, Simon Partner. University of California Press, 1999.

Civilization and Monsters: Spirits of Modernity in Meiji Japan, by Gerald Figal. Duke University Press, 1999.

The Logic of Japanese Politics: Leaders, Institutions, and the Limits of Change, Gerald L. Curtis. Columbia University Press, 1999.

Contesting Citizenship in Urban China: Peasant Migrants—The State and Logic of the Market, Dorothy Solinger. University of California Press, 1999.

Bicycle Citizens: The Political World of the Japanese Housewife, Robin LeBlanc. University of California Press, 1999.

Alignment Despite Antagonism: The United States, Japan, and Korea, Victor Cha. Stanford University Press, 1999.